Praise for the First Edition of *Your Child's Health*

"This terrific reference sets a new standard for child-care books."
> —Daniel D. Broughton, M.D., Consultant in Pediatrics,
> The Mayo Clinic

"Barton Schmitt has proved himself to be a worthy successor to Spock.... At this time I recommend the book to parents as my 'number one choice.'"
> —Gunnar B. Stickler, M.D., Department of Pediatrics,
> The Mayo Clinic and Mayo Foundation,
> in *Clinical Pediatrics*

"A book that parents will really find helpful. Dr. Schmitt has brought his considerable experience in general pediatrics to the writing of a text that is clear and well organized and that emphasizes both preventive care and common sense."
> —Betsy Busch, M.D., Department of Pediatrics,
> New England Medical Center,
> in the *American Journal of Diseases of Children*

"The book's strength is not only in its content, which is complete, but also in its organization, which allows readers to find what they want to know easily and quickly.... *Your Child's Health* has the potential to become a classic."
> —Edward W. Collins, M.D., Brown University,
> in the *Journal of the American Medical Association*

"The most remarkable aspect of this book, and one which sets it apart from other similar child care books, is the coverage given to developmental and behavioral issues.... Dr. Schmitt's sections on discipline are particularly clear, sensible, and well-referenced."
> —Robin Hansen, M.D., Department of Pediatrics,
> University of California, Davis,
> in *Developmental and Behavioral Pediatrics*

YOUR CHILD'S HEALTH

The Parents' Guide to Symptoms, Emergencies, Common Illnesses, Behavior, and School Problems

Barton D. Schmitt, M.D., F.A.A.P.

*Director of General Consultative Services, The Children's Hospital of Denver
Professor of Pediatrics, University of Colorado School of Medicine*

 BANTAM BOOKS
NEW YORK · TORONTO · LONDON · SYDNEY · AUCKLAND

AUTHOR'S NOTE

The information contained in this book is intended to complement, not substitute for, the advice of your child's physician. Before starting any medical treatment or medical program you should consult with your own physician, who can discuss your individual needs with you and counsel you about symptoms and treatment.

YOUR CHILD'S HEALTH: THE PARENTS' GUIDE TO SYMPTOMS, EMERGENCIES, COMMON ILLNESSES, BEHAVIOR, AND SCHOOL PROBLEMS

A Bantam Book / September 1987
Revised edition / September 1991

Library of Congress Cataloging-in-Publication Data

Schmitt, Barton D., 1937–

    Your child's health : the parents' guide to symptoms, emergencies, common illnesses, behavior, and school problems / Barton D. Schmitt.
    —*Rev. ed.*
    p.   cm.
    Includes index.
    ISBN 0-553-35339-X
    1. Pediatrics—Popular works. 2. Children—Diseases—Treatment.
3. Children—Health and hygiene. I. Title.
RJ61.S365 1991
618.92—dc20

    91-19595
    CIP

Published simultaneously in the United States and Canada

Bantam Books are published by Bantam Books, a division of Random House, Inc. Its trademark, consisting of the words "Bantam Books" and the portrayal of a rooster, is Registered in U.S. Patent and Trademark Office and in other countries. Marca Registrada. Bantam Books, 1540 Broadway, New York, New York 10036.

PRINTED IN THE UNITED STATES OF AMERICA

BVG 20 19

This book is dedicated to the inner strength of families:
To my parents for believing in me.
To Mary for her enduring love and encouragement.
And to Dave, Elaine, Becky, and Mike for everything they
taught me about fractured femurs, sea urchins, wolf spiders,
pill-swallowing, ATVs, hypothermia, and having fun.
And to Calvin, for taking me on so many walks I would
have missed.

CONTENTS

IV. HEALTH PROMOTION: KEEPING YOUR CHILD HEALTHY

FEEDING AND EATING   145

GROWTH, DEVELOPMENT, AND SAFETY   200

PREVENTING INFECTIONS   211

MEDICINES   227

V. BEHAVIOR: PREVENTING AND SOLVING PROBLEMS

SKIN: LOCALIZED PINK OR RED RASHES   444

SKIN: CONDITIONS WITHOUT A RASH   469

BRAIN   493

EYES   502

EARS   514

NOSE   533

INTRODUCTION

Dear Parents,

Welcome to the universal joys and challenges of parenthood. These guidelines were written to help you provide better health care and nurturing for your child. I have emphasized the common illnesses, injuries, and behavior problems that befall the majority of children. When possible, I have stressed the healthy life-styles and preventive measures you can take to keep your child physically and psychologically well. When appropriate, I have cautioned you about the limitations of surgery and drugs. The table of contents, cross-references in the text, and the index have been organized and interwoven so you can find needed advice quickly. And finally, the topics are covered in depth, so you can find answers to almost all of your questions in one book.

To help you use this book, information relating to each of the topics or diseases is organized in the following way:

SYMPTOMS AND CHARACTERISTICS

- What are the symptoms?

- What does it look like?

- What's normal?

Causes

- Is it caused by virus, bacteria, allergy, injury, heredity, stress, or some other factor?

- Is it contagious?

Expected Course

- How long will it last?
- How bad will it get?
- What are the possible complications?

GUIDELINES FOR CALLING YOUR CHILD'S PHYSICIAN

- How can you recognize serious symptoms and emergencies?
- Should you call immediately?
- Can you safely wait to call during office hours?
- Can your child safely be treated at home without a call?

HOME CARE RECOMMENDATIONS

- What first aid measures can you take for emergencies?
- For nonemergencies, what can you do to make your child comfortable?
- How can you prevent similar infections or injuries in the future?
- How can you speed recovery?
- What are the nuts and bolts of home care?
- How can you improve your child's behavior?

The desire to be better informed about child rearing and childhood illnesses is universal. These guidelines are meant to supplement the health education provided by your child's physician. Most parents also receive ongoing health advice from friends, relatives, newspapers, magazines, radio, and television. Unfortunately, information from the media or nonprofessionals may be confusing, conflicting, or downright alarming. One of the main purposes of this book is to help bridge the information gap with accurate, up-to-date, and straightforward health facts and advice. *Your Child's Health* is the only book of its kind that has been carefully reviewed by 26 successful parents and pediatricians. The guidelines for when to call your child's physician have been tested by hundreds of physicians and nurses across the country who use my earlier book, *Pediatric Telephone Advice.*

One sound rule of child rearing is: Don't do anything for

your child that he can do for himself (such as feeding or dressing). The same advice can easily be applied to parents with regard to health care decision-making. You are an important member of the health care team. You have innate common sense and you know your child better than anyone else. Observe your child's symptoms. Use this book as your reference and make informed decisions. As your ability to differentiate (triage) between serious and nonserious illnesses increases, so will your confidence. The common illnesses and behavior of childhood will come into perspective as something you can competently manage. You will become a smart parent. Don't underestimate your abilities.

Best wishes for enjoyable and successful parenting during these exciting years.

—BARTON D. SCHMITT, M.D.

Director of General Consultative Services
The Children's Hospital

Professor of Pediatrics
University of Colorado School of Medicine
Denver, Colorado

ACKNOWLEDGMENTS

I am immeasurably indebted to my pediatric and parent reviewers for their careful examination of my text for accuracy, safety, objectivity, clarity, and completeness. Their ongoing efforts have been extraordinary and their feedback invaluable.

Pediatric Review Board
Joseph H. Banks, M.D., Columbus, Ohio
John M. Benbow, M.D., Concord, North Carolina
Daniel D. Broughton, M.D., Rochester, Minnesota
Rosemary D. Casey, M.D., Philadelphia, Pennsylvania
David M. Christopher, M.D., Renton, Washington
Jessie R. Groothuis, M.D., Denver, Colorado
Robin L. Hansen, M.D., Sacramento, California
David L. Kerns, M.D., San Jose, California
Bruce J. McIntosh, M.D., Jacksonville, Florida
Robert D. Mauro, M.D., Denver, Colorado
Cajsa J. Schumacher, M.D., Albany, New York
Daniel R. Terwelp, M.D., Austin, Texas
Wallace C. White, M.D., Denver, Colorado

Parent Review Board
Lynnette Baer, Bowmar, Colorado
Elizabeth T. Berk, Concord, Massachusetts
Gayle N. Ebel, Bowmar, Colorado
Candy Ergen, Bowmar, Colorado
Nancy Gary, Child Health Associate, Denver, Colorado
Doris L. Klein, Child Life Worker, Denver, Colorado
Carol J. Markley, Bowmar, Colorado

Christina Podolak, Bowmar, Colorado
Sara Rotbart, Denver, Colorado
Mary C. Schmitt, Bowmar, Colorado
Lynne M. Weaver, Littleton, Colorado
Sandra Wilday, Bowmar, Colorado
Marjorie S. Wise, Englewood, Colorado

My appreciation and admiration to the following pediatric subspecialists and pediatric surgeons who have graciously helped me with specific topics and questions in their areas of expertise:

General Pediatrics: Drs. Robert Mauro, Steven Poole, Richard Krugman, Stephen Berman, Richard Shiffman, and Burris Duncan
Adolescent Medicine: Drs. David Kaplan, Kathleen Mammel, Ida Nakashima, and Henry Cooper
Emergency Pediatrics: Dr. Michael Clemmens
Infectious Disease: Drs. James Todd, Mary Glode, Mark Abzug, and Brian Lauer
Dermatology: Dr. William Weston
Allergy: Drs. James Lustig, Allen Bock, David Pearlman, James Shira, and Fred Leffert
Psychology: Drs. Edward Christophersen, Jeffrey Dolgan, and Andrea Van Steenhouse
Neonatology: Drs. Jacinto Hernandez and Susan Niermeyer
Breast-Feeding: Drs. Marianne Neifert, Joy Seacat, and Jack Newman
Cardiology: Drs. James Wiggins, Robert Wolfe, Henry Sondheimer, and Reginald Washington
Pulmonology: Drs. Leland Fan and Frank Accurso
Gastroenterology: Drs. Arnold Silverman, Ronald Sokol, Judy Sondheimer, and Sharon Taylor
Neurology: Dr. Paul Moe
Ear, Nose, and Throat: Drs. James Jaskunas, Nigel Pashley, and Ray Wood
Ophthalmology: Drs. Robert King and Robert Sargent
Dentistry: Drs. William Mueller and Richard Abrams
Urology: Dr. Martin Koyle
Orthopedics: Drs. Robert Eilert, Frank Chang, and Gerard Glancy

My special thanks to Toni Burbank, my editor and advocate at Bantam Books. Her intelligence, experience, insight, and patience are everything an author could ask for. In addition, the following good people at Clinical Reference Systems, a medical software company in Denver, have helped this project from behind the scenes: Richard Thompson, David Steinman, Robert Bruegel, Janice Burley, and Ray Gardner. So have Karen Bardossi and Jeffrey Forster at Contemporary Pediatrics. Finally, my deep gratitude goes out to the many physicians, nurses, students, and parents who have shared ideas and questions with me over the last 24 years—especially my wonderful colleagues who practice medicine in the mile-high city.

THE READER'S RESPONSIBILITY

The contents of this book have been carefully reviewed for accuracy.

If you have any questions as to the correct diagnosis or proper treatment for your child, call your child's physician for help.

If you feel your child's condition has become serious, don't be reluctant to recontact your physician. Trust your intuition; you know your child better than anyone else.

YOUR CHILD'S HEALTH

I.

EMERGENCIES

I. EMERGENCIES

EMERGENCY TELEPHONE CALLS

LIFE-THREATENING EMERGENCIES
Dial 911 or "0" (Operator).

In larger cities, this call will dispatch an emergency vehicle staffed by a rescue squad. In smaller towns and counties, the operator will connect you with an emergency ambulance service. The direct number for this service is usually found on the inside front cover of your telephone directory. In areas that use 911, children and the elderly should be taught to dial this number for crises. Increasingly, 911 is being linked to a computer system ("enhanced 911") that can determine the address of the incoming call even if the caller can't speak.

NON-LIFE-THREATENING EMERGENCIES
Call your child's physician.

If you don't have a physician, call the nearest emergency room. Always call in first, rather than simply going to an emergency room. Usually the physician will be able to provide you with critical first aid instructions by phone (e.g., for burns, animal bites, or fractures). Your physician can help you decide whether a rescue squad should be sent out or if it is safe for you to come in. Your physician can also tell you where to take your child for the best emergency care.

POISONING
Call your child's physician or the nearest Poison Control Center. (Each region has a toll-free number.)

3

HOW TO CUT THROUGH RED TAPE

When you call in, always state assertively, "This is an emergency." Do not let the answering service or receptionist put you on hold before talking with you. If you are put on hold, hang up and call back immediately.

EMERGENCY TRANSPORTATION

LIFE-THREATENING OR MAJOR EMERGENCIES

Call your rescue squad (911) or ambulance service.

Definition of a Major Emergency • Children who may need resuscitation en route (for instance, those with severe breathing difficulty, severe choking, or not breathing) must be looked on as "5-minute emergencies." Other potentially life-threatening emergencies are loss of consciousness (coma), continuing seizure, or bleeding that can't be stopped by direct pressure. Children with major trauma or possible neck injury need splinting before transportation.

The Staff of Emergency Vehicles • Emergency vehicles are staffed by EMTs (Emergency Medical Technicians). These people are trained in Basic Life Support: cardiopulmonary resuscitation (CPR), splinting, bandaging, and so on. Paramedics are EMTs with additional training in Advanced Life Support: drawing blood, starting IVs, intubation, recording EKGs, and so on. Training ranges from 300 to 600 hours. EMTs are all certified by the National Association of EMTs, which has 20,000 members. While providing emergency care, they are linked by two-way radio to an emergency room physician at their base hospital.

Rescue Squads versus Ambulance Services • In larger cities, rescue squads are often available through local fire departments. Usually rescue squads can respond more rapidly than ambulances, and their service is free. After the patient's condition has been stabilized, they will often call an ambulance company for transport to the hospital if it is warranted. In general the police do not transport sick people, so don't call them for medical emergencies.

NON-LIFE-THREATENING EMERGENCIES

Go to the nearest hospital offering emergency services. Try to call your child's physician first.

Definition of Less Severe Emergencies • These concern children who need to be seen as quickly as possible but whose condition is currently stable or at least does not pose a danger of suddenly needing resuscitation. Examples are poisonings, slow bleeding controlled by pressure, severe pain, and seizures that have stopped. These can be looked on as "20-minute emergencies."

Advantage of Car over an Ambulance • A private car is quicker and less expensive than an ambulance. Another option is to call a taxi.

Driving in to Seek Emergency Care • If you are going by private car, don't leave until you know the exact location of the emergency room you will be going to. It is a good idea to rehearse the drive by the fastest route before an emergency occurs. Keep your sick child in a car safety seat, or if he must lie down, in the back seat. Try to have a friend or neighbor accompany you and do the driving. Some parents are too shaken by their child's injury to drive safely.

What to Bring with You to the Emergency Room

- Your child's immunization record.
- Your health insurance card.
- Your pharmacy's telephone number.
- Any medicines your child is taking (or a list of drugs and dosages).
- Your child's security object or favorite toy.
- If your child has been poisoned, bring the container.
- If your child has passed blood in the urine, stool, or vomited material, bring a sample for testing.
- If your child has painful urination, bring a urine sample (see page 612).

EMERGENCY SYMPTOMS

All the conditions discussed in this chapter are emergencies. I'm sure you won't overlook or underestimate the importance of life-threatening emergencies such as major bleeding, choking, a convulsion, or coma. The following emergency symptoms, however, are highlighted because they are either difficult to recognize or not considered serious by some parents. If your child has any of the following symptoms, contact your child's physician immediately.

SICK NEWBORN

If your baby is less than one month old and sick in any way, the problem could be serious.

SEVERE LETHARGY

To be tired during an illness is normal, but if your child stares off into space, won't smile, has no interest in playing, is too weak to cry, is floppy, or is hard to awaken, these are serious symptoms.

SEVERE PAIN

If your child cries when you touch him or move him, this can be a symptom of meningitis. Such children also don't want to be held. Constant screaming or the inability to sleep also point to severe pain.

CAN'T WALK

If your child has learned to walk and then loses the ability to stand or walk, the most likely reason is that he or she has a serious injury to the legs or an acute problem with balance. If your child walks bent over, holding his abdomen, he probably has a serious abdominal problem such as appendicitis.

TENDER ABDOMEN

Press on your child's belly while he or she is sitting up in your lap and looking at a book. Normally you should be able to press an inch or so in with your fingers in all parts of the belly without resistance. If he pushes your hand away or screams, this is an important finding. If the belly is also bloated and hard, the condition is even more dangerous. (See ABDOMINAL PAIN, page 583.)

TENDER TESTICLE OR SCROTUM

The sudden onset of pain in the groin area can be due to twisting (torsion) of the testicle. This requires surgery within 8 hours to save the testicle.

LABORED BREATHING

You should assess your child's breathing after cleaning out the nose and when he is not coughing. If your child is working hard at breathing, has tight croup, or has obvious wheezing, he or she needs to be seen immediately. Other signs of respiratory difficulty are a breathing rate of more than 60 breaths per minute, bluish lips, or retractions (pulling in between the ribs). (See BREATHING DIFFICULTY, SEVERE, page 34.)

BLUISH LIPS

Bluish lips or cyanosis can indicate a reduced amount of oxygen in the bloodstream. (See BLUISH LIPS, page 470.)

DROOLING

The sudden onset of drooling or spitting, especially associated with difficulty in swallowing, can mean that your child has a serious infection of the tonsils, throat, or epiglottis (top part of the windpipe).

DEHYDRATION

Dehydration means that your child's body fluids are at a low level. Dehydration usually follows severe vomiting and/or diarrhea. Suspect dehydration if your child has not urinated in 8 hours, crying produces no tears, the mouth is dry rather than moist, or the soft spot in the skull is sunken. Dehydration requires immediate fluid replacement by mouth or intravenously.

BULGING SOFT SPOT

If the anterior fontanel is tense and bulging, the brain is under pressure. (See SOFT SPOT, BULGING, page 501.) Since the fontanel normally bulges with crying, assess it when your child is quiet and in an upright position.

STIFF NECK

To test for a stiff neck: With your child lying down, lift his head until the chin touches the middle of the chest. If he is resistant to this, place a toy or other object of interest on his belly so he will have to look down in order to see it. A stiff neck can be an early sign of meningitis.

INJURED NECK
Any injury to the neck, regardless of symptoms, should be discussed with your physician because of the risk of damage to the spinal cord.

PURPLE SPOTS
Purple or blood-red spots on the skin can be a sign of a serious bloodstream infection. Explained bruises don't count. (See PURPLE SPOTS, page 439.)

FEVER OVER 105° F
All the preceding symptoms are stronger indicators of serious illness than is the level of fever. All of them can occur with low fevers as well as high ones. Serious infections become a special concern only when the temperature rises above 105°F. In infants a rectal temperature less than 97.5°F (36.5°C) can also be serious.

SUICIDE CONCERNS
Because of the marked increase in suicide attempts in adolescence, parents should be alert to any of the following warning signs: preoccupation with thoughts of death or suicide; themes of death in writing or conversation; abrupt withdrawal from friends and family; abrupt loss of interest in favorite pastimes; abrupt decline in schoolwork; reckless risk-taking behavior; depressed mood. Either call the suicide hotline or your child's physician.

CHILD ABUSE CONCERNS
Call your child's physician or the child abuse hotline if you are afraid you might hurt your child, if someone has injured your child, or if someone has shaken your child. Child abuse has a tendency to escalate, so protect your child by seeking help early. Infants are at the greatest risk for a serious reinjury.

RELATED TOPICS

THE SICK NEWBORN: SUBTLE SYMPTOMS, (see page 125)
THE SICK INFANT: JUDGING THE SEVERITY OF ILLNESS, (see page 126)

RESUSCITATION (Mouth-to-Mouth Breathing)

If your child has stopped breathing or is gasping for breath (e.g., from choking, croup, carbon monoxide poisoning, drowning, or head trauma), you won't have time to read these guidelines. So read them now. And take an approved CPR (cardiopulmonary resuscitation) or first aid course. You can't learn external cardiac massage purely from reading. Fortunately, more than 90 percent of children who stop breathing still have a pulse and heartbeat (unlike heart attack victims) and they need only artificial respiration to revive them. The steps in mouth-to-mouth breathing are as follows:

PREPARATION

Rescue Squad • Have someone call a rescue squad (911) immediately. You're going to need help.

Clear the Mouth • Look for any gum, food, foreign object, or loose orthodontic retainer. If present, remove them with your fingers or a Heimlich maneuver (see CHOKING, *Heimlich Maneuver*, page 11.) If any liquid is in the mouth, remove it by turning your child on one side and using gravity.

Position the Head • With your child lying faceup, put a folded blanket or towel (½ inch to 2 inches thick) directly under the back of your child's head. Do not put anything under the shoulders or neck. This "sniffing," head-forward position opens the airway and closes the esophagus (thereby keeping air out of the stomach). The jaw and chin can also be pulled forward to open the airway more. (Note: Some adolescents and adults may require slight extension of the neck for optimal breathing.)

MOUTH-TO-MOUTH BREATHING

Pinch your child's nostrils closed with one hand and seal the mouth with yours. (In small children, an adult can often seal both the child's nostrils and mouth with his mouth.) Blow air with a steady pressure into your child's lungs until you see the chest rise (the smaller the child, the smaller the volume of your puff). Then remove your mouth and your child will automatically blow the air out without any help. During this time, take a breath and refill your lungs. Repeat this at the following rates:

- Under 2 years old: 20 times per minute (once every 3 seconds)
- 2 to 12 years old: 15 times per minute (once every 4 seconds)
- Over 12 years old: 12 times per minute (once every 5 seconds)

Occasionally, take several quite deep breaths to bring plenty of oxygen into your lungs. (Note: If it is impossible to open the victim's mouth, cover the mouth and give mouth-to-nose breathing.) If 4 or 5 breaths don't move the chest, assume the airway is blocked and perform a Heimlich maneuver 6 to 10 times in rapid succession (see CHOKING, p. 10).

CHOKING

Choking is the coughing spasm and sputtering that follows getting liquids or solids on the vocal cords or into the airway. Most children choke on liquids that go down the wrong way or mucus from sniffing back nasal secretions. Temporary choking following vomiting is also common. The child's cough reflex will clear the windpipe of aspirated liquid within 10 to 30 seconds. Complete blockage occurs when solid food (a piece of hot dog, for instance) or a foreign object becomes lodged in the voice box. (It can also occur with severe croup.) Under these conditions, the child is unable to breathe, cry, or speak. The child will be in a state of panic, and if the obstruction isn't relieved in 1 or 2 minutes, the child will pass out and have a convulsion due to lack of oxygen.

FIRST AID FOR CHOKING
Call the rescue squad (911) immediately in all cases of choking on a solid object. In general, choking on liquids is temporary and harmless. For liquids, call the rescue squad if your child turns blue, becomes limp, or passes out.

Encourage Coughing • As long as your child is breathing and coughing, do nothing except encourage him to cough the material up by himself. Reassure him that it will come out. The main purpose of your child's cough reflex is to clear the windpipe. Don't offer anything to drink, unless your child is choking on something dry and flaky. In general, fluids just worsen the problem by taking up some of the space needed for the passage of air.

Heimlich Maneuver If Breathing Stops in a Child over 1 Year Old •
If your child can't breathe, cough, or make a sound, proceed
with high abdominal thrusts. Grasp your child from behind,
just below the lower ribs but above the navel, in bear-hug
fashion. Make a fist with one hand and fold your other hand
over it. Give a sudden upward jerk at a 45-degree angle to try
to squeeze all the air out of the chest and pop the lodged
object out of the windpipe. Repeat this upward abdominal
thrust 6 to 10 times in rapid succession. If your child is too
heavy for you to suspend from your arms, lay him on his back
on the floor. Put your hands on both sides of the abdomen,
just below the ribs, and apply sudden, strong bursts of upward pressure.

Back Blows and Chest Compressions for Children Under 1 Year Old •
If your infant is under 1 year old, use back blows *before*
applying the Heimlich maneuver. Place him or her facedown
in a 60-degree incline over your knees or on your forearm.
(You need gravity to help propel the object out.) Deliver 4
hard blows with the heel of your hand between the shoulder
blades in rapid succession. If breathing has not resumed, lay
your child on the floor and apply 4 rapid chest compressions
over the lower breast bone (sternum) using 2 fingers. (These
revised first aid measures were recommended by the American Academy of Pediatrics in July, 1986.)

Resuscitation If Your Child Passes Out • The rescue squad should
be on its way. Quickly open the mouth and look inside with a
light to see if there is an object that can be removed with a
sweep of your finger or a tweezers (usually there is not).
Don't put your fingers into your child's mouth unless you can
already see the object and think you can sweep or pull it out.
Probing blindly can wedge an object deeper into the voice
box (larynx). If you know how, begin mouth-to-mouth breathing. (Otherwise, see the guideline on RESUSCITATION, page 9.)
Air can usually be forced past the foreign object. If mouth-to-
mouth breathing doesn't move the chest, repeat the abdominal thrusts or chest compressions.

PREVENTION OF CHOKING ON FOODS AND OTHER OBJECTS
Choking can be life-threatening, so try to prevent its happening again. Choking on foods kills as many children each year
as accidental poisonings.

- Foods that are likely to be aspirated into the lungs are nuts of any kind, sunflower seeds, orange seeds, cherry pits, watermelon seeds, gum, hard candies, popcorn, raw carrot, raw peas, and raw celery. These hard foods should not be given to children under 4 years of age because molars are needed to chew them and knowledge is needed to spit them out.

- The soft foods that most commonly cause fatal choking by completely blocking the windpipe are hot dogs, sausage, grapes, and caramels (especially if the child is in a hurry). These dangerous soft foods must be chopped up before serving.

- Warn baby-sitters and older siblings not to share these foods with small children.

- In general, teach your child to chew all foods thoroughly before attempting to swallow them.

- Don't allow your child to fill his cheeks with food like a chipmunk.

- An especially dangerous time is the morning after parties when some of these foods may be found on the floor by a toddler. Clean up early.

- Choking on a rubber balloon is the leading cause of choking deaths from objects other than foods. Most incidents occur while children are chewing on a deflated balloon and suddenly inhale it. Warn your child never to chew or suck on pieces of rubber balloons. Even teenagers have died from this freak accident. Chewing on an inflated balloon is also dangerous because it could burst. While Mylar helium balloons are safer, rubber balloons are fine when used with supervision.

- Don't give a young child a toy with small, detachable parts. In 5 minutes you'll find the missing part in the mouth (if you're lucky).

- Periodically check your child's environment for small objects (anything with a diameter less than 1.25 inch) that your child could choke on. Ask older children to protect younger siblings by checking the carpet for missing small pieces from toys or games.

- Dispose of button batteries carefully.

- Remind people of all ages not to run or play sports with gum or other material in their mouths.

ALLERGIC REACTION, SEVERE (ANAPHYLACTIC REACTION)

SYMPTOMS AND CHARACTERISTICS

- Immediate symptoms within 30 minutes
- Wheezing, croupy cough, hoarseness, or difficulty breathing
- Tightness in the chest or throat
- Widespread hives, swelling, or itching
- Dizziness or passing out
- Previous allergic reaction to the same item is added evidence
- Usually caused by a bee-sting, drug, or food

FIRST AID

Call your physician immediately, even if you're not certain if a severe reaction is in progress. Call the rescue squad if your child is having difficulty breathing or passes out. Have your child lie down with the feet elevated to prevent shock.

Epinephrine and Antihistamines • If you have an anaphylactic kit, give an injection of epinephrine (adrenaline) 0.01 ml per kilogram of body weight (a 20-pound child gets 0.1 ml, 40 pounds gets 0.2 ml, 60 pounds gets 0.3 ml, and adults get 0.4 ml). Inject it into the subcutaneous (fat) layer by angling the needle about 45 degrees. Check to see whether you have an antihistamine or cold medication containing antihistamines at home. If you do, give 1 dose immediately by mouth in addition to the epinephrine.

Bee Sting Treatment—For Severe Reactions • If a stinger is still present in the wound, remove it. Do this by scraping it off with the edge of a knife blade or credit card rather than squeezing it. Once a reaction has begun, a tourniquet is not helpful, according to the American College of Emergency Physicians in 1985. Rub the bite for 15 minutes with a cotton ball soaked in a meat tenderizer/water solution while seeking medical care.

Transportation • If you can't reach your physician and your child is stable, go to the nearest emergency room (see EMERGENCY TRANSPORTATION, page 4).

PREVENTION OF SEVERE ALLERGIC REACTIONS

Children with anaphylactic reactions need to be evaluated by an allergist. Since the reactions can be fatal, you should keep emergency kits containing epinephrine preloaded in a syringe at home and in the glove compartment of your car. (These are available by prescription only.)

All these children must carry a card in pocket or purse listing their name, parent's home and work phone numbers, physician's name, physician's phone number, and type of allergy. Ideally, your child should wear a medical identification necklace or bracelet that records the insect, food, or drug allergy. Some can be found in pharmacies. They can also be ordered from Medic Alert Foundation, P.O. Box 1009, Turlock, CA 95381, or National Identification Company, P.O. Box 9438, Denver, CO 80223.

BITES, ANIMAL OR HUMAN

The following three types of bites are covered in the next few pages. Go directly to the one that applies to your child.

BITES, WILD ANIMAL
BITES, PET ANIMAL
BITES, HUMAN

BITES, WILD ANIMAL

There are two basic types of wild-animal bites: rabies-prone bites and safe ones.

Rabies-Prone Bites • Rabies is a fatal disease. Bites or scratches from a bat, skunk, raccoon, fox, coyote, or large wild animal are especially dangerous. Squirrels rarely carry rabies. These animals can transmit rabies even if they themselves have no symptoms.

Safe Wild-Animal Bites • Rodents such as mice, rats, moles, gophers, chipmunks, and rabbits fortunately are considered free of rabies. In the Southwest, prairie dogs can carry plague, and people should not handle them. Campers should avoid placing bedrolls over rodent burrows.

CALL YOUR CHILD'S PHYSICIAN IMMEDIATELY IF

• The bite was by a dangerous wild animal.

• The bite penetrated the skin (even a puncture from one tooth).

• You have other urgent questions.

FIRST AID FOR SUSPECTED RABIES CONTACT

Washing the wound immediately with soap and water for 10 to 15 minutes is critical. If possible, flush the wound thoroughly under a faucet. If a wild animal is still on the premises, call the police department immediately. If the animal is captured or dead, avoid all contact with it. Saliva from a rabid animal can cause rabies by getting into a cut. In the future, teach your child to avoid direct contact with any wild animal (even healthy ones).

BITES, PET ANIMAL

Most of these bites are from dogs or cats. Bites from domestic animals such as horses can be handled using these guidelines. Small indoor pets (such as gerbils, hamsters, guinea pigs, and white mice) are at no risk for rabies. Dogs and cats are free of rabies in many metropolitan areas. The main risk in pet bites is serious wound infection, not rabies. Cat bites become infected five times more frequently than dog bites. Puncture wounds are more likely to become infected than cuts. Claw wounds are treated the same as bite wounds, since they are contaminated with saliva.

CALL YOUR CHILD'S PHYSICIAN IMMEDIATELY IF

• The teeth or claws went through the skin (i.e., a puncture wound). Caution: Cat bites of the hand can become infected rapidly and need prompt attention.

• The skin is split open (i.e., a laceration) and probably needs sutures.

• There are superficial cuts *and* the animal seemed to be sick, the attack was unprovoked, or the animal was a stray.

• There are superficial cuts *and* the animal is one without rabies shots. (Exception: a known, healthy, friendly dog who was teased or became frightened.)

• You have other urgent questions.

HOME CARE FOR PET-ANIMAL BITES

First Aid for Puncture Wound or Laceration (Deep Cut) • Wash the area with a liquid soap and running water for 10 minutes before going to the physician's office. Immediate, vigorous flushing under a faucet is the best protection against wound infection. Also check your child's immunization status for tetanus.

Scrapes and Superficial Cuts • For wounds that don't penetrate the skin, wash the area with lots of water and a liquid soap for 5 minutes. You can leave it exposed to the air, or put a dressing on it for 12 hours if it's on an area that easily gets dirty. No antiseptic is necessary.

Observation of the Pet • If there is any possibility of rabies, the pet should be carefully watched for any signs of sickness and isolated from contact with humans for 10 days. If the animal belongs to another family and they are not cooperative, report the incident to the police so they can deal with the problem. Too many pets are left to roam without supervision.

Call Your Child's Physician Later If

• The wound begins to look infected.

• The pain increases after the second day.

• The redness increases after the second day.

PREVENTION OF PET-ANIMAL BITES

• Choose a pet that is friendly and tolerates children. Pit bull terriers are extremely dangerous. German shepherds, Dobermans, and St. Bernards are not good dogs for children.

• Teach your dog the commands of "down" and "sit." Teach your child how to give these commands.

• Teach your children not to touch strange animals, break up dogfights, go near a dog that's eating, or touch a sleeping dog.

• Children under 4 years of age should always be supervised around dogs and cats. Never allow them to tease a pet.

• Infants under 1 year of age should never be left alone in a room with a pet. Some have been attacked, possibly due to the pet's jealousy. There are rare reports of a sleeping newborn being *smothered* by a cat.

• Protect your pet against rabies by yearly rabies shots. The first shot is normally given when your pet is 3 to 4 months old.

• Teach your child not to run from a strange dog. Rapid movement can trigger a dog's predatory instinct.

• Never keep wild animals as pets. For example, ferrets have caused disfiguring bites to the faces of young children.

BITES, HUMAN

Most of these bites occur during fighting. In younger children, the bite is usually deliberate and on the arm or hand. In older children, sometimes a fist is cut when it strikes a tooth. Human bites are more likely to become infected than any other animal bite. Bites on the hands are at increased risk of complications.

CALL YOUR CHILD'S PHYSICIAN IMMEDIATELY IF

• The teeth went through the skin.

• The skin is split open and probably needs sutures.

• You have other urgent questions.

HOME CARE FOR HUMAN BITES

First Aid for Puncture Wound or Laceration • Wash the area with a liquid soap and running water for 10 minutes before going to the physician's office. Also check your child's immunization status for tetanus.

Scrapes and Superficial Cuts • Wash the area with lots of water and a liquid soap for 5 minutes. You can leave it exposed to the air, or put a bandage on it for 12 hours if it's on an area that easily gets dirty. No antiseptic is necessary.

Children Who Bite • See the guideline on BITING, p. 299.

Call Your Child's Physician Later If

• The wound begins to look infected.

• The pain increases after the second day.

• The redness increases after the second day.

BITES, INSECT

The following 4 types of insect bites and stings are covered. A bite involves biting with the insect's mouth parts and removing a drop of blood from the human. A sting involves injecting a poison into the human from the insect's stinger. Go directly to the one that applies to your child.

BEE STINGS (see page 18)
ITCHY INSECT BITES (see page 19)
PAINFUL INSECT BITES (see page 21)
TICK BITES (see page 21)

If your child has difficulty breathing, difficulty swallowing, hives, or other worrisome symptoms within 30 minutes following an insect bite (especially with stings) or had a previous severe allergic reaction, turn directly to ALLERGIC REACTION, SEVERE, page 13.

BEE STINGS

Your child was stung by a honeybee, bumblebee, hornet, paper wasp, or yellow jacket. Over 95 percent of stings are from yellow jackets. These stings cause immediate painful red bumps. While the pain is usually better in 2 hours, the swelling may increase for up to 24 hours. Multiple stings (more than 10) can cause vomiting, diarrhea, a headache, and fever. This is a toxic reaction related to the amount of venom received (i.e., not an allergic reaction). A sting on the tongue can cause swelling that interferes with breathing.

CALL YOUR CHILD'S PHYSICIAN IMMEDIATELY IF

• Breathing or swallowing is difficult.

• Hives are present.

• There are 10 or more stings.

• A sting is inside the mouth.

HOME CARE

Treatment • If you see a little black dot in the wound, the stinger is still present. (This means your child was stung by a honeybee.) Remove it by scraping it off with the edge of a knife blade or credit card. If only a small fragment remains, use a tweezers or sterile needle just as you would to remove a sliver. Then rub each sting with a meat-tenderizer-and-water solution. This will neutralize the venom and relieve the pain. If meat tenderizer is not available, apply an ice cube while you obtain some.

Call Your Child's Physician During Office Hours If

- You can't remove the stinger.

- The swelling continues to spread after 24 hours.

- Swelling of the hand (or foot) spreads past the wrist (or ankle).

- You want the sting looked at.

PREVENTION OF BEE STINGS

Some bee stings can be prevented by avoiding gardens, clover fields, orchards in bloom, perfumes, and going barefoot. Also teach your young children how to identify nests. Insect repellents are not effective against these stinging insects.

ITCHY INSECT BITES

Bites of mosquitoes, chiggers (harvest mites), fleas, and bedbugs usually cause itchy red bumps. The size of the swelling following a mosquito bite means very little. Mosquito bites near the eye always cause massive swelling for 2 days. Clues to a bite's being due to a mosquito are itchiness, a central raised dot in the swelling, bites on surfaces not covered by clothing, summertime, and the child's being an infant. Some mosquito bites in sensitive children form hard lumps that last for months. In contrast to mosquitoes, fleas and bedbugs don't fly; therefore, they crawl under clothing to nibble. Flea bites often turn into little blisters in young children. Some children appeal to these insects more than other children and repeatedly acquire numerous bites.

HOME CARE

Treatment • Apply calamine lotion or a baking soda solution. If the itch is severe (as with chiggers), apply nonprescription ½ percent hydrocortisone cream. Oral antihistamines do not help.

Another way to reduce the itch is to apply firm, sharp, direct, steady pressure to the bite for 10 seconds. A fingernail, pen cap, or other object can be used.

Encourage your child not to scratch because it increases the itching. Encourage your child not to pick at the bites or they will leave marks and could become infected.

Call Your Child's Physician Later If

- Itching interferes with sleep.

- The bites become infected due to scratching.

PREVENTION OF ITCHY INSECT BITES

Mosquitoes and Chiggers • Many of these bites can be prevented by applying an insect repellent sparingly to the clothing or exposed skin before going outdoors or into the woods. Repellents are essential for infants (especially those less than 1 year of age), because their inability to bat away the pesky critters leaves them helpless targets.

Precautions with DEET Insect Repellents • Excessive application of repellents containing DEET can cause seizures or coma through absorption across the skin. Younger children have experienced reactions from licking it off the skin. To prevent harmful reactions, take the following precautions:

- Apply repellent mainly to clothing and shoes.

- Don't apply it to the hands, to prevent contact with the mouth or eyes.

- Don't apply it to areas of sunburn or other rashes because absorption is increased in these areas.

- Warn older children who apply their own repellent that 3 or 4 drops can protect the body.

- Since one application lasts 4 to 8 hours, apply twice a day.

- If it's applied on the skin, wash it off after coming indoors.

Bedbugs • Beds and baseboards can be sprayed with 1 percent malathion, which can be obtained from any garden supply store. Keep young children away from the area until it dries, because this substance is somewhat poisonous. You may need to call in an exterminator.

Fleas • Usually you will find the fleas on your dog or cat. If the bites started after you moved into a different house or apartment, fleas from the previous owner's pet are the most common cause. Fleas can live in carpeting for several months without a meal. Fleas can often be removed by bringing a dog or cat inside the house for 2 hours to collect the fleas—they prefer the dog or cat to living in the carpet. In either case, apply flea powder or soap to your animal outdoors. Careful vacuuming will usually capture any remaining fleas. Malathion bug spray (see BEDBUGS, above) can be used for persistent cases.

PAINFUL INSECT BITES

Bites of horseflies, deerflies, sandflies, gnats, fire ants, harvester ants, cone-nosed bugs, blister beetles, and centipedes usually cause a painful (sometimes burning) red bump. Within a few hours, fire ant bites change to blisters or pimples.

HOME CARE

Treatment • Rub the bite area with a cotton ball soaked in meat-tenderizer-and-water solution. This will relieve the pain. Ammonia rubbed on the area is helpful if you have no meat tenderizer. If these substances are not available, an ice cube applied to the area may help.

Call Your Child's Physician Later If

• The bites are from fire ants.

• Pain interferes with sleep.

• The bites become infected.

PREVENTION

Apply insect repellent sparingly to exposed parts and clothing. (See precautions on page 20.)

TICK BITES

A tick is a brown insect that attaches to the skin and sucks blood for 3 to 6 days. The bite is usually painless and also doesn't itch. Therefore, your child will usually be unaware of its presence. The wood tick (or dog tick) that transmits Rocky Mountain spotted fever and Colorado tick fever is up to ½ inch in size. The deer tick that transmits Lyme disease is the size of a pinhead.

Lyme Disease • Lyme disease is the disease most frequently spread by a tick bite. About 7,000 cases are reported each year in our country. It's not carried by the usual ticks, only by the tiny deer ticks, which are harder to notice. In most states, only 2 percent of ticks carry the disease. But in the New England states, Wisconsin, and Minnesota, up to 50 percent of ticks are infected. Within 1 to 3 weeks of the bite, 70 percent to 80 percent of people develop a unique rash where they are bitten. The rash (*erythema migrans*) consists of a red ring or bull's-eye that expands in size. The rash is neither painful nor itchy. At this stage, Lyme disease is easily treatable with an antibiotic. So watch for the rash, but don't panic. Complications are rare. It's not yet time to give up picnics, hikes, and camping because of this pest.

HOME CARE

Tick Removal • The simplest and quickest way to remove a tick is to pull it off. Use a tweezers to grasp the tick as close to the skin as possible (try to get a grip on its head). Apply a steady upward traction until it releases its grip. Do not twist the tick or jerk it suddenly because these maneuvers can break off the tick's head or mouth parts. Do not squeeze the tweezers to the point of crushing the tick, because the secretions released may spread disease. If you have no tweezers, pull the tick off in the same way, using your fingers, a loop of thread around the jaws, or a needle between the jaws for traction. Some tiny ticks need to be scraped off with a knife blade or the edge of a credit card.

If the body is removed but the head is left in the skin, it must be removed. Use a sterile needle (as you would to remove a sliver). Dispose of the tick by returning it to nature or flushing it down the toilet. You don't need to save the tick for positive identification by your doctor; he's seen more than his share of them. If you are unsure if it's a dog tick or a deer tick, measure it but don't save it. Don't crush ticks with your hands, since this practice increases your chances of getting a disease. Wash the wound and your hands with soap and water after removal.

A recent study by Dr. G. R. Needham showed that embedded ticks do not back out when covered with petroleum jelly, fingernail polish, or rubbing alcohol. We used to think that this would block the tick's breathing pores and take its mind off eating. Unfortunately, ticks breathe only a few times per hour. The application of a hot match to the tick failed to cause it to detach, and also carried the risk of inducing the tick to vomit infected secretions into the wound. (Yuck!)

Call Your Child's Physician Later If

- You can't remove the tick.

- The tick's head remains embedded.
  (Note: If the tick is moving, you got it all out.)

- A fever or rash occurs in the week following the bite.

- You think your child has some of the symptoms of Lyme disease.

- You think your child has been bitten by a deer tick and it was probably attached for more than 18 hours. (Note: You do not need to call if your child was bitten by a tick and it was removed promptly.)

PREVENTION

Ticks like to hide in underbrush and shrubbery. They don't drop out of the trees; they come aboard from ground level. Children and adults who are hiking in tick-infested areas should wear long clothing and tuck the end of the pants into the socks. Apply an insect repellent to shoes and socks. During the hike, perform tick checks using a buddy system every 2 to 3 hours to remove ticks on the clothing or exposed skin. Immediately after the hike or at least once a day, do a bare-skin check. A brisk shower at the end of a hike will also remove any tick that isn't firmly attached. Because the bite is painless and doesn't itch, the child will usually be unaware of its presence. Favorite hiding places for ticks are in the hair, so carefully check the scalp, neck, armpit, and groin. Removing ticks promptly may prevent infection, because transmission of Lyme disease requires 18 to 24 hours of feeding. Also, the tick is easier to remove before it becomes firmly attached. To prevent the spread of Lyme disease from your dog, wash him with an antitick soap during the spring and summer months.

Perform tick checks on him if he accompanies you on a hike. Pull off any that are found.

BITES, MARINE ANIMAL

The following five types of marine bites are covered in the next few pages. Go directly to the one that applies to your child.

JELLYFISH OR PORTUGUESE MAN-OF-WAR REACTIONS
VENOMOUS FISH REACTIONS (as from stingray, stonefish, scorpion fish, catfish)
CUTS OR LACERATIONS (as from moray eels, sharks, barracudas)
SEA URCHIN STINGS
SHOCKS (e.g., from electric eels)

Clearly, all of these unpleasantries occur in saltwater. But the dangers of the deep are a small price to pay for the rejuvenating qualities of an ocean vacation. Go to a beach with lifeguards and observe all warning signs or flags.

JELLYFISH OR PORTUGUESE MAN-OF-WAR REACTIONS

The jellyfish and Portuguese man-of-war have long, stinging tentacles (called nematocysts). Fragments of tentacles washed up on the beach after a storm can still cause sharp stings. They produce lines of redness and burning pain. Sometimes they cause generalized symptoms of weakness, dizziness, nausea, and headache. Sea anemones (sea nettle) cause similar local reactions for 24 to 48 hours.

FIRST AID

- Wipe off any stinging tentacles with a thick towel or sand. Be careful to protect your hands, since the stingers can even penetrate gloves. Rinse the wound with seawater.

- Neutralize the venom with the continuous application of alcohol (in any available form) for 30 minutes. Meat tenderizer is a second-choice agent for deactivating the toxin.

- Apply a ½ percent hydrocortisone cream (no prescription needed) 4 times a day for a few days to reduce itching.

CALL A PHYSICIAN IMMEDIATELY IF

• Any generalized symptoms have occurred.

VENOMOUS FISH REACTIONS

These creatures always cause localized pain and redness. They also commonly cause weakness, sweating, fever, vomiting, muscle cramps, paralysis, or even shock. The stinging fish usually have venom in dorsal spines. The stingray has one or more venomous spines on its tail. Because of its powerful strike, the stingray often also causes a laceration.

FIRST AID

Fortunately, the venom of all these fish can be destroyed by heat.

• Rinse the area with lots of seawater to dilute the venom.

• Remove any particles of stingray spine left in the wound.

• Immerse the damaged extremity in water as hot as can be tolerated (but under 120°F) until the pain completely subsides (30 to 90 minutes).

CALL A PHYSICIAN IMMEDIATELY IF

• Any generalized symptoms have developed.

For stingrays:

• The skin is split open.

• The barb needs to be removed.

CUTS OR LACERATIONS, MARINE ANIMAL

Some fish cause a bite mark of varying severity without injecting any venom.

CALL A PHYSICIAN IMMEDIATELY IF

• Bleeding won't stop after 10 minutes of direct pressure.

• The skin is split open.

• A puncture wound is present.

FIRST AID

Wash the area with lots of seawater. Later, wash with soap and water for 10 minutes.

SEA URCHIN STINGS

A sea urchin usually causes localized burning pain if part of a venomous spine breaks off in the skin. If not removed, it may be dissolved by the body or it may persist and cause irritation and swelling (a "foreign-body reaction").

FIRST AID

First, stop the flow of venom by pulling out any spine that protrudes from the skin. Neutralize the venom with a meat tenderizer/water solution or alcohol for 30 minutes. (Unfortunately, none of these are of proven benefit.) Then wash the area off carefully with soap and water. If any large fragment of a sea urchin barb remains beneath the skin, try to remove it with a sterile needle and tweezers as you would for a splinter. A mild acid such as vinegar can dissolve small pieces of spine that you can't get out. If purplish discoloration remains after the spine is removed, it's merely due to dye from the spine and is unimportant.

SHOCKS, MARINE ANIMAL

Your child may feel shocked, stunned, or partially paralyzed after contact with an electric eel.

FIRST AID

Reassurance should be offered. Your child will be feeling and acting normal in 20 to 30 minutes. No treatment is necessary except lying down with the feet elevated.

BITES, SNAKE

The following three types of snakebites are covered in the next few pages. Go directly to the one that applies to your child.

SNAKEBITES, POISONOUS
SNAKEBITES, NONPOISONOUS
SNAKEBITES, UNIDENTIFIED

SNAKEBITES, POISONOUS

In the United States the poisonous snakes are rattlers, copperheads, cottonmouths (water moccasins), and coral snakes. Over 90 percent of snakebites occur on the leg. In about 30 percent of poisonous snakebites, luckily, no venom is injected (dry bites). If the venom was injected (envenomation), the fang marks will begin to burn, hurt, and swell within 5 minutes. Therefore, begin first aid only if these signs develop.

CALL YOUR CHILD'S PHYSICIAN IMMEDIATELY IN ALL CASES

FIRST AID

Transportation • Go to the nearest hospital emergency room as rapidly as possible. The most important part of therapy is antivenin, and it needs to be given within 4 hours. Have your child lie quietly, and carry him or her when necessary to reduce absorption of the venom. If the bite is on the arm, remove any rings or bracelets before swelling occurs.

Incision and Suction • If you are more than 60 minutes from the hospital, you are certain the snake was poisonous (except for coral snakes), and the fang marks begin to swell or hurt, take 10 minutes to try to remove some of the venom. Use a knife or razor blade, preferably cleaned with alcohol or a flame. Make a single cut in the long direction of each fang mark (don't make cross incisions), ¼ to ½ inch long and deep enough to go through the skin to the depth of the bite mark (about ⅛ inch). First squeeze out the venom for 1 to 2 minutes. Then try suction with a suction cup or your mouth for at least 5 minutes. After suction, wash the incisions vigorously with soap and water. Suction is not useful after 30 minutes.

Lymphatic Tourniquet for Bites on Arm or Leg • If you are more than 2 hours from the hospital, put a lymphatic tourniquet between the bite and the heart, at least 2 inches above the bite (but not around a joint). Use a wide band such as elastic wrap or a stocking. Make it snug but not tight enough to stop blood flow in the veins or arteries. If the veins stand out, the tourniquet is too tight. If the hand or foot turns white and cold, or the pulse disappears, the tourniquet is much too tight and may damage normal tissue. Once applied, the American Red Cross recommends you not release the tourniquet until after antivenin is given. Never apply ice, since ice can cause frostbite, which increases the risk of tissue damage.

SNAKEBITES, NONPOISONOUS

Most nonpoisonous bites are from garter snakes during attempted capture or from pet snakes. All are harmless.

HOME CARE FOR NONPOISONOUS SNAKEBITES

Treatment • Usually, the small teeth of a snake leave a scrape that doesn't even puncture the skin. Wash it well with soap and water. A bandage isn't necessary. If the skin is punctured, call in for a tetanus booster if your child hasn't had one in over 5 years.

Call Your Child's Physician Later If

• Your child develops any symptoms in the next 6 hours.

SNAKEBITES, UNIDENTIFIED

Sometimes the snake has disappeared by the time the parent has been notified. In other cases, the snake has been killed but is hard to identify. (If your child needs to be seen by a physician, bring the snake with you after you're certain it is dead.) Most bites are from harmless snakes, and you can assume this to be the case unless the bite mark burns or swells within 5 minutes.

CALL YOUR CHILD'S PHYSICIAN IMMEDIATELY IF

• One or two puncture (fang) marks are present.

• The bite area burns or hurts.

• The bite area is swollen.

• Blood blisters or purple spots are present in the bite area.

• Your child is acting sick in any way.

• You have other urgent questions.

HOME CARE FOR UNIDENTIFIED SNAKEBITES

See *Home Care for Nonpoisonous Snakebites*, above.

BITES, SPIDER OR SCORPION

The following five types of bites are covered in the next few pages. Go directly to the one that applies to your child.

SCORPION BITES
SPIDER BITES, BLACK WIDOW
SPIDER BITES, BROWN RECLUSE
SPIDER BITES, NONDANGEROUS
SPIDER BITES, UNIDENTIFIED

SCORPION BITES

Scorpions belong to the same class as spiders—called the arachnids. They are found in desert areas. About twenty different kinds occur in the southwestern United States. Scorpions have a poisonous stinger in the tail. Over 90 percent of scorpion bites are on the hands. Most of the bites cause symptoms similar to those of black widow spiders, namely immediate local pain with slight swelling. In the United States, only one scorpion *(C. sculpturatus)* can cause serious or fatal reactions. It is small (1 to 3 inches), uniformly yellow, and without stripes.

CALL YOUR CHILD'S PHYSICIAN IMMEDIATELY IN ALL CASES

FIRST AID

See *First Aid* for black widow spider bites, below.

SPIDER BITES, BLACK WIDOW

The black widow is a shiny, jet-black spider with long legs and a red (or orange) hourglass-shaped marking on its underside. It is about an inch in length, including the legs, and is easy to recognize. The black widow and brown recluse spiders are the only highly venomous spiders in North America. Black widow bites cause immediate local pain and swelling. Because the symptoms begin rapidly, the spider is usually still in the vicinity. Muscle cramps also occur for 6 to 24 hours. They rarely cause death (except in younger children or when the victim is bitten by several spiders).

CALL YOUR CHILD'S PHYSICIAN IMMEDIATELY IN ALL CASES

FIRST AID

Apply an ice cube or ice pack to the bite for 20 minutes to reduce the spread of the venom. Then go to the nearest emergency room or wherever your physician directs you. A tourniquet is not helpful. Antivenin is available for severe bites in young children, and other medicines can relieve muscle pain.

SPIDER BITES, BROWN RECLUSE

The brown recluse is brown, has long legs, and has a dark, violin-shaped marking on its head. It is about ½ inch in length, including the legs, and is difficult to recognize. Brown recluse spider bites cause delayed local pain and blister formation in 4 to 8 hours. The center of the reaction becomes bluish and depressed (i.e., the opposite of swollen). The skin damage may require grafting. The bites are rarely fatal.

CALL YOUR CHILD'S PHYSICIAN IMMEDIATELY IN ALL CASES

FIRST AID

Wash the bite thoroughly with soap and water. Bring the spider with you if possible. (Brown recluse spiders may be hard to identify.)

SPIDER BITES, NONDANGEROUS

More than fifty types of spiders in the United States can cause local but nondangerous reactions (such as golden garden spiders). The bites are painful and mildly swollen for 1 or 2 days, much like a bee sting. In fact, spiders are probably responsible for many of the single, unexplained, tender bites that occur on children during the night. (Mosquito bites, on the other hand, are usually multiple and itchy rather than painful.) Many people are unduly concerned about the tarantula, a black, hairy spider that is 2 to 3 inches long. The tarantula is not dangerous. Its mild venom also causes a local reaction resembling a bee sting.

HOME CARE FOR NONDANGEROUS SPIDER BITES

Treatment • Wash the bite thoroughly with soap and water. Then rub the area with a cotton ball soaked with a meat tenderizer/

water solution for 15 minutes. If meat tenderizer is not available, an ice cube applied to the area often helps.

Call Your Child's Physician Later If

• Muscle spasm occurs in the bite area.

• The bite turns into a blister or purple spot.

• A sore occurs that doesn't heal.

• Other new symptoms occur.

SPIDER BITES, UNIDENTIFIED

Although most of these bites are harmless, an occasional one may be due to a black widow spider.

CALL YOUR CHILD'S PHYSICIAN IMMEDIATELY IF

• The bite area burns or hurts.

• Muscle spasm occurs in the bite area.

• The bite has turned into a blister or purple spot.

• Your child is acting sick.

Try to capture the spider (dead or alive) in a jar and bring it along to the physician's office. Don't bludgeon it beyond recognition.

HOME CARE FOR UNIDENTIFIED SPIDER BITES

Treatment • Wash the bite thoroughly with soap and water.

Call Your Child's Physician Later If

• A sore occurs that doesn't heal.

• Any new symptoms develop, especially muscle spasm in the area of the bite.

PREVENTION OF SPIDER BITES

• Don't work in woodpiles, rock piles, rubbish heaps, or dark corners of outdoor buildings without wearing gloves.

• Spray with insecticides any area where black widow spiders are seen.

• Spiders normally come indoors with the onset of cold weather. Prevent this fall migration into your house by repairing cracks and spraying near outside doors with insecticide.

BLEEDING, SEVERE

This guideline covers arterial (from an artery) bleeding or major venous (from a vein) bleeding. In arterial bleeding, the blood pumps or spurts from the wound with each heartbeat. In major venous bleeding, the blood just runs out of the wound at a steady rate. The arterial bleeding is bright red compared to the darker red of venous bleeding. Minor bleeding (from capillaries), however, can also be bright red. For minor bleeding, see the guidelines on TRAUMA, SKIN, page 80, or NOSEBLEED, page 544.

FIRST AID FOR ARTERIAL BLEEDING

Prevent Shock • Have your child lie down with the feet elevated 10 to 12 inches to prevent symptoms of shock (low blood pressure). If your child is pale and the hands and feet are cold, shock is imminent.

Apply Direct Pressure • If you know the arterial pressure points, apply strong, direct pressure to the artery between the wound and the heart until help arrives. If you do not know the arterial pressure points, place several sterile dressings or the first clean cloth at hand (towels, sheets, shirts, or handkerchiefs) over the wound and apply direct pressure immediately. The pressure must be forceful and continuous, often applied with the palm of the hand. Act quickly, because the ongoing blood loss can cause shock.

Rescue Squad • Have someone call a rescue squad (911) immediately while you tend to the bleeding. (See EMERGENCY TRANS-PORTATION, page 4.)

Arterial Tourniquet • A tourniquet is needed only under the following unusual circumstances: the bleeding is arterial; it is from the arm or leg; it cannot be controlled by direct pressure (as with an amputated or mangled limb); and the patient is located at a significant distance from emergency facilities. A tourniquet should be avoided if at all possible since it can damage the uninjured tissues. In 1985 the American College of Emergency Physicians recommended that once an arterial tourniquet is applied, it should be released for 15 minutes of every hour. During this time, direct pressure must be used to prevent excessive blood loss. Apply a tourniquet as follows:

- If you have a blood pressure cuff, use it as a tourniquet. The second choice is a tight elastic bandage. If these items are unavailable, use a piece of cloth (such as a bandanna or stocking).

- Tie it around the limb above the wound.

- Lay a 4- to 5-inch piece of wood or an eating utensil above the knot and tie the tourniquet again.

- Twist the wooden or metal handle until the tourniquet is tight enough to stop the bleeding.

- Tie the stick in place so it won't unwind before you reach the hospital.

FIRST AID FOR VENOUS BLEEDING

Prevent Shock • Have your child lie down with the feet elevated to prevent symptoms of shock. If your child is pale and the hands and feet are cold, shock is imminent. Act quickly.

Apply Direct Pressure

- Place two or three sterile dressings (or a clean towel or sheet) over the wound immediately.

- Apply direct pressure to the wound for 8 to 10 minutes, using your entire hand. Direct pressure can always stop venous bleeding if it is applied to the right spot.

- Then bandage the dressings tightly in place (an elastic bandage gives excellent compression) and leave them there until arrival at the emergency room.

Seek Emergency Care • Go to the nearest emergency room. Exception: Call for a rescue squad (911) if your child is clearly in shock. (See EMERGENCY TRANSPORTATION, page 4.)

FIRST AID FOR OPEN ABDOMINAL WOUNDS

Cover the wound with a sterile dressing. If a knife or other weapon protrudes from the wound, don't remove it before reaching the hospital. When it is removed, the cut it leaves could bleed uncontrollably. Call a rescue squad (see EMERGENCY TRANSPORTATION, page 4).

FIRST AID FOR OPEN CHEST WOUNDS

A sucking wound of the chest is one that goes through to the pleural space or lung. It can be recognized by the sound of air being sucked into the chest with each effort to breathe in. This type of wound quickly collapses the lung if it is not treated properly.

First Aid • Seal the opening as quickly as possible. Use several sterile dressings or pieces of clean cloth and lots of adhesive tape or plastic wrap to make it airtight. If possible, apply the seal while your child is breathing out. If one part of the chest bulges out when your child breathes out, there are several broken ribs in that area (flail chest). Have your child lie with the bulging part down, or hold a pillow or towel over it to keep it from bulging. If a knife or other weapon protrudes from the wound, don't remove it before reaching the hospital. When it is removed, the cut it leaves could bleed uncontrollably. Call a rescue squad (see EMERGENCY TRANSPORTATION, page 4).

BREATHING DIFFICULTY, SEVERE

STOPPED BREATHING, PERSISTENT

- Call the rescue squad (911).
- Begin mouth-to-mouth resuscitation if you know how. (Otherwise, go to the guidelines on RESUSCITATION, page 9.)

BREATHING, VERY SLOW AND WEAK

- Call the rescue squad (911).

STOPPED BREATHING, TRANSIENT; AND NOW NORMAL BREATHING

• Call your child's physician immediately or go to the nearest emergency room.

• Note: In an infant, prolonged periods without breathing (apnea), especially if accompanied by turning blue or limpness, can be a forerunner of crib death and should always receive a careful medical evaluation. On the other hand, breathing pauses of less than 6 seconds (periodic breathing) in infants from birth to 3 months are normal. Occasionally, normal pauses can last for 15 seconds, but check with your physician.

CHOKING
Turn directly to page 10.

CROUP
Turn directly to page 574.

BREATHING FAST

Rapid Breathing Rates • The following rates are abnormal:

2 months or younger:	more than 60 per minute
2 to 12 months:	more than 50 per minute
1 to 5 years:	more than 40 per minute
6 to 12 years:	more than 30 per minute
12 years or older:	more than 20 per minute

These rates apply to children who are not crying. The breathing rate normally goes up 10 to 20 breaths per minute in children who are upset or crying. Also, healthy infants occasionally pant and have higher rates. If your infant seems well, recheck the rate while asleep.

Rapid and Labored • Call your child's physician immediately.

With Wheezing • Call your child's physician immediately.

With Fever • With fever, the rate of breathing rises by 3 for each degree Fahrenheit of elevation (or by 6 for each degree Centigrade). If the rate is appropriate for the level of fever, all is probably well. If it is considerably higher, call your child's physician immediately.

With Snorting • Clean the nose with warm water drops and a rubber suction bulb. If that doesn't help and the breathing rate remains high, call your child's physician immediately.

RELATED TOPICS

BREATH-HOLDING SPELLS (see page 331)
BREATHING, NOISY (see page 567)

BURNS, CHEMICAL

Chemical burns are external burns from lye, acids, or other tissue-damaging chemicals splashed on the skin. Most of these accidents cause only first-degree burns, which may peel like a sunburn during the following week. A mild irritation and burning of the scalp has been caused by some home permanent solutions. A few of the stronger chemicals may cause deep burns.

FIRST AID

Remove contaminated clothing and rinse off the burned part of your child's body with clear water for 20 minutes, using the shower or tub. Don't rub the skin during this rinse. Don't apply any burn ointments because washing them off will cause pain. Also, don't apply butter; it only increases the infection rate. If the burned area is large, cover it loosely with a wet clean sheet.

CALL YOUR CHILD'S PHYSICIAN IMMEDIATELY

Call in all cases, after carrying out first aid instructions. The physician will probably need to examine your child if there are any blisters, facial burns, or extensive burns.

RELATED TOPICS

EYE, CHEMICAL IN (see page 48)
POISONING (see page 55)

BURNS, THERMAL

Most of these burns are from hot water or hot drinks. A few are from hot ovens, stoves, electric or kerosene space heaters, exhaust pipes, grease, hair-curling irons, clothes irons, heating grates, and cigarettes. Usually the burn is first degree (reddened skin without blisters) or second degree (with blisters). Neither of these leave any scars. Second-degree burns take up to 3 weeks to heal. A third-degree burn is deep and leaves pain-free areas of black (leathery) or white skin. During healing it usually needs a skin graft to prevent bad scarring if it is larger than a quarter.

FIRST AID FOR THERMAL BURNS

Immediately (don't take time to remove clothing) put the burned part in cold tap water or pour cold water over it for 10 minutes. If you are outdoors, the nearest garden hose will do. If the burn is small, massage it with an ice cube. This will lessen the depth of the burn and relieve pain. Don't apply any butter or ointments.

If the burned area is large, cover it loosely with a clean sheet or plastic wrap. The covering will keep the burn clean and reduce pain until you reach a medical facility.

CALL YOUR CHILD'S PHYSICIAN IMMEDIATELY IF

• Three or more blisters are present.

• A blister is larger than 1 inch (i.e., won't fit under a Band-Aid).

• The burn is on the face, neck, hands, feet, or genitals.

• Areas of charred or white skin are present.

• An extremely hot substance caused the burn.

• It was an electrical burn.

• An explosion caused the burn.

• You have other urgent questions.

HOME CARE FOR THERMAL BURNS

Treatment • Wash the area gently with liquid soap twice a day. Don't open any blisters—the outer skin still protects the burn from infection. For any open burns (second degree), apply an antibiotic ointment (such as Bacitracin or Betadine) and cover it with a Band-Aid. Change the dressing daily. For pain, apply cold compresses and take acetaminophen every 4 hours. Do not apply any butter or burn ointments. Note: Once the blisters break open, the dead skin needs to be removed (debrided) with a fine scissors. Otherwise the hidden pockets become an ideal breeding ground for infections.

Call Your Child's Physician Later If

• Any blisters break open.

• The burn starts to look infected.

• Tenderness or redness increases after day 2.

• The burn hasn't healed after 10 days.

• You feel your child is getting worse.

PREVENTION

Think about how you can prevent similar accidents in the future.

• Never drink anything hot (such as coffee, tea, or cocoa) while holding a young baby. The baby will grab for it, spill it, and probably get burned.

• On the stove, try to use the back burners and keep handles turned in.

• Once your child can walk, keep hot substances away from the edge of the table or stove (such as a pan of boiling water, a coffee pot, a curling iron, or an iron). The burn from a crockpot usually causes scarring because the contents are sticky and at high temperature.

• Always supervise young children in the bathtub. Don't let a young child touch the faucet handles. He or she may turn on the hot water and be scalded.

• Lower your hot-water heater setting to 130°F or to the "low medium" setting. Higher settings can cause burns in 2 or 3 seconds. You can test the temperature of your hot water by using a candy or meat thermometer.

• Use cool humidifiers, not hot steam vaporizers. A vaporizer can cause severe burns if a child overturns it or puts his face too close to it.

• Supervise children around fires, stoves, and heaters of any kind.

- Use flame-resistant sleepwear.

- Give up smoking, or at least dispose of used cigarettes conscientiously. Cigarettes are the most common cause of residential fires.

- Keep cigarette lighters away from children. Even a 2-year-old can ignite one by inverting it and pushing it across the floor.

- Install smoke detectors in your home on every floor. Check them monthly for proper functioning. More people die from smoke inhalation than from burns. Smoke alarms detect smoke long before your nose can.

- Teach your children not to hide if a house fire occurs, but to go outside. Have a fire drill and rehearse it.

- Before placing a child under 1 year old in a car seat, check the seat's temperature. Hot straps or buckles have caused second-degree burns. Whenever you park in direct sunlight, cover the car seat with a towel or sheet.

- Avoid fireworks, or allow older children to use them only with close adult supervision. In addition to burns, fireworks (especially bottle rockets) cause 300 cases of blindness per year.

COMA

A child who is unconscious, cannot be fully awakened, or is very difficult to awaken is in a coma. The causes are many, including drug overdose, poisoning, head injury, encephalitis, and low blood sugar. In all cases, you should contact your child's physician immediately.

CALL A RESCUE SQUAD FOR ASSISTANCE AND TRANSPORTATION FOR A COMATOSE CHILD IF

- Your child can't be awakened at all.

- The head or neck may be injured.

- A severe allergic reaction to a bee sting or medication is possible.

- Your child is not breathing.

- Breathing is slow or weak.
- Breathing is labored (croup, wheezing, choking, etc.).
- The lips are bluish or dusky.

TAKE YOUR CHILD TO THE NEAREST EMERGENCY ROOM

- In all other cases, if your child is breathing normally.
- If your child starts to vomit, place him on the side or abdomen.

CONVULSIONS WITH FEVER (FEBRILE SEIZURES)

Febrile (fever-related) convulsions are seizures triggered by high fever. They are the most common type of convulsion (occurring in 4 percent of children) and in general are harmless. The children are usually between 6 months and 4 years of age. Most first seizures occur by 2 years of age. The average temperature at which they occur is 104°F, although some occur at lower or higher levels of fever. Everyone has a convulsion threshold. For most children the threshold is 106° or 107°F, so they never have a febrile seizure. The fever itself can be caused by an infection in any part of the body, including a simple cold or ear infection.

During a seizure, the child becomes unconscious. The eyes stare or roll upward. The arms and legs become stiff or jerk. Each febrile seizure usually lasts 1 to 10 minutes without any treatment. Most of these children have just 1 febrile seizure in a lifetime. The other 40 percent of children with febrile seizures have 2 or 3 recurrences over the years. Recurrences are more likely if the initial seizure occurred with a low-grade fever (less than 103°F). They usually stop occurring by age 5 or 6. While seeing a seizure may be frightening, there is no cause for alarm. The seizure does not cause any brain damage or epilepsy. Occasionally a child will hurt himself during a fall. Only a few children (3 percent) will go on to have seizures without fever (epilepsy) at a later age.

FIRST AID FOR FEBRILE CONVULSIONS

Reduce the Fever • Bringing your child's fever down as quickly as possible will shorten the seizure. Remove most clothing and apply cold washcloths to the forehead and neck. Sponge the body surface with cool water (but avoid rubbing alcohol, which could cause a coma). As the water evaporates, the temperature will fall. Don't put your child in a bathtub, however; that could be dangerous during the seizure. When the seizure is over and your child is fully awake, give the appropriate dose of acetaminophen. (For dosage, see FEVER, page 407) and encourage cool fluids.

Protect Your Child's Airway • If he has anything in his mouth, clear it with a finger to prevent choking. Place him on his side or abdomen (facedown) to help drain secretions. If he vomits, help clear the mouth. If available, use a suction bulb. If breathing becomes noisy, pull the jaw and chin forward by placing two fingers behind the corner of the jaw on each side (this will automatically bring the tongue forward).

Common Mistakes in First Aid for Convulsions • During the seizure, don't try to restrain your child or stop the seizure movements. Once started, the seizure will run its course no matter what you do. Don't try to resuscitate your child just because breathing stops momentarily for 5 to 10 seconds. Instead, try to clear the airway. Don't try to force anything into your child's mouth. This is unnecessary and can cut the mouth, injure a tooth, cause vomiting, or result in a serious bite of your finger. Don't try to hold the tongue. While children may rarely bite the tongue during a convulsion, they can't "swallow the tongue."

CALL YOUR CHILD'S PHYSICIAN IMMEDIATELY IF

• The febrile convulsion lasts more than 10 minutes. (Start timing the length of the seizure as soon as it begins.)

• In all other cases, after the seizure has stopped.

If you are told to bring your child to your physician's office or the nearest emergency room, keep the fever down during transport. Dress your child lightly and continue sponging if necessary. (Warning: Prolonged seizures due to persistent fever have been caused by bundling up sick infants during a long drive. A seizure lasting more than 30 minutes can be harmful.)

HOME CARE FOR FEBRILE CONVULSIONS

If your physician decides the seizure can be treated safely at home, the following information may help you.

Oral Fever-Reducing Medicines • If your physician agrees, place your child on acetaminophen at the regular dosage every 4 hours for the next 48 hours (or longer if the fever persists). For dosages, turn to FEVER, page 407.

Fever-Reducing Suppositories • Have some acetaminophen suppositories on hand in case your child ever has another febrile seizure (same dosage as oral medicine). Since your pharmacist may keep these suppositories refrigerated, you may have to ask for them. When your child awakens fully, you can give the other fever-reducing medicine by mouth.

Call Your Child's Physician Later If

• Another seizure occurs.

• The neck becomes stiff. (Note: The inability to touch the chin to the chest is an early symptom of meningitis.)

• Your child becomes confused or delirious.

• Your child becomes difficult to awaken.

• You feel your child is getting worse.

PREVENTION OF FEBRILE CONVULSIONS

The only way to prevent future convulsions completely is for your child to take an anticonvulsant medicine daily until age 3 or 4. Since anticonvulsants have side effects and febrile seizures are generally harmless, anticonvulsants are rarely prescribed anymore unless your child has other neurologic problems. Your physician will discuss this decision with you.

Try to control fever more closely than is necessary for children without febrile seizures. Begin acetaminophen at the first sign of any fever (temperatures over 100°F rather than 102°F). Febrile convulsions usually occur during the first day of an illness. Because fever is common after DPT immunizations, begin acetaminophen in the physician's office and continue it for at least 24 hours. If your child has a fever at bedtime, awaken him once during the night to give antifever medicine. Avoid more than 1 blanket, since bundling during sleep can push the temperature up 1 or 2 extra degrees.

RELATED TOPICS

FEVER (see page 407)
DELIRIUM (see page 44)

CONVULSIONS WITHOUT FEVER

During a convulsion (seizure), a child becomes unconscious and falls, the eyes stare or roll upward, the body stiffens, and the arms and legs jerk. Most seizures last less than 5 minutes. Convulsions without fever occur in 0.4 percent of children. If they become recurrent, the child is said to have epilepsy. While the causes are many, the usual one is a small scar in the brain tissue that triggers seizures. Recurrent seizures can usually be controlled with special medicines called anticonvulsants.

FIRST AID FOR CONVULSIONS WITHOUT FEVER

Your child should be left on the floor or ground. Move him only if he is in a dangerous place.

Protect Your Child's Airway • See CONVULSIONS WITH FEVER, page 41.

Common Mistakes in First Aid • See CONVULSIONS WITH FEVER, page 41.

CALL YOUR CHILD'S PHYSICIAN IMMEDIATELY IF

• The seizure lasts more than 5 minutes. (If the seizure lasts more than 15 minutes, you probably should call an ambulance. In general, a seizure won't hurt the brain unless it continues for at least 30 minutes.)

• It's the first one.

• Seizures are occurring frequently.

HOME CARE FOR CONVULSIONS WITHOUT FEVER

Treatment for Previously Diagnosed Convulsions • After the seizure is over, let your child sleep if he wishes. The brain is temporarily exhausted, and there is no point in trying to keep your child awake. Since recurrent seizures are common, work out a plan with your child's physician in advance. Some will want you to give your child an extra dose of anticonvulsants at this time. If you have recently missed giving a dose, twice the usual dose may be in order. There is no need to bring your child to an emergency room for every seizure.

Precautions • While most sports are safe, be certain your child avoids activities that would be unsafe if he suddenly had a seizure. These include heights (e.g., climbing a tree or rope), cycling on a highway, or swimming alone. Wind surfing, scuba diving, and hang gliding must also be avoided. Have him take showers instead of baths, and only when someone else is in the house.

Call Your Child's Physician Later If

• Another seizure occurs.

• Your child stays confused or groggy for more than 2 hours.

DELIRIUM

Delirium is the sudden onset of disorientation (talking crazy), strange behavior (acting "wild"), and visual hallucinations (seeing things that aren't there). Judgment and memory are also impaired. Commonly, the child's confused thinking comes and goes (fluctuates). Children mainly get delirium with fevers over 104°F. It usually goes away once the fever is lowered. Illegal drugs can cause delirium. So can cold and cough medicines, especially if two are given together or one is given in too large a dose. Brief delirium can occur when a child awakens in strange surroundings, as on the first night of a vacation. If your child has no fever and has recently sustained head trauma, see the guideline on HEAD TRAUMA, page 73.

CALL YOUR CHILD'S PHYSICIAN IMMEDIATELY IF

• Your child's temperature is normal or less than 102°F.

• Your child is on any medicine that could cause delirium (like antihistamines).

- Poisoning is a possibility.

- Your child may be using drugs.

- Head trauma recently occurred. (Unobserved head trauma with amnesia should be considered.)

- The neck is stiff.

- Your child is also vomiting.

- Before the delirium, your child was acting very sick.

HOME CARE FOR FEBRILE DELIRIUM

Fever-Reducing Therapy • Give your child acetaminophen. Remove the clothing and apply cold washcloths to the forehead and neck. Sponge the body surface with cool water. If your child shivers, raise the water temperature. Don't put your child in the bathtub, however; that could be dangerous. See FEVER for details, page 407.

Delirium Therapy • Keep the lights on in your child's room. Be sure a familiar person stays with your child at all times until he or she feels better. It's best if you reassure your child by touching and talking to him. Tell him where he is, who you are, and that he will feel better soon.

Call Your Child's Physician Later If

- The delirium lasts for over an hour.

- The delirium is still present after you lower the fever below 102°F.

- The delirium clears up but your child develops other symptoms that worry you.

DROWNING

FIRST AID
Have someone call a rescue squad (911) immediately. (See EMERGENCY TRANSPORTATION, page 4.)

Resuscitation • Begin mouth-to-mouth breathing as soon as possible. (Review RESUSCITATION, page 9.) This should be started immediately—in the boat, in a life preserver, or at the latest when the rescuer reaches shallow water. It should be continued until the child is brought to a medical facility, since children have survived long submersions (especially in cold water).

Neck Injury • If there is any possibility of a neck injury (for example, a diving accident), protect the neck from any bending or twisting. If the child is still in the water, he or she can be helped to float on the surface until a spine board is applied or until several people can remove him while supporting the head and back as a unit.

Vomiting • Vomiting is common because the stomach is usually filled with water in drowning. If vomiting occurs, quickly turn the child on his or her side, or facedown, and try to keep the water from entering the lungs. The lungs are usually free of water because they are protected by spasm of the vocal cords. Avoid pressure on the stomach during resuscitation because it can trigger vomiting.

PREVENTION

• Never leave a child less than 3 years old unattended in the bathtub or a wading pool. Toddlers can drown in 2 inches of water.

• Never leave a toddler unattended near a 5-gallon industrial bucket with any water inside. If they peer inside, they may fall in and drown because these large buckets don't easily tip over.

• Never leave children who can't swim well unattended near a swimming pool or hot tub. (More children drown in backyard swimming pools than at beaches or public pools.)

• Make sure that neighborhood pools are fenced off and the gates are kept locked.

• Try to arrange swimming lessons for your child before age 8. (Children are often ready by age 4.)

• Caution children of all ages to check the depth of the water before diving in and to avoid any diving in the shallow end of a pool.

- Caution children not to overbreathe as a way to stay underwater longer. This practice can lead to passing out underwater.

- Caution the accomplished swimmer to continue to swim with a buddy.

INFANT OR TODDLER "SWIMMING" PROGRAMS

Toddler swimming lessons are very popular, especially in the Sunbelt. Most pediatricians remain opposed to them for the following reasons:

- If your child is pushed or hurried, he can develop a fear of water.

- If he is not being held and happens to go under, he can inhale enough water in the first 10 seconds to cause drowning.

- Swallowed pool water can also be dangerous. An excessive intake of water can lower the body sodium and cause seizures. Infant programs that encourage submersion of the head for more than a few seconds should be avoided for this reason.

- Even if your child can be taught how to swim, he cannot learn to save himself. Children are not able to understand the basic elements of water safety and cannot be made "water safe" before 4 years of age. Don't allow the ability to dog-paddle give you a false sense of security.

If you want to acquaint your infant or toddler with water, do so in a wading pool and concentrate on having fun, not learning how to swim. Infant water programs held in pools should also teach water fun. You can enroll your youngster in true swimming lessons at age 4 or 5. If you have already taught him to enjoy the water, he may learn to swim quickly.

ELECTRIC SHOCK OR LIGHTNING INJURY

Electrocution (death from electricity) usually occurs from contact with high-tension wires that have fallen or which the child has climbed up to. Household current can cause severe electric shock if your child is standing in water at the time contact is made. Electric shock usually stops breathing and the heartbeat. Rapid resuscitation can lead to a full recovery.

FIRST AID

Breaking Contact • If your child is still in contact with a live wire, turn off the electricity or break contact with the wire. Be sure to use a nonconducting object (such as a wooden pole).

Call the Rescue Squad Immediately • (See EMERGENCY TRANSPORTATION, page 4.)

Resuscitation • Begin mouth-to-mouth breathing as soon as possible if breathing has stopped. (Review RESUSCITATION, page 9.) Often external cardiac massage will also be needed. Take a CPR course in advance.

PREVENTION

• Cover all electrical outlets with plastic safety caps.

• Unplug appliances, such as hair dryers and curling irons, when not in use.

• Keep electrical cords away from toddlers who might chew on them. (Note: This accident could burn off part of the lip or the end of the tongue.)

• Teach your child not to turn on lights or electrical appliances while standing on wet floor or ground.

• Teach your child never to touch an electrical appliance, such as a hair dryer or radio, while in a bathtub. (Note: This mistake can result in immediate electrocution if the appliance is plugged into the socket, even with the switch turned to "off.")

• Teach your child to avoid open water, tall trees, high ground, or metal objects (e.g., a shovel) during thunderstorms. Cars and houses are safe.

EYE, CHEMICAL IN

Acids (e.g., toilet bowl cleaners) and alkalis (e.g., drain cleaners) splashed into the eye can severely damage the cornea, the clear part of the eye. However, most chemicals (such as alcohol or hydrocarbons) just cause temporary stinging and superficial irritation. All should be treated as emergencies until your physician or a Poison Control Center expert tells you otherwise.

FIRST AID FOR CHEMICAL IN EYE

Immediate and thorough irrigation of the eye with tap water is essential to prevent damage to the cornea. (Do not use antidotes such as vinegar.) This irrigation should be performed at home and as quickly as possible. Either hold your child faceup under a gently running water tap or have your child lie down and continuously pour lukewarm water into the eye from a pitcher or glass. It is very important to hold the eyelid open during this process. For most chemicals, the eye should be irrigated for 5 minutes; for acids, 10 minutes; and for alkalis, 20 minutes. If one eye is not burned, cover it while irrigating the other. Any chemical particles that can't be flushed away should be wiped away with a moistened cotton swab. Call your physician immediately after irrigating the eye.

RELATED TOPIC

For mild irritants like soap or food, see the guideline on EYES, RED OR PINK EYE, page 505.

EYE, FOREIGN BODY IN

The most common objects that get in the eye are an eyelash or a piece of dried mucus (sleep). Particulate matter such as sand, dirt, sawdust, or cinders also can be blown into the eyes. The main symptoms are irritation, pain, and tears. Rubbing the eye can lead to the foreign object's scratching the cornea (clear part). See also EYE, CHEMICAL IN, above.

Some parents needlessly worry that the foreign body can get lost behind the eyeball. This is impossible, since the space where the object is hidden is a dead end. The space on the sides and beyond the eyelids goes back ¼ inch and then stops.

FIRST AID FOR GLASS FRAGMENTS ON THE EYELIDS

Have your child bend forward and try to get flakes of glass off the skin by blowing on the closed eyelids. A few pieces can often be removed from the eyelids by touching them with a piece of Scotch tape. Pour water over the eyelids and face to get off any remaining glass. Cover the eyes with a wet washcloth and go to your physician's office. The eye should not be rubbed.

CALL YOUR CHILD'S PHYSICIAN IMMEDIATELY IF

- Any particle is stuck to the eyeball (especially the cornea).
- Fluid or blood is coming from the eyeball.
- The object hit the eye at high speed (e.g., a particle from striking metal on metal, or from a lawn mower).
- The foreign object is sharp.
- You have other urgent questions.

HOME CARE FOR FOREIGN BODY IN EYE

Treatment for Numerous Particles • If there are numerous particles in the eye (such as dirt or sand), clean around the eye with a wet washcloth first. Then have your child try to open and close the eye repeatedly while submerging that side of the face in a pan of water. If you are at the beach, have your child open and close the eyes while swimming underwater to clear sand from the eyes. If your child is too young to cooperate with this, hold him or her faceup under a gently running warm-water tap. The eyelids must be held open during the irrigation and this usually requires the help of another person.

Treatment for Particle in a Corner of the Eye • If the particle is in the corner of the eye, try to get it out with the corner of a clean handkerchief, a moistened cotton swab, or a piece of Scotch tape.

Treatment for Particle Under the Lower Lid • If the particle is under the lower eyelid, pull the lower lid out by depressing the cheek, and touch the particle with a moistened cotton swab. If that doesn't work, try pouring water on the speck while holding the lid out.

Treatment for Particle Under the Upper Lid • If the particle can't be seen, it's probably under the upper lid, the most common hiding place. Try having your child open and close the eye several times while it is submerged in a pan or bowl of water. If you have an eye cup, use it. If this fails, pull the upper lid out and draw it over the lower lid. This maneuver, and tears, will sometimes dislodge the particle.

Call Your Child's Physician Later If

- This approach does not remove all the foreign material from the eye—i.e., if the sensation of "grittiness" or pain persists.

  First Aid: While waiting to be seen by the physician, cover the eye with a wet washcloth or bandage it shut to relieve discomfort. If eye movement causes pain, cover both eyes.

- The vision does not return to normal after the eye has been allowed to rest for an hour.

- The foreign object has been removed, but tearing and blinking persist for more than 2 hours.

FROSTBITE

Frostbitten skin is cold, white, painful, tingly, or numb. The most common sites are toes, fingers, tip of the nose, outer ear, or cheeks. The nerves, blood vessels, and skin cells are temporarily frozen. The windchill temperature determines how quickly it occurs. The frostbite is much worse if the skin and clothing are also wet at the time of cold exposure. Touching bare hands to cold metal or volatile products (like gasoline) stored outside during freezing weather can cause immediate frostbite. Frostbite of the cheeks can occur in the summertime when a toddler keeps a Popsicle in his mouth too long. Cold injuries are painful and sometimes dangerous. Severe cold exposure (hypothermia) with shivering and sleepiness is an emergency.

CALL YOUR CHILD'S PHYSICIAN IMMEDIATELY IF

- Three or more areas are involved.

- A large area is involved.

- The frostbite resulted from severe cold exposure.

- Your child's temperature is less than 95°F.

- Severe shivering is present.

- Speech is slurred or confused.

- You have other urgent questions.

HOME CARE

Treatment • The main treatment for frostbite is to rewarm the area rapidly with wet heat. Bring your child into a warm room. Place the frostbitten part in very warm water or cover it with warm wet compresses. A bath is often the quickest approach. The water should be very warm (104° to 108°F, or 40° to 42°C) but not hot enough to burn. Immersion in this warm water should continue until a pink flush signals the return of circulation to the frostbitten part (usually 30 minutes). At this point, the numbness should disappear. If your child has lots of frostbite, the last 10 minutes of rewarming is usually quite painful. The rest of your child's body should also be kept warm by plenty of blankets. If there is any pain, your child can take aspirin or acetaminophen. Offer warm fluids to drink.

Common Mistakes • A common error is to apply snow to the frostbitten area or to massage it; both can cause damage to thawing tissues. Do not rewarm with dry heat, such as a heat lamp or electric heater, because frostbitten skin is easily burned.

PREVENTION

- Be sure your child dresses in layers for cold weather. The first layer should be thermal underwear, and the outer layer needs to be waterproof. The layers should be loose, not tight. Mittens are warmer than gloves.

- Have your child wear a hat, because over 50 percent of heat loss occurs from the head.

- Set limits on the time spent outdoors when the windchill temperature falls below 0.

- Teach your child to recognize the earliest warnings of frostbite. Tell him that the tingling and numbness are reminders that he is not dressed adequately for the weather and needs to go indoors.

Call Your Child's Physician Later If
- The color and sensation don't return to normal after 60 minutes of rewarming.

- The frostbitten part develops blisters.

HEAT REACTIONS

There are three main reactions to an extremely hot environment. All three are caused by excessive loss of water through sweating. They mainly occur in people who are exercising during hot weather. Infants are at added risk because they are less able to sweat with heat stress. For treatment, select the type of heat reaction that pertains to your child. A rectal temperature is more reliable than an oral temperature for these disorders.

HEATSTROKE OR SUNSTROKE
Hot, flushed skin; high fever (at least 105°F); the absence of sweating; confusion or unconsciousness; and shock (low blood pressure) are present. The onset is usually rapid.

HEAT EXHAUSTION
Cold, pale skin; no fever (temperature less than 100°F); profuse sweating; and dizziness, fainting, or weakness are present. The onset is usually gradual.

HEAT CRAMPS
Severe cramps in the limbs (especially calf or thigh muscles) and abdomen, with no fever, are present.

FIRST AID FOR HEATSTROKE OR SUNSTROKE
- Call the rescue squad (911) immediately.

- Heatstroke can be life-threatening. The high fever is a serious emergency. Cool your child off as rapidly as possible. Move him or her to a cool place. Keep the feet elevated. Place ice packs in the armpits and groin. Sponge your child with cool water (as cold as is tolerable), and fan him. If your child is unconscious, immersion in cold water could be lifesaving. (Note: aspirin or acetaminophen is of no help.)

- If your child is conscious, give as much cold water to drink as he or she can tolerate.

FIRST AID FOR HEAT EXHAUSTION

- Call your child's physician immediately.

- Put your child in a cool place. Have him or her lie down with the feet elevated. Cover your child with cold wet towels.

- Give as much cold water to drink as your child can tolerate until he or she feels better.

- Your physician will probably want to examine your child's state of hydration. You can drive in, but keep your child lying down in the back seat during the drive and provide unlimited amounts of water.

HOME CARE FOR HEAT CRAMPS

Heat cramps are the most common reaction to excessive heat. They are never serious. Give your child as much cold water to drink as he can tolerate until he feels better. Your child will not need to be seen by the physician.

PREVENTION OF HEAT REACTIONS

- When your child is working or exercising in a hot environment, have him or her drink large amounts of cool water. Water is the ideal solution for replacing lost sweat. Very little salt is lost. Special glucose-electrolyte solutions offer no advantage over water unless you are exercising for longer than an hour.

- Have your child take 5-minute water breaks every 25 minutes in the shade. Encourage him to drink water even if he's not thirsty. Thirst is often delayed until a person is almost dehydrated. Tell your child he can't drink too much water during hot weather.

- Avoid salt tablets, because they slow down stomach emptying and delay the absorption of fluids.

- Have your child wear a single layer of lightweight clothing. Change it if it becomes wet with perspiration.

- Athletic coaches recommend that exercise sessions be shortened and less vigorous if the temperature exceeds 82°F, especially if the humidity is high.

- When using a hot tub, limit exposure to 15 minutes and have a "buddy" system in case a heat reaction suddenly occurs. Hot tubs and saunas should be avoided by people with a fever, or following vigorous exercise when the body needs to release heat.

- Protect infants with fevers from heatstroke by not bundling them in blankets or excessive clothing.

POISONING

First, sweep any pills or solid poisons out of your child's mouth, using your finger. If your child swallowed a chemical, immediately give him 1 glass of water or milk to rinse the esophagus (not necessary for swallowed medicines). Then call the nearest Poison Control Center (or your child's physician) immediately for *all* ingestions. Don't induce vomiting until you are certain it is necessary and safe. About 10 percent of poisoning is with substances (such as acids) that can cause harm if they are vomited. Also, more than 50 percent of ingestions are of poisonous substances taken in a nontoxic amount or of nonpoisonous substances. In addition, ipecac is rarely helpful if more than 1 hour has passed since the ingestion (activated charcoal is used instead). Always suspect poisoning if your child is 1 to 4 years old and has the abrupt onset of unexplained symptoms (without fever). Be prepared to answer the following questions:

- What was swallowed?

- How much was swallowed? (Estimate the maximal amount.)

- When was it swallowed?

- Does your child have any symptoms? (For COMA or CONVULSIONS, go directly to those guidelines, pages 39–44.)

In the meantime, select from the following three guidelines the one that applies to your child's ingestion.

ACIDS, ALKALIS, OR PETROLEUM PRODUCTS

OTHER POISONOUS SUBSTANCES
PROBABLY HARMLESS SUBSTANCES

Some products have first aid for their ingestion listed on the label.

ACIDS, ALKALIS, OR PETROLEUM PRODUCTS
These include toilet bowl cleaners, drain cleaners, lye, Clinitest tablets, ammonia, bleaches, kerosene, gasoline, benzene, furniture polish, and lighter fluid. If these agents are vomited, additional damage can occur to the esophagus or lungs.

FIRST AID
Don't Induce Vomiting
Have your child drink 1 to 2 glasses of milk (or water) to wash out the esophagus. Keep your child sitting or standing to protect the esophagus. Don't let your child lie down. Your physician will decide where to see you. Bring with you the container the poison was in.

OTHER POISONOUS SUBSTANCES
Poisonous substances include most drugs, chemicals, and plants. The most dangerous prescription drugs of all (in overdosage) are barbiturates, clonidine, digitalis products, narcotics, Lomotil, Darvon, Tofranil, and other trycyclic antidepressants. Very dangerous over-the-counter medicines are iron and aspirin.

FIRST AID
Induce Vomiting If Approved by a Physician
The best way to cause vomiting is with syrup of ipecac. Give 1 tablespoon (3 teaspoons) to children 1 to 6 years old; 2 tablespoons to those over age 6. For infants under 12 months old, give 2 teaspoons (10 ml). Also, give your child about 6 ounces or more of water or other clear fluid. Keep your child walking about to make the ipecac work faster. If your child hasn't vomited in 30 minutes, gagging with a spoon may help. If not, give a second tablespoon of ipecac. Once vomiting begins, repeat the clear fluids until the vomited material comes back clear. Then rest the stomach and give nothing by mouth for 2 hours. If you do not have ipecac at home, you can probably get some from a neighbor. Otherwise rush your child to a pharmacy and give it there. If no pharmacy or physician

is within 30 minutes of your home, give your child 2 table-spoons of a liquid dishwashing soap, such as Joy, Ivory, or Palmolive. (**Caution:** Never use soaps intended for automatic dishwashers or clothes washers.) It can induce vomiting almost as well as ipecac. If you can get someone else to drive, take a large mixing bowl or a pail and induce vomiting in the car while driving to the nearest emergency room or your physician's office. Bring the poison container with you.

PROBABLY HARMLESS SUBSTANCES

Fortunately, most children will ingest nonedible substances that do not produce any serious symptoms. It is unnecessary to induce vomiting for these. Some examples of nontoxic substances are candles, chalk, crayons, ballpoint pens, felt-tip pens, lead pencils (which are actually graphite), cosmetics (except hair dye or nail polish remover), dog or cat food, deodorants, detergents (exception: automatic dishwasher detergent), dirt, soaps, greases, oils, hairsprays, hand lotions, 3 percent hydrogen peroxide, lipstick, perfumes, petroleum jelly, rouge, shampoos, shaving cream, and suntan lotions. Some children like to chew on newspaper but don't swallow it. In general, the inks used in newspapers are harmless. The exception is that some of the colored inks are harmful, but one serving of the comic strips requires no intervention. Some harmless drugs are birth control pills, antacids, laxatives, stool softeners, and vitamins (unless they contain iron). Call your physician to be sure.

PREVENTION OF POISONING

You were lucky this time, but it's time to poison-proof the house.

• Remember to keep drugs and chemicals locked up, or out of reach. Review where you keep drain cleaners, furniture polish, drugs, and insecticides, since these are the most common dangerous poisons.

• Also, remember that alcoholic beverages have caused serious poisonings. As little as 3 ounces of hard liquor has been fatal to a 2-year-old child. Remember that most mouthwashes contain 15 percent to 25 percent alcohol.

• Whenever you or your child are prescribed a new drug, remember to keep the safety cap on and carefully check the dosage before giving it.

- Don't leave drugs on countertops, especially when you are called to the door or telephone.

- Don't leave drugs in a purse, because children often search them for candy or gum. When you have guests, keep purses out of reach of children.

- Learn the names of all your house plants and remove any (e.g., dieffenbachia) that would cause more than vomiting or diarrhea. Teach your child never to put leaves, stems, seeds, or berries from any plant into the mouth.

- Don't store any chemicals in soft-drink bottles.

- Even with good planning, keep some syrup of ipecac (periodically check the expiration date) and the telephone number of the Poison Control Center handy.

SUFFOCATION

Suffocations mainly occur in infants who are placed facedown on a soft surface that they sink into. The age group at risk is mainly birth to 3 months. These young infants don't have the strength to lift the head and turn the face away. Many of these deaths occur when a baby naps at the home of a friend who doesn't have a crib. These tragic deaths are preventable if you avoid the following surfaces with young infants:

- Water beds

- Sheepskin rugs or mattress covers

- Soft pillows such as beanbag or bead-filled pillows

- Mattresses covered with plastic bags

To be extra safe, place your young infant in a crib with a firm mattress and on his back or side. As of 1992, this is the sleep position recommended by the American Academy of Pediatrics for healthy infants.

These suffocation deaths are different from crib deaths. Despite extensive research, the exact cause of crib deaths remains unknown. Crib deaths can't be predicted or prevented. However, one other cause of suffocation in young infants should be mentioned: Small babies have been smothered by mothers who inadvertently fell asleep on top of them. If you nurse your baby in your bed at night, be careful.

Older infants and toddlers can be suffocated from plastic bags or sheets of plastic. The accidents usually occur when they pull the plastic over their heads or crawl into plastic bags. Carefully dispose of the following products or keep them away from this age group:

- Plastic dry-cleaning bags
- Plastic shopping bags
- Plastic garbage bags

II.

TRAUMA (INJURIES)

II. TRAUMA (INJURIES)

BONE, JOINT, AND MUSCLE TRAUMA

This guideline covers injuries to bones, joints, and muscles. The legs are more commonly injured than the arms. *Fractures* (broken bones) and *dislocations* (bones out of joint) obviously need treatment by a physician. Stretches and tears of ligaments (*sprains*) are due to sudden twisting injuries and require medical attention unless they are very mild. By contrast, most stretches and tears of muscles (*strains*) are due to overexertion and can be treated at home. Excessive jumping gives muscle pain in the front of the upper leg. Excessive running (especially uphill) gives muscle pain in the front of the lower leg (called shin splints). A *muscle bruise* (called a charley horse) is the most common injury in contact sports and can also be treated at home. *Bone bruises* usually follow direct blows to the bone in exposed areas, like the elbow, hip, or knee, and are usually minor injuries.

Similar Condition • If appropriate, turn directly to the guideline for FINGER AND TOE TRAUMA, page 69.

FIRST AID FOR SUSPECTED FRACTURE OR SEVERE SPRAIN

Suspected Fracture • If you suspect a broken bone, take your child in for a medical exam and an X ray. Don't let your child put pressure or weight on it. Splint the fracture before moving your child so the fracture edges won't damage blood vessels. Note: If your child sustains a fracture, be sure he is

63

consuming a normal amount of calcium (800 to 1,200 mg) each day.

- *Shoulder or arm:* Use a sling made of a triangular piece of cloth to support the forearm at an 80- to 90-degree angle. At a minimum, support the injured part with the other hand.

- *Leg:* After placing a towel between the legs, use the uninjured leg as a splint by binding the thighs and legs together. At a minimum, carry your child and don't permit any weight bearing on the injured leg. Transportation can be by car.

- *Neck:* Protect the neck from any turning or bending. Do not move your child until a neck brace or spine board has been applied. Call a rescue squad (911) for transportation.

Suspected Sprained Ankle or Knee • Treat most sports injuries with R.I.C.E. (rest, ice, compression, and elevation) for the first 24 to 48 hours. Apply continuous compression with a snug, wet elastic bandage. Numbness, tingling, or increased pain means the bandage is too tight. Apply crushed ice in a plastic bag for 20 minutes out of every hour while awake. Ice and compression reduce bleeding, swelling, and pain (all of which slow healing). Keep the injured ankle or knee elevated and at rest for 24 hours. While mild sprains could be cared for at home, most injuries to ligaments need to be evaluated by your physician. Transportation can be by car. (Note: Sprains are mainly seen in adults. Under age 12 or 14, suspect a fracture.)

CALL YOUR CHILD'S PHYSICIAN

Immediately If

- Your child is under 6 months old.

- The bone is deformed or crooked.

- Your child won't move an arm normally
  (especially if the injury followed someone's pulling on the arm; young children who won't straighten the elbow or turn the palm up usually have a subluxed radius, a partial dislocation of the elbow).

- Your child won't stand (bear weight) on the legs.

- A severe limp is present.

- The joint nearest the injury can't be moved fully.

- The pain is extreme.

- A "snap" or "pop" was felt at the time of an injury to the knee.

During Office Hours If

- Your child can't walk without pain.

- There is a large area of swelling
(especially if it appeared within 30 minutes).

- The pain interferes with sleep.

- You have other questions.

HOME CARE FOR BONE AND JOINT TRAUMA

Treatment of a Bruised Muscle or Bone

- Apply an ice bag or massage the area with ice for 20 to 30 minutes. Repeat this 3 to 4 times the first day. (Note: Water in a Styrofoam cup can be placed in the freezer. After it is frozen, the cup can be peeled away and the piece of ice used for massage.)

- Give your child acetaminophen or ibuprofen 4 times a day for pain. Acetaminophen is readily available for children. Ibuprofen is especially helpful for injuries and is available without a prescription in pill form, but is approved only for use in youngsters over age 12. Some of the brand names are Advil, Medipren, and Nuprin. (Avoid aspirin in anyone with soft-tissue bleeding. Since aspirin is an anticoagulant, one aspirin can increase the tendency to bleed easily for up to a week.)

- Have your child rest the injured part as much as possible.

- The pain usually starts to ease after 48 hours, but there may be some discomfort for 2 weeks.

Treatment of Strained Muscles • These guidelines apply if several muscles hurt after a strenuous practice, athletic game, or long hike. Most muscle injuries can safely be cared for at home. Massage the sore muscles with ice for 20 to 30 minutes. Repeat this 3 to 4 times the first day. Also give your child acetaminophen or ibuprofen 4 times a day for at least 48 hours. If stiffness persists after 48 hours, have your child soak in a hot bath for 20 minutes and gently massage the sore muscles. If the pain is localized, use a heating pad or hot compresses. Repeat this several times a day until improvement occurs. Have your youngster learn about stretching exercises and return to exercise gradually. Next time, he or she should be in better condition before going full throttle. Getting back in condition takes at least 7 days.

Acetaminophen and Ibuprofen Dosage Chart

		AGE (YEARS)				
TYPE	STRENGTH	2–3	4–5	6–8	9–11	12+
Children's acetaminophen	80-mg. tablets	2	3	4	5–6	8
Adult acetaminophen	325-mg. tablets	—	—	1	1–1½	2
Ibuprofen	200-mg. tablets	—	—	—	—	1–2

Call Your Child's Physician Later If

• A limp lasts more than 72 hours.

• The pain is not improving by 72 hours.

• The pain is not gone by 2 weeks.

• Other questions come up.

RELATED TOPIC
For the home care of cuts and scrapes, and guidelines on tetanus boosters, see SKIN TRAUMA, page 80.

EAR TRAUMA

This guideline covers injuries to the outer ear (pinna) or ear canal (the channel that carries sound down to the eardrum). Most external injuries are bruises and scratches. If the ear is severely swollen, a blood clot is present which could permanently damage the ear's shape if it is not treated by a physician. Most bleeding from within the ear canal is from a scratch on the lining caused by a fingernail, cotton swab, or physician's otoscope. These scratches just bleed a few drops and then heal nicely. Long, pointed objects, such as pencils, sticks, straws, or wires, carry the risk of puncturing the eardrum or doing even greater damage.

CALL YOUR CHILD'S PHYSICIAN

Immediately If

- The skin is split open and probably needs sutures.

- The ear is very swollen.

- The pain is severe.

- A pointed object was inserted into the ear canal (e.g., a pencil, stick, straw, or wire).

- More than 4 drops of blood have come from the ear canal.

- Any clear fluid is draining from the ear canal.

- Walking is unsteady.

During Office Hours If

- The injury caused an earache.

- The hearing is decreased on that side.

- You have other questions.

HOME CARE FOR SUPERFICIAL CUTS AND SCRAPES TO THE EAR
Wash the wound vigorously with soap and water for 5 minutes. Then apply pressure for 10 minutes with a sterile gauze to stop bleeding. Leave the area exposed to the air. (See SKIN TRAUMA, page 80, for more details.)

EYE TRAUMA

This guideline covers injuries to the eye, eyelid, and area around the eye. Brushing against a small twig often causes more damage than collision with a large object like a door. The main concern is if the vision has been damaged. Older children can tell us if their vision is blurred or out of focus. Test them at home by covering each eye in turn and having them look at a distant object. Children under 3 years old usually need to be examined to answer this question.

CALL YOUR CHILD'S PHYSICIAN

Immediately If

- The skin is split open and probably needs sutures.
- Any cut is present on the eyelid or eyeball.
- The pain is severe.
- The eyes are constantly tearing or blinking.
- Your child keeps the eye covered and won't open it.
- Vision is blurred or lost in either eye.
- Your child has double vision or can't look upward.
- The pupils are unequal in size.
- Blood or clouding is present behind the cornea (clear part).
- An object hit the eye at high speed (such as from a lawn mower).
- A sharp object hit the eye (such as a metallic chip).

During Office Hours If

- Your child is less than 3 years old *and* there are any findings of injury (like a black eye or bleeding in the white of the eyeball).
- You have other questions.

HOME CARE FOR EYE TRAUMA

Superficial Cuts or Scrapes • Protect the eye with a clean cloth, then wash the wound vigorously with soap and water for 5 minutes. Then apply pressure for 10 minutes with a sterile gauze to stop bleeding. Leave the area exposed to the air. (See TRAUMA, SKIN, page 80, for more details.)

Swelling or Bruises with Intact Skin • Swelling usually follows injury to the soft tissues or bone around the eye. Apply ice for 20 minutes. Give your child acetaminophen if necessary for pain. Don't be surprised if a black eye develops over the next 2 days. A black eye is harmless and needs no special treatment. A subconjunctival hemorrhage (flame-shaped bruise of the sclera or white of the eyeball) also shouldn't cause undue concern. These unsightly bruises do not spread to inside the eye. They generally last for 2 weeks and their disappearance cannot be hurried by any medicine or home remedy.

Call Your Child's Physician Later If

• There are any complaints about vision.

PREVENTION OF EYE TRAUMA

• Objects that penetrate the eyeball often result in loss of vision. Don't buy your child an air-powered gun (BB gun).

• Don't allow your child to play nearby when someone is using a lawn mower.

FINGER AND TOE TRAUMA

This guideline covers injuries to the fingers or toes. Usually the impact simply causes a bruise or swelling of the soft tissues and underlying bone (as when a heavy object falls on a toe or when a hand is bumped against a wall). However, if the end of a straightened finger or thumb receives the blow (usually from a ball), the energy is absorbed by the joints' surfaces and the injury occurs there (a jammed finger). For jammed fingers, always check carefully that the end of the finger can be fully straightened. In crush injuries (as from slammed car or screen doors), usually the last digit receives a few cuts. Occasionally the nail is damaged. Rarely is there any fracture of the small underlying bone.

CALL YOUR CHILD'S PHYSICIAN

Immediately If

• The skin is split open and probably needs sutures.

• Any bleeding won't stop after 10 minutes of direct pressure.

• The pain is severe.

• Blood collects under a nail *and* becomes quite painful.

• The fingernail is damaged following a crush injury.

• There is any dirt or grime in the wound that you can't get out.

- A finger joint can't be opened (straightened) and closed (bent) completely.

During Office Hours If

- The finger or toe is quite swollen.

- You have other questions.

HOME CARE FOR FINGER AND TOE TRAUMA
The following topics are covered. Go directly to the part that pertains to your child:

BRUISED FINGER OR TOE
JAMMED FINGER
SMASHED OR CRUSHED FINGERTIP
TORN NAIL
SUPERFICIAL CUTS
SKINNED KNUCKLES
RING CAUGHT ON SWOLLEN FINGER

For puncture wounds, go to the guideline on SKIN TRAUMA, page 80.

Bruised Finger or Toe: Treatment • Soak it in ice water for 20 minutes. Give your child acetaminophen as necessary for the pain. Call your physician later if the pain is not improving by 3 days or if your child is not using the finger or toe normally after a week.

Jammed Finger: Treatment • Soak the hand in ice water for 20 minutes. Give acetaminophen as necessary for the pain. The finger will be sensitive for the next week, so protect it by "buddy-taping" it to the next finger. A splint could be used but often makes it more prone to getting bumped. Call your physician later if the pain is not improving by 3 days or if your child isn't using the finger normally within 2 weeks. If this problem is recurrent, tape the involved fingers (so the painful joints can't bend) before sports for 3 or 4 weeks. To prevent future jammed fingers, have your child build up the small muscles of the fingers by daily squeezing exercises with a hand grip.

Smashed or Crushed Fingertip: Treatment • Before taking care of this yourself, recheck the guidelines for when to consult a physician. Soak the hand in ice water for 20 minutes. Give your child acetaminophen as necessary for the pain. Wash the finger well with a liquid soap while soaking it. Trim any small pieces of torn skin with a sterile scissors. If there's a chance of a cut getting dirty, cover it with a Band-Aid. Change the dressing every 24 hours. The injured area will be sensitive for the next week, so protect it from re-injury. Call your physician later if the pain isn't improving by 3 days, any signs of infection develop, or your child isn't using the finger normally in 1 week.

Torn Nail: Treatment • These recommendations apply to a nail that has been torn by catching on something. If the nail was torn by a crush injury, your child needs to see a physician. If the nail is cracked but there are no rough edges, leave it alone. If the nail is almost torn through or there is a large flap of nail, use sterile scissors or nail clippers to cut along the line of the tear. Pieces of nail taped in place will catch on objects. Soak the finger for 20 minutes in cold water. Apply an antibiotic ointment (such as Bacitracin or Betadine) and cover it with a Band-Aid. Each day, remove the dressing and soak the finger in a warm salt solution (½ teaspoon of salt to a pint of water) for 20 minutes once a day. By the seventh day, the nailbed should be covered with new skin, and both the soaking and the bandaging can be stopped. A new nail will grow in over the next 1 to 2 months. Call your physician later for any signs of infection.

Superficial Cuts: Treatment • Wash the wound vigorously with soap and water for 5 minutes. Then apply pressure for 10 minutes with a sterile gauze to stop bleeding. Leave the area exposed to the air.

Skinned Knuckles: Treatment • These wounds are deep scrapes of the upper surfaces of fingers or toes. Wash the wound vigorously for 5 minutes with a liquid soap and water. Scrubbing with a sterile gauze may be necessary to get all the dirt out. Flaps of skin (especially if they are dirty) should be cut off with sterile scissors or nail clippers. When clean, apply pressure for 10 minutes with a sterile gauze to stop any bleeding. Apply an antibiotic ointment and cover with a Band-Aid. Remove the dressing and clean the wound each day. Call your physician for any signs of infection.

Ring Caught on Swollen Finger: Treatment • Call your physician immediately if the finger has turned blue or numb. In most cases, a high priority is to save the ring. The key to removing the ring is reducing the swelling of the finger. This approach requires patience. At 5-minute intervals, alternate soaking the hand in ice water and holding it (with all the fingers straightened) high in the air. At 30 minutes (after the hand has been elevated for the third time), mineral oil or cooking oil can be applied to the finger. While the hand remains elevated, steady upward pressure can be applied until the ring slides off. If it won't slide off, call your physician before the swelling becomes worse.

Swollen Toe in Infant • An unexplained swelling of a toe requires medical attention. Fine human hair or a thin strand of thread can inadvertently become wrapped around a toe (occasionally a finger or penis). As your infant grows and the tourniquet of hair doesn't stretch, the blood supply from the toe is gradually cut off. A sharply demarcated groove with a swollen toe beyond it are the main findings. You will need medical help in removing this ring of hair.

GENITAL TRAUMA

This guideline covers injuries to the female or male genital area. Most are bruises (with swelling) or minor cuts that heal rapidly in 3 or 4 days.

CALL YOUR CHILD'S PHYSICIAN IMMEDIATELY IF

- The skin is split open and probably needs sutures.

- Any external bleeding won't stop after 10 minutes of direct pressure.

- The pain is severe.

- Passing the urine is difficult.

- Blood is in the urine.

- Your child is a male *and* the scrotum is swollen.

- Your child is a female *and* there is any bleeding from inside the vagina.

- Your child is a female *and* the injury was from an object that could have penetrated the vagina.

- Your child feels dizzy or faints with standing up.

- Sexual abuse could be the cause.

- You have other urgent questions.

HOME CARE FOR GENITAL TRAUMA

For minor cuts, wash the area vigorously with soap and water for 5 minutes. Then apply pressure for 10 minutes with a sterile gauze to stop bleeding. For swelling, apply ice for the next 20 minutes (if tolerated). (See SKIN TRAUMA, page 80, for additional information.) Call your physician later if passing the urine becomes difficult.

HEAD TRAUMA

SYMPTOMS AND CHARACTERISTICS

- History of a blow to the head
- Scalp trauma (cut, scrape, bruise, or swelling)
- Crying and holding the head

Cause • Every child sooner or later strikes his head. Falls are especially common when your child is learning to walk.

Expected Course • Most head trauma simply results in a scalp injury. Big lumps can occur with minor injuries because the blood supply to the scalp is so plentiful. For the same reason, small cuts here can bleed profusely. Most bruises occur on the forehead. Sometimes black and blue eyes appear after 3 days because the bruising spreads downward by gravity. Only 1 to 2 percent get a skull fracture. Since the presence of a simple skull fracture neither increases the chances of a complication nor changes the treatment, skull X-rays are rarely helpful and not routinely ordered. Usually there are no associated symptoms except for a headache at the site of impact. Children with concussions need to be examined by a physician, but concussions are uncommon following head trauma.

Unless there is temporary unconsciousness, confusion, or amnesia, your child has not had a concussion.

CALL YOUR CHILD'S PHYSICIAN IMMEDIATELY IF

(Call a rescue squad if your child is unconscious, having difficulty breathing, or has a neck injury.)

- The skin is split open and probably needs sutures.

- The accident was a severe one involving great force.

- Your child is under 1 year old.

- The crying lasted more than 10 minutes after the injury.

- Your child had a seizure (convulsion).

- Your child was unconscious or confused after the injury.

- Your child can't remember the accident (amnesia).

- A severe headache is present. (Young children with severe headaches either cry or are extremely restless.)

- Vomiting has occurred 3 or more times.

- Your child is unusually sleepy and difficult to awaken.

- Speech is slurred.

- Vision is blurred or double.

- Walking or crawling is unsteady.

- The arms are weak.

- There is any neck pain.

- Blood or watery fluid is coming from the nose or ears.

- The eyes are crossed.

- There are other symptoms that concern you.

HOME CARE FOR HEAD TRAUMA

Wound Care • If there is a scrape, wash it off with soap and water. Then apply pressure with sterile gauze or a clean cloth for 10 minutes to stop any bleeding. For swelling, apply ice for 20 minutes. Although the swelling will go down in 3 to 4 days, the bruise may last for 2 to 4 weeks.

Observe During First 2 Hours Following Injury • Encourage your child to lie down and rest until all symptoms have cleared. Your child can be allowed to sleep; trying to keep your child awake continuously is unnecessary. Just have him or her sleep nearby so you can observe him. Awaken him after 2 hours of sleeping to check his ability to walk and talk.

Diet • Give only clear fluids (ones you can see through) until your child has gone 6 hours without vomiting. Vomiting is common after head injuries and there is no need to have him vomit up his dinner.

Avoid Pain Medicines • Don't give acetaminophen or aspirin, because you need to closely follow your child's reaction to the injury. If the headache is bad enough to need a pain medicine, your child should be checked by a physician. In addition, aspirin increases the tendency to bleed easily.

Special Precautions and Awakening • Although your child is probably fine, watching your child for 48 hours will insure that no serious complication is missed. Close observation is especially important during the first 8 hours after the injury. After 48 hours, however, your child should return to a normal routine and full activity.

Awakening at Night • Awaken your child twice during the night: once at your bedtime and once four hours later. (Awakening him every hour is unnecessary and next to impossible.) Arouse him until he is walking and talking normally. Do this for two nights and also sleep in the same room with your child. If his breathing becomes abnormal or his sleep is otherwise unusual, awaken him to be sure a coma is not developing. If you can't awaken your child, call your physician immediately.

Checking Pupils • This is unnecessary. Some physicians may ask you to check your child's pupils (the black centers of the eyes) to make sure they are equal in size and become smaller when you shine a flashlight on them. Unequal pupils are never seen before other symptoms like confusion and difficulty walking. In addition, this test is difficult to perform with uncooperative children or dark-colored irises. In general, pupil checks are only necessary on children with severe head injuries, and they will be hospitalized.

Call Your Child's Physician Later If

• The headache becomes severe.

• Vomiting occurs 3 or more times.

• Your child becomes difficult to awaken or confused.

• Walking or talking becomes difficult.

• Your child's condition worsens in any other way.

PREVENTION OF HEAD TRAUMA

• When driving, place your child in a car safety seat. After your child's weight reaches 40 pounds, use a booster safety seat. Don't use the regular car seat and lap belt until your child weighs over 60 pounds. (See page 118 for details.) All states now have child-restraint laws, and with good reason: They reduce injuries by 80 percent and deaths by 90 percent.

• To prevent pedestrian accidents, teach your child to "look both ways" before crossing and while crossing. Teach him to use crosswalks and not to run across the street. Most children cannot safely cross the street alone until age 7 or 8.

• Never leave an infant of any age alone on a high place like a bed, sofa, changing table, or an exam table in the doctor's office. Your baby may unexpectedly roll over for the first time or wiggle off and fall on his head.

• Always keep the side rails up on the crib. Once your child can pull to standing in the crib, lower the mattress.

• Don't buy a bunk bed. If you already have one, keep children under age 6 out of the top bunk and use a side rail. Be sure the bed frame is strong enough to keep the mattress from falling through. And don't let your children jump on beds.

• Don't buy a baby walker (see page 124). They do not accelerate development and 35 percent of infants using them have an accident requiring emergency care.

• Don't leave your child unattended in a shopping cart.

• Place a sturdy gate at the top of stairways. Keep the stairway cleared of clutter. When your child starts to climb stairs, teach him to hold on to the banister when descending.

• For doors leading to the basement or outdoors, keep them closed and secure with an extra latch above the child's reach.

- If you live on an upper floor of a building, install window locks or guards.

- Don't leave younger children under the supervision of an aggressive sibling.

- Always supervise your child's outside play until he or she can be trusted to stay in the yard (age 4 or 5). Three-year-olds can't be expected to keep promises not to go near the street.

- Don't teach your child how to ride a bicycle until your child is old enough (age 7 or 8) to understand such safety issues as emergency stops and rules about right of way.

- Never allow your child to ride a bike unless she is wearing a bicycle helmet. ATV and motorcycles are too unsafe to ride, even with a helmet.

- Forbid trampolines. Serious accidents have occurred even with close supervision.

MOUTH TRAUMA

Small cuts and scrapes inside the mouth heal up beautifully in 3 or 4 days—twice as fast as skin injuries. Infections of mouth injuries are rare. You'll have difficulty finding where the injury was in a few weeks. Cuts of the tongue and insides of the cheeks due to accidentally biting oneself during eating are the most common mouth injury. Cuts and bruises of the lips are usually due to falls. A tear of the piece of tissue connecting the upper lip to the gum is very common. It can look terrible and bleed profusely until pressure is applied, but it is harmless. The potentially serious mouth injuries are those to the tonsil, soft palate, or back of the throat (as from falling with a pencil in the mouth). Prevent these by teaching your child not to run or play with any long object in the mouth. Cuts in the mouth usually don't require suturing except for loose flaps of tissue or gaping wounds of the tongue.

Similar Condition • If appropriate, turn directly to the guideline for TEETH TRAUMA, page 85

CALL YOUR CHILD'S PHYSICIAN IMMEDIATELY IF

• Any bleeding won't stop after 10 minutes of direct pressure.

• A deep or gaping cut is present and probably needs sutures.

• The injury is to the back of the throat.

• It resulted from falling down with a stick or other long object in the mouth.

• The pain is severe.

• You have other urgent questions.

HOME CARE FOR MOUTH TRAUMA

Stop Any Bleeding • Stop any bleeding by pressing the bleeding site against the teeth or jaw for 10 minutes. For bleeding from the tongue, squeeze the bleeding site with a sterile gauze or piece of clean cloth. Don't release the pressure until 10 minutes are up. Once bleeding from inside the lip stops, don't pull the lip out again to look at it. Every time you do, the bleeding will start again.

Pain Relief • The area will probably hurt for 1 or 2 days. Apply a piece of ice or a Popsicle as often as necessary. If there is pain at bedtime, give acetaminophen. Avoid aspirin because it increases the tendency to bleed easily. For a day or so, offer your child a soft diet. Avoid any salty or citrus foods that might sting. Keep food out of the wound by rinsing the area well with water immediately after meals.

Call Your Child's Physician Later If

• You feel the area is becoming infected, especially increasing pain or swelling after 48 hours. (Keep in mind that any healing wound in the mouth is normally white for several days.)

• A fever (over 100°F) occurs.

• Other questions come up.

NOSE TRAUMA

Most blows to the nose result in a bloody nose or swelling and bruising of the nose but no fracture. Even when a fracture is present, nasal X rays often show nothing conclusive. The best course of action is to wait until day 4, when the swelling is gone. If the nose then appears to be crooked, you will probably be referred to an ear, nose, and throat surgeon. For mild fractures of the nose, this delayed correction leads to the best cosmetic results because the surgeon can see what he is changing. Severe fractures of the nose are often reset immediately.

CALL YOUR CHILD'S PHYSICIAN IMMEDIATELY IF

• The nose is definitely broken or crooked.

• The skin is split open and probably needs sutures.

• A nosebleed won't stop after 10 minutes of pinching the nostrils closed.

• Clear fluid is draining continuously from the nose.

• Pain is severe.

• Breathing is blocked on one side (when you close the other nostril with your finger) or both sides.

• A swelling of the septum (central dividing wall) is visible inside one nostril.

• You have other urgent questions.

HOME CARE FOR NOSE TRAUMA

Bruises or Swelling • Apply ice to the area for the next hour. Give acetaminophen as necessary for pain. (Aspirin should be avoided, since it can increase the body's tendency to bleed easily and make nosebleeds worse.)

Superficial Cuts or Abrasions • Wash the area vigorously with soap and water for 5 minutes. Then apply pressure for 10 minutes with a sterile gauze to stop bleeding. Leave the area exposed to the air. To stop bleeding from the nostrils, see the guideline on NOSEBLEED, page 544.

Call Your Child's Physician Later If

• The shape of the nose has not returned to normal in 4 days.

• A yellow discharge, increasing tenderness, fever, or other signs of infection occur.

• Other questions come up.

SKIN TRAUMA

The following four skin injuries are covered. Go directly to the type of injury that pertains to your child.

Bruises
Cuts and Scratches
Puncture Wounds
Scrapes (Abrasions)

BRUISES

Bleeding into or under the skin from damaged blood vessels gives a black-and-blue mark. Since the skin is not broken, there is no risk of infection. Bruises usually follow trauma with blunt objects. Unexplained bruises can indicate a bleeding tendency. (Exception: Bruises overlying the shins don't count, since children so commonly bump this area and then forget about it.)

CALL YOUR CHILD'S PHYSICIAN IMMEDIATELY IF

• Bruises are unexplained *and* several in number.

HOME CARE FOR BRUISES

Bruises • Apply ice for 20 minutes. No other treatment should be necessary. Give acetaminophen for pain. Avoid aspirin, since it may prolong the bleeding. Avoid massage. Bruises clear in 2 to 4 weeks after undergoing yellow, green, and brown color changes.

Blood Blisters • Do not open blisters; it will only increase the possibility of infection. They will dry up and peel off in 1 to 2 weeks.

RELATED TOPIC

Bone, Joint, and Muscle Trauma (see page 63)

CUTS AND SCRATCHES

Most cuts are superficial and extend only partially through the skin. They are caused by sharp objects. The cuts that need sutures (stitches) are deep, go through the skin to the fat layer, have fat protruding from the wound, and leave the skin edges separated. Another rule of thumb is that cuts need sutures if they are longer than ½ inch (¼ inch if on the face).

CALL YOUR CHILD'S PHYSICIAN

Immediately If

• Bleeding won't stop after 10 minutes of direct pressure.

• The skin is split open and probably needs sutures.

• The cut is deep (e.g., you can see bone or tendons).

• There is any dirt in the wound which you can't get out. Note: Lacerations must be sutured within 12 hours of the time of injury, and the infection rate is far lower if they are closed within 2 or 3 hours.

During Office Hours If

• Your child hasn't had a tetanus booster in more than 10 years (5 years for dirty cuts).

HOME CARE FOR CUTS AND SCRATCHES

Treatment • Wash your hands. Then wash the wound vigorously for at least 5 minutes with soap and water. Thorough washing is more important than the type of soap; a liquid soap provides more cleansing penetration. Rinse the wound well. Leave small cuts exposed to the air. If the area is one that will probably get dirty (such as the hands or feet), cover it with a Band-Aid or sterile gauze and adhesive tape for several days. Change the dressing daily. Antiseptic ointments or sprays are unnecessary. Don't use alcohol or Merthiolate on open wounds. They sting and damage the normal tissue. Hydrogen peroxide also is not used, because it can break down normal clots and is a feeble germ-killer.

Common Mistakes • Teach your children that kissing an open wound is dangerous, because the wound will become contaminated by the many germs in the human mouth. Let the scab fall off by itself; picking it off may cause a scar.

Call Your Child's Physician Later If

• The cut looks infected (pus is visible, for instance).

- Pain, redness, or swelling increases after 48 hours.

- The wound doesn't heal within 10 days.

RELATED TOPICS

BITES, ANIMAL OR HUMAN (see page 14)
WOUND INFECTIONS (see page 88)
SUTURE REMOVAL (see page 88)

PUNCTURE WOUNDS

The skin has been completely punctured by an object that is pointed and narrow. The most common puncture wound follows stepping on a nail. The wound is not wide enough to need sutures. Since puncture wounds usually seal over quickly and are not cleansed by any active bleeding, wound infections of all kinds are more common with this type of skin injury. Puncture wounds of the upper eyelid (as from a sharp pencil) are especially dangerous and can result in a brain abscess. A deep infection of the foot can begin with swelling of the top of the foot 1 to 2 weeks after the puncture. Tetanus (lockjaw) can occur if your child is not immunized.

CALL YOUR CHILD'S PHYSICIAN

Immediately If

- A dirty object caused the puncture.

- The skin was quite dirty at the time.

- The object went through a shoe.

- You can see some debris (crud) in the wound after soaking.

- The tip of the object could have broken off in the wound.

- The puncture is on the head, chest, abdomen, or overlying a joint.

- Your child has never received a tetanus shot.

During Office Hours If

- Your child hasn't had a tetanus booster in more than 5 years.

HOME CARE FOR PUNCTURE WOUNDS

Treatment • Soak the wound in hot water and a liquid soap for 15 minutes to promote circulation and cleansing. Cut off any flaps of loose skin. If you can make the wound rebleed, that would be helpful. A Band-Aid and antibiotic ointment on the wound for 12 hours will help keep the opening clean.

Call Your Child's Physician Later If

• The wound looks infected.

• Pain, redness, or swelling increases after 48 hours.

RELATED TOPIC

Wound Infections (see page 88)

SCRAPES (ABRASIONS)

An abrasion is an area of superficial skin that has been scraped off during a fall—a "skinned" knee from skidding on gravel, for instance. The mild ones are often called friction burns (such as a rope burn or floor burn).

CALL YOUR CHILD'S PHYSICIAN

Immediately If

• There is any dirt or grime in the wound which you can't get out.

• It was a bicycle-spoke injury.

• It was a washing machine wringer injury.

• It is quite deep. (Note: If the complete layer of skin is removed, a skin graft may be necessary.)

• It involves a very large area.

• The pain is severe.

During Office Hours If

• Your child hasn't had a tetanus booster in more than 10 years.

HOME CARE FOR SCRAPES

Cleaning the Scrape • First, wash your hands. Then wash the wound vigorously for at least 5 minutes with a liquid soap and warm water. The area will probably need to be scrubbed several times with a wet gauze to get all the dirt out. You may have to remove some dirty particles (e.g., gravel) with a tweezers. If there is tar in the wound, it can often be removed by rubbing it with petroleum jelly, followed by soap and water again. A detergent cuts grease better than bar soap. Pieces of loose skin (especially if they are dirty) should be cut off with a sterile scissors. Rinse the wound well.

Dressing the Scrape • If it is small, leave it exposed to the air. If it is large, cover it with a nonsticking dressing. Change this in 12 hours, and after 24 hours leave the wound open. Exception: Scrapes on the hands and feet need to be kept covered until healed. See the next paragraph about daily dressing changes.

Antibiotic Ointment • Antiseptic ointments or sprays in general are unnecessary. However, abrasions overlying the elbow, knee, or hand undergo constant stretch. To prevent cracking and reopening of these, apply an antibiotic ointment to keep the crust soft. Use Bacitracin or Betadine ointment. Cleanse the area once a day with warm water, then reapply the ointment.

Aspirin or Acetaminophen • Since abrasions can hurt badly, use acetaminophen for the first day. (For dosage, see chart on page 411.)

Call Your Child's Physician Later If

• The scrape looks infected.

• The scrape increases in size or spreads to good skin.

• The scrape doesn't heal within 2 weeks.

RELATED TOPIC

WOUND INFECTIONS (see page 88)

TAILBONE TRAUMA

The tailbone (or coccyx) is the small bone at the lower end of the spine. The tailbone is usually injured during a fall onto a hard surface, such as ice or stairs. The pain usually is due to bruising of the bone or stretching of the ligaments. Fractures of the tailbone are rare and they heal fine, so an X ray is unnecessary for this injury. Dislocations of the tailbone are also rare, but they need to be put back in place by a physician. Tailbone injuries can be diagnosed by finding tenderness of the bone located in the upper part of the groove between the buttocks.

HOME CARE FOR TAILBONE TRAUMA

A bruised tailbone will usually hurt for 3 to 4 weeks. Give your youngster acetaminophen for 2 or 3 days (for dosage, see chart on page 66). Sitting on a large rubber ring or a cushion placed forward on the chair will take pressure off the tailbone. A heating pad may also help. Occasionally bowel movements will cause enough discomfort that 1 or 2 tablespoons of mineral oil will temporarily be needed twice a day. (See also CONSTIPATION, page 586, regarding a nonconstipating diet.) Call your physician if the pain is severe.

TEETH TRAUMA

This guideline covers injuries to the teeth (usually the front ones). Often, the only noticeable injury is bleeding from the gums. The tooth has been jarred and perhaps slightly loosened. These minor injuries heal in 3 days. The next most common injury is tooth displacement (usually pushed inward). It usually returns to its normal position within a few weeks without any treatment. Chipped (or fractured) teeth need to be seen by a dentist. Permanent teeth that are knocked out (avulsed) constitute an emergency.

First Aid for Replacing a Permanent Tooth • Although primary teeth can't successfully be reimplanted, permanent (second) teeth need to be returned to their sockets and the gumline as soon as possible. Best results occur if the tooth is reimplanted within 15 minutes. After 2 hours, replacement is worthless. Ideally, the tooth should be returned to the socket at the scene of the accident.

• Rinse off the tooth with saliva or water.

• Replace it in the socket facing the correct way.

• Press down on the tooth with your thumb until the crown is level with the adjacent tooth.

- Have your child bite down on a wad of cloth to stabilize the tooth until you can reach your dentist.

CALL YOUR CHILD'S DENTIST

(Call your physician only if your dentist can't be reached and you are dealing with an emergency.)

Immediately If

- A permanent tooth has been knocked out. (If you haven't been able to replace it, bring it with you in a cup in some of your child's saliva or some milk.)

- A large piece of tooth has been chipped off.

- A red dot is visible inside a fractured tooth.

- The pain is severe.

- Any bleeding won't stop after 10 minutes of direct pressure. (For bleeding with missing teeth, have your child chomp down on a piece of gauze.)

During Office Hours If

- A baby tooth has been knocked out by trauma.

- A small piece of tooth has been chipped off.

- You can see a fracture line in the tooth.

- The tooth is sensitive to cold fluids.

- The tooth has been pushed out of its usual position.

- The tooth is more than slightly loose.

- You have other questions.

HOME CARE FOR TEETH TRAUMA

Treatment • Apply a piece of ice or a Popsicle to the injured gum area, unless it increases the pain. If it still hurts, give your child some acetaminophen. Avoid aspirin, because it increases the bleeding tendency. If any teeth are loose, put your child on a soft diet for 3 days. If a tooth is out of its normal position, try to reposition it with a little finger pressure. If a tooth is broken and dental care must be delayed, temporarily seal the sensitive area with melted candle wax. A delay of several days, however, may lead to a root-canal infection.

Prevention • Prevent tooth trauma in children who play contact sports by having them wear a mouth guard.

Call Your Child's Dentist Later If

- Any new symptoms develop.

- The tooth becomes sensitive to hot or cold fluids during the next week.

- The tooth becomes a darker color.

TETANUS BOOSTER FOLLOWING TRAUMA

The need for a tetanus booster depends on the type of wound (whether or not it is tetanus-prone) and your child's immunization status. All puncture wounds and all cuts (breaks in the skin) caused by an unclean object pose a risk of tetanus. Cuts from a clean knife, piece of glass, etc., are not tetanus-prone wounds unless they become contaminated afterwards. Neither are minor burns or scrapes, because these injuries are so superficial that they have adequate exposure to air. The tetanus bacteria can multiply only if buried in a wound where no air is present. Most children have scrapes from time to time; tetanus boosters for all of these wounds would be impractical.

CALL YOUR CHILD'S PHYSICIAN DURING OFFICE HOURS FOR

- Any puncture wound or dirty cut in children who have had no tetanus booter in more than 5 years.

- Any wound in patients who have had no tetanus booster in more than 10 years. (All immunized children and adults need a tetanus booster every 10 years.)

The administration of a tetanus booster is not an emergency. It can wait 24 hours without increasing the risk of tetanus. Most physicians give a Td booster at these times to help maintain adequate protection against diphtheria as well.

Cautions: If your child has not been immunized against tetanus and sustains a wound, he needs to be seen immediately. Also, if a wound needs suturing, it should be treated as soon as possible.

SUTURE REMOVAL

The following guidelines can serve as a reminder that sutures (stitches) are ready for removal at different times, depending on the site of the wound.

AREA	NUMBER OF DAYS
Face	3–4
Neck	5
Scalp	6
Anterior chest or abdomen	7
Arms and back of hands	7
Legs and top of feet	10
Back	12
Palms and soles	14

If any sutures come out early, call your child's physician. In the meantime, reinforce the wound with tape. Stitches removed too late can leave unnecessary skin marks or even scarring.

If your child needed sutures, he will develop a scar. All wounds heal by scarring. The scar can be kept to a minimum by taking the sutures out at the right time, preventing wound infections, and protecting the wound from being reinjured during the following month. The healing process goes on for 6 to 12 months; only then will the scar assume its final appearance.

WOUND INFECTIONS

Most contaminated wounds that are going to become infected do so 24 to 72 hours after the initial injury. An infected wound develops redness, tenderness, and pus. Keep in mind that a 2 mm to 3 mm rim of pinkness or redness, confined to the edge of a wound, can be normal, especially if the wound is sutured. However, the area of redness should not be spreading. Pain and tenderness also occur normally, but the pain and swelling are at a peak during the second day and thereafter diminish. If the infection spreads beyond the wound, it will follow the lymph channels and cause a red streak. If the infection reaches the bloodstream ("blood poisoning"), a fever will be present. The healing process can normally cause mild swelling and tenderness of the lymph nodes that drain the injured area.

CALL YOUR CHILD'S PHYSICIAN

Immediately If

• The wound is extremely tender.

• An unexplained fever (over 100°F) occurs.

• A red streak runs from the wound.

• The wound infection is on the face.

Within 24 Hours If

• You can see pus in the wound, or there is pus draining from it.

• A pimple starts to form where a stitch comes through the skin.

• The wound is becoming more tender than it was on the second day.

• You have other questions or concerns.

HOME CARE

Treatment of Mild Redness • Use warm salt water soaks or compresses (1 tablespoon of table salt per quart of water) on the wound for 15 minutes, 3 times a day. Dry the area thoroughly afterward.

Call Your Child's Physician Later If

• The wound becomes more tender.

• Pus or drainage develops.

• The redness starts to spread.

• You feel your child is getting worse.

III.

NEW BABY CARE

NORMAL NEWBORNS

FIRST DAYS IN THE HOSPITAL: GETTING ACQUAINTED

PRENATAL TASKS

Childbirth-preparation classes are especially important during the first pregnancy. These classes reduce the amount of fear that normal parents harbor about labor. They also teach mothers various techniques to control the pain of labor and delivery. In addition they introduce the parents to the world of hospital obstetrics. If at all possible, both parents-to-be should attend these classes, which ideally (though not essentially) will be taught by a husband-and-wife team. During the prenatal period you will have carefully considered the following five questions:

- Will the father be present at labor and delivery? Most fathers find this a memorable experience, and most mothers are grateful to have their husbands present for emotional support. In general, siblings should not be present at the delivery because some of them become frightened by the birth process.

- What baby equipment will you buy? (See NEWBORN EQUIPMENT AND SUPPLIES, page 118.)

- What will you name your baby? Try to narrow your list down to two male and two female names by the time of delivery.

- Will you breast-feed or bottle-feed? (See BREAST-FEEDING, page 145, and FORMULA-FEEDING, page 151.) In some communities, breast-feeding preparation classes are available.

93

- If your newborn is a boy, will you have him circumcised? (See THE CIRCUMCISION DECISION: PROS AND CONS, page 113.)

- If you have other children, who will baby-sit while you are in the hospital? Who will help you during the first weeks after you come home from the hospital? (See page 97.)

DELIVERY- OR BIRTHING-ROOM CONTACT WITH YOUR BABY

Parent bonding to an infant is one of the strongest human ties. This bonding gets off to a good start if the mother and father have close contact with their newborn during the first day of life. After your baby has been dried off and placed in a warm blanket, both parents can have some private time with the infant until he or she falls asleep. The period of wakefulness usually lasts from 30 to 60 minutes. Many studies over the past decade have found that early contact (preferably 6 hours during the first day) increases the parents' ability to soothe the baby, increases the likelihood of successful breast-feeding, enhances language development, and maximizes the sense that the baby belongs to the parents. This information underscores the importance of the father's being involved with his baby on the day of birth.

ROOMING-IN WITH YOUR BABY

Most hospitals now have units on the maternity ward where the mother and baby can constantly be together, with backup by the nursing staff. Increasing numbers of hospitals have gone over to this arrangement entirely. Others allow modified rooming-in, in which the baby is with the mother whenever the mother is awake. Rooming-in promotes bonding and a better feeding schedule. In this manner, the mother is quite familiar with her newborn by the time she is discharged. The nursing staff is available to help rather than replace the mother.

FEEDING: GETTING STARTED

Getting breast-feeding off to a good start will help guarantee success. During the first 30 minutes of quiet alert behavior after delivery, many babies will be interested in nursing at the breast. For others, the first real attempt at breast-feeding will occur when the baby awakens from his or her initial sleep, at 3 to 6 hours after delivery. Early sucking on the breast stimulates it to begin producing milk. Your baby should nurse for 10 minutes on the first breast and as long as he wants on the second breast.

Ask your nurse for help with correct breast-feeding positioning. Your baby's face and abdomen should be against your body so he doesn't have to turn his head to nurse. This position is 90 degrees different from the bottle-feeding position. Also keep his nose clear of the breast for breathing. Breast-feeding should be repeated on demand, approximately every 2 hours, including night feedings. Have your infant brought to your room at night to nurse if he or she is not rooming in with you around the clock. Supplementary formula or glucose water should not be offered during the first 6 weeks, because it interferes with sucking and milk production. Supplementation during the first week of life (especially in the newborn's nursery) is the most common cause of inadequate breast milk production. Any mother who needs to be supplementing also needs to be pumping her breasts.

Don't expect a full milk supply until your milk "comes in" on the second to fourth day after delivery. A common error during this period of engorgement is failing to compress the areola so that the infant can grasp the nipple correctly. Take advantage of the brief hospital stay to get as much help with breast-feeding as possible before going home.

Healthy formula-fed babies should be offered formula as soon as they display an interest in feeding, which is usually 3 to 6 hours after delivery when they awaken from their first sleep. Bottle-fed babies typically take ½ ounce (15 ml) at the first feeding. By 3 days of age, full-term infants will usually take 2 ounces every 3 to 4 hours.

LEARNING PARENTING SKILLS

During the hospital stay, both parents should take a crash course in caring for their newborn. Many of the skills will be demonstrated by the nursing staff. Some will be reviewed by video tapes or audio tapes. Your child's physician may give you written instruction-sheets on some of these topics. Be certain that someone has taught you how to carry out each of the following tasks before you are discharged:

Feeding your baby (see BREAST-FEEDING, page 145, or FORMULA-FEEDING, page 151)
Soothing your baby with touching or holding when he or she is crying (see CRYING BABY [COLIC], page 239)
Normal skin care and bathing (see page 110)
Cord care (see page 112)
Circumcision care (see page 115)

Foreskin care (see page 116)

Diapering (see DIAPER RASH, page 128)

Taking a temperature (rectal and armpit) and reading a thermometer (see FEVER, page 407)

Using a suction bulb (see under COLDS, page 533)

Using an approved car safety seat (see ACCIDENT PREVENTION, page 205)

Dealing with siblings (see SIBLING RIVALRY TOWARD A NEWBORN, page 322)

Helping your baby sleep on the back to avoid suffocation (see page 58)

You should also be aware there is nothing out of the ordinary about spitting up, loose bowel movements, bowel-movement straining, and unexplained crying.

NEWBORN TESTS AND TREATMENTS

During your hospital stay, your physician will examine your new baby and answer any questions you might have about your baby's appearance (see THE NORMAL NEWBORN'S APPEARANCE, page 102). He will also review normal newborn behavior (see page 101), and symptoms to look for in the sick newborn (see page 125). During the hospital stay your baby will receive a vitamin K injection, which prevents hemorrhagic disease of the newborn, a condition that otherwise could cause severe bleeding in the first 7 days of life. Antibiotic eyedrops will be placed in each eye within one hour of birth to prevent eye infections with gonorrhea or chlamydia, two germs that can be present in the birth canal without any symptoms. A blood test to screen for metabolic diseases that could cause mental retardation will be performed from a heel stick. These genetic disorders (such as phenylketonuria or hypothyroidism) cannot be detected on a regular physical exam. Your baby's blood type will be determined only if the mother is blood group O or Rh negative. **Caution:** All of these conditions may go untreated or undetected with a home delivery. If your baby is born at home and is well, arrange medical care for the baby within 24 hours of birth.

VISITORS—FRIENDS, RELATIVES, AND CHILDREN

The father is the most important visitor. He should come as often and stay as long as possible. He should hold his baby each day. Many hospitals now allow visits by siblings. Studies show that children who visit their mothers after the birth of a newborn are more responsive to their mother and the new baby than nonvisiting children are. Children should be supervised by parents or a responsible adult during the entire hospital visit. Siblings should not visit if they have an acute illness, a fever, or recent exposure to a contagious disease. Hospital visitors, however, can wear the mother out. People should telephone before they come by. If you are tired, consider temporarily canceling all visits (except from your husband).

DISCHARGE FROM THE HOSPITAL

In our country most normal full-term newborns are discharged from the hospital with their mothers by 48 to 72 hours of age. Early discharge is defined as discharge before 24 hours of age. Some parents desire early discharge because of limited insurance coverage, a need for the mother to be home with siblings, or personal preference. A baby should not be discharged before the temperature, pulse, and respirations have stabilized, the baby has urinated, and two successful feedings have occurred. (In a successful feeding, the baby demonstrates normal sucking, swallowing, and stomach-emptying mechanisms—all necessary for weight gain.) Babies who are discharged early should be seen on the third day of life to check them for weight, jaundice, and general health. The first blood sample for phenylketonuria (PKU) should also be collected at this time. Close medical follow-up is essential for infants who are discharged early. And finally, be sure to make your baby's first ride a safe ride. Leave the hospital with your infant in a car safety seat. It's illegal not to.

FIRST WEEKS AT HOME: GETTING HELP

PREVENTING FATIGUE AND EXHAUSTION

For most mothers the first weeks at home with a new baby are often the hardest in their lives. You will probably feel overworked, even overwhelmed. Inadequate sleep will leave you with the feeling of fatigue. Caring for babies can be a lonely and stressful responsibility. You may wonder if you will ever catch up on your rest or work. The solution is asking for help. No one should be expected to care for a young baby alone. Every baby awakens one or more times a night. The way to avoid sleep deprivation is to know the total amount of sleep you need per day and to get that sleep in bits and pieces. Go to bed earlier in the evening. When your baby naps, you must also nap. Your baby doesn't need you hovering over him while he's asleep. If he is sick he will have symptoms. While you are napping, take the telephone off the hook and put up a sign on the door stating MOTHER AND BABY SLEEPING. If your total sleep remains inadequate, hire a baby-sitter or bring in a relative to allow yourself a good nap. (See the role of helpers and the father, page 99.) If you don't take care of yourself, you won't be able to take care of your baby.

THE POSTPARTUM BLUES

More than 50 percent of women experience postpartum blues on the third or fourth day after delivery. The symptoms include irrepressible crying, tiredness, sadness, and sometimes difficulty in thinking clearly. The main cause of this temporary reaction is probably the sudden decrease of maternal hormones. The full impact of being totally responsible for a dependent newborn may also be a contributing factor. If caring for your baby leads to a state of exhaustion, you may find yourself in a downward spiral. Many mothers feel guilty about these symptoms, because they have been led to believe they should be overjoyed about caring for their newborn. In any event, these symptoms usually clear in 1 to 3 weeks as the hormone levels return to normal and as the mother develops routines and a sense of control over her life.

There are several ways to cope with the postpartum blues. First, acknowledge your feelings. Discuss them with your husband or a close friend, as well as your sense of being trapped, and that these new responsibilities are insurmountable. Don't feel you need to suppress crying or put on a "Supermom show" for everyone. Second, get adequate rest. Third, get help with all your work. Fourth, mix with other people; don't become isolated. Get out of the house at least once a week—going to the hair dresser, shopping, or visiting friends. By the third week, setting aside an evening a week for a "date" with your husband is also helpful. If you don't feel better by the time your baby is 1 month old, see your physician about the possibility of needing counseling for depression.

HELPERS: RELATIVES, FRIENDS, SITTERS

As already emphasized, everyone needs extra help during the first few weeks alone with a new baby. Ideally, you were able to make arrangements for help before your baby was born. The best person to help is usually your mother or mother-in-law. If not, teenagers or adults can come in several times a week to help with housework or look after your baby while you go out or get a nap. If you have other young children, you will need daily help. Clarify that your role is looking after your baby. Your helper's role is to shop, cook, houseclean, and wash clothes and dishes. If your newborn has a medical problem that requires special care, ask for home visits by a public health nurse.

RECOMMENDED READING FOR GRANDPARENTS
Linda B. White, *The Grandparent Book*
  (San Francisco: Gateway Books, 1990).

THE FATHER'S ROLE
The father needs to take time off from work to be with his wife during labor and delivery, as well as on the day she and his child come home from the hospital. If the couple has a relative who will temporarily live in and help, the father can continue to work. However, when the relative leaves, the father can take saved-up vacation time as paternity leave. At a minimum he needs to work shorter hours until his wife and baby have settled in. The age of noninvolvement of the father is a thing of the past. Not only does the mother need the father to help her with household chores, but the baby also needs the father to develop a close relationship with him. Today's fathers get involved with feeding, changing diapers, bathing, putting to bed, reading stories, dressing, disciplining, helping with homework, playing games, and calling the physician when the child is sick. Some fathers avoid interacting with the baby during the first year of life because they are afraid they will hurt their baby or, if the baby cries, that they won't be able to calm the baby. The longer they go without learning these skills, the harder it becomes to master them. At a minimum, fathers should hold and comfort their babies at least once a day (something commonly overlooked in our culture).

RECOMMENDED READING FOR FATHERS
Martin Greenburg, *The Birth of a Father*
  (New York: Continuum, 1985).
T. Berry Brazelton, *Families, Crisis and Caring*
  (New York: Ballantine Books, 1989).

VISITORS

During the first month at home, only close friends and relatives should be allowed to visit. They should call before they visit to be sure that it is a convenient day. They should not visit if they are sick. To prevent unannounced visitors, the parents can put up a sign stating MOTHER AND BABY SLEEPING. NO VISITORS. PLEASE CALL FIRST. Friends without children may not understand your needs. During visits, the visitor should pay special attention to older siblings (see SIBLING RIVALRY TOWARD A NEWBORN, page 322).

FEEDING: ACHIEVING WEIGHT GAIN

Your main assignments during the early months of life are loving and feeding your baby. All babies lose a few ounces during the first few days after birth. However, they should never lose more than 7 percent of the birth weight (about 8 ounces). Most bottle-fed babies are back to birth weight by 10 days of age, and breast-fed babies by 14 days of age. Then, infants gain approximately an ounce per day during the early months. If milk is provided liberally, the normal newborn's hunger drive sees to it that enough weight is gained.

Breast-feeding mothers often wonder if their baby is getting enough calories, since they can't see how many ounces the baby takes. Your baby is doing fine if he or she demands to nurse every 1½ to 2½ hours, appears satisfied after feedings, takes both breasts at each nursing, wets 6 or more diapers each day, and passes 4 or more soft stools per day. Whenever you are worried about your baby's weight gain, take your baby to your physician's office for a weight check. Feeding problems detected early are much easier to remedy than those of longstanding. A special weight check 1 week after birth is a good idea for infants of first-time breast-feeding mothers or those concerned about their milk supply. (See BREAST-FEEDING, page 145, or FORMULA-FEEDING, page 151.)

DEALING WITH CRYING

Crying babies need to be held. They need someone with a soothing voice and a soothing touch. You can't spoil your baby during the early months of life. Overly sensitive babies may need a more gentle kind of touch. For additional help on this subject, see CRYING BABY (COLIC), page 239, or PREVENTION OF SLEEP PROBLEMS, page 243.

TAKING YOUR BABY OUTDOORS

Your baby can be taken outdoors at any age; just dress for the weather. You already took him outdoors when you left the hospital, and you will be going outside again when you take him for the two-week checkup. Dress him with as many layers of clothing as an adult would wear for the outdoor temperature. The most common mistake is overdressing babies in the summertime. (See also SUNBURN, page 484.) In the wintertime, babies need a hat because they often don't have much hair to protect against heat loss. The idea that cold air or winds can cause ear infections or pneumonia is a myth. Camping and crowds should probably be avoided during the first month of life. Also try to avoid close contact with sick people during the first year of life.

THE TWO-WEEK MEDICAL CHECKUP

This checkup is probably the most important medical visit during the first year of life. Any physical condition that was not detectable during the hospital stay will usually have developed symptoms by 2 weeks of age. From your baby's height, weight, and head circumference, your child's physician will be able to judge how well your child is growing. This is also the time during which your family is under the most stress of adapting to a new baby. Try to develop a habit of jotting down questions about your child's health or behavior at home. Bring this list with you to office visits for discussion with your child's physician. Most physicians welcome the opportunity to address your agenda, especially if your questions are ones not easily answered by reading or talking with other mothers. If at all possible, have your husband join you on these visits to the physician's office. Most physicians prefer to get to know the father during a checkup rather than during the crisis time of an acute illness. If you think your newborn is sick between health supervision visits, be sure to call your physician for help (see THE SICK NEWBORN: SUBTLE SYMPTOMS, page 125).

THE NORMAL NEWBORN'S BEHAVIOR

Some findings in newborns that concern parents are not signs of illness. The best evidence that these behaviors are harmless is that the infant does not seem to mind them. Most of these reflexes are due to an immature nervous system and will disappear in 2 or 3 months:

- Chin trembling

- Lower lip quivering

- Hiccups

- Irregular breathing (It's normal, if your baby is content, the rate is less than 60 breaths per minute, a pause is less than 6 seconds, and your baby doesn't turn blue). Occasionally infants take rapid, progressively deeper, stepwise breaths to expand their lungs completely.

- A seesaw motion of the chest and abdomen with breathing due to the diaphragm moving up and down.

- Passing gas (not a temporary behavior). (See GAS, EXCESSIVE, page 599.)

- Sleep noise from breathing and moving

- Sneezing

- Spitting up or belching. (See SPITTING UP, page 133, for details.)

- Startle reflex or brief stiffening of the body (also called the Moro or embrace reflex) following noise or movement

- Straining with bowel movements

- Throat clearing (or gurgling sounds of secretions in the throat)

- Trembling or jitteriness of arms and legs during crying. Jittery babies are common. Convulsions are rare. During convulsions, babies also have jerking or blinking of the eyes, rhythmic sucking of the mouth, and they don't cry. If your baby is trembling and not crying, give her something to suck on. If the trembling doesn't stop during sucking, call your child's physician immediately.

- Yawning

THE NORMAL NEWBORN'S APPEARANCE

Even after your child's physician assures you that your baby is normal and has all his parts, you may find that he looks a bit odd. He does not have the perfect body you have seen in baby books. Be patient. Most newborns have some peculiar characteristics. Fortunately they are temporary. Your baby will begin to look normal by 1 to 2 weeks of age.

The discussion of these temporary newborn characteristics is arranged by parts of the body. A few minor congenital defects that are harmless but permanent will also be included (marked by an asterisk). Talk with your child's physician if you are not sure that what you see on your baby matches what is described on this list. Better yet, find out when he is coming to the hospital so he can examine your baby in your presence.

HEAD

Molding • Molding refers to the long, narrow, cone-shaped head that results from passage through a tight birth canal. This compression of the head can temporarily hide the fontanel. The head returns to a normal shape in a few days.

Caput • This refers to swelling on top of the head or throughout the scalp due to fluid squeezed into the scalp during the birth process. Caput is present at birth and clears in a few days.

Cephalohematoma • This is a collection of blood on the outer surface of the skull. It is due to friction between the skull and the pelvic bones during the birth process. The lump is usually confined to one side of the head. It first appears on the second day of life and may increase in size for up to 5 days. It doesn't resolve completely until 2 or 3 months of age.

Anterior Fontanel • The "soft spot" is found in the top front part of the skull. It is diamond-shaped and covered by a thick fibrous layer. Touching this area is quite safe. The purpose of the soft spot is to allow rapid growth of the brain. The soft spot will normally pulsate with each beat of the heart. It normally closes over with bone between 9 and 12 months of age.

EYES

Swollen Eyelids • The eyes may be puffy due to pressure on the face during delivery. They may be puffy and reddened if silver nitrate eyedrops are used. This irritation should clear in 3 days.

Subconjunctival Hemorrhage • A flame-shaped hemorrhage on the white of the eye (sclera) is not uncommon. It's harmless and due to birth trauma. The blood is reabsorbed in 2 to 3 weeks.

Iris Color • The iris generally comes in variations of four colors: blue, green, gray, or brown. The permanent color of the iris is often uncertain until your baby reaches 6 months of age. White babies are usually born with blue-gray eyes. Black babies are usually born with brown-gray eyes. Children who are going to have dark irises often change color early (by 2 months of age). Children who are going to have light-colored irises usually change closer to 5 or 6 months of age.

Tear Duct, Blocked • See page 135.

EARS

Folded Over • The ears of newborns are commonly soft and floppy. Sometimes one of the edges is folded over. The outer ear will assume normal shape as the cartilage hardens over the first few weeks.

Earpits • About 1 percent of normal children have a small pit or dimple in front of the outer ear. This minor congenital defect is of no importance unless it becomes infected.

NOSE

Flattened • The nose can become misshapen during the birth process. It may be flattened or pushed to one side. It will look normal by 1 week of age.

MOUTH

Sucking Callus (or blister) • Sucking callus occurs in the center of the upper lip and is due to constant friction at this point during bottle- or breast-feeding. It will disappear when your child begins cup feedings. Children may also develop a sucking callus on the thumb or wrist.

Tongue-Tie • The normal tongue in newborns has a short, tight band that connects it to the floor of the mouth. This band normally stretches with time, movement, and growth. I have never seen a baby with symptoms from tongue-tie (see page 561).

Epithelial Pearls • Little cysts (containing clear fluid) or shallow white ulcers can occur along the gumline or on the hard palate. These are due to blockage of normal mucous glands. They disappear by 1 to 2 months of age.

Teeth • The presence of a tooth at birth is a rare event. Approximately 10 percent of them are extra teeth without a root structure. The other 90 percent are prematurely erupted normal teeth. The distinction can be made with an X ray. The extra teeth must be removed by a dentist. The normal teeth need to be removed only if they become loose (with a danger of choking) or if they cause sores on your baby's tongue.

BREASTS

Breast Engorgement • Swollen breasts are present during the first week of life in many girl and boy babies. They are caused by the passage of female hormones across the mother's placenta. Swollen breasts generally last for 4 to 6 months, but longer in breast-fed and girl babies. One breast may become less swollen before the other one by a month or more. Never squeeze the breast because this can cause infection. Be sure to call your child's physician if the swollen breast develops any redness, streaking, or tenderness.

GENITALS, GIRLS

Swollen Labia • The labia minora can be quite swollen in newborns due to the passage of female hormones across the placenta. The swelling will resolve in 2 to 4 weeks.

Hymenal Tags • The hymen can also be swollen due to maternal estrogen and have smooth ½-inch projections of pink tissue. These normal tags occur in 10 percent of newborn girls and slowly shrink over 2 to 4 weeks.

Vaginal Discharge • As the maternal hormones decline in the baby's blood, a clear or white discharge can flow from the vagina during the latter part of the first week of life. Occasionally the discharge will become pink or blood-tinged (false menstruation). This normal discharge should not recur once it stops.

GENITALS, BOYS

Hydrocele • The newborn scrotum can be filled with clear fluid. This fluid is squeezed into the scrotum during the birth process. (See SWELLING, GROIN OR SCROTUM, page 620, for details.)

Undescended Testicle • The testicle is not in the scrotum in about 4 percent of full-term newborns. Many of these testicles gradually descend into the normal position during the following months. By 1 year of age only 0.7 percent of all testicles are undescended. These need to be brought down surgically.

Tight Foreskin • Most uncircumcised babies have a tight foreskin that doesn't allow one to see the head of the penis. This is normal and should not be retracted. (See FORESKIN CARE AND PROBLEMS, page 116, for details.)

Erections • Erections occur commonly in the newborn infant, as they do at all ages. They are usually triggered by a full bladder. Erections demonstrate that the nerves to the penis are normal.

Urine Stream • The normal urine stream is forceful and may travel 2 feet at the speed of light. If your son's stream is weak or dribbly or he has to strain down to urinate, he needs to see his physician to be sure he doesn't have an obstruction (posterior urethral valves).

BONES AND JOINTS

Tight Hips • Your child's physician will test how far your child's legs can be spread apart to be certain the hips are not too tight. Bending the upper legs outward until they are horizontal is called 90 degrees of spread. (Less than 50 percent of normal newborn hips permit this much spreading.) As long as the upper legs can be bent outward to 60 degrees and are the same on each side, they are fine. The most common cause of a tight hip is a dislocation.

Tibial Torsion • The lower legs (tibia) normally curve in because of the cross-legged posture that your baby was confined to while in the womb. If you stand your baby up, you will also notice that the legs are bowed. Both of these curves are normal and will straighten out after your child has been walking for 6 to 12 months.

Feet Turned Up, In, or Out • Feet can turn any which way because of the cramped quarters inside the womb. As long as the feet are flexible and can be easily moved to a normal position, they are normal. The direction of the feet will become more normal between 6 and 12 months of age.

Long Second Toe • The second toe is longer than the great toe by heredity in some ethnic groups that originated along the Mediterranean, especially Egyptians.

"Ingrown" Toenails • Many newborns have soft nails that easily bend and curve. However, they are not truly ingrown because they don't curve into the flesh.

HAIR

Scalp Hair • Most hair at birth is dark-colored. This hair is temporary and begins to shed by 1 month of age. Some babies lose it gradually while the permanent hair is coming in; others lose it rapidly, and temporarily become bald. The permanent hair will appear by 6 months. It may be an entirely different color from the newborn hair.

Body Hair (lanugo) • Lanugo is the fine, downy hair that is sometimes present on the back and shoulders. It is more common in premature infants. It is rubbed off with normal friction by 2 to 4 weeks of age.

SKIN

See NEWBORN RASHES AND BIRTHMARKS, page 108.
Some bruises on the head or face from the birth process are not unusual. They don't require any treatment.

MINOR BIRTH DEFECTS

Minor defects of the body surface are found at birth in over 13 percent of newborns. Most of them have no medical significance (e.g., an extra toe). A few are markers for major internal abnormalities. Examples are an ear tag, which can be accompanied by deafness, or a birthmark overlying the lower back, which can be accompanied by spinal cord defects. Such children need a hearing test and spinal X rays, respectively.

NEWBORN RASHES AND BIRTHMARKS

After the first bath, your newborn will normally have a ruddy complexion due to the extra high count of red blood cells. He can quickly change to a pale- or mottled-blue color if he becomes cold, so keep him warm. During the second week of life, the skin will normally become dry and flaky. In this guideline, the following seven rashes and birthmarks are covered. Save time by going directly to the one that pertains to your baby.

ACNE
DROOLING RASH
ERYTHEMA TOXICUM
FORCEPS OR BIRTH CANAL TRAUMA
MILIA
MONGOLIAN SPOTS
STORK BITES (PINK BIRTHMARKS)

ACNE

More than 30 percent of newborns develop acne of the face—mainly small red bumps. This neonatal acne begins at 3 to 4 weeks of age and lasts until 4 to 6 months of age. The cause appears to be the transfer of maternal hormones just prior to birth. Since it is temporary, no treatment is necessary. Baby oil or ointments make it worse.

DROOLING RASH

Many babies have a rash on the chin or cheeks that comes and goes. This is often due to contact with food and acid that has been spit up from the stomach (especially prolonged contact during sleep). Rinsing the face with water after all feedings can help. Having babies sleep on the back has also reduced the frequency of face rashes.

Other temporary rashes on the face are heat rashes in areas held against the mother's skin during nursing (especially in the summertime). Change your baby's position more frequently and put a cool washcloth on the area. No baby has perfect skin. The babies in advertisements wear makeup.

ERYTHEMA TOXICUM

More than 50 percent of babies get a rash called erythema toxicum on the second or third day of life. The rash is composed of ½-inch to 1-inch red blotches with a small white lump in the center. They look like insect bites, but are not. They can be numerous, keep occurring, be present anywhere on the body surface (except the palms and soles), and look terrible. Their cause is unknown, they are harmless, and they resolve by 2 weeks of age (rarely, 4 weeks).

FORCEPS OR BIRTH CANAL TRAUMA

If your baby's delivery was difficult, a forceps may have been used to help him through the birth canal. The pressure of the forceps on the skin can leave bruises, scrapes, or damaged fat tissue anywhere on the head or face. Skin overlying bony prominences (such as the sides of the skull bone) can become damaged even without a forceps delivery by pressure from the birth canal. Fetal monitors can also cause scrapes and scabs on the scalp. The bruises and scrapes will be noted on day 1 or day 2 and disappear by 1 to 2 weeks. The fat tissue injury (subcutaneous fat necrosis) won't be apparent until day 5 to day 10. A firm coin-shaped lump, attached to the skin and sometimes with an overlying scab, is the usual finding. This lump may take 3 or 4 weeks to resolve. If it becomes tender to the touch, soft in the center, or shows other signs of infection, call your child's physician.

MILIA

Milia are tiny white bumps that occur on the faces of 40 percent of newborn babies. The nose and cheeks are most often involved, but milia are also seen on the forehead and chin. Although they look like pimples, they are smaller and not infected. They are blocked-off skin pores and will open up and disappear by 1 to 2 months of age. No ointments or creams should be applied to them.

Any true blisters or pimples (especially of the scalp) that occur during the first month of life must be examined and diagnosed quickly. If they are caused by the herpes virus, treatment is urgent.

MONGOLIAN SPOTS

A Mongolian spot is a bluish-green or bluish-gray flat birthmark that is found in over 90 percent of Native American, Oriental, Hispanic, and black babies. They are also seen in 10 percent of Caucasians, especially those of Mediterranean descent. They occur most commonly over the back and buttocks, although they can be present on any part of the body. They vary greatly in size and shape. They have no relationship to any disease. Most fade away by 2 or 3 years of age, although a trace may persist into adult life.

STORK BITES (PINK BIRTHMARKS)

Flat pink birthmarks (also called capillary hemangiomas or salmon patches) occur over the bridge of the nose, the eyelids, or the back of the neck ("stork bites") in more than 50 percent of newborns. The ones in front are often referred to as "an angel's kiss." All the birthmarks on the bridge of the nose and eyelids clear completely. Those on the eyelids clear by 1 year of age; those on the bridge of the nose may persist for a few additional years. Most birthmarks on the nape of the neck also clear, but 25 percent can persist into adult life. Talk with your child's physician during regular visits about bloodvessel birthmarks that are raised or increasing in size (strawberry hemangiomas). These run a small risk of bleeding with trauma. They persist until 6 to 8 years of age but go away without any treatment.

NEWBORN SKIN CARE AND BATHING

BATHING

Bathe your baby daily in hot weather, once or twice a week in cool weather. Keep the water level below the navel or give sponge baths until 2 days after the cord has fallen off. (Reasons: Sitting in poopy bath water can cause a cord infection. Also submerging the cord may interfere with its drying out and falling off. Getting it a little wet doesn't matter.) Use tap water without soap or use a nondrying soap (such as Dove) sparingly. Don't forget to wash the face; otherwise, chemicals from milk or other foods can build up and cause an irritated rash. Also rinse off the eyelids with clean water. The ear canals don't need cleaning. Putting cotton swabs in them just pushes the earwax back in and leads to blockage and possible hearing problems. The earwax moves outward naturally; just pick off flakes of earwax as they come to the surface. Don't forget to wash the genital area. The male genitals can be washed with either plain water or a mild soap. However, when you wash the inside of the female genital area (the vulva), never use soap. This tissue is very sensitive to any soap. Rinse the area with plain water, wiping from front to back. This practice and the avoidance of any bubble baths before puberty may prevent many urinary tract infections and vaginal irritations. At the end of the bath, rinse your baby well; soap residue can be irritating.

RELATED TOPICS

CIRCUMCISION CARE AND PROBLEMS (see page 115)
FORESKIN CARE AND PROBLEMS (see page 116)

CHANGING DIAPERS

After wet diapers are removed, just rinse your baby's bottom off with a wet washcloth. After soiled diapers, rinse the bottom under running warm water. After you finish the rear, cleanse the genital area by wiping front to back with a wet cloth. In boys, carefully clean the scrotum; and in girls, the creases of the vaginal lips (labia).

RELATED TOPIC

DIAPERS: REUSABLE VS. DISPOSABLE (see page 119)

SHAMPOO

Wash your baby's hair once or twice a week with a special baby shampoo that doesn't sting the eyes. You can use an adult shampoo if you are careful about the eyes. Don't be concerned about hurting the anterior fontanel (soft spot). It is well protected.

RELATED TOPIC

CRADLE CAP (see page 127)

LOTIONS, CREAMS, AND OINTMENTS

Newborn skin normally does not require any ointments or creams. Especially avoid the application of any oil, ointment, or greasy substance, since this will almost always block the small sweat glands and lead to pimples and/or a heat rash. If the skin starts to become dry and cracked, use a baby lotion, hand lotion, or moisturizing cream twice a day, just as you would for yourself. For deep cracks (as around the ankles), petroleum jelly is better. Cornstarch powder can be used to prevent rashes in areas of friction (as under the diaper). But avoid talcum powders because of the risk of a serious chemical pneumonia if your baby inhales some into the lungs.

UMBILICAL CORD

Try to keep the cord dry. Apply rubbing alcohol to the base of the cord (where it attaches to the skin) twice a day (including after the bath) until 1 week after it falls off. Clean underneath the cord with rubbing alcohol and a cotton swab by lifting it and bending it to each side. Air exposure also helps with drying and separation, so keep the diaper folded down below the cord area or use a scissors to cut away a wedge of the diaper in front.

RELATED TOPICS

UMBILICAL CORD, DELAYED SEPARATION (see page 139)
UMBILICAL CORD, OOZING (see page 140)

FINGERNAILS

Cut the toenails straight across to prevent ingrown toenails, but round off the corners of the fingernails to prevent scratches. Trim the nails once a week after a bath when the nails are softened. Long nails can cause unintentional scratches to your baby or others. Occasionally a baby scratches the clear part of the eye (causing a corneal abrasion), screams bloody murder, and needs the eye checked and patched by your physician for 1 or 2 days. Use a nail clipper, special baby scissors, or a fine emery board. This job usually takes two people unless you do it while your child is asleep. If you don't hold the finger still, you can cause a nasty cut of the fingertip.

THE CIRCUMCISION DECISION: PROS AND CONS

Circumcision means cutting off the foreskin or ring of tissue that covers the head (glans) of the penis. This surgical procedure is usually performed on newborns on the second day of life. In a 1986 survey, 60 percent of American newborn males were reported circumcised that year. (The rate has declined from 90 percent in 1979.) The following information should help you decide what is best for your son.

CULTURAL ASPECTS
Followers of the Jewish and Moslem faiths perform circumcision for religious reasons. Nonreligious circumcision became popular in English-speaking countries between 1920 and 1950, in hopes it would prevent sexually transmitted diseases. It never caught on in Asia, South America, Central America, or most of Europe. Over 80 percent of the world's male population is not circumcised. The circumcision rates have fallen to 1 percent in Britain, 10 percent in New Zealand, and 40 percent in Canada.

PURPOSE OF THE FORESKIN
The presence of the foreskin is not some cosmic error. The foreskin protects the glans against urine, feces, and other types of irritation. Although rare events, infections of the urinary opening (meatitis) and scarring of the opening (meatal stenosis) almost exclusively occur in the circumcised penis. The foreskin may also serve a sexual function, namely protecting the sensitivity of the glans. (See FORESKIN CARE AND PROBLEMS, page 116, for information on hygiene.)

BENEFITS OF CIRCUMCISION
In 1989 the American Academy of Pediatrics issued a new statement on circumcision, clarifying that the procedure carried small potential risks and benefits that parents needed to consider. According to a recent study by Dr. T. E. Wiswell, circumcision may protect against a 1 percent occurrence of urinary tract infections during the first year of life. But should we circumcise all infants to prevent urinary tract infections (which are treatable) in 1 percent of them? Probably not. Removal of the foreskin also prevents infections under the foreskin (posthitis) and a persistent tight foreskin (phimosis). Both of these uncommon conditions, however, are probably due to

excessive and/or unclean attempts to retract the foreskin. (See page 117.) In general, circumcision does not prevent sexually transmitted disease later in life. While it does protect against cancer of the penis, good hygiene offers equal protection against this rare condition.

Another argument for circumcision is "so he will look like other boys in his school," or "like his father." The psychological harm from "being different," however, has never been documented. In my experience, boys don't mind being different from other males in their family. They do mind, however, being harassed in the locker room or shower, which may occur if over 95 percent of their buddies are circumcised. It's emotionally painful to be a trailblazer about the appearance of one's genitals. In the final analysis, nonreligious circumcision is mainly cosmetic surgery.

RISKS OF CIRCUMCISION

Like any surgical procedure, a circumcision can end in complications (in less than 1 percent of cases). Among these are skin infections, bloodstream infections, bleeding, gangrene, scarring, and various surgical accidents. In a recent study, 1 in 500 newborns suffered a serious side effect. In addition, the procedure itself causes some pain, although this pain can be minimized if physicians use a local anesthetic to block the nerves of the foreskin. Finally, the cost of circumcision in the United States is $200 million each year (at $100 per procedure). You may have to pay for this procedure yourself because many medical insurance companies don't cover the costs of this cosmetic surgery.

RECOMMENDATIONS

Circumcision for religious purposes will continue. Circumcision for other boys is open to question. Just because a father was circumcised doesn't mean that this elective procedure must be performed on the son. Since the foreskin comes as standard equipment, I lean toward leaving it intact, unless your son will be attending a school where everyone else is likely to be circumcised. But I don't feel strongly about it. The risks and benefits are both too small to swing the vote either way. This is a parental decision, not a medical decision.

CIRCUMCISION CARE AND PROBLEMS

A circumcision is the removal of part of the normal male foreskin. The incision is initially red and tender; the tenderness should be minimal by the third day. The scab at the incision line comes off in 7 to 10 days. If a Plastibel ring was used, it should fall off by 14 days (10 days on the average). While it cannot fall off too early, don't pull it off, because you may cause bleeding. Any cuts, scrapes, or scabs on the head of the penis may normally heal with yellowish-colored skin if your baby has been jaundiced. This bilirubin in healing tissue is commonly mistaken for an infection or pus.

CALL YOUR CHILD'S PHYSICIAN

(The following statements apply to recent circumcisions.)

Immediately If

- The urine comes out in dribbles.

- The urine stream is weak.

- The head of the penis is blue or black.

- The incision line bleeds more than a few drops.

- The normal skin of the penis becomes red or tender.

- Your baby develops a fever over 100°F (37.8°C) rectally.

- Your baby is acting sick.

During Office Hours If

- The circumcision looks abnormal to you.

- The Plastibel ring has been attached for more than 14 days. (Note: It can't fall off too early.)

- You have other questions.

HOME CARE FOR CIRCUMCISION PROBLEMS

Treatment

- Plastibel type. Gently cleanse the area with water 3 times a day or whenever it becomes soiled. Soap is usually unnecessary. Petroleum jelly or Bacitracin antibiotic ointment can be applied to the incision line after cleansings to keep it soft during healing.

- Gomco type (i.e., no plastic ring is present). Remove the dressing (which is usually gauze with petroleum jelly) with warm compresses 48 hours after the circumcision was done. Then care for the area as described for the Plastibel.

Call Your Child's Physician Later If

- It looks infected.

- It bleeds more than a few drops.

- The Plastibel ring does not fall off by day 14.

FORESKIN CARE AND PROBLEMS

At birth the foreskin is normally attached to the head of the penis (glans) by a layer of cells. Over the next 5 or 10 years the foreskin will naturally separate from the head of the penis without any help from us. It gradually loosens up (retracts) a little at a time. Normal erections during childhood probably cause most of the change by stretching the foreskin.

The foreskin generally causes no problems. However, overzealous retraction can cause it to get stuck behind the head of the penis (the glans) and cause severe pain and swelling. If retraction causes bleeding, scar tissue may form and interfere with natural retraction. Occasionally the space under the foreskin becomes infected. Most of these problems can be prevented.

CALL YOUR CHILD'S PHYSICIAN

Immediately If

- The foreskin is pulled back and stuck behind the head of the penis.

- Your child can't pass any urine.

- The foreskin is red or tender to the touch.

- A fever (over 100°F) is present.

During Office Hours If

- The foreskin is swollen.

- Any pus is coming out of the end of the foreskin.

- The urine stream is weak or dribbly.

- You have other questions.

NORMAL FORESKIN RETRACTION

Some physicians feel that parents should not engage in any attempts at retraction, but this runs the risk of smegma collection and infection. In general, the foreskin requires minimal care. The following suggestions are a modest attempt to assist the natural process and maintain good hygiene.

- Only the outside of the foreskin needs to be cleaned during the first year. Gentle partial retraction can begin at 1 or 2 years of age. It can be done once a week during bathing. Perform retraction by gently pulling the skin on the shaft of the penis downward toward the abdomen. This will make the foreskin open up, revealing the end of the glans.

- During retraction, the exposed part of the glans should be cleansed with water and dried carefully. Wipe away any whitish material (smegma) that you find there. Smegma is simply the accumulation of dead skin cells that are normally shed from the glans and lining of the foreskin throughout life. Do not use soap or leave soapy water under the foreskin, because this can cause irritation and swelling. (Note: a collection of smegma that is seen or felt through the foreskin, but which lies beyond the level to which the foreskin is retractable, should be left alone until normal separation exposes it.)

- After cleansing, always pull the foreskin forward to its normal position.

- Avoid vigorous retraction, because this can cause the foreskin to become stuck behind the head of the penis (paraphimosis). Retraction is excessive if it causes any discomfort or crying.

- By age 5 or 6, teach your son to retract his own foreskin and clean beneath it once a week during bathing to prevent poor hygiene and infection. Gentle reminders are necessary in the early years.

- In summary, foreskin retraction is overdone in our country.

Keep in mind that any degree of foreskin movement is normal as long as your boy has a normal urine stream. There should be no rush to achieve full retraction. Full retraction always occurs naturally by puberty. As the foreskin becomes retractable on its own, cleanse beneath it to prevent infections.

NEWBORN EQUIPMENT AND SUPPLIES

Before the baby is born, most parents prepare a special room. They buy a layette including clothing, a place to sleep, feeding equipment, bathing equipment, and changing supplies. This preparation is called nesting behavior. The most common mistake parents on a limited budget can make during this time is buying something they don't need at all or buying an expensive (often fancy) version of an essential piece of equipment. Sometimes parents can borrow some of the equipment from friends or relatives. The first list describes essential equipment. It may also come in handy next time you need a shower gift. The second list includes helpful but nonessential items. The final list reviews items that are unnecessary for most families.

ESSENTIAL EQUIPMENT

Car Safety Seat • Child restraint seats are essential for transporting your baby in a car. They are required by law in most states. Consider buying one that is convertible and usable until your child reaches 40 pounds and 40 inches. Until your child weighs more than 20 pounds, the car seat faces backward; after that time it is moved to a forward-facing position. While car seats must conform to federal safety standards, they are also ranked by consumer magazines. Many hospitals have a rental program for car seats which can save you money unless you are going to have several children. (See CAR SAFETY, page 206, on how to select and use a car seat.)

Crib • Since your baby will spend so much unattended time in the crib, make certain it is a safe one. Federal safety standards require that all cribs built after 1974 have spaces between the crib bars of 2⅜ inches or less. This restriction is to prevent a child from getting the head or body stuck between the bars. If you have an older crib, be sure to check this distance, which is approximately the width of 3 fingers. Also check for any defective crib bars. The mattress should be the same size as the crib so that your baby's head can't get caught in the gap. It should also be waterproof. Bumper pads are unnecessary because infants rarely strike their head on the railings. The pads have the disadvantage of keeping your baby from seeing out of the crib; they are also something to climb on at a later stage. During the first 2 or 3 months of life it may be more convenient to have your baby sleep in a drawer, a cardboard box, or a basket that is well padded with towels or blankets.

Bathtub • Small plastic bathtubs with sponge linings are available. A large plastic dishpan will also suffice for the purpose. A molded sponge lining can be purchased separately. As a compromise, a kitchen sink works well if you are careful about preventing your child from falling against hard edges or turning on the hot water, thereby causing a burn. Until the umbilical cord falls off, keep the water level below the navel. Most children can be bathed in a standard bathtub by 1 year of age.

Bottles and Nipples • If you are feeding your baby formula, you will need about ten 8-ounce bottles. While clear plastic bottles cost twice as much as glass ones, you will be glad you bought the unbreakable type the first time you or your baby drop one. You will also need a corresponding number of nipples. If you prepare more than one bottle at a time, you will need a 1-quart measuring cup and a funnel for mixing a batch of formula.

Diapers: Reusable vs. Disposable • Disposable diapers have become extremely popular in our country. Ecologists remind us that disposable diapers use up valuable natural resources and after one use are thrown into already overflowing landfills. Let's compare disposable diapers to cloth diapers. The rate of diaper rashes is about the same. If you're concerned about using safety pins, worry not. Modern cloth diapers come with Velcro straps. The main advantage of disposable diapers is that they are very convenient—freeing the family to travel easily and daycare centers to operate efficiently. The superabsorbent gel diapers have the advantage of not letting urine leak out of the diaper. The main disadvantage of disposable diapers is that they cost more. Disposable diapers average about 20 cents per diaper versus 12 cents per diaper from the diaper service or 3 cents per diaper if you wash your own diapers (after their initial purchase). A diaper service will save you over $500 per child and washing your own will save you over $1,200 per child. Another smaller disadvantage of disposable diapers is that if you are breast-feeding and trying to use the frequency of wetting to assess the adequacy of breast-feeding, often you won't be able to tell if your child has passed any urine.

If you have an automatic washer and dryer, you may prefer to use cloth diapers. You will need 3 dozen to 6 dozen cloth diapers as well as several pairs of plastic pants. You will also need a diaper pail for storing dirty diapers until washtime. Regardless of the type of diaper you use, bowel movements should be scraped into the toilet for sanitary purposes.

Which type of diaper to use is a controversial issue. My advice is to take advantage of both options. Use cotton diapers when you are at home. Use disposable diapers when you are traveling or as a backup if you are out of the home. Use disposables when your child has diarrhea because they prevent leakage of watery stools. (Some parents prefer disposables at night because they are leakproof.) During the first 2 or 3 months of life, when most mothers are exhausted by new-baby care, consider a diaper service rather than washing the diapers yourself. You will find that modern diaper services are very efficient, provide excellent sterilized diapers, and pick them up once a week.

Pacifier • A pacifier is useful in soothing many babies. To prevent choking, the pacifier's shield should be at least 1½ inches in diameter and the pacifier should be one single piece. Some of the newer ones are made of silicone (instead of rubber), which lasts longer because it doesn't dry out. The orthodontic-shaped pacifiers are accepted by some babies but not by others. (See PACIFIERS, page 329, for additional information.)

Nasal Suction Bulb • A suction bulb is essential for helping young babies with breathing difficulties due to sticky or dried nasal secretions. A suction bulb with a blunt tip is more effective than the ones with long tapered tips (which are used for irrigating ears). The best ones on the market have a small clear plastic tip (mucus trap), which can be removed from the rubber suction bulb for cleaning. (See under COLDS, page 533, for proper use.)

Thermometer • A rectal thermometer is most helpful if your baby becomes sick. The digital thermometers that display the temperature in 30 seconds are worth the extra few dollars. If you buy a glass thermometer, the ones with four color zones are easiest to read.

Humidifier • A humidifier will be helpful in dry climates or areas with cold winters. The new ultrasonic humidifiers are quieter and have other advantages. Do not buy a vaporizer (a gadget that produces steam) because it can cause burns in children and doesn't deliver humidity at as fast a rate as a humidifier.

Diaper and Bottle Bag • For traveling outside the home with your baby, you will need an all-purpose shoulder bag to carry the items that allow you to feed your baby and change diapers.

Highchair • During the first 6 months of life your baby can be held when he or she is being fed. Once your child can sit unsupported and take solid foods, a highchair is needed. The most important feature is a wide base that prevents tipping. The tray needs to have a good safety latch. The tray should also have adjustable positions to adapt to your infant's growth. A safety strap is critical. Plastic or metal chairs are easier to clean than wooden chairs. Small, portable, hook-on highchairs that attach directly to the tabletop are gaining in popularity. They are convenient and reasonably priced. The ones with a special clamp that keeps your child from pushing the chair off the tabletop with his feet have a good safety record.

Food Grinder • The time comes when your baby must make the transition from baby foods to table foods. A baby-food grinder takes the work out of mashing up table foods. It's as effective as a blender, easier to clean, and less expensive. Food processors have the advantage of allowing you to make larger quantities faster than in a grinder.

Training Cup • By the time your child is 1 year old, he will want to hold his own cup. Buy a spillproof one with a weighted base, double handles, a lid, and a spout.

Bib • To keep food off your baby's clothes, find a molded plastic bib with an open scoop on the bottom to catch the mess.

Safety Gadgets • Once your child is crawling, you will need electric-outlet safety plugs, cabinet door safety locks, bathtub spout protectors, plastic corner guards for sharp table edges, and so forth.

HELPFUL EQUIPMENT
The following items mainly provide your child with forms of transportation or special places to play. While they all have some advantages, if none of them are available, your child could also be carried and permitted to play on a blanket on the floor.

Changing Table • Diapers need to be changed 10 to 15 times a day. While a bed can be used for changing, performing this task without bending over prevents back strain. An old dining table or buffet can work as well as a special changing table.

Automatic Swing • While swings are entertaining to most babies, they are especially helpful for crying babies. They come in windup-spring, pendulum-driven, or battery-powered models. The latter two have quieter mechanisms. Again, a sturdy base and crossbars are important for safety.

Front-Pack or Carrier • Front-packs are great for new babies. They give your child a sense of physical contact and warmth. In fact, they have been shown to promote bonding. They allow you freedom to use your hands. Buy one with head support. Carrying a baby in front after 5 or 6 months of age can cause a backache for the parent.

Backpack • Backpacks are useful in carrying babies who are 5 or 6 months old and have good head support. They are an inexpensive way to carry your baby outside when you go shopping, hiking, or walking anywhere. The inner seat can usually be adjusted to different levels.

Stroller • Another way to transport a baby who has outgrown the front-pack is in a baby stroller. The most convenient ones are the umbrella type, which fold up. A safety belt is important to keep your baby from standing up and falling.

Infant Seat • An infant seat is a good place to keep a young baby when he or she is not eating or sleeping. Infants prefer this inclined position so they can see what is going on around them. Buy one with a safety strap, but don't substitute it for a car seat. Once children reach 3 to 4 months of age, they can usually tip the infant seat over, so discontinue using it.

Playpen • A playpen is a handy and safe place to leave your baby when you need uninterrupted time to cook a meal or do the wash. Babies like playpens because the slatted or mesh sides afford a good view of the environment. Playpens can be used both indoors and outdoors. As with cribs, the slats should be less than 2⅜ inches apart. The playpens with a fine-weave netting are also acceptable although sometimes older infants can climb out of them. Bottomless playpens are gaining in popularity. Your baby should be introduced to the playpen by 4 months of age so that he or she builds up positive associations with it. It is very difficult to introduce a playpen after a baby has learned to crawl. Avoid stringing any objects on a cord across the playpen, because your baby could become entangled in them and strangle.

Gates • A gate is essential if your house has stairways that your baby must be protected from. A gate also helps to keep a child in a specific room with you and out of the rest of the house, as when you are working in the kitchen. Many rooms can be closed off with doors. All gates should be climb-resistant. The strongest gates are spring-loaded.

UNNECESSARY EQUIPMENT

Some baby equipment is usually not worth the investment, but your judgment may be different. You can bathe your baby without a special bathinette. Nursery monitors or intercoms will not prevent crib deaths and may interfere with the learning of self-comforting behavior. Baby carriages or buggies generally have been replaced by baby strollers, front-packs, or backpacks.

You can determine if your baby is being fed enough without a baby scale (see BREAST-FEEDING, page 145, and FORMULA-FEEDING, page 151). An infant feeder is a bottle with a nipple on one end and a piston on the other, used to feed young babies strained foods. They are advertised as a "natural" step between bottle- and spoon-feeding. Since babies don't need any food except formula or breast milk until at least 4 months of age (at which time spoon-feeding works quite nicely), this item is unnecessary and can lead to forced feedings. You can prepare warm formula without a bottle warmer.

Finally, shoes are not needed until your child has to walk outdoors (see SHOES, page 208).

POTENTIALLY HARMFUL EQUIPMENT: WALKERS

Infants like to be in a walker. But is it worth it? Over 40 percent of children who use walkers have an accident requiring medical attention. They get skull fractures, concussions, dental injuries, and lacerations. There have even been some deaths. Most of the serious walker injuries occur from falling down a stairway. When a crawling child falls down some unprotected steps, he tumbles and breaks his fall. When a child goes down a stairway in a walker, he accelerates and crash-lands at the bottom.

Why, then, do parents use walkers? Mainly because children like to be upright, especially after they have learned to sit with support but can't sit alone. Once they learn to crawl, however, they usually prefer to be out of the walker. Some parents believe walkers help children learn to walk. On the contrary, walkers can delay both crawling and walking if used over 2 hours a day.

I prefer that you simply not buy a walker. But if you have one, remember that walkers and stairways don't mix. Be sure to keep the door to any stairway locked. And don't trust a gate. Children in walkers have crashed right through them.

NEWBORN PROBLEMS

THE SICK NEWBORN: SUBTLE SYMPTOMS

A newborn is a baby less than 1 month old. Newborns mainly eat, sleep, cry a little, and need lots of love and their diapers changed frequently. If a newborn is ill, the symptoms can be subtle. Also, a newborn can deteriorate quickly. If a newborn is sick at all, the illness can be serious.

CALL YOUR CHILD'S PHYSICIAN IMMEDIATELY IF

- Your baby is less than 1 month old and sick in any way (e.g., cough, poor color, vomiting, or diarrhea).

- Your newborn's appetite or suck becomes poor.

- Your newborn sleeps excessively—for instance, past feeding times.

- Your newborn cries excessively. (See also CRYING BABY [COLIC], page 239.)

- Your newborn develops a fever over 100°F (37.8°C) rectally or over 98.6°F (37.0°C) axillary.

- Your newborn's temperature drops below 97.5°F (36.5°C) rectally, or below 96.5°F (36°C) axillary. (Note: In general, do not take an infant's temperature unless he feels hot or looks sick.)

- You have other urgent questions.

125

RELATED TOPIC

THE NORMAL NEWBORN'S BEHAVIOR (see page 101)

THE SICK INFANT: JUDGING THE SEVERITY OF ILLNESS

In the first 2 years of a child's life, most parents feel inexperienced and inadequate in determining how sick their child is during a cold or other infection. Since these children can't talk, they can't help much with diagnosis. How sick your child looks or acts is much more relevant than the level of fever. Also, some children look much better 30 to 40 minutes after the fever is reduced with medicine.

GUIDELINES TO SEVERE ILLNESS

CALL YOUR CHILD'S PHYSICIAN IMMEDIATELY IF

- Your child is a newborn (less than 1 month old) with any sign of illness (exception: mild nasal congestion).
- Your child looks or acts very sick.
- Your child cannot be made to smile, or hardly responds.
- Your child refuses to play.
- Your child is too weak to sit up or stand.
- Your child cries constantly for more than 3 hours.
- Your child cries when you touch him or hold him.
- The cry becomes high-pitched and strange-sounding.
- The cry becomes a weak whimper or moan.
- Your child cannot sleep for more than 30 minutes at a time.
- Your child cannot be comforted for more than 30 minutes at a time.
- Your child cannot be fully awakened.
- The breathing becomes labored.
- The mouth and lips become bluish.
- The skin becomes grayish.

RELATED TOPICS

CRYING BABY (COLIC) (see page 239)
FEVER (see page 407)
THE SICK NEWBORN: SUBTLE SYMPTOMS (see page 125)

CRADLE CAP

Cradle cap consists of oily, yellow scales and crusts on the scalp. It begins in the first weeks of life and is probably caused by adult hormones that crossed the placenta before birth. Without treatment it can last for months; with treatment it usually is cleared up in a few weeks. Cradle cap is not contagious and does not recur.

CALL YOUR CHILD'S PHYSICIAN DURING OFFICE HOURS IF

• A weepy, raw rash is present behind the ears.

• The rash has spread beyond the scalp.

• You have other questions.

HOME CARE FOR CRADLE CAP

Antidandruff Shampoo • Buy an antidandruff shampoo (no prescription needed) at the drugstore. Wash your baby's hair with it once a day. Wh... with it once a day. Wh... baby's scalp with a s... minutes. Don't worry ... cradle cap has cleared ... week.

Softening Thick Crusts • If t... oil or mineral oil on the... the crust. Wash all the ... cradle cap.

Resistant Cases • If the ras... percent hydrocortisone c... a day for 4 days.

Call Your Child's Physician Later If

• The cradle cap lasts more than 2 weeks with treatment.

DIAPER RASH

SYMPTOMS AND CHARACTERISTICS

• Any rash in the skin area covered by a diaper

Causes • Almost all children get diaper rashes. Diaper rashes are more common in children with fair, sensitive skin, especially in redheads. Most of them are due to the prolonged contact with wetness, bacteria, digestive enzymes, and ammonia that comes with wearing diapers. The skin irritants are made by the action of bacteria from bowel movements on certain chemicals in the urine. Bouts of diarrhea cause rashes in almost all children. Diaper rashes occur equally with cloth and disposable diapers. You don't have to switch diapers to clear up a diaper rash. Diaper rashes are worse with airtight plastic pants, so avoid them until your baby makes enough urine to soak through the diaper. In societies where diapers aren't worn, babies don't acquire diaper rashes.

Allergies to soaps, detergents, whiteners, and bleaches are very rare, and you needn't worry about these.

Expected Course • With proper treatment these rashes are usually better in 3 days. If they do not respond, a yeast infection (*Candida*) has probably occurred. Suspect this if the rash becomes bright red and raw, covers a large area, and is surrounded by red dots. Your physician will have to prescribe a special cream for yeast.

CALL YOUR CHILD'S PHYSICIAN

Immediately If

• The diaper rash has any big (larger than 1 inch across) blisters or open sores.

• The surface is bright red and tender to the touch.

• Your child is acting very sick.

Within 24 Hours If

- The diaper rash is a solid bright-red.

- Open, weeping sores are present.

- The rash is raw or bleeding.

- Pimples, blisters, boils, or crusts are present.

- An unexplained fever (over 100°F) is present.

- The rash causes enough pain to interfere with sleeping.

- The rash has spread beyond the diaper area.

- Your child is male and circumcised *and* the end of the penis has a sore or scab (meatal ulcer).

- You have other questions.

HOME CARE FOR DIAPER RASH

Change Diapers Frequently • The key to successful treatment is keeping the area dry and clean so it can heal itself. Check the diaper about every hour, and if it is wet or soiled, change it immediately. Exposure to stools causes most of the skin damage.

Increase Air Exposure • Leave your baby's bottom exposed to the air as much as possible each day. Practical times are during naps or after bowel movements. Put a towel or diaper under your baby. When the diaper is on, fasten it loosely so that air can circulate between it and the skin. Avoid airtight plastic pants until the rash is gone. Put a towel between you and your baby's bottom instead. If you use disposable diapers, punch holes in them to let the air circulate, and avoid the type with tight leg bands. Warm air from a hair dryer for 3 minutes on the low setting can encourage healing.

Rinse the Skin with Warm Water • All you need is warm tap water. Washing with soap following every diaper change will damage the skin. A mild soap (like Dove) is needed only after bowel movements to help remove the film of bacteria left on the skin. After using a soap, rinse thoroughly and pat dry. If the diaper rash is quite raw, use lukewarm water soaks in a tub for 15 minutes 3 times a day. Adding 1 or 2 tablespoons of baking soda to the water may help healing. (Note: Running water is far superior to disposable diaper wipes. Disposable wipes should be used only for traveling, but avoid those containing alcohol.)

Nighttime Care of Diaper Rashes • Awaken once during the night to change your baby's diaper until the rash is better. Avoid plastic pants at night.

Creams and Powders • Creams and powders are optional. Most babies don't need any cream unless the diaper rash becomes infected with yeast. In addition, unless the hygiene measures outlined above are carried through, creams can't help the rash. If your baby's skin is dry and cracked, apply an ointment after a diaper change to protect the skin. A barrier protection ointment is also needed when your child has diarrhea. If your child develops a heat rash, change to a cream.

After the diaper rash is healed, cornstarch powder can be used to prevent the shiny pink diaper rash that comes from friction against the diaper. Recent studies show that cornstarch does not encourage yeast infections. Avoid talcum powders because of the risk of serious pneumonia if your baby breathes some in.

Washing Cloth Diapers • If you wash cloth diapers yourself, you will need to use bleach (such as Clorox, Borax, or Purex) to sterilize them. During the first wash cycle, use the hot temperature setting and any detergent. During the second cycle, use warm water and 1 cup of bleach. Unlike bleach, vinegar is not effective in killing germs.

Call Your Child's Physician Later If

• The rash isn't much better in 3 days.

• Any pimples, blisters, boils, or crusts develop.

• The rash spreads beyond the diaper area.

PREVENTION OF DIAPER RASHES

• Change the diapers frequently, especially after bowel movements (BMs).

• Rinse the skin with plenty of warm water after BMs.

• Fasten the diaper loosely, so air can circulate under the diapers.

• Give your child some genes for industrial-strength skin.

JAUNDICE OF THE NEWBORN

Jaundice is a yellow (or orange) color of the skin and the whites of the eyes (the sclera). The yellow coloration is due to increased amounts of a pigment in the body called bilirubin. Bilirubin is produced by the normal breakdown of red blood cells. Bilirubin accumulates if the liver doesn't excrete it into the intestines at a normal rate.

TYPES OF JAUNDICE

Physiological Jaundice • Physiological (normal) jaundice occurs in more than 50 percent of babies. An immaturity of the liver leads to a slowdown in the processing of bilirubin. The jaundice first appears at 2 to 4 days of age. By 5 or 6 days, the liver kicks in. The jaundice usually disappears by 1 to 2 weeks of age and the levels reached are harmless. In prematures, jaundice occurs more commonly and lasts longer.

Breast-Milk Jaundice • Breast-milk jaundice occurs in 1 to 2 percent of breast-fed babies. It is caused by a special substance that some mothers produce in their breast milk. This substance (an enzyme) increases the resorption of bilirubin from the intestines. This type of jaundice starts at 4 to 7 days of age, and may last from 3 to 10 weeks normally.

Blood-Group Incompatibility (Rh or ABO Problems) • If a baby and mother have different blood types, sometimes the mother produces antibodies that destroy the newborn's red blood cells. This causes a sudden buildup in bilirubin in the baby's blood. This type of jaundice usually begins during the first 24 hours of life. High levels of bilirubin may be reached. Rh problems formerly caused the most severe form of jaundice but now are preventable with an injection of Rho GAM to the mother within 72 hours after delivery which prevents her forming antibodies that might endanger her subsequent babies.

TREATMENT OF SEVERE JAUNDICE

High levels of bilirubin (usually above 20 mg. percent) can cause deafness, cerebral palsy, or brain damage in some babies. High levels usually occur with blood-type problems. These complications can be prevented by lowering the bilirubin using phototherapy (blue light that breaks down bilirubin in the skin). In many communities, phototherapy can be used in the home. In rare cases where the bilirubin reaches dangerous levels, an exchange transfusion may be used. This technique replaces the baby's blood with fresh blood. Physiological jaundice does not rise to levels requiring this type of treatment.

Treatment of Breast-Milk Jaundice • The bilirubin level can rise above 20 in less than 1 percent of children with breast-milk jaundice. Almost always elevations to this level can be prevented by more frequent feedings. Nurse your baby every 1½ to 2½ hours. Since the bilirubin is carried out of the body in the stools, passing frequent BMs is helpful. If your baby sleeps more than 5 hours at night, awaken him for a feeding. If your baby goes more than 24 hours without a BM, insert a lubricated thermometer carefully into the anus and gently move it from side to side a few times to stimulate a BM.

Occasionally the bilirubin will not come down with frequent feedings. In this situation the bilirubin level can be reduced by alternating each breast-feeding with formula-feeding for two or three days. Supplementing with glucose water is not as helpful as formula for moving the bilirubin out of the body. (Talk to your baby's physician for the latest instructions on lowering bilirubin in these babies.) Whenever you miss a nursing, be sure to use a breast pump to keep your milk production flowing. Breast-feeding should never be permanently discontinued because of breast-milk jaundice. Once the jaundice clears, you can return to full breast-feeding and you needn't worry about the jaundice coming back.

CALL YOUR BABY'S PHYSICIAN

Immediately If

• Jaundice is noticed during the first 48 hours of life.

• The jaundice involves the arms or legs.

• Your baby develops a fever over 100°F (37.8°C) rectally.

• Your child also starts to look or act sick (see page 125).

During Office Hours If

• The color gets deeper after day 7.

• The jaundice is not gone by day 14.

• Your baby is not gaining weight well.

• You are concerned about the amount of jaundice.

Since newborns are going home earlier than formerly, the parent must be more involved with observations about the degree of jaundice. The amount of yellowness is best judged by viewing your baby unclothed in natural light by a window. The best way to check for yellow skin is to press on it with your finger, then assess the underlying color before the pink color returns.

SPITTING UP (REGURGITATION)

SYMPTOMS AND CHARACTERISTICS
Regurgitation is the effortless spitting up of 1 or 2 mouthfuls of stomach contents. Following overfeeding, the amount can be larger. It is usually seen shortly after feedings. It occurs mainly in children under 1 year of age and begins in the first week of life. More than half of all children have it to some degree.

Similar Condition • If appropriate, turn directly to the guideline for VOMITING, page 608. Vomiting is more forceful and involves larger amounts.

Cause • A lack of closure of the valve at the upper end of the stomach is responsible. This condition is also called gastroesophageal reflux (GE reflux) or chalasia.

Expected Course • It improves with age. By the time your baby has been walking for 3 months, it should be totally cleared up. Many babies are better by 8 to 10 months of age after learning to sit well.

CALL YOUR CHILD'S PHYSICIAN
Immediately If

• Any blood is seen in the spit-up material.

• The spitting up causes your child to choke or cough.

During Office Hours If

• Your baby is not gaining weight normally.

- Your baby is frequently cranky.

- Your baby has been walking for more than 3 months and is still spitting up.

- You have other questions.

HOME CARE FOR SPITTING UP

Feed Smaller Amounts • Overfeeding always makes spitting up worse. If the stomach is filled to capacity, spitting up is more likely. Give your baby smaller amounts (at least 1 ounce less than you have been), especially if he is somewhat overweight. Keep the total feeding time to less than 20 minutes. Your baby doesn't have to finish a bottle. If you are breast-feeding and have a plentiful milk supply, try nursing on 1 side and pumping the other side. Walt at least 2½ hours between feedings, because it takes that long for the stomach to empty itself. Don't add food to a full stomach.

Cut Back On Pacifier Time • Constant sucking can pump the stomach up with air.

Burp Your Child to Prevent Spitting Up • Burp your baby several times during each feeding. Do it when he pauses and looks around. Don't interrupt his feeding rhythm in order to burp him. Burp each time for less than a minute. Keep in mind that burping is less important than giving smaller feedings.

Avoid Pressure on the Abdomen • Avoid tight diapers and the sitting position. They put added pressure on the stomach. Don't double him up during diaper changes. Don't let people hug him or play vigorously with him right after meals.

After-Meals Position • After meals, try to hold your baby in the upright position using a front-pack, backpack, or swing. Avoid infant seats because they increase the contact of stomach acid with the lower esophagus. After your child is over 6 months old, a walker can be helpful for maintaining the upright posture after meals. To make the walker safe, try to remove the wheels. Make sure stairways are closed off securely.

Sleeping Position • If spitting up causes choking, coughing, or difficulty breathing, have your baby sleep stomach down.

Otherwise have him lie on his back like normal babies. A recent study by Dr. S. R. Orenstein showed that sleeping flat was as helpful as sleeping with the head of the bed elevated.

Cleaning Up • One of the worst aspects of spitting up cow's milk was the odor. This was caused by the effect of stomach acid on the butterfat The odor was eliminated by the use of commercial formulas, because they contain vegetable oils. To protect carpets from stains, try to confine your baby to areas without rugs, such as the kitchen. Also, don't pick your baby up when you're wearing your best clothes. Milk spots are more easily cleaned using soda water or tap water with a pinch of baking soda. Also use the powdered formulas; they stain the least.

Call Your Child's Physician Later If
• Your baby doesn't seem to improve with this approach.

TEAR DUCT, BLOCKED

SYMPTOMS AND CHARACTERISTICS

• A continuously watery eye.

• Tears run down the face even without crying.

• During crying, the nostril on the blocked side remains dry.

• Onset at birth to 2 months of age.

• The eye is not red and the eyelid is not swollen (unless the soggy tissues become infected).

If your child's symptoms are different, call your physician for help.

Cause • Your child probably has a blocked tear duct (dacryostenosis). This means that the channel that normally carries tears from the eye to the nose is blocked. Although the obstruction of the tear duct is present at birth, the occasional delay in onset of symptoms can be explained by the delay in tear production until the age of 3 or 4 weeks in a few babies.

Expected Course • This is a common condition that affects 6 percent of newborns. Both sides are blocked 30 percent of the

time. Over 90 percent of tear ducts open up spontaneously by
the time the child is 12 months of age. If the obstruction
persists beyond 12 months of age, an ophthalmologist can
open it using a special probe.

CALL YOUR CHILD'S PHYSICIAN

Immediately If

• The eyelids are red or swollen.

• A red lump appears at the inner lower corner of the eyelid.

Within 24 Hours If

• The eyelids are stuck together with pus after naps.

• Lots of yellow discharge is present.

During Office Hours If

• Your child is over 12 months old.

• The cornea (clear part) becomes cloudy.

• You have other questions.

HOME CARE FOR BLOCKED TEAR DUCT

Preventing Infections • Because of poor drainage, eyes with blocked
tear ducts easily become infected. The infected eye produces
a yellow discharge. To keep the eye free of infection, massage
the lacrimal sac (where tears collect) twice a day. Always
wash your hands carefully before doing this. The lacrimal sac
is in the inner lower corner of the eye. This sac should be
massaged to empty it of old fluids and to check for infection.
Start at the inner corner of the eye and press *upward*, using a
cotton swab. (**Caution:** Massaging downward is not helpful
and may lead to infection.) If the eye becomes infected, it is
very important to begin antibiotic eyedrops.

Call Your Child's Physician Later If

• The eye becomes infected.

• Your child reaches 12 months of age and the eye is still
watering.

• Other questions come up.

RELATED TOPIC

Eye, Yellow Discharge (see page 508)

THRUSH

SYMPTOMS AND CHARACTERISTICS

- White, irregularly shaped patches

- Coats the insides of the mouth and sometimes the tongue. (If the only symptom is a uniformly white tongue, it's due to a milk diet, not thrush.)

- Adherent to the mouth (cannot be washed away or wiped off easily like milk curds)

- Your child is bottle-fed or breast-fed

If your child's symptoms are different, call your physician for help.

Cause • Thrush is caused by a yeast (called *Candida*) that grows rapidly on the lining of the mouth in areas abraded by prolonged sucking (as when a baby sleeps with a bottle or pacifier). A large pacifier or nipple can also injure the lining of the mouth. Broad-spectrum antibiotics also make a child susceptible by eliminating the normal bacteria in the mouth. Note: Thrush is not contagious, since it does not invade normal tissue.

CALL YOUR CHILD'S PHYSICIAN DURING OFFICE HOURS IF

- An unexplained fever (over 100°F) is present.

- You have other questions.

HOME CARE FOR THRUSH

Nystatin Oral Medicine • The drug for clearing up thrush is Nystatin oral suspension. It requires a prescription. Call your physician during office hours with the name and telephone number of your pharmacy. Some physicians will want to examine the child before prescribing. Give 1 ml of Nystatin 4 times a day. Place it in the front of the mouth on each side (it doesn't do any good once it's swallowed). If the thrush isn't responding, rub the Nystatin directly on the affected areas with a cotton swab or a gauze wrapped on your finger. Apply it after meals, or at least don't feed your baby anything for 30 minutes after application. Keep this up for at least 7 days, or until all thrush has been gone for 3 days. If you are breast-feeding, apply Nystatin to any irritated areas on your nipples. Thrush is not a reason to stop nursing.

Decrease the Sucking Time • If eating and sucking are painful for your child, temporarily use a cup and spoon. In any event, reduce sucking time to no more than 20 minutes per feeding.

Restrict the Pacifier to Bedtime • Eliminate the pacifier temporarily, except when it's really needed for going to sleep. If your infant is using an orthodontic pacifier, switch to a smaller, regular one. Soak all nipples in water at 130°F (the temperature of most hot tap water) for 15 minutes. If the thrush recurs and your child is bottle-fed, switch to a nipple with a different shape and made from silicone.

Diaper Rash Associated with Thrush • If your child has an associated diaper rash, assume it is due to yeast. Request Nystatin cream and apply it 4 times a day. (Also see the guideline on DIAPER RASH, page 128.)

Call Your Child's Physician Later If

• Your child refuses to eat.

• The thrush becomes worse on treatment.

• The thrush lasts more than 10 days.

• An unexplained fever (over 100°F) occurs.

UMBILICAL CORD, BLEEDING

A few drops of blood at the point of separation of the cord is common. The area may bleed a few times from the friction of the diaper or your baby's normal movements.

HOME CARE

The bleeding usually stops by itself or can easily be stopped by direct pressure with a sterile gauze.

CALL YOUR CHILD'S PHYSICIAN IMMEDIATELY IF

• The tie has come undone and the cord is bleeding.

• Any bleeding spot is the size of a quarter or greater.

• Bleeding doesn't stop after 10 minutes of direct pressure.

• Rebleeding continues for more than 3 days.

UMBILICAL CORD, DELAYED SEPARATION

Although most cords fall off between 10 and 14 days of age, an occasional cord may stay for 3 weeks. Cords can also hang by a strand of tissue for 2 or 3 days. Eventually they all fall off by themselves, so just be patient about it. In the meantime:

HOME CARE

Clean the base of the cord (where it attaches to the skin) with rubbing alcohol twice a day. To do this properly, you must lift the cord stump away from the body surface. Also help the cord dry faster by keeping the diaper folded below it. An easier approach is to cut off a wedge of diaper (if disposable) with a scissors so the cord is uncovered.

Call Your Child's Physician Later If

• The cord is still attached after 3 weeks. (Note: The cord can't fall off too early.)

• You have any other questions.

RELATED TOPIC

If the cord begins to look infected, see UMBILICAL CORD, OOZING, page 140

UMBILICAL CORD, OOZING

The umbilicus (navel) is oozing, moist, or may even have some dried pus on the surface. Sometimes the cord has already fallen off; more often it is still attached and contributes to the problem. Your baby probably has a superficial infection of the navel from surface bacteria. It usually can be cleared up fairly quickly. Infection of the umbilicus must be treated with respect because of the risk of spreading to the liver or the abdominal cavity.

CALL YOUR CHILD'S PHYSICIAN

Immediately If

• Red streaks develop on the normal skin surrounding the navel.

• Pimples or blisters appear around the navel.

• Lots of drainage is coming out of the navel.

• Your baby develops a fever over 100°F (37.8°C) rectally.

• Your baby acts sick.

During Office Hours If

• There is a nubbin of tissue inside the navel that looks abnormal to you.

• You have other questions.

HOME CARE FOR UMBILICAL CORD OOZING

Cleansing the Umbilicus • Six times a day, clean the area with rubbing alcohol for several minutes. Use a cotton swab and be vigorous about it. The umbilical area does not have any sensation, so the alcohol won't sting. If the cord is still present, you must clean underneath it by lifting it and bending it to each side. If the cord has fallen off, you can pour some alcohol into the depression and remove it after 2 or 3 minutes. It takes that long to kill all the bacteria. Air exposure and dryness help healing, so be sure to keep the diaper folded down below the cord area or cut off a wedge of diaper (if disposable) with a scissors.

Common Mistakes • Do not put talcum powder on the umbilicus; it can cause irritation and tissue reaction (talc granulomas).

Ointments should be avoided, because they delay drying and healing.

Call Your Child's Physician Later If

• The infection seems to spread.

• The umbilical area is not completely dry and clean by 48 hours on this treatment.

• Your baby begins to act sick.

RELATED TOPICS

UMBILICAL CORD, BLEEDING (see page 138)
UMBILICAL CORD, DELAYED SEPARATION (see page 139)

UMBILICAL HERNIA

An umbilical hernia is a navel that bulges ("pops out") with crying or straining. The bulge may disappear when your baby is quiet. If you feel the area with your finger, you will find a small round opening in the muscles of the abdominal wall. During pregnancy, the umbilical cord's blood vessels pass through this ring, and normally it closes off after birth. Umbilical hernias are very common. They are not painful and they never break. Crying does not make them any bigger or last any longer. Most close spontaneously by school age. Half of the persistent ones close by adolescence.

TREATMENT

No treatment is needed unless the hernia persists beyond age 5 or 6. At that age, day (outpatient) surgery can be performed to close the defect if the hernia presents a cosmetic problem or the defect is larger than 2 cm (about 1 inch) across. The smaller ones usually continue to close. Covering them with tape, a coin, or a "belly band" does not speed healing, but can lead to a skin rash or infection. Your child's physician will be glad to check the hernia on regular office visits. The only complication (which occurs in less than 1 percent of cases) is getting a loop of intestine stuck in the opening. If you think this has happened (if, for instance, the hernia becomes hard, tender, and won't go back in), call your child's physician immediately for help.

RELATED TOPIC

SWELLING, GROIN OR SCROTUM (see page 620)

IV.

HEALTH PROMOTION: KEEPING YOUR CHILD HEALTHY

FEEDING AND EATING

BREAST-FEEDING

Babies who are breast-fed have fewer infections (especially diarrhea) and allergies during the first year of life than babies who are fed formula. Breast milk is also inexpensive, sterile, and served at the perfect temperature. Breast-feeding becomes especially convenient when a mother is traveling with her baby. Overall, breast milk is nature's best food for young babies. Even if you need to return to work early, breast-feeding for 1 month can be beneficial for your baby. After you return to work, breast-feeding can be continued or discontinued, depending on your situation.

HOW OFTEN TO FEED

The baby should nurse for the first time in the delivery room. The second feeding will usually be at 4 to 6 hours of age, after he awakens from a deep sleep. Until your milk supply is well established and your baby is gaining weight (usually 2 weeks), nurse your infant whenever he cries or seems hungry ("demand feeding"), usually 1½ hours or greater. After your baby is 1 month of age and your milk supply is in, babies can receive adequate breast milk by nursing every 2 to 2½ hours. If your baby cries and less than 2 hours have passed, he can be rocked or carried in a front-pack. However, waiting more than 2½ hours can lead to swollen breasts (engorgement), which causes discomfort and decreases milk production. (Feeding less frequently is okay at night, but no more than 5 hours should pass between feedings during the first 4 weeks.) Your baby will not gain adequately unless he nurses 8 or more times per day initially. The risks of continuing to nurse at short intervals (less than 1½ hours) is that "grazing" will become a habit, your baby won't be able to sleep through the night, and you won't have much free time. Although your baby's appetite will determine feeding intervals, the guidelines for bottle feedings per day (see page 153) generally also apply to breast-feeding after the first 2 months of life.

HOW LONG PER FEEDING

Nurse your baby 10 minutes on the first breast and as long as he wants on the second breast. Your goal is to have your baby nurse for a total of about 30 minutes at each feeding. Remember to alternate which breast you start with each time. Once your milk supply is well established (about 2 to 3 weeks after birth), 10 minutes of nursing per breast is fine when you are in a hurry (since your child usually gets over 90 percent of the milk in this time). However, try not to nurse for periods shorter than 20 minutes because it may lead to more frequent feedings and more nighttime awakenings.

HOW TO KNOW YOUR BABY IS GETTING ENOUGH BREAST MILK

In the first couple weeks, if your baby has 4 or more bowel movements per day and 6 or more wet diapers per day, he is receiving a good supply of breast milk. (**Caution:** Infrequent bowel movements are not normally seen before the second month of life.) In addition, most babies will act satisfied after completing a feeding. Your baby should be back to birth weight by 10 to 14 days of age if breast-feeding is going well. Therefore, the 2-week checkup by your baby's physician is very important. The presence of a letdown reflex is another indicator of good milk production.

THE LETDOWN REFLEX

A letdown reflex develops after 2 to 3 weeks of nursing and is indicated by tingling or milk ejection in the breast just before feeding (or when you are thinking about feeding). It also occurs in the opposite breast while your baby is nursing. Letdown is enhanced by adequate sleep, adequate fluids, a relaxed environment, and reduced stress (such as lower expectations about how much housework needs to be done). If your letdown reflex is not present yet, take extra naps and ask your husband and friends for more help. Also consider calling the local chapter of La Leche League (a support group for nursing mothers) or a lactation nurse at your hospital.

SUPPLEMENTAL BOTTLES

Do not offer your baby any bottles during the first 4 to 6 weeks after birth because this is when you establish your milk supply. Good lactation depends on frequent emptying of the breasts. Supplemental bottles take away from sucking time on the breast and reduce the appetite. If your baby is not gaining well, see your physician or a lactation specialist for a complete evaluation.

After your baby is 6 weeks old and nursing is well established, you may want to offer your baby a bottle of expressed milk or water once a day so he can become accustomed to the bottle and the artificial nipple. Once your baby accepts bottle feedings, you can occasionally leave your baby with a sitter and go out for the evening or return to work outside the home. You can use pumped breast milk that has been refrigerated or frozen. Keep 1 or 2 bottles of expressed breast milk (or ready-to-use formula) handy in case you are unexpectedly delayed and your baby is hungry. If practical, supplement with pumped breast milk rather than commercial formula, since taking formula will cancel some of the advantages that breast milk provides.

EXTRA WATER

Babies do not routinely need extra water. Even when they have a fever or the weather is hot and dry, breast milk provides enough water.

PUMPING THE BREASTS TO RELIEVE PAIN OR COLLECT MILK

Severe engorgement (severe swelling) of the breasts decreases milk production. To prevent engorgement, nurse your baby more often. Also, compress the area around the nipple (the areola) with your fingers at the start of each feeding to soften the areola. For milk release, your baby must be able to grip and suck on the areola as well as the nipple. Every time you miss a feeding (e.g., if you return to work outside the home), pump your breasts. Also, whenever your breasts hurt and you are unable to feed your baby, pump your breasts until they are soft. If you don't relieve engorgement, your milk supply can dry up in 2 to 3 days.

A breast pump is usually unnecessary because pumping can be done by hand. Ask someone to teach you the Marmet technique. If you use a breast pump, you will also need some initial assistance.

Collect the breast milk in plastic containers or plastic bottles because some of the immune factors in the milk stick to glass. Pumped breast milk can be saved for 24 hours in a refrigerator or up to 3 months in a freezer. To thaw frozen milk, put the plastic container of breast milk in the refrigerator (it will take a few hours to thaw) or place it in a pan of warm water until it has warmed up to the temperature your baby prefers. Never warm it up in a microwave or boiling water; this would destroy the protective antibodies.

SORE NIPPLES

Clean a sore nipple with water after each feeding. Do not use soap or alcohol, because they remove natural oils. At the end of each feeding, the nipple can be coated with some breast milk to keep it lubricated. Try to keep the nipples dry with loose clothing, air exposure, and nursing pads.

Sore nipples usually are due to poor latching on and a feeding position that causes undue friction on the nipple. Position your baby so he directly faces the nipple without turning his neck. At the start of the feeding, compress the nipple and areola between your thumb and index finger so your baby can latch on easily. Throughout the feeding, hold your breast from below so the nipple and areola aren't pulled out of your baby's mouth by the weight of the breast. Slightly rotate your baby's body so his mouth applies pressure to slightly different parts of the areola and nipple at each feeding.

Start your feedings on the side that is not sore. If one nipple is extremely sore, temporarily limit feedings to 10 minutes on that side.

VITAMINS/FLUORIDE FOR THE BABY

Breast milk contains all the necessary vitamins and minerals except vitamin D and fluoride. Most full-term light-skinned babies who are breast-fed receive adequate vitamin D from its natural production in their skin during sun exposure. To prevent inadequate vitamin D and soft bones (rickets), all premature babies need 400 units of vitamin D each day. Full-term dark-skinned babies regardless of the climate and light-skinned babies who have little sun exposure (less than 15 minutes of sun exposure twice a week) also probably need vitamin D supplements. The usual dose is 1 ml. of ADC drops (vitamin D drops are usually not available as a separate product).

Breast milk doesn't contain fluoride. From 2 weeks to 12 years of age, children need fluoride to prevent tooth decay. Some pediatricians don't begin fluoride supplements until 6 months of age in breast-fed babies. I begin at 2 weeks of age because fluoride is safe and it probably improves the tooth enamel, even at this young an age. Give 0.25 mg of fluoride drops each day. In the United States this is a prescription item that you can obtain from your child's physician. When you discontinue breast-feeding, also stop the fluoride supplements if your municipal water supply contains fluoride and your baby drinks 4 to 8 ounces of water per day.

Breast milk contains adequate iron during the first 6 months of life. To prevent iron deficiency anemia, add iron-containing solid foods (e.g., cereals) to your infant's diet after 6 months of age.

VITAMINS FOR THE MOTHER
A nursing mother can take a multivitamin tablet daily if she is not following a well-balanced diet. She especially needs 400 units of vitamin D and 1,200 mg of both calcium and phosphorus per day. A quart of milk (or its equivalent in cheese or yogurt) can also meet this requirement.

THE MOTHER'S MEDICATIONS
Almost any drug a breast-feeding mother consumes will be transferred in small amounts into the breast milk. Therefore, try to avoid any drug that is not essential, just as you did during pregnancy. Fortunately, the dose your baby receives via breast milk is much less than he or she would receive if we were prescribing it for the baby. Therefore, side effects are uncommon.

Some commonly used drugs that are safe for you to take while nursing are acetaminophen, penicillins, erythromycin, stool softeners, antihistamines, mild sedatives, cough drops, nose drops, eyedrops, and skin creams. Aspirin and sulfa drugs can be taken once your baby is beyond 2 weeks of age *and* not jaundiced. Acceptable drugs should nonetheless be taken immediately following breast-feedings so that their level in the breast milk at the time of the next feeding is low. A high intake of caffeine-containing beverages or herbal teas (or excessive smoking of cigarettes) can cause restlessness, crying, even diarrhea. Excessive alcohol can cause drowsiness. Diarrhea in the baby can also be caused by some laxatives (but not by chocolate). Used in moderation, these products shouldn't cause any symptoms. The effect on the baby of foods in the mother's diet is overrated.

Some of the dangerous drugs that *can* harm your baby are tetracyclines, chloramphenicol, antithyroid drugs, anticancer drugs, or any radioactive substance. Women who must take these drugs should not be breast-feeding or should request a safer form of therapy. Another group of drugs that should be avoided because they can suppress milk production are ergotamines (for migraine), birth control pills with a high estrogen content (most are okay), vitamin B_6 (pyridoxine) in large doses, and many antidepressants. Overall, most drugs can be taken while breast-feeding.

BURPING

Burping is optional. While it may decrease spitting up, air in the stomach does not cause pain. Burping twice during a feeding and for about 1 minute is plenty. Try burping your baby when switching from the first breast to the second and at the end of the feeding.

CUP-FEEDING

Introduce your child to a cup at approximately 6 months of age. Total weaning to a cup will probably occur somewhere between 9 and 18 months of age, depending on your baby's individual preference (see WEANING, page 157). Regardless of when you start, weaning should proceed gradually. If you discontinue breast-feeding before 9 months of age, switch to bottle-feeding first. If you stop breast-feeding after 9 months of age, you may be able to go directly to cup-feeding.

CALL YOUR CHILD'S PHYSICIAN DURING OFFICE HOURS IF

- Your baby doesn't seem to be gaining adequately (a weight check at 1 week is a good idea for babies of mothers who are breast-feeding for the first time).

- Your baby has less than 6 wet diapers per day.

- During the first month, your baby has less than 4 bowel movements per day.

- You suspect your baby has a food allergy.

- You need to take a medication that was not discussed.

• Your breasts are not full (engorged) before feedings by day 5.

• You have painful engorgement or sore nipples that do not respond to the recommended treatment.

• You have a fever (also call your obstetrician).

FORMULA-FEEDING

Breast milk is best for babies, but breast-feeding isn't always possible. Use an infant formula if:

• You decide not to breast-feed.

• You need to discontinue breast-feeding and your infant is less than one year of age.

• You need to supplement your infant's diet occasionally after breast-feeding is well established.

• Note: If you want to breast-feed but feel your milk supply is insufficient, don't discontinue breast-feeding. Instead seek help from your physician or a lactation nurse.

COMMERCIAL FORMULAS

Infant formulas are a safe alternative to breast milk. Infant formulas have been designed to resemble breast milk and fulfill the nutritional needs of your infant by providing all known essential nutrients in their proper amounts. Most formulas are derived from cow's milk. A few are derived from soybeans and are for infants who may be allergic to the type of protein in cow's milk. Bottle-feeding can provide your child with all the emotional benefits and many of the health benefits of breast-feeding. Bottle-fed babies grow as rapidly and are as happy as breast-fed babies. A special advantage of bottle-feeding is that the father can participate.

Use a commercial formula that is iron-fortified to prevent iron deficiency anemia, as recommended by the American Academy of Pediatrics. The amount of iron in iron-fortified formula is too small to cause any symptoms. The formulas that are not iron-fortified (called low-iron formulas) are not appropriate for any infant and will eventually be removed from the market.

Most commercial infant formulas are available in three

forms: powder, concentrated liquid, and ready-to-serve liquid. Powder and ready-to-serve liquid are the most suitable forms when formula is used to supplement breast milk. Powder and concentrated liquid formulas are less expensive per feeding than ready-to-serve formulas.

PREPARING COMMERCIAL FORMULAS

The concentrated formulas are mixed 1:1 with water. The powdered formulas are mixed 2 ounces of water per each level scoop of powder. Never make the formula more concentrated by adding extra powder or extra concentrated liquid. Never dilute the formula by adding more water than specified. Careful measuring and mixing ensure that your baby is receiving the proper formula.

If you make one bottle at a time, you can use warm water directly from the tap rather than boiled water. This method saves you the time of warming or cooling down the formula. Most city water supplies are quite safe. If you have well water, either boil it for 10 minutes (plus one minute for each 1,000 feet of elevation) or use distilled water until your child is 6 months of age. If you prefer to prepare a batch of formula, you must use boiled or distilled water and closely follow the directions printed on the side of the formula can. This prepared formula should be stored in the refrigerator and must be used within 48 hours.

HOMEMADE FORMULAS FROM EVAPORATED MILK

If necessary, you can make your own formula temporarily from evaporated milk. Evaporated-milk formulas have some of the same risks as whole cow's milk. This formula needs supplements of vitamins and minerals. It also requires sterilized bottles because it is prepared in a batch. While 30 cents less expensive per quart than liquid commercial formulas, it saves little over powdered commercial formulas. If you must use it in a pinch, mix 13 ounces of evaporated milk with 19 ounces of boiled water and 2 tablespoons of corn syrup. Place this mixture in sterilized bottles and keep them refrigerated until use.

WHOLE COW'S MILK

Whole cow's milk should not be given to babies before 12 months of age because of increased risks of iron deficiency anemia and allergies. The ability to drink from a cup doesn't mean you should switch to cow's milk. While it used to be acceptable to introduce whole cow's milk after 6 months of age, recent studies (by Drs. W. W. Tunnessen, F. A. Oski, and others) have shown that infant formula is the optimal food for nonbreast-fed babies during the first year of life. (Note: Evaporated milk mixed with water becomes whole milk.)

Skim milk or 2 percent milk should not be given to babies before 2 years of age, because the fat content of regular milk (approximately 3.5 percent butterfat) is needed for rapid brain growth. (Note: Powdered milk mixed with water becomes skim milk.) The American Academy of Pediatrics recommends that parents not use raw (even though certified) milk for children because of the risk of transmitting serious infectious diseases. Stay with the safety record of pasteurized milk products.

TRAVELING

When traveling, use powdered formula for convenience. Put the required number of scoops in a bottle, add warm tap water, and shake. A more expensive alternative is to use throwaway bottles of ready-to-use formula. This product can be stored at room temperature and avoids problems with contaminated water.

FORMULA TEMPERATURE

In the summertime, many children prefer cold formula. In the wintertime, most prefer warm formula. By trying various temperatures, you can find out which your child prefers. If you do warm the formula, be certain to check the temperature of a few drops on your skin before giving it to your baby. If it is too hot, it will burn your baby's mouth. Microwave heating deserves special caution, as high temperatures can be reached quickly.

AMOUNTS AND SCHEDULES

The amount of formula that most babies take per feeding (in ounces) can be calculated by dividing your baby's weight (in pounds) in half. Another way to calculate the ounces per feeding is to add 3 to your baby's age (in months), with a maximum of 8 ounces per feeding at 5 or 6 months of age. The maximal amount per day is 32 ounces. Overfeeding during the first 6 months of life can cause vomiting or diarrhea from overfilling the stomach and intestines. If your baby needs more than 32 ounces and is not overweight, start solids.

If your baby is not hungry at some of the feedings, the feeding interval should be increased. Although the feeding schedule should be flexible, the following guidelines apply to most babies:

From Birth to 1 Month

- 6 to 8 milk feedings per day
- no more than every 2½ hours
- To reduce night feedings, awaken your baby if he naps for more than 3 consecutive hours during the day.

From 1 to 3 Months

- 5 or 6 milk feedings per day
- no more than every 3 hours

From 3 to 6 Months

- 4 or 5 milk feedings per day
- no more than every 4 hours

By 6 Months

- 4 milk feedings a day (solids with 3 of these)
- 4-hour intervals

By 9 Months

- 3 milk feedings a day (solids with all meals)
- 5-hour intervals
- 1 or 2 snacks per day (see SOLID [STRAINED] FOODS, page 162)

LENGTH OF FEEDING

A feeding shouldn't take more than 20 minutes. If it does, you are overfeeding your baby or the nipple is clogged. A clean nipple should drip about 1 drop per second when the bottle of formula is inverted. At the end of each feeding, discard any formula left in the bottle, because it is no longer sterile.

EXTRA WATER

Babies do not routinely need extra water. They should be offered a bottle of water twice a day, however, when they have a fever or the weather is hot and dry.

FEEDING POSITION

Feeding should be a relaxing time—a time for you to provide both food and comfort for your baby. Make sure that both you and the baby are comfortable:

• Your arm supported by a pillow.

• Your baby in a semisitting position supported in the crook of your arm.

• The bottle titled so that the nipple and the neck of the bottle are always filled with formula. (This prevents your baby from taking in too much air.)

BURPING

Burping is optional. While it may decrease spitting up, air in the stomach does not cause pain. If you burp your baby, be sure to wait until he reaches a natural pause in the feeding process. Burping 2 times during a feeding and for about 1 minute is plenty. More burping may be needed if your baby is a "spitter" (see SPITTING UP, page 133). To reduce the amount of swallowed air, hold the bottle tipped at an angle that keeps the nipple full of formula.

VITAMINS/IRON/FLUORIDE

Commercial formulas with iron contain all of your baby's vitamin and mineral requirements except for fluoride. (Note: All soy-based formulas are iron-fortified.) In our country, the most common cause of anemia in children under 2 years old is iron deficiency (largely because it's not present in cow's milk). Iron also can be provided at 4 months of age by adding iron-fortified cereals to the diet.

From 2 weeks to 12 years of age, children need fluoride to prevent dental caries. If the municipal water supply contains fluoride and your baby drinks some water each day, this should be adequate. Otherwise, fluoride drops or tablets (without vitamins) should be given separately. This is a prescription item that can be obtained from your child's physician. Try to give fluoride on an empty stomach because mixing it with milk reduces its absorption to 70 percent. Added vitamins are unnecessary after your child has reached one year of age and is on a regular balanced diet, but continue the fluoride.

CUP FEEDING

Introduce your child to a cup at approximately 4 to 6 months of age. Total weaning to a cup will probably occur somewhere between 9 and 18 months of age, depending on your baby's individual preference (see WEANING, page 157).

BABY-BOTTLE CARIES: PREVENTION

Sleeping with a bottle of milk, juice, or any sweetened liquid in the mouth can cause severe decay of the newly erupting teeth. The sugar in these drinks is converted to acid by the normal bacteria of the mouth. Since liquids tend to pool in the mouth during sleep, the acid etches the enamel. Prevent this tragedy by not using the bottle as a daytime or nighttime pacifier. If you cannot discontinue the nighttime bottle or replace it with a pacifier, fill it with water. This approach will prevent tooth decay, although it may not improve sleep problems. Of note, dental decay has also resulted when a mother repeatedly falls asleep with her baby asleep on the breast.

NIGHTTIME FEEDINGS

The first weeks are crazy. Your baby will probably need to be fed every 2 to 3 hours. His voracious appetite precludes any schedule. You'll be up for feedings at least twice each night. But by 1 month of age you can start to shape his feeding behaviors. Here are some tips:

- Keep daytime feeding intervals to at least 2 hours for newborns. More frequent daytime feedings (such as hourly) lead to frequent awakenings at night. For every time you nurse your baby, there should be 4 or 5 times that you snuggle him without nursing. Don't let him get into the bad habit of eating every time you hold him. That's called grazing.

- Place your baby in the crib drowsy but awake. His last waking memory needs to be of the crib, not of the breast or bottle. If he learns how to put himself back to sleep, then the only reason he will cry at night is if he's hungry.

- Make middle-of-the-night feedings brief and boring, compared to daytime feedings. Don't turn on the lights or talk to him. Feed your child quickly and quietly. Provide that extra rocking and playtime during the day.

- With this approach and a little luck, your baby will give up middle-of-the-night feedings between 2 and 4 months of age.

WEANING, NORMAL

The definition of weaning is: replacing the bottle or breast (i.e., nipple feedings) with cup-drinking and solid foods. Weaning occurs easily and smoothly unless the breast or bottle has become overly important to the child. Then we have to deal with weaning resistance (see page 159).

HOW TO PREVENT WEANING PROBLEMS

Children normally develop a reduced interest in breast and bottle feedings between 6 and 12 months of age if they are also taking cup and spoon feedings. Brazelton has found that the onset of crawling (at 7 or 8 months) and walking (at 11 or 12 months) are associated with a diminished interest in breast-feeding. Both of these bursts in motor development provide a natural time to start weaning. Between 12 and 18 months of age the parent often has to initiate weaning, but the child is still receptive. After 18 months of age, weaning is usually resisted because the child has become overly attached to the breast or bottle. If your child shows a lack of interest in nipple feedings at any time after 6 months of age, start to phase them out.

You can tell that your baby is ready to begin weaning when he or she throws the bottle down, takes only a few ounces of milk and then stops, chews on the nipple rather than sucking it, refuses the breast, or nurses for only a few minutes, then wants to play. The following steps make early natural weaning at 9 to 12 months most likely:

- Keep formula feedings to 4 times a day or less after your child reaches 6 months of age. (Some breast-fed babies may need 5 feedings per day until 9 months of age.) Even at birth, milk feedings should be kept to 8 times per day or less.

- Give older infants their daytime milk at mealtimes with solids. Once your child is on just 4 milk feedings a day, be sure 3 of them are given at mealtime with solids (rather than as part of a prenap-time ritual). Your child can have the fourth feeding prior to going down for the night.

- After your baby is 6 weeks old and breast-feeding is well established, offer him a bottle of expressed breast milk or water once a day. This experience will help your baby become accustomed to a bottle so that you can occasionally leave him with a sitter. This step is especially important if you will be returning to work or school. The longer after 2 months you wait to introduce the bottle, the more strongly your infant will initially reject it. If you wait until 4 months of age, the transition period may take up to 1 week. Once bottle feedings are accepted, you will need to continue them at least 3 times a week.

• Hold your child for discomfort and stress rather than nursing him or her. Try to separate simple holding from holding with nursing. You can comfort your child and foster a strong sense of security and trust without nursing every time he or she is upset. If you don't follow this guideline, your child will learn to eat whenever he is upset and you may become an "indispensable mother."

• Don't let the bottle or breast substitute for a pacifier. Learn to recognize the need for nonnutritive sucking when your young baby is not hungry. At these times encourage him to suck on a pacifier or thumb rather than giving him food. Feeding your baby every time he or she needs to suck can lead to obesity.

• Don't let the bottle or breast become a substitute for a transitional (security) object at bedtime. Your child should be able to go to sleep at night without having a breast or bottle in his mouth. He needs to learn how to put himself to sleep. If he doesn't, he will develop sleep problems that require the parents' presence during the night.

• Don't let your child hold the bottle or take it to bed. Your child should think of the bottle as something that belongs to you; hence, he won't protest giving it up, since it never belonged to him in the first place.

• Don't let a bottle become a daytime toy. Don't let your child carry a bottle around as a companion during the day. This habit will keep him or her from engaging in more stimulating activities.

• Offer your child formula or breast milk in a cup by 6 months of age. For the first few months your child will probably accept the cup only after he or she has had some milk from bottle or breast. However, by 9 months of age your child should be offered some milk from a cup before bottle feedings.

• Help your baby become interested in foods other than milk by 4 months of age. Introduce solids by spoon by 4 months of age in bottle-fed babies, and by 6 months in breast-fed. Introduce finger foods by 8 months of age. As soon as your child is able to use finger foods, have him or her sit with the family during mealtime. This custom will stimulate your child to ask for other foods that he sees you eating. Consequently, his or her interest in exclusive milk feedings will diminish.

WEANING PROBLEMS

When Is Weaning Delayed or Abnormal? • Breast-feeding or bottle-feeding can be considered prolonged after about 18 months of age. The older toddler who only occasionally nurses or bottle-feeds doesn't necessarily need any pressure to give up the breast or bottle. Delayed weaning should be considered abnormal only if it is causing one or more of the following types of harm:

• refusal to eat any solids after 6 months of age;

• anemia confirmed on a routine screening test at 1 year of age;

• tooth decay (baby-bottle caries);

• obesity from overeating;

• daytime withdrawal and lack of interest in play because the child is always carrying a bottle around;

• frequent awakening at night for refills of a bottle;

• inability to stay with a baby-sitter because the child is exclusively breast-fed and refuses a bottle or cup.

  If any of these criteria apply to your baby, proceed to the following section. Otherwise, continue to nipple-feed your baby when he or she wants to (but 4 times or less a day) and don't worry about complete weaning at this time.

How to Eliminate Excessive Breast- or Bottle-Feeding

To decrease breast- or bottle-feedings to a level that won't cause any of the preceding side effects, take the following steps:

• *Reduce milk-feedings to three or four a day.* When your child comes to you for additional feedings, give him extra holding and attention instead. Get your child on a schedule of three main meals per day plus two or three nutritious snacks.

- *Introduce cup-feedings if this was not done at 6 months of age.* Cup-feedings are needed as substitutes for breast- or bottle-feedings regardless of the age at which weaning occurs. The longer the infant goes without using a cup, the less willing he will be to try it. Starting daily cup-feedings by 5 or 6 months of age is a natural way to keep breast- or bottle-feedings from becoming overly important.

- *Immediately stop allowing your child to carry a bottle around during the day.* The companion bottle can interfere with normal development that requires speech or two-handed play. It also can contribute to problems with tooth decay. You can explain to your child that "It's not good for you" or "You're too old for that."

- *Immediately stop allowing your child to take a bottle to bed.* Besides causing sleep problems, taking a bottle to bed carries the risk of causing tooth decay. You can offer the same explanations as above.

Once you have made these changes, you need not proceed further unless you wish to eliminate breast- or bottle-feedings completely. Attempt total weaning only if your family is not under stress (such as might be caused by moving or some other major change) and your child is not in crisis (e.g., from illness or trying to achieve bladder control). Weaning from breast or bottle to cup should always be done gradually and with love. The "cold turkey," or abrupt withdrawal, approach will only make your child angry, clingy, and miserable. While there is no consensus about the best time to wean, there is agreement about the appropriate technique.

How to Eliminate Breast-Feeding Completely

- *Offer formula in a cup before each breast-feeding.* If your child refuses formula, offer expressed breast milk. If that fails, add some flavoring he likes to the formula. If your child is older than 12 months, you can use whole milk. Some infants won't accept a cup until they've nursed for several minutes. (Note: If your child is less than 9 months of age and you wish to discontinue breast-feeding, follow this procedure but switch to bottle-feedings rather than a cup.)

- *Gradually eliminate breast-feeding.* First, eliminate the feeding that is least important to your child (usually the midday one). Replace it with a complete cup-feeding. About once a week drop out one more breast-feeding. The bedtime nursing is usually the last to be given up, and there's no reason why you can't continue it for months if that's what you and your child want. Some mothers prefer to wean by decreasing the length of feedings. Shorten all feedings by 2 minutes each week until they are 5 minutes long. Then eliminate them one at a time.

- *Relieve breast engorgement.* Since the breast operates on the principle of supply and demand, reduced sucking time eventually reduces milk production. In the meantime, express just enough milk to relieve breast pain resulting from engorgement. (This is better than putting your baby to the breast for a minute, because she probably won't want to stop nursing.) Remember that complete emptying of the breast increases milk production. An acetaminophen product also may help relieve discomfort.

- *If your child asks to nurse after you have finished weaning, respond by holding her instead.* You can explain that "the milk is all gone." If she has a strong sucking drive, more pacifier time may help.

How to Eliminate Bottle-Feeding Completely

- *Offer formula in a cup before each bottle-feeding.* Use whole milk if your child is 1 year of age or older.

- *Make the weaning process gradual.* Eliminate 1 bottle-feeding every 3 to 4 days, depending on your child's reaction. Replace each bottle-feeding with a cup-feeding and extra holding.

- *Eliminate bottle-feedings in the following order: midday, late afternoon, morning, and bedtime.* The last feeding of the day is usually the most important one to the child. When it is time to give up this feeding, gradually reduce the amount of milk each day over the course of a week.

- *After you have completed the weaning process, respond to requests for a bottle by holding your child.* You can explain that bottles are for little babies. You may even want to have your child help you carry the bottles to a neighbor's house. If your child has a strong need to suck, offer a pacifier.

CALL YOUR CHILD'S PHYSICIAN DURING OFFICE HOURS IF

- Your child is over 6 months of age, won't eat any food except milk, and won't drink from a cup.

- Your child has tooth decay.

- You think your child has anemia.

- This approach to weaning has not been successful after trying it for 1 month.

- Your child is over 3 years old.

- You have other questions or concerns.

SOLID (STRAINED) FOODS

AGE FOR STARTING SOLID FOODS

The best time to begin using a spoon is when your baby can sit with some support and voluntarily move his head to engage in the feeding process—i.e., when he or she is ready. This time is usually between 4 and 6 months of age. From a nutritional standpoint, breast milk and iron-fortified formulas meet all of your baby's needs until 4 to 6 months of age. He or she needs nothing else. Introducing strained foods early just makes feeding more complicated. The current recommendation of the American Academy of Pediatrics is that bottle-fed babies not be introduced to solids until 4 months of age and breast-fed babies or allergic babies not until 6 months of age. Waiting also reduces the likelihood of food allergies in your baby. By all means, don't give strained foods in a bottle; wait until your child can accept spoon feedings. An exception to the above guideline is to start solids at 3 months of age if your baby is drinking more than 1 quart of formula per day and remains quite hungry.

A common myth is that solids at bedtime will help your baby sleep through the night. Three research studies have shown this is not true. The only exceptions are those few breast-fed babies who are not receiving enough calories or gaining adequately. If your baby is not sleeping through the night, see PREVENTION OF SLEEP PROBLEMS, page 243.

TYPES OF SOLID FOODS

Between 4 and 8 months of age, introduce your baby to strained foods and cereals. The order is not very important. While most books recommend starting with cereals, it is often helpful to begin with a fruit (bananas, for instance) so that your baby immediately builds a positive association with the spoon. Giving a little milk first also helps with this transition. When your child is very hungry, he or she is intolerant of trying new substances. After 1 or 2 weeks of fruits, go to cereals, usually starting with rice cereal. The cereals are helpful at this time if your child has no other source of iron. Cereal can be mixed with water, fruit juice, or milk. The amount of solid food can gradually be increased. The first few times your baby may just want a taste. Then go to a few small spoonfuls. Eventually work up to 2 tablespoons of each food.

Introduce only 1 new food at a time and no more than 3 per week. Since your baby is receiving plenty of protein in the milk, meats can be introduced last.

Between 8 and 12 months of age, introduce your baby to mashed table foods or junior foods (though the latter are probably unnecessary). If you make your own baby foods in a baby-food grinder or electric blender, be sure to add enough water to get a consistency that your baby can easily swallow. For convenient individual portions, these homemade baby foods can be poured into ice cube trays, frozen, removed, and stored in plastic freezer bags.

Avoid sweet foods and desserts in the first year of life, since they may interfere with your baby's willingness to try other new, unsweet foods.

Although there is controversy about them, egg whites, wheat, peanut butter, fish, and orange juice may be more likely to cause allergies than other solids and should be avoided until 1 year of age (especially in infants with allergies).

SPOON-FEEDING

Spoon-feeding is begun at 4 to 6 months of age. By a year of age, most children want to try to feed themselves, and can do so with finger foods. By 15 to 18 months of age, most children can use a spoon independently for foods they can't pick up with their fingers, and the parent is no longer needed in the feeding process. Here's how to start:

• Be sure to place food on the middle of the tongue. If you place it in front, your child will probably push it back at you.

Some infants get off to a better start if you place the spoon between their lips and let them suck off the food.

- Some children constantly bat at the spoon or try to get a grip on it during feedings. These children need to be distracted with finger foods (such as Cheerios) or by having a spoon of their own to play with.

- If your child previously liked spoon-feeding and now clamps his mouth shut when the spoon approaches, he's probably not hungry or someone has tried to force him to eat more than he wants. Only spoon-feed your child when he is hungry. If he turns his head away more than once, mealtime should be over.

- Spoon-feeding can be very messy in the beginning. Use a small baby spoon and a scooped-out bib to catch the dribble. Also, put down newspapers under the high chair to reduce your cleanup time.

FINGER FOODS

Finger foods are small, bite-size pieces of soft foods. Most babies love to feed themselves and gain this added sense of independence. Finger foods can be introduced between 9 and 10 months of age or whenever a child develops a pincer grip (finger-thumb pickup). Since most babies will not be able to feed themselves with a spoon until 15 months of age, finger foods keep them actively involved in the feeding process. Good finger foods are dry cereals (Cheerios are hard to beat), toast, cheese wedges, pieces of scrambled egg, cooked vegetable strips, slices of canned fruit (peaches, pears, or pineapple), slices of banana, crackers, cookies, and breads. With each passing month, try to increase the amount of finger foods and decrease the amount of mashed foods that require a spoon.

SNACKS

Once your baby goes to 3 meals a day or 5-hour intervals, small snacks will often be necessary to tide him over to the next meal. Most babies go to this pattern between 6 and 9 months of age. The midmorning and midafternoon snack should be a nutritious, nonmilk food. Fruits and dry cereals are recommended. If your child is not hungry at mealtime, the snacks should be made smaller or eliminated.

TABLE FOODS

Your child should be eating the same meals as you do by approximately 1 year of age. This assumes that your family consumes a well-balanced, low animal-fat diet, and that you carefully dice any foods that would be difficult for your baby to chew. Avoid foods like raw carrots that could be aspirated into the lungs. (See under CHOKING, page 10, for a list of dangerous foods.)

HEATING SOLID FOODS

Overheated foods can cause mouth burns. Be careful. Test them before serving to an infant. Microwaves have the disadvantage of heating from the inside out, leaving some parts of the food hotter than others. The cooler temperature of the container can also be misleading. Stir microwave-heated food to distribute the heat evenly before testing it.

VITAMINS

Added vitamins are unnecessary after your child has reached 1 year of age and is on a regular balanced diet. If he's a picky eater, give him 1 chewable vitamin pill per week.

POOR EATERS, POOR APPETITES

SYMPTOMS AND CHARACTERISTICS

- You think your child "doesn't eat enough," "is never hungry," "won't eat unless you feed him," or "eats slower than anyone else."

- Your child is between 1 and 5 years of age.

- Your child's energy level remains normal.

- Your child is growing normally.

- Your child is not losing weight.

Causes • Between 1 and 5 years of age, many children normally gain only 4 or 5 pounds per year, in contrast to the 15 pounds gained during the first year of life. Children in this age range can normally go 3 or 4 months without any weight gain. This normal slowdown in growth results in a reduced need for calories and a normal decline in appetite (called physiological anorexia). Food intake is governed by the appetite center in the brain. Kids eat as much as they need for growth and energy. Any hungry child will eat if food is available. No child will voluntarily starve himself at this age.

The appetite may decrease even further if parents try to force the child to eat more than he needs (even though he is of normal height and weight). They may apply pressure because they fear that decreased eating might cause poor health or a nutritional deficiency—neither of which is true. But forced feedings interfere with the normal pleasure of eating and actually decrease the appetite. If the child is going through a normal phase of negativism, the struggle can accelerate.

Two other reasons that parents attempt to force their children to eat are short stature and normal shifting linear growth. The 3 percent of children under the third percentile in height are said to have short stature. The majority of them are well nourished. Feeding them more cannot increase their height—but it can make them fat as well as short. Children with shifting linear growth concern their parents, because their growth rate falls off before 1 year of age. Many children with short parents are born with average height. During the second half of the first year of life, however, they may shift to a lower height percentile (or line on the growth curve) because it corresponds to the height of their parents. Once they get to the new growth channel, they continue to grow along it at a normal rate. They never appear to be underweight during any of this gradual shifting.

Expected Course • Once you allow your child to control his own food intake, the "problem" will disappear in a matter of 2 to 4 weeks. Rest assured, your child's appetite will reach gigantic proportions by adolescence.

IMPROVING POOR APPETITES

Put Your Child in Charge of How Much He Eats. Trust Your Child's Appetite Center • The most common reason for never appearing hungry is that your child has received enough snacks that he never becomes truly hungry. You have stayed one meal ahead of his appetite. Let your child miss 1 or 2 meals if he chooses and then watch his appetite return. Skipping a meal is harmless.

Never Feed Your Child If He Is Capable of Feeding Himself • The greatest tendency for parents of a child with a poor appetite is to pick up the utensils, load up the spoon, smile, and try to trick or coerce the child into taking it. Once your child is old enough to use a spoon (usually age 12 to 15 months), never again pick it up for him. If your child is hungry, he will feed himself. Forced feeding is the main cause of eating power struggles.

Offer Finger Foods • Finger foods can be started at 6 to 8 months of age. They allow your child a major role in self-feeding even if he is not yet able to use a spoon.

Limit Milk Intake to Less Than 16 Ounces Per Day • If your child eats cheese or yogurt, reduce milk by an equivalent amount. Most children in our society receive excessive milk, which fills kids up and dulls the appetite. Milk is a food and contains as many calories as most solid foods.

Limit Snacks to Two Per Day • Offer small-sized snacks of nutritious foods. Provide them only if your child requests them and offer some food choices. If your child is thirsty between meals, offer water to quench the thirst. Keep juice to less than 6 ounces per day. If your child skips the majority of a meal, cancel the next snack. Some of these children do quite well on only 2 meals a day and no snacks.

Serve Small Portions of Food • A child's appetite is decreased by being served more food than he could possibly eat. Serving a small amount (less than you think he will eat) on a large plate leads to a sense of accomplishment. If your child seems to want more, wait for him to ask for seconds.

Consider Giving Your Child Daily Vitamins If Food Intake Is Borderline • Although vitamins are probably unnecessary, they are not harmful in normal dosages and may allow you to relax about your child's eating patterns. However, they won't increase the appetite.

Make Mealtimes Pleasant • Draw your children into the conversation. Tell them what's happened to you today and ask about their day. Talk about fun subjects unrelated to food. Avoid making it a time for criticism or struggle over control.

Avoid Conversation About Eating at Any Time • Don't discuss food intake in your child's presence. Trust the appetite center to look after your child's food needs. Don't provide praise for appropriate eating. Don't give bribes or rewards for meeting your eating expectations. Children should eat for themselves. Occasionally the child can be praised for trying new foods that he does not like the taste or texture of.

Don't Extend Mealtime • Don't keep your child sitting at the dinner table after the rest of the family is done. This only causes your child to develop unpleasant associations with mealtime.

COMMON MISTAKES

Parents who are worried that their child isn't eating enough may initiate some irrational patterns of feeding. Some awaken the child at night to feed him or her. Some offer the child snacks at 15- or 20-minute intervals throughout the day. Some try to make the child feel guilty by talking about other children in the world who are starving. Others threaten that "If you don't eat what I cook, it means you don't love me." Some parents force the child to sit in the high chair or at the table for long periods of time after the meal has ended. The most common mistake, of course, is picking up a spoon or fork and trying various ways to get food into the child's mouth. Another mistake is cooking special foods for the child. Although the child may eat these, the total calories consumed per day will probably not increase (since it does not need to increase).

PREVENTION

The main way to prevent feeding struggles is by teaching your child how to feed himself or herself from as early an age as possible. You needn't wait until your child is old enough to use a spoon independently. For the young child, you can allow your child to initiate the feeding (by reaching or leaning forward) and to pace the feeding (by turning the head or gesturing). Food should not be placed in the mouth just because it is inadvertently open. The hands should be free and not pinned down during feedings. Do not insist that your child empty the bottle, finish a jar of baby food, or clean the plate. By the time your child is 6 to 8 months old, start giving her finger foods. By 12 months of age your child should start to learn how to use a spoon and should be completely self-feeding by 15 months of age.

RESPECT SPECIFIC FOOD DISLIKES

Children of all ages (and adults) commonly have a few food dislikes. Usually, parents of these children are not concerned about the amount of calories consumed but about their child missing some essential food or nutrient. The complaints are usually about vegetables, a greatly overrated food. Vegetables are in the same food group as fruits and can be entirely replaced by fruits without any harm to the child. There are no essential foods, just essential food groups.

If your child has a few strong food dislikes (e.g., something that makes her gag), she should not be served them when they are prepared as part of the family meal. A minimal-amount rule can be put into effect for other food dislikes. For example, the preschool-age child must taste each food, and the parents should trust her word that she has done so. By school age, most children will take 1 bite per year of age (for example, a 7-year-old will eat 7 peas).

An unnecessary area of friction for these children is a ruling that if they don't clean their plates, they are not allowed to have dessert. Since desserts are not harmful, a better approach is to allow your child 1 serving of dessert if she complies with the minimal-amount rule for foods she dislikes.

CALL YOUR CHILD'S PHYSICIAN DURING OFFICE HOURS IF

- Your child has not had a medical checkup in the last year.

- Your child is losing weight.

- Your child has not gained any weight in 6 months.

- Your child has associated symptoms of illness (such as diarrhea or fever).

- Your child gags on or vomits some foods.

- Someone is punishing your child for not eating.

- This approach has not improved mealtimes in your house within 1 month.

- You have other questions or concerns.

RELATED TOPICS

MEDICINES: HELPING CHILDREN SWALLOW THEM (see page 230)
OVERWEIGHT: PREVENTION IN INFANTS (see page 190)

A HEALTHY DIET

HEALTH PROBLEMS RELATED TO DIET

In the United States, at least six health conditions have been proven to relate to diet. The first four problems occur in children as well as in adults. The last two primarily occur in adults.

Iron Deficiency Anemia • This type of anemia usually occurs between 6 months and 2 years of age. The main symptoms are fatigue and delayed motor development. Iron deficiency anemia can also cause behavioral symptoms such as restlessness, irritability, and poor attention span.

Overweight • Obesity is one of the most common nutritional problems in our country (see OVERWEIGHT: PREVENTION IN INFANTS, page 190). Obesity is also one of the most important contributing factors in heart disease, hypertension, and some cancers.

Tooth Decay • Tooth decay is accentuated by the intake of sugars in association with poor tooth-brushing habits (see TOOTH DECAY PREVENTION, page 183).

Intestinal Symptoms • Too little fiber intake can cause intestinal symptoms such as constipation, abdominal discomfort, appendicitis, gallstones, and some intestinal cancers.

Coronary Artery Disease • An increased intake of animal fats (especially cholesterol) contributes to coronary artery disease. This disease hardly exists in poor countries where the population subsists on low-fat, high-carbohydrate diets. It is also less common among vegetarians.

High Blood Pressure • High blood pressure has been associated with an increased salt intake or a decreased calcium intake in some susceptible individuals. Most individuals, however, get rid of extra salt through their kidneys and don't develop hypertension.

RECOMMENDATIONS FOR A HEALTHY DIET

Learn the Four Food Groups • Food can be divided into four basic groups: Milk products, meats/eggs, grains, and fruits/vegetables.

- Milk products include milk, cheese, yogurt, and ice cream.

- Meats include red meats, poultry, fish, and eggs. Eggs have the highest cholesterol content of any of the commonly eaten foods. The cholesterol in one egg is equivalent to the cholesterol in 14 ounces of beef, 1½ quarts of whole milk, or 1 quart of ice cream.

- Grains include breads, cereals, rice, pasta, and so forth.

- Fruits and vegetables may be consumed as solids or juices.

- A healthy diet should consist of 20 percent milk, meat, and eggs, and 80 percent vegetables, fruits, and grains. (Fiber is found in grains, fruits, and vegetables.) This is similar to the recommendations that children receive 55 percent of their calories from carbohydrates, 30 percent from fats, and 15 percent from protein.

Eat Three Meals a Day • Breakfast is essential for children. Skipping breakfast can compromise performance at school. For dieters, skipping breakfast usually doesn't lead to weight loss. All meals should contain fruits or vegetables, and grains as well. Meat or milk should be included in two of the meals.

Eating snacks is largely a habit. Snacks are unnecessary for good nutrition but harmless unless your child is overweight. If your child likes snacks (and most children do), encourage fruits, vegetables, yogurt, dry cereal, corn chips, and crackers but don't give them if it is close to mealtime.

Decrease the Intake of Fat (Meat and Milk Products) • Americans eat excessive amounts of meat and dairy products. Although cholesterol is important for rapid growth, after age 2 it should be consumed in moderation (not eliminated). To decrease the intake of fat, follow these guidelines:

- Remember that one serving of meat per day is adequate for normal growth and development. (Don't serve meat more than twice a day.)

- Serve more fish and poultry and fewer red meats, since the latter have the highest cholesterol levels. Lean meats are lean ground beef, pork loin, veal, and lamb.

- Trim the fat off meats and remove the skin from poultry.

- Don't serve bacon, sausages, spareribs, pastrami, and other meats that have a high fat content. Cut back on hot dogs, lunch meats, and corned beef.

- Limit the number of eggs to 3 or 4 per week.

- Use 2 percent milk instead of whole milk (after 2 years of age).

- Decrease milk intake to 2 or 3 cups per day. (Encourage water for satisfying thirst.) On the other hand, teenage girls may need to be reminded to consume adequate milk products (the equivalent of 3 glasses of milk) to lay down the bone mass to prevent osteoporosis later in life.

- Use margarine instead of butter.

- Keep in mind that red meats may be hard to give up because of the widespread misconception that red meat helps to build muscle mass and strength.

Increase the Intake of Fruits, Vegetables, and Grains • Children should consume at least five servings of fruits and vegetables per day. (In actuality 50 percent of American children eat only one fruit or vegetable per day.)

- Try to serve a fruit at every meal.

- Offer fruits as dessert and snacks.

- Start every day with a glass of fruit juice. (**Caution:** Limit fruit juices to 2 cups per day to prevent diarrhea.)

- Since fruits and vegetables are interchangeable, don't force children to eat vegetables they don't like.

- When making casseroles, increase the amount of vegetables and decrease the amount of meat.

- Serve more soups.

- Encourage more cereals for breakfast.

- Use more whole-grain bread in making sandwiches.

Maintain an Adequate Iron Intake • Throughout our lives we need an adequate amount of iron in our diets to prevent anemia. Everyone should know which foods are good sources of iron. Red meats, fish, and poultry are best. Having one serving per day will provide adequate iron. Although liver is a good source of iron, it contains 16 times more cholesterol than beef and should be avoided. For those young children who refuse meats in general, low-fat luncheon meats can be provided as a meat source. Adequate iron is also found in iron-enriched cereals, beans of all types, peanut butter, raisins, prune juice, sweet potatoes, spinach, and egg yolks. The iron in these foods is better absorbed if the meal also contains fruit juice or meat.

Avoid Excessive Salt • Salt is not usually harmful for people without high blood pressure. However, we can discourage a taste for excessive salt in infants by not adding it to their foods. The salt shaker can be removed from the dinner table. Other herbs and spices can be used instead of salt. Salty foods such as potato chips and pretzels can be purchased sparingly.

Avoid Excessive Pure Sugars • See SUGAR AND SWEETS, page 180.

Eating Before Exercise • The best foods to consume before prolonged exercise are complex carbohydrates. These include bread, pasta (noodles), potatoes, and rice. These should be consumed 3 to 4 hours before the athletic event so they have passed out of the stomach. Water consumption continues to be important right up to the time of participation and every 20 to 30 minutes during the activity. Eating meat does not improve athletic performance.

FOOD MYTHS

Some Americans consider a faulty diet to be the cause of most health problems. If this were true the practice of medicine would become relatively easy. Unfortunately, most diseases do not respond to a change in the diet. The following misleading statements have received some attention in the media.

"Everyone Needs Vitamin Supplements." • In general in our society vitamins are overused (the "once a day" vitamin habit). Vitamins do not improve a child's appetite, prevent infections, or increase pep and energy. Added vitamins are unnecessary once your child has reached 1 year of age, if he consumes a regular balanced diet from all 4 food groups. Keep in mind that vitamins and minerals are already present in foods. Vitamin supplements may be helpful in special situations (for instance, if your child is a picky eater, is dieting, or has a chronic disease). Some vitamins taken in excess (mainly vitamins A and D) are stored in the body and can cause symptoms (such as headaches and kidney stones). The danger of overdosage is a good example of "more is not better." Any extra vitamin B or C is quickly passed in the urine.

"Natural Foods Are Better." • Natural or organic foods are those grown without pesticides or artificial fertilizers, and processed without preservatives, food colorings, or food additives. Natural foods have no nutritional advantages. They have no higher level of vitamins or minerals. Foods grown in worn-out soil are no different in food value from those grown in rich soil. Foods grown with chemical fertilizers are just as healthy as foods grown with natural fertilizers. The chemicals used to preserve food do not take away from its nutritional or health value. The main difference between these two types of foods is that natural foods are more costly.

"Junk Foods Are Bad." • Junk foods are an area of great confusion. Some people consider any meal served at a fast-food restaurant to be junk food. In truth these meals often contain foods from all four groups (although they may be heavy on fat and low on fiber). Fast-food meals are fine if they aren't eaten daily. More commonly, some people define any sweet or dessert as a junk food. They claim that these foods "lack nutritional value" or "contain empty calories." In truth, they contain plenty of calories, mainly as sugars. *Empty calories* is a meaningless term. (See SUGAR AND SWEETS, page 180.)

CHOLESTEROL SCREENING OR TESTING

Cholesterol is the normal way fat is carried in the bloodstream. Cholesterol has become a health issue because high cholesterol levels carry an increased risk of coronary heart disease (CHD). A 1 percent decrease in blood cholesterol leads to a 2 percent decrease in risk of CHD in adults. Societies with low serum cholesterol usually have a low incidence of CHD. The amount of cholesterol and saturated fats we eat contributes to the level of cholesterol in our bloodsteams. The level of cholesterol in childhood tends to persist (track) into adulthood in about 50 percent of children. This ability of the child's level of cholesterol to predict the adult level increases in adolescence. Furthermore, reducing the cholesterol and saturated fat in the diet does reduce the level of cholesterol in the bloodstream. One major goal of preventive medicine is to lower cholesterol to healthy levels.

Types of Cholesterol • Cholesterol is composed of high-density lipoproteins (HDL), low-density lipoproteins (LDL), and triglycerides. The HDL is called the "good" cholesterol because it carries cholesterol away from the arteries and to the liver for elimination. LDL is referred to as the "bad" cholesterol. An excess of LDL deposits cholesterol on the inner walls of the arteries over time. In addition to reducing total cholesterol levels, we would like to see you increase your HDL and decrease your LDL. A 1 percent rise in HDL may give a 3 percent reduction in CHD in adults.

Normal and Abnormal Cholesterol Levels • Normal cholesterol levels remain rather constant, between 120 and 170, throughout childhood. After age 18 they tend to rise about 1 point per year of age. For total cholesterol and LDL, a healthy or desirable level is below the 75th percentile. A borderline high level is between the 75th and 95th percentiles. A high or abnormal level is above the 95th percentile. In general, levels above the 75th percentile should be lowered because the normal values in our country are considerably higher than normal values in countries with a low incidence of CHD.

		Children	Adults
Total cholesterol	>95th	>200	>240
	>75th	>170	>200
	Desirable	<170	<200
LDL	>95th	>130	>160
	>75th	>110	>130
	Desirable	<110	<130

The desired level for HDL, which we want to be high since it is protective, is above the 25th percentile. A borderline low value is between the 5th and 25th percentiles. A low or abnormal value is below the 5th percentile.

		Children	**Adults**
HDL	<5th	<35	<30
	<25th	<45	<40
	Desirable	>45	>40

High-Risk Children: At What Age to Test? • The American Academy of Pediatrics and the American Heart Association are in complete agreement that all children who have risk factors for CHD should be screened soon after age 2. The reason children aren't tested before age 2 is that during this period of rapid growth and development, the diet needs to be high in fat. Two main risk factors should be considered: (1) a family history of high blood cholesterol and (2) a family history of CHD. The first factor includes an early (less than 50 years of age in men or less than 60 years of age in women) history of heart attack, angina, stroke, or bypass surgery. The family history is considered positive if these diseases have occurred in parents, grandparents, aunts, or uncles. Information must be obtained about the grandparents, since the parents are often too young to have entered the high-risk age group for CHD. By screening these high-risk children, over 50 percent of children with high cholesterols are identified.

All Other Children: At What Age to Test? • The practice of performing cholesterol testing on all children is controversial. The main reason for universal testing is to identify all children with high cholesterols. Good eating and exercise patterns in children need to be established early if these patterns are to be followed throughout life. The main arguments against testing all children are that testing is costly, high cholesterol levels do not persist into adulthood 50 to 60 percent of the time, and healthy diets can be started on all children without knowing cholesterol levels. If routine testing is done, it's usually performed between ages 2 and 5 years, often upon school entry.

Retesting Children with High Cholesterols • If your child's cholesterol value is borderline high or high, the test will be repeated in one to two weeks to confirm that the value is high. There is some normal day-to-day variation in cholesterol levels. If the level remains high, it's assumed to be accurate. Children with confirmed high total cholesterols (greater than the 95th percentile) will then have blood drawn for a lipid profile or panel. This test measures not only total cholesterol but also LDL, HDL, and triglycerides. Depending on the results, treatment will be initiated and the level retested in approximately

2 to 4 months. If your child has a high normal total cholesterol level (greater than the 75th percentile), treatment can be started without additional tests. The test for total cholesterol will probably be repeated yearly. The reason we don't obtain routine lipid panels on all children is that the test costs approximately $50, in contrast to $15 for a total-cholesterol test. In addition, the lipid panel requires drawing blood from a vein (which can be a more difficult procedure in children) rather than a simple fingerstick.

Retesting Children with Normal Cholesterols • Children with cholesterols below the 75th percentile do not need their cholesterol rechecked until they reach adolescence. Most physicians who monitor adult levels repeat tests for cholesterols every 5 years as long as the levels remain within normal range.

Testing Family Members • If your child's value is high (greater than the 95th percentile), we recommend that you have everyone else in your family tested for total cholesterol. If a child has a high level, other family members also have high values in over 80 percent of cases. This will provide you with additional reasons to start your family on a healthier diet and exercise program. If your child's cholesterol level is high or high-normal, see the information sheet on treating high cholesterol levels.

TREATING HIGH CHOLESTEROL LEVELS

If your child's cholesterol level is high or borderline high, start the programs listed below. (If your child's cholesterol level is normal, it still would be a good idea to place your family on the same programs.) High cholesterols are not the only risk factor for coronary heart disease (CHD). The following risk factors are just as harmful as being on a high cholesterol diet: physical inactivity, obesity, and smoking. The more risk factors that you and your child have, the higher the risk of CHD. Living a long and healthy life requires healthy eating and exercise patterns. It is easier to start these habits as a child than to have to adopt them as an adult. Review with your family the following checklist of ways to reduce cholesterol levels. If you already are carrying out the majority of these recommendations, you are protecting your child's heart and blood vessels.

1. **Low-fat diet.** The American Heart Association recommends that all children over age 2 be on a low-cholesterol, low-saturated-fat diet. Currently most Americans take in 40 percent of their daily calories as fat. A healthy (prudent) diet keeps fat to 30 percent of total calories. The goal is eating fat in moderation, not eliminating fat entirely. Lowering your child's fat intake to 30 percent of daily calories carries no risk for children over age 2. (None of the following recommendations applies to children under age 2.)

Foods of plant origin such as fruits, vegetables, and grains do not contain cholesterol. Foods of animal origin such as meats, eggs, and milk products do contain cholesterol. Our blood cholesterol is raised by consuming cholesterol itself, or by eating saturated fats that stimulate the production of cholesterol. Even without any fat intake, the liver produces a small amount of cholesterol each day. Therefore we will always have a blood cholesterol level. Serving a low-fat diet in your house is rather easy:

- Serve more fish, turkey, and chicken, since they have less fat than red meats. Buy lean ground beef for hamburgers. Use lean ham or turkey for sandwiches.

- Trim the fat from meats and remove the skin from poultry before eating.

- Avoid meats with the highest fat content, such as bacon, sausages, salami, pepperoni, and hot dogs.

- Limit the number of eggs eaten to 3 or 4 per week.

- Limit the amount of all meats to portions of moderate size.

- Use 1 percent or skim (0.5 percent) milk instead of whole milk (which is 3.5 percent).

- Use a margarine product instead of butter.

- Avoid deep-fat fried food or food fried in butter or fat. If you prefer to fry meats, use margarine or nonstick cooking sprays.

- Increase your child's fiber intake. Fiber is found in most grains, vegetables, and fruits.

2. **Family exercise program.** Exercise is the best way to raise your HDL level. Your goal should be 20 to 30 minutes of

vigorous exercise three times per week. Vigorous exercise must involve the large muscles of the legs and cause your heart to beat faster (aerobic exercise). Vigorous exercise also improves your heart's response to work. A child is much more likely to exercise if you exercise with him. Try the following forms of exercise:

- Encourage walking or biking instead of riding in a car.
- Encourage using stairs instead of elevators.
- Encourage taking the dog for a walk, jumping rope, or playing ball if your child appears to be bored.
- Encourage your child to join a team (e.g., soccer) or learn a new sport (e.g., roller skating) that requires vigorous (aerobic) activity. Swimming and jogging are sports that burn lots of calories. Sports such as baseball and football do not give the heart much of a workout.
- Encourage exercising to a videotape or music on TV.
- Limit TV and video game time to 2 hours or less per day. These sitting activities interfere with physical fitness.
- Encourage using an exercise bike, dancing, or running in place while watching TV.
- Support better physical education programs and aerobics classes in your schools.

   3. **Ideal body weight.** Children who are overweight tend to have a low HDL and a high LDL. Helping your child return to ideal body weight will improve his blood cholesterol levels. When people decrease the fat in the diet, they automatically decrease the calories they consume each day because fat has twice as many calories as the same amount of protein or carbohydrates. A low-fat diet *and* exercise are the key ingredients for losing weight. If your child is overweight, also see the guideline on overweight.

   4. **Smoke-free home.** A good way to raise your HDL level is to stop smoking. Also avoid exposing your child to passive smoking. If someone in your home has a problem with smoking, see the guideline on passive smoking.

   5. **Set a good example.** If your child needs to lower his cholesterol level, he will need help from his family. You cannot put him on a special diet without putting the entire family on it. You cannot put him on a special exercise program

without having other family members participate. Eat healthy foods and snacks so your child will eat similarly. Play more sports and watch less TV sports—as you would like your child to do.

6. **Medications to lower cholesterol.** Such medications are rarely used in children unless they have a rare form of high cholesterol, relating to disease rather than diet. If your child's level remains high despite your initial efforts, request a consultation with a nutritionist regarding special diets. Also, join an exercise program at a local gym or fitness center. These additional steps will usually help your child.

7. **When to recheck your child's cholesterol level.** Generally, for high cholesterols (above the 95th percentile) the level is rechecked approximately 2 to 4 months after starting a program to lower it. If the cholesterol level is borderline high (above the 75th percentile), it is usually rechecked yearly.

SUGAR AND SWEETS

A popular misconception suggests that eating sugar is harmful or even sinful. Many well-educated parents worry needlessly about sugar, candy, and desserts. Sweets are not bad. They just need to be eaten in moderation. If you want to protect your child's health, get after the Cholesterol Monster, not the Sugar Monster and the Cookie Monster.

The Normal "Sweet Tooth" • Soon after birth, infants show a preference for sweet solutions (such as breast milk) over unsweetened solutions. Many humans are born with a "sweet tooth," probably on a genetic basis. Most adults also naturally seek out and enjoy sweets. Giving candy as a gift for holidays or birthdays is a common symbol of affection. Many members of the animal kingdom also show a craving for sweets.

People forget that the recommended daily amount of calories from carbohydrates (sugar and starches) is 55 percent. The amount from refined sugars (sucrose) should not exceed 10 percent of the daily calories. Sugar is present in most foods except the meat group.

Lactose is the sugar present in milk, fructose is the sugar present in fruits, and maltose is the sugar present in grain products. Sucrose, the sugar in sugarcane and sugar beets, has no greater adverse effect on body functioning than any of the other sugars.

Side Effects of Sugar • The main risk of sugar is its ability to increase tooth decay. It is also the only permanent harm from consuming too much sugar. This risk can be greatly reduced if the teeth are brushed after sugar-containing foods are eaten. The foods causing the most dental cavities (caries) are those that stick to the teeth (e.g., raisins carry considerable risk). The greatest risk factor for causing severe dental caries is falling asleep or walking around with a bottle of sugar solution in the mouth. The solution can be fruit juice, Kool-Aid, or milk. This type of tooth decay is called "baby-bottle caries."

A temporary side effect may be seen 2 hours after excessive sugar consumption. A withdrawal reaction consisting of sweating, hunger, dizziness, tiredness, or sleepiness may be felt. This reaction to a sugar binge is brief, harmless, and can be relieved by eating some food. The sleepiness is caused by serotonin, which is produced by the body in response to the high level of blood sugar that follows eating refined sugar (sucrose).

Myths About Sugar • Eating sugar is basically not harmful. Candy does not cause cancer, heart disease, or diabetes mellitus. The following are some common overconcerns: (1) Obesity. Obesity is due to overeating in general and not specifically to eating sugars. Fatty foods have twice the calories per amount as sugar and are much more related to obesity. (2) Hyperactivity. Extensive research has shown that sugar does not cause hyperactivity. In fact, 10 teaspoons of refined sugar (as found in the usual 12 ounces of soft drink) usually causes drowsiness one or two hours later. (3) "Junk food." The term "junk food" has led to considerable confusion in our country. Some people define any sweet or dessert as a "junk food." Others define fast foods as "junk foods." Let's junk this negative term, which implies that if a food is sweet or purchased from a fast-food chain, it's bad for your health.

Recommendations for the Safe Use of Sugar

1. *Allow sugar in moderation.* In general, eating foods in moderation is healthy, but eating foods in excess is unhealthy. One precaution is to avoid sweets if possible during the first year of life. If they are introduced too early,

they may interfere with a willingness to try new foods.
(Note: These guidelines about sugar in moderation may not
apply to children with diabetes mellitus.)

2. *Don't try to forbid sugar.* Some parents do this in hopes of
preventing a preference for sweet foods. Since this preference is present at birth, we have little influence over it. If
we forbid sweets entirely, children may become fascinated
with them. With candy and other sweets so readily available in stores and vending machines, a sugar embargo
cannot be monitored and becomes unenforceable as a child
grows up. If we make an issue of it, this becomes an
unnecessary battleground.

3. *Limit the amount of sweets you buy.* The more sweets
there are in the house, the more your child will eat.

4. *Limit how much sweets are eaten.* While one candy bar is
fine, eating an entire bag of candy at one time is unacceptable. Try to eliminate binging on candy or other sweets. Do
this mainly by setting a good example. Exceptions of allowing extra candy can be on Halloween, other holidays, birthday parties, and other parties. The worst that could happen
is that your child could become extra sleepy or have a mild
stomachache.

5. *Allow sweets for desserts.* As stated earlier sweets only
cause symptoms if they are eaten in excess. As long as they
follow a well-balanced meal, they cause no symptoms. An
acceptable dessert, therefore, can be just about anything,
including a candy bar.

6. *Discourage sweets for snacks.* Candy, soft drinks, or other
sweets are not a good choice for a snack. Since very little
else is eaten with the snack, consuming mainly refined
sugar can cause a withdrawal reaction one or two hours
later. Teach your child that if he does take a soft drink or
Kool-Aid as a snack, he should eat something else from the
grain or fruit food groups along with it. An occasional
sweet drink with a sugar substitute is fine. Stock up on
nutritious snacks (such as juices), and set a good example
by what you eat for snacks.

7. *Insist that the teeth are brushed after sweets are eaten.*
Unless you encourage this good habit, a "sweet tooth" will
become a "decayed tooth."

Special Benefits of Sugar • Using candy occasionally as a reward
is not habit-forming. The joy of eating sweets is a natural
preference, not enhanced by this practice. Candy and other

sweet treats are a powerful incentive. Whether we like it or not, the best motivators are always items that children crave. In addition, candy is inexpensive and easy to purchase. Because of the many types of candy, the child also has many choices. Candy may bring about a breakthrough with a negative child who has not responded to other approaches. Star charts and praise should be used simultaneously for improved behavior and continued after the candy has been phased out.

Second, sugar can be useful in helping a finicky eater try an essential new food. Some children who have breast-fed until almost a year of age will not accept any milk products. One way of helping them make this transition is by sweetening the cow's milk temporarily with honey or other flavorings. (**Caution:** Avoid giving honey before 1 year of age because of the small risk of botulism for this age group). After the child is drinking adequate amounts of milk the sweetener can be gradually phased out.

Third, some children will take bitter medicines easier when they are mixed with a sweet flavoring such as Kool-Aid powder or chocolate pudding.

CALL YOUR CHILD'S PHYSICIAN DURING OFFICE HOURS IF

• You think your child has a problem with sugar.

• You have other questions or concerns.

TOOTH DECAY PREVENTION

Tooth decay causes toothaches, lost teeth, malocclusion, and costly visits to the dentist. With present knowledge, 80 to 90 percent of tooth decay can be prevented.

FLUORIDE

• Fluoride builds strong, decay-resistant enamel. Fluoride is needed from 2 weeks to 12 years of age. Drinking fluoridated water (containing 0.7 to 1.2 parts per million) or taking a prescription fluoride supplement is the best protection against tooth decay, reducing cavities by 70 percent.

• If fluoride is consumed in drinking water, a child must take at least 1 pint per day (preferably 1 quart per day by school age).

- If your city's water supply doesn't have fluoride added or you are breast-feeding, ask your physician for a prescription for fluoride drops or tablets during your next routine visit. The dosage of fluoride is 0.25 mg per day in the first 2 years, 0.5 mg from 2 to 3 years of age, and 1.0 mg over age 3. Try to give fluoride on an empty stomach, because mixing it with milk reduces its absorption to 70 percent.

- Bottled water usually doesn't contain adequate fluoride. Call the producer for information. If your children drink bottled water containing less than 0.7 part per million of fluoride, ask your child's physician for a fluoride supplement.

- Fluoride is safe. Over half of all Americans drink fluoridated water. *Consumers Report* (July/August 1978) states: "The simple truth is that there is no scientific controversy over the safety of fluoridation. The practice is safe, economical and beneficial. The survival of any controversy is one of the major triumphs of quackery over science in our generation."

- One concern about fluoride is white spots or mottling on the teeth (called fluorosis). This can occur when a child ingests 2 mg or more per day. The preventative dose is 1 mg or less. Children can ingest excessive fluoride if they receive supplements when it is already present in the city water supply. Occasionally they ingest it by eating their toothpaste. A ribbon of toothpaste contains about 1 mg. of fluoride. Therefore, people of all ages should use only a drop of toothpaste the size of a pea. This precaution and encouraging your child not to swallow most of the toothpaste will prevent fluorosis.

- A recent concern has been raised about fluoride causing bone cancer or osteosarcoma. This misleading information comes from a study wherein rats received high intakes of fluoride. This resulted in a 2 percent to 4 percent rate of bone cancer. For an adult human to consume an equivalent amount of fluoride we would have to drink 24 to 42 gallons of water per day. This is another example of something we didn't need to worry about receiving media attention. The bone cancer rate has not changed over the past 20 years, during which fluoride has been present in our water supplies.

TOOTH-BRUSHING AND FLOSSING

The purpose of tooth-brushing is to remove plaque from the teeth. Plaque is the invisible scum that forms on the surface of teeth. Within this plaque, mouth bacteria change sugars to acids, which in turn etch the enamel.

• Tooth-brushing or wiping with a damp cloth should begin before 1 year of age.

• Try to brush after each meal, but especially after the last meal or snack of the day.

• Brush the molars (back teeth) extra carefully. Decay usually starts in the pits and crevices of the molars.

• To prevent the mouth bacteria from changing food caught in the teeth into acid, tooth-brushing must occur within the first 5 to 10 minutes after meals.

• Help your child brush the teeth at least until age 6. Most children don't have the coordination or strength to brush their own teeth adequately before then.

• If your child is negative about tooth-brushing, have him brush your teeth first before you brush his.

• A fluoride toothpaste is beneficial. People of all ages tend to use too much toothpaste; an amount the size of a pea is all that is needed.

• If your child is in a setting where he can't brush his teeth, teach him to rinse his mouth with water after meals instead. Chewing on sugar-free gum (or even regular gum) for 10 minutes after meals gets the saliva flowing enough to clean the teeth.

• Dental floss is very useful for cleaning between the teeth where a brush can't reach. This should begin when your child's molars start to touch. In the early years, most of the teeth have spaces between them.

DIET

A healthy diet from a dental standpoint is one that keeps the sugar concentration in the mouth at a low level. The worst foods contain sugar and also stick to the teeth.

• Prevent baby-bottle caries by not letting your infant sleep with a bottle of milk, juice, or any sweetened liquid in the mouth. Once the teeth erupt, if your baby must have a bottle at night, it should contain only water. Preferably you should put your child to bed after he or she has finished with the bottle.

- Discourage prolonged contact with sugar (e.g., hard candy) or any sweets that are sticky (e.g., caramels or raisins).

- Avoid frequent snacks.

- Give sugar-containing foods only with meals.

- Parents worry needlessly about soft drinks. The sugar in these products does not bind to the teeth and is cleared rather rapidly from the mouth with normal saliva flow.

- Since we can't keep children away from candy completely, try to teach your child to brush after eating candy.

VISITING THE DENTIST AND DENTAL SEALANTS

- The American Dental Association recommends that dental checkups begin at age 3 (sooner for dental symptoms or abnormal-looking teeth). Prepare your child for this visit by taking her with you on one of your dental visits (if it doesn't involve drilling or teeth-cleaning). The latest breakthrough in dental research is dental sealing of the pits and grooves (fissures) of the biting surfaces of the molars. Fluoride does little to prevent decay on these surfaces. A special plastic seal can be applied to the top surfaces of the permanent molars at about age 6, when the first molars erupt. The seal may protect against decay for a lifetime. Ask your child's dentist about the latest recommendations.

FOOD ALLERGIES

While food allergies tend to be overdiagnosed, about 5 percent of children have true reactions to foods. Suspect that your child may have a food allergy if the following three characteristics are present:

1. Your child has allergic symptoms after eating certain foods. The most common reactions involve the mouth (e.g. swelling), GI tract (e.g., diarrhea), or skin (e.g., hives). Rarely a child has a severe allergic reaction (anaphylactic reaction) that may be life-threatening. Common anaphylactic symptoms are a rapid onset of difficulty breathing, difficulty swallowing, or a fall in blood pressure (shock).

2. Your child has other allergic conditions, such as eczema, asthma, or hay fever. Children with these conditions have a much higher rate of associated food allergies than nonallergic children.
3. Other family members (parents or siblings) have food allergies. Food allergies are often inherited.

Cause • Allergic children produce antibodies against certain foods. When these antibodies come in contact with the allergic foods, the reaction releases numerous chemicals that cause the symptoms. The tendency to be allergic is inherited. If one percent has allergies, about 40 percent of the children will develop allergies. If both parents have allergies, about 75 percent of the children will. Sometimes the child is allergic to the same food as the parent.

Expected Outcome • At least half of the children who develop a food allergy during the first year of life outgrow it by age 2 or 3. Some food reactions (e.g., to milk) are more commonly outgrown than others. Whereas 3 percent to 4 percent of infants have a cow's milk allergy, less than 1 percent of them develop a lifelong allergy to cow's milk. Allergies to peanuts, tree nuts, fish, and shellfish (shrimps, crab, and lobster) often persist for life.

Common Symptoms of Food Allergies • The following symptoms are all commonly seen with food allergies. In some cases the food aggravates the underlying allergic condition:

• lips, tongue, or mouth swelling

• diarrhea or vomiting

• hives

• itchy red skin (especially with underlying eczema)

Some less common symptoms are:

• sore throat or throat-clearing

• nasal congestion, runny nose, sneezing, or sniffing (especially with underlying hay fever)

An occasional child with asthma, migraine headaches, colic, or recurrent abdominal pain may have some attacks triggered by food allergies. These children, however, also have some of the typical symptoms (listed above) that occur with food reactions. Attention-deficit disorder and behavioral disorders, as isolated symptoms, have not been scientifically linked to food allergies.

Common Allergic Foods • Overall, the most allergic food is the peanut. In infants, egg and milk products are more common. The following 5 foods account for over 80 percent of food reactions: peanuts (and peanut butter), eggs, cow's milk products, soybeans (and soy formula), and wheat. Eight foods (fish, shellfish, tree nuts, and the preceding 5 foods) account for over 95 percent of food reactions. Four foods (chocolate, strawberries, corn, and tomatoes) are highly overrated as triggers of symptoms. While commonly mentioned, they rarely cause any allergic symptoms.

Diagnosing a Food Allergy

1. *Keep a diary of symptoms and recently eaten foods.* If the ingestion of a particular food is clearly the cause of particular symptoms, go directly to step 2. Otherwise be a good detective and keep a symptom/food diary for 2 weeks. Any time your child has symptoms, write down the foods he ate during the preceding meal. After 2 weeks, examine the diary for foods that were repeatedly consumed on days your child had symptoms. Expect some inconsistency, depending on the amount of food consumed. While anaphylactic reactions can be triggered by small amounts of allergic foods, other symptoms (e.g., diarrhea) usually increase as the amount of the allergic food increases, but not to the point of being serious. Reactions to food may be worse when a child is also reacting to other substances in the environment such as pollens. Therefore, food allergies may flare up during pollen season.
2. *Eliminate the suspected food from the diet for 2 weeks.* Record any symptoms that occur during this time. If you have eliminated the correct food, all symptoms should disappear. Most children improve within 2 days, and almost all of them improve after a week of avoiding the allergic food.
3. *Rechallenge your child with the suspected food.* (**Caution:** This step should never be carried out if your child has experienced a severe or anaphylactic reaction to a food.) The purpose of rechallenging is to prove that the suspected

food is definitely the cause of your child's symptoms. Give your child a small amount of the suspected food. The same symptoms should appear 10 minutes to 2 hours after the food is consumed. Call your child's physician before doing this.

Treatment of Food Allergies (if confirmed by your child's physician)

1. *Avoid the allergic food.* This should keep your child free of symptoms. If you are breast-feeding, eliminate the food your child is allergic to from your diet until breast-feeding is discontinued. Food allergens can be absorbed from your diet and enter your breast milk. Talk to a nutritionist if you have questions.
2. *Consider avoiding other foods in that food group.* Some children are allergic to 2 or more foods. Occasionally the foods belong to the same food group. The most common cross-reaction involves children allergic to ragweed pollen. They commonly react to watermelon, cantaloupe, musk-melon, honeydew melon, or other foods in the gourd family. Children allergic to peanuts may rarely cross-react with soybeans, peas, or other beans. Surprisingly, most tree nuts are unrelated to each other and do not cross-react with peanuts.
3. *Provide a substitute for any missing vitamins or minerals.* Eliminating single foods usually does not cause side effects. If a major food group (such as milk products) is eliminated, however, your child will develop vitamin D and calcium deficiency unless he receives appropriate supplements. Talk to your physician or a nutritionist about this.

Preventing Food Allergies in High-Risk Children • High-risk or allergy-prone children have parents or siblings with asthma, eczema, severe hay fever, or documented food allergies. The risk is highest if both parents are allergic to foods. The onset of allergies in these children may be delayed by being some-what careful about their diet. If possible they should breast-feed during the first year of life. The mother should avoid milk products, peanuts, and eggs in her diet during this time. If the mother cannot breast-feed, there are two choices: a formula made from protein hydrolysate (known as an elemental formula), or a soy protein formula. The allergy-prone child should avoid all solid foods until 6 months old. Try to avoid milk products, eggs, peanut butter, soy protein, fish, wheat, and citrus fruits during the entire first year of life. Try to avoid the most allergic foods (peanuts and fish) until age 2.

CALL AN EMERGENCY RESCUE SQUAD (911) IMMEDIATELY IF

- Your child develops any serious symptoms such as wheezing, croupy cough, difficulty breathing, passing out, tightness in the chest or throat.

CALL YOUR CHILD'S PHYSICIAN

Immediately If

- Widespread hives, swelling, or itching occur.

- Other mild symptoms occur within 30 minutes of eating a suspected food.

During Office Hours If

- You suspect your child has a food allergy.

- You want to rechallenge your child with a food you suspect.

- You have other questions or concerns.

RECOMMENDED READING
S. Allan Bock, *Food Allergy: A Primer for People* (New York: Vantage Press, 1988).

OVERWEIGHT: PREVENTION IN INFANTS

Definition • A fat baby is not necessarily a healthy baby. On the other hand, only 10 percent of overweight 1-year-olds go on to become overweight adults. The ones who continue to be overweight usually have parents, siblings, or grandparents who are overweight. Any infant with a strong family tendency toward obesity needs help. Some physicians wait until such a child shows signs of being overweight before making any alterations in the diet, but prevention is easier than treatment.

DIETARY PRECAUTIONS TO PREVENT AN EXCESSIVE WEIGHT GAIN IN INFANTS

If your family has a problem with easy weight gain, consider the following dietary precautions to help your baby:

- From the beginning, try to teach your child to stop eating before she reaches a point of satiation. Help her stop before she has a sense of complete fullness and a reluctance to eat another bite.

- Try to breast-feed. Breast-fed babies tend to be lighter in weight.

- If you are breast-feeding, avoid grazing. Grazing is nursing at frequent intervals, sometimes hourly. Such infants learn to eat when they are upset and to use food as a stress-reliever.

- If you are bottle-feeding, don't allow your child to keep a bottle as a companion during the day or night. Children who are allowed to carry a bottle around with them learn to eat frequently and use food as a comforting device.

- Don't feed your baby every time he cries. Most crying babies want to be held and cuddled or may be thirsty and just need some water.

- Also teach your infant to use human contact (rather than food) to relieve stress and discomfort.

- Don't assume a sucking baby is hungry. Your baby may just want a pacifier or help with finding her thumb.

- Don't mistake thirst for hunger. Fussing in hot weather may mean that your baby is thirsty and needs some water.

- Don't insist that your baby finish every bottle. Unless your baby is underweight, he knows how much formula he needs.

- Don't enlarge the hole in the nipple of a baby bottle. The formula will come out of the bottle too fast.

- Feed your infant no more often than every 2 hours at birth, and no more often than every 3 hours from 2 to 6 months of age.

- Feed your child slowly rather than rapidly.

- Avoid solids until your child is 4 months old (6 months old in breast-fed babies).

- Change to 3 meals a day by 6 months of age.

- Don't insist that your child clean his plate or finish a jar of baby food.

- Don't encourage your child to eat more after she signals she is full, by turning her head or not opening her mouth.

- Discontinue breast- and bottle-feeding by 12 months of age.

- Avoid sweets until at least 12 months of age.

- Don't give your child food as a way to distract him or keep him occupied. Instead, give him something to play with when you need free time.

- Use praise and physical contact instead of food as rewards for good behavior. Use food for rewards only in solving special problems such as difficult toilet training.

- **Caution:** Don't put your baby on 2 percent milk or skim milk before 2 years of age. Your baby's brain is growing rapidly and needs the fat content of whole milk.

OVERWEIGHT: A WEIGHT-REDUCTION PROGRAM

SYMPTOMS AND CHARACTERISTICS

- Your child has an overweight appearance

- Your child weighs more than 20 percent over the ideal weight for her height

- The skin fold thickness of her arm's fat layer is more than 1 inch (25 millimeters)

- Occurs in 25 percent of American children

- Also called obesity

Causes • The tendency to be overweight is usually inherited. If one parent is overweight, 50 percent of the children will be overweight. If both parents are overweight, 80 percent of the children will be overweight. If neither parent is overweight, less than 10 percent of the children will be overweight. Heredity alone (without overeating) accounts for most mild obesity (less than 30 pounds overweight as an adult).

Moderate obesity is usually due to a combination of heredity, overeating, and underexercising. However, some overeating is normal in our society. People like to eat because it makes them feel good. But only those who have the tendency to be overweight will gain weight. It is therefore not reasonable to blame your child for being overweight. Perhaps 10 percent of overweight adults eat excessively because they are depressed.

Less than 1 percent of obesity has a physical cause. Your physician can easily determine this by a simple physical examination. While obesity is not your child's fault, something can be done about it.

Expected Course • Losing weight is very difficult. Keeping the weight off is also a chore. The best age for losing weight is over 15 years, or whenever appearance becomes critical to your child. The self-motivated teenager can follow a diet and lose weight regardless of what the family eats. The second-best age for helping your child lose weight is before 5 years. At this age, you are still in control of what foods are being served. The younger your child, the more influence you have. However, the diet must be acceptable to your child at any age.

Trying to help your child lose weight between 5 and 15 years of age is like trying to push water uphill. Once children are outside the home, they have access to so many foods that trying to impose a diet is fruitless. In the long run, the most important factor is how easily a particular child gains weight (i.e., genetics).

HOW TO HELP OLDER CHILDREN AND TEENAGERS LOSE WEIGHT

Readiness and Motivation • Children are usually not ready to lose weight until they reach the teenage years. Teenagers can be helped with motivation by joining a weight-loss club such as TOPS, Weight Watchers, or Overeaters Anonymous. Sometimes schools have a special class or gym class for helping with weight loss. Often the school nurse will talk with overweight children both in groups and individually once a week, as well as weigh them. Children are also better motivated if the diet and exercise programs are undertaken by the entire family. Competing with a parent to see who can lose weight faster can be helpful.

Weight loss is not healthy during the rapid growth spurt of the first 2 years of life or early adolescence. During these years any attempt to change weight should try to slow down the rate of gain without actually losing any weight.

Protecting Your Child's Self-Esteem • Self-esteem is more important than an ideal body weight. If your child is overweight, he is probably already disappointed in himself. He needs his family to support him and accept him as he is. The self-esteem can be reduced or destroyed by parents who become overconcerned about their child's weight. Avoid the following pitfalls:

- Don't tell your child he's "fat." Use terms such as "big" or "a little on the heavy side." Don't discuss his weight unless he brings it up.

- Never try to put your child on a strict diet. Diets are unpleasant and should be self-imposed.

- Never deprive your child of food if he says he is hungry. Withholding food eventually leads to overeating.

- Don't nag him about his weight or eating habits.

Setting Weight-Loss Goals • Pick a realistic target weight, depending on your child's bone structure and degree of obesity. The loss of 1 pound per week is an attainable goal. Your child will have to work quite hard to maintain this rate of weight loss for several weeks. Weigh your child once per week at the most. Daily weighings generate too much false hope or false disappointment. When losing weight becomes a strain, have your child take a few weeks off. During this time, help your child hold his or her weight constant.

Once your child has reached the target weight, the long-range goal is to try to maintain that weight within 5 pounds in either direction. Staying at a particular weight is possible only through a permanent moderation in eating. The tendency to gain weight easily will probably be with your child for a lifetime. It's important for your child to understand this.

Diet: Decreasing Calorie Consumption • Your child should eat 3 well-balanced meals a day and average-sized portions. There are no forbidden foods. Your child can have a serving of anything his family or friends are eating. However, there are forbidden amounts. While your child is reducing, he must leave the table a bit hungry. There's no question about it, dieting is painful. Your child can't eat until he's satiated (full) and hope to lose weight. Shortcuts such as fasting, crash dieting, or diet pills rarely work and may be dangerous. Calorie counting is helpful for some people but it is usually too time-consuming. Consider the following guidelines on what to eat:

- Fluids: Have your child take all milk as skim or 2 percent milk. Limit milk to 16 ounces per day, as it has lots of calories. All other fluid intake should be either water or diet drinks. Encourage drinking 6 glasses of water per day.

- Meals: Encourage average portions. Discourage seconds.

- Desserts: Encourage smaller-than-average portions. Encourage more Jell-O and fresh fruits as desserts. Avoid rich desserts. No seconds.

- Snacks: Limit snacks to 2 or fewer per day. Serve only special low-calorie foods such as raw vegetables (carrot sticks, celery sticks, raw potato sticks, pickles, etc.), raw fruits (apples, oranges, cantaloupe, etc.), popcorn, or diet soft drinks.

- Types of food: Serve fewer fatty foods. Fat has twice as many calories as the same portion of protein or carbohydrate. Trim the fat off meats. Serve more baked, broiled, boiled, or steamed foods (fewer fried foods). Serve more fruits, vegetables, salads, and grains. Unfortunately, no food is a particularly good appetite suppressant.

- Vitamins: Give your child one multivitamin tablet per day while reducing.

Eating Habits • In order to counteract the tendency to gain weight, your youngster must be taught eating tips and habits that will last for a lifetime. The following habits can make keeping off pounds easier:

- Discourage skipping any of the 3 basic meals.

- Encourage drinking a glass of water before meals.

- Serve smaller portions. Don't serve adult helpings to children before adolescence.

- Suggest chewing the food slowly, paying more attention to flavors and textures.

- Offer second servings only if your child has waited for 10 minutes after finishing the first serving. It takes at least 20 minutes from the start of the meal for the sensation of fullness to occur.

- Discourage the need to consume all the food in the serving bowls. Leftovers can be placed in the refrigerator.

- Don't purchase high-calorie snack foods such as potato chips, candy, or regular pop.

- Do purchase and keep available diet soft drinks, fresh fruits, and vegetables.

- Leave only low-calorie snacks out on the counter—fruit, for instance. Put away the cookie jar.

- Store food only in the kitchen. Keep it out of other rooms.

- Offer no more than 2 snacks per day. Discourage your child from continual snacking ("grazing") throughout the day. The number of snacks we eat each day is a matter of habit. A person can learn to go through a day with no snacks without developing symptoms.

- Allow eating in your home only while sitting at the kitchen or dining room table. Discourage eating while watching TV, studying, riding in a car, or shopping in a store. Once eating becomes associated with these events, the body learns to expect it.

- Discourage eating alone.

- Help your child reward herself for hard work or studying with a movie, TV, music, or book, rather than food.

- Put up reminder cards on the refrigerator and bathroom mirror which state: EAT LESS.

Exercise: Increasing Calorie Expenditure • Small changes in activity level will burn up a surprising number of calories. Daily exercise to the point of breathing hard will have a major impact on the rate of weight loss as well as the sense of physical well-being. Diet and exercise together are the only effective way to lose weight and maintain your new weight. As your child loses weight, exercise will become less tiring because he or she will be in better condition and have less weight to move about. Try the following forms of exercise:

- Encourage walking or biking instead of riding in a car.

- Encourage using stairs instead of elevators.

- Encourage learning new sports such as roller-skating or jumping rope. Swimming and jogging are the sports that burn the most calories. Your child's school may have an aerobics class.

- Encourage taking the dog for a long walk.

- Encourage spending 30 minutes a day exercising or dancing to records or music on TV.

- Encourage using an exercise bike or Hula Hoop while watching TV.

- Limit TV sitting time to 2 hours or less per day.

Social Activities: Keeping the Mind off Food • The more outside interests your child participates in, the easier it will be for him or her to lose weight. Spare time fosters nibbling in everyone. Most snacking occurs between 3:00 and 6:00 P.M. Help your child fill after-school time with activities such as music, drama, sports, scouts, or other clubs. A part-time job after school may help. If nothing else, encourage your child to call or visit a friend. An active social life almost always leads to weight reduction.

EATING PROBLEMS: OTHER STRATEGIES

Doesn't Eat Enough • See POOR EATERS, POOR APPETITES, page 165.

Stands Up in the High Chair
The rule: "Don't stand up in your chair. Stay seated until the meal is over." This is an important safety issue.
Discipline technique: Some children can be confined to their high chair with the safety strap; others can wiggle out of it. Logical consequences of being put down and having the meal end can teach your child not to stand up.
Praise your child: For staying in his chair at future meals.

Plays with Food
Definition: During the early months of learning self-feeding, many children will make a mess of their high-chair tray and of themselves. They may also make a mess because they mix their food with hand or spoon. Children should not be punished for this normal behavior.
The rule: "Don't throw or drop your food. Don't put food on your body. Eat without making a mess."
Discipline technique: When your child throws food, take him

out of the high chair and put him in timeout in the playpen for 2 minutes. Then let him return to the table. If he repeats the misbehavior, assume he has had enough to eat and put him down permanently. To deal with some of the normal sloppiness of young eaters, put down newspapers and offer your child small amounts of food at any one time. A dog also comes in handy.

Praise your child: For eating without making a mess.

Eats Too Slowly

Definition: Some of these children are not hungry. Others are being negative. The problem arises when a child has not finished eating but the rest of the family has completed their meal.

The rule: "The meal is over when everyone else is done eating, because we have to clean up."

Discipline technique: Natural consequences. Clear away your child's plate and put her down after a reasonable amount of time. Don't give her any between-meal snacks if she only eats part of her meal. Serve her smaller portions.

Praise your child: For not playing or wasting time during meals.

Eats Too Fast

Definition: Most of these children are in a hurry to go back to their play. They may gulp their food in an unsavory manner.

The rule: "Mealtime lasts for at least ten minutes (or whatever length of time the parents decide on) whether you're done earlier or not. Mealtime is a special time when our family gets together."

Discipline technique: Logical consequences. Children will learn that finishing quickly does not allow them to leave the dinner table sooner.

Praise your child: For eating slowly, chewing food with the mouth closed, and eating with good manners.

Demands Frequent Snacks

Definition: Some children want a snack, fruit juice, or soda pop every 30 minutes. Frequent snacking leads to tooth decay, is disruptive, and can't be continued when the child enters school.

The rule: "Don't ask for a snack until snack time. We only have one snack in the morning and one snack in the afternoon."

Discipline technique: Ignore your child's requests for snacks before snack time. If he persists, send him to timeout.

Takes Food from the Refrigerator or Cupboards

The rule: "You're not permitted to open the refrigerator until you're five years old. Ask a grown-up if you need something out of the refrigerator."

Discipline technique: If your child opens the refrigerator without your permission, send her to timeout. Put a stop sign on the refrigerator door as a reminder. If your child gets into food cupboards, also send her to timeout. With a persistent child, you may need to put locks on the doors or move snack foods to higher cupboards.

Leaves the Kitchen a Mess

The rule: "Whoever makes a mess in the kitchen cleans it up."

Discipline technique: Logical consequences. If you find the kitchen messy, call your child to clean it up. If your child is not at home, cancel the snack privilege for the next day. As a reminder, put up a sign: CLEAN UP AFTER YOURSELF, in the kitchen.

Praise your child: For cleaning up the kitchen.

Model: Cleaning up after yourself in the kitchen area.

Messes Up the Rest of the House with Food

The rule: "We only eat in the kitchen."

Discipline technique: Logical consequences. If you find crumbs or dirty dishes outside the kitchen area, call your child to clean it up. If your child starts to walk around the house eating food, send your child back to the kitchen.

Model: Not taking food outside the kitchen.

GROWTH, DEVELOPMENT, AND SAFETY

NORMAL GROWTH

Normal growth is one of the best indicators of good health and nutrition. Normal heights and weights, however, are difficult to define. Short parents tend to have short children. Tall parents tend to have tall children. For any given height, an ideal weight can be determined from a growth chart. An infant with failure-to-thrive is one who is underweight for his height. A child with obesity is one who is overweight for his height.

Your child's physician weighs and measures your child on each visit. These numbers are plotted on a standard growth chart. Your child's growth rate over time tells us the most about his physical health. The following facts and figures may answer some of your questions about normal growth.

AVERAGE NEWBORNS (FULL-TERM)
Weight: 7 pounds, 5 ounces (normal range: 6 to 10 pounds)
Length: 20 inches (50 cm) (normal range: 18½ to 21½ inches)
Head circumference: 13.8 inches (35 cm) (normal range: 33 to 37 cm)
A premature baby weighs less than 5½ pounds (2.5 kilograms)

AVERAGE WEIGHTS AT DIFFERENT AGES
5 months: double birthweight
12 months: triple birthweight
2 years: quadruple birthweight
1 to 6 years: weight in pounds = (age × 5) + 17
7 to 12 years: weight in pounds = (age × 7) + 5
Remember: 1 pound = 16 ounces; 1 kilogram = 2.2 pounds.

AVERAGE HEIGHTS AT DIFFERENT AGES

4 years: double birth length
13 years: triple birth length
2 to 14 years: height in inches = (age × 2½) + 30
Remember: 1 foot = 12 inches; 1 inch = 2.5 centimeters

PREDICTING ADULT HEIGHTS

	BOYS		GIRLS	MULTIPLY BY
½ adult height is reached at	27	months	20	2
⅔ adult height is reached at	6	years	5	1.5
¾ adult height is reached at	9	years	7	1.3

Another formula is: adult height (boys) = 1.87 × height at age 3
adult height (girls) = 1.73 × height at age 3

NORMAL DEVELOPMENT

The most rapid changes in development occur during the first year of life. Your baby will go from a helpless, unresponsive little bundle to a walking, talking, unique personality. Almost all parents worry if their baby is developing fast enough, especially if a sibling or neighbor's child is progressing differently. Keep in mind that there is a wide variation in normal development. While the average child walks at 12 months of age, the normal range for walking is any time between 9 and 16 months of age. All of these children are normal. Motor development occurs in an orderly sequence starting with lifting the head, then rolling over, sitting up, crawling, standing, and walking. Although the sequence is predictable and follows the maturation of the spinal cord downward, the rate varies and it can't be accelerated.

Again, for speech development the sequence goes from cooing and gurgling to babbling, to imitating speech sounds, to first words, to using words together. The rate, however, can normally vary considerably. The most reassuring characteristics of normal development are the presence of alert eyes, alert facial expressions, and curiosity about the environment.

STIMULATION: ENCOURAGING NORMAL DEVELOPMENT

From birth on, the main determinant of an infant's social, emotional, and language development is the amount of positive contact he has with his parents. His strong attachment to you (that begins at 3 or 4 months of age) will make him eager to learn from you. Your role in stimulating your child should be fun for both of you. The following recommendations may be helpful:

- Hold your baby as much as possible. Touching and cuddling is good for your baby. Give him or her lots of eye contact, smiles, and affection at these times. Use feedings to emphasize these warm personal contacts.

- Talk to your baby. Babies enjoy being talked and sung to from birth onward. Babies must first receive language before they are able to express language. You don't need a scriptwriter— just put into words whatever you are thinking and feeling.

- Play with your baby. If this doesn't come easy for you, try to loosen up and rediscover your free spirit. Respond to your baby's attempts to initiate play. Provide your baby with various objects of interest. Toys need not be expensive; for example, mobiles, rattles, spools, pots and pans, and various packages that things come in. Encourage your baby's efforts at discovering how to use his or her hands and mind.

- Read to your baby. Even six-month-olds enjoy looking at pictures in a book. Cut out interesting pictures from old magazines and put them in a scrapbook for your baby. Look at the family photo album. Keep these sessions brief.

- Show your baby the world. Enrich his or her experience. Babies don't need to visit a museum yet. They need a guide to point out the leaves, clouds, stars, and rainbows. Don't forget trains, airplanes, and fire trucks. Help your child describe what he or she is experiencing. These first encounters can be exhilarating and unforgettable.

- Provide your child with social experience with other children by age 2. If he or she is not in daycare, consider starting a play group. Young children can learn wonderful lessons from one another, especially how to get along with other people.

- Avoid formal teaching until age 4 or 5. Some groups in our country have recently overemphasized academic (cognitive) development of young children. Trying to create "superkids" through special lessons, drills, computer programs, and classes has put undue pressure on many young children and may result in "early burnout." Old-fashioned creative play and spontaneous learning are much more beneficial during the early years. If it's not fun, your child won't follow through the way you would like.

SYMPTOMS REQUIRING A DEVELOPMENTAL EVALUATION

The following developmental milestones (reprinted with the permission of William K. Frankenburg, M.D., University of Colorado School of Medicine, 1986) are listed by the age at which 80 to 90 percent of normal children are able to perform them. If your child has reached the listed age (corrected for any prematurity by subtracting the months early from the actual age) and is not able to perform the listed tasks, he or she should be seen by your child's physician for a developmental checkup. While failing one of these items does not mean that your child's development is abnormal, it is a warning sign that deserves attention.

3 months

- When your baby is lying on his back, he can move each of his arms as easily as the other and each of his legs as easily as the other. If your child makes jerky or uncoordinated movements with one or both of his arms or legs, this is abnormal.

- Your child can make sounds such as gurgling, cooing, babbling, or other noises, in addition to crying.

6 months

- Your child plays with his hands by touching them together.

- Your child has rolled over at least two times from stomach to back or from his back to his stomach.

9 months

- When your child is playing and you come up quietly behind him, he turns his head as though he heard you. He responds to quiet sounds or whispers in this manner. (Loud sounds do not count.)

- When you hold your baby under his arms, he tries to stand on his feet and supports some of his weight on his legs.

12 months

- When you hide behind something (or around a corner) and then reappear again, your baby eagerly looks for you to reappear.

- Your baby makes "ma-ma" or "da-da" sounds.

18 months

- Your child uses a regular cup or glass without help and drinks from it without spilling.

- Your child walks all the way across a large room without falling or wobbling from side to side.

24 months

- Your child can say at least three specific words (other than "da-da" and "ma-ma") that mean the same thing each time they are said.
- Your child can take off clothes such as pajamas or pants. (Diapers, hats, and socks do not count.)

36 months

- Your child can name at least one picture when you look at animal books together.

- Your child can throw a ball overhand (not sidearm or underhand) toward your stomach or chest from a distance of five feet.

4 years

- Your child can pedal a tricycle at least 10 feet forward.

- Your child can play hide-and-seek, or other games where he takes turns and follows rules.

5 years

- Your child can button some of his clothing or his doll's clothes. (Snaps do not count.)

- Your child is comfortable when you leave him with a baby-sitter. (He does not become overly upset.)

6 years

- Your child can dress himself completely without help.

- Your child can catch a small ball (such as a tennis ball) using only his hands. (Large balls do not count.)

RECOMMENDED READING

T. B. Brazelton, *Infants and Mothers: Differences in Development* (New York: Dell, 1983).

ACCIDENT PREVENTION

INFANT SAFETY

During the first 3 years of life, children have little sense of danger or self-preservation. They are totally dependent on adults to look after their safety. They cannot be left unattended on a table or bed; they may roll off it and strike their head. For the same reason, crib railings must always be kept in an upright position. A small child cannot be given toys with small parts, because of the danger that the child may put them in his or her mouth and choke on them. Mattresses should not be covered with pieces of thin plastic, because children may get the plastic caught on the face and be smothered by it. Children cannot be left alone in a bathtub while a parent answers the doorbell, because they could drown. Talcum powder should not be used on them because they may breathe it in and develop severe chemical pneumonia. A pacifier or teething ring should not be tied about the neck because it could catch on something and strangle them. And babies should not be left to sleep in a car, because they could develop a life-threatening heatstroke.

Unfortunately this is only a partial list of the accidents that can befall a young infant. Adult supervision and vigilance are essential.

ACCIDENT PREVENTION OVERVIEW

The prevention of various accidents is discussed throughout this book, along with the first aid for these same accidents. For details on the prevention of any of the following accidents, turn to the appropriate pages.

CAR SAFETY

WHY USE A CAR SAFETY SEAT?

The number one killer and crippler of children in the United States is motor vehicle crashes. Approximately 700 children under the age of 5 are killed each year, and about 60,000 are injured. Proper use of car safety seats can reduce traffic fatalities by at least 80 percent. Laws have been passed in all 50 states that require children to be sitting in an approved child passenger safety seat. One common myth is that a baby can be protected by being held tightly in a parent's arms. During a 30-mile-per-hour crash, the baby will either be crushed between the parent's body and the dashboard or be ripped from the parent's arms with a force of almost 300 pounds. Another myth is that children not belted in may be thrown free of the crash and saved. Actually, a child thrown from a car has a 25-times greater chance of dying than if he were kept in the car by a safety seat. Riding in a car seat also has the advantage of reducing children's misbehavior, motion sickness, and the accident rate caused by children's distracting the driver.

HOW TO CHOOSE ONE

Since January 1981, all manufacturers of child safety seats must meet stringent government safety standards, including crash-testing. Look for a seat marked as having met Federal Motor Vehicle Safety Standard 213, with the date of manufacture being 1981 or later. If the seat was manufactured between 1971 and 1981, it may or may not meet the government safety standard. When in doubt, contact the National Highway

Traffic Safety Administration hotline, (800) 424-9393, for information. The American Academy of Pediatrics also publishes a yearly updated list of infant/child safety seats. This list can be obtained by writing the American Academy of Pediatrics, Division of Public Education, 141 Northwest Point Boulevard, P.O. Box 927, Elk Grove Village, Illinois 60007.

Car safety seats come in three types. Infant safety seats are rear-facing only and are useful from birth to approximately 20 pounds. Convertible safety seats can be used in both rear- and forward-facing positions. Booster safety seats are forward-facing and have a removable shield. Whenever possible put the car seat in the back seat, which is much safer than the front seat.

MATCHING CAR SEATS WITH YOUR CHILD'S WEIGHT

- Birth to 20 pounds: Use an infant safety seat until your child is over 20 pounds and able to sit up by himself. Keep your child facing backward as long as possible, because it protects him from neck injuries.

- Over 20 pounds: Use a convertible car seat in the forward-facing position.

- Over 40 pounds and over 40 inches: Use a booster safety seat. This will also help your child see out the window.

- Over 60 pounds: Use the regular car seat without a booster seat and with a lap belt low on the hips. Another rule of thumb is to discontinue a safety seat when the tops of your child's ears are above the top of the safety seat.

- Over 4 feet (48 inches): Add a shoulder strap. Using a shoulder strap before your child is 4 feet tall can cause neck injuries. If it runs across the neck (rather than the shoulder), put it behind your child. Never put the shoulder belt under both arms.

HOW TO USE ONE

Your child's car safety seat can be a lifesaver. But to protect your child, the seat must be used consistently and properly. Most children accept the use of car seats and seat belts as a routine necessity; however, at various times children need some special attention to keep them well protected. Your attitude toward the use of safety belts and child safety seats is of prime importance. If you treat buckling up as a normal part of living—something to be done automatically—your children generally will follow your lead. To keep your kids safe and happy:

- Always use the safety seat, and use it correctly. Start the use of safety seats on the first ride home from the hospital, and keep on using them for every ride.

- Allow NO exceptions for older kids and adults. Everyone buckles up! If adults ride unprotected, the child quickly decides that safety is just kid stuff.

- Give frequent praise for appropriate behavior in the car.

- Remember that a bored child can become a disruptive one. Keep a supply of favorite soft toys and munchies on hand.

- NEVER let a fussy child out of the car seat or safety belt while the car is in motion. If your child needs a break, STOP the car. Don't reward complaints by allowing your child to ride unprotected. That's a disastrous decision, and one that will make it harder to keep him in the seat on the next ride.

- If a child tries to get out of the seat, stop the car and firmly but calmly explain that the car won't go until he is back in place—buckled in the car seat.

- Make a vinyl seatpad more comfortable in hot weather by covering it with a cloth pad or towel.

- When your child travels in another person's car (such as a baby-sitter or grandparent) insist that the driver also use the car safety seat.

- For long-distance trips, plan for frequent stops, and try to stop before the children get restless. Cuddle young children and let older children snack and run around for 10 to 15 minutes.

(Reprinted with the permission of the American Academy of Pediatrics, 1986)

SHOES

The following information may help you make more rational decisions about buying shoes for your young infant.

SHOES VS. BAREFOOT

- The only purpose of shoes is to protect from injury, cold, or burns (from asphalt surfaces). No shoes are needed until your child begins to walk in rough terrain. Children who are walking inside a house or outside on sand or grass do not require shoes.

- Before the age of walking, keep your child's feet warm with booties or socks during the winter.

- Once your child begins to walk, he will prefer to walk bare-footed because it gives him a better sense of where his feet are and enables him to use his toes for balance. Shoes may interfere with learning to walk.

TYPES OF SHOES

- When your child finally needs a shoe, buy tennis shoes (sneakers) or some other shoe with a softer flexible sole, such as moccasins, which allow free movement of the foot. Sneakers have the advantage over leather shoes of being comfortable, ventilated, easy to wash, inexpensive, and good for traction. During the first year of walking, moccasins are usually better. Toddlers in sneakers may have too much traction, catch the rubber sole on things, and fall.

- Hand-me-down shoes are fine if they are still in good condition (the sole is still skidproof) and fit. The suggestion that shoes with a previous wear pattern on the heels will cause leg or foot pains is a myth.

- Expensive shoes have no advantage at any age for 99 percent of children. Arches do not "fall." Save your money for something more important.

- Heels are not essential at any age, and they can cause tripping during the first 2 years.

- High-top shoes are not useful, and children who wear them are often teased. Occasionally a toddler will need high-top sneakers because his or her feet continually slip out of low-cut ones.

- Even children with flat feet rarely need a special shoe or heel. Tennis shoes are fine for most of these children.

SHOE SIZE AND FIT

- With a little practice, most parents can determine whether or not a shoe fits. Check proper fit with your child putting weight on the shoes. The length should be approximately ½ inch (an index finger) longer than the big toe. The width should allow you to grasp a small piece of shoe at the widest portion of the foot (the pinch test). The heel area should be snug enough to keep the shoe from flopping up and down during walking. Also, maximum flex should be where the foot flexes and not in the middle of the shoe.

• In young, growing children, shoes commonly become too tight before they wear out.

• During the second and third year of life, shoe size can change three times a year, so check the fit every few months.

• Fluoroscopy should not be used in fitting shoes because of the radiation exposure. Hopefully, all of these machines have been banished from shoe stores.

PREVENTING INFECTIONS

THE PREVENTION OF INFECTIONS

Public health measures have had the greatest impact in preventing the spread of infectious diseases. Proper sewage disposal and safe water supplies have largely eliminated epidemics such as typhoid fever and cholera. Immunizations and vaccinations constitute the other aspect of modern medicine that has controlled infectious diseases like smallpox and polio. Precautions within the home can limit the spread of gastrointestinal illnesses. Unfortunately, controlling the spread of colds, coughs, and sore throats within a family unit is impractical if not impossible.

HOW DIFFERENT INFECTIOUS DISEASES ARE SPREAD

- Nose, mouth, and eye secretions are the most common sources of respiratory infections. These secretions are usually spread by contaminated hands or occasionally by kissing. Toddlers are especially prone to spreading these infections because of their habits of touching or mouthing everything.

- Droplet spread from coughing or sneezing is a less common means of transmission of respiratory infections. Droplets can travel up to 6 feet.

- Fecal contamination of hands or other objects accounts for the spread of most diarrhea, as well as infectious hepatitis.

Unlike urine, which is usually sterile, bowel movements are composed of up to 50 percent bacteria.

- The discharge from sores such as chicken pox and fever blisters can be contagious. However, most red rashes without a discharge are not contagious by skin contact.

- Contaminated food or water accounted for many epidemics in earlier times. Even today, some foods frequently contain bacteria that cause diarrhea. (For example, over 50 percent of raw turkey or chicken contains Campylobacter or salmonella. By contrast, only 1 percent of raw eggs are contaminated with salmonella.)

- Contaminated utensils such as bottles and dishes can occasionally be a source of respiratory or intestinal infections.

- Contaminated objects such as combs, brushes, and hats can lead to the spread of lice, ringworm, or impetigo.

HOW TO PREVENT OR REDUCE THE SPREAD OF INFECTIOUS DISEASES

The following preventive actions can help reduce the spread of disease within your household.

- *Encourage hand washing. Hand washing helps to prevent the spread of gastrointestinal infections more than all other approaches combined.* Rinsing the hands vigorously with plain water is probably as effective as using soap and water. Hand washing is especially important after using the toilet, changing diapers, and contact with turtles or aquarium water. Choose a daycare center where the staff practices good hand washing after changing diapers. Young children must be supervised in their use of toilets and sinks. A surprising finding of recent studies was that hand washing is also the mainstay in preventing the spread of respiratory disease. (Wash the hands after blowing or touching the nose.)

- Clean a public toilet seat off before sitting on it, if it appears wet or soiled. Sitting on toilet seats does not spread infection if you teach your child always to wash the hands afterward.

- *Discourage habits of touching the mouth and nose.* Again, this is helpful in preventing the spread of respiratory infections to others. Also, touching the eyes after touching the nose is a common cause of eye infections.

- *Don't smoke around your children.* Passive smoking increases the frequency and severity of colds, coughs, croup, ear infections, asthma, etc. (See Passive Smoking, page 218.)

- *Discourage the kissing of pets.* Pets (especially puppies) can transmit bloody diarrhea, worms, and more. Pets are for petting.

- *Cook all poultry thoroughly.* Undercooked poultry is a common cause of diarrhea. If it is frozen, thaw it in the refrigerator rather than at room temperature to prevent multiplication of the bacteria. After preparation, carefully wash your hands and any object that comes in contact with raw poultry (such as the knife and cutting board) before using them with other foods. Never serve chicken that is still pink inside (a common problem with outdoor grilling). Don't place the cooked meat on the same platter that the uncooked meat was removed from.

- Use a plastic cutting board. Germs can't be completely removed from wooden cutting boards.

- Avoid eating raw eggs. Don't undercook your eggs. If you make your own eggnog or ice cream, use pasteurized eggs.

- *Choose a small daycare home over a daycare center.* Daycare provided in private homes has a lower rate of infectious disease. Children who are cared for in their own homes by baby-sitters have the lowest rate of infection. Since colds have more complications during the first year of life, try to arrange for home-based daycare if your child is in this age group.

- *Clean contaminated areas with disinfectants.* These products kill most bacteria, including staph. Disinfecting the diaper-changing area, cribs and strollers, play equipment, and food service items is effective in limiting intestinal diseases at home and in daycare centers.

- Don't share cups. When playing team sports, tell your child to use a disposable cup. Don't drink directly from a community water bottle.

- Don't share towels. In public places, use paper towels.

- *Contact your child's physician if your child is exposed to meningitis or hepatitis.* Antibiotics are useful in preventing some types of bacterial meningitis in exposed children under 4 years of age. An injection of gamma globulin is helpful in preventing hepatitis in those who have had intimate contact (i.e., greater than 4 hours) with someone having this disease.

- Keep your child's immunizations up-to-date (see below).

- *Don't attempt to isolate your child.* Isolation is mentioned last because its value within a family unit is questionable. By the time a child shows symptoms, he or she has already shared the germs with the family. Also, from a practical stand-point, isolation at home is impossible to enforce.

IMMUNIZATION SCHEDULE

These immunizations protect your child against serious, life-threatening disease. Check the recommended schedule. If your child's shots are not up-do-date, call your physician for an appointment. Ask for an immunization record card, keep it up-to-date, and bring it with you to health checkups and school enrollment.

IMMUNIZATION SCHEDULE
This is the schedule recommended by the American Academy of Pediatrics. The abbreviations are explained below.

AGE	IMMUNIZATION
Birth	HBV
2 months	DTP, OPV, Hib, HBV
4 months	DTP, OPV, Hib
6 months	DTP, OPV, Hib, HBV
12 months	TB
12–15 months	MMR, Hib, chickenpox
18 months	DTP
4–6 years	DTP, OPT
11–12 years	MMR
14–16 years	Td

Explanation of Abbreviations
DTP; diphtheria, tetanus, pertussis (whooping cough)
Hib: *Hemophilus influenzae type* b
HBV:Hepatitis B virus
MMR:measles, mumps, rubella
OPV:oral polio virus (drops, not a shot)
(Note: An OPV at the 6-month visit is optional.)
TB: tuberculosis skin test (tine test)

Td: adult tetanus and diphtheria (Note: Continue Td every 10 years throughout life.)

MEASLES REVACCINATION

In 1989 the American Academy of Pediatrics recommended that all children receive a second MMR vaccine prior to entering middle school (approximately age 11 or 12 years). The best age for giving this MMR booster is controversial, and in some settings it is given as young as 5 years of age. This change in policy was needed because of recent outbreaks of measles in high schools and colleges. The measles, mumps, and rubella vaccine is being used rather than a single measles vaccine because cases of mumps have also increased in recent years. If your child has been exposed to measles and has not received 2 MMR vaccines after 12 months of age, call your child's physician during office hours for additional information.

HEMOPHILUS INFLUENZAE TYPE B VACCINE

Hemophilus influenzae is a bacterium that causes several life-threatening diseases (e.g., meningitis, epiglottitis, and pneumonia) in young children. At one time, over 10,000 children developed Hemophilus meningitis each year; thanks to a recently developed vaccine, meningitis and its complications are now rare. The first Hib vaccine became available in 1985 and was only effective in children over 2 years of age. In late 1990 a new Hib vaccine was approved that could be started in infants as young as 2 months of age. The complete series of 4 Hib vaccines gave up to 99 percent protection against these devastating diseases. The side effects are minor (a sore injection site and low-grade fever) and occur in only 1.5 percent of children. If your child is over 15 months of age, the vaccine can still be helpful if given through age 5. This vaccine does not protect against viral influenza or viral meningitis.

TUBERCULOSIS SKIN TESTING

While not an immunization, the tuberculosis skin test is an important part of infectious-disease prevention. Early detection permits treatment and prevents spread of this serious lung disease. The frequency of repeat skin tests depends on the incidence of TB in your community and is a judgment best made by your child's physician. Not uncommonly, it is repeated at the 12-year visit.

Read your child's TB test 48 to 72 hours after it was placed.

Call your child's physician for bumps at any of the 4 prong marks (not for redness). The test is positive if 2 bumps or more are touching.

SMALLPOX VACCINE

Smallpox has been eradicated from the world and vaccination is no longer necessary. The elimination of polio is our next challenge.

IMMUNIZATION REACTIONS

RARE, SERIOUS REACTIONS

These vaccines protect children against terrible, life-threatening diseases. (It is worth noting that without protection, the death rate for tetanus and the paralysis rate for polio are both 50 percent.) Most of these diseases do not have an antibiotic or other medicine for treating them. The occurrence of all these diseases has been greatly reduced in our country. With these benefits, however, came a small risk of severe complications. (For example, following the polio vaccine, 1 person in 3 million actually gets polio.) During office visits for immunizations, your child's physician will probably provide you with information sheets describing the possible reactions to vaccines. Read these informed consent forms carefully and ask questions. Keep in mind that after careful thought, almost all physicians have decided to immunize themselves and their own children.

COMMON, NONSERIOUS REACTIONS

DTP Vaccine • DTP vaccines commonly produce fever, local tenderness, redness, and swelling for 24 to 48 hours. These symptoms can be reduced by giving acetaminophen by mouth and applying cold compresses to the tender area. If your child has severe pain with the first DTP, with future ones give acetaminophen at the time of the injection and continue it for 4 or 5 dosages.

• Call your child's physician immediately if your child cries for more than 3 hours, has a fever over 105°F, or has any other unusual reaction.

• Call during office hours if the redness becomes larger than 2 inches, spreads after 24 hours, persists over 48 hours, or if the fever lasts for more than 48 hours. A few children develop a small, painless lump (or nodule) at the injection site 1 to 2 weeks after the shot. This DTP nodule is harmless and disappears in about 2 months. Call your child's physician if it becomes red or tender to the touch.

Measles Vaccine • The measles vaccine can result in a fever and rash about 7 to 10 days following the injection. The fever is between 101°F and 103°F for 2 to 3 days in 10 percent of children. The rash is mainly on the trunk and lasts 2 to 3 days. No treatment is necessary. For details, see MEASLES VACCINE RASH, page 439.

Polio, Mumps, Rubella and *Hemophilus influenzae* Type B Vaccines • There are no common reactions to polio, mumps, rubella, or Hib vaccine. A small percentage of older children have brief joint pain or swelling about 14 days following the rubella vaccine. Children with poor immunity or living with adults who have poor immunity (e.g., AIDS) should receive the inactivated polio vaccine (IPV) rather than the live oral polio vaccine (OPV).

Egg Allergy • Children who are allergic to eggs can receive all the routine immunizations except those for measles and mumps. These vaccines are grown in chick cell cultures, and cross-reactions have occurred. If the reaction to eggs was mild and delayed, the measles vaccine can be given. If the reaction to eggs occurred rapidly (within 2 hours of ingestion) or was severe (e.g., difficulty breathing or swallowing), your child should be skin-tested by an allergist to determine if the measles vaccine would be safe.

PERTUSSIS VACCINE CONCERNS

The pertussis vaccine scare has made some parents postpone their child's immunizations. Keep in mind that pertussis (whooping cough) is a highly dangerous disease, especially for infants. (For infants with whooping cough disease, the death rate is 1 percent and the brain damage rate is 0.5 percent.) The chance of getting whooping cough for a child not protected by the vaccine is 1 in 3,000; whereas the risk of having neurological damage with the vaccine was reported as 1 in 2 million. A new study (1990) by Dr. M. R. Griffin found no brain damage or epilepsy caused by the pertussis vaccine. The pertussis vaccine panic may all have been a tempest in a teapot. In the meantime, this risk for developing pertussis increases as the number of immunized children decreases.

The American Academy of Pediatrics has stated clearly that "the risk of suffering and death caused by whooping cough is far greater than the possible side effects of the vaccine." The pertussis vaccine should be withheld initially only in children with epilepsy or serious neurologic disease. One false claim blamed pertussis vaccine for some crib deaths. Several studies proved that such an association did not exist. If you remain opposed, at least give your child the benefits of the tetanus and diphtheria (Td) vaccine.

PASSIVE (INVOLUNTARY) SMOKING

Nonsmoking children who live in homes with smokers are involuntarily exposed to cigarette smoke. The smoke comes from two sources: secondhand smoke and sidestream smoke. Secondhand smoke is exhaled by the smoker. Sidestream smoke rises off the end of a burning cigarette and accounts for most of the smoke in a room. Sidestream smoke contains two or three times more harmful chemicals than secondhand smoke because sidestream smoke does not pass through the cigarette filter. At its worst, a child in a very smoky room for 1 hour with several smokers inhales as many bad chemicals as he would by smoking 10 or more cigarettes. In general, children of smoking mothers absorb more smoke into their bodies than children of smoking fathers because the children spend more time with their mothers. Children who are breast-fed by a smoking mother are at the greatest risk because chemicals are found in the breast milk as well as in the surrounding air.

HARMFUL EFFECTS OF PASSIVE SMOKING ON CHILDREN

Children who live in a house where someone smokes have an increased rate of all respiratory infections. Their symptoms are also more severe and last longer than those of children who live in a smoke-free home. The impact of passive smoke is worse during the first five years of life, when children spend most of their time with their parents. The more smokers there are in a household and the more they smoke, the more severe a child's symptoms. Passive smoking is especially hazardous to children who have asthma. Exposure to smoke causes more severe asthma attacks, more emergency-room visits, and increased admissions to the hospital. These children are also less likely to outgrow their asthma. The following conditions are worsened by passive smoking:

- pneumonia
- coughs or bronchitis
- croup or laryngitis
- wheezing or bronchiolitis
- asthma attacks
- influenza
- ear infections
- middle-ear fluid and blockage
- colds or URIs
- sinus infections
- sore throats
- eye irritation
- crib deaths (SIDS)
- school absenteeism for all of the above

HOW TO PROTECT YOUR CHILD FROM PASSIVE SMOKING

1. *Give up active smoking.* Sign up for a stop-smoking class or program. Giving up smoking is even more urgent if you are pregnant, because your unborn baby has twice the risk for prematurity and complications of the newborn if you smoke during pregnancy. It is also important to avoid smoking if you are breast-feeding, because smoke-related, harmful chemicals get into your breast milk. You can stop smoking if you get help. If you need self-help reading materials, call your local American Lung Association or American Cancer Society office. The surgeon general would like us to become a smoke-free society by the year 2000. For more information, call the National Cancer Institute on their toll-free line: 1-800-4-CANCER. If you want your child not to smoke, set a good example.

2. *Never smoke inside your home.* Some parents find it difficult to give up smoking, but all parents can change their smoking habits. Restrict your smoking to times when you are away from home. If you feel you have to smoke when you are home, smoke only in your garage or on the porch. If these options are not available to you, designate a smoking room within your home. Keep the door to this room closed, and periodically open the window to let fresh air into the room. Wear a special overshirt in this room to protect your underlying clothing from collecting the smoke. Never allow your child inside this room, and don't smoke in other parts of the house. Apply the same rules to visitors.

3. *Never smoke while holding your child.* If you feel your smoking habit cannot be controlled to the degree mentioned above, at a minimum protect your child from smoking when you are close to him. This precaution will reduce his exposure to smoke and protect him from cigarette burns. Never smoke in a car when your child is a passenger. Never smoke when you are feeding or bathing him. Never smoke in your child's bedroom. Even doing this much will help your child to some degree.

4. *Avoid leaving your child with a caretaker who smokes.* Inquire about smoking when you are looking for daycare centers or baby-sitters. If your child has asthma, this safeguard is crucial.

CONTAGIOUS DISEASES AND INCUBATION PERIODS

Young children are afflicted with infectious diseases 10 to 15 times per year. The attack rate decreases with age because with each new infection we build up antibodies against future ones. Most of these infections are due to viruses or bacteria, but occasionally fungi or parasites are involved. Your child's symptoms are probably due to an infection if fever is present or the illness spreads to others. The following information is intended to improve your understanding of contagious diseases. (See pages 222 and 223 for details.)

THE INCUBATION PERIOD
The incubation period is defined as the time interval between exposure to a contagious disease and the onset of symptoms. This information should help answer the questions (1) "When

will my child come down with it?" and (2) "Should we cancel our weekend plans?"

If the outer time limit of the incubation period passes and your child is still well, he or she has probably escaped that infection for now (or has previous antibodies against it).

THE CONTAGIOUS PERIOD

The contagious period is defined as that time interval during which a sick child's disease is contagious to others. Knowing the period of contagion helps answer the question "How long does my child have to stay home from school or daycare?"

For major illnesses (such as hepatitis), a child will need to remain in isolation at home or in the hospital until all chance of spread has passed. For minor illnesses (like the common cold) we are less strict. Most physicians would agree that a child should stay home at least until he feels well enough to return to school, and the fever has been gone for 12 hours.

INFECTIONS THAT ARE NOT CONTAGIOUS

Try not to become preoccupied with infections. Some of the more serious ones are not even contagious. Some infections are due to blockage of a passageway followed by an overgrowth of bacteria. Examples of these are ear infections, sinus infections, and urinary tract infections. Lymph node and bloodstream infections are also rarely contagious. Pneumonia is a complication of a viral respiratory infection in most cases and is usually not contagious. While exposure to meningitis requires consultation with your child's physician, most children exposed to this disease do not become infected. Venereal (genital) diseases are usually noncontagious unless there is sexual contact or shared bathing arrangements.

FREQUENT INFECTIONS

Some children seem to have the constant sniffles. They get one cold after another. Many a parent wonders: "Isn't my child having too many colds?" Children start to get colds after about 6 months of age. During infancy and the preschool years, they average 7 or 8 colds a year. During the school-age years, they average 5 or 6 colds a year. During adolescence they finally reach an adult level of approximately 4 colds a

GUIDELINES FOR COMMON CONTAGIOUS DISEASES

DISEASE	INCUBATION PERIOD (DAYS)	CONTAGIOUS PERIOD (DAYS)
Skin Infections:		
Chicken pox	14–16	2 days before rash until all sores have crusts (7)
Fifth disease (*Erythema infectiosum*)	10–14	7 days before rash until rash begins
Hand, foot, and mouth disease	3–6	Onset of mouth ulcers until fever gone
Impetigo (strep or staph)	2–5	Onset of sores until 24 hours on antibiotic
Lice	7	Onset of itch until 1 treatment
Measles	10–12	4 days before rash until rash gone (7)
Roseola	10–15	Onset of fever until rash gone (2)
Rubella (German measles)	14–21	7 days before rash until rash gone (4)
Scabies	30	Onset of rash until 1 treatment
Scarlet fever	3–6	Onset of fever or rash until 24 hours on antibiotic
Shingles (contagious for chicken pox)	14–16	Onset of rash until all sores have crusts (7) (Note: No need to isolate if sores can be kept covered.)
Warts	30–180	*
Respiratory Infections:		
Bronchiolitis	4–6	Onset of cough until 7 days
Colds	2–5	Onset of runny nose until fever gone
Cold sores (herpes)	2–12	†
Coughs (viral)	2–5	Onset of cough until fever gone
Croup (viral)	2–6	Onset of cough until fever gone
Diphtheria	2–5	Onset of sore throat until 4 days on antibiotic
Influenza	1–2	Onset of cough until fever gone
Sore throat, strep	2–5	Onset of sore throat until 24 hours on antibiotic

DISEASE	INCUBATION PERIOD (DAYS)	CONTAGIOUS PERIOD (DAYS)
Sore throat, viral	2–5	Onset of sore throat until fever gone
Tuberculosis	14–70	Until 2 weeks on drugs (Note: Most childhood TB is not contagious.)
Whooping cough	7–10	Onset of runny nose until 5 days on antibiotic

Intestinal Infections:

Diarrhea, bacterial	1–5	‡
Diarrhea, giardia	7–21	‡
Diarrhea, traveler's	1–6	‡
Diarrhea, viral (Rotavirus)	1–3	‡
Hepatitis A	14–50	2 weeks before jaundice begins until jaundice resolved
Hepatitis B	50–180	Same
Pinworms	21–28	*
Vomiting, viral	2–5	Until vomiting stops

Other Infections:

Infectious mononucleosis	30–50	Onset of fever until fever gone (7)
Meningitis, bacterial	2–10	7 days before symptoms until 24 hours on IV antibiotics in hospital
Mumps	16–18	5 days before swelling until swelling gone (7)
Pinkeye without pus (viral)	1–5	*
Pinkeye with pus (bacterial)	2–7	Onset of pus until 1 day on antibiotic eyedrops

*Staying home is unnecessary because the infection is very mild and/or minimally contagious.

†Cold sores: Less than 6 years old, stay home until sores are dry, 4–5 days. (No isolation if sores are on part of body that can be covered.)
More than 6 years old, no isolation necessary if beyond touching, picking stage.

‡Diarrhea: Less than 6 years old, stay home until stools are formed.
More than 6 years old, stay home until fever is gone, diarrhea is mild, and child has control over loose BMs.

References:
(1) Incubation periods are from American Academy of Pediatrics, Committee on Infectious Diseases, 1988 Red Book, 21st edition, Evanston, Illinois.
(2) Isolation recommendations are from Garner, J.S., and Simmons, B.P. "Guideline for Isolation Precautions in Hospitals, Infection Control 4" (Suppl.), 1983, pp. 245–325.

year. Colds account for more than 50 percent of all acute illnesses with fever. A young child who has 8 colds a year (each lasting 10 to 14 days) actually is sick almost a third of that year.

In addition, children can have diarrhea illnesses (with or without vomiting) 2 or 3 times per year. Some children are especially worrisome to their parents because they tend to get high fevers with most of their colds or they have a sensitive gastrointestinal (GI) tract and develop diarrhea with the majority of their colds. These repeatedly ill children cause their parents a great deal of consternation.

Similar Condition • If your child is over age 3, sneezes a lot, has a clear nasal discharge that lasts over a month, doesn't have a fever, doesn't spread the symptoms to other people, and especially if these symptoms occur during pollen season, your child probably has a nasal allergy and you should refer to the guideline on HAY FEVER, page 540.

Causes • The main cause of all these infections is that your child is being exposed to new viruses. There are at least 200 different cold viruses. The younger the child, the less the previous exposure and subsequent protection. Your child is exposed more if he or she attends daycare, play group, a church nursery, or a preschool. Your child has more indirect exposures if he has older siblings in school. Therefore, colds are more common in large families. The rate of colds triples in the wintertime when people spend more time crowded together indoors breathing recirculated air. In addition, smoking in the home increases your child's susceptibility to colds.

WHAT DOESN'T CAUSE FREQUENT INFECTIONS

Most parents are worried that their repeatedly ill child has some serious underlying disease. Children with immune system diseases (inadequate antibody or white blood cell production) don't experience any more colds than the average child. Instead, they have two or more bouts per year of pneumonia, sinus infection, draining lymph nodes, or boils. They also heal slowly from these infections. In addition, most children with serious disease do not gain weight adequately. Tell your physician if your family is worried about a particular diagnosis so your physician can discuss this concern with you. Also, recurrent ear infections don't mean that your child has a serious health problem, only that his eustachian tubes don't drain properly.

Other parents worry that they have in some way neglected their child or done something wrong to cause frequent colds. On the contrary, having all these colds is an unavoidable part of growing up. Colds are the one infection we can't prevent yet. From a medical standpoint, colds are an educational experience for your child's immune system.

DEALING WITH FREQUENT INFECTIONS

Look at Your Child's General Health • If your child is vigorous and gaining weight, you don't have to worry about his or her health. Your child probably is no sicker than the average child of her age. Children get over colds by themselves. While you can do something to reduce the symptoms, you can't shorten the course of each cold (see COLDS, page 533). Your child will just have to muddle through like every other child. The long-term outlook is good. The number of colds will decrease over the years as your child's body builds up a good antibody supply to the various viruses. To help put infections in perspective, a recent survey found that on any given day, 10 percent of children have a cold, 8 percent have a fever, 5 percent have diarrhea, and 3 percent have an ear infection.

Send Your Child Back to School as Soon as Possible • The main requirement for returning your child to school is that the fever is gone and the symptoms are not excessively noisy or distracting to classmates. It doesn't make sense to keep a child home until we can guarantee that he or she is no longer shedding any viruses (as this could take 2 or 3 weeks). If isolation for respiratory infections were taken seriously, insufficient days would remain to educate children. Also the "germ warfare" that normally occurs in schools is fairly uncontrollable. Most children shed germs during the first days of their illness before they even look sick or have symptoms. In other words, contact with respiratory infections is unavoidable in group settings, such as schools or daycare. Also, as long as your child's fever has cleared, there is no reason not to attend parties, play with friends after school, and go on scheduled trips. The overexertion of gym and team sports may need to wait a few extra days.

Try Not to Miss Work • When both parents work, these repeated colds are extremely inconvenient and costly. Since the complication rate is low and the improvement rate is slow, don't hesitate to leave your child with someone else at these times. If your baby-sitter is willing to accept the care of a child with a fever, take advantage of the offer. If your child is in daycare or a preschool, send him or her back once the fever is gone. No need to prolong the recovery at home if you need to return to work. Early return of a child with a respiratory illness won't increase the complication rate for your child or the exposure rate for other children.

Likewise, you don't need to cancel an important social engagement because your child has a minor acute illness. There will be many more of these. You also don't need to take your child out of preschool or daycare permanently because of the nuisance aspect of all these repeated illnesses. Because there are so many more working mothers, "sick child" daycare programs are starting to spring up around the country.

WHAT DOESN'T HELP

There are no instant cures for recurrent colds and other viral illnesses. Antibiotics are not helpful unless your child develops complications such as an ear infection, sinus infection, or pneumonia. Since the colds are not caused by bad tonsils, having your child's tonsils removed is not helpful (see TONSIL AND ADENOID SURGERY, page 562). Colds are not caused by poor diet or lack of vitamins. They are not caused by bad weather, air conditioners, or wet feet. Again, the best time to have these infections and develop immunity is during childhood.

RELATED TOPICS

PREVENTION OF COLDS (see page 539)

MEDICINES

MEDICINES: GENERAL INSTRUCTIONS

OVERUSE OF MEDICINES

We are a greatly overmedicated society. Many people believe that there is a drug for every symptom. Some physicians prescribe a drug during every office visit. These habits can convey to our young people that drugs are the answer to life's discomforts. More than $4 billion per year is spent on nonprescription drugs for fever, colds, and coughs—many of them unnecessary. Drugs for vomiting and diarrhea are largely ineffective, and these symptoms respond best to dietary changes. Remember that mild symptoms do not require any medication, and moderate symptoms often respond to home remedies. Drugs are not essential to recovery from most illnesses. Life is not a drug-deficient state.

VIRAL INFECTIONS AND ANTIBIOTICS

Let's set the record straight about antibiotics:

- More than 90 percent of infections are due to viruses (as with colds, coughs, croup, and diarrhea).

- Antibiotics ("wonder drugs") kill bacteria.

- Unfortunately, *antibiotics have no effect on viruses;* they don't even slow viruses down.

- *Repeated use of antibiotics increases the likelihood of an*

227

allergic reaction. The more they are used, the more likely the body will develop an allergy to them. That's why 5 to 10 percent of adults are allergic to penicillin.

- All antibiotics have additional side effects—such as wiping out your normal protective bacteria and replacing them with bacteria resistant to the antibiotic.

- *Antibiotics can neither shorten the source of viral illnesses nor reduce symptoms.*

- Fortunately, the body's antibodies, once produced, can kill viruses.

- Use home remedies or nonprescription medicines for the symptoms of viral illnesses.

COMMON SYMPTOMS AND NONPRESCRIPTION MEDICINES

- When your child is sick with a viral illness, your goal is to make him as comfortable as possible.

- If your child is playing and sleeping normally, nonprescription medicines are not needed.

- Give medicines only for symptoms that are causing discomfort, disrupting sleep, or really bothering your child—coughing spasms, for instance.

- Medicines for symptoms can only partially relieve those symptoms (e.g., a fever will be lowered but not normal).

- Medicines for symptoms do not shorten the course of an illness.

- Nonprescription (over-the-counter) medicines also can have side effects.

GUIDELINES FOR SAFE USE OF MEDICINES

- Most medicines can cause poisoning. Keep them out of reach of children. Keep the child-proof caps on.

- Give the correct amount (dosage) for your child. Read the directions on the label carefully. Measure the dose out exactly. Use a measuring spoon or device. A 1-teaspoon measuring spoon should hold 5 ml (or 5 cc). Tableware teaspoons hold varying amounts (2 to 7 ml) and should not be used.

• Give the medicine at the correct time intervals. If you forget a dosage, give it as soon as you remember it, and give the next one at the correct interval following the late dosage. Generally, "4 times a day" does not mean you have to awaken your child, unless he sleeps more than 8 hours.

• If you think your child is having a reaction to the medicine, call your physician before discontinuing it. Drug allergies tend to be overdiagnosed (see AMPICILLIN RASH, page 423). Many drug symptoms, such as nausea or jitteriness, disappear when the dosage is reduced.

• Continue antibiotics until the bottle is empty. Your physician will prescribe the correct amount of antibiotic to kill all the bacteria. Stopping the antibiotic early can result in a flare-up.

• Give symptomatic medicines only when your child is having lots of symptoms (e.g., hacking cough) or is uncomfortable (e.g., fever over 102° or 103°F). These medicines do not need to be given continuously. If you decide to use them continuously, however, be certain to stop them once the symptoms have cleared for more than 12 hours.

• Don't give a prescription medicine to anyone except the person it was prescribed for—not to brothers or sisters, for instance. Some adult medicines are never prescribed for children because of their special side effects on the growing body, such as staining the teeth.

• Don't use outdated medicines. They lose their strength over time and some may be harmful. Most liquid antibiotics are worthless after 4 weeks, so discard them if any is left. Most other medicines are potent for 1 to 4 years. While pills usually last longer than liquid medicines, check the label for an expiration date.

RELATED TOPICS

Giving ear drops—see under EAR, SWIMMER'S, page 528
Giving eye drops—see under EYES, YELLOW DISCHARGE, page 508
Giving nose drops—see under COLDS, page 533

MEDICINES: HELPING CHILDREN SWALLOW THEM

A PREVENTIVE APPROACH

When your child is sick, he may need to take some medicines. For liquid medicines, a plastic syringe or dropper is easier to use than a spoon with infants or struggling children. If you have only a spoon, keep a towel handy for spills.

Approach your child in a matter-of-fact way with an expectation that he will take it without resistance. Some children will respond better to an enthusiastic "Mary Poppins" approach.

Position your child sitting up and pour or drip the medicine onto the back of the tongue. Don't squirt it into the pouch inside the cheek, because it won't go down when your child swallows. You must place the liquid beyond the teeth or gumline. Also, if you're using a syringe, don't squirt it forcefully into the back of the throat, because of the danger of its going into the windpipe and causing choking. If you drip the medicine in slowly, you can avoid gagging or choking.

MEDICINES THAT TASTE BAD: DISGUISING THE TASTE

Bitter medicines will often lead to refusal unless some of the following preventive steps are taken:

- Have your child suck on a Popsicle beforehand to numb the mouth partially.

- Serve the medicine cold to reduce the taste.

- Mix it with a strong flavor (such as Kool-Aid powder or chocolate pudding) to hide the bad taste.

- Dilute the medicine as much as possible (e.g., 1 dose mixed in 2 glasses of cold apple juice) if you're certain your child can drink it all.

- Mix crushed pills with one of your child's favorite foods that doesn't require chewing. Consider ice-cream toppings (especially chocolate syrup), honey, maple syrup, applesauce, ice cream, sherbet, or yogurt. Before adding the medicine, have your child practice swallowing the food alone without chewing it—since chewing would bring out the bad taste of the medicine.

- Have a glass of your child's favorite cold drink ready to rinse his mouth afterward—a sort of "chaser."

- Praise and hug your child for all cooperation.

- The older your child is, the more you can ask for his or her suggestions.

- Some respond to being given complete control of the spoon or syringe.

REFUSAL OF LIQUID MEDICINES

Some 1- to 4-year-old children vigorously refuse to take medicines, even after you have tried to hide the taste. If the medicine is not essential to recovery (such as most nonprescription medicines for coughs, colds, and fever), discontinue it. If you are uncertain of the importance of the medicine, call your physician for advice. If the drug is essential (such as most antibiotics), apply the following recommendations:

- Be honest and sympathetic ("I'm sorry it tastes bad. We can mix it with anything you like").

- Be firm and give a reason ("You have to take it, or you won't get well").

- Give your child a time-out in the corner to think about it. Every 5 minutes, ask him, "Are you ready yet?" If 15 minutes pass, take action.

- Immobilize your child. Two people are usually needed. Have your friend position your child on the lap, holding the arms with one hand and the head with the other. You can use one hand to hold the medicine and the other to open your child's mouth. If you are alone, first wrap your child with a sheet. Ask the office nurse to show you how this is done.

- Be sure your child is not lying flat, to prevent choking.

- Open your child's mouth by pushing down the chin or running your finger inside the cheek and pushing down on the lower jaw.

- Insert the syringe between the teeth and drip the medicine onto the back of the tongue.

- Keep the mouth closed until your child swallows. Gravity can help if you have your child in an upright position. However, swallowing can't occur if the head is bent backward.

- Afterward, apologize and review the alternative: "I'm sorry we had to hold you. If you cooperate next time, we won't have to."

- Give your child a hug.

- Forcing your child in this way to take an important medicine will teach him you mean business and will eventually bring cooperation.

- Don't attack self-esteem—for instance, by saying, "You're acting like a baby."

- Don't punish, as with spanking or yelling.

- If your child vomits or spits out the medicine, estimate the amount lost and repeat it.

REFUSAL OF PILLS OR CAPSULES
Some children have difficulty swallowing pills and capsules.

- The easiest approach is to convert it to a liquid form. Empty out the capsules or crush the pills. This approach is acceptable unless the product is a slow-release or enteric-coated pill. (Check with your physician if you are uncertain what you can do.)

- Slow-release capsules can be emptied as long as the contents are swallowed without chewing. Since capsules usually contain medicines with a bitter taste, the contents need to be mixed with a sweet food.

- Pills are usually made as a convenient alternative to the liquid form, and they may not taste bad. Pills can be crushed between two spoons. Crushing is made easier by first moistening the pill with a few drops of water and letting it soften for 15 minutes.

- Place the pill or capsule far back on the tongue and have your child quickly drink water or Kool-Aid through a straw. If your child concentrates on swallowing (even gulping) the liquid, the pill will follow downstream without a hitch.

- If your child is over 7 or 8 years old and unable to swallow pills, he should practice this skill when he's not sick or cranky. (Some children can't accomplish pill-swallowing until age 10, however.) Start with small pieces of candy or ice and progress to M & M's. Try to use substances that will quickly melt if they get stuck. If necessary, first coat them with butter.

Use the liquid and straw technique. Once candy pellets are mastered, pills will usually be manageable. For extra confidence, split the pill into halves or quarters.

CALL YOUR CHILD'S PHYSICIAN IF

• Your child vomits the medicine more than once.

• You are unable to get your child to take an essential medicine.

The next time your physician prescribes a medicine, be sure to mention that your child has this common problem. He may be able to prescribe one that tastes better.

FIRST AID KIT

The first aid kit may be needed at home, on a vacation, or while hiking or camping. Therefore, the contents should be kept in a small box that is portable. Medicines are usually not included.

• Band-Aids

• Sterile gauze pads—both regular and nonstick type

• Adhesive tape, ½-inch wide

• Steristrips or butterfly Band-Aids (for closing minor lacerations)

• Soap—small sample bar (note: Hydrogen peroxide solution is unnecessary. It's no better than soap and water for cleaning wounds.)

• Alcohol wipes (individually wrapped packets)

• Elastic bandage (for sprained ankle)

• Triangular bandage (for arm injury)

• Tourniquet (can use the triangular bandage)

• Needle and tweezers without teeth (for removing slivers or ticks)

• Razor blade (for poisonous snakebite)

• Small scissors

• Papain (meat tenderizer powder for bee stings)

- Insect repellent

- Sunscreen

- Adrenalin and syringes (optional: needed if family member has a severe bee-sting allergy) (See ALLERGIC REACTION, SEVERE, page 13 for details.)

- Optional medicines for camping: antibiotic ointment, hydrocortisone cream, antihistamines, acetaminophen

- Extra supplies for hiking or camping: compass, whistle, flashlight, matches

HOME MEDICINE CHEST (NONPRESCRIPTION MEDICINES)

This list of nonprescription drugs and supplies will be sufficient to relieve symptoms in the majority of acute illnesses that affect every family. Since these medicines will not shorten the course of the illnesses, give them only when symptoms are really bothering your child. See the specific guidelines for more details on using these drugs. (**Caution:** Keep these medicines locked up and away from children.)

- Acetaminophen: for fever or pain

- Aspirin: for pain only

- Ibuprofen: for pain relief from injuries

- Thermometer, rectal and oral types

- Rubber suction bulb: for stuffy, blocked nose, after using warm water nose drops

- Vasoconstrictor nose drops: for severely blocked nose

- Butterscotch hard candies: for sore throat

- Cough drops or corn syrup: for mild coughs

- Dextromethorphan-containing (cough-suppressant) cough syrup: for severe coughs

- Humidifier (cool mist type): for coughs or croup

- Ice bag: for injured muscles, bones, and joints

- Long-acting vasoconstrictor eye drops: for irritated, reddened eyes
- Antibiotic eye drops: for bacterial eye infections with a yellow discharge (Note: This is the only prescription item on this list.)
- Cotton balls: for cleaning infected eyes
- Sunscreen (cream and lip balm)
- Hydrocortisone, ½ percent: for itchy skin conditions such as mosquito bites and poison ivy
- Bacitracin or Betadine antibiotic ointment: for skin infections
- Acetone (nail polish remover): for removing tape from the skin
- Rubbing alcohol (70 percent isopropyl alcohol): for sterilizing the skin or needles
- Ipecac, syrup of (30-ml bottle): for inducing vomiting in some types of poisoning
- Antihistamine medicine (e.g., Chlortrimeton—4-mg tablets or 2-mg per teaspoon syrup): for hives, hay fever, and eye allergies (optional: needed if family members have allergies)
- Dramamine tablets: for motion sickness (optional if family member has this condition)
- Gastrointestinal medicines: Vomiting and diarrhea respond best to dietary changes, and the numerous nonprescription medicines that are available are unnecessary or harmful. Acute constipation may occasionally require some milk of magnesia, but most children, again, respond to dietary change.
- Tincture of time: cures the majority of self-limited illnesses
- TLC (tender loving care): makes the time pass more quickly for most symptoms

FAILURE TO IMPROVE ON ANTIBIOTICS

If your child is taking an antibiotic for an ear infection, sinus infection, pneumonia, urinary tract infection, etc., he should begin to improve between 24 and 48 hours. If not, he may have a complication or a resistant bacteria.

CALL YOUR CHILD'S PHYSICIAN
Immediately If

- The fever continues for more than 48 hours despite use of the antibiotics.
- Your child develops a stiff neck.
- Your child starts to act very sick.

During Office Hours If

- The fever goes away for 24 hours or more and then returns
- Symptoms other than fever (e.g., headache or earache) have not improved after 48 hours on the antibiotic.
- You have other questions or concerns.

HOME CARE

Bacterial infections usually do not respond to the first dose of antibiotics. While some infections (such as strep) respond fast, most take 24 to 48 hours before we see any improvement.

V.

BEHAVIOR: PREVENTING AND SOLVING PROBLEMS

SLEEP

CRYING BABY (COLIC)

SYMPTOMS AND CHARACTERISTICS OF FUSSY CRYING (COLIC)

- Unexplained crying
- Healthy child (not sick or in pain)
- Well-fed child (not hungry)
- Usually cries 1 to 2 hours at a time
- Cries once or twice per day
- Acts fine (happy or contented) between bouts of crying
- Usually consolable when held and comforted
- Onset usually under 2 weeks of age
  (Crying that begins after 4 weeks of age is not colic)
- Resolution by 3 months of age

  If your child's symptoms are different, call your physician for help.

Cause • Normally infants do some crying during the first months of life. When babies cry without being hungry, overheated, or in pain, we call it colic. About 10 percent of babies have colic. While no one is certain what causes colic, these babies seem to want to be cuddled or to go to sleep. Colic tends to occur in high-needs babies with a sensitive temperament. Colic is not the result of bad parenting, so don't blame yourself. Colic is also not due to excessive gas, so don't bother with extra burping or special nipples. Cow's milk allergy may cause crying in a few babies, but only if your baby also has diarrhea and/or vomiting. Colic is not caused by abdominal pain. The reason the belly muscles feel hard is that a baby needs these muscles to cry. Drawing up the legs is also a normal posture for a crying baby, as is flexing the arms.

Expected Course • This fussy crying is harmless for your baby. The hard crying spontaneously starts to improve at 2 months and is gone by 3 months. Although the crying can't be eliminated, the minutes of crying per day can be dramatically reduced with treatment. In the long run, these children tend to remain more sensitive and alert to their surroundings.

CALL YOUR CHILD'S PHYSICIAN

Immediately If

- It seems to be a painful cry rather than a fussy one.

- Your baby has been crying constantly for more than 3 hours.

- You can't find a way to soothe your baby (inconsolable crying).

- Your baby is under 2 months old *and* acts sick.

- You have shaken your baby. (Note: Shaking an infant can cause severe bleeding in the brain.)

- You are afraid you might hurt your baby.

During Office Hours If

- The colic-type crying occurs 3 or more times per day.

- The crying began after 1 month of age.

- Your baby is over 3 months old.

- Diarrhea, vomiting, or constipation occur with the crying.

- Your baby is not gaining and may be hungry.

- You are exhausted from all this crying.

- Your baby mainly cries when you're trying to sleep.

- You have other questions.

HOME CARE FOR A CRYING BABY

1. *Cuddle and rock your baby whenever he cries.* A soothing, rhythmic activity is the best approach to helping a baby relax, settle down, and go to sleep. You can't spoil a baby during the first 3 or 4 months of life. Consider using the following:

- Cuddling your child in a rocking chair.

- Rocking your child in a cradle.

- Placing your child in a baby-carrier or sling (which frees your hands for housework).

- A wind-up swing or a vibrating chair.

- A stroller (or buggy) ride—outdoors or indoors.

- Anything else you think may be helpful (e.g., a pacifier, a warm bath, or massage).

    If all else fails, Sleep Tight is a new device that attaches under the crib and simulates the motion and sound of a moving car. This gadget has lessened colicky behavior in over 90 percent of babies. It costs about $70. For more information call 1–800–662–6542.

2. *A last resort: Let your baby cry himself to sleep.* If none of these measures quiets your baby after 30 minutes of trying and he has been fed recently, your baby is probably trying to go to sleep. He needs you to minimize outside stimuli while he tries to find his own way into sleep. Wrap him up and place him on his back or side. He will probably be somewhat restless until he falls asleep. Close the door, go into a different room, turn up the radio, and do something you want to do. Even consider earplugs or earphones. Save your strength for when your baby definitely needs you. But if he cries for over 15 minutes, pick him up and again try the soothing activities.

3. *Prevent later sleep problems.* Although babies need to be held when they are crying, they don't need to be held all the time. If you overinterpret the advice for colic and rock your baby every time he goes to sleep, you will become indispensable to your baby's sleep process. Your baby's colic won't resolve at 3 months of age. To prevent this from occurring, when your baby is drowsy but not crying, place him in the crib and let him learn to self-comfort and self-induce sleep. Don't rock or nurse him to sleep at these

times. While colic can't be prevented, secondary sleep problems can be.

4. *Promote nighttime sleep (rather than daytime sleep).* Try to keep your infant from sleeping excessively during the daytime. If your baby has napped 3 hours, gently awaken him and entertain or feed him, depending on his needs. In this way the time when your infant sleeps the longest (often 5 hours) will occur during the night.

5. *Try these feeding strategies.* Don't feed your baby every time he cries. Being hungry is only one of the reasons babies cry. It takes about 2 hours for the stomach to empty, so wait that long between feedings. For breast-fed babies, however, nurse them every time they cry until your milk supply is well established and your baby is gaining weight (usually 2 weeks). Babies who feed too frequently during the day become hungry at frequent intervals during the night. If you are breast-feeding, avoid drinking or taking coffee, tea, colas, and other stimulants. Suspect a cow's milk allergy if your child also has diarrhea, vomiting, eczema, wheezing, or a strong family history of milk allergy. If any of these factors are present, try a soy formula for 1 week. Soy formulas are nutritionally complete and no more expensive than regular formula. If you are breast-feeding, avoid all forms of cow's milk in your diet for 1 week. If the crying dramatically improves when your child is on the soy formula, call your child's physician for additional advice about keeping him on the formula. Also, if you think your child is allergic but he doesn't improve with soy formula, call about the elemental formulas.

6. *Get rest and help for yourself.* While the crying can be reduced, what's left must be endured and shared. Avoid fatigue and exhaustion. Get at least one nap a day, in case the night goes badly. Ask your husband, a friend, or a relative for help with other children and chores. Caring for a colicky baby is a two-person job. Hire a baby-sitter so you can get out of the house and clear your mind. Talk to someone every day about your mixed feelings. The screaming can drive anyone to desperation.

Common Mistakes • If you are breast-feeding, don't stop. If your baby needs extra calories, talk with a lactation consultant about ways to increase your milk supply. Don't place your baby facedown on a water bed or sheepskin rug. While these surfaces can be soothing, they also run the risk of suffocation.

A young infant may not be able to lift the head adequately to breathe. The available medicines are ineffective and many (especially those containing phenobarbital) are dangerous for children of this age. The medicines that slow intestinal activity (the anticholinergics) can cause fever or constipation. The ones that remove gas bubbles have been shown not to help the crying in most studies, but they are harmless. Inserting a thermometer or suppository into the rectum to "release gas" does nothing except irritate the anal sphincter. Stay with TLC (tender loving care) for best results.

Call Your Child's Physician Later If

- The crying continues after your baby reaches 3 months of age.

- Your baby seems to be in pain.

- Your baby cries constantly for more than 3 hours.

- You can't find a way to soothe your baby.

RECOMMENDED READING
Bruce Taubman, *Curing Infant Colic*
(New York: Bantam Books, 1990).

SLEEP PROBLEMS, PREVENTION OF

It is far easier to prevent sleep problems than it is to treat them later. Consider the following guidelines if you want your child to sleep through the night.

NEWBORNS

- *Place your baby in the crib when he is drowsy but awake.* This step is very important. Without it, the other preventive measures will fail. Your baby's last waking memory should be of the crib, not of you or of being fed. He must learn to put himself to sleep without you. Don't expect him to go to sleep as soon as you lay him down. It often takes 20 minutes of restlessness for a baby to go to sleep. If he is crying, rock him and cuddle him. But when he settles down, try to place him in the crib before he falls asleep. Handle naps in the same way. This is how your child will learn to put himself back to sleep after normal awakenings. Don't help your infant when he doesn't need help.

- *Hold your baby for all fussy crying during the first 3 months.* All new babies cry some during the day and night. If your baby cries excessively, the cause is probably colic. A crying baby should always be responded to. Gentle rocking and cuddling seems to help the most. Remember, babies can't be spoiled during the first 3 or 4 months of life. But even colicky babies have a few times each day when they are drowsy and not crying. On these occasions place your baby in the crib and let him learn to self-comfort and self-induce sleep.

- *Carry your baby for at least 3 hours a day when he or she isn't crying.* This practice will reduce fussy crying. In cultures where babies are carried almost continually, crying is rarely seen. A recent Montreal study showed that supplemental carrying reduces crying by over 50 percent. While extra carrying did not increase the hours of sleep per day, it did increase the hours of contented awake time per day.

- *Don't let your baby sleep for more than 3 consecutive hours during the daytime.* Attempt to awaken him gently and entertain him. In this way, the time when your infant sleeps the longest will occur during the night. In general, keep him busy during the day rather than encouraging sleep at this time.

- *Keep daytime feeding intervals to at least 2 hours for newborns.* More frequent daytime feedings (such as hourly) lead to frequent awakenings for small feedings at night. Crying is the only form of communication newborns have. Crying does not always mean your baby is hungry. He may be tired, bored, lonely, or too hot. Hold your baby at these times or put him to bed. Don't let feeding become a pacifier. For every time you nurse your baby, there should be 4 or 5 times that you snuggle your baby *without* nursing. Don't let him get into the bad habit of eating every time you hold him. That's called grazing.

- *Make middle-of-the-night feedings brief and boring.* You want your baby to think of nighttime as a special time for sleeping. When he awakens at night for feedings, don't turn on the lights, talk to him, or rock him. Feed him quickly and quietly. Provide extra rocking and playtime during the day. This approach will lead to longer periods of sleep at night.

- *Don't awaken your infant to change diapers during the night.* Babies can survive until morning with a wet diaper. The exceptions to this rule are soiled diapers at night (which are uncommon) or times when you are treating a bad diaper rash.

If you must change your child, use a flashlight, do it quietly, and don't provide any entertainment.

• *Don't let your baby sleep in your bed.* Once your baby has gained such a privilege, change will be extremely difficult. In addition, a very young infant may fall out of the bed or be hurt by a parent who rolls over upon him. For the first 2 or 3 months, you can keep your baby in a crib next to your bed.

• *Give the last feeding at your bedtime (10 or 11 P.M.).* Try to keep your child awake for the 2 hours before this last feeding. Regularity of bedtime helps your baby organize his sleep. When your baby begins to sleep more than 8 hours, you can shift the bedtime to an earlier hour.

2-MONTH-OLD BABIES

• *Move your baby's crib to a separate room.* By 2 months of age at the latest, your baby should be sleeping in a separate room. This arrangement will help keep the parent who is a light sleeper from being awakened by the rustlings and noises that all babies make during the night. Also, your baby may forget that her parents are available if she can't see you when she awakens. If separate rooms are impractical, at least put up a screen or cover a crib railing with a blanket so your baby can't see your bed.

• *Try to delay middle-of-the-night feedings.* By now, your baby should be down to one feeding during the night. Before preparing a bottle, try holding your baby briefly to see if that will satisfy her. If you must feed her, give 1 or 2 ounces less formula than you would during the day. If you are breast-feeding, nurse for less time at night. As your baby gets close to 4 months of age, try nursing on just one side at night. Never awaken your baby at night for a feeding except at your bedtime.

4-MONTH-OLD BABIES

• *Try to discontinue the 2:00 A.M. feeding before it becomes a habit.* By 4 months of age, your baby does not need to be fed more than 4 times a day (5 times a day for breast-fed babies). If you do not eliminate the night feeding at this time, it will invariably become more difficult to stop with each passing month. Remember to give the last feeding at 10 or 11 P.M. If your child cries during the night, don't feed him; just comfort him with a back rub and some soothing words instead of with a feeding. (Note: Some breast-fed babies who are not gaining well may need to be supplemented with formula or cereal several times during the day to help them go without nursing at nighttime.)

• *Don't allow your baby to hold the bottle or take it to bed with her.* Babies should have the idea that the bottle belongs to the parents. A bottle in bed leads to middle-of-the-night crying, since your baby will inevitably reach for the bottle and find it empty or on the floor.

• *Make any middle-of-the-night contacts brief and boring.* Comfort your child as little as possible between 10 P.M. and 6 A.M. All children have 4 or 5 partial awakenings each night. They need to learn how to go back to sleep on their own. If your baby cries for more than 5 minutes, visit him but don't turn on the light, play with him, or take him out of his crib. Comfort him with a few soothing words and stay for less than 1 minute. This brief contact usually will not be enough to encourage your baby to keep waking you up every night. If your child is standing in the crib, don't try to make him lie down. He can do this himself. If the crying continues, you can check your baby every 15 to 20 minutes, but do not take him out of the crib nor stay in the room until he goes to sleep. (Exceptions: You feel your baby is sick or afraid.)

6-MONTH-OLD INFANTS

• *Provide a friendly, soft toy for your child to hold in the crib.* Six months is the age when separation anxiety begins. If you haven't already helped your child bond with a teddy bear or "horsey," it's time to do so. This security object will provide comfort when your child awakens during the night.

• *Leave the door to your baby's room open.* Children with separation anxiety become very fearful when they are in a closed space and are not sure that their parents are still available to them.

• *During the day, respond to separation fears with holding and reassurance.* The extra physical contact will reduce nighttime fears. This step is especially important for mothers who work outside the home.

• *For middle-of-the-night fears, make contacts prompt and reassuring.* For mild nighttime fears, check on your child promptly and be reassuring, but keep the interaction as brief as possible. If your child panics when you leave or vomits with crying, stay in your child's room until she is either calm or goes to sleep. Do not take her out of the crib, but provide whatever else she needs for comfort, keeping the light off and not talking too much. At most, sit next to the crib with your hand on her. These measures will calm even a severely upset infant.

- *Don't put your baby to sleep before she has met the baby-sitter.* If a young infant unexpectedly awakens during the night and is responded to by a baby-sitter she doesn't know, she will usually become extremely fearful and develop sleep problems that continue for several weeks. If you are using a new sitter, bring him or her over during the day to play with your child or at least 1 hour before your time of departure.

1-YEAR-OLD CHILDREN

- *Establish a pleasant and predictable bedtime ritual.* While bedtime rituals can start in the early months, they become very important to the child by 1 year of age. Children need a familiar routine and a pleasant story. Both parents can be involved at bedtime, taking turns with reading stories or making them up. Both parents should kiss and hug the child good-night. Finish the bedtime ritual before your child falls asleep.

- *Once put to bed, your child should stay there.* Some older infants have bedtime temper tantrums. They may protest about bedtime or even refuse to lie down. You should overlook these protests and leave the room. You can ignore any ongoing questions or demands your child makes and solely enforce the rule that your child can't leave the bedroom. If your child comes out, return him quickly and avoid any conversation. If you respond to his protests in this way every time, he will learn not to try to prolong bedtime.

- *If your child has nightmares or bedtime fears, sit with her briefly and reassure her.* In contrast to manipulative behavior, never punish or ignore fears. Everyone has 4 or 5 dreams a night. Some of these are good dreams and some are bad dreams. If nightmares become frequent, the cause is often that your child has watched a violent television show or an R-rated movie.

- *Don't worry about noises or movements during your child's sleep.* During dreams, children often display face-twitching, fist-clenching, or even eye-rolling. Many people have muscle jerks while dozing off to sleep. Keep in mind how a dog acts as it chases a rabbit during its dream state. Overall, anything short of not breathing is probably normal sleep behavior.

- *Don't worry about the amount of sleep your child is getting.* Sleep requirements vary greatly among different people and at different ages. The best assurance that your child is getting adequate sleep is that he or she is not fatigued or tired during the day. Naps are important to young children, but keep them less than 2 hours each. Children give up their morning naps between 1½ and 2 years of age and their afternoon naps between 3 and 6 years of age. Some children may choose to substitute a "rest period" for the afternoon nap. If the "rest period" is discontinued before 5 years of age, most children can't stay awake (or "civilized") until their regular bedtime.

- *Switch from a crib to a bed at age 2 or 2½.* Change sooner if your child learns how to climb out of a crib with the springs at the lowest setting. Climb-proofing a crib can't be done. The next attempt at climbing out could result in a serious head injury. Until you find a bed, keep the crib railing down and place a chair next to the crib so your child can descend safely. Don't buy bunk beds. They have a terrible accident rate with children of all ages. A good first bed is a mattress and box spring placed on the floor without a frame.

NIGHT AWAKENING IN OLDER INFANTS

CHARACTERISTICS

- Your child is 4 to 24 months old. Babies normally awaken at night 1 or more times during the first 4 months of life

- Awakens and cries once or several times per night

- Receives food, attention, or entertainment at this time

- Usually occurs every night

- Usually has been present since birth

- Occurs in 10 percent to 15 percent of babies

• You would like to help your baby sleep through the night

If your child's symptoms are different, call your child's physician for help.

Similar Topic • If colic is suspected, save time by turning directly to the guideline for CRYING BABY (COLIC), page 239.

Causes • The causes of resisting sleep or nighttime crying are many. While all children (especially during the first year of life) awaken several times per night following dreams, most can put themselves back to sleep. The ones who have not learned how to do this will instead cry for a parent. If the parent does too much (for instance, rocking), the infant becomes dependent on the parent for help in returning to sleep. If the parent plays with the baby at these hours (which is a secondary gain), the child may elect to have such fun and games every night. These infants can be called "trained night criers" (see ROCKING and PROVIDING ENTERTAINMENT, below). The infants who demand to be fed as well as held can be called "trained night feeders" (see the first three paragraphs below). After 6 months of age, many infants have their normal separation fears accentuated at bedtime and during the night (see SEPARATION FEARS, below). These infants can be called "fearful night criers." The last three causes mentioned below can contribute to all three types of sleep problems.

Frequent Daytime Feedings • Some mothers misinterpret *demand feedings* to mean "feed the baby every time he cries." This can lead to feeding every 30 to 60 minutes. The stomach becomes conditioned to being fed small amounts frequently, instead of waiting at least 2 hours between feedings at birth (and at least 4 hours by 4 months of age). This problem usually occurs in breast-fed babies if nursing is offered for any distress and the breast becomes a pacifier.

Leaving a Bottle in the Bed • Periodically during the night the child sucks on the bottle. When it becomes empty, he or she awakens fully and cries for a refill. In addition to sleep problems, bottles in bed (unless they contain only water) can lead to severe dental caries—known as "baby-bottle caries"—or ear infections.

Nursing the Baby to Sleep • If the last memory before sleep is sucking, the breast or bottle can become the infant's transitional object. (A transitional object is something that helps a waking child cross over into sleep—a teddy bear, for instance.) When he reawakens, the child may think that he cannot return to sleep without being on the breast.

Rocking the Baby to Sleep • Rocking your baby as part of the bedtime routine is great. However, some mothers continue to rock their infants until they go to sleep, even when they are not crying. Infants who have rarely been placed in their cribs while still awake expect their mothers to appear and help them go back to sleep when they awaken normally during the night. Instead of going back to sleep on their own, they cry. Since they customarily fall asleep away from their cribs, they never learn to associate the crib with sleeping.

Providing Entertainment During the Night • The awakening and crying behavior can become frequent if it leads to major secondary gain, such as being walked, rocked, played with, or enjoying other prolonged contact with the parent. Sleeping in the parents' bed reinforces the problem. Trained night crying can also follow an acute illness (e.g., blocked nasal passages) or a change in the infant's sleep environment (perhaps while traveling) during which the parents temporarily provide increased nighttime attention. Many infants quickly settle back into their previous sleep patterns, but some enjoy the nighttime contact so much that they continue in their demands.

Separation Fears • Separation anxiety normally occurs between 6 months and 2 years of age. It is seen during the day whenever the child loses sight of the mother or is left with a sitter, and these fears are often accentuated at bedtime and during the night. Separation fears can become the main content of nightmares.

Changing Diapers During the Night • Some parents check the baby's diaper during the night. If it is wet, they change it. The infant learns to find wetness uncomfortable, and thereafter cries at night whenever he or she is wet.

Excessive Daytime Naps • A baby can sleep only a certain number of hours a day.

Sleeping in the Same Room • Some babies are noisy sleepers. Also, many parents are light sleepers and respond to these normal baby noises. The father who wants his sleep may also pressure the mother to quiet the baby immediately. In addition, a baby who can see his or her parents has an incentive to continue trying to arouse them.

Expected Course • Most babies from birth to 2 months normally awaken twice a night for feedings. Between 2 and 3 months, most need 1 middle-of-the-night feeding. By 4 months of age, some 90 percent can sleep more than 8 consecutive hours without feeding. The remainder can learn to sleep through the night if the recommendations given below, under HELPING YOUR BABY SLEEP THROUGH THE NIGHT, are implemented. Improvement usually occurs in 2 weeks. The older the child, the harder his habits are to change. Infants over 1 year of age will vigorously protest any change and may cry for hours. Without treatment, however, these children don't start sleeping through the night until 3 or 4 years of age, when busy daytime schedules finally exhaust them.

HELPING YOUR BABY SLEEP THROUGH THE NIGHT

Select the aspects of treatment that correspond with the causes of your baby's sleep problem. If your baby is fed during the night, deal with this first (see TRAINED NIGHT FEEDERS, below). If he or she does not awaken for food, go directly to TRAINED NIGHT CRIERS. If your baby is very fearful, vomits, or cries nonstop for hours, start with FEARFUL NIGHT CRIERS. The last group of recommendations below apply to all three types.

Trained Night Feeders • If your child is over 4 months of age and wants to be fed during the night, deal with this problem first.

1. *Lengthen the time between daytime feedings to 4 hours or more.* Nighttime feeding intervals cannot be extended if the daytime intervals are short. If a baby's stomach is conditioned to expect frequent feedings during the day, he will have hunger pangs during the night. This bad habit is called grazing. It often happens to mothers who don't separate holding from nursing. For every time you nurse your baby, there should be 4 or 5 times that you snuggle your baby without nursing. Gradually postpone daytime feeding times until they are more normal for your child's age. If you currently feed your baby hourly, go to 1½ hours. When this is accepted, go

to 2 hours. When he cries, provide cuddling or a pacifier. Your goal for formula-fed babies is 4 meals each day by 4 months of age. (Breast-fed babies often need 5 feedings each day until 6 months of age, when baby foods are introduced.)

2. *Place your baby in the crib drowsy but awake.* When your baby starts to act drowsy, stop feeding him and place him in the crib. His last waking memory needs to be of the crib, not of the breast or bottle. He needs to learn to put himself to sleep. He will need this self-quieting skill to cope with normal awakenings at night. This change will require some crying. For crying, go to your child every 15 minutes, but don't feed him or lift him out of the crib. Give him a hug and leave. Stay for less than a minute. Help him learn to self-initiate sleep at naps and bedtime, when you can better tolerate the crying. For middle-of-the-night crying, you can rock him to sleep for now.

3. *Discontinue any bottle in bed immediately.* If you feed your child at bedtime, don't let her hold the bottle. Also feed her in a different room than the bedroom. Try to separate mealtime and naptime. If your baby needs to suck on something to help her go to sleep, offer a pacifier or help her find a thumb. Also encourage attachment to a favorite stuffed animal or blanket.

4. *Phase out night feedings.* For now, after the 10 or 11 P.M. last feeding of the day, only feed your baby once during the night, and make it brief and boring. If it takes more than 20 minutes, handling or burping is excessive. For other awakenings at night, rock your child to sleep.

After the daytime feeding intervals are normal, gradually start to reduce the amount you feed your baby at night. For bottle-fed babies, the amount of formula you give can be decreased by one ounce every few nights until your infant no longer has a craving for food at night. Nurse breast-fed babies on just one side and for fewer minutes.

Trained Night Criers • If your baby is over 4 months of age, cries during the night, calms down when you hold her, and doesn't need to be fed, you have a trained night crier.

1. *Place your baby in the crib drowsy but awake at naps and bedtime.* It's good to hold babies. But when your baby starts to look drowsy, place him in the crib. His last waking memory needs to be of the crib, not of you. He needs to learn to put himself to sleep. If your baby is very fussy, rock him until he settles down or is almost asleep, but stop before he's fully asleep.

2. *For crying at naps and bedtime, make brief contact every 15 minutes.* Infants cannot learn to self-comfort without some crying. This crying is not harmful. If the crying continues, visit your baby in the crib every 15 minutes. Don't stay longer than 1 minute. Act sleepy. Whisper, "Shhh, be quiet, everyone's sleeping." Add a few reassuring comments and give some gentle pats. Do not turn on the lights or remove your child from the crib. Do not rock or play with the baby, bring her to your bed, or stay in the room for more than 1 minute. Most young infants will cry for 30 to 90 minutes and then fall asleep. If the crying persists, you may recheck your baby every 15 minutes, for 1 minute or less each visit. This brief contact will not reward your baby sufficiently to perpetuate the behavior.

3. *For middle-of-the-night crying, rock your baby to sleep temporarily.* Until your child learns how to put himself to sleep at naps and bedtime, make the middle of the night as easy as possible. Take your crying child out of the crib and rock him to sleep. However, don't talk to him, leave the room, or turn on the lights. After he has learned to quiet himself for naps and bedtime, you can place the same demands on him for middle-of-the-night crying—namely, go to him every 15 minutes, but make your contact brief and boring. By then this problem can be turned around in a few nights.

Fearful Night Criers. • If your child is between 6 and 18 months of age and has daytime separation fears when you leave him, treat his sleep problem as follows:

1. *Stay with your child if he is fearful.* At bedtime and naptime, put your child in the crib drowsy but awake. Stay as long as it takes to calm him, but don't lift him out of the crib. At the most, sit in a chair next to the crib with your hand on his body. A headphone with some good music may help you pass the time. Make a few reassuring comments initially, then don't talk to him. If it's the middle of the night, consider going to sleep in a sleeping bag in your child's room.

2. *Leave briefly every 15 minutes.* Leave for 1 or 2 minutes every now and then to teach your child that separation is tolerable because you do come back. Leave the door open and a night light on if your child has separation fears.

3. *Provide lots of holding during the day.* During the day, respond to your child's fears with lots of hugs and comforting. Young babies may need more time being carried about in a

front sling or backpack. Children of mothers working outside the home need extra attention and cuddling in the evenings. Also play separation games like peekaboo, hide-and-seek, or chase me. Fears and insecurities can be completely treated during the day.

Steps to Take for All Types of Sleep Problems • Whether your baby's problem is trained night feeding, trained night crying, or fearful night crying, the following measures should be helpful:

1. *Move the crib to another room.* If the crib is in your bedroom, move it to a separate room. If this is impossible, cover one of the side rails with a blanket so your baby can't see you when he awakens.
2. *Eliminate long daytime naps.* If your baby has napped for more than 2 hours, awaken her. If she is in the habit of taking 3 naps during the day, try to change her habit to 2 naps each day.
3. *Don't change wet diapers during the night.* Change the diaper if it is soiled or if you are treating a bad diaper rash. If you must change your child, use as little light as possible (e.g., use a flashlight), do it quietly, and don't provide any entertainment.
4. *If he's standing up in the crib, leave him in that position.* Don't try to get him to lie down every time you go in. He will just spring back up as you start toward the door. He can lie down without your help. Soon encouraging him to lie down becomes a game.

CALL YOUR CHILD'S PHYSICIAN DURING OFFICE HOURS IF

• You feel the crying has a physical cause (e.g., an earache).

• Your child acts sick.

• Someone in your family can't tolerate any crying.

• Your infant's sleeping habits aren't improved after 2 weeks with this approach.

• You have other questions or concerns.

RECOMMENDED READING
Joanne Cuthbertson and Susanna Schevill, *Helping Your Child Sleep Through the Night*
(Garden City, N.Y.: Doubleday, 1985).

Richard Ferber, *Solve Your Child's Sleep Problem*
(New York: Simon & Schuster, 1985).

BEDTIME RESISTANCE

CHARACTERISTICS

- Children over age 2 who refuse to go to bed or stay in the bedroom.

- These children can come out of the bedroom because they no longer sleep in a crib.

- In the usual form, the child goes to sleep while watching TV with the parent or sleeps in the parent's bed.

- In a milder form, the child stays in his bedroom but prolongs the bedtime interaction with ongoing questions, unreasonable requests, protests, crying, or temper tantrums.

- In the morning, these children sleep late or have to be awakened.

- Over age 2.

Cause • These are attempts to test the limits, not fear. Your child has found a good way to postpone bedtime and receive extra entertainment and is stalling and taking advantage of your good nature. If given a choice, over 90 percent of children would stay up until their parents' bedtime. These children also often try to share the parents' bed at bedtime or sneak into their parents' bed during the middle of the night. By contrast, the child who comes to the parents' bed if he is frightened or not feeling well should be supported at these times.

ENDING BEDTIME RESISTANCE

Start the Night with a Pleasant Bedtime Ritual • Provide a bedtime routine that is pleasant and predictable. Most prebedtime rituals last about 30 minutes and include taking a bath, brushing teeth, reading stories, talking about the day, saying prayers, and other interactions that relax your child. Try to keep the same sequence each night because familiarity is comforting for children. Try to have both parents take turns in creating this special experience. Never cancel this ritual because of misbehavior earlier in the day. Before you give your last hug and kiss and leave your child's bedroom, ask, "Do you need anything else?"

Establish a Rule That Your Child Can't Leave the Bedroom at Night • Enforce the rule that once the bedtime ritual is over and your child is placed in the bedroom, he cannot leave that room. Your child needs to learn to put himself to sleep for naps and at bedtime in his own bed. Do not stay in the room until he lies down or falls asleep. Parents can't force a child to fall asleep. Establish a set bedtime and stick to it. Make it clear that your child is not allowed to leave the bedroom between 8:00 at night and 7:00 in the morning (or whatever sleep time you decide upon). Obviously, this change won't be accomplished without some crying or screaming for a few nights.

If your child has been sleeping with you, tell him "Starting tonight, we sleep in separate beds. You have your room, we have our room. You have your bed, we have our bed. You are too old to sleep with us anymore."

Ignore Verbal Requests • Despite ongoing questions or demands from the bedroom, do not engage in any conversation with your child. All of these requests should have been dealt with during your prebedtime ritual. Don't return or talk with your child, unless you think he is sick. Some exceptions: If your child says he needs to use the toilet, tell him to take care of it himself. If your child says his covers have fallen off and he is cold, promise him you will cover him up after he goes to sleep. You will usually find him well covered.

Close the Bedroom Door if Your Child Screams • For screaming from the bedroom, tell your child, "I'm sorry I have to close your door. I'll open it as soon as you're quiet." If he pounds on the door, you can open it after 1 or 2 minutes, and suggest that he go back to bed. If he does, you can leave the door open. If he doesn't, close the door again. For continued screaming or pounding on the door, reopen it approximately every 15 minutes and tell your child that if he quiets down the door can stay open. Never spend more than 30 seconds reassuring him.

Close the Bedroom Door if Your Child Comes Out • If your child comes out of the bedroom, return him immediately to his bed. During this process, avoid any lectures and skip the hug and kiss. Get good eye contact and remind him again that he cannot leave his bedroom during the night. Warn him that if he comes out again, you're sorry but you will need to close the door. If he comes out, close the door. Tell him, "I'll be happy to open your door as soon as you're in your bed." If your child says he's in his bed, open the door. If he says nothing, every 10 to 15 minutes open the door just enough to ask your child if he's in his bed now.

Barricade or Lock the Bedroom Door for Repeated Coming Out • If your child is very determined and continues to come out of the bedroom, consider putting a barricade in front of his door, such as a strong gate. A half-door or plywood plank may also serve this purpose. If your child makes a ruckus at night, you can go to him without taking him out of his bedroom and say, "Everyone is sleeping, I'll see you in the morning."

If your child learns to climb over the barricade, a full door may need to be kept closed until morning with a hook, piece of rope, or chain lock. While you may consider this step extreme, it can be critical for protecting children less than 5 years old who wander through the house at night without an understanding of dangers (such as the stove, hot water, electricity, knives, going outdoors, etc.).

If your child does not get into trouble at night, you can open the door as soon as he falls asleep. Reassure him that you will do this. Also, each night give him a fresh chance to stay in the bedroom with the door open. (**Caution:** If your child has bedtime fears, don't close his door. Get him some counseling.)

Return Him to His Bed if He Comes into Your Bed at Night • For middle-of-the-night attempts to crawl into your bed, unless your child is fearful, sternly order your child back to his own bed. If he doesn't move, escort him back immediately without any physical contact or pleasant conversation. If you are asleep when your child crawls into your bed, return him as soon as you discover his presence. If he attempts to come out again, temporarily close his door. If you are a deep sleeper, consider using some signaling device that will awaken you if your child enters your bedroom (such as a chair placed against your door or a loud bell attached to your doorknob). Some parents simply lock their bedroom door. Remind your child that it is not polite to interrupt other people's sleep. Tell him that if he awakens at night and can't go back to sleep, he can read or play quietly in his room, but he is not to bother his parents.

Help the Roommate • If the bedtime screaming wakes up a roommate, have the well-behaved sibling sleep in a separate room until the nighttime behavior has improved. Tell your child with the sleep problem that his roommate cannot return until he stays in his room quietly for 3 consecutive nights. If you have a small home, have the sibling sleep in your room temporarily; this will be an added incentive for your other child to improve.

Praise Appropriate Sleeping Behavior • Praise your child in the morning if he stayed in his bedroom all night. Tell him that people are happier when they get a good night's sleep. If he fought bedtime and fell asleep late, wake him up at the regular time so he will be tired earlier the next evening.

Start Bedtime Later if You Want to Minimize Bedtime Crying • The later the bedtime, the more tired your child will be and the less resistance he will offer. For most children, you can pick the bedtime hour. For children who are very stubborn and cry a lot, you may want to start the bedtime at 10:00 P.M. (or whenever your child naturally falls asleep). If the bedtime is at 10:00 P.M., start the bedtime ritual at 9:30 P.M. After your child learns to fall asleep without fussing at 10:00 P.M., move the bedtime back by 15 minutes every week. In children who can't tell time, you can gradually (over 8 weeks or so) achieve an 8:00 P.M. bedtime in this way with much less tantrums (this technique was described by Adams and Rickert in 1989). However, don't let your child sleep late in the morning or you won't be able to advance the bedtime.

CALL YOUR CHILD'S PHYSICIAN DURING OFFICE HOURS IF

- Your child is not sleeping well after trying this program for 2 weeks.

- Your child needs to be locked in the bedroom for more than 7 nights. (He probably needs some counseling.)

- Your child is frightened at bedtime.

- Your child has lots of nightmares.

- Your child also has several discipline problems during the day.

- You have other questions or concerns.

SLEEPING WITH THE PARENTS (BED-SHARING)

In general, I don't recommend bed-sharing. While it's not harmful for your children to sleep with you, it's unnecessary. And it may be bad for you. Once begun, it's rather hard to undo, so don't start until you have all the facts.

1. *Your child doesn't need this arrangement to be secure and happy.* Children's fears and insecurities can be dealt with during the day. The majority of children in our country sleep happily in their own bed. In poor countries, families sleep together by necessity.
2. *Bed-sharing is not quality time.* If your child is asleep in your bed, it is neutral time. If your child is crying and keeping you awake, it is aggravating time. So there is really no quality time here.
3. *Several studies have shown that over 50 percent of children who sleep with parents resist going to bed and awaken several times at night.* Most parents who bed-share have to lie down with their child for 30 minutes to get them to sleep. Most of these parents also do not get a good night's sleep.
4. *Bed-sharing is never a long-term solution to sleep problems.* Your child will not learn to sleep well in your bed and then decide on his own to start sleeping in his bed. With every passing month, the habit becomes harder to change.

Prevention of Bed-Sharing

- Place your child in the crib drowsy but awake. In this way he will learn to put himself back to sleep following normal awakenings.

- Make middle-of-the-night feedings brief and boring. This is hard to do if you are sleeping with your child.

- Put your child in his own room by 3 or 4 months of age. Have a rule that he does not leave the crib at night, and after age 2, that he does not leave the bedroom. Most children in our country follow these guidelines and do just fine.

Putting an End to Bed-Sharing • If you are sleeping with your child and want to change it, here are some suggestions:

- Tell your child the new rule. "You are too old to sleep with us anymore. You have your bed, and we have our bed. Starting tonight, we want you to stay in your bed during the night."

- If your child leaves his bedroom, return him immediately. If he does it again, close the door until he's in his bed.

- If he crawls into your bed during the night, order him back to his own bed, using a stern voice. If he doesn't move, escort him back immediately without any conversation.

- If you are asleep when he crawls into your bed, return him as soon as you discover him. If he attempts to come out again, temporarily close his door. If you are a deep sleeper, consider using some signaling device that will awaken you if your child enters your bedroom (such as a chair placed against your door or a loud bell attached to your doorknob). Some parents simply lock their bedroom door. Remind your child that "it is not polite to interrupt people who are sleeping."

- Expect some crying. Young children normally cry when they don't get their way.

NIGHTMARES

Definition • Nightmares are scary dreams that awaken a child. Occasional bad dreams are normal at all ages after about 6 months of age. When infants have a nightmare, they cry and scream until someone comes to them. When preschoolers have a nightmare, they usually cry and run into their parents' bedroom. Older children begin to understand what a nightmare is and put themselves back to sleep without waking their parents.

Cause • Everyone dreams 4 or 5 times each night. Some dreams are good, some are bad. Dreams help the mind process complicated events or information. The content of nightmares usually relates to developmental challenges: Toddlers have nightmares about separation from their parents; preschoolers, about monsters or the dark; and school-age children, about death or real dangers. Frequent nightmares may be caused by violent TV shows or movies.

Dealing with Nightmares

1. *Reassure and cuddle your child.* Explain to your child that she was having a bad dream. Sit on the bed until she is calm. Offer to leave the bedroom door open (never close the door on a fearful child). Provide a night-light, especially if your child has fears of the dark. Most children return to sleep fairly quickly.

2. *Help your child talk about the bad dreams during the day.* Your child may not remember what the dream was about unless you can remind him of something he said about it when he woke up. If your child was dreaming about falling or being chased, reassure him that lots of children dream about that. If your child has the same bad dream over and over again, help him imagine a good ending to the bad dream. Encourage your child to use a strong person or a magic weapon to help him overcome the bad person or event in the dream. You may want to help your child draw pictures or write stories about the new, happier ending for the dream. Working through a bad fear often takes several conversations about it.

3. *Protect your child against frightening movies and TV shows.* For many children, violent or horror movies cause bedtime fears and nightmares. These fears can persist for months or years. Absolutely forbid these movies before 13 years of age. Between 13 and 17 years, the maturity and sensitivity of your child must be considered carefully in deciding when he is ready to deal with the uncut versions of R-rated movies. Be vigilant about slumber parties or Halloween parties. Tell your child to call you if the family he is visiting is showing scary movies.

CALL YOUR CHILD'S PHYSICIAN DURING OFFICE HOURS IF

- The nightmares become worse.
- The nightmares are not minimal after using this approach for 2 weeks.
- The fear interferes with daytime activities.
- Your child has several fears.
- You have other concerns or questions.

NIGHT TERRORS

Definition

- Your child is frightened but cannot be awakened or comforted.

- Your child is agitated and may sit up or run helplessly about, possibly screaming or talking wildly.

- Your child doesn't appear to realize that you are there. Although the eyes are wide open and staring, your child looks right through you.

- Your child may mistake objects or persons in the room for dangers.

- The episode lasts from 10 to 30 minutes.

- Your child cannot remember the episode in the morning (amnesia).

- The child is usually 1 to 8 years old.

Cause • Night terrors are an inherited disorder in which a child tends to have dreams during deep sleep from which it is difficult to awaken. They occur in 2 percent of children and usually are not caused by psychological stress. Getting overtired can trigger night terrors, so be sure your child goes to bed at a reasonable time. For younger children, consider having them return to a daily nap.

Expected Course • Night terrors usually occur within 2 hours of bedtime. Night terrors are harmless, and each episode will end of its own accord in deep sleep. The problem usually disappears by age 12 or sooner.

Dealing with Night Terrors

1. *Try to help your child return to normal sleep.* Your goal is to help your child go from agitated sleep to a calm sleep. You won't be able to awaken your child, so don't try to. Turn on the lights so he is less confused by shadows. Make soothing comments such as "You are all right. You are home in your own bed. You can rest now." Speak slowly and repetitively. Such comments are usually better than silence. Some children like to have their hand held during this time, but most will

pull away. Hold your child only if it seems to help him feel better. There is no way to shorten the episode abruptly. Shaking or shouting at your child will just cause him to become more agitated and will prolong the attack.

2. *Protect your child against injury.* During a night terror, a child can fall down a stairway, run into a wall, or break a window. Gently try to direct your child back to bed.

3. *Prepare baby-sitters or overnight leaders for these episodes.* Explain to people who care for your child what a night terror is and what to do if one happens. Understanding this will prevent them from overreacting if your child has a night terror.

4. *Try to prevent night terrors with prompted awakenings.* If your child has frequent night terrors, Dr. B. Lask of London has found a new way to eliminate this distressing sleep pattern in 90 percent of children. For several nights, note how many minutes elapse from falling asleep to the onset of the night terror. Then awaken your child 15 minutes before the expected time. Keep your child fully awake and out of bed for 5 minutes. Carry out these prompted awakenings for 7 consecutive nights. If the night terrors return, repeat this 7-night program.

CALL YOUR CHILD'S PHYSICIAN DURING OFFICE HOURS IF

- Any drooling, jerking, or stiffening occurs.

- The episodes occur two or more times per week after doing the 7 prompted awakenings.

- Episodes last longer than 30 minutes.

- Your child does something dangerous during an episode.

- Episodes occur during the second half of the night.

- Your child has several daytime fears.

- You feel family stress may be a factor.

- You have other questions or concerns.

SLEEPWALKING

Definition

- Your child walks while asleep.

- Your child's eyes are open but blank.

- Your child is not as well coordinated as when awake.

- Your child may perform semipurposeful acts such as dressing and undressing, opening and closing doors, or turning lights on and off.

- The episode may last 5 to 20 minutes.

- During this time the child cannot be awakened no matter what the parent does.

- The child is usually 4 to 15 years old.

Cause • Sleepwalking is an inherited tendency to wander during deep sleep. About 15 percent of normal children sleepwalk.

Expected Course • Sleepwalking usually occurs within 2 hours of bedtime. Children stop sleepwalking during adolescence.

Dealing with Sleepwalking

1. *Gently lead your child back to bed.* First, steer your child into the bathroom, because he may be looking for a place to urinate. Then guide him to his bedroom. The episode may end once he's in bed. Don't expect to awaken him, however, before he returns to normal sleep.
2. *Protect your child from accidents.* Although accidents are rare, they do happen, especially if the child wanders outside. Sleepwalkers can be hit by a car or bitten by a dog, or they may become lost. Put gates on your stairways and special locks on your outside doors (above your child's reach). Avoid having your child sleep in the upper part of a bunk bed.
3. *Help your child avoid exhaustion.* Fatigue and lack of sleep can lead to more frequent sleepwalking. So be sure your child goes to bed at a reasonable hour, especially when ill or exhausted.
4. *Try prompted awakenings to prevent sleepwalking.* If your child has frequent sleepwalking, try to eliminate this distress-

ing sleep pattern. For several nights, note how many minutes elapse from falling asleep to the onset of the sleepwalking. Then awaken your child 15 minutes before the expected time. Keep your child fully awake for 5 minutes. Carry out these prompted awakenings for 7 consecutive nights. If the sleepwalking returns, repeat this 7-night program.

EARLY-MORNING RISER

Some children awaken before their parents do, usually between 5:00 and 6:00 A.M. The children are well rested and raring to go. They come out of their room or call out from the crib and want everyone to wake up. They are excited about the new day and want to share it with you. If people don't respond, they make a racket. Such a child is a morning person.

Causes • Most of these children have received plenty of sleep. They are no longer tired. They are not awakening early on purpose. Most of them were put to bed too early the night before, had too many naps, or had naps that were too long. Some of them have a reduced sleep requirement—one that is below the average of 10 to 12 hours a night. Such children often have a parent who needs only 6 hours or so of sleep at night. Other children may begin awakening early in the springtime because of sunlight streaming through their window. (This scenario is easily remedied with dark shades or curtains.) Finally, those children who are fed an early breakfast or allowed to come into their parents' bed early in the morning develop a bad habit that persists after the original cause is removed.

Home Care

1. *Reduce naps.* Assume your child is getting too much sleep during the day. Most children over 1 year of age need only one nap (unless they are sick). If cutting back to one nap doesn't help, shorten the nap to 1½ hours maximum. Also make sure your child gets plenty of exercise after his nap, so he'll be tired at night.
2. *Delay bedtime until 8:00 P.M. or 9:00 P.M.* These two steps should cure your child unless he has a below-average sleep requirement.

3. *Establish a rule.* "You can't leave your bedroom until your parents are up. You can play quietly in your bedroom until breakfast." Also tell your child, "It's not polite to wake up someone who is sleeping. Your parents need their sleep."

4. *If your child is in a crib, leave him there until 6:00 A.M.* Put some toys in his crib the night before (but not ones he can stand on). If he cries, go in once to reassure him and remind him of the toys. Don't include any surprises or treats in his toy bag, or he'll awaken early, as children do on holiday mornings. If he makes loud noises with the toys, remove those particular toys. If he cries, ignore it. If crying continues, visit him briefly every 15 minutes to reassure him that all is well and most people are sleeping. Don't turn on the lights, talk much, remove him from his crib, or stay more than 1 minute.

5. *If your child is in a floor-level bed, keep him in his bedroom until 6:00 A.M.* Get him a clock radio and set it for 6:00 A.M. Tell him he can't leave his bedroom until the music comes on. Tell him he can play quietly until then. Help him put out special toys or books the night before. If he comes out of his room, put up a gate or close the door. Tell him that you'll be happy to open the door as soon as he is back in his bed. If this is a chronic problem, put up the gate the night before.

6. *If you meet strong resistance, change the wake-up time gradually.* Some children protest a great deal about the new rule, especially if they have been coming into your bed in the morning. In that case, move ahead a little more gradually. If he's been awakening at 5:00 A.M., help him wait until 5:15 for 3 days. Set the clock radio for that time. After your child has adjusted to 5:15, change the clock radio to 5:30. Move the wake-up time forward every 3 or 4 days.

7. *Praise your child for not waking other people in the morning.* A star chart or special treat at breakfast may help your child wait more cooperatively.

8. *Change your tactics for weekends.* Many parents want their child to sleep in on Saturday and Sunday mornings. If this is your preference, keep your early-morning riser up an hour later the night before. If you are using a clock radio with your program, turn it off or reset the time for an hour later. As a last resort, put a breakfast together for your child the night before and allow him to watch a preselected videotape.

SLEEP PROBLEMS: OTHER STRATEGIES

Climbs Out of the Crib

Premise: Once a child climbs out of a crib with the springs on the lowest setting, he or she will definitely try to climb out again and eventually will fall and possibly get hurt.

Response: Correct this hazard on the same day your child climbs out. One solution is to put your child's mattress on the floor. Another is to leave your child in the crib with the crib railing down and a chair next to the bed so he or she can easily get out. Eventually you can transfer your child to a floor-level bed.

Won't Take a Nap

The rule: "Don't leave your room during quiet time." Every day after lunch, you or your child's caretaker can expect him to spend 60 to 90 minutes resting in his room. During this time he may read but not turn on the radio or TV.

Discipline technique: Return your child to his room if he comes out before 60 to 90 minutes is up. If he comes out a second time, close the door temporarily.

Is Negative at Bedtime

Examples: Your child refuses to put on her pajamas, lie down, close her eyes, or stay in bed.

The rule: "Stay in your bedroom after we put you to bed."

Discipline technique: Natural consequences. Your child will eventually become tired and go to sleep. Your child can't be forced to fall asleep. Insisting on any of the actions mentioned above is unnecessary—it doesn't matter if your child sleeps on the floor in her daytime clothing.

Two Children Play and Talk in the Bedroom After Bedtime

The rule: "After bedtime you have to be quiet so that your mind will be able to go to sleep."

Discipline technique: Logical consequences. For every night that children stay up, fight, play, or make noise, they will be put to bed 15 minutes earlier the following night. If one child in particular tries to keep the other one up, that child can be sent to bed 1 hour earlier.

Praise your children: (On the following morning) for going to sleep without a fuss.

Wanders or Prowls About During the Night

Examples: Some children awaken during the night and move about the house getting into trouble. They may raid the refrigerator or leave it open. They may watch TV, or turn on the stove or water faucet. Unlike sleepwalkers, they are awake.

The rule: "If you wake up during the night, except for going to the bathroom, you have to stay in your room."

Discipline technique: Nighttime restriction to the bedroom. Because of the safety issues, until children are safety-conscious, (namely, at 4 or 5 years of age) they need a barricade to keep them in their bedrooms. This can be a gate, plywood plank, or locked door. A chain lock (hotel lock) can keep your child in the room yet allow him to open the door partially in case he needs to cry out for someone. If your child is one who needs to urinate during the night, a pot can be placed in his room. After 4 years of age most children will stay in their rooms if they awaken early and have been told they're expected to stay and play quietly.

Wants to Choose His or Her Own Bedtime

Assumption: Adolescents should be able to take care of their own sleep requirements before going off to college.

The rule: "Stay up as late as you want, but it's your responsibility to get yourself up in the morning with an alarm clock and to get to school on time. Also, you can't make any noise after the rest of the family has turned in."

Discipline technique: Natural consequences.

DISCIPLINE

DISCIPLINE BASICS

GOALS OF DISCIPLINE

The first goal of discipline is to protect your child from danger. Another very important goal is to teach your child an understanding of right from wrong. Good discipline gradually changes a self-centered child into a mature adult who is responsible, thoughtful, and respectful of others, assertive without being hostile, and in control of his or her impulses. Reasonable limit-setting keeps us from raising a spoiled child (see pages 271–277). Discipline means to teach, not to punish. To teach respect for the rights of others, first teach your child to respect your rights. Children need a parent who is "in charge." Begin external controls by 4 months of age when you gradually change from a demand schedule of feeding to fitting your child into your schedule. Children don't start to develop internal controls (self-control) until 3 or 4 years of age. They continue to need external controls (in gradually decreasing amounts) through adolescence.

HOW TO BEGIN A DISCIPLINE PROGRAM

If your child has several discipline problems or is out of control, start here. If you are reading to learn more about normal discipline, go directly to GUIDELINES FOR SETTING RULES, on page 271.

1. *List problem behaviors.* What do you want to change? Take 3 or 4 days to note and write down your child's inappropriate or annoying behavior traits.

2. *Set priorities on correcting the problem behavior.* Some modes of behavior need immediate attention—for instance, those that might cause harm to your child or others. Some are too annoying or obnoxious to be ignored (such as not going to bed). Some instances of unpleasant behavior (such as negativism) are normal and must be tolerated (see TERRIBLE TWOS AND STUBBORN TODDLERS, page 290). Some families who have an out-of-control child have too many rules and need to rethink what can be overlooked.

3. *Write house rules concerning the most important kinds of misbehavior* (see GUIDELINES FOR SETTING RULES, below).

4. *Devise a discipline response for each type of misbehavior* (see DISCIPLINE TECHNIQUES [INCLUDING CONSEQUENCES], page 272). All behavior, regardless of cause, can be changed. Behavior is predominantly shaped by consequences. If the consequence is pleasant (a reward or praise), behavior is more likely to be repeated. If the consequence is unpleasant (a punishment), behavior is less likely to be repeated. Young children usually do not respond to lectures or reminders. The best way to get your child to stop doing something is to take action. The most helpful actions are ignoring the misbehavior, redirecting to appropriate behavior, or putting your child into timeout.

5. *Discontinue any physical punishment* (see REASONS TO LIMIT OR AVOID PHYSICAL PUNISHMENT, page 277). Most out-of-control children are already too aggressive. Physical punishment teaches them that aggression is acceptable for solving problems.

6. *Discontinue any yelling.* Yelling and screaming teach your child to yell back, thereby legitimizing shouting matches. They also convey that you are not in charge. Yelling often escalates the disagreement and turns it into a win-lose battle. Your child will respond better in the long run to a pleasant tone of voice and words of diplomacy.

7. *Don't take your child to public places until his or her behavior is under control at home.* Misbehaving children are usually more difficult to control in a shopping mall or supermarket. Leave your child with a baby-sitter or spouse when you need to go to these places.

8. *Take daily breaks from your child.* Ask your spouse to spell you from supervising your young child, to take over

all the discipline for a few hours. If this is impossible, hire a teenager a few times a week to look after your child while you go out. Also make a "date" for a weekly night out with your spouse.

9. *Give your child more positive feedback* (see GUIDELINES FOR POSITIVE REINFORCEMENT, page 279). Children respond to discipline from people they feel loved by and want to please. Every child needs daily praise, smiles, and hugs. Give your child this increased attention when he is not demanding it, especially if he is behaving in an adaptive way. When all is quiet in your house, make the rounds and catch your child being good. If your child receives more negative comments and criticisms each day than positive responses, you need to restore an emotionally healthy balance by reducing the rules, reducing the criticism, and increasing the positive contacts. Many experts feel that it takes several positive contacts to counter one negative one.

10. *Protect your child's self-esteem.* Your child's self-esteem is more important than how well disciplined he or she is. Don't discuss his discipline problems and your concerns about him when he is around. Correct your child in a kindly way. Sometimes begin your correction with "I'm sorry I can't let you ————." Don't label your child a "bad girl" or "bad boy." After punishment is over, accept your child back into the family circle, convey that all is forgiven, and give him a clean slate.

GUIDELINES FOR SETTING RULES
1. *Begin discipline after 4 months of age.* Prior to 4 months of age, infants don't need any discipline. Starting at this age, however, parents can begin to clarify their own rights. If your child kicks and wiggles during a diaper change, making the process difficult, you can say firmly, "No, help Mommy change your diaper." By the time they start to crawl (8 months of age), all children need rules for their safety.
2. *Express each example of misbehavior as a clear and concrete rule.* Vague descriptions of misbehavior (such as "hyperactive," "irresponsible," or "mean") are not helpful. The younger the child, the more concrete the rule must be. Examples of clear rules are: "Don't push your brother" and "Don't interrupt me on the telephone."
3. *Also state the acceptable, desired, adaptive, or appropriate behavior.* Your child needs to know what is expected of

him or her. Examples are: "Play with your brother," "Look at books when I'm on the telephone," or "Walk, don't run." Praise your child at these times. Make your praise specific (e.g., "Thank you for being quiet").

4. *Ignore unimportant or irrelevant misbehavior.* The more rules you have, the less likely your child is to listen. Constant criticism is usually ineffective. Behavior such as swinging the legs, poor table manners, or normal negativism are unimportant during the early years.

5. *Use rules that are fair and attainable.* Rules must be age-appropriate. A child should not be punished for clumsiness when he or she is learning to walk, nor for poor pronunciation when learning to speak. In addition, a child should not be punished for behavior that is part of normal emotional development, such as thumbsucking, separation fears, and toilet training confusion.

6. *Concentrate on two or three rules initially.* The highest priority is given to issues of safety, such as not running into the street. Of equal importance is the prevention of harm to others—parents, other children and adults, or animals. Destructive behavior toward property is of the next importance. Then come all the annoying behavior traits that wear you down.

7. *Avoid trying to change "no-win" power struggles through punishment.* This type of misbehavior usually involves a body part. Examples are wetting, soiling, hair-pulling, thumbsucking, body rocking, masturbation, not eating enough, not going to sleep, and refusing to complete schoolwork. No-win behavior is usually uncontrollable by the parent if the child decides to continue it. The first step in resolving a power struggle is to withdraw from the conflict. Then apply positive feedback (see GUIDELINES FOR POSITIVE REINFORCEMENT, page 279).

8. *Apply the rules consistently.* After the parents agree on the rules, it may be helpful to print them out and post them in a conspicuous place in the home.

DISCIPLINE TECHNIQUES (INCLUDING CONSEQUENCES)

Techniques to Use for Different Ages

(The techniques mentioned here are further described after this list.)

• From birth to 4 months: no discipline necessary

- From 4 to 8 months: mild verbal disapproval

- From 8 to 18 months: structuring the environment, distracting, ignoring, verbal and nonverbal disapproval, physically moving or escorting, and temporary timeout in a playpen

- From 18 months to 3 years: the preceding techniques plus temporary timeout in a chair

- From 3 years to 5 years: the preceding techniques plus temporary timeout in a room, natural consequences, logical consequences, restricting places where the child can misbehave

- From 5 years to adolescence: the preceding techniques plus delay of a privilege, negotiation and family conferences, and "I" messages

- Adolescence: mainly logical consequences, family conferences about house rules, and "I" messages. We can't discipline adolescents the way we discipline preschoolers (and vice versa). By the time your child is an adolescent you should discontinue manual guidance and timeout techniques (see ADOLESCENTS: DEALING WITH NORMAL REBELLION, page 398).

Structuring the Home Environment • The surroundings can be modified so that an object or situation that could potentially cause a problem is eliminated. Examples are: putting breakables out of reach, fencing in a yard, setting up gates, putting locks on a special desk, or locking certain rooms.

Distracting, Redirecting, or Diverting Your Child from Misbehavior • Distracting a child counteracts one temptation with a different temptation. Distraction is especially helpful with young children when they are in someone else's house, a physician's office, or a store where other options for discipline (such as timeout) would be difficult to employ. It also can be used preventively if you're going to be busy at home with guests, the telephone, or feeding a baby. Most children can be distracted with toys or food. School-age children may need books, games, or other activities to keep their attention.

Ignoring the Misbehavior • Ignoring, or extinction, is a technique that is helpful for eliminating unacceptable behavior that is harmless, such as tantrums, sulking, whining, quarreling, or interrupting. The proper way to ignore is to move away from your child, turn your back, avoid eye contact, and stop any conversation with your child. Ignore any protests or excuses. At times, you may need to leave the area where your child is misbehaving.

Verbal and Nonverbal Disapproval • Mild disapproval is often all that is required to stop a young child's misbehavior. The proper technique is to move close to your child, obtain eye contact, assume a stern facial expression, and give a brief, direct instruction such as "no" or "stop." Your comments can be made in a soft but disapproving tone, since you are close to your child. Also show your child what you want him to do (the adaptive behavior). You may want to underscore your serious intent by pointing or shaking your finger. The most common mistake in using this technique is smiling or laughing.

Physically Move or Escort (Manual Guidance) • Manual guidance is the process of moving a child from one place to another against his or her will. Sometimes children must be physically removed, from a place where they are causing trouble, to a timeout chair. Other children must be physically taken to the bed, bath, or car when they refuse to go. The correct technique is guiding your child by the hand or forearm. If he refuses to be led, pick him up from behind and carry him.

Temporary Time-out or Social Isolation • Temporary time-out is the most effective discipline technique available to parents for dealing with misbehaving infants and young children. See THE TIME-OUT TECHNIQUE (page 281) for details. Time-out should be applied briefly, on the order of 1 minute per year of age.

Natural Consequences • Natural consequences are the negative results of your child's own actions. They permit your child to learn from the natural laws of the physical world. Examples are: Coming to dinner late means the food will be cold; not dressing properly for the weather means your child will be cold or wet; not wearing mittens while playing in the snow will lead to cold hands; running on ice will usually lead to falling down; putting sand in the mouth leads to an unpleasant taste; breaking a toy means it's no longer playworthy; and going to bed late means being sleepy in the morning. Although it is very helpful for children to learn from their mistakes, it is important that they not be allowed to engage in behavior that could be harmful, such as playing with matches or running into the street.

Restricting Places Where a Child Can Misbehave • This technique is especially helpful for behavior problems that can't be eliminated. Allowing the misbehavior in your child's room prevents an unnecessary power struggle. Indications include: thumbsucking, nose picking, and masturbation. Roughhousing can be restricted to outdoors. The child's tricycle can be restricted to the basement in the wintertime.

Delay of a Privilege • This technique requires that a less preferable activity be completed before a more preferable one is allowed ("work before play"). Examples are: "After you clean your room, you can go out and play"; "When you finish your homework, you can watch TV"; and "When you have tasted all your foods, you can have your dessert."

Temporary Removal of a Privilege or Possession (Logical Consequences) • Logical consequences permit children to learn from the reality of the social order. These consequences should be logically related to the unacceptable behavior. Many logical consequences are simply the temporary removal of a possession or privilege. Examples are: removal of toys or crayons that are mishandled, not replacing a lost toy, not repairing a broken toy, sending your child to school partially dressed if she won't dress herself, having your child clean up milk he has spilled or a floor he has tracked mud on, having your child clean up underwear if she has soiled it, and turning off the TV if siblings are quarreling about it. In addition, TV, telephone, shopping, bicycle, and car privileges can all be temporarily suspended if they are misused. The schoolteacher will provide appropriate logical consequences if your child does not complete homework assignments.

Some mistakes made by parents in the area of providing consequences are depriving children of: basic essentials, such as a meal; of activities with an organized peer group, like a team or scout troop; or of greatly anticipated events, such as going to the circus. The main thrust of logical consequences is to make your child accountable for his or her problems and decisions. It is important for children to learn from experience and not be sheltered from realities.

"I" Messages • When your child misbehaves, preface your correction by telling your child how you feel. Say "I am angry" or "I am upset when you do such and such." Your child is more likely to listen to this than a message that starts with "you." You messages usually trigger a defensive reaction. (For details see ADOLESCENTS: DEALING WITH NORMAL REBELLION, page 398.)

Negotiation and Family Conferences • As children become older they need more communication and discussion with their parents. A parent can initiate such a conversation by stating: "We need to change these things. Where do you want to start?" Discussions involving the whole family (family conferences) also become helpful (see ADOLESCENTS: DEALING WITH NORMAL REBELLION, page 398). Don't forget to reward acceptable (desired) behavior (see page 279).

GUIDELINES FOR GIVING CONSEQUENCES (PUNISHMENTS)

• *Be unambivalent.* Mean what you say and follow through. Be stern and tough. You know the rules, so take charge.

• *Correct with love.* Talk to your child the way you would want to be talked to. Avoid yelling or using a disrespectful tone of voice. For example, say, "I'm sorry you left the yard, but now you must stay in the house."

• *Precede the consequence by one warning or reminder.* After the rule is clearly understood, this warning is unnecessary and you can punish your child without a warning. Avoid repeated threats of consequences if your child doesn't stop what he is doing.

• *With aggressive behavior, punish your child for clear intent.* Interrupt your child before someone is hurt or damage is done. An example would be that you see your child raising a toy to hit a playmate. Intervene before the friend is injured.

• *Apply the consequence immediately.* Delayed consequences are less effective, because young children forget why they are being punished. Punishment should occur close in time to the misdeed and be administered by the adult who witnessed the misbehavior. An exception for children older than 4 or 5 years of age is when they misbehave outside the home, thereby taking advantage of you. You may put check marks on your child's hand with a felt-tip pen to indicate the number of punishments to be meted out when you get home. Punishment might be 5 minutes of time-out or 30 minutes of lost TV time for each check mark.

- *Make a one-sentence comment about the rule* during correction. However, avoid making a long speech.

- *Ignore your child's arguments during correction.* This is the child's way of delaying punishment. Especially under 3 years of age, children mainly understand action, not words.

- *Make the punishment brief.* Toys can be taken out of circulation for no more than 1 or 2 days. Time-out should be on the order of 1 minute per year of age.

- *Keep the consequence in proportion to the misbehavior.* Also try to make the consequence relate to the misbehavior (see LOGICAL CONSEQUENCES, page 275).

- *Follow the consequence with love and trust.* Welcome your child back into the family circle and do not comment upon the previous misbehavior or require an apology for it.

- *Direct the punishment against the misbehavior,* not the person. Avoid degrading comments such as "You never do anything right."

- *Don't be surprised* if your child temporarily shows an increased frequency of bad behavior once you start disciplining your child more consistently. Children who are out of control initially go through a phase of testing their parents before they comply with the new system. This testing usually lasts 2 or 3 days.

REASONS TO LIMIT OR AVOID PHYSICAL PUNISHMENT

The American Academy of Pediatrics and the National Education Association are strongly opposed to spanking. We can raise children to be agreeable, disciplined, responsible, productive adults without ever spanking them. (I didn't say without ever correcting them.) All children need discipline on hundreds of occasions but there are alternatives to spanking. A parent can just as readily "clear the air" by sending a child to his or her room. Spanking carries the risk of triggering the unrelated pent-up anger that many adults carry inside them. This anger can start a chain reaction ending in child abuse. Parents who turn to spanking as a last resort for "breaking their child's will" may find that they have underestimated their child's determination. In addition, physical punishment makes aggressive behavior worse. It teaches a child to lash out when he or she is angry. Other forms of discipline are more constructive in that they leave a child with some guilt and the early formation of a conscience.

We might ponder why physical punishment by parents is prohibited by law in Sweden, Finland, Norway, Denmark, and Austria. Physical punishment by school personnel is illegal in all countries except the United States and South Africa. (The same holds true for 20 of our fifty states.) At this time, however, over 50 percent of American parents use some physical punishment in child-rearing, and most of them are not ready to give up this type of power over their children.

Spanking children is on the way out. But if you have not changed your mind after reading the facts, certain guidelines for safe physical punishment should be followed.

- Hit only with an open hand. Hitting your child with any instrument interferes with your ability to measure the amount of force you are applying. Paddles and belts commonly cause bruises, some not intended.

- Hit only on the buttocks, legs, or hands. Hitting a child on the face is demeaning as well as dangerous; in fact, slapping the face is inappropriate at any age.

- Give only one swat; that's enough to change behavior. Hitting your child more than once is more to relieve your anger than to teach your child anything additional.

- Don't spank children less than a year of age. Spanking is inappropriate before your child has learned to walk. An upper age limit of 5 to 6 years makes sense, because negotiation and discussion should be used to resolve most differences with school-age children.

- Don't use physical punishment more than once per day. The more your child is spanked, the less effect it will have.

- Don't use physical punishment for aggressive misbehavior such as biting, hitting, or kicking. Physical punishment under such circumstances teaches a child that it is all right for a bigger person to strike a smaller person. Aggressive children need to be taught restraint and self-control. They respond best to timeout and an opportunity to think about the pain they have caused.

- Never shake a child because it causes internal bleeding and blood clots on the brain (subdural hematomas).

- Learn alternatives to physical discipline. Time-out or brief social isolation is much more civilized and effective. Learn the fine points of implementing it (see THE TIME-OUT TECHNIQUE, page 281).

- Don't allow baby-sitters and teachers to spank your children. You may wish to clarify this.

- Never spank your child when you are out of control, scared, or drinking. A few parents can't stop hitting their child once they start. They can't control their rage and need help for themselves, such as from Parents Anonymous groups. They must learn to walk away from their children and never initiate physical punishment.

GUIDELINES FOR POSITIVE REINFORCEMENT OF DESIRED BEHAVIOR

Most parents don't give enough positive reinforcement—especially touching and hugs. Dr. Edward Christophersen, an eminent pediatric psychologist, calls these brief, nonverbal physical contracts "time-in" (in contrast to time-out). Don't take good behavior for granted. Watch for behavior you like, then praise your child by saying such things as "I like the way you ————," or "I appreciate ————." When you give positive social reinforcement (positive strokes), move close to your child, look at him or her, smile, and be physically affectionate. Although it takes little time or energy, a parent's affection and attention is the favorite reward of most children.

Social reinforcement should principally be used when your child behaves in an adaptive or desired way. Praise the behavior, not the person. Examples are: sharing toys, demonstrating good manners, doing chores, playing cooperatively, treating the baby gently, petting the dog, being a good sport, cleaning the room, or reading a book. Your child can also be praised for trying, such as trying to use the potty or attempting something difficult, like a puzzle. Positive reinforcement will increase the frequency of desired behavior.

You should try to "catch" your child being good, and comment on it three or more times for every one time you discipline or criticize your child. Although difficult, it can be achieved. Some families with teenagers have increased everybody's ability to pay attention to positives by providing each member with ten thank-you cards, one of which is given to a family member whenever one is helpful to another. This increases everybody's awareness of working cooperatively. Social reinforcers are especially helpful when a child is having a bad day.

Special material reinforcers are often candy, animal crackers, money, or video time. While these tangible reinforcers tend to be overused by many parents, other parents are completely opposed to them. They consider them to be bribes. To my way of thinking, a bribe is when something like candy is given to a child for not doing something bad. This type of misbehavior could be dealt with by isolation or some other form of punishment. When I suggest material reinforcers, they are as incentives rather than bribes. As incentives they are used for increasing the frequency of more responsible behavior. Incentives may be helpful in overcoming inertia when children need to engage in an unpleasant behavior, such as eating less for weight loss. They may be useful in overcoming resistance when children are entrenched in power struggles around "no-win" behaviors (e.g., soiling). These reinforcers should be used for only one problem behavior at a time and when praise alone hasn't worked. They should be phased out and replaced by natural (social) reinforcers as soon as possible.

CALL YOUR CHILD'S PHYSICIAN DURING OFFICE HOURS IF

• The misbehavior is dangerous.

• The instances of misbehavior seem too numerous to count.

• Your child is also having behavior problems at school.

• Your child doesn't seem to have many good points.

• Your child seems depressed.

• The parents can't agree on discipline.

• You can't give up physical punishment. (Note: Call immediately if you are afraid you might hurt your child.)

• The misbehavior does not improve in one month using this approach.

RECOMMENDED READING

Glenn Austin, *Love and Power: Parent and Child*
(Rolling Hills, Calif.: Robert Erdmann Publishing, 1988).

Edward R. Christophersen, *Little People: Guidelines for Common Sense Child Rearing*
(Kansas City, Mo.: Westport Publishers, 1988).

————, *Beyond Discipline*
(Kansas City, Mo.: Westport Publishers, 1990).

Don Dinkmeyer and Gary D. McKay, *Parenting Young Children*
(Circle Pines, Minn.: American Guidance Service, 1989).

Michael Popkin, *Active Parenting*
(San Francisco, Calif.: Harper & Row, 1987).

Jerry Wyckoff and Barbara C. Unell, *Discipline Without Spanking or Shouting* (Deephaven, Minn.: Meadowbrook, 1984).

THE TIME-OUT TECHNIQUE

Time-out is a technique used to interrupt unacceptable behavior by removing your child from the area of trouble and placing your child in a chair or room that is more or less isolated. Time-out has the advantage of providing a cooling-off period to allow both child and parent to regain control of their emotions. It prevents the parent from feeling guilty afterward about excessively punishing the child. A child over age 2 or 3 is given a chance to think about the misbehavior and feel a little remorseful about it. This thinking time is the beginning of the formation of a conscience. For a child less than 2 years of age, time-out mainly establishes who is in charge.

Some parents ask what they should do if time-out doesn't work. That shouldn't happen. There's nothing better than time-out for most of the irrational behavior of toddlers. It's much more effective than threatening, shouting, or spanking your child. If used appropriately and repeatedly, it can change any childhood misbehavior. Time-out is your trump card.

Misbehavior that responds to time-out may be aggressive, harmful, or disruptive behavior that cannot be ignored. Time-out is unnecessary for most temper tantrums. Time-out is not needed until at least 8 months of age, when children begin to crawl. By 6 years of age, it can gradually be replaced with logical consequences. By 10 or 12 years of age, time-out is no longer appropriate or accepted.

CHOOSING A PLACE FOR TIME-OUT

Playpens or Cribs • Playpens or cribs are convenient places for time-out with infants. The playpen is preferable because most infants are frightened if they are not in the same room as their parents. If a crib is used, it should have the spring support positioned at the lowest setting. Once a child is able to climb out of the crib or playpen, it can no longer be used for time-out.

Chairs or Corners • A child can be told to sit in a chair if he or she is cooperative. The chair should be placed in a dull, uneventful setting. The chair can be placed facing toward a corner. Some parents prefer to have their child stand facing the corner. A chair is often a good choice for punishment when the child is in a public place such as a store, restaurant, or swimming pool area.

Rooms with the Door Open • Many parents prefer a room for time-out because it offers more confinement and isolation than a chair. Until 2 years of age, most children become frightened if they are put in a room with a closed door. Other ways to barricade your child in a room without completely closing it off are with a gate, a heavy dresser that blocks the lower part of the door frame, or a plank of plywood that goes halfway up the door and is dropped between some runners. Occasionally a parent with carpentry skills can put a half-door or screen door on the time-out room.

The most convenient room for time-out is the child's bedroom. There are two misconceptions about using the bedroom for time-out: namely that the association with punishment will cause sleep problems, and that the toys and distractions in most bedrooms will interfere with time there being considered a punishment. Both of these concerns are unfounded. When a child is put in the bedroom (assuming it doesn't have a TV or radio), the child initially is upset about being excluded from the mainstream and can't focus on playing. Bathrooms and kitchens are a poor choice for time-out because they contain potentially dangerous objects. Dark closets or basements are poor choices because they can be scary for the child.

Closing or Locking the Bedroom Door • Most children under 2 years of age, when sent to the bedroom, will stay there until they are told they can come out. However, some children with poor self-control will come out just as soon as they are put in. If you cannot devise a barricade, then the door must be closed. You can hold the door closed for the 3 to 5 minutes it takes to complete the time-out period. If you don't want to hold the door, you can put a latch on the door that allows it to be temporarily locked. Your child should not be forgotten and kept in time-out longer than a few minutes.

Other Sites for Time-Out • If your child is over age 5 and might damage his room, he can be sent outside to the porch or yard. This is also a good place to send a child who is misbehaving at someone else's home. Sometimes your child can be sent to stand or sit in the hallway. If you are in a public place, use a bench or a rest room for time-out. If your child is outdoors with you and misbehaves, he or she can be requested to stand facing a tree.

Other examples of using time-out are: if you are holding your child when he or she misbehaves (e.g., pulls your hair), the child can be put down. If your child misbehaves with a friend, the friend can be sent home. For older children you may leave the room and say, "That's all I have to say on that subject."

HOW TO ADMINISTER TIME-OUT

Deciding the Length of Time-out • Time-out should be short enough so that your child has many chances to go back to the original situation and learn the acceptable behavior. A good rule of thumb is 1 minute per year of age with a maximum of 5 minutes. A kitchen timer is often helpful and can be set for the required number of minutes in time-out. Place the timer where your child can see or hear it. By age 6 most children can be sent to their room "until you can behave," allowing them to choose how long they stay there. If your child leaves time-out early ("escapes"), he or she should be returned to time-out and the timer reset. If your child must be escorted to time-out (once she has reached an age where she usually goes by herself), the time-out time can be doubled. If your child quickly repeats the misbehavior after being released from time-out, the next punishment should also be for an extended time.

Putting Your Child in Time-Out • If your child misbehaves, state the rule briefly and send him or her to the time-out chair or room. If he doesn't go immediately, lead him there with manual guidance or, if necessary, carry him there facing him away from you. Expect your child to cry, protest, or have a tantrum on the way to time-out. Don't lecture or spank on the way. Also, don't answer his pleas.

Keeping Your Child in Time-Out • Once children understand time-out, most of them will stay there until the time is up. However, you will have to keep an eye on your child. If she gets up from a chair, put her back quickly without spanking. Reset the timer. If your child comes out of the room, intercept her and reset the timer. Also threaten to close the door if she comes out a second time. If your child is a strong-willed 2- or 3-year-old and you are introducing the time-out approach, you may initially need to hold her in the chair with one hand on her shoulder for the entire 2 minutes. Don't be discouraged; this does teach her that you mean what you say. No one should talk with your child while she is in time-out. In fact, no one should be around her (unless she's the hardheaded kind you need to hold in the chair). Isolation and silence are part of the lesson. If your other children touch the timer or tease the child in time-out, they should also be placed in time-out.

Releasing Your Child from Time-Out • Make it clear that you are in charge of when time-out ends. After you place your child in time-out, listen carefully for the timer or keep an eye on your watch. Go to your child and state, "Time-out is over. You can get up now." Then treat your child normally and give him a clean slate. Don't review the rule your child broke. Try to notice some positive behavior on your child's part and praise him for it as soon as possible. If your child repeats the problem behavior, quickly repeat the entire process.

Some parents don't start the timer until their child is completely quiet. If the child yells or cries during time-out, the previous time doesn't count. From my experience, as long as the child remains in time-out, it really doesn't matter whether or not he's quiet. If he's having a temper tantrum in time-out, ignore it. The important thing is that he stay there for a certain time period. Your child will not be able to understand the need for quietness until at least 3 years of age, so don't expect this of him before then.

Dealing with a Child Who Messes Up the Time-out Room • Children who are out of control can become destructive of their rooms. They may write on the walls, empty out their drawers, or take their beds apart. Your response can include having your child clean up the mess before she leaves the room or taking any toys out of circulation that have been misused. If your child is older, have her pay for the repair of any damage. Some damage may be prevented by removing any scissors or crayons from your child's room in advance.

Practicing Time-out with Your Child • If you have not used time-out before, go over it with your child in advance. Tell your child it will replace spanking, yelling, and other forms of discipline. Review the kinds of negative behavior that will lead to placement in time-out. Also review the positive behavior that you would prefer. Then pretend with your child that he has broken one of the rules. Take him through the steps of time-out so he will understand your directions when you send him to time-out in the future. Also teach this technique to your baby-sitter.

SPOILED CHILDREN, PREVENTION OF

Definition • A spoiled child is undisciplined, manipulative, and unpleasant to be with. He has many of the following behaviors:

- doesn't follow rules or cooperate with suggestions
- doesn't respond to "no," "stop," or other commands
- protests everything
- doesn't know the difference between his needs and his wants
- insists on having his own way
- makes unfair or excessive demands on others
- doesn't respect other people's rights
- tries to control other people
- has a low frustration tolerance
- frequently whines or throws tantrums
- constantly complains about being bored

Causes • The main cause of spoiled children is a lenient, permissive parent who doesn't set limits and gives in to tantrums and whining. If the parent gives the child too much power, he will become more self-centered. Such parents also rescue the child from normal frustrations. Occasionally the child of working parents is left with a nanny or baby-sitter who spoils the child by providing constant entertainment and giving in to unrealistic demands.

The reason some parents are overly lenient is that they confuse the child's needs (e.g., for demand feeding) with the child's wants or whims (e.g., for demand play). They do not want to hurt their child's feelings or to cause any crying. In the process, they may take the short-term solution of doing whatever prevents crying, which, in the long run, causes more crying. The child's ability to cry and fuss deliberately to get something usually doesn't begin before five or six months of age. There may be a small epidemic of spoiling in our country because some working parents come home feeling guilty about not having enough total time for their children and so spend their free time together trying to avoid any friction or limit-setting.

Confusion exists about the differences between giving attention to children and spoiling children. In general, attention is good for children. Attention can become harmful if it is excessive, given at the wrong time, or always given immediately. Attention from you is excessive if it interferes with your child's learning to play by himself or with other children. An example of giving attention at the wrong time is when you are busy and your child is demanding attention. Another wrong time is when a child has just misbehaved and needs to be ignored. If attention is always given immediately, your child won't learn to wait.

Holding is a form of attention that some parents unnecessarily worry about. Holding babies is equivalent to loving them. Most cultures hold their babies much more than we do. Lots of holding by the mother and father does not cause a spoiled infant or child.

Expected Outcome • Without intervention, spoiled children run into trouble by school age. Other children do not like them because they are too bossy and selfish. Adults do not like them because they are rude and make excessive demands on them. Eventually they become hard for even the parent to love because of their behaviors. As a reaction to not getting along well with other children and adults, spoiled children eventually become unhappy. Spoiled children may show reduced motivation and reduced perseverance in schoolwork. There is also an association with risk-taking behaviors, such as drug abuse. Overall, spoiling a child prepares him poorly for life in the real world.

How to Avoid Spoiling a Child

1. *Provide age-appropriate limits or rules for your child.* Parents have the right and the responsibility to take charge and make rules. Adults must keep their child's environment safe. Age-appropriate discipline must begin by the age of crawling. Saying "no" occasionally is good for children. Children need external controls until they develop self-control and self-discipline. Your child will still love you after you say "no" to him.
2. *Require cooperation with your important rules.* It is important that your child be in the habit of responding properly to your demands long before he enters school. Important rules include staying in the car seat, not hitting other children, being ready to leave on time in the morning, going to bed, and so forth. These adult decisions are not open to negotiation. Do not give your child a choice when there is none.

   Child decisions, however, involve such things as which cereal to eat, book to read, toys to take into the tub, clothes to wear, etc. Make sure your child understands the difference between areas in which he has choices (control) and your rules (demands). Try to keep your important rules to no more than 10 or 20 items, and be willing to go to the mat about these. Also, be sure that all adult caretakers consistently enforce these rules.
3. *Expect your child to cry.* Distinguish between needs and wants. Needs include crying from pain, hunger, or fear. In these cases, respond immediately. Other crying is harmless. Crying usually relates to your child's wants or whims. Crying is a normal response to change or frustration. When the crying is part of a tantrum, ignore it. Don't punish him for crying, tell him he's a crybaby, or tell him he shouldn't cry. While not denying him his feelings, don't be moved by his crying. To compensate for the extra crying your child does during a time when you are tightening up on the rules, provide extra cuddling and enjoyable activities when he is not crying or having a tantrum. There are times when it is

necessary to withhold overt affection temporarily to help your child learn something important.

4. *Do not allow tantrums to work.* Children throw temper tantrums to get your attention, to wear you down, to change your mind, and to get their way. The crying is to change your "no" vote to a "yes" vote. Tantrums may include whining, complaining, crying, breath-holding, pounding the floor, shouting, or slamming a door. As long as your child stays in one place and is not too disruptive, you can leave him alone at these times. By all means don't give in to tantrums.

5. *Don't overlook discipline during quality time.* If you are working parents, you will want to spend part of each evening with your child. This special time needs to be enjoyable but also reality-based. Don't ease up on the rules. If your child misbehaves, remind him of the existing limits. Even during fun activities, you occasionally need to be the parent.

6. *Don't start democratic child-rearing until your child can participate as an adult.* Don't give away your power as a parent. At age 2, be careful not to talk too much with your toddler about the rules. Toddlers don't play by the rules. By age 4 or 5, you can begin to reason with your child about discipline issues, but he still lacks the judgment necessary to make the rules. By ages 14 to 16, an adolescent can be negotiated with as an adult. At that time you can ask for his input about what rules or consequences would be fair.

   The more democratic the parents are during the early years, the more demanding the children tend to become. Generally, young children do not know what to do with power. Left to their own devices, they usually spoil themselves. If you have given away your power, take it back. You don't have to explain the reason for every rule. Sometimes it is just because "I said so."

7. *Teach your child to get himself unbored.* Your job is to provide toys, books, and art supplies. Your child's job is to play with them. Assuming you talk and play with your child several hours a day, you do not need to become his constant playmate. Nor do you need to provide him with an outside friend constantly. When you're busy, expect your child to amuse himself. Even 1-year-olds can keep themselves occupied for 15-minute blocks of time. By 3 years, most children can entertain themselves half the time. Sending your child outside to "find something to do" is doing him a favor. Much good creative play, thinking, and daydreaming come out of

solving boredom. If you can't seem to resign as social director, enroll your child in a playschool.

8. *Teach your child to wait.* Waiting helps children better deal
with frustration. All jobs in the adult world carry some
degree of frustration. Delaying immediate gratification is a
trait your child must gradually learn, and it takes practice.
Don't feel guilty if you have to make your child wait a few
minutes now and then (e.g., don't allow your child to interrupt your conversations with others in person or on the
telephone). Waiting doesn't hurt him as long as he doesn't
become overwhelmed or unglued by waiting. His perseverance and emotional fitness will be enhanced.

9. *Don't rescue your child from normal life challenges.* Changes
such as moving and starting school are normal life stressors.
These are opportunities for learning and problem-solving.
Always be available and supportive, but don't help your child
if he can handle it himself. Overall, make your child's life as
realistic as he can tolerate for his age, rather than going out
of your way to make it as pleasant as possible. His coping
skills and self-confidence will benefit from this practice.

10. *Don't overpraise your child.* Children need praise, but it can
be overdone. Praise your child for good behavior and following the rules. Encourage him to try new things and work on
difficult tasks. But teach him to do things for his own reasons, too. Self-confidence and a sense of accomplishment
come from doing and completing things he is proud of.
Praising your child while he is in the process of doing
something may make him stop at each step and want more
praise. Giving your child constant attention can make him
"praise-dependent" and demanding. Avoid the tendency (so
common with the firstborn) to overpraise your child's normal development.

11. *Teach your child to respect parents' rights and time together.*
The needs of your children for love, food, clothing, safety,
and security obviously come first. However, your needs should
come next. Your children's wants (e.g., for play) and whims
(e.g., for an extra bedtime story) should come after your
needs are met and as time is available on that day. This is
especially important for working parents where family time
is limited. It is both the quality and quantity of time that you
spend with your children that is important. Quality time is
time that is enjoyable, interactive, and focused on your child.
Children need some quality time with their parents every
day. Spending every free moment of every evening and week-

end with your child is not good for your child or your marriage. You need a balance to preserve your mental health. Scheduled nights out with your mate will not only nurture your marriage but also help you to return to parenting with more to give. Your child needs to learn to trust other adults and that he can survive separations from you. If your child isn't taught to respect your rights, he may not respect the rights of other adults.

THE TERRIBLE TWOS AND STUBBORN TODDLERS

From 18 months to 3 years of age many children are in the "Terrible Twos." Stubbornness, opposition, or outright defiance may principally characterize their behavior. They normally are noisy (not quiet), busy (not still), distractible (not focused), impulsive (not cautious), and negative (not cooperative). No matter how calm and gentle a parent you are, your child will throw some temper tantrums. Your child will say no to many of your reasonable requests. You may feel helpless and at your child's mercy. Not until adolescence will you again be put through such an ordeal.

The Terrible Twos are a normal phase in child development. Your child is not deliberately trying to irritate you. Negativism is a normal step in becoming independent. Temper tantrums are a normal step in becoming more verbal. The children who have the most severe form of the Terrible Twos usually are "difficult" children by temperament. From birth they stand out as infants who resist anything new, react intensely, and are unpredictable in their behavior. Occasionally a parent makes the Terrible Twos worse by being excessively strict or having unreasonable expectations. Fortunately all children pass through this phase into a more cooperative one.

DEALING WITH STUBBORN TODDLERS

Negativism is a normal phase seen in most children between 18 months and 3 years of age. It begins when children discover they have the power to refuse other people's requests. Once the Terrible Twos are in full swing, children become more stubborn and less cooperative. They respond negatively to many requests (including pleasant ones). They delight in refusing a suggestion, be it to get dressed or take off their clothes, take a bath or get out of the bathtub, go to bed or get up. Unless understood, this behavior can become extremely frustrating for parents. Handled appropriately, it lasts about a year. As a bonus, the better you handle this phase, the fewer temper tantrums your child will have. Consider the following guidelines for helping your child through this phase.

- *Don't take this normal phase too personally.* To your child, "No" means "Do I have to?" or "Do you mean it?" A negative response should not be confused with disrespect. Also, it is not meant to annoy you. This phase is critical to the development of independence and identity. Try to look at it with a sense of humor and amazement.

- *Don't punish for saying "No."* Punishment should be for what your child does, not what he or she says. Since saying "No" is not something you can control, ignore it. If you argue with your child about saying "No," you will probably prolong this behavior.

- *Give your child plenty of choices.* This is the best way to increase your child's sense of freedom and control, so that he or she will become more cooperative. Examples of choices are letting your child choose between a shower or a bath, choose which book is read, which toys go in the tub, which fruit is eaten for a snack, which clothes or shoes will be worn, which breakfast cereal eaten, which game played, whether inside or outside, in the park or in the yard, and so forth. Even for a task your child doesn't like, he can be given a say in the matter by asking him, "Do you want to do it slow or fast?" or "Do you want me to do it, or you?" The more quickly your child gains a feeling that he is a decision-maker, the sooner he will become cooperative.

- *Don't give your child a choice when there is none.* Safety rules are not open to discussion. Taking a bath, going to bed, or going to daycare also are not things that can be negotiated. Don't ask a question when there's only one answer. When a request such as this must be made, it can be presented in as kind a way as possible (e.g., "I'm sorry, but now you have to go to bed."). Directives ("Do this or else") should be avoided.

- *Give transition time when changing activities.* If your child is having fun and must change to another activity, he or she probably needs a transition time. For example, when playing with trucks as dinnertime approaches, your child needs a 5-minute warning. A kitchen timer sometimes helps a child accept the change better. Set the timer and say, "In five minutes, it will be time to stop playing and come to eat dinner."

• *Eliminate excessive rules.* The more rules you have, the less likely it is that your child will be agreeable about them. Eliminate unnecessary expectations and arguing about wearing socks, cleaning one's plate, or sleeping in bed. Help your child feel less controlled by making your positive contacts greater than your negative contacts each day.

• *Avoid responding to your child's requests with excessive "No"s.* Be for your child a model of agreeableness. When your child requests something and you're unsure, try to say "Yes," or postpone your decision by saying, "Let me think about it." If you're going to grant a request, do it right away, before your child whines or begs for it. When you must say "No," say you're sorry and give your child a reason.

TEMPER TANTRUMS

Temper tantrums are immature ways of expressing anger. There are several types of temper tantrums. Some are to get something, others are to avoid doing something. Try to teach your child that temper tantrums don't work, that you don't change your mind or give in because of them. By 3 years of age, you can begin to teach your child to verbalize his feelings ("You feel angry because ———"). We need to teach children that anger is normal but that it must be channeled appropriately. By school age, temper tantrums should be rare. During adolescence, tantrums reappear, but your teenager can be reminded that blowing up creates a bad impression. Teach your teenager how to keep temper tantrums in check by counting to ten or pausing long enough to regain control.

PHYSICAL TEMPER TANTRUMS OF YOUNGER CHILDREN
Overall, praise your child when he controls his temper, verbally expresses his anger, and is cooperative. Be a good model by staying calm and not screaming or having adult tantrums. Avoid spanking for tantrums because it conveys to

your child that you are out of control. Try using the following responses to the different types of temper tantrums.

Support and Help Children Having Frustration- or Fatigue-Related Tantrums • Children normally have temper tantrums when they are frustrated with themselves. They may be frustrated because they can't put something back together. Young children may be frustrated because their parents cannot understand their speech. Older children may be frustrated with their inability to do their homework.

At these times your child needs encouragement and a parent who listens. Put an arm around him and say something brief that shows understanding, such as "I know it's hard, but you'll get better at it. Is there something I can do to help you?" Also give praise for not giving up. Some of these tantrums can be prevented by steering your child away from tasks he can't do well.

Temper tantrums also normally increase when children are tired (for instance when they've missed a nap) or exhausted (as during a party), because they are less able to cope with frustrating situations. At these times put your child to bed. Hunger can also contribute to temper tantrums. If you suspect this, give your child a snack. Temper tantrums also increase during sickness. Mood is clearly affected by a child's physical state.

Ignore Attention-Seeking or Demanding-Type Tantrums • Young children commonly throw temper tantrums to get their way. They may want something to eat right before dinner, want to go with you rather than be left with the baby-sitter, want candy, want to empty a desk drawer, or want to go outside in bad weather. They don't accept rules for their safety. As long as your child stays in one place during the tantrum and is not too disruptive, you can leave him alone. Harmless behavior can be ignored.

If you recognize that a certain event is going to push your child over the edge, try to shift his attention to something else. However, don't give in to your child's demands. During the temper tantrum, ignore it completely. Once a tantrum has started, it rarely can be stopped.

Move away, even to a different room; you are thereby removing the child's audience. Don't talk to or try to reason with your child; it will only make the tantrum worse. Simply state, "I can see you're very angry. I'll leave you alone until

you cool off. Let me know if you want to talk." Don't hold
your child during the temper tantrum. And by all means, don't
give in to your child's demands. Let your child regain control.
After the tantrum, be friendly and try to return things to
normal. You can prevent some of these tantrums by saying
"No" less often.

The following types of temper tantrum can be ignored:

• Crying and screaming to get attention

• Whining to get attention. (See WHINING, page 296.)

• Minor displays of anger such as slamming a door, sticking out
the tongue, or making a face. These harmless releases of
anger when your child is overruled should be permitted.

• Temper tantrum with pounding and kicking the floor, wall, or
door. The only limitation is if your child is damaging property.

• A temper tantrum with head banging. You can assume your
child won't hurt herself, since children don't like pain. If she
has such a complete loss of control that she throws herself
backward and has caused a bump on the back of her head, as
a last resort you can throw a glass of water on her when she
starts to have a temper tantrum, and then leave the room.
Don't rush to her to try to prevent her falls, since this will
lead to more frequent tantrums.

• Temper tantrums with breath-holding. While your child will
turn blue and pass out for 30 to 60 seconds, he won't hurt
himself (see BREATH-HOLDING SPELLS, page 331).

**Physically Move Children Having Refusal-Type or Avoidance-Type
Tantrums** • If your child refuses something unimportant (such
as a snack or lying down in bed), let it go before a tantrum
begins. However, if your child must do something important,
such as going to bed or to daycare, he should not be able to
avoid it by having a tantrum.

Some of these tantrums can be prevented by giving your
child a 5-minute warning instead of asking him suddenly to
stop what he is doing. Once a tantrum has begun, let your
child have the tantrum for 2 or 3 minutes. Try to put his
displeasure into words: "You want to play some more, but
it's bedtime." Then take him to the intended destination
(e.g., the bed), helping him as much as is needed (including
carrying). And change the bedtime ritual to a brief, no-frills
type.

Use Time-outs for Disruptive Tantrums • Some temper tantrums are too disruptive or aggressive for the parents to ignore. On such occasions, children need to be sent or taken to their rooms for 2 to 5 minutes (see THE TIME-OUT TECHNIQUE, page 281). Examples are:

• Clinging to you or following you around during the tantrum. This type of interruption should not be tolerated.

• Hitting you during the temper tantrum. This is no longer a temper tantrum but has become aggressive behavior and should be treated as such.

• Throwing something or damaging property during a temper tantrum.

• Prolonged screaming or yelling that gets on your nerves. (See SCREAMING AND SHOUTING, page 297.)

• Having a temper tantrum in a public place such as a restaurant or church. Move your child to another place for his time-out. The rights of other people need to be protected.

Hold Children Having Harmful or Rage-Type Tantrums • If your child is totally out of control and screaming wildly, consider holding him. His loss of control probably scares him. Also hold your child when he is having tantrums that carry a danger of self-injury (such as if he is violently throwing himself backward).

Take your child in your arms, tell him you know he is angry, and offer him your sense of control. Hold him until you feel his body start to relax. This usually takes 1 to 3 minutes. Then let him go. This comforting response is rarely needed after 3 years of age.

Some children won't want you to comfort them. Hold your child only if it helps. If your child says "Go away," do so. After the tantrum subsides, your child will often want to be held briefly. This is a good way to get him back into family activities.

CALL YOUR CHILD'S PHYSICIAN DURING OFFICE HOURS IF

• Your child has hurt himself or others during tantrums.

• The tantrums occur 5 or more times per day.

• The tantrums also occur in school.

• Your child has several other behavior problems.

- One of the parents has tantrums or screaming bouts and can't give them up.

- This approach does not bring improvement within 2 weeks.

- You have other questions or concerns.

VERBAL TEMPER TANTRUMS OF OLDER CHILDREN

Verbal disagreement (normal arguing) is healthy; so is the expression of feelings. We want children to express their anger through talking. Some talking back to parents is also normal. When a school-age child challenges our decisions in a logical way, we need to listen. As long as your child is reasonable, he or she needs to be heard. However, if a rule is important to the parent (for instance, not paying to see the same movie twice), the parent can cut off the discussion in 3 to 5 minutes by saying something like: "I've heard your side of it, but the rule stands and now leave me to get back to my work." Try to teach your child to argue without whining, screaming, exaggerating, being rude, or swearing.

Whining • The whining child keeps asking and bugging us to do something he's been told he can't do. He may want an extra snack or to go outside after dark. Usually his voice is high-pitched and irritating. There's nothing mysterious about what causes whining. Whining is a low-grade, minor-league type of temper tantrum. It's the opposite of a screaming tantrum. You must teach your child that whining never works. Dealing with whining now is important to prevent complaining behavior in adults. Here's how to eliminate whining:

- Tell your child what you expect: "I can't understand you when you're whining. Come back to me when you can talk in your normal voice."

- If whining continues, ignore your child completely. No eye contact and no conversation. Don't try to reason with your child. If necessary, go to a different room.

- If the whining is loud or nerve wracking, tell your child to take a 3-minute time-out in the "whining chair." That should be somewhere boring and at the other end of the house.

- Give your child lots of positive attention when he's not whining.

Screaming and Shouting • Screaming is a super-duper temper tantrum, unleashed by a youngster with exceptional vocal cords and lungs. Screaming tends to recur because it usually works. It either gets the parent to hand over an unconditional surrender or it causes the parent to scream back. Try this instead:

• Clarify the house rule for your child: "We don't scream in this house. Either talk in a calm voice or go to your room."

• If the screaming continues, take your child to her bedroom for a brief time-out. Don't try to ignore this disruptive tantrum. Close the door to the "screaming room" to preserve your sanity.

• Every 4 or 5 minutes, open the door and tell your child, "I hope you feel good enough to come out now." Give her lots of chances to rejoin the family. But if she comes out screaming, return her.

• Be sure none of the adults who care for your child yells or screams. Kids are marvelous copycats.

Giving Excuses • Without being abusive, your child may present outlandish comments in order to postpone his punishment. In young children less than 3 years of age, these stalling tactics can be ended by saying: "For the last time, go to your room." If they don't go, they can be taken there. Other children may try to put their parents on a guilt trip by saying: "Everyone else does it," "You never listen to me," or "You don't love me." Your response can be: "Of course I love you, but that has nothing to do with this," and then stick to your guns about the consequence.

Making Threats or Hurtful Comments • When young children are angry, they scream or throw a tantrum. As they become older, they say hurtful things, like "I hate you." When they're mad, they go right for the jugular. Such remarks are called "showstoppers." How should you respond?

• Respect your child's need to express angry feelings. Don't take these exaggerated comments personally. You can reply: "Well, I love you anyway, but you still need to take that time-out." Don't allow her comment to change the rule.

• At a later time, discuss anger with your child. Explain how people who live together normally have both positive and negative feelings about each other. You can add, "Sometimes I get angry with you, but I always care about you."

- If your youngster threatens to run away, you can calmly state, "That would make me very sad." Most children then drop the subject. An adolescent who threatens to run away needs to be taken more seriously.

- Do children try to play psychological games on us? What do you think?

Rudeness and Insults • Verbal abuse can be defined as making derogatory comments about the parent. These include calling the parent stupid, a liar, or a jerk. The parent should not tolerate such comments. If the young person is allowed to continue this type of behavior, he or she will have difficulty keeping friends or pleasing other adults. You can give an "I" message, such as "I feel very hurt when you say rude things like that," in a nonangry voice. You can then send your child to his or her room, or outside. It's very important that you not retaliate with a similar verbal attack. Try to present a model of objective, constructive disagreement. Don't forget to praise your child when she uses politeness and diplomacy in stating her case.

Swearing • Swearing has become commonplace in our society—largely due to TV and the movies—not to mention bumper stickers. Children today hear in grade school bad language that used to start in high school. But that doesn't mean you have to listen to it. Here are some suggestions:

- Have a rule that "swearing is not allowed in our house." You can enforce that, but define in advance any words you allow (e.g., "damn"). And tell him not to swear around teachers or other adults. Enforcing this is more complicated but back up the school. Then accept the fact that how your youngster talks with his friends in private is something you can't control.

- If your youngster swears around you or other adults, send him to his room for a time-out. If he does it repeatedly, ground him for a day. But don't wash his mouth out with soap; that's too barbaric and it doesn't work.

- When your child is angry at someone, suggest he tell you about it without swearing. If he can't, suggest he swear in his room or hit a pillow.

- Praise your child for not swearing when he gets mad.

- Clean up your act. You won't be able to get your youngster to give up any four-letter words that you continue to use. Have you tried "darn it" lately? How about "rats"?

BITING

Biting another child is one of the more unacceptable aggressive behaviors in our society. The parent of the child who has been bitten is usually very upset and worried about the risk of infection. If it happens in a childcare setting, the other parents may want the biter to be expelled. If it happens in another's home, the child is often told never to return. Most children first learn to bite by doing it to their parents playfully. It is very important to interrupt this primitive behavior at this early stage.

Causes • Biting is usually a chance discovery around 1 year of age, at a time when teething and mouthing are normal behaviors. It often continues because the parents initially think it is cute and the child considers it a type of game to get attention. Later, children may use it when they are frustrated and want something from another child. At this age, when children have minimal verbal skills, biting becomes a primitive form of communication. Only after age 2 or 3 can it become a deliberate way to express anger and intimidate others.

Recommendations

1. *Establish a rule.* "We never bite people." Give your child a reason for the rule—that biting hurts. Other reasons (that won't interest him at his age) are that bites can lead to infection or scarring.
2. *Suggest a safe alternative behavior.* Tell your child that if he wants something he should come to you and ask for help or point to it, rather than biting the person who has it. If he bites when he is angry, tell him "If you are mad, come to me and tell me." If your child is at the chewing-everything stage (usually less than 18 months), help him choose a toy he can bite rather than telling him he cannot bite anything. A firm toy or teething ring will do. Encourage him to carry his "chewy" with him for a few days.

3. *Interrupt biting with a sharp "No."* Be sure to use an un-friendly voice, and look him straight in the eye. Try to interrupt him when he looks like he might bite somebody but before he actually does it, leaving the victim hurt and screaming. Extra-close supervision may be necessary until the biting has stopped.

4. *Give your child a time-out if he bites others.* Send him to a boring place for approximately 1 minute per year of age. If he attempts to bite you while you are holding him, say "No," always put him down immediately, and walk away (a form of time-out). If time-out does not work, take away a favorite toy for the remainder of the day.

5. *Never bite your child for biting someone else.* Biting back will make your child upset that you hurt him and may teach him that it is okay to bite if you are bigger. Also do not wash the mouth out with soap, pinch the cheek, or slap the mouth. In fact, if your child tends to be aggressive, avoid physical punishment in general (e.g., spanking). Also eliminate "love-bites," since your child will be unable to distinguish them from painful biting.

6. *Praise your child for not biting.* The most important times to praise him is when he is in situations where or with particular children whom he used to bite frequently. Give him a kind reminder just prior to these high-risk visits. Then praise him afterward for good behavior.

7. *Prevention.* The best time to stop a biting behavior from becoming a habit is when it first starts. Be sure that no one laughs when he bites and that no one treats it like a game (this includes older siblings). Also never "give in" to your child's demands because of biting. Since biting not uncommonly occurs in childcare settings, be sure the providers understand your approach and are willing to apply it.

CALL YOUR CHILD'S PHYSICIAN

Immediately If

- Biting causes a puncture or a cut that completely breaks the skin.

During Office Hours If

- Biting behavior lasts for more than four weeks with this approach.

- Your child bites or hurts himself.
- Your child has several other behavior problems.
- You have other questions or concerns.

HURTING ANOTHER CHILD

Some aggressive behaviors that children experiment with are hitting, slapping, pinching, scratching, poking, hair-pulling, biting, kicking, shoving, and knocking down. Since these behaviors are unacceptable in the adult world and potentially harmful, they should not be allowed between children.

Causes • Many children fight when they are angry. They do not like something another child did, and they retaliate. They want something another child has and see force as the easiest way to get it. Most children try aggressive behaviors because they see this behavior in playmates or on TV. If children get their way through hitting, it will only become more frequent. Occasionally children become excessively aggressive because they receive lots of spankings at home or witness spouse or sibling abuse.

Recommendations

1. *Establish a rule.* "Do not hit, because it hurts. We do not hurt people."
2. *For aggressive behavior give your child a brief time-out in a boring place.* Being in a time-out helps a child learn to cool down (rather than blow up) when he is angry. When it looks as if your child might hurt someone, intervene immediately. Stop the behavior at the early threatening or shoving stage. Do not wait until the victim is hurt or screams. If a time-out does not seem to be effective, also take away your child's favorite toy or television time for the remainder of the day.
3. *Suggest acceptable ways to express anger.* In the long run you want your child to be able to verbalize his anger in a calm but assertive way. Encourage your child to come to you when he's angry and talk about it until he feels better. A second option is to teach your child to stop and count to 10 before doing anything about his anger. A third option is to help him

learn to walk away from a bad situation. Giving your child a time-out is one way of teaching him to walk away from anger.

Younger children with limited expressive language (less than 3 or 4 years old) need time to develop these skills. When they are in a time-out, don't be surprised if they pout, mutter to themselves, yell in their room, or pound on their door. If these physical outlets for anger are blocked, a more aggressive outburst may occur. As long as the behavior is not destructive, ignore it. Teaching your child how to control anger provides him with a valuable resource.

4. *Verbalize your child's feelings for him.* If your child can't talk about his anger, put it into words for him: "I know that you feel angry." It is unrealistic to expect your child not to feel anger. You may need to make an understanding statement such as "You wish you could punch your brother, but we cannot hurt other people."

5. *Teach your child acceptable ways to get what he wants.* Teach him how to negotiate (ask for) what he wants, rather than taking it. Teach him how to take turns or how to trade one of his toys to gain use of another child's toy.

6. *Give special attention to the victim.* After putting your child in a time-out, pick up the child who has been injured and give him extra sympathy and attention. It is especially helpful if you can rescue the victim before he is hurt. In your child's mind the attention he wanted is now being given to the other person, and that should give him some "food for thought." If fighting is a pattern with certain playmates or siblings, be sure the "victim" isn't "setting up" the "perpetrator" to gain attention.

7. *Never hit your child for hitting someone else.* Hitting your child only teaches that it is fine to hit if you are bigger. If your child tends to be aggressive, it's critical to eliminate all physical punishment (such as spanking). You can use many other consequences (such as a time-out) to teach your child right from wrong.

8. *Praise your child for friendly behavior.* Praise him for being nice to people, playing with agemates in a friendly way, sharing things, and helping other children. Remind your child that people like to be treated kindly, not hurt. Some children respond to a system of receiving a treat or star chart for each day they go without any "hitting"-type behavior.

9. *Prevention.* Set a good example. Show self-control and verbal problem-solving. Avoid playmates who often tease or other situations where your child frequently gets into fights. And

when your child becomes tired or hungry, leave the play setting until these needs are met.

CALL YOUR CHILD'S PHYSICIAN DURING OFFICE HOURS IF

- The aggressive behavior is very frequent.
- Your child has seriously hurt another child.
- Your child can't keep friends.
- Your child seems very angry.
- The misbehavior lasts more than 4 weeks with this approach.
- You have other questions or concerns.

SIBLING ARGUING AND QUARRELING

Most siblings argue and bicker occasionally. They fight over possessions, space on the sofa, time in the bathroom, the last doughnut, etc. Quarreling is an inevitable part of sibling relationships. On some days, brothers and sisters are rivals and competitors. But on most days they are friends and companions. This ambivalence between love and hate is part of all close relationships, and it becomes more intense in siblings because both of them want to gain their parents' attention and be their parents' favorite. The positive side of this sibling rivalry is that it gives children a chance to learn to give and take, share, and stand up for their rights.

Recommendations

1. *Encourage children to settle their own disagreements.* Have a rule: "Settle your own arguments, but no hitting, property damage, or name-calling." The more you intervene, the more you will be called upon to intervene. When possible, stay out of disagreements as long as they remain verbal. Children can't go through life having a referee to resolve their differences. They need to learn how to negotiate with people and find common ground. Arguing with siblings and peers provides this experience. The only exception is if they are both under age 2 or 3 and one of them is aggressive. At this age they do not understand the potential dangers of fighting and need to be supervised more closely.

2. *If they come to you, try to stay out of the middle.* Try to keep your children from bringing their argument to you for an opinion. Remind them again to settle it themselves. If you do become involved, help them clarify what they are arguing about. To achieve this, try to teach them to listen better. Encourage each child to describe the problem for a minute or 2 without being interrupted by the other. If they still don't understand the issue, reframe it for them. Unless there's an obvious culprit, do not try to decide who is to blame, who started it, or who is right. Interrogation in this area can be counterproductive because it may cause them to exaggerate or lie. Also do not impose a solution. Since it's their problem, let them find their own solution whenever possible.

3. *If an argument becomes too loud, do something about it.* If the arguing becomes annoying or interferes with your ability to think, go to your children and tell them "I do not want to hear your arguing. Please settle your differences quietly or find another place to argue." If they do not change at that point, send them to the basement, outdoors, or to time-out in separate rooms. If they are arguing over an object such as the TV, take it away. If they are arguing over who gets to sit in the front seat of the car, have them both sit in the backseat. If they are arguing about going somewhere, cancel the trip for both.

4. *Do not permit hitting, breaking things, or name-calling.* Under these circumstances, punish both of your children. If they are hurting each other, send them both to time-out in separate places no matter who you see doing the hitting when you come on the scene. That may not be the person who took the first swing or provoked it. Name-calling or teasing hurts people's feelings and should never be allowed (e.g., calling a child who is not good in school "dummy," one who is not athletic "clumsy," or one who has a bed-wetting problem "smelly"). Derogatory comments such as these can be harmful to self-esteem and should not be permitted.

5. *Stop any arguing that occurs in public places.* If you are in a shopping mall, restaurant, or movie theater and your children begin arguing, you need to stop them because it is annoying to other people. If the arguing continues after a warning, separate them (e.g., by sitting between them). If that doesn't work, give them a brief (2 to 5 minutes) time-out outside or at an out-of-the-way spot. If they are over age 4 or 5, you can sometimes tell them to stop or they'll get a 30-minute time-out (or a 30-minute loss of TV time) upon arrival at home. Some-

times you will have to leave the public setting and take them home.

6. *Protect each child's personal possessions, privacy, and friendships.* When children argue over toys, if the toy belongs to one of the children, return it to that child. Although children don't have to share their possessions, warn them that sharing works both ways. For family "toys" (such as video games or board games), teach taking turns. Also teach sharing toys when friends come over. Sharing is a skill they will need in order to have friends and to get along in school. Younger siblings often intrude on older siblings' friendships and play. It is helpful if the younger sibling is provided with a playmate or special activity when your older child has a friend over. Your child's study time also deserves protection from interruption. Designating a study room often helps.

7. *Avoid showing favoritism.* It is critical that all punishments for arguing or fighting be "group punishments." Parents must avoid the myth that fighting is always started by the brother rather than the sister, by the older child rather than the younger one, or by one child who is the "troublemaker." Rivalry will be intense if the parent shows favoritism. Try to treat your children as unique and special individuals. Do not take sides. Do not compare them, and do not polarize them into good ones and bad ones. Do not listen to tattling. And if one of your children complains about you not being fair, either ignore this comment or restate the rule that has been broken. If you're feeling guilty, remind yourself that "it all balances out."

8. *Praise cooperative behavior.* Catch your children "being good" —namely, playing together in a friendly way. Give "group praise" whenever possible. Compliment them for helping each other and settling disagreements politely.

9. *Prevent fighting or name-calling.* First, help your children acknowledge their feelings. Let them know it is all right to be angry toward a sibling but that they should not vent their anger by fighting or name-calling. Give them useful alternatives to hurtful arguing, such as talking to you about it. Second, provide access to outside friends and different settings, rather than expecting your children to play constantly with each other. Third, avoid showing favoritism toward one child over another. Try to talk with each child every day and to schedule a special individualized activity once or twice a week. Most importantly, show your child how to settle disagreements peacefully and in a calm voice. Try not to act disrespectful, disagreeable, or ill-tempered to your children or to other people.

CALL YOUR CHILD'S PHYSICIAN DURING OFFICE HOURS IF

- Sibling interactions have not improved after using this approach for 6 weeks.
- Your children constantly fight with each other.
- Your children have several other behavior problems.
- One of your children constantly teases the other.
- One of your children has physically harmed the other.
- You have other questions or concerns.

DISCIPLINE PROBLEMS: OTHER STRATEGIES

These guidelines cover specific types of misbehavior and how to deal with them. Most of these discipline problems can occur in well-adjusted children with self-disciplined parents. Each type of misbehavior includes recommendations on how to phrase the rule, the preferred discipline technique, the adaptive behaviors that should be praised, and the parent behaviors that should be modeled to help your child behave better. Refer to DISCIPLINE BASICS (page 269) or THE TIME-OUT TECHNIQUE (page 281) for details on how to implement the different types of punishment or praise recommended in this guideline. The areas of misbehavior are described in the following order: Safety, Aggression, Siblings or Peers, Pets, Destructive Behavior Toward Property, Public Places, Interrupting Others, Delaying or Ignoring Others, Dressing, Sleep, Eating, Washing and Bathing, and Miscellaneous. Specific recommendations for dealing with negativism and different types of temper tantrums are reviewed in THE TERRIBLE TWOS AND STUBBORN TODDLERS and TEMPER TANTRUMS (pages 290 and 292).

SAFETY MISBEHAVIOR

Runs Out of the House or Yard
The rule: "Don't go outside," or "Don't leave your yard."

Until age 3 or 4 most children can't be trusted to stay in their yards. They may wander off and may be harmed on a street, railroad track, pond, or swimming pool.

Discipline technique: Structure your child's environment so that you do not have to supervise him or her to prevent this misbehavior. Lock the outside doors to keep children inside. Leave them outside alone only if you have a safe, fenced-in yard.

Runs Away from the Parent When Walking

The rule: "Stay on the sidewalk or path when you're walking with me," and "Hold my hand when we cross the street."
Discipline technique: If your child starts to run off, catch him immediately. Make this a very serious matter and tell him sternly: "Never run off again." Don't let your child tease you about this or allow running off to become a game. Say firmly, "That's not funny."

- If your child repeats running off, routinely hold his hand when you go walking.

- If this is unsuccessful, take a children's harness with you when you go walking. The harness can be put on if your child breaks the rule and taken off after approximately 5 minutes. If your child breaks the rule a second time, the harness can be put on for 10 minutes. Using a harness occasionally is harmless.

Praise your child: For staying close to you.
Model: Cross streets carefully.

Plays with Electricity or Gas

The rule: "Never touch that, because you can get hurt."
Examples: Chewing on electrical cords, playing with electrical outlets, or turning the knobs on the stove.
Discipline technique: Give your child strong verbal disapproval. Don't let this behavior become something your child can tease you about. Also, put your child in time-out. Some of these hazards can be eliminated by using safety plugs or rerouting electrical cords. Since chewing on an electrical cord can cause severe burns to the mouth, you may wish to underscore your special concern about this behavior by slapping your child once on the hand.

Lights Matches

The rule: "Don't play with matches. They can start fires."
Discipline technique: Remove all matches from your child's reach. Consider teaching your child how to use matches properly after 8 years of age.
Model: The appropriate use of matches.

Climbs Trees or Fences

The rule: "Don't climb trees or fences, because you can fall and be seriously hurt."

You might specify that your child can climb certain trees after reaching an appropriate age, such as 6.

Discipline technique: Time-out. To help your child through this phase, consider designating a safe place to practice climbing, such as on an old sofa or a jungle gym at the playground.

Unfastens Seat Belts in the Car

The rule: "We don't drive unless everyone is buckled up."

Discipline technique: Immediate time-out. Don't start the car until all passengers have buckled their seat belts. As soon as anyone unbuckles, pull your car off the road into a boring place, such as a parking lot. Read a book until your child puts the seat belt on. Children usually want to go somewhere rather than sit in the car.

Praise your child: For keeping the seat belt buckled.

Model: Buckling yourself in.

Rides Bicycle Unsafely

The rule: "Obey the bicycle safety rules."

Discipline technique: Logical consequences of not being able to use the bike for 2 or 3 days.

Praise your child: For riding a bike safely.

Model: Appropriate use of your bicycle and wearing your bike helmet.

AGGRESSION

Hurting Another Child (see page 301)

Two Children Physically Fight with Each Other

Definition: Two children are angry with each other and hitting, kicking, or shoving. This is not wrestling. In wrestling, children are not angry with each other but are practicing their physical skills. Wrestling is fine as long as it's done outside or in a recreation room and the opponents are reasonably well matched.

The rule: "Don't fight with each other, because disagreements can't be settled by hitting."

Discipline technique:

- Intervene at the early shoving stage.

- Separate the children without interrogation.

- Send both to time-out in separate rooms or separate corners. Another option is to send one child home.

- See SIBLING ARGUING AND QUARRELING (page 303) for details.

Refuses to Fight • While you can have a rule against fighting in your home and yard, you can't control what goes on in the neighborhood or school. Some parents teach their children to fight (but fight fair). Another option is to teach your child to say "I don't believe in fighting" and to walk away from aggressors. Although the chance of being seriously hurt in a fight is slim, it can happen. Sometimes it's better to be smart than to be brave. Most disagreements can be settled by words, and most bullies can be ignored. You don't have to teach your child to defend himself or herself physically.
Praise your child: For playing with other children in a friendly way and settling verbal disagreements themselves.
Model: Problem-solving without hitting or yelling. Spouse abuse condones physical fighting among children. Also avoid favoritism, which contributes to sibling fighting.

Spits
The rule: "Don't spit. It doesn't look nice."
Discipline technique: If your child spits on another person, use immediate time-out. If your child spits for attention-seeking purposes, restrict the places where it is permitted (such as in the toilet, sink, or outdoors). If your child spits anywhere else, place him or her in time-out.
Praise your child: For not spitting in situations where he or she previously spit.
Model: Nonspitting behavior in your own life. Take a position against chewing (smokeless) tobacco.

Yells, Threatens, Insults, or Swears (i.e., Verbal Aggression) • See THE TERRIBLE TWOS AND STUBBORN TODDLERS and TEMPER TANTRUMS, pages 290 and 292.

MISBEHAVIOR TOWARD SIBLINGS OR PEERS

Fights Physically • See HURTING ANOTHER CHILD, page 301.

Hurts the Baby • See SIBLING RIVALRY TOWARD A NEWBORN, page 322.

Teases or Calls Names
Examples: Calling a child who is not good in school, "dummy"; one who is not athletic, "clumsy"; or one who has a bed-wetting problem, "smelly." These derogatory comments can be harmful to the self-esteem, especially if they are true.
The rule: "Teasing and name-calling are not allowed, because they are unfair and hurt someone's feelings."

Discipline technique: Immediate time-out.
Model: The parent should avoid teasing as well.

Tells on Another ("Tattletale")

Definition: Children report their siblings' or others' misbehavior to get them into trouble—a form of oneupmanship.
The rule: "Don't tell me about your brother's misbehavior unless it's dangerous. It hurts your friendship."
This rule is based on the premise that bad news gets around, and if it's important, you'll hear about it.
Discipline technique: Give verbal disapproval: "I don't want to hear about it." You can also remind your child: "Tattletales don't have friends," and "Brothers are supposed to stand up for each other."
Praise your child: For looking after, standing up for, or telling you something good about the sibling or friend.
Model: Being supportive of others and avoiding gossip.

Takes Toys Away from Others

The rule: "Don't grab toys that other people are playing with."
Discipline technique: Use logical consequences and return the toy immediately to the child who owns it or had it. Never let the aggressive child keep a toy he or she has taken away. If the misbehavior recurs, use time-out.
Praise your child: For asking another child if he or she may use a toy, and also for returning a toy when requested.

Doesn't Share Toys

Premise: Children can't be expected to share toys until 3 or 4 years of age. Generosity has to be the child's decision. But you can plant the idea with statements such as "If you share with other children, they will usually share with you."
Discipline technique: A child should not be punished for not sharing his or her toys. Some problems can be prevented by allowing your child to take only one toy to the playground until she reaches an age where she can share. When she's not playing with her toy, pick it up so that other children won't take possession of it. For toys that belong to the family rather than an individual, temporarily put it away if two children can't take turns with it.
Praise your child: For any sharing. Encourage your child to share.
Model: Sharing in your home. Sharing your food, drink, and possessions with your child. Lending household objects to friends. Mention to your child that this is sharing.

Is a Poor Friend or Poor Sport

Examples: Some children are bossy and dominant with their friends, causing the friends to leave unhappily. Others show off so much that their friends find them boring. Others are poor sports or bad losers and try to change the rules of a game or sport.

Discipline technique: Natural consequences. Peer pressure will eventually shape your child's behavior into what is acceptable in the peer group. In the meantime your child will lose some friends until he or she has learned how to treat other children better. Occasionally ask your child: "What could you do to be a better friend?" Overall, let peers work out these disagreements themselves.

Praise your child: For being courteous, agreeable, and a good sport about losing.

Model: Stop being critical and bossy of your child if this applies. Don't argue with referees at your child's athletic events.

MISBEHAVIOR TOWARD PETS

Hurts Pets

The rule: "Don't hurt your pet, because animals feel pain and sadness just like people." Sometimes preschoolers are unduly rough with pets because they equate them with toys.

Discipline technique: Verbal disapproval followed by time-out.

Praise your child: For playing gently with a pet.

Model: Gentleness with animals.

Doesn't Feed the Pet

The rule: "Pets must be fed or they will starve."

Discipline technique: Give an "I" message, such as: "I really feel sorry for Charlie when you don't feed him." In addition, help your child come up with a reminder system, such as a small note on his mirror to help him remember to feed the pet. Sometimes delaying a privilege and linking it with the chore can be helpful (e.g., "No dinner for you until Charlie's been fed.").

Praise your child: For feeding the pet in a timely manner.

Model: Feeding your child in a timely manner.

DESTRUCTIVE BEHAVIOR TOWARD PROPERTY

Touches Things That Shouldn't Be Touched

Examples: Stereo, television, plants, breakables, or valuables.

The rule: "Don't touch the stereo, because it is only for grownups. Ask me for help if you want it turned on."

Discipline technique: Mainly restructure the environment. Put away valuable or dangerous objects, use gates, and lock doors to make certain areas off limits. For objects that can't be removed, use clear verbal disapproval. If this fails, use temporary time-out.

Caution: Much of this exploratory behavior is normal and contributes to your child's development. In general, encourage this normal curiosity. Allow exploration of some closets or shelves. For example, give your child a drawer of his own in the kitchen where he can keep some utensils you no longer use. As he becomes older, teach your child to explore objects with his eyes rather than his hands.

Praise your child: For asking you to turn on the television or stereo.

Damages or Destroys Property Deliberately

Imitators: Some children take toys or other objects apart out of curiosity. Sometimes children break something accidentally. Since people are more important than property, these children need sympathy and help with their dilemma, not punishment.

The rule: "Don't break things, because they cost money and/or are hard to fix."

Discipline technique: Time-out. In addition, use logical consequences. If the object belongs to the child, don't replace it. If the object is yours and your child is over age 6, have him or her pay for part of it out of allowance money.

Praise your child: For taking good care of your possessions and his or her own.

Model: Show care in handling other people's belongings.

Jumps on Furniture

The rule: "Don't jump on the furniture or bed, because you might break it or get hurt."

Discipline technique: Redirect your child to some other play—if possible, one that involves jumping.

Praise your child: For playing in the bedroom without jumping on the bed.

Draws on the Walls

The rule: "Don't put any marks on the walls, because it's hard to get them clean."

Discipline technique: Logical consequences of having your child clean up the mess he or she has caused, as well as temporarily removing the privilege of using paints, crayons, or markers.

Praise your child: For drawing on paper.

Steals

Definition: Taking toys, food, or money from parents, friends, or a store.

Goal: Parents should try to teach ownership. Children are not developmentally able to learn the difference between what is "mine" and what is "yours" before age 4 or 5. Prior to that age they consider everything "mine" or that they have "borrowed it." Fortunately, they can't conceal stealing well before this age. Parents must also teach that it is wrong to borrow something without the owner's consent.

The rule: "Don't take things that don't belong to you, because they belong to somebody else, who will miss them and feel sad."

Discipline technique: Logical Consequences.

- Don't accept fabrications of where your youngster found the new possession.

- Have your child take the stolen object back to the teacher, storekeeper, friend, or other rightful owner. The embarrassment of doing this with you present often prevents future stealing.

- If the object has been broken or the food has been consumed, help your child think of ways to earn money to pay the owner back.

- Be suspicious when your child suddenly "finds" a new possession. And it's good if you catch your child stealing at a young age. The sooner he learns that stealing doesn't work, the easier it will be for him to give it up.

- Give your child opportunities to earn money so he or she has less need to steal.

- Also try to teach that people can't have everything they want.

Praise your child: For honesty.
Model: Honesty.

Breaks or Throws Toys

The rule: "Don't break toys, because they cost money. Don't throw toys, because you might break something in the house."
Discipline technique: Logical consequences.

- If the toy is not broken, take it out of circulation for 2 days. The toy has to go back into circulation in order to teach proper behavior.

- If the toy is broken, delay the repair for at least 2 days. Teach that things can't be fixed until you have some free time.

- If the toy can't be repaired, either don't replace it or have your child use his or her own money to replace it.

Praise your child: For taking good care of possessions.

MISBEHAVIOR IN PUBLIC PLACES

Touches Objects That Shouldn't Be Touched
Example: Grabs food off the shelves in a grocery store.
The rule: "Don't touch anything without my permission, because everything here belongs to the store and some things can break."
Discipline technique: Mainly, distract your child on arrival by getting her a snack, such as animal cookies.

- Keep her involved by giving her safe foods to carry or having her push the grocery cart.

- If she's sitting in the grocery cart seat, hand her foods to place in the basket.

- Talk with your child as you shop so that she feels involved.

- Avoid taking your 2-year-old to a store with lots of breakables, such as a glass shop.

Praise your child: For helping.

Has a Temper Tantrum in a Public Place
Example: Often, children have temper tantrums when they beg for a toy or candy at the store and are not given it.
The rule: "We buy only food at the grocery store, not toys."
Discipline technique: Ignore your child and remain firm. If your child is having a temper tantrum in a safe place, walk on and he will stand up and follow you. If your child is near breakable objects or is a reckless child, take him outside for time-out. If he is annoying other people (as in a restaurant or church), also take him outside.
Model: No yelling or tantrums in the store.

Runs Away from the Parent in a Store
The rule: "Stay close to me in the store so you won't get lost."
Discipline technique: Time-out. First try putting your child in the grocery cart for 2 or 3 minutes if she doesn't stay near to you. If she won't stay in the grocery cart, take her outside and put her in time-out facing the wall of the building or sitting inside your car while you stand by. Consider buying a harness

and bringing it with you to the store. Harness your child only if she wanders off. Remove it every 5 minutes, giving her a chance to prove that she can control herself in a public setting. As a last resort, leave your child at home with a sitter and be sure to tell her before you go to the grocery store that she can't come this time because she didn't stay near to you. *Praise your child:* For following you through the store.

Resists Going to the Doctor's Office

Does your child dread going to the doctor's office? If so, the following tips may make it easier:

• Schedule an appointment at a time when your youngster won't be needing a nap. Also feed him beforehand so he won't be hungry.

• Bring a stuffed animal, security blanket, pacifier, or snack with you to keep him busy in the waiting room. These may also help him quiet down during parts of the exam.

• To make the physical exam go easier, practice at home holding still for looking in the ears, opening his mouth really wide, and taking deep breaths through an open mouth. By all means, don't let anyone tickle him; this will interfere with ever getting a good exam of the abdomen.

Finally, if he is over 2 years of age and fearful because of previous shots or procedures, try to help him reassociate the doctor's office with more pleasant events. Whenever you are in the neighborhood, drop in to say hello to the nurses and doctors. Just stay for a few minutes, but encourage your youngster to give people some hugs. Then give him a treat. This approach will gradually make him look forward to the visits.

INTERRUPTING OTHERS

Demands Constant Entertainment and Attention

Example: Some children demand that their parents play with them all the time. When a parent is reading, watching TV, fixing her hair, or thinking, the child complains of boredom, or sadness, or wants to be picked up. This situation is an example of the invasion of parents' rights, assuming the parent talks to the child and plays with the child at other times. Even parents of 1- and 2-year-olds can reasonably insist on several 15-minute blocks of personal time each day while the child is awake.

The rule: "Don't interrupt me when I'm busy."

Discipline technique: First, redirect your child by stating: "I'm going to read the newspaper now. What are you going to do?" Suggest some toys, books, or crayons. If your child keeps talking, say: "I can't listen now. We'll play when I'm done with the newspaper." If your child continues to talk or makes demands, either ignore the child or make temporary use of time-out.

Praise your child: For entertaining himself or herself when you are busy.

Interrupts the Parent on the Telephone

The rule: "Don't interrupt me when I'm on the telephone, because I can't hear what the other person is saying."

Discipline technique: Redirect your child by giving him or her some toys to play with. Have your child select these special toys in advance and keep them near the telephone. If your child continues to be disruptive, put the caller on hold (or hang up) and place your child in time-out. Then return to the telephone.

Praise your child: For being quiet and waiting while you are on the telephone. Smile at your child while you are on the telephone. Do something afterward with your child.

Prevention: Place most of your telephone calls during your child's nap or after bedtime. Keep calls to less than 5 minutes when your child is awake.

Interrupts Guests

Premise: When your child has friends over, you don't interrupt them. Children don't have the right to interrupt their parents' friends. After an initial greeting and some brief attention, your child should not be allowed to crawl on guests or interrupt adult conversations.

The rule: "Don't interrupt me when I'm talking to my friend, because it makes it hard for us to talk."

Discipline technique: For a younger child, distract him with special toys or games. For an older child, tell her she has to find something to do. If your child persists in interrupting, don't feel guilty about sending her to her room or, if it's near bedtime, to bed. Children should be able to take a back seat to guests. Other adults will approve of your insisting on this.

Praise your child: For good behavior when guests are over.

Interrupts Family Conversations with Incessant Talking and Questioning
> *The rule:* "Don't talk when other people are talking. Don't change the topic." Although we like children to talk, they need to wait their turn if someone else is talking.
> *Discipline technique:* Ignore the child who is interrupting and continue your conversation with the other person. If the interruption continues, tell the interrupting child that you will be glad to talk with him when you are finished talking with the other person. Suggest he do something else for now. If he continues to be disruptive, send him to time-out.
> *Praise your child:* For not interrupting and for waiting.
> *Model:* Not interrupting other people and listening carefully when they speak.

DELAYING OR IGNORING OTHERS

Doesn't Come When Called
> *Example:* This condition is also called "parent deafness" or "tuning out the parents." This behavior occurs when children don't want to listen or follow through with a parent's suggestion. A child does not need his hearing tested if the "deafness" only occurs in selected circumstances.
> *The rule:* "Listen to what I say, because I'll only tell you once."
> *Discipline technique:* If you have something important to tell your child, go to her and elicit eye contact before giving your instruction. If she doesn't follow through, use logical consequences, such as cold food for getting to dinner late.
> *Praise your child:* For coming when called.
> *Model:* Discontinue shouting from the other room. Discontinue lectures or commands. Listen carefully to your child and respond promptly. Discontinue repeated reminders.

Doesn't Come Home on Time
> *The rule:* "Come home on time."
> *Discipline technique:* Logical consequences of grounding for one day or having your child come home earlier in the future.
> *Praise your child:* For keeping deadlines.
> *Model:* Being punctual.

Doesn't Get Ready to Go Somewhere on Time
> *The rule:* "Don't be late when we have to go somewhere."
> *Discipline technique:* Give your child some lead time. If the

activity is not essential, have your child miss that activity. If the activity is important, use manual guidance to interrupt your child's dawdling.

Praise your child: For being ready on time.

Model: Don't make your child wait for you. Show your child how you get ready in a hurry.

DRESSING MISBEHAVIOR

Doesn't Cooperate When the Parent Tries to Dress the Child or Change a Diaper

The rule: "Hold still when I'm trying to dress you."

Discipline technique: Give your child strong disapproval if she doesn't cooperate while you're getting her dressed. Don't smile, talk to her, or allow this behavior to become a game.

Praise your child: For helping you get her dressed.

Won't Dress Himself Though Able To

Premise: Once a child is old enough to dress himself, the parent should never need to dress him again. Avoid situations where you feel that you are pressured into becoming involved in the dressing process.

The rule: "You're old enough to dress yourself."

Discipline technique: If you're going to stay at home, don't allow your child to watch TV or go outdoors until he is completely dressed. Also, avoid buying clothing which is hard to get on.

Procrastinates Dressing When the Parent Is Trying to Leave

Examples: You need to take your child to school, daycare, the store, or on some other errand. Your child won't dress herself (despite being able to) and eats breakfast slowly.

The rule: "You must be ready to leave the house by eight-thirty each morning, because we can't be late to school."

Discipline technique: Logical consequences.

- Give your child 10 minutes' warning before departure, preferably using a kitchen timer. Encourage your child to "beat the timer."

- If your child is not dressed at departure time and you are driving somewhere, put her clothes and shoes in a bag and take her to the car dressed as she is. If she likes, she can try to get dressed in the car, though that will be difficult with the seat belt on. If your child is going to school, try to get there a few minutes late to provide some additional pressure to speed up on the next morning. If your child misses a school bus, take her to school yourself, but be sure again that she's a few minutes late.

- Provide breakfast in the morning, but if your child is not finished with breakfast at the time of departure, that is her problem.
- Don't nag during the time your child is stalling and dawdling. By all means don't dress your child at the last minute.

Praise your child: For trying to dress herself, completely dressing herself, dressing herself promptly, or being ready to leave for school or other appointments on time.
Model: Dress before breakfast. Show your child how you sometimes dress in a hurry.

Doesn't Dress Appropriately for the Weather
The rule: "It's up to you to dress so that you won't be too hot or too cold. This is today's weather forecast."
Discipline technique: Natural consequences.
Model: Preparedness for weather variation during the day.

WASHING AND BATHING MISBEHAVIOR

Procrastinates About Washing, Bathing, or Toothbrushing
The rule: "We wash our hands before meals. We have a clean face and smell good before going places. We brush our teeth after meals and before bed."
Discipline technique: Logical consequences. Your child is not allowed to have his dinner until he has washed his hands. Your child is not allowed to go to school until he is clean, even if this means he will be late for school. You decide whether or not his body or teeth are clean enough, by doing a recheck after your child has had an opportunity to brush his teeth or wash again. For infants, use more distraction (such as storytelling) and enthusiasm to make your child feel positive about the cleaning process.
Praise your child: For spontaneously brushing teeth or washing. Also compliment him on how he looks and smells afterward.
Model: Have good hygiene habits yourself.

Wets or Soils During the Day • See Toilet-Training Resistance, page 338.

Smears Fecal Material

Definition: A child in diapers takes fecal material and smears it on the bed, walls, bathroom, and so on. Rather than being deliberate, usually this behavior arises from a chance discovery by a bored child, perhaps one who is left in bed too long. Unlike the parents, the child is usually not repulsed by feces.

The rule: "Don't get any poo-poo on your bed or the walls. Poo-poo is messy. Poo-poo goes in the toilet."

Discipline technique: For fecal smearing, give clear verbal disapproval without yelling or showing anger. Clean up your child without any entertainment or conversation. Then clean the room, with your child's help if possible. Avoid any physical punishment, because if you overrespond to the first few times your child does this, you may initiate a power struggle. If you are also toilet training your child at this time, reduce any pressure about his or her performance.

Prevention: Supervise your child more closely. Don't leave him alone for more than 10 minutes at a time. When he awakens from his nap, lift him out of bed promptly. Leave him some toys in the bed to play with if he awakens early. Put his diapers on tightly so he can't easily get his hands inside.

Praise your child: For telling you when his pants are full and he needs to be changed.

MISCELLANEOUS

Won't Talk When Able to

Definition: Some children point at things, pull on their parents' sleeves, and play dumb rather than talking.

The rule: "If you want something, tell me."

Discipline technique: Ignore your child after stating once: "I don't know what you want unless you tell me."

Praise your child: For talking.

Won't Confess or Apologize

Definition: Children can't be made to confess or apologize. This expectation is too high for many normally stubborn children.

Discipline technique: Rather than turning this into a power struggle, eliminate it as a problem by not asking for apologies or confessions.

Model: Demonstrate that you can sometimes apologize, such as stating: "I'm sorry that I said such and such when I corrected you."

Lying

Premise: Children usually lie to try to avoid punishment. Hence the saying "Ask me no questions and I'll tell you no lies." These are called self-protective lies. During the first 5 years of life, children go through a normal phase of trying to cover up by lying. They stop lying when they learn it doesn't convince anyone. Excessive lying is almost always due to harsh punishment, frequent punishment, trying to please adults with high expectations, or a parent's preoccupation with lying.

The rule: "Don't lie. Tell me the truth."

Discipline technique:

- Punish your child based on the available evidence. For example if a dish is broken and your child has just been in the kitchen, you don't need Sherlock Holmes. Don't ask your child what happened, when you already know what he did. Children aren't good at testifying against themselves.

- For misbehavior without any evidence (e.g., you think your child watched a TV show you told her not to), overlook it. Trying to investigate it will just bring you grief.

- When you confront your child about misbehavior and she spontaneously denies she had anything to do with it, show your disapproval. Tell her "I really feel badly when you lie to me and I hope you'll tell me the truth next time." Then give her a double time-out if she lies compared to the amount of time she has to spend there if she doesn't lie (i.e., 2 minutes instead of 1 per year of age).

- Don't try to catch your child in a lie or make her confess. These just lead to bigger and better lies.

Praise your child: For telling the truth.

Model: Being truthful yourself and lying as little as possible (including tactful lies).

INFANTS, TODDLERS, AND PRESCHOOLERS

SIBLING RIVALRY TOWARD A NEWBORN

Sibling rivalry refers here to the natural jealousy of older siblings toward the arrival of a new baby. The peak age for sibling rivalry is 1 to 3 years, but it also can be seen in 4- and 5-year-olds. Not surprisingly, most children prefer to be the only child during these years. Basically, they don't want to share your time and affection. The arrival of a new baby is especially stressful for the firstborn. The jealousy stems from the sibling's viewpoint that the newcomer receives all the attention, visitors, gifts, and special handling. The most common symptom is lots of demands for attention. The sibling wants to be held and carried about, especially when the mother is busy with the newborn. Other symptoms include regressive behavior, such as thumbsucking, wetting, or soiling. Aggressive behavior, such as handling the baby roughly, can also occur. All of these symptoms are normal. While some can be prevented, the remainder can be improved within a few months.

PREVENTION

During Pregnancy

- Prepare the older sibling for the newcomer. Talk about the pregnancy. Have him or her feel your baby's movements.

- Try to find a hospital that provides sibling classes where children can learn about babies and sharing parents.

- Try to give your older child a chance to be around a new baby so that he has a better idea of what to expect.

- Encourage your older child to help you prepare the baby's room.

- Move your older child to a different room or big bed several months before the baby's birth so she won't feel pushed out by the new baby. If he or she will be enrolling in a play group or nursery school, start it well in advance of the delivery.

- Praise your older child for mature behavior, like talking, using the toilet, feeding or dressing himself, and playing games.

- Don't make any demands for new skills (such as toilet training) during the months just preceding the delivery. Even if your child appears ready, postpone these changes until your child has made a good adjustment to the new baby.

- Tell your child where she'll go and who will care for her when you go to the hospital if she won't be home with her father.

- Read books together about what happens during pregnancy as well as after the baby is born.

- Look through family photographs and talk about your older child's first year of life.

In the Hospital

- Call your older child daily from the hospital.

- Try to have your older child visit you and the baby in the hospital. Many hospitals are accepting this practice.

- If your older child can't visit you, send him a picture of the new baby.

- Encourage Dad to take your youngster on some special outings at this time (e.g., to the park, zoo, museum, or fire station).

Coming Home

- When you enter your home, spend your initial moments with the older sibling. Have someone else carry the new baby into the house.

- Give the sibling a gift "from the new baby."

- Ask visitors to give extra notice to the older child. Have your older child unwrap the baby's gifts.

- From the beginning, refer to your newborn as "our baby."

The First Months at Home

- Give your child the extra attention he needs. Help him feel more important. Try to provide at least 30 minutes a day of exclusive, uninterrupted time. Hire a baby-sitter and take your older child outside or look through his baby album with him. Make sure that the father and relatives spend extra time with him during the first month. Give him lots of physical affection throughout the day. If your older child wants more outings than you can provide, ask a relative or hire a sitter to take him places.

- Encourage your older child to touch and play with the new baby in your presence. Allow him to hold the baby while sitting in a chair with side arms. Avoid such warnings as "Don't touch the baby." Newborns are not fragile and it is important to show your trust. However, you can't allow your older child to carry the baby until he reaches school age.

- Enlist your older child as a helper. Encourage him to help with baths, dry the baby, get a clean diaper, find a pacifier, or fetch toys. At other times encourage him to feed or bathe a doll as you do the same for the baby. Emphasize how much the baby "likes" the older sibling. Make comments such as: "Look how happy she gets when you play with her," or "You can always make her laugh."

- When you are busy attending to the baby, try to include your older child by talking with him. When you are nursing or bottle-feeding, read a story, play a game, or do a puzzle with your older child.

- Accept regressive behaviors (such as thumbsucking or cling- ing) as things your child needs to do temporarily. Do not criticize them.

- Intervene promptly for any aggressive behavior. Tell him "we never hurt babies." Send your child to "time-out" for a few minutes. Don't spank your child or slap her hand at these times, because if you hit her, she will eventually get back at the baby. For the next few weeks don't leave the two of them alone.

- If your child is old enough, encourage her to talk about her mixed feelings about the new arrival. Give her an alternative behavior: "When you're upset with the baby, come to me for a big hug."

Spacing Children • The ideal spacing between children is 2 or more years. Children less than 2 years apart tend to have a greater number of negative interactions. Another reason for spacing children is that a separate, special early childhood enhances development. More importantly, spacing children increases the ability of the parents to cope successfully with child-rearing. The care of three or more preschoolers can be overwhelming, with all their needs to be fed, toileted, dressed, and entertained.

CALL YOUR CHILD'S PHYSICIAN DURING OFFICE HOURS IF

- Your older child tries to hurt the baby.

- Regressive behavior doesn't improve by 1 month.

THUMBSUCKING

CHARACTERISTICS

- Sucking on the thumb when not hungry
- Finger sucking or fist sucking in some children
- A security object, such as a blanket, may become part of the ritual
- Mainly occurs when tired, bored, sick, or upset
- Mainly occurs when not using the hands to play
- Occurs in 80 percent of infants
- Onset before birth or by 3 months of age at the latest

Causes • A desire to suck on the breast or bottle is a drive that is essential for survival. In addition, more than 80 percent of babies also do some extra sucking when they are not hungry (called nonnutritive sucking). Many fetuses are observed on ultrasound to suck while still in the uterus. This extra sucking ability probably becomes important if the breast milk supply decreases and the infant needs to suck more minutes per day. Thumbsucking also appears to help with normal comforting and quieting and often increases when breast- or bottle-feedings decrease. It does not point to insecurity or emotional problems in your child.

Expected Outcome • The sucking need is strongest during the first 6 months of life. In a study by Dr. T. Berry Brazelton, only 6 percent of thumbsucking babies continued the habit past 1 year of age and only 3 percent continued beyond the age of 2 years. A different study found that 15 percent of 2-year-old children still sucked their thumbs. Most children give up thumbsucking by 4 years of age, except those who become involved in a power struggle in the early years with a parent who tries to stop their thumbsucking at too young an age. These children may become fixated on the thumbsucking and persist in the behavior to underscore their independence. Occasionally it simply persists as a bad habit. Thumbsucking must eventually be dealt with because if continued after the permanent teeth erupt, it can lead to an overbite (buck teeth). Even before age 6, frequent thumbsucking can lead to some minor complications. These include paronychia (fingernail infections), and a swollen abdomen with increased passage of gas (secondary to increased air swallowing). Children should also be helped to give up the habit before they enter school to prevent the teasing they would otherwise receive there. By adolescence, all normal children abandon thumbsucking because of peer pressure.

HOW TO OVERCOME THUMBSUCKING

Before 4 Years of Age, Distract Your Child or Ignore the Thumbsucking • It should be considered normal in this age range and completely ignored, especially when your child is tired or sick. In fact, during the first 6 months of life it can be encouraged as a means of self-comforting. However, if your child is over 1 year of age and it occurs when she is bored, try to distract her. Give her something to do with her hands without mentioning your concern about the thumbsucking. Occasionally praise your child for not thumbsucking. Until your child reaches an age of reason, any pressure you apply to stop thumbsucking will only lead to resistance and lack of cooperation.

After 4 Years of Age, Help Your Child Give Up Thumbsucking During the Day • Pick a time when your child is not unhappy, sick, or coping with new stresses. First get your child's commitment to giving up thumbsucking by showing him what thumbsucking is doing to his body. Show him the gap between his upper and lower teeth with a mirror. Have him look at the wrinkled rough skin (callus) on his thumb. Appeal to his sense of pride. At this point most children will agree they would like to stop thumbsucking.

If your child wants to stop, ask him if it would be all right if you reminded him in case he forgets. Do this gently with comments such as "Guess what?" and put an arm around your child as he remembers that he was sucking on his thumb again. Encourage your child to use a visual reminder. Self-reminders include painting a star on the thumb with a Magic Marker, putting a Band-Aid on the thumb, or applying fingernail polish for girls. Your child should put these reminders on himself. Praise your child whenever you notice he is not sucking his thumb in situations where he previously did. Also, give her a star on her chart and a reward (such as a dime, a snack, or an extra story) at the end of any day during which she did not suck her thumb at all. Share your plan with other caretakers.

After Daytime Control Is Established, Help Your Child Give Up Thumbsucking During Sleep • Thumbsucking during naps and nighttime is usually an involuntary process. Your child can be told that although it's not her fault, she can learn to not suck the thumb during sleep by putting something on the thumb to remind her. A glove, sock, splint (thumb guard), or piece of adhesive tape that runs up one side and down the other can be used. Another technique is to wrap an elastic bandage around the arm from a few inches below to a few inches above the elbow. Apply it while the elbow is straight. Then whenever your child starts to bring the thumb toward the mouth, the pressure increases at the elbow and reminds him to return the arm to the straight position. Your child should be in charge of putting on whatever material is used to prevent thumbsucking or asking you for assistance. Help your child look upon this intervention as a clever invention rather than any kind of penalty.

Bitter-Tasting Medicines • A recent study by Dr. P. C. Friman demonstrated a high success rate in 1 to 3 nights using a bitter-tasting solution called Stop-zit (no prescription neces-sary) in combination with a reward system. Only use it with your child's permission, after 4 years of age and after other methods have failed. Don't use it as a punishment. Present it as a reminder that "other kids like to use it." Help your child apply Stop-zit to the thumbnail (1) before breakfast; (2) before bedtime; (3) whenever thumbsucking is observed day or night.

- Observe your child every 30 minutes after his bedtime until you retire. Awaken your child if it needs to be applied.

- After 5 nights without thumbsucking, discontinue the morning Stop-zit.

- After 5 more nights without the habit, discontinue the bedtime Stop-zit.

- For recurrences, repeat this program.

Bring Thumbsucking to the Attention of Your Child's Dentist at Least by 6 Years of Age • By the time the permanent teeth come in, thumbsucking carries the danger of causing an overbite. Den-tists have a variety of approaches to thumbsucking. By the time a child is 7 or 8, dentists can place a reminder bar in the upper mouth that interferes with the ability to suck. This helpful appliance does not cause any pain to your child but may spare you the future economic pain of $2,500 of orth-odontic treatment.

PREVENTION OF PROLONGED THUMBSUCKING

Prolonged thumbsucking can usually be prevented if you avoid pulling your child's thumb out of his mouth. Also, don't com-ment in your child's presence about your dissatisfaction with the habit. Obviously, scolding, slapping the hand, or other punishments will only make your child dig in his heels about thumbsucking. If you can wait, your child will usually give up the thumbsucking naturally. If you turn it into a showdown, you will lose, since the thumb belongs to your child. The best prevention is to get your newborn to take up the pacifier instead of the thumb. (See page 329.)

CALL YOUR CHILD'S PHYSICIAN DURING OFFICE HOURS IF

- Your child is over 4 years old and sucks the thumb constantly.

- Your child is over 5 years old *and* doesn't stop if peers tease him.

• Your child is over 6 years old *and* does any thumbsucking.

• Your child also has emotional problems.

• The thumbsucking does not improve after trying this approach.

• You have other concerns or questions.

RELATED TOPICS
FINGERNAIL INFECTION (PARONYCHIA) (see page 473)
PACIFIERS

RECOMMENDED READING
Susan M. Heitler, *David Decides About Thumbsucking*,
  (Reading Matters, P.O. Box 300309, Denver, CO 80203).

PACIFIERS

Babies vary in how much extra sucking they do when they are
not feeding. This extra sucking is a beautiful self-comforting
behavior. Some babies almost constantly suck on their thumb
or fingers. If you have a baby like this, you may want to try to
interest him or her in a pacifier. The pacifier has to be
introduced during the first month or two of life for it to
substitute for the thumb. While the orthodontic type of pacifier is preferred because it prevents tongue-thrusting during
sucking, the regular type usually causes no problems. By trial
and error, let your baby choose the shape.

Advantages of a Pacifier Over Thumbsucking • The main advantage of a pacifier is that if you can get your child to use one,
he won't be a thumbsucker. Thumbsucking can cause a severe overbite if it is continued after the permanent teeth come
in. The pacifier exerts less pressure on the teeth and causes
much less overbite than the thumb. In addition, the pacifier's
use can be controlled as your child grows older. You can
decide when it's reasonable to discontinue it. By contrast,
thumbsucking can't be stopped when you want it to, because
the thumb belongs to your child.

When to Offer the Pacifier • The peak age for sucking is 2 to 4
months. During the following months, the sucking drive nor-

mally decreases. A good age to make it less available is when your child starts to crawl. A pacifier can interfere with normal babbling and speech development. This is especially important after 12 months of age when speech should take off. It's hard to talk with a pacifier in your mouth. To prevent problems with pacifiers, make sure your child doesn't become overly attached to one (e.g., walks around with one in his mouth). Consider the following recommendations for preventing excessive use and a "pacifier habit":

• During the first 6 months of life, give the pacifier to your baby whenever she wants to suck. But don't use it whenever your baby cries. See CRYING BABY (COLIC), page 239, to review other causes of crying besides hunger and sucking needs.

• After 6 months of age (or when your infant starts crawling), keep the pacifier in your child's crib. She can use it for naptime and bedtime. After your infant falls asleep, remove it from her mouth if it doesn't fall out. If you allow her to use it all the time, her interest in it will increase rather than decrease. If your child seems to want a security object while awake, offer her alternatives such as a stuffed animal.

• When your older infant is stressed, try to hold and cuddle her more rather than using the pacifier for this purpose. Some infants like massage. Try not to use the pacifier while you are comforting her.

• Reminder: If your baby likes the pacifier, don't forget to take it with you when you travel. Keeping a spare pacifier in the car is helpful. For air travel, sucking or swallowing fluids during descent can prevent ear pain.

Pacifier Safety • Some cautions regarding the pacifier should be observed.

• Use a 1-piece commercial pacifier, not a homemade one. Avoid using one that comes apart (such as made from the nipple and taped to a plastic bottle cap). These can be pulled apart, become caught in your baby's throat, and cause choking.

• Don't put the pacifier on a string around your baby's neck, which could cause strangulation. Use a "catch-it-clip."

• Don't use pacifiers with a liquid center. (Some have been found to be contaminated with germs.)

- Don't coat the pacifier with any sweets, which may cause dental cavities if teeth have erupted.

- Don't coat the pacifier with honey, which may cause a serious disease called botulism in children less than one year of age.

- Rinse off the pacifier each time your baby finishes using it or if it drops to the floor.

- Replace the pacifier if it becomes damaged.

Stopping Use of the Pacifier • If the pacifier's use has been confined to naptime and bedtime, you can usually obtain her permission to give it up completely by the age of 3 or 4. Pick a time when your child is not coping with new stresses or fears. Sometimes giving it up on a birthday, holiday, or other celebration makes it easier. Give your child a choice such as throwing it away, leaving it out for Santa Claus or the "pacifier fairy," etc. Saving it somewhere in the house is usually not a good idea, because your child will be more likely to ask for it during periods of stress. At such times, offer to cuddle your child instead. Help your child talk about how she misses the pacifier. Praise your child for this sign of growing up.

Make the transition as pleasant as possible. Sometimes incentives are needed. If your child seems especially attached to it, help her give it up at naptime first. Use a star chart to mark her progress. When that goal is accomplished, offer to replace the nighttime pacifier with a new stuffed animal or encourage her to trade it for something else she wants. Never force her to give up the pacifier through punishment or humiliation.

BREATH-HOLDING SPELLS

SYMPTOMS AND CHARACTERISTICS

- Preceded by an upsetting event, such as falling down, being frustrated or angry, or being frightened

- Your child gives out 1 or 2 long cries

- Then holds his breath in expiration until the lips become bluish

- Then passes out (One third of children occasionally progress to having a few twitches or muscle jerks.)

- Then resumes normal breathing and becomes fully alert in less than 1 minute

- Onset between 6 months and 2 years of age

- Occurs only when child is awake

If your child's symptoms are different, call your physician for help.

Cause • Five percent of children have an abnormal reflex that allows them to hold their breath long enough to actually pass out. Holding the breath (when angry) and becoming bluish without passing out is so common in young infants, it is not considered abnormal.

Expected Course • The attacks occur from 1 or 2 times a day to 1 or 2 times a month, and are gone by age 4 or 5 years. They are not dangerous, and they don't lead to epilepsy or brain damage.

CALL YOUR CHILD'S PHYSICIAN

Immediately—Call a Rescue Squad (911)—If

- There is no breathing or air flow for more than 1 minute.

- Your child is less than 6 months old and turns blue.

- Your child turns white rather than bluish.

During Office Hours If

- Your child was unconscious for more than 1 minute (by the clock).

- Any muscle jerks occured during the attack.

- More than 1 spell occurs per week (so we can prevent them from becoming more frequent).

- You have other questions.

HOME CARE FOR BREATH-HOLDING SPELLS

Treatment During Attacks • These attacks are harmless and always stop by themselves. Breath-holding spells look terrible and cause some parents to panic. If this is your child's diagnosis, however, try to be calm. Don't worry about crib deaths—they are different, and most occur before 6 months of age (all by 1 year). Have your child lie flat to increase blood flow to the brain. (This position may prevent some of the muscle-jerking.) Apply a cold, wet washcloth to your child's forehead until he or she starts breathing again. Time the length of a few attacks, using a watch with a second hand, since it's difficult to estimate the length of an attack accurately.

Don't start resuscitation or call 911; it's unnecessary. Also, don't put anything in your child's mouth; it could cause choking or vomiting. Above all, don't shake your baby, because it could lead to bleeding in the brain (subdural hematomas).

Treatment After Attacks • Give your child a brief hug and go about your business. A relaxed attitude is best. If you are frightened, don't let your child know it. If your child had a temper tantrum that progressed to a breath-holding spell because she wanted her way over something, don't give in to her after the attack. Breath-holding attacks should not result in any payoff for your child, any more than a temper tantrum should.

Prevention of Breath-Holding Spells • Most attacks from falling down or a sudden fright can't be prevented. Neither can most attacks that are triggered by anger. However, if your child is having daily attacks, he probably has learned to trigger the attacks himself. This happens when parents run to the child and pick him up every time he starts to cry, or when they give him his way as soon as the attack is over. Avoid these responses, and your child won't have an undue number of attacks.

Call Your Child's Physician Later If

- The attacks become more frequent.

- You have other questions about breath holding.

TOILET-TRAINING BASICS

Toilet training can be considered achieved when your child can walk to the potty, undress, urinate or defecate, and pull up his or her pants without any reminder or assistance from anyone. Some children will learn to control their bladders first; others will start with bowel control. Both can be worked on simultaneously. Bladder control through the night normally happens several years later than daytime control. The gradual type of toilet training discussed here can usually be completed in 2 weeks to 2 months.

TOILET-TRAINING READINESS

Don't begin training until your child is clearly ready. Readiness doesn't just happen; readiness includes concepts and skills you can teach your child from 12 months of age onward. Reading some of the special toilet learning books to your child can help (see Mack and Lansky). Most children with normal development can be made ready for toilet training by 24 months of age, many by 18 months. By age 3, your child will probably have trained himself. If the following indications are present, your child is ready.

• Your child understands what "pee, poop, dry, wet, clean, messy, and potty" mean. Teach him the vocabulary.

• Your child understands what the potty is for. Teach this by having your child watch parents, older siblings, and peers use the toilet correctly.

• Your child prefers dry, clean diapers. Change your child frequently.

• Your child likes to be changed. As soon as he is able to walk, teach him to come to you immediately whenever he is wet or dirty to have his diaper changed. Praise him for telling you.

• Your child understands the connection between dry pants and using the potty. "If you go pee-pee in the potty, your pants will stay nice and dry."

• Your child can recognize the sensation of a full bladder and the urge to have a bowel movement—that is, he paces, jumps up and down, holds his genitals, pulls at his pants, squats down, grunts, pushes, or tells you. Clarify for him what these signals mean: "The poop (or pee) wants to come out. It needs your help." Try to teach your child to come to you at these times.

• Your child has the ability to postpone briefly the urge to go. He may go off by himself and come back wet or soiled, or he wakes up from naps dry.

THE TOILET-TRAINING PROCESS

The main approach to training must be encouragement, patience, praise, and making the process fun. Avoid any pressure or punishment. Your child must feel in control of the process.

Buy Supplies

- Potty chair (floor-level type). Having the feet reach the floor during training gives your child leverage for pushing and a sense of security. It also offers the freedom of getting on and off at will. This type is also portable.

- Favorite treats (fruit slices, raisins, animal crackers, cookies, and the like) for rewards.

- Stickers or stars, for rewards.

Make the Potty Chair One of Your Child's Favorite Possessions • Several weeks before you plan on beginning toilet training, take your child with you to purchase a potty chair. Make it very clear that this is your child's own special chair. Help your child put his name on it. Allow your child to decorate it or even paint it a different color. Then have your child sit on it fully clothed until he is comfortable with using it as a chair. Have your child use it while watching TV, eating snacks, playing games, or looking at books. Keep it in the room in which your child usually plays—often the kitchen. Only after your child is clearly friendly toward the potty chair (for at least one week), proceed to actual toilet training.

Encourage Practice Runs to the Potty • Do a practice run whenever your child gives a signal that looks promising, such as a certain facial expression, grunting, holding the genital area, pulling at his pants, pacing, squatting, squirming, or passing gas. Other good times are after naps or 20 minutes after meals. Say encouragingly, "The poop (or pee) wants to come out. Let's use the potty." Encourage your child to walk to the potty and sit there with his diapers or pants off. Your child can then be told: "Try to go pee-pee in the potty." If your child is reluctant to cooperate, he can be encouraged to sit on the potty by doing something that is fun—you might read a story, for instance. If your child still wants to get up after 1 minute of encouragement, permit it. *Never* force your child to sit there. *Never* physically hold your child there. Even if your child seems to be enjoying it, end each session after 5 minutes, unless something is happening.

Praise or Reward Your Child for Cooperation or Any Success

• All cooperation with these practice sessions should be lavishly praised with words: "Johnny is sitting on the potty just like Daddy," perhaps, or "You're trying real hard to make pee-pee in the potty."

• If your child urinates into the potty, he can be rewarded with treats or stickers, as well as praise and hugs. While a sense of accomplishment is enough for some children, others need treats to stay focused.

• The big rewards (like going to the ice-cream store) should be reserved for when your child spontaneously walks over to the potty and uses it, or asks to go there with you and then uses it.

• Once your child uses the potty spontaneously on two or more occasions, you can stop the practice runs. For the following week, continue to praise your child frequently for dryness and using the potty. (Note: Practice runs and reminders should not be used for more than 1 or 2 months.)

• While you're at all this, train your child early in the good habit of rinsing the hands each time he finishes using the toilet.

Change Your Child for Urine or BM Accidents • Change your child as soon as it's convenient, but respond sympathetically. Say something like: "You wanted to make pee-pee in the potty, but you made pee-pee in your pants. I know that makes you sad. You like to be dry. You'll get better at this." If you feel a need to be critical, keep it to mild verbal disapproval and use it rarely (e.g., "Big boys don't go pee-pee in their pants," or mention the name of another child whom he likes and who is trained). Then your child should be changed into a dry diaper or training pants in as neutral and nonangry a way as possible. Avoid physical punishment, yelling, or scolding. Pressure or force can turn the normally negative child of this age into a completely uncooperative one. Also, keeping your child in wet or soiled pants for punishment is counterproductive.

Introduce Training Pants After Your Child Starts Using the Potty • Switch from diapers to training pants after your child is cooperative about sitting on the potty chair and passes about half of her urine and bowel movements there. She definitely needs training pants if she comes to you to help her take off her diaper so she can use the potty. Take your child with you to buy the underwear and make it a reward for her success. Buy loose-fitting ones that she can easily lower and pull up by herself. Once you start using training pants, use diapers only for naps and nighttime. Disposable pull-ups come in handy for travel.

Review the Following Guideline on Toilet-Training Resistance If

- Your child won't sit on the potty or toilet.
- Your 2-year-old child is negative about toilet training.
- Your child holds back BMs.
- You begin to use force or punishment.
- Your child is over 3 years old and not daytime toilet-trained.
- This approach isn't working after 2 months.

RECOMMENDED READING

Joanna Cole, *The Parents Book of Toilet Teaching* (New York: Ballantine Books, 1983).

Vicki Lansky, *Koko Bear's New Potty* (New York, Bantam Books, 1986).

Alison Mack, *Toilet Learning* (Boston: Little, Brown, 1978).

Katie Van Pelt, *Potty Training Your Baby* (New York: Avery, 1988).

PREVENTION OF TOILET-TRAINING PROBLEMS

Some Dos

1. Change your child frequently.
2. Teach your child to come to you when he needs to be changed.
3. Help your child spend time with children who are trained and watch them use the toilet or potty chair.
4. Read toilet-learning books to your child.

5. Initially keep the potty chair in the room your child usually plays in. This easy access markedly increases the chances he will use it without you asking him to. Consider owning 2 potty chairs.
6. Teach him how the toilet works.
7. Mention using the toilet or potty chair only if your child gives a cue that he needs to go.
8. Give suggestions, not demands.
9. Give your child an active role, and let him do it his way.
10. Be supportive.
11. Keep a sense of humor.
12. Keep the process fun and upbeat. Be positive about any interest your child shows.

Some Don'ts
1. Don't start when your child is in a stubborn or negative phase.
2. Don't use any punishment or pressure.
3. Don't force your child to sit on a potty chair.
4. Don't keep your child sitting on a potty chair against his will.
5. Don't flush the toilet while your child is sitting on it.
6. Don't lecture or remind your child.
7. Avoid any friction.
8. Avoid battles or showdowns.
9. Don't try to control what you can't control.
10. Never escalate your response; you will always lose.
11. Don't act overconcerned about these normal body functions. Try to appear casual and relaxed during the training.
12. After your child uses the toilet, don't expect a perfect performance. Some accidents occur for months.

TOILET-TRAINING RESISTANCE

Children who refuse to be toilet-trained either wet themselves, soil themselves, or try to hold back their bowel movements (thus becoming constipated). Many of these children also refuse to sit on the toilet or will use the toilet only if a parent brings up the subject and marches them into the bathroom. Any child who is over 2½ years old and not toilet trained after several months of trying can be assumed to be resistant to the process, rather than untrained. Consider how capable your child is at delaying a BM until he or she is off the toilet or you are on the telephone. More practice runs, such as you used in toilet training, will not help. Your child's control is already impressive. Instead, your child now needs full responsibility and some incentives.

The most common cause of not being toilet trained is that the child was reminded or lectured too much. Some of the children have been forced to sit on the toilet against their will, occasionally for long periods of time. A few have been spanked or punished in other ways for not cooperating. Many parents make these mistakes, especially if they have a strong-willed child.

Occasional small amounts of wetting and soiling can be normal. If your child has small amounts of wetting that occur while trying to pull down underwear or undo a zipper, this is normal and no special intervention is needed. Occasionally a girl will have some leakage of urine because she stands up too quickly after urinating. She simply needs to sit there an extra 10 seconds. Also, some of the children with small smears of stool in their underwear simply need a careful review of how to wipe themselves "until clean."

Most children less than 5 or 6 years of age with soiling (encopresis) or daytime wetting (without any other symptoms) are simply engaged with you in a power struggle. These children can be helped with the following suggestions. If your child holds back bowel movements and becomes constipated, medicines will also be needed, so first talk with your child's physician. If your child also has bed-wetting, work on the daytime wetting first, because it will be much easier to change.

HELPING THE CHILD WITH DAYTIME WETTING OR SOILING

Transfer All Responsibility to Your Child • Your child will decide to use the toilet only after he realizes that he has nothing left to resist. Have one last talk with him about this subject. Tell your child that his body makes "pee" and "poop" every day and it belongs to him. Explain that his "poop" wants to go in the toilet and his job is to help the "poop" get out. Tell him you're sorry you punished him, forced him to sit on the toilet, or reminded him so much. Tell him from now on you won't try to help him, because he doesn't need any help and he's "in charge." Then stop talking about this subject with your child or with others when your child is present. When your child stops receiving so much attention and conversation for non-performance (not going), he will eventually decide to perform for attention.

Stop All Reminders About Using the Toilet • Let your child decide when she needs to go to the bathroom. He should not be reminded to go to the bathroom, nor asked if he needs to go. Reminders are a form of pressure, and pressure doesn't work. Your child should not be made to sit on the toilet against his will, because this will foster a negative attitude about the whole process. He knows when his rectum needs to be emptied (the defecation urge), when his bladder is full, and where the bathroom is. If your child doesn't respond when he needs to, the best reminder of wetness is urine dripping down the leg, and the best reminder of soiling is the odor.

Give Incentives for Using the Toilet • If your child stays clean and dry, he or she needs plenty of positive reinforcement. This reinforcement should include praise, smiles, and hugs from everyone in the family. This positive response should occur every time your child passes his bowel movement or urine into the toilet. For the child who soils or wets himself on some days and not others, this recognition should occur whenever he is clean for a complete day. Better yet, on successful days a parent should take 20 minutes to play a special game with the child or take him for a walk.

For turning around a resistant child, special incentives (such as jelly beans, chocolates, or video time) are invaluable—especially under age 5. Take your child to the grocery store to select 2 bags of favorite candies. For using the toilet, err on the side of giving too much (e.g., a handful each time). If you want a breakthrough, make your child "an offer he can't refuse."

Give Stars for Using the Toilet • Get a calendar for your child and post it in a conspicuous location. Place a star on it for every BM or urination into the toilet. This record of progress should be kept until your child has gone 2 weeks without any accidents.

If Your Child Has Never Sat on the Toilet, Try to Change His Attitude • First, give him choices by asking if he wants to use the big toilet or the potty chair. If he chooses the potty chair, be sure to keep it in the room he usually plays in. For wetting, the presence of the chair and the promise of treats will usually bring about a change in behavior. For soiling, your child may need a pleasant reminder once a day when he is clearly holding back. You can say "The poop is trying to get out and go in the toilet. The poop needs your help." A few children temporarily may need treats for simply sitting on the toilet and trying. However, don't accompany your child into the bathroom or stand with him by the potty chair. He needs to get the feeling of success that comes from doing it on his own, and then finding you to tell you what he did.

Remind Your Child to Change Clothing If He Wets or Soils Himself • Don't ignore soiled or wet clothes. As soon as your child is noted to be soiled or wet by odor or behavior, remind him to clean himself up immediately. The main role you have in this program is to enforce the rule "You can't walk around wet or with a mess in your pants." Don't expect your child to confess to being wet or soiled, nor ask him a question he will probably answer with a lie. If he is wet, he can probably change into dry clothes by himself. This makes it more boring, which is good. Also have your child rinse the wet underwear in the sink and then hang it on the side of the bathtub to dry. If your child is soiled, he will probably need your help with cleanup, but keep him involved. Have your child rinse the soiled underwear in the toilet. This may be "yucky," which is also good. Then store them until washday in a bucket of water with a lid. Your child may also need a 5-minute soak in the bathtub if he is soiled. If he wets or soils himself when you are out in public places, always have him carry a brown bag with extra clothes in it. If your child has an accident, find a public restroom and put him through his paces.

Don't Punish or Criticize Your Child for Accidents • Respond gently to accidents. Your child should not be criticized or punished. In addition, siblings should not be allowed to tease. Your child should never be put back into diapers unless he needs to be on laxatives or stool softeners. If there is anyone in your family who wants to "crack down" on your youngster, have that person talk to your child's physician, because this kind of pressure will only delay a cure and it could cause secondary emotional problems. Try to keep your family optimistic about this problem. Eventually all children want to be "grown up" and will use the toilet.

Ask the Preschool Staff to Apply the Same Strategy • Children who soil or wet themselves at school need access to the bathroom at school, especially if they are shy. Remind your child it's fine to leave the classroom to go to the bathroom. Send the school a note requesting unlimited privileges to go to the school bathroom anytime your child wants to without raising his hand and also during recess. If the problem is significant, you might also temporarily supply the school with an extra set of clean underwear.

CALL YOUR CHILD'S PHYSICIAN DURING OFFICE HOURS IF

- Your child is over 5 years old.

- Your child is constipated or holds back BMs.

- Your child has diarrhea.

- Urinary tract infections occurred previously.

- Passing the urine causes pain or burning.

- The urine stream is weak or dribbly.

- Your child's underwear is constantly damp.

- Your child wets while running to the toilet.

- Your child wets during laughter.

- Your child drinks excessive fluids.

- The symptoms are not improved by 1 month on this program.

- The symptoms are not cleared by 3 months.

SEX EDUCATION FOR PRESCHOOLERS

By age 4, most children develop a healthy sexual curiosity. They ask a variety of questions and need honest, brief answers. If they don't ask sexual questions by age 5, it is your job to bring up this subject. If you don't, they may acquire a lot of misinformation from their schoolmates.

Promoting Good Sex Education

- Teach the differences in anatomy, and the proper names for body parts. This is easy to do during baths with siblings or friends.

- Teach about pregnancy and where babies come from. The easiest way is to get a pregnant friend to volunteer and have your child feel her baby moving about.

- Explain the birth process. Tell your child that the baby comes out through a special passage called the vagina. Help him understand the process by seeing the birth of some puppies.

- Also, explain sexual intercourse. Many parents who discuss everything else keep postponing this topic. Get past this hurdle by reading your child some picture books on sex education. If you cover these topics by age 5, your child will find it easy to ask you more about them as he grows older.

Normal Sexual Play • A common part of normal sexual development between ages 3 and 5 is for children to get undressed together and look at each other's genitals. This is their attempt to learn about sexual differences. There's no reason why you can't turn this discovery into a positive one.

- After your child's friends have gone home, read him a book about sex education. Help him talk about how boys' and girls' bodies differ.

- Tell your child that genitals are private. That's why we wear clothes. Clarify some basic rules. It's okay to see other people's genitals but not to touch them or stare at them. It's not acceptable to show someone your genitals deliberately.

- In the future, supervise the play a little more closely. If the children occasionally expose their bodies to each other, just ignore it. But if it seems to be becoming more frequent, tell the children it's not polite and has to stop. If this doesn't get your message across, give them a 5-minute time-out in separate rooms, or send the visiting child or children home for the day. But don't give any major punishment or act horrified.

- It's up to parents to put the brakes on undressing games. If you don't, they usually escalate into touching and poking. But keep your response low-key.

Nudity and Your Child • Feelings about nudity vary from family to family. Exposure to nudity with siblings or the parent of the same sex is fine and continues indefinitely (e.g., in locker rooms). But nudity with the parent or sibling of the opposite sex probably should be phased out between ages 4 and 5. Some reasons for this are the following:

- Your child will soon be entering school, and nudity is clearly not accepted there.

- Most families in our society practice modesty, so a child who is interested in looking at other people's bodies can get into trouble.

- It is more comfortable for children to learn genital anatomy from siblings and agemates than from seeing their parents nude.

If you agree with these comments, then between ages 4 and 5 begin to teach a respect for privacy.

- Stop any showering and bathing with your children (especially those of the opposite sex).

- Close the bathroom door when you use the toilet.

- Close the bedroom door when you get dressed and suggest they do the same.

Wasn't that easy?

CALL YOUR CHILD'S PHYSICIAN DURING OFFICE HOURS IF

- Your child won't stop touching other children's genitals.

- Your child won't stop exposing his or her genitals.

- Your child has an excessive interest in sex or nudity.

- You have other questions or concerns.

MASTURBATION IN PRESCHOOLERS

SYMPTOMS AND CHARACTERISTICS

Masturbation is self-stimulation of the genitals for pleasure and self-comfort. Children may rub themselves with a hand or other object. During masturbation, a child usually appears dazed, flushed, and preoccupied. Masturbation is more than the normal inspection of the genitals commonly observed in 2-year-olds during baths. The frequency varies from once a week to several times per day. Masturbation occurs more commonly when a child is sleepy, bored, watching television, or under stress.

Cause • Occasional masturbation is a normal behavior of many infants and preschoolers. Up to a third of children in this age group discover masturbation while exploring their bodies. It continues simply because it feels so good. Some children masturbate frequently because they are unhappy about something, such as having their pacifier taken away. Others are reacting to punishment or pressure to stop completely. Masturbation has no medical causes. Irritation in the genital area causes pain or itching; it doesn't cause masturbation.

Expected Course • Once masturbation begins, it will seldom stop completely. It may decrease in frequency if associated power struggles or unhappiness are remedied. By age 5 or 6, most children can learn some discretion and masturbate only privately. Masturbation becomes almost universal at puberty with normal surges in hormones and sexual drive.

Common Misconceptions • Masturbation does not cause any physical injury or harm to the body. It is not abnormal or excessive unless it is deliberately done in public places after age 5 or 6. It does not mean your child will be oversexed, promiscuous, or sexually deviant. Masturbation can cause emotional harm (such as guilt and sexual hangups) only if adults overreact to it and make it seem dirty or wicked.

COMING TO TERMS WITH MASTURBATION IN PRESCHOOLERS

Set Realistic Goals • It is impossible to eliminate masturbation. Accept the fact that your child has learned about it and enjoys it. All that a parent can control is where it occurs. A reasonable goal is to permit it only in the bedroom or bathroom. Clarify for your child "It's okay to do that in your bedroom when you're tired." Don't ignore it completely or your child will think he or she can do it freely in any setting, leading to criticism by other adults.

Ignore Masturbation at Naptime and Bedtime • Leave your child alone at these times. Stay out of your child's room. Avoid surveillance or checking up. Do not forbid lying on the abdomen and do not ask if your child's hands are between the legs.

Distract or Discipline Your Child for Masturbation Outside Her Bedroom • Intervene as soon as possible. First try to distract your child with a toy, game, or other activity. Suggest your child run an errand within the house. If that fails, explain to your child: "I know that rubbing yourself feels good, but you can't do that around other people. It's okay to do it in your room or the bathroom, but not in the rest of the house. It's something we do when we're alone." Eventually this will help children become sensitive to other people's feelings. Often this can't be accomplished readily before age 4 or 5. The younger child may need to be sent to his or her room to masturbate.

Discuss This Approach with All of Your Child's Caretakers • If your child masturbates at daycare or preschool, ask that they try to keep their responses consistent with yours. First they should try to distract the child. If that is not effective, they should catch the child's attention with comments such as "We need to have you join us now." Masturbation should be tolerated at school only at naptime.

Increase Physical Contact with Your Child • Some children will masturbate less if they receive extra hugging and cuddling throughout the day. Try to be sure that your child receives at least 1 hour per day of special time together and physical affection from the parents.

Common Mistakes • The most common mistake that parents make is to try to completely eliminate masturbation. This leads to an all-out power struggle which the parents inevitably lose. Parents must also discontinue any physical punishment, yelling, or lecturing about masturbation. They should not label masturbation as bad, dirty, evil, or sinful (the "moral approach"). They should avoid tying the hands or using any kind of restraints. All of these approaches lead only to resistance and, possibly, later sexual inhibitions.

CALL YOUR CHILD'S PHYSICIAN DURING OFFICE HOURS IF

- Your child continues to masturbate when other people are around.

- You suspect that your child has been taught to masturbate by someone.

- Your child tries to masturbate others.

- You feel your child is unhappy.

- You cannot accept any masturbation by your child.
- This approach does not bring improvement within 1 month.
- You have other questions or concerns.

STUTTERING VS. NORMAL DYSFLUENCY

CHARACTERISTICS OF TRUE STUTTERING

- Also called stammering
- Repetitions of sounds, syllables, words, or phrases
- Hesitations and pauses in speech
- The absence of smooth speech flow
- Increases when tired, excited, or stressed
- Fear of talking
- Occurs in boys 4 times more frequently than in girls

CHARACTERISTICS OF NORMAL DYSFLUENCY AND DYSARTHRIA

"Normal dysfluency" and "psuedostuttering" are the terms used to describe the normal repetition of words or phrases children make when they are learning to speak between 18 months and 5 years of age. "Normal dysarthria" and "mispronunciation" are the terms used to describe the incorrect pronunciation of many children as they learn to speak; sounds are substituted or left out, so that some words become hard to identify.

CAUSES OF DYSFLUENCY, DYSARTHRIA, AND TRUE STUTTERING

Normal dysfluency occurs because the mind is able to form words faster than the tongue can produce them. The cause of normal dysarthria is usually genetic. In most cases, true stuttering develops when a child with normal dysfluency and/or dysarthria is pressured to improve and in the process becomes sensitive to his inadequacies. Soon thereafter the child begins to anticipate speaking poorly and struggles to correct it. The child becomes tense when he speaks, and the more he attempts to control his speech, the worse it becomes (a vicious circle). The repetitions become multiple rather than single. Temporary stuttering can occur at any age if a person becomes overly critical and fearful of his own speech. Although it is normal for us to be aware of what we are saying, how we are saying it is normally subconscious. Genetic factors also play a role in stuttering.

Normal dysfluency occurs in 90 percent of children, in contrast to true stuttering, which occurs in only 1 percent of children. Approximately 70 percent of children pronounce words clearly from the onset of speech; however, the other 30 percent of children between ages 1 and 4 years have normal dysarthria and say many words that are unintelligible to their parents and others.

EXPECTED COURSE OF DYSFLUENCY, DYSARTHRIA, AND TRUE STUTTERING

Normal dysfluency lasts for approximately 2 or 3 months if handled correctly. Unlike normal dysfluency, normal dysarthria is not a brief phase but instead shows very gradual improvement over several years as development unfolds. The speech of 90 percent of the children who have dysarthria becomes completely understandable by age 4, and 96 percent by age 5 or 6. Without treatment, true stuttering will become worse and persist in adulthood.

HELPING YOUR CHILD COPE WITH NORMAL DYSFLUENCY AND DYSARTHRIA

These recommendations should prevent progression to true stuttering in these children.

Encourage Conversation • Keep the content pleasant and enjoyable. Sit down and talk with your child at least once a day. However, avoid requests for verbal performance or reciting. Keep speaking time low-key and fun.

Don't Correct Your Child's Speech • Avoid any disapproval, such as "Stop that stuttering" or "Think before you speak." Remember that this is your child's normal speech for his age and is not controllable. Avoid attempts to improve your child's grammar, verb tense, or enunciation. Also avoid praise for good speech—which implies that your child's previous speech wasn't up to standard.

Don't Interrupt Your Child's Speech • Give your child ample time to finish what he is saying. Don't complete sentences for him. Try to pause 2 seconds between the end of your child's sentence and the start of yours. Don't allow siblings to interrupt one another.

Don't Ask Your Child to Repeat Himself or Start Over • If possible, guess at the message. Try to become a careful listener when your child is speaking. Only if you don't understand a comment and it appears to be an important one should you ask your child to restate it.

Don't Ask Your Child to Practice a Certain Word or Sound • This just makes the child more self-conscious about his speech.

Don't Ask Your Child to Slow Down When He Speaks • Try to convey to your child that you have plenty of time and are not in a hurry. Model a relaxed rate of speech. A rushed type of speech is a temporary phase that can't be changed by orders from the parent.

Don't Label Your Child a Stutterer • Labels tend to become self-fulfilling prophecies. In fact, don't discuss in your child's presence that he or she has any kind of speech problem.

Ask Other Adults Not to Correct Your Child's Speech • The preceding instructions must be shared with baby-sitters, teachers, relatives, neighbors, and visitors. Don't allow siblings to tease or imitate your child who stutters. If they do so, send them to their room for time-out. Encourage your child to talk about frustrations. If your child becomes quite upset while speaking, say something sympathetic like "That's a hard word." Then ask him about his feelings and help him express them. Reassure him that his speech will become better.

Help Your Child Relax and Feel Accepted in General • Try to increase the hours of fun and play your child has each day. Try to slow down the pace of your family life. Avoid situations that seem to bring on stuttering. If there are any areas in which you have been applying strict discipline, try to back off.

CALL YOUR CHILD'S PHYSICIAN DURING OFFICE HOURS IF

- Your child is over age 5.

- Your child has true stuttering.

- Your child has associated facial grimacing or tics.

- Your child has become self-conscious or fearful about his or her speech.

- Your family has a history of stuttering in adulthood.

- Speech is also delayed (no words by 18 months or no sentences by 2½ years).

- Speech is totally unintelligible to others *and* your child is over age 2.

- Speech is more than 50 percent unintelligible to others *and* your child is over age 3.

- Speech is 10 percent unintelligible to others *and* your child is over age 4.

- Dysfluency doesn't improve after trying this program for 2 months.

- You have other questions or concerns.

SCHOOL AGE CHILDREN

SCHOOL PHOBIA OR REFUSAL

SYMPTOMS AND CHARACTERISTICS

- Your child experiences vague physical symptoms such as stomach aches, headaches, sore throats, nausea, or dizziness.
- Your child has missed 5 or more days of school for these symptoms.
- The symptoms mainly occur in the morning.
- The symptoms worsen at the time of departure for school or on arrival at school.
- There are usually minimal symptoms on weekends and holidays.
- Your child misses you while at school and wants to go home.
- The symptoms began during kindergarten or first grade.
- The symptoms start in September or October.
- Your child otherwise seems healthy and vigorous.

  If your child's symptoms are different, call your physician for help.

Causes • A school-phobic child is usually afraid of leaving home in general, rather than afraid of anything in particular at school. For example, he may experience homesickness when

351

staying at a friend's house. Often the first test of a child's independence comes when he must attend school daily. Aside from poor attendance, these children usually are good students and well behaved at school. The parents are typically good parents who are conscientious and loving. Such parents are sometimes overly protective and close, and the child finds it difficult to separate from them (separation anxiety). He may lack the self-confidence that comes from handling life's normal stresses without his parents' help.

Sometimes a change of schools, a strict teacher, hard tests, a learning problem, or a bully add to the problem. When such factors are present, they are usually just part of the problem, and your child should still go to school while they are being settled.

Expected Course • Without intervention, the physical symptoms and the desire to stay home become more frequent. The longer your child stays home, the harder it will be for him or her to return. Your child's future social life and education may be at stake. If full school attendance is enforced, the problem will improve dramatically in 1 to 2 weeks.

CALL YOUR CHILD'S PHYSICIAN DURING OFFICE HOURS IF

- You think the cause of the symptoms may be physical rather than emotional.

- Your child is over 12 years old.

- Your child is withdrawn in general or seems depressed.

- Your child is on homebound teaching.

- You have other questions.

OVERCOMING SCHOOL PHOBIA

Insist On an Immediate Return to School • The best therapy for school phobia is to be in school every day. Fears are overcome by facing them as soon as possible. Daily school attendance will cause most of your child's physical symptoms to improve magically. At least they will become less severe and occur less often. Your child will eventually enjoy school again. But in the beginning, your child will test your determination to send her every day. You must make school attendance a nonnegotiable, ironclad rule. It won't be effective if handled in a hesitant way. Be optimistic with your child and reassure him that he will feel better after he gets to school.

Be Extra Firm on School Mornings • In the beginning, mornings may be a difficult time. Never ask your child how she feels, because it may just encourage her to complain. If your child is well enough to be up and around the house, she is well enough to go to school. If your child spontaneously complains of physical symptoms but they are the usual ones, she should be promptly sent to school with minimal discussion. When there is doubt about your child's health, try to err on the side of sending her to school. If things change during the day, the school nurse can reevaluate your child.

If your child is late, she should go to school anyway. In case your child misses the school bus, you should have a prearranged alternative plan of transportation. If your child wanders home during lunch or recess, she should be sent back promptly. Sometimes a child may cry and scream and absolutely refuse to go to school. In that case, after talking with your child about his fears, he has to be taken there. One parent may be better at enforcing this than the other. Sometimes a relative can take charge of this for a few days.

Have Your Child See His Physician on Any Morning He Stays Home • If your child has a new physical symptom or seems quite sick, you will probably want him to stay home. However, keep in mind that anxiety can cause a wide variety of symptoms. If you are puzzled, your child's physician will usually be able to determine the exact cause. Call the physician as soon as the office opens. The physician will try to see your child that morning. If the symptom is from a disease, appropriate treatment can be started. If the symptom is from anxiety, your child should be back in school before noon. Working closely with your child's physician in this way can solve even the most difficult problems.

Some symptoms that might keep your child at home are: fevers (over 100°F), vomiting (more than once), frequent diarrhea, a frequent cough, a widespread rash, earaches, or toothaches. The physician should be called about all of these problems, and many need to be seen. On the other hand, children with a sore throat, moderate cough, runny nose, or other cold symptoms (but without fever) can be sent to class. Children with mild stomachaches, headaches, or leg pains can also usually go to school. Children should not be kept home for "looking sick," "poor color," or "tiredness."

Ask the School Staff for Assistance • Schools are usually very understanding about school phobia once they are informed of the diagnosis, because this problem is such a common one. Usually the school nurse will let your child lie down for 5 to 15 minutes in her office and regroup (if the child's symptoms act up at school), rather than sending him or her home. It is often helpful if you talk to your child's teacher about the situation. If your child has special fears like reciting in class, the teacher will usually make special allowance for these.

Talk With Your Child About School Fears • At a time other than a school morning, talk with your child about her problems. Encourage her to tell you exactly what upsets her. Ask her what is the worst possible thing that could happen to her at school or on the way to school. If there's a situation you can change, tell her you will work on it. If she's worried about the physical symptoms becoming worse at school, reassure her she can lie down for a few minutes in the nurse's office as needed. After listening carefully, tell her you can appreciate how she feels, but it's still necessary to attend school while she's getting better.

Help Your Child Spend More Time with Other Children • Outside of school hours, school-phobic children have a tendency to prefer to be with their parents, play indoors, be alone in their rooms, watch a lot of TV, and so on. Many of them cannot stay overnight at a friend's home without developing overwhelming homesickness. They need encouragement to have more peer contact and less parent contact. This is a difficult task for parents who enjoy their child's company, but it is the best course of action in the long run. Your child can be encouraged to join clubs and athletic teams. Noncontact sports like baseball may be preferred initially. Your child can be sent outside more, or to other children's homes. Your child's friends can be asked to join the family for outings or for overnight stays. Help your child learn to stay overnight with relatives and friends. If he or she can handle weekend camping, a summer camp experience can be a turning point.

Call Your Child's Physician Later If

- The school phobia is not resolved by 2 weeks on this approach.

- The school phobia recurs.

- Your child continues to have other fears or separation problems.

PREVENTION OF SCHOOL PHOBIA

- School phobia tendencies can be reduced or prevented by helping your child develop a sense of independence. Acquiring independence must occur in gradually increasing amounts; your child can't avoid it and then suddenly catch up.

- Start baby-sitter contact by 6 months of age at the latest. Being apart from you and then having you return builds security and confidence in your child. Baby-sitter contact is also important for helping your child develop a sense of trust in other adults.

- Begin peer contact by at least 1 year of age, even though the children don't play cooperatively. From 3 years of age onward, your child should be able to interact with peers without your being present. This is a good age for starting shared play groups for children.

- Enroll your child in a preschool by 3 or 4 years of age. This is especially helpful for children who show tendencies to be overly dependent on their parents. Always refer to the school as a "fun place" and the teachers as "nice people."

- Help your child adjust to kindergarten. Over half of children entering kindergarten have transient discomfort and crying for 2 to 5 days. Their symptoms resolve as long as the child returns to school each day and the teacher is supportive. You can sometimes help with the transition by temporarily staying at school (but in the background) for the first hour. By all means, don't take your child out of school, even if he or she is among the 5 percent that urgently want to leave and never return. These children (sometimes labeled "immature" by the teaching staff) need preschool and kindergarten the most.

ATTENTION DEFICIT DISORDER (SHORT ATTENTION SPAN)

CHARACTERISTICS

- Short attention span. Normal attention span is 3 to 5 minutes per year of age. A child in kindergarten needs a 15-minute attention span, and first- and second-graders need a 20-minute span to do the work. (Note: The attention span while watching TV doesn't count.)

- Symptoms of short attention span include the following: The child hasn't learned to listen when someone talks, wait his or her turn, complete a task, or return to a task if interrupted. (Caution: these characteristics can be normal until 3 or 4 years of age.)

- The short attention span has been verified by two or more adults (e.g., parent and teacher)

- Some children (80 percent of boys and 50 percent of girls) also have associated hyperactivity (increased motor activity) with symptoms of being restless, impulsive, and in a hurry

- Some children (50 percent) also have an associated learning disability. The most common one is an auditory processing deficit (i.e., they can't understand complex instructions)

- Intelligence is usually normal

- Occurs mostly in males

- Attention Deficit Disorder (A.D.D.) is also called ADHD (the *H* standing for Hyperactivity), or the Hyperactive Child

Similar Conditions • Disruptive children, children who don't mind, and aggressive children are sometimes included under the broad definition of hyperactivity. Many problem 2-year-olds are referred to as being "hyperactive." These children should be looked upon as children with behavior problems and approached with appropriate discipline techniques (see THE TERRIBLE TWOS AND STUBBORN TODDLERS AND TEMPER TANTRUMS, pages 290 and 292).

Causes • Attention Deficit Disorder (A.D.D.) is the most common developmental disability. It occurs in 3 percent to 5 percent of children. *Developmental* means that the cause is immaturity of brain development. This delay results in poor self-control, requiring external controls by the parents for a longer period of time. Often this type of temperament and short attention span is hereditary. Your style of child rearing did not cause your child to have this limitation. Remind your friends and relatives that there is no simple way to "straighten out" your child. A small percent of children with A.D.D. are reacting to chaotic home environments. Despite controversy, minor brain damage has not been proven to be a cause of A.D.D.

Expected Course • The children with A.D.D. on a developmental basis can expect an excellent outcome if the parents and teachers provide understanding and direction, and preserve the child's self-esteem. Many of these children as adults have good attention spans but remain restless, have to keep busy, and, in a sense, have not entirely outgrown the problem. However, not only does society learn to tolerate such traits in adults but in some settings the person with endless energy is prized. Children with severe A.D.D. may need vocational counseling as adults.

CALL YOUR CHILD'S PHYSICIAN FOR REFERRAL TO A CHILD PSYCHIATRIST OR PSYCHOLOGIST IF

- Your child shows unprovoked aggression and destructiveness.

- Your child has repeated accidents.

- Your child has been suspended or expelled from school.

- Your child can't make or keep any friends.

- You have "given up" hope of improving your child.

- You can't stop using physical punishment on your child.

- You are at your wit's end.

  Premise: All children with A.D.D. should already have been evaluated by their physician and, if of school age, by the school's special education teacher or psychologist.

GUIDELINES FOR LIVING WITH A CHILD HAVING ATTENTION DEFICIT DISORDER (SHORT ATTENTION SPAN)

A.D.D. is a chronic condition that needs special parenting and school intervention. If your child seems to have a poor attention span and is over 3 years of age, these recommendations may assist you in helping your child. Your main obligations will involve organizing your child's home life and improving discipline. Only after your child's behavior has improved will you know for certain if your child also has a short attention span. If he does, specific interventions to help him learn to listen and complete tasks ("stretch" his attention span) can be initiated. Even though you can't be sure about poor attention span until your child is 3 or 4 years of age, you can detect and improve behavior problems at any time after 8 months of age.

• **Accept your child's limitations.** Accept the fact that your child is intrinsically active and energetic and possibly always will be. The hyperactivity is not intentional. Don't expect to eliminate the hyperactivity but merely bring it under reasonable control. Any criticism or other attempt to change an energetic child into a quiet or model child will cause more harm than good. Nothing is more helpful for the hyperactive child than having a tolerant, patient, low-keyed parent.

• **Provide an outlet for the release of excess energy.** This energy can't be bottled up and stored. Daily outdoor activities such as running, sports, and long walks are good outlets. A fenced yard helps. In bad weather your child needs a recreational room where he can play as he pleases with minimal restrictions and supervision. If no large room is available, a garage will sometimes suffice. Your child's toys should not be excessive in number, for this can accentuate his distractibility. They should also be ones that are safe and relatively unbreakable. Encourage your child to play with one toy at a time.

Although the expression of hyperactivity is allowed in these ways, it should not be needlessly encouraged. Don't initiate roughhousing with your child. Siblings should be forbidden to say "Chase me, chase me," or to instigate other noisy play. Rewarding hyperactive behavior can lead to its becoming your child's main style of interacting with people.

• **Keep your home well organized.** Household routines help the hyperactive child to accept order. Make wake-up, mealtimes, snacks, chores, naps, and bedtime as consistent as possible. Try to keep your environment on the quiet side, since this encourages thinking and listening. In general, leave the radio and TV off. Predictable daily events help your child become more predictable in his or her responses.

• **Try not to let your child become fatigued.** When a hyperactive child becomes exhausted, his self-control often breaks down and the hyperactivity becomes worse. Try to have your child sleep or rest when he is fatigued. If he can't seem to "turn off his motor," hold and rock him in a rocking chair.

- **Avoid taking your child to formal gatherings.** Settings where hyperactivity would be extremely inappropriate and embarrassing (such as churches or restaurants) can be completely avoided except for special occasions. To avoid some friction you also may wish to reduce the number of times you allow your child to accompany you to stores and supermarkets. Not only will you be able to shop more efficiently, but the store manager will also be grateful. After your child develops adequate self-control at home, he can gradually be introduced to these situations. Be sure to praise your child when he plays independently rather than interrupting you when you are talking to guests or on the telephone.

- **Maintain firm discipline.** These children are unquestionably difficult to manage. They need more carefully planned discipline than the average child. Rules should be formulated mainly to prevent harm to your child and to others. Aggressive behavior should be no more accepted in the hyperactive child than in the normal child. Unlike the expression of hyperactivity, you can try to eliminate aggressive behaviors, such as biting, hitting, and pushing. Unnecessary or unattainable rules should be avoided—don't expect your child to keep his hands and feet still. Hyperactive children tolerate fewer rules than the normal child. Set down a few clear, consistent, important rules and add other rules at your child's pace. Avoid constant negative comment like "Don't do this," and "Stop that."

- **Enforce rules with nonphysical punishment.** Physical punishment should be avoided in these children, since we want to teach them to be less aggressive rather than to make aggression acceptable. You will need an isolation or time-out room to back up your attempts to enforce rules if a show of disapproval doesn't work. This room can be your child's bedroom or a time-out chair. Your child should be sent there for about 1 minute per year of age. Without a time-out room, overall success is unlikely. Because of your child's short attention span, apply punishment for misbehavior immediately. Your child also needs adult models of control and calmness. Try to correct your child in a friendly, matter-of-fact voice. If you yell, your child will be quick to imitate you (see THE TIME-OUT TECHNIQUE, page 281).

- **Stretch your child's attention span.** Praising attentive (non-hyperactive) behavior is the key to preparing your child for school. Increased attention span and persistence with tasks can be taught at home. Don't wait until your child is of school age and expect the teacher to change him. By age 5 he needs at least a 25-minute attention span to perform adequately in school.

    Set aside several brief periods each day to teach your child listening skills through reading. Start with picture books, and gradually progress to reading stories. Coloring of pictures can be encouraged and praised. Games of increasing difficulty can be taught to your child, starting with building blocks and progressing to puzzles, dominoes, card games, and dice games. Matching pictures is an excellent way to build your child's memory and concentration span. Later, consequence games such as checkers or tic-tac-toe can be introduced. When your child becomes restless, stop, and return for another session later. This process is slow but invaluable in preparing your child for school.

- **Buffer your child against any overreaction by neighbors.** Neighbors with whom your child has contact should be enlisted as helpers. If your child is labeled by some adults as a "bad" kid, it is important that this doesn't carry over into his or her home life. At home the attitude that must prevail is that your child is a "good child with excess energy." It is extremely important that you don't give up on him. Your child must always feel loved and accepted within the family. As long as a child has this, self-esteem and self-confidence will survive. If school is not rewarding, help your child gain a sense of success through a hobby in an area of strength.

- **From time to time, get away from it all.** Exposure to some of these children for 24 hours a day would make anyone a wreck. Periodic breaks help parents to tolerate hyperactive behavior. In a family in which only the father goes out to work, when he comes home he should try to look after the child, not only to give his wife a deserved break but also to understand better what she must contend with during the day. A baby-sitter an afternoon a week and an occasional evening out with her husband can salvage an exhausted mother. Preschool is another helpful option. Parents need a chance to rejuvenate themselves so that they can continue to meet their child's extra needs.

- **Utilize special programs at school.** Try to start your child in preschool by age 3 to help him organize his thoughts and ability to focus. On the other hand consider enrolling your child in regular school a year later (i.e., at age 6 rather than 5) to allow the added maturity to help him fit in better with his classmates. Once your child enters school, the school is responsible for providing appropriate programs for your child's attention deficit disorder and any learning disability he might have. Some standard approaches that teachers use to help children with A.D.D. are smaller class size, isolated study space, spaced learning techniques, and inclusion of the child in tasks like erasing the blackboard or passing out books as outlets for excessive energy. Many of these children spend part of their day with a learning disability teacher who helps improve their skills and confidence.

  If you feel your child has A.D.D. and he has not been tested by the school's special education team, you can request an evaluation. Usually you can obtain the help your child needs by working closely with the school through parent-teacher conferences and special meetings. Your main job is to continue to help your child improve his attention span, self-discipline, and friendships at home.

- **Medications are sometimes helpful.** Some stimulant drugs can improve the powers of concentration. The use of drugs is a matter for you and your child's physician to discuss. In general, medications should not be prescribed before school age. They should also not be prescribed until after your child has received a medical and school evaluation, an individualized educational plan (I.E.P.) is in effect at school, and the preceding guidelines are in effect at home. Medications without special education and home management programs have no long-term benefit. They need to be part of a broader treatment program.

RECOMMENDED READING

Barbara Ingersoll, *Your Hyperactive Child* (New York: Doubleday, 1988).

Melvin D. Levine, *Keeping a Head in School: A Student's Book About Learning Abilities and Learning Disorders* (Educators Publishing Service, 75 Moulton St., Cambridge, MA 02138-1104).

SCHOOLWORK RESPONSIBILITY: HOW TO INSTILL IT

Taking responsibility for schoolwork helps children grow up to be responsible adults who keep their promises, meet deadlines, and succeed at their jobs. Responsible children finish schoolwork, homework, and long-term projects on time. They remember their assignments and turn in papers. They occasionally ask for help (e.g., with a spelling list) but usually like to think through their work by themselves.

HOW TO ENCOURAGE SCHOOLWORK RESPONSIBILITY

The following suggestions should help you cultivate the trait of responsibility in your child and avoid problems with schoolwork that may be difficult to correct later on:

1. *Encourage learning and responsibility in the preschool years.* Listen attentively to your child's conversation. Encourage him to think for himself. Take your child to the library and read to him regularly. Watch educational programs together and talk about them. Be a role model of someone who reads, finds learning exciting, enjoys problem-solving, and likes to try new things. Ask your preschool child to help you with chores (e.g., clearing the table or putting away clean clothes).

2. *Show your child that you are interested in his school performance.* Ask your child about his school day. Look at and comment positively on the graded papers he brings home. Praise your child's strong points on his report card. Show interest in the books your child is reading. Help your child attend school regularly; don't keep him home for minor illnesses. Go to regular parent-teacher conferences and tell him about them. If you feel discouraged, rather than conveying this to your child, schedule an extra conference with his teacher.

3. *Support the school staff's recommendations.* Show respect for both the school system and the teacher, at least in your child's presence. Verbal attacks on the school may pit your child against the school and give him an excuse for not working. Even when you disagree with a school policy, encourage your child to conform to school rules, just as they will need to conform to the broader rules of society.

4. *Make it clear that schoolwork is between your child and the teacher.* When your child begins school, she should

understand that homework, school〉
strictly between her and her teache〉
set goals for better school perform〉
Your child must feel responsible for
in school. People take more pride
they feel fully responsible for then
sponsible for their child's school
door for the child to turn his responsibilities o...
Occasionally, elementary-school teachers may ask you to
review basic facts with your child or see that your child
completes work that was put off at school. When your
child's teacher makes such requests, it's fine for you to
help, but only as a temporary measure.

5. *Stay out of homework.* Asking if your child has homework,
helping nightly, checking the finished homework, or drilling your child in areas of concern all convey to your child
that you don't trust him. If you do your child's homework,
your child will have less confidence that he can do it
himself. If your child asks for help with homework, help
with the particular problem only. Your help should focus
on explaining the question, not on giving the answer. A
good example of useful help is reading your child's spelling
list to him while he writes the words, but then letting him
check his own answers. A chief purpose of homework is to
teach your child to work on his own.

6. *Avoid dictating a study time.* Assigning a set time for your
child to do homework is unnecessary and looked on as
pressure. The main thing parents can do is provide a quiet
setting with a desk, a comfortable chair, and good lighting.
If any, the only rule should be, "No television until homework is done." Without checking, accept your child's word
that the work is done. For long-term assignments, help
your child organize his work the first few times if he seems
overwhelmed. Help him estimate how many hours he thinks
the project will take. Then help him write a list of the days
at home he will work on the project.

7. *Provide home tutoring for special circumstances.* Occasionally a teacher will request parental assistance when a
child has lots of makeup work following a prolonged absence or a transfer to a new school. If your child's teacher
makes such a request, ask her to send home notes about
what he or she wants you to help your child with (e.g.,
multiplication for 2 weeks). By using this approach you are
still not taking primary responsibility for your child's school-

work, because the assignments and request for help come from the teacher. Provide this home instruction in a positive, helping way. As soon as your child has met the teacher's goal for improvement, remove yourself from the role of tutor. In this way you have provided temporary tutoring to help your child over an obstacle that the school staff does not have the time or the resources to deal with fully.

8. *Request special help for children with learning problems.* Some children have learning problems that interfere with learning some of the basic skills (e.g., reading). The comments so far have assumed that your child has no learning limitations. If a child with a reading disability slips too far behind in class, the child may lose confidence in his ability to do schoolwork. If you have concerns about your child's ability to learn, set up a conference with your child's teacher. At that time, inquire about an evaluation by your school's special education team. With extra help, children with learning disabilities can preserve their self-esteem and sense of competency.

HOMEWORK PROBLEMS (SCHOOL UNDERACHIEVER)

CHARACTERISTICS

- Performs below his or her potential at school.

- Has average or better intelligence, with no learning disabilities.

- Doesn't finish schoolwork or homework.

- "Forgets" to bring homework home.

- "Forgets," loses, or doesn't turn in finished homework.

- "Doesn't remember" what parents have taught.

- Gets a poor report card.

- Doesn't want any help.

Causes

Some children get into bad habits with their homework because they become preoccupied with TV programs or video games. Some middle-school children become sidetracked by their hormones or by sports. Other children who find school-work difficult would simply rather play. If parents help these children cut back other activities to reasonable amounts and count on the teacher to grade the child's efforts on school-work and homework, most of these children will improve. Motivation for good grades eventually comes from a desire to please the teacher and be admired by peers, enjoyment in knowing things, ability to see studying as a pathway to a future career, knowledge that she needs a 3-point average to get into college, and her own self-reproach when she falls short of her goals.

When parents overrespond to this behavior and exert pressure for better performance, they can start a power struggle around schoolwork. "Forgetfulness" becomes a game. The child sees the parents' pressure as a threat to his independence. More pressure brings more resistance. Poor grades become the child's best way of proving that he is independent of his parents and that he can't be pushed. Good evidence for this is the child doing worse in the areas where he receives the most help. If parental interference with a child's school-work continues for several years, the child becomes a school "underachiever."

HELPING YOUR CHILD REGAIN RESPONSIBILITY FOR SCHOOLWORK

1. *Get out of the middle regarding homework.* Clarify that completing and turning in homework is between your child and the teacher. Remember that the purpose of homework is to teach your child to work on his own. Don't ask your child if he has any. Don't help with homework except at your child's request. Allow the school to apply natural consequences for poor performance. Walk away from any power struggles. Your child can learn the lesson of school-work accountability only through personal experience. If possible, apologize to your youngster, saying, for example, "After thinking about it, we have decided you are old enough to manage your own affairs. Schoolwork is your business, and we will try to stay out of it. We are confident you will do what's best for you."

   The result of this "sink or swim" approach is that arguments will stop, but your child's schoolwork may temporarily worsen. Your child may throw caution to the winds to see if you really mean what you have said. This period of doing nothing but waiting for your child to find her own reason for doing well in school may be very agonizing. However, children need to learn from their mistakes. If you can avoid "rescuing" your child, her grades will show a dramatic upsurge in 2 to 9 months. This planned withdrawal of parental pressure is best done in the early grades, when marks are of minimal importance but the development of the child's own personal reason for learning is critical.

2. *Avoid reminders about schoolwork.* Repeatedly reminding your child about schoolwork promotes rebellion. So do criticizing, lecturing, and threatening your child. Pressure is different from parental interest and encouragement. If pressure works at all, it works only temporarily.

We can never force children to learn or to be productive. Learning is a process of self-fulfillment. It is an area that belongs to the child and one that we as parents should try to stay out of, despite our yearnings for our children's success.

3. *Coordinate your plan with your child's teacher.* Schedule a parent-teacher conference. Discuss your views on schoolwork and homework responsibility. Tell your child's teacher you want your child to be responsible to the teacher for homework. Clarify that you would prefer not to check or correct the work, because this has not been helpful in the past. Tell them you want to be supportive of the school and could do this best if the teacher sent home a brief, weekly progress report. If the teacher thinks your youngster needs extra help, encourage her to suggest a tutoring program. In middle school, peer tutoring is often a powerful motivator.

4. *Limit TV until schoolwork improves.* While you can't make your child study, you can increase the potential study time. Eliminate all TV and video game time on school nights. Explain to your child that these privileges will be reinstated after the teacher's weekly report confirms that all homework was handed in and the overall quality of work (or grades) is improving. Explain that you are doing this to help him better structure his time.

5. *Consider adding incentives for improved schoolwork.* Most children respond better to incentives than to disincentives. Ask your youngster what he thinks would help. Some good incentives are taking your child to a favorite restaurant, amusement park, video arcade, sports event, or the movies.

Sometimes earning "spending money" by working hard on studies will interest your child. The payments can be made weekly, based on the teacher's progress reports. A's, B's, and C's can receive a different cash value. What your child buys with this money should be his business (music, toys, etc). Rewarding hard work is how the adult marketplace works.

6. *Consider removing other privileges for falloff in schoolwork.* You have already eliminated school night TV-viewing because it obviously interferes with studying. If the school reports continue to be poor, you may need to eliminate all TV and video games. Other privileges that may need to be temporarily limited should be those that matter to your child (e.g., telephone, bike, outside play, or visiting friends). If your teenager drives a car, this privilege may need to be curtailed until his grades are at least a 3-point (B) average. For youngsters who have fallen behind in their work, grounding (i.e., no peer contact) for 1 to 2 weeks may be required until they "catch up." Avoid severe punishment, however, because it will leave your youngster angry and resentful. Canceling something important (like membership in Scouts or an athletic team) or taking away something they care about (like a pet) because of poor marks is unfair and ineffective. Being part of a team is also good for motivation.

Call Your Child's Teacher For a Conference If

- Your child's schoolwork and grades do not improve within 2 months.

- Homework is still an issue between you and your child after 2 months.

- You think your child has a learning problem that makes school difficult.

Call Your Child's Physician If

- You think your child is preoccupied with some stresses in his life.

- You think your child is depressed.

- You have other questions or concerns.

Note: If these attempts to motivate your child fail, he may need an evaluation by a child psychologist or child psychiatrist.

TELEVISION: REDUCING THE NEGATIVE IMPACT

TV has a tremendous influence on how children view our world. Youngsters spend more hours watching TV from birth to age 18 than they spend in the classroom. The positive aspects include seeing different life-styles and cultures and entering school more knowledgeable than children did before the era of TV. Television also presents some positive, even heroic, role models. In addition, TV has great entertainment value, providing humor, excitement, and other types of diversion. While TV can be a good teacher, many children watch TV excessively and therefore experience some of its negative consequences.

HARMFUL ASPECTS OF TV

* *TV displaces active types of recreation.* It decreases time spent with peers, when games and other creative activities are experienced. It decreases daydreaming and thinking time. It takes away the practice time required to become competent in sports, art, or music. Television is especially dangerous for children who already tend to be shy or withdrawn.

* *TV interferes with conversation and discussion time,* especially if kept on during meals. It reduces social interactions with family and friends.

* *TV discourages reading.* Reading requires much more brain activity and thinking than television. Reading improves a youngster's vocabulary. A falloff in reading scores may be related to excessive TV time.

* *Heavy TV viewing (more than 4 hours a day) definitely reduces school performance.* This much TV interferes with study, reading, and thinking time. If watching television prevents adequate sleep, the children will not be alert enough to learn well on the following day.

* *TV discourages exercise.* An inactive life-style leads to poor physical fitness. If accompanied by frequent snacking, watching TV may contribute to weight problems. A recent study found that for each additional hour of television watched per week, the tendency toward obesity was increased by 1 percent.

* *TV advertising encourages a demand for material possessions.*

Particular toys are highlighted in such a way that young children pressure their parents to buy them. TV portrays materialism as the "American way."

- *TV advertising teaches poor eating habits.* Sweets (such as sugared cereals) tend to be emphasized for young children.

- *TV advertising teaches a magical trust in health products, drugs, and vitamins.* TV suggests that there is a pill for every symptom.

- *TV fosters a poor reality base.* Young children through age 10 have some difficulty separating fact from fantasy. Television frequently presents a distorted view of the world in which most problems have easy solutions. Game shows may give children the sense that they can suddenly become rich and that hard work and delayed gratification is unnecessary.

- *TV depicts unrealistic stereotypes of human beings.* Men outnumber women 3 to 1 on television shows. Minority groups, elderly people, common occupations, and middle-class lifestyles are underrepresented.

- *TV is sexually seductive.* Television programs and commercials depict relationships that rapidly progress to sexual activity. The risks and ethics of promiscuity are seldom addressed. Some programs (such as MTV) may portray sexual violence toward women. Many of the lead characters also smoke and drink heavily.

- *TV violence creates its own set of problems.* Crime and violence occurs on television ten times as often as in real life. Viewing violence may cause pessimism regarding personal safety and the future. Several studies have shown that TV violence can lead to apathy toward violence. TV violence may numb the normal sympathy toward victims of human suffering. Young children may be more aggressive in their play after seeing violent television shows. While TV violence does not increase aggressive behavior toward people in most children, it may do so in disturbed or impulsive children.

THE PREVENTION OF TV ADDICTION

- *Encourage active recreational outlets.* Help your child become interested in sports, games, hobbies, and music. Occasionally turn off the television and take a walk or play a game with your child.

- *Read to your children.* Begin reading to your child by 1 year of age and encourage him to read on his own as he becomes older. Some parents help children earn TV or video-game time by equivalent reading time. Help him improve his conversational skills by spending more of your time talking with him.

- *Limit TV time to 2 hours per day or less.* Allowing children to view excessive amounts of television is probably an even greater problem in our country than watching violence on TV. Another alternative is to limit TV to 1 hour on school nights and 2 or 3 hours per day on weekends. You occasionally may want to allow extra viewing time for special educational programs. If you cut back your child's TV watching, don't be surprised if he initially complains. Excessive TV watching is a habit that, once established, is hard to break. Suggest other activities to fill the free time.

- *Don't use TV as a distraction or a baby-sitter for preschool children.* Preschoolers' viewing should be limited to special TV shows and videotapes that are produced for young children. Use your VCR to save good programs for rainy days. Because the difference between fantasy and reality is not clear for this age group, regular TV shows may cause fears.

- *If your child is doing poorly in school, limit TV time to 1 half hour each day.* Make a rule that homework and chores must be finished before television is watched. If his favorite show is on earlier, try to record it for later viewing.

- *Set a bedtime for your child that is not altered by TV shows that interest her.* Children who are allowed to stay up late to watch television are usually too tired the following day to remember what they were taught in school. By all means, don't permit your child to have a TV set in her bedroom because this eliminates your control over TV viewing.

- *Turn off the TV set during meals.* Family time is too precious to be squandered on TV shows. After your children are grown up and have left home, you will probably regret it if your mealtimes were not protected and your children were allowed to disappear into their private TV worlds while they ate. In addition, don't use television as a background sound in your house. If you don't like a quiet house, leave a radio or record player on playing music without lyrics. Television is too engrossing a medium. It demands to be seen as well as heard. Also turn off the TV set for visitors or study time.

- *Set a bedtime deadline* that is not altered by TV shows that interest your child. Children who are allowed to stay up late and watch television may be tired the following day and perform poorly in school.

- *Teach critical viewing.* Turn the TV on only when a specific program is going to be watched. Don't turn it on at random and scan for something interesting. Teach your child to look first in the program guide. On some nights, nothing worthwhile or entertaining is on television.

- *Teach your child to turn off the TV set* at the end of a show. If it is allowed to stay on, your child will probably become interested in the following show and then it will be difficult to turn it off.

- *Encourage your child to watch some shows that are educational* or teach human values. Point out characters who care about others. Encourage watching documentaries, real-life dramas, or programs about great artists. Look at what public television has to offer (including the absence of advertising). Use programs about love, sex, family disputes, drinking, and drugs to open family discussions on these difficult topics.

- *Try to be present with your child* the first time he or she watches a new program. Help decide whether or not this is a program you wish to allow your child to watch on a weekly basis.

- *Forbid violent TV shows.* This means you have to know what your child is watching and turn off the TV set when you don't approve of the program. Develop separate lists of programs that are okay for older and younger kids to watch. Make your older children responsible for keeping the younger ones out of the TV room at these times. If not, the show is turned off. The availability of cable television and videocassette recorders means that any child of any age has access to the uncut versions of R-rated films. Many children under 13 years of age develop daytime fears and nightmares after watching vicious movies. Children in elementary school should not be allowed to watch R-rated movies or music video channels.

- *Discuss the consequences of violence* if you allow your older child to watch violent shows. Point out how violence hurts both the victim and his family. Be sure to discuss any program that has content which upsets your child.

- *Discuss commercials with your children.* Help them identify high-pressure selling and exaggerated claims. If your child wants a toy that is a look-alike version of a TV character, ask him how he would use it at home. The response will probably convince you that the toy will be added to a collection of rarely used toys rather than become a catalyst for much active play. Point out foods that cause cavities.

- *Discuss the differences between reality and make-believe.* This type of clarification can help your child enjoy a show and yet realize that what is happening doesn't happen in real life.

- *Set a good example.* If you are a TV addict, you can be sure your child will become one. The types of programs you watch also sends a clear message to your child. Consider starting yourself on a TV diet.

For more information on children's programming, write Action for Children's Television (ACT), 20 University Road, Cambridge, MA 02138.

VIDEO GAMES

Home video games have swept the country. Over 30 percent of American homes have a computerized game system hooked up to the television set. Over 500 different game cartridges are available. Video games are currently the most popular toy in our country. Portable video games are the latest option. Every day more 6 -to 16-year-olds become part of Nintendo mania.

VIDEO GAMES VS. TELEVISION
Compared to watching television, video games are a better form of entertainment. Video games are interactive. Your child's mind has to be turned on and working. The following are some potential benefits of the better games:

- Promotes paying attention to details (e.g., to clues), memory, sequencing, and strategizing

- Promotes eye-hand (visual motor) coordination

- Improves visual perception (spatial awareness)

DISADVANTAGES OF VIDEO GAMES
The drawbacks of video games are similar to the ones we see with TV (see page 368):

- Video games can dominate your child's leisure and study time. Video games can eliminate time needed to develop competence in sports, music, or art. If reading and homework are displaced, school performance can be affected.

- Video games can be a solitary activity, reducing social interactions with family and friends. Your youngster can become a junior hermit interacting with friends only to pump them for pieces of information about hidden passages or secret trap doors. Encourage playing video games with other children.

- Violent video games can teach an acceptance of violent behavior in real life.

- Overall, realize that your child is overdosing on video games if his grades have fallen, he doesn't finish his homework, he gets inadequate sleep, he doesn't play outdoors, he has become a loner, or he is preoccupied with karate chops or other aggressive behavior that is part of one of his video games.

TAKE A STAND ON VIDEO GAMES

Don't expect your youngster to limit the time allocated to this mesmerizing form of entertainment. Given his own way, he might play Nintendo every waking moment. You are responsible for protecting your child from harm. You must decide on rules that are appropriate for your child. If the rules are broken, the game (or control panel) needs to be put away for 1 or more days.

Allow video games only after homework and chores are completed. Access to video game time can even be presented as an incentive for finishing these tasks properly.

Limit video game time. Two hours a day or less is a reasonable goal. An alternative is to limit it to one hour on school nights and two or three hours a day on weekends. Some parents allow the system to be used only on weekends. If your child is doing poorly in school, temporarily eliminate video game time on school nights. Some parents have their children earn video game time by putting in equivalent reading time.

Don't allow your child to postpone bedtime because he wants to finish a video game. Remember that children who are allowed to stay up late are usually too tired the next day to remember what they are taught in school. Don't allow your child to have a video game set in her bedroom because this eliminates your control over the hours of play. When bedtime is drawing near, give your child a 10-minute warning.

Encourage your children to settle their own disputes over using the video game. When possible, stay out of disagreements, as long as they remain verbal. Children can't go through life having a referee to resolve their differences. If the argument becomes too loud, remove the control panel until your children work out a schedule.

Help your child buy video games that are not excessively violent. Encourage him to buy or rent sports, puzzle, maze, or adventure games. Avoid games that contain lots of murder, combat, and destruction. Since your child is an active participant in the mayhem on video games, research suggests they have a greater impact on his aggressive behavior than violent TV shows, in which he is strictly an observer. If your child borrows a video cartridge from a friend, have a rule that you have to approve of its contents before he uses it.

If you own a computer, take advantage of some of the educational games. These tap the motivational power of the arcade games to help your child learn. They combine academics and entertainment. They also teach computer skills. If you have a choice, buy computer games rather than video games.

Try to channel your child's leisure time into a variety of activities. Video games are not bad for children. They can teach skills. They are more educational than TV. And, if you try to forbid video games, your child will play them at another child's home. So help your child learn to use them in moderation after the first weeks of normal infatuation have passed. Encourage more reading, music, hobbies, sports, and playing with friends.

R-RATED MOVIES: PROTECTING OUR CHILDREN

The following symptoms have all been reported in children after watching violent, R-rated movies:

- bedtime fears

- recurrent nightmares

- daytime flashbacks of something frightening

- disruption of concentration and study

- a fearful view of the world

Since these movies were made to frighten teenagers and

adults, this information should come as no surprise to you. Frequent exposures to violent material can also cause a child to become insensitive to human suffering. The impact of these movies on disturbed children may go a step farther: Some of them try to imitate the movies.

Causes • Most bad reactions are to R-rated movies containing horror, graphic violence, or sexual violence. The content of violent movies has changed over the last 10 years. Mutilation is the message. Thanks to improved special effects, we can now see the details of torture or brutality in slow, agonizing close-up. Recent movies show a head being chopped off, a brain being blown up, the disfigurement of a face with a knife, a neck being slashed, or a hypodermic needle being plunged into an eyeball.

The 12-and-under age group is most at risk for severe reactions. Most elementary-school children don't have the adult defense mechanisms needed to cope with these movies. They are most threatened by movie villains who seem real and play on their deepest fears (e.g., surprise attack, kidnapping, torture, or death). They are especially vulnerable if they identify with the victim in the movie. Some of these mad slashers (unlike real people) are portrayed as indestructible and leave the young viewer feeling helpless. Children less than 7 or 8 also think concretely. If it can happen on the screen, it could happen to them tonight.

Access to these violent movies has also changed. The uncut versions of violent movies are now readily available through cable TV and video rentals. Parents say "I didn't know she was watching that. I can't keep track of everything she sees." A popular party game in middle school involves renting a horror movie and seeing how much of it your friends can watch before becoming ill.

Most of the research done on the impact of violence on children has used TV violence. This research shows that TV affects children's behavior. No research review committee will ever approve a study in which children are exposed to R-rated movies. You don't have to be a psychiatrist to know that viewing graphic violence in movies (which is much more powerful than anything on TV) is harmful to children. Yet some parents allow it.

Expected Course • Without treatment, these fears and preoccupations can last 1 to 6 months. With treatment, they usually improve over a few weeks.

Protecting Your Child from Movie Violence

1. *Understand the movie rating system.* Don't lump all R-rated movies together. The R rating means that children under 17 are not admitted without a parent. It is given for nudity, profanity, violence, *or* a combination of the above. Nudity, depending on the context, may be harmless. Profanity in the movies has contributed to the common use of profanity on elementary-school playgrounds, and this trend is probably irreversible. It is the violence in the movie that has the disturbing impact on children. In fact, if one reads the ratings carefully, the degree of violence is also often listed (e.g., "graphic" violence or rape).

2. *Forbid all R-rated movies before age 13.* Never allow a child who is less than 13 years of age to see any R-rated film, no matter how liberal you may be about nudity and profanity. Between 13 and 17, the maturity and sensitivity of your child must be carefully considered in deciding when he is ready to deal with some of these movies. Don't allow your child to see movies with personal or sexual violence (graphic violence) before age 17. These movies are not a required part of life experiences at any age.

3. *Select your child's movies.* Don't let your child see a movie unless you know the rating and have read a review. Don't give in to their pressure to see something that is potentially harmful (that's an adult decision). Keep a list of movies you approve of. Look at the reviews of Colleen Harty, who is a PTA-sanctioned movie reviewer. She reviews films through the eyes of a parent and has a unique rating system that describes various aspects of the content of the movie, including cruelty to animals.

4. *Monitor what your child is watching on cable TV and network TV.* Don't allow him to turn on the cable movie channel unless he has your permission to view a specific program. Even some of the edited versions of movies on network TV can be too frightening for young children. Don't let your younger children watch the programs that you have approved only for your older children (including the evening news). Young children who have viewed fires, tornadoes, earthquakes, warfare, or terrorism on the news have become worried about their personal safety.

5. *Warn your child about violent movies outside the home.* Protect your youngster from being unintentionally victimized by film violence. Be especially vigilant about slumber parties

or Halloween parties. Tell your child to call you if the family he is visiting or a baby-sitter is showing any scary movies. Teach him to walk out of movies that make him scared or upset. Warn him to obey theater policies and not to sneak into R-rated movies.

6. *Discuss any movie that upsets your child.* Respect your child's fears; don't make fun of them. Help him talk about what scared him. Help him gradually come to grips with the situation.

7. *Prevention.* Protect your child's mental health from unnecessary fears. R-rated movies are never harmless for children in elementary school. Use the movie ratings and your common sense to choose age-appropriate movies for your child. Never let your child see anything that frightens you.

TICS (TWITCHES)

SYMPTOMS AND CHARACTERISTICS

- Rapid, repeated muscle twitches (also called habit spasms)
- Eye-blinking, facial-grimacing, forehead-wrinkling, head-jerking, or shoulder-shrugging are most common types
- Tics increase with stress
- Tics decrease with relaxation
- Tics disappear during sleep
- Occur in 20 percent of children
- Occur in boys 3 times more frequently than in girls
- Peak age is 6 to 10 years

Causes • Tics reflect the spilling over of emotional tension. They mean your child is under pressure. They are involuntary, not deliberate.

Tics usually occur in normal, bright, sensitive children. Tics are more severe in children who are shy or overly conscientious. Tics can be accentuated by critical parents who nag, pressure for achievement beyond the child's ability, or draw negative comparisons to siblings.

Expected Outcome • If tics are ignored, they will usually disappear in 2 months to 1 year's time. If extra effort is made to help the child relax, they will usually improve more quickly. Without intervention, most children with tics have spontaneous improvement or clearing at adolescence. Approximately 3 percent of children with tics develop incapacitating tics if they are not handled appropriately.

HOW TO HELP YOUR CHILD WITH TICS

Help Your Child Relax in General • Tics are a barometer of inner tension. Make sure your child has free time and fun time every day. If he or she is overscheduled with activities, try to lighten the commitments. If your child is unduly self-critical, praise him more and remind him to be a good friend to himself.

Identify and Remove Specific Environmental Stresses • Keep a tic diary. Whenever your child has a flurry of tics, write down the date, time, and the preceding event. From this diary, you should be able to identify some of your child's pressure points. (Note: Your child shouldn't be aware you are keeping this diary.) In any event, reduce the amount of criticism that your child receives about grades, music lessons, sports, keeping his or her room clean, table manners, and so forth. Avoid stimulant medications (such as decongestants), which can lower the threshold for tics.

Ignore Tics When They Occur • When your child is having tics, don't call his or her attention to them. Reminders imply that they are bothering you. If your child becomes worried about the tics, then every time they occur, the child will react with tension rather than acceptance. The tension in turn will trigger more tics (a vicious cycle). Don't allow siblings or others to tease your child about the tics. Be sure that relatives, friends, and teachers also abide by this approach. When tics occur, people should say nothing and back off from any pressure they may be applying.

Don't Talk About Tics When They Are Not Occurring • Stop all family conversation about tics. The less said about them, the less your child will be apprehensive about their occurring. If your child brings up the topic, reassure him that he will regain control over his facial muscles and the tics will go away.

Avoid Any Punishment for Tics • Some parents have the mistaken idea that tics are a bad habit that can be broken. This idea is absolutely false. Also having children practice tic control in front of a mirror usually makes them realize they can't control the tics. Any facial exercises or massage should also be discontinued, because they just draw undue attention to the problem.

CALL YOUR CHILD'S PHYSICIAN DURING OFFICE HOURS IF

- The tics interfere with friendships or studies at school.
- The tics involve sounds, words, or profanity.
- The tics involve coughing.
- The tics involve parts of the body other than the head, face, or shoulders.
- The tics become frequent (more than 10 each day).
- The tics have lasted for more than a year.
- The tics are not better after trying this program for 1 month.
- You have other questions or concerns.

BED-WETTING (ENURESIS)

SYMPTOMS AND CHARACTERISTICS

Enuresis is the involuntary passage of urine during sleep more than once a month. This very common problem occurs in 60 percent of children at age 3, in 40 percent at age 4, in 20 percent at age 5, in 10 percent at age 6, in 7 percent at age 8, in 3 percent at age 12, and in 1 percent by age 18. Therefore, we consider it normal until at least age 6.

Causes • Most of these children have inherited small bladders, which cannot hold all the urine produced in a night. In addition, they don't awaken to the signal of a full bladder. The kidneys are normal. Physical causes are very rare, and your physician can easily detect them. Emotional problems do not cause enuresis, but they can occur if it is mishandled.

Expected Course • Most children with bed-wetting overcome it between ages 6 and 10. If one of the parents was a bed-wetter, the child will probably become dry at the same age the parent did. Even without treatment, all children eventually get over it. Therefore, treatments that might have harmful complications should not be used. On the other hand, treatments without side effects can be started as soon as your child has achieved complete daytime bladder control for 6 to 12 months.

CALL YOUR CHILD'S PHYSICIAN DURING OFFICE HOURS IF

• Passing the urine causes pain or burning.

• The urine stream is weak or dribbly.

• Wetting occurs days as well as nights.

• Your child drinks excessive fluids.

• Bed-wetting is a new problem (your child used to be dry).

• Your child is over 12 years old.

• You have other questions.

HOME CARE FOR A CHILD OF ANY AGE WHO IS BED-WETTING

Encourage Your Child to Get Up to Urinate During the Night • This advice is more important than any other. Tell your child at bedtime, "Try to get up when you have to pee." Leaving a light on in the bathroom may help. Some preschoolers prefer to use a potty chair left next to the bed.

Encourage Postponing Urination • Encourage your child to urinate infrequently during the daytime. If your child urinates often, sometimes encourage him to wait, but don't make an issue of it. Don't remind him to use the bathroom except at bedtime.

Encourage Intake of Daytime Fluids • Encourage fluid intake during the morning and early afternoon. The more fluids your child drinks, the more urine your child will produce, and more urine leads to larger bladders.

Discourage Intake of Evening Fluids • Discourage your child from drinking more than 2 ounces during the 2 hours before bedtime. Give gentle reminders about this, but don't worry about a few extra swallows of water.

Protect the Bed from Urine • Your child should wear extra-thick underwear in addition to his pajamas. This keeps much of the urine from getting through to the sheets. Diapers or plastic pants should no longer be used by age 4. Odor becomes a problem if urine soaks into the mattress or blankets. Protect the mattress with a plastic mattress cover.

Establish a Morning Routine for Wet Pajamas and Wet Bedding • On wet mornings, your child can rinse his pajamas and underwear in the sink until the odor is gone. If your child smells of urine, he will need to take a quick rinse in the shower so he won't be teased at school. You can cut down on the laundry by placing a dry towel under your child's bottom each night. This can be rinsed each morning and saved until you do your wash. If a wet bed is left open to the air, the wet sheets will usually be dry by noon. Because of odor, sheets may need to be washed a few extra times each week.

Respond Positively to Dry Nights • Praise your child on mornings when he wakes up dry. A calendar with gold stars or "happy faces" for dry nights may also help.

Respond Gently to Wet Nights • Your child does not like being wet. Most bed-wetters feel quite guilty and embarrassed about this problem. They need sympathy, not blame or punishment. Siblings should not be allowed to tease bed-wetters. Punishment or pressure will delay a cure and cause secondary emotional problems.

ADDITIONAL HOME CARE WHEN YOUR CHILD REACHES AGE 6

Follow the previous recommendations in addition to the guidelines given below:

Self-Awakening Program for Children with Small Bladders • Children with small bladders cannot stay dry unless they get up to urinate one or more times every night. Make sure your child understands this. His goal should be getting up, not holding his urine until morning. Getting up can keep a person dry regardless of how small the bladder is or how much fluid he drinks. To help your child learn to awaken himself at night, encourage him to practice the following pep talk at bedtime:

• Lie on your bed with your eyes closed.

• Pretend it's the middle of the night.

- Pretend your bladder is full.

- Pretend it's starting to hurt.

- Pretend it's trying to wake you up.

- Pretend it's saying: "Get up before it's too late."

- Then run to the bathroom and empty your bladder.

- Remind yourself to get up like this during the night.

Encourage Changing Wet Clothes During the Night • If your child wets at night, he should try to get up and change himself. First, if your child feels any urine leaking out, he should try to stop the flow of urine. Second, he should hurry to the toilet to see if he has any urine left in his bladder. Third, he should change himself and put a dry towel over the wet part of the bed. This step can be made easier if dry pajamas and towels are always kept on a chair near the bed. The child who shows the motivation to carry out these steps is close to being able to awaken from the sensation of a full bladder.

Determine the Capacity (Size) of Your Child's Bladder • Do this by having your child hold his urine as long as possible on at least three occasions. Each time have your child urinate into a container. Measure the amount of urine in ounces. The largest of the three measurements can be considered your child's bladder capacity. The normal capacity is 1 or more ounces per year of age. In a 6-year-old, a capacity of 5 ounces or less is small; a capacity of 6 to 8 ounces is normal and means that the bladder can hold a night's urine production until morning. Normal adult bladder size is 14 to 16 ounces.

Encourage Bladder-Stretching Exercises • These can gradually enlarge the size of the bladder so that it can hold more urine at night. Just as importantly, waiting 10 to 15 minutes during the day can help the bladder wait at night until your child can get out of deep sleep and wake up. To stretch the bladder, encourage your child to hold his urine as long as possible during the daytime. Whenever your child feels the urge to go, he can try to distract himself for the 10 seconds or so it takes for the bladder spasms to stop. Learning to resist the first urge to urinate is especially important. At least once a day, have your child urinate into a measuring cup to see if he has maintained or even beaten his previous record (in ounces). Mark the highest volume achieved with a piece of masking tape on the cup. These exercises should be introduced only if your child wants to try them; for some children this won't occur before age 8.

Help Your Child Assume Responsibility • Your child should feel responsible for solving this problem. The bladder exercises, self-awakening program, control of fluid intake, and record-keeping need your child's involvement and commitment. By all means, don't try to awaken your child at night. As long as you are doing it, your child is less likely to do it for himself. Your child should look upon his parents and physician as people who can provide suggestions and support but who do not take responsibility for the bed-wetting.

ADDITIONAL INTERVENTION WHEN YOUR CHILD REACHES AGE 8

Follow the previous recommendations. Talk with your physician about the possibility of using alarms or drugs as well, as follows:

Bed-Wetting Alarms • Alarms are used to teach a child to awaken when he needs to urinate during the night. They have the highest cure rate (about 70 percent) of any available approach. They are the treatment of choice for any bed-wetter with a small bladder who can't otherwise train himself to awaken at night. The new transistorized alarms are small, lightweight, sensitive to a few drops of urine, not too expensive (about $50), and easy for a child to set up by himself. Children using alarms still need to work on the self-awakening program.

Directions for the Youngster on Using a Bed-Wetting Alarm

• This is your alarm. It can help you cure your bed-wetting only if you use it correctly. Remember, the main purpose of the alarm is to help you get up during the night and use the toilet. The alarm won't work unless you listen for it carefully and respond to it quickly. It's the backup system for your self-awakening program.

• Hook up the alarm system by yourself. Trigger the buzzer a few times by touching the sensors with a moist finger and practice going to the bathroom as you will do if it goes off during the night.

- Have a night-light or flashlight near your bed so it will be easy to see what you are doing when the alarm sounds.

- Go through your self-awakening pep talk at bedtime. Try to "beat the buzzer" by waking up when your bladder feels full but before any urine leaks out. If the buzzer does go off, try to wake up and stop urinating at the first moment that you think you hear the alarm—even if you think you are hearing it in a dream.

- As soon as you hear the alarm, jump out of bed and stand up. After you are standing and awake, turn off the buzzer's sound by removing the metal strip from the little pocket in your underwear (if you have a Wet-Stop) or disconnect the clips (if you have a Nytone) and dry them off.

- Hurry to the bathroom. Empty your bladder and see how much urine you were able to hold back.

- Put on dry underwear and pajamas, and reconnect the alarm. Put a dry towel over the wet spot on your bed.

- In the morning write on your calendar DRY, WET SPOT (if you got up after the alarm went off), or WET (if you didn't get up).

- Use the alarm every night until you go 3 or 4 weeks without bed-wetting. This usually takes 2 to 3 months, so try to be persistent.

The Parents' Role with Bed-Wetting Alarms • If your child doesn't awaken immediately to the sound of the buzzer, he needs your help. You may need to be involved every night for the first 2 to 3 weeks.

- Go to your child's room as quickly as you can. Turn on the light and say loudly, "Get out of bed and stand up."

- If that doesn't work, get your child to a sitting position and run a cold washcloth over his face to bring him out of his deep sleep.

- Only after your child is standing, remind him to turn off the alarm. By all means, don't turn off the buzzer for him. Your child has to learn to carry out this step for himself.

- Make sure your child is wide awake and walks into the bathroom before you leave him. If necessary, ask him questions to help awaken him.

- Your goal is to help your child awaken immediately and get out of bed when the buzzer goes off. Phase out of your child's alarm program as soon as possible. Going to bed with the radio *off*, going to bed at a reasonable hour, and using a night-light can help your child respond faster to the alarm.

How to Order Enuresis Alarms • Alarms and information can be ordered from:

- Nytone Alarm: Nytone Medical Products, 2424 South 900 West, Salt Lake City, UT 84119, or call 801-973-4090.
- Potty Pager Silent Alarm, Ideas for Living, 1285 N. Cedarbrook, Boulder, CO 80304 or call 1-800-497-6573
- Wet-Stop Alarm: Palco Laboratories, 8030 Soquel Ave., Santa Cruz, CA 95062, or call 800-346-4488.

Alarm Clock • If your child is unable to awaken himself at night and you can't afford a bed-wetting alarm, teach him to use an alarm clock or clock radio. Set it for 3 or 4 hours after your child goes to bed. Put it beyond arm's reach. Encourage your child to practice responding to the alarm during the day while lying on the bed with eyes closed. Have your child set the alarm each night. Praise your child for getting up at night, even if he isn't dry in the morning.

Drugs • Most bed-wetters need extra help with staying dry during slumber parties, camping trips, vacations, or other overnights. Some take an alarm clock with them and stay dry by awakening once at night. Some are helped by temporarily taking a drug at bedtime. One drug (given by nasal spray) decreases urine production at night and is quite safe. Another, older drug (taken as a pill) temporarily increases bladder capacity. It is safe at the correct dosage but dangerous if too much is taken or a younger sibling gets into it. If you do use a drug, be careful about the amount you use and where you store the drug, and be sure to keep the safety cap on the bottle. The drawback of these medicines is that when their use is stopped, the bed-wetting usually returns. They do not cure bed-wetting. Therefore, children on drugs for enuresis should also be using an alarm and learning to get up at night.

Call Your Child's Physician Later If

- Your child is over 6 years of age and is not better after 3 months using this treatment program.

RECOMMENDED READING
Alison Mack, *Dry All Night* (Boston: Little, Brown, 1989).

FAMILY ISSUES

THE WORKING MOTHER: JUGGLING CHILDREN, HOME, AND CAREER

THE DECISION TO WORK

Reasons for Working • At this time only 10 percent of American households have a full-time homemaker-mother. More than 50 percent of mothers with infants are working outside the home. The frequency is even higher for mothers of preschoolers.

The reasons for working outside the home are many. In some families, it is financial need, as in a single-parent family. Other mothers work because two incomes are needed to sustain a middle-class life-style. For some mothers it is the personal preference of work over "housekeeping and mothering." For others it is essential for staying up-to-date in a fast-changing career, as well as for the fulfillment work brings. It has often been said that a satisfied parent makes a better parent.

The question of returning to work versus staying at home has no easy or correct answer. The decision is one that each parent must make based on her particular circumstances. Children can do well with either approach; the family's needs are the main issue.

Pros and Cons for Your Child • If you can provide your child with a consistent nurturing caretaker, there is no evidence that your return to work will cause your child any harm. Children of working mothers develop as well emotionally as do other children. Working does not weaken the mother-child bond. In fact, there are some benefits for your child in having a working mother. These include increased independence, responsibility, and maturity. Young children of working mothers learn to trust other adults and to negotiate with peers. (The stay-at-home mother must provide extra adult and peer contact to achieve similar social skills.) Other advantages include, for girls, having higher career aspirations and, for boys, learning that fathers share in housework. Each parent must decide how important it is for her to be present during her child's early years. Research does not document any dire consequences to the children of working mothers, except daycare brings increased infections (but usually minor ones, such as colds).

Timing the Return to Work • A mother should try to remain at home for 6 to 8 weeks after the birth of her baby in order to recover physically from normal childbirth and establish breastfeeding. A preferred maternity leave might extend to 4 months after the birth, at which time the mother would have developed greater confidence regarding her mothering skills and have a baby who sleeps through the night. Unfortunately, few mothers can return to work at the time of their preference. Many mothers need to return to work because of financial realities and the limits of subsidized leave. At this time only 40 percent of jobs provide any paid maternity leave, and a smaller percent guarantee job security through unpaid leave until the baby is 4 months of age. In fact, the United States is the only advanced nation without federal legislation guaranteeing maternity leave. (Over 100 nations do have such leave.)

The optimal length of maternity leave is unknown and should probably be based upon individual preference. Some authorities suggest that mothers should attempt to be a full-time parent during the first 2 or 3 years of their babies' life. In the best of all worlds I would agree, but the advantages of this commitment remain unproven. Mothers should not feel guilty about returning to work when their babies are 2 to 4 months of age. But during the early years, try to find part-time or at-home employment.

CHILD-CARE RESOURCES

Types of Child Care • Several types of child care are available in most communities. During the first 2 years of life, children often do better with individual care or family daycare because they need more cuddling and personal attention. The child-care arrangements are listed in descending order of preference for younger infants.

• *Individual Care in Your Own Home.* This is the preferred arrangement for infants. The care is usually provided by a grandmother or professional sitter. Often the parents will need to advertise in the local newspaper. The applicant's references need to be carefully checked, especially for characteristics that are important to you. While most professional sitters provide part-time services, some are available as live-ins (a nanny).

• *Individual Care in Someone Else's Home.* This arrangement is very similar to the previous one except that your child will not have the extra stability of being cared for in his or her own home. In addition, you will need to pack diapers, bottles, and toys, as well as to transport your child to the sitter's home.

• *Family Daycare Homes.* In these settings a mother may care for 2 to 5 children in her home. This is the most common type of daycare used for young children and it's usually less expensive than center-based care. Disadvantages are that the children do not usually receive as much individual attention, and many of these homes are not licensed or monitored by the state.

• *Center-Based Daycare.* In these settings 30 or more children may be cared for. Because of the numbers, many children do not adapt well to these large centers until they are over age 2 or 2½ years. Optimal daycare centers are workplace-based, but they remain uncommon in our country. Daycare centers are state-licensed and must comply with certain standards. If you are looking for a daycare center, assemble a list from friends or by looking in the Yellow Pages under "Child Care" or "Day Nurseries and Child Care."

The Substitute Caregiver: Choosing the Right Person • The most important factor in your decision about choosing a child-care resource is finding a caretaker who understands and meets children's emotional needs. Choose someone who is warm, affectionate, sympathetic, plays with the children, and has a sense of humor. Avoid someone who is harsh, fussy, nagging, regimented, or overly concerned with neatness, cleanliness, and order. Try to find someone who understands children's normal emotional development. Look for someone who listens to and complies with your expectations (e.g., no spanking, and similar toilet-training methods). Form a close partnership with your child's caregiver. Choose a center that has a staff with a positive attitude toward parents, and then support that staff for what they provide for your child. Competition and rivalry are unnecessary if you've chosen well. Be sure that no more than two consistent caregivers are assigned to your child. More than three or four parent-equivalents (including the parents) can cause confusion and lack of security for a young child.

Choosing the Right Child-Care Environment • Don't make your final decision about a child-care center until you have visited it for at least half a day. Children deserve high standards of care. During your visit review the following checklist.

• The ratio of staff to children should be 1:3 for infants (especially for those who don't feed themselves) and 1:4 to 1:6 for preschool children, depending upon their age. By and large these ratios are regulated by each state.

• Each child has a regular primary caregiver assigned.

• The staff turnover is low.

• The playground is safe.

• Sinks and toilets are adequate.

• Diapers are changed promptly, not on some schedule.

• Space and time are adequate for rest and naps.

• Staff members wash their hands after changing diapers and before handling food.

• The staff doesn't smoke on the premises.

• A TV or VCR with tapes is absent or viewed minimally.

• The center's atmosphere is positive when one enters it.

• The children appear happy and busy.

• The children receive individualized attention.

• The children receive plenty of verbal stimulation. (Be concerned if the setting is too quiet.)

- The preschoolers receive some learning activities.

- The staff works through praise and suggestion rather than criticism and punishment.

- Staff members are warm, affectionate, and not afraid to hug the children.

- The staff welcomes you as a visitor at any time.

- The staff welcomes your suggestions and questions.

- The staff provides feedback about each child at the time of pickup, especially if anything significant has happened.

Helping Your Child Adjust to Daycare • All parents occasionally need to leave their child with another caretaker while they go to an appointment, go shopping, or go out for an evening. Daycare is simply an extension of this concept. However, your child will not be ready to adjust to a daycare setting unless the child has had previous successful experiences with a baby-sitter within your home. Also, before beginning daycare, your child should have had ample opportunity to visit with other children in friends' homes. Because of the separation fears that children normally experience between 6 months and 2½ years of age, being left at daycare can initially be somewhat stressful during this time. Talk about the daycare center before you actually go there. Then visit it briefly, pointing out the positive aspects.

When you take your child to daycare for the first day, plan on spending that day there. Let your child gradually reach out and become involved with the other children and staff. On the second day, stay 5 or 10 minutes while your child makes a transition to interacting with a member of the daycare staff. Leave a familiar toy or security object with your child. If the daycare center is near your workplace, visit your child during the day. When you leave, do so with a cheerful attitude and let your child know you are leaving—don't sneak away. Don't be surprised if your child gets teary on the first days that you depart from the daycare center. When you pick your child up, there may also be tears. For the first week your child may talk about not wanting to return. Remain firm in your decision and your child will gradually adapt to the change. Some children take as long as 1 or 2 months to look forward to attending daycare. Usually, this process cannot be hurried.

Dealing with a Sick Child • The onset of illness can be a major disruption for the working mother. Many daycare centers will not accept sick children. Your options are: staying home with your child, using your sick leave; having your spouse take time off from work and stay home with your child; or having your child stay with a friend or relative who has agreed in advance to be a backup for illness care. Rarely, a parent may have the type of job in which an employer will allow an employee to work at home for a day under these conditions. Sick-care programs for children are springing up across the country to help working parents deal with this situation. Many of these services are based in a special sick wing of a large daycare center. Some agencies offer sick-care baby-sitters who come into the home and look after children for the working mother. Care for sick children is more expensive than regular child care.

When a child becomes sick, the parents first have to decide whether or not their child needs to see a physician. Refer to the guidelines in this book that pertain to your child's symptoms to help answer this question. If your child becomes sick during the working day and your review of his illness indicates that he needs to see a physician, try to arrange for a late-afternoon appointment by calling before 3:00 P.M. In addition, many physicians are scheduling evening clinic hours to accommodate the high numbers of working parents.

A second decision that a working parent must make is when is the child well enough to return to daycare. Children with a sore throat, moderate cough, runny nose, or cold symptoms (but without a fever or breathing difficulties) can usually return to daycare. In the first place, daycare is where they acquired the infection. In the second place, the spread of colds cannot be prevented. The return should be based mainly on how well your child feels. Children with fevers (over 100°F), chicken pox, vomiting, or diarrhea cannot return to a regular daycare setting. Children with a strep throat or an eye infection can usually return after 24 hours on an antibiotic. Many child-care centers have their own rules about which children will be excluded, and you should become familiar with these rules (see CONTAGIOUS DISEASES AND INCUBATION PERIODS, page 220).

Latchkey Children (Self-Care) • A latchkey child is a school-age child who is left alone either before or after school while his parent is at work. The name comes from the wearing of a house key around the neck. This practice of self-care has been estimated to occur for 3 million children between 6 and 12 years of age, and 7 million children between 12 and 18 years of age. Elementary-school-age children often develop fears from being left alone. They feel unsafe, lonely, and neglected.

The following recommendations may make the practice more acceptable.

• Children shouldn't be left alone unless they are over 10 years of age.

• They should not spend more than 2 hours per day alone—which means they should not be left alone during school holidays or when they are sick.

• They should be taught how to handle household emergencies and what telephone numbers to call for assistance.

• A safe play area should be designated.

• They should not be left with too many chores, because they need time for schoolwork and entertainment.

• Sometimes the availability of pets will provide a sense of protection and companionship.

• The parents should be available by telephone and periodically call the children during this time. Children should also have a backup adult who lives close by and whom they can call or visit if they have any questions.

• The parents should be punctual about the time at which they promise they will come home.

Since the latchkey-child practice is clearly a compromise, the availability of after-school services for these children in schools or churches is a welcome development.

SURVIVING EACH DAY AS A WORKING MOTHER

Being a working mother is always harder and more stressful than being a full-time mother, because the other roles are never completely absorbed by other people. The following recommendations may help to lessen the burden:

Look for a Supportive Employer and Workplace • If it's financially acceptable, try to find part-time work. Some employers offer flexible schedules, with a set number of hours per week fulfilled during different times of the day. Other jobs allow the employee to work in her home. Job sharing by two women, each working 20 hours per week, is another alternative. Clearly the options are changing rapidly in our country. However, many women with financial needs or career obligations continue to work 40 or more hours per week.

Avoid Fatigue • If you can't get enough sleep, nothing else will seem to turn out right. You won't have the initiative to nurture your children at the end of the day. You won't have the energy necessary to maintain a marriage or friendships. Pick a reasonable bedtime and stay with it. Cut corners in other areas but protect your sleep time.

Provide Quality Time with Your Child • Working parents spend a lot of energy trying to make up to their children for not being with them all day. Research had shown that both the quality and quantity of time you spend with your child is important. If you interact with your child, actively listen to him, talk with him, and keep it pleasant, that's quality time. Children need some quality time with their parents every day. Let's look at how you can turn scattered moments during a typical day into quality time:

• Talk with your child during the drive to and from childcare.

• Include your child in adult activities such as shopping, cooking, and home repair. As long as you make him feel important or even helpful, this is quality time.

• When you first get home from work, try to snuggle with your kids for 5 minutes (giving them the first 30 minutes, as some experts suggest, is usually impractical unless you are still breast-feeding). Then give them something to do and look after yourself. Your day was probably much more stressful than theirs, and you may need to regroup as well as prepare dinner.

• Make dinner a pleasant, unhurried time, with the TV off.

• Use the 30 minutes before bedtime to discuss the day's events at your child's pace. End with your usual bedtime ritual.

• If you're providing some of this quality contact every day, you're doing great.

• A common mistake of working parents is to think that bed-sharing is quality time. This isn't a good choice. If your child is asleep in your bed, we could call this neutral time. If your child is awake and crying, it's aggravating time. If you want to provide extra quality time with your child, set aside some special half days on the weekend for child-centered activities.

Reduce Your Housework Time • If you can afford it, hire a house-keeper. In any case, try to simplify your home life. A spotless house must become a low priority. Do less cooking. Make triple recipes and freeze leftovers.

Ask Other Family Members for Help • It is imperative that the spouse share with the housework and child care. The father must actively participate in what was formerly considered the mother's responsibilities. He must be more than "available" or a "backup." He must look after more than outside work and the car. Child care and housework tasks must be redistributed to prevent the mother from becoming overworked. The father can help buy a son's clothing, do car-pooling, cook, and do housecleaning chores. School-age children can also be assigned some chores.

Watch Out for Guilt • Try to understand that the "Supermom" is a myth. You can't do everything singlehandedly or perfectly. You need help and deserve help. Don't compare yourself to your mother or necessarily expect support from her or other relatives for your pursuit of a career. You don't need to apologize to anyone for not doing well enough. If you have chosen a good child-care resource, you should be comfortable during the day with your child's well-being. And despite your best efforts, your child will sometimes cry when dropped off at daycare, become sick, or "fall apart" when picked up. Try not to rethink your career decision every time this happens.

Nurture Your Marriage • One major loss for a working mother is recreational time with her husband. Try to compartmentalize your life. You deserve a break from your endless list of unfinished work. Make a date for a night out with your husband at least once a week. A strong marriage is an important underpinning for a working mother. Relaxation time is essential, not frivolous or wasteful. Plan it and savor it.

Single-Parent Families: Extra Help • Try to find a friend with a child close in age to yours. Share shopping, overnight and weekend visits, baby-sitting, car-pooling, and other responsibilities with your friend. Trading services will, in this way, save you money. Sometimes, living with another single mother is mutually beneficial. It's crucial that you spend time with other adults and do something for yourself once in a while. Consider joining an organization for single parents.

RECOMMENDED READING

T. Berry Brazelton, *Working and Caring* (Reading, Mass.: Addison-Wesley, 1987).

Earl A. Grollman and Gerri L. Sweder, *The Working Parent Dilemma* (Boston, Mass.: Beacon Press, 1986).

Helen L. Swan and Victoria Houston, *Alone After School: A Self-Care Guide for Latchkey Children and Their Parents* (Englewood Cliffs, N. J.: Prentice-Hall, 1985).

DIVORCE'S IMPACT ON CHILDREN

More than 1 million children are affected by divorce each year. Over a third of U.S. marriages end in divorce. Our primary goal should be to minimize the emotional harm to these children. The main way to achieve this is to help them maintain a close and secure relationship with both parents. The following recommendations may help your child cope with divorce:

- *Keep your child informed.* Tell your child about the separation or divorce before the actual departure of one parent. Preferably, both parents and all children should be present at that meeting. The following topics may serve as a good agenda.

- *Reassure your children that both parents love them.* Clarify that although you are unhappy with each other and disagree about many things, the one subject you both completely agree on is "We love you." Demonstrating this love by time together is even more important. Preschoolers need lots of cuddling from both parents, but don't start bad habits like letting your child sleep with you.

- *Keep constant as many parts of your child's world as you can.* The fewer changes, the better your child will cope with the stress of divorce. Try to keep your child in the same home or neighborhood. If this is impossible, at least try to keep your child in the same school with the same teachers, friends, and teams (even if it's on a temporary basis). Reassure your child that although your standard of living will decrease some, that you will continue to have the basic necessities of living (i.e., food, clothing, and shelter).

• *Reassure your child that the noncustodial parent will visit.* Young children are confused by divorce and fear that one parent may abandon them. Children need to know that they will have ongoing contact with their father (or mother, if the father has custody). The custodial parent should strongly support the visiting schedule. Your child needs both parents. Have a scheduled predictable time for visiting. One full day every 1 or 2 weeks is usually preferable to more frequent, rushed, brief visits. Your child will eagerly look forward to visiting, so the visiting parent must keep promises, be punctual, and remember birthdays and other special events. If there is more than one child, all should spend equal time or the same time with the noncustodial parent to prevent favoritism. Try not to do too much in one day. Even more important, both parents should work to make these visits pleasant. Allow your child to tell you he had a good time during the visit with your ex-spouse. Children should also be provided with the telephone number of the noncustodial parent and encouraged to call at regular intervals. If the noncustodial parent has moved to a distant city, telephone calls and letters become essential to the ongoing relationship.

• *If the noncustodial parent becomes uninvolved, find substitutes.* Turn to relatives and Big Brother or Big Sister volunteers to spend more time with your son or daughter. Explain to your child that "Your dad [or mom] is not capable right now of being available for you. He's sorting out his own problems. There's not much we can do to change that." Help your child verbalize his or her sense of disappointment and loss. If your child is a teenager, writing and calling may eventually reengage the absent parent.

• *Help your child talk about painful feelings.* At the time of separation and divorce, many children experience symptoms of anxiety, depression, and anger, as would be seen with any crisis. They are frequently on the brink of tears, sleep poorly, have stomachaches, experience a decline in school performance, and so forth. To help these symptoms pass, encourage your child to talk about these unhappy feelings and respond with understanding and support. A divorce discussion group at school can help children counter the isolation and shame they often feel. Allow feelings to be expressed honestly. But if anger turns into disruptive behavior, limits must be imposed while you help your child put the anger into words. Books about other children of divorce who deal with feelings of sadness but ultimately emerge stronger can provide reassurance.

• *Make sure your child understands that he is not responsible for the divorce.* Children often feel guilty, believing that they somehow caused the divorce. Your children need reassurance that they did not in any way cause the divorce.

• *Clarify that the divorce is final.* Some children hold on to a wish to reunite the parents and pretend that the separation is temporary. Clarifying that the divorce is final can help children mourn their loss and move on to more adaptive functioning.

• *Try to protect your child's positive feelings about both parents.* If possible, mention the good points about the other parent. Don't be overly honest about your negative feelings toward your ex-spouse. (You need to unload these feelings on another adult, not your children.) Devaluing or discrediting the other parent in your child's presence can reduce your child's personal self-esteem and create greater stress.

  Don't ask your child to take sides. A child does not need to have a single loyalty to one parent. Your child should not have to choose between parents. Your child should be able to love both of you, even though you don't love each other.

• *Maintain normal discipline in both households.* Children need consistent child-rearing practices. Overindulgence or leniency by one parent makes it more difficult for the other parent to get the child to behave. Constant competition for the child's love through gifts or special privileges leads to a spoiled child. The general ground rules regarding discipline should be set by the custodial parent.

• *Don't argue about your child in the child's presence.* Children are quite upset by seeing their parents fight. Most important, avoid any arguments regarding visiting, custody, or child support in your child's presence. Try to resolve your remaining differences in a civilized way.

- *Try to avoid custody disputes.* Your child badly needs a sense of stability. Challenge custody only if the custodial parent is causing obvious harm or repeated distress to your child. False accusations of physical abuse or sexual abuse cause great emotional anguish for the child. If possible, don't split siblings unless they are adolescents and state a clear preference for living in different settings.

CALL YOUR CHILD'S PHYSICIAN DURING OFFICE HOURS IF

- Your child has symptoms that interfere with schoolwork, eating, or sleeping for more than 2 weeks.

- You feel your child is depressed.

- Your child has any physical symptoms, due to the divorce, lasting for more than 6 months.

- Your child continues to believe that the parents will come back together again, even though over a year has passed since the divorce.

- You feel the other parent is harming your child.

- Your child refuses visits with the noncustodial parent.

RECOMMENDED READING

Mitchell A. Baris and Carla B. Garrity, *Children of Divorce* (Dekalb, IL: Psytec, Inc., 1988).

Linda B. Francke, *Growing Up Divorced* (New York: Fawcett Crest, 1983).

Richard A. Gardner, *The Boys and Girls Book About Divorce* (New York: Bantam Books, 1970).

Richard A. Gardner, *The Parents Book About Divorce* (New York: Bantam Books, 1976).

ADOLESCENTS: DEALING WITH NORMAL REBELLION

The main task of adolescence in our culture is to become psychologically emancipated from the parents. The teenager must cast aside the dependent relationship of childhood. Before he can develop a new adult relationship with his parents, the adolescent must first distance himself from the parents of his past and gain control of his life. This process is characterized by a certain amount of intermittent normal rebellion, defiance, discontent, turmoil, restlessness, and ambivalence. Emotions usually run high. Mood swings are common. Even teenagers who have a mild transition into adolescence hurt their parents' feelings repeatedly with clear messages of "Leave me alone" and "I don't need you."

This stage usually starts at ages 12 to 14. Under the best of circumstances, this adolescent rebellion continues for approximately 2 years. Not uncommonly it continues for 4 to 6 years. Rebellion can be accentuated or prolonged for the teenager who is doing poorly in school and is unsure of his or her adult role. The teen with a difficult temperament (who had a terrible phase of negativism in the preschool period) is also likely to have a difficult adolescence. Parental high standards or expectations also cause teens to overreact. Defiance will become very intense if the parent tries to eliminate any signs of normal rebellion and regain control over the teenager.

PRACTICAL APPROACHES TO LIVING WITH AN ADOLESCENT

Treat Your Teenager as an Adult Friend • Whatever relationship you would like to have with your child as an adult, start working on it by age 12. Treat your child the way you would like him or her to treat you as an adult. Your goal is mutual respect, support, and having fun together. Strive for relaxed, casual conversations during bicycling, hiking, playing catch, fishing, cooking, working, driving, and especially at mealtime. Use praise and trust to help build self-esteem. Recognize and validate your child's feelings by listening carefully and making nonjudgmental comments. Remember that listening doesn't mean you have to solve your teen's problems. The friendship model is the best basis for family functioning. In this model people do things for each other out of caring and loyalty. (It doesn't mean bending your behavior or values in an attempt to be popular with your teenager.)

Avoid Criticism About "No-Win" Topics • Most negative parent-adolescent relationships are caused by too much criticism and pressure to change. Much of the objectionable behavior merely reflects conformity with the current preferences of the youngster's peer group. Peer-group immersion is one of the essential stages of adolescent development. Dressing, talking,

and acting differently from adults help your child feel independent from you. So back off, as your teenager would say.

Try not to attack your teenager's clothing, hair style, makeup,
music, dance steps, friends (unless they're in trouble with the
law), recreational interests (such as movies, television, or
hobbies), room decorations, how money or free time is spent,
speech, posture, manners, religion, and philosophy. Allowing
your teen to rebel in these minor areas often prevents testing
in major areas—such as experimentation with drugs, truancy,
or stealing. Intervene and try to make a change only if the
behavior is harmful, illegal, or infringes on your rights (see
HOUSE RULES, below). Another error is to criticize your teen's
mood, attitude, or facial expression. A negative or lazy attitude can only be changed through good example and praise.
The more you dwell on these nontraditional (even strange)
behaviors, the longer they will last.

**Let Society's Rules and Consequences Teach Responsibility Outside
the Home** • Your teenager must learn from trial and error. As
she experiments, she will learn to take responsibility for her
decisions and actions. The parent should speak up only if the
adolescent is going to do something dangerous or illegal.
Otherwise, the parent must rely on self-discipline, positive
peer pressure, and logical consequences (the school of hard
knocks).

City curfew laws will help to control late hours. The requirement for punctual school attendance will influence when
your teen goes to bed at night. If he has trouble getting up in
the morning, buy him an alarm clock. School grades will
usually hold your teenager accountable for homework and
other aspects of school performance. (Prevent confusion by
making clear your support for the rules imposed by the school
and community. But it's not your job to check the homework.)
If your teen has bad work habits, she will lose her job. If she
selects an excessively violent movie, she may have nightmares. If your teenager makes a poor choice of friends, she
may find her confidences broken or that she gets into trouble.
If she doesn't practice hard for a sport, she will get pressure
from the team and coach to do better. If she misspends her
allowance or earnings, she will run out of money before the
end of the month. If she abuses her freedom to choose clothes,
her fixed clothing allowance will be spent before she buys
something she needs, such as a bathing suit. (By age 16, your
teenager should have a summer job. These earnings should

cover most of the year's expenses, and any allowance can be discontinued.) If your teenager's mood or attitude is negative, she will lose friends.

If by chance your teenager asks you for advice about these problem areas, try to cover the pros and cons in a brief, impartial way. Ask some questions to help her think about the main risks. Then wrap up your remarks with a comment such as "Do what you think is best." Teenagers need plenty of opportunity to learn from their own mistakes before they leave home and have to solve problems without a support system.

Clarify the House Rules and Consequences • You have the right and the responsibility to make rules regarding your house and other possessions. Written ones cut down on misunderstandings. A teenager's preferences can be tolerated within his own room but they need not be imposed on the rest of the house. You can forbid loud music or incoming telephone calls after 10:00 P.M. that interfere with other people's concentration or sleep. You can forbid a TV set in his bedroom. While you should make your teen's friends feel welcome in your home, clarify the ground rules about parties or where snacks can be eaten. Your teen can be placed in charge of cleaning his own room, washing his clothes, and ironing his clothes. You can insist upon clean clothes and enough showers to prevent or overcome body odor. You must decide whether to loan out your car, bicycle, camera, radio, TV, clothes, and other possessions. To borrow the car, he must ask in advance, tell you his destination, clean the car after using it, and promise not to drive it if he drinks any alcohol.

Reasonable consequences for breaking house rules include loss of telephone, TV, stereo, and car privileges. (Time-out is rarely useful in this age group, and physical punishment can escalate to a serious breakdown in your relationship.) If your teenager breaks something, he should repair it, pay for its repair or replacement, or work for you until his debt is paid off. If he makes a mess, he should clean it up. If your teen is doing poorly in school, you can restrict TV time. You can also put a limit on telephone privileges and weeknights out. If your teen stays out too late or doesn't call you when he's delayed, you can ground him for a day or a weekend. In general, grounding for more than a few days is looked upon as unfair and is hard to enforce.

Use Family Conferences for Negotiating House Rules • Some families find it helpful to have a brief meeting after dinner once a week. At this time your teenager can ask for changes in the house rules or bring up family issues that are causing problems. You can also bring up issues (such as the demand to drive your teen to many places and your need for his or her help in arranging car pools). The family unit often functions better if the decision-making is democratic. The objective of negotiation should be that both parties win. The atmosphere can be one of: "Nobody is at fault; we have a problem. How can we solve it?"

Give Space to a Teenager Who Is in a Bad Mood • Generally when your teenager is in a bad mood, he or she won't want to talk about it with you. If teenagers want to discuss a problem with anybody, it will probably be with a close friend. In general, it is advisable at this time to give your teen lots of space and privacy. This is a poor time to talk to your teenager about anything, pleasant or otherwise.

Use "I" Messages for Rudeness • Some talking back is normal. We want our teenagers to express their anger through talking and to challenge our opinions in a logical way. We need to listen. Expect your teenager to present his case passionately, even unreasonably. Let the small stuff go; it's only words. But don't accept disrespectful remarks such as calling you a "jerk." Unlike a negative attitude, these mean remarks should be addressed. You can respond with a comment like "I really hurt inside when you put me down or don't answer my question." Make your statement in as nonangry a way as possible. If your adolescent continues to make angry, unpleasant remarks, leave. Don't get into a shouting match or game of uproar with your teenager because this behavior is not adaptable to outside relationships. Set a good example of the ability to express disapproval without insult or attack. If angry or rude remarks come up in the context of a complaint about something, try to overlook the rudeness and directly engage your teen in a discussion of the issue. If you can focus on objective problem-solving and keep a courteous tone of voice, often your teenager will be able to regain control over his or her emotions and remarks.

What you are trying to teach is that one has the right to disagree and even to express anger. However, screaming and rude conversation are not allowed in your house. When your teen is angry about something, he or she can explain what it is, but in a calm voice. Family friends and other visitors are also to be treated with respect. You can prevent some rude behavior by role-modeling politeness, constructive disagreement, and the ability to apologize.

CALL YOUR TEENAGER'S PHYSICIAN DURING OFFICE HOURS IF

• You think your teenager is depressed, suicidal, drinking or using illegal drugs, or going to run away.

• Your teenager is taking undue risks (e.g., reckless driving or unsafe sex).

• Your teenager has no close friends.

• Your teenager's school performance is declining markedly.

• Your teenager is skipping school frequently.

• Your teenager's outbursts of temper are destructive or violent.

• You feel your teenager's rebellion is excessive.

• Your family life is seriously disrupted by your teenager.

• You find yourself escalating the criticism and punishment.

• Your relationship with your teenager does not improve within 3 months using this approach.

• You have other questions or concerns.

RECOMMENDED READING

Peter H. Buntman and E. M. Saris, *How to Live with Your Teenager* (New York: Ballantine Books, 1982).

Lois Davitz and Joel Davitz, *How to Live (Almost) Happily with a Teenager* (New York: Signet, 1983).

Don Dinkmeyer and Gary D. McKay, *Parenting Teenagers* (Circle Pines, Minn.: American Guidance Service, 1990).

Kathleen McCoy and Charles Wibbelsman, *The Teenage Body Book* (New York: Simon & Schuster, 1984).

———, *Crisis-Proof Your Teenager* (New York: Bantam Books, 1991).

VI.

COMMON SYMPTOMS AND ILLNESSES

GENERAL SYMPTOMS OF ILLNESS

FEVER

DEFINITION OF FEVER

- Rectal temperature over 100.4°F (38.0°C) is a fever

- Oral temperature over 99.5°F (37.5°C) is a fever

- Axillary (armpit) temperature over 98.6°F (37.0°C) is a fever

- While the body's average temperature is 98.6°F (37°C) orally, it normally fluctuates during the day from a low of 97.6°F in the morning to a high of 99.5°F in the late afternoon (called normal diurnal variation)

- Mild elevations of 100.4 to 101.2°F (38 to 38.5°C) can be caused by exercise, excessive clothing, a hot bath, or hot weather. Warm food or drink can elevate an oral temperature. If you suspect one of these causes, retake the temperature in a half hour, after eliminating the possible cause

Similar Conditions • For CONVULSIONS or DELIRIUM (acting very confused), go directly to those guidelines (see pages 40, 43, and 44). Both symptoms should stop if you reduce the fever below 102°F with medicine and sponging. Then return to this guideline.

TAKING THE TEMPERATURE
If you have questions about how to take your child's temperature, see page 413.

407

CAUSES OF FEVER

Fever is a symptom, not a disease. Fever is the body's normal response to infections and it plays a role in fighting them. Fever turns on the body's immune system, thereby increasing the release and activity of white blood cells and other germ-killing substances. The usual fevers (100° to 104°F) that all children get are not harmful. Most are due to viral illnesses; some are due to bacterial ones. Most "fevers" that stay under 101°F are simply due to hot weather or overdressing. Teething does not cause fever.

EXPECTED COURSE OF FEVER

Most fevers associated with viral illnesses range between 101° and 104°F and last for 2 to 3 days. In general, the height of the fever doesn't relate to the seriousness of the illness. How sick your child acts is what counts. Fever causes no symptoms until it reaches 102° or 103°F. Fever causes no permanent harm (such as brain damage) until it reaches 107° or 108°F. Fortunately, the brain's thermostat keeps untreated fevers due to infections below 105° or 106°F. While all children get fevers, only 4 percent develop a brief febrile convulsion. Since this type of seizure is generally harmless, it is not worth worrying about, especially if your child has experienced high fevers without one.

CALL YOUR CHILD'S PHYSICIAN

Immediately If

- Your child is under 2 months old.

- The fever is over 105°F.

- Your child is crying inconsolably or whimpering.

- Your child cries if you touch him or move him.

- Your child is difficult to awaken.

- The neck is stiff. (Note: The inability to touch the chin to the chest is an early symptom in meningitis.)

- Any purple spots are present on the skin.

- Breathing is difficult *and* no better after you clear the nose.

- Your child is drooling saliva and is unable to swallow anything.

- A convulsion has occurred.

- Your child acts or looks very sick. (Note: If your child hasn't received acetaminophen, recheck his condition 1 hour after giving him a proper amount.)

Within 24 Hours If

- Your child is 2 to 4 months old (unless fever is due to a DTP shot).

- The fever is between 104° and 105°F (especially if your child is under 2 years old).

- Burning or pain occurs with urination.

- The fever has been present more than 24 hours without an obvious cause or location of infection.

During Office Hours If

- The fever went away for more than 24 hours and then returned.

- The fever has been present more than 72 hours.

- Your child has a history of febrile seizures.

- You have other questions.

HOME CARE FOR FEVER

Fever Phobia and the Overtreatment of Fever • Fever phobia is a term I coined in 1980 to describe the unwarranted fears many parents hold about normal fevers that all children experience. My study found that 80 percent of parents thought fevers between 100°F and 106°F could cause brain damage. Some 20 percent of parents thought that if they didn't treat the fever, it would keep going higher. Neither of these statements is true. Because of these misconceptions, many parents treat low-grade fevers with unnecessary medicines and sponging. They also spend many sleepless nights worrying about their child's fever. Try to keep fever in perspective (see page 408) as you treat your child's fever.

Fever-Reducing Medicines: Acetaminophen • Children older than 2 months of age can be given one of the acetaminophen products listed on page 411. Remember: Fever is helping your child fight the infection. Use drugs if the fever is over 102°F (39°C), but preferably only if your child is also uncomfortable. Give the correct dosage for your child's weight or age every 4 to 6 hours, but no more often. Acetaminophen will reduce the fever by 2° to 3°F by 2 hours after it is given. Medicines do not bring the temperature down to normal, unless the fever was low-grade to begin with. The drug often needs repeating, since the fever will go up and down as it pleases until the disease runs it course. If acetaminophen is needed at all, my custom is to continue it for 24 hours because the fever usually stays at an uncomfortable level for the first day and the continuous medicine prevents the fever from making big swings. Thereafter, give it only for symptoms. If your child is sleeping, don't awaken him or her for medicines. If the fever is high enough to need an antipyretic, your child will awaken. In general, these medicines are overused in our country.

CAUTIONS:

• Do not use these drugs for more than 3 days *or* in children less than 4 months old without consulting your physician.

• Since all these drugs are poisonous if taken in overdosage, keep them out of the sight and reach of children.

Liquid Ibuprofen • In 1989, ibuprofen received FDA approval for treating fever in children 6 months to 12 years of age. It's available only by prescription. (Ibuprofen pills, a nonprescription product, have been used for many years to treat menstrual cramps and sports injuries.) Ibuprofen and acetaminophen are similar in their ability to lower fever and their safety records. One advantage of ibuprofen over acetaminophen is that ibuprofen has a longer duration of effect (6 to 8 hours vs. 4 to 6 hours). When the issue is fever control, acetaminophen is still the drug of choice for most conditions. Children with special problems requiring a longer period of fever control, however, may do better with ibuprofen.

Cautions About Aspirin • The American Academy of Pediatrics has recommended that children (through age 21 years) not receive aspirin if they have chicken pox or influenza (any cold, cough, or sore throat symptoms). This recommendation stems from several studies that have linked aspirin to Reye's syndrome, a severe encephalitis-like illness. Most pediatricians have stopped using aspirin for fevers associated with any illness. On the other hand, aspirin may be a better drug than acetaminophen for pain relief with muscle and bone pains, menstrual cramps, and sunburn. (Aspirin and acetaminophen are given at the same dosage.) If you have teenagers, be sure they are aware of this warning about aspirin and fevers, since they tend to self-medicate. **Caution:** A hidden source of aspirin that is commonly overlooked is Pepto-Bismol. Don't give your child Pepto-Bismol if he has a fever.

Sponging for Fever • Sponging is usually unnecessary. Never sponge without giving acetaminophen first. Sponge immediately only

ACETAMINOPHEN DOSAGES

TYPE AND BRAND	STRENGTH	CHILD'S WEIGHT (POUNDS)			AGE (YEARS)				
		6–11	12–17	18–23	2–3	4–5	6–8	9–11	12+
Total amount (mg.)		40 mg.	80	120	160	240	325	485	650
Acetaminophen drops (Tylenol, Anacin-3, Liquiprin, Panadol, or Tempra)	80-mg/dropper	½ dropper	1	1½	2	3	—	—	—
Acetaminophen syrup	160/5 ml (1 tsp.)	—	½ tsp.	¾	1	1½	2	2½	4
Chewable acetaminophen*	80-mg tablets	—	—	1½	2	3	4	5–6	8
Adult acetaminophen	325-mg tablets	—	—	—	—	—	1	1–1½	2

*Chewable acetaminophen also comes as 120-mg tablets. Use half the number of tablets listed for the 80-mg size. Note: Acetaminophen comes in 120, 325, and 650 mg suppositories. They are useful in febrile children with vomiting or in children with febrile seizures. The rectal dose is the same as the oral dose. Since the drug is dispersed uniformly throughout the newer suppositories, they can be cut.

for emergencies such as heat stroke, delirium from fever, a seizure from fever, or any fever over 106°F (41.1°C). For other children, sponge only if the fever is over 104°F (40°C), it stays above that level when you retake it 20 minutes after acetaminophen has been given, and your child is uncomfortable. Until acetaminophen has taken effect (by resetting the body's thermostat), sponging will just cause shivering, which is the body's way of trying to raise the temperature.

Sponge your child in lukewarm water (85°F to 90°F or 29°C to 32°C). (Use slightly cooler water for emergencies.) Sponging works much faster than immersion, so sit your child in 2 inches of water and keep wetting the skin surface. If your child shivers, raise the water temperature or wait for the acetaminophen to take effect. Don't expect to get the temperature down below 101°F. Don't add rubbing alcohol to the water; it can cause a coma or seizure if breathed in. Never leave your child alone in the tub; accidents can happen quickly. If your child is seizing or thrashing about, sponge him in a safer place than the bathtub.

Retaking the Temperature • In general, take the temperature once a day in the morning until the fever is gone. Take it more often if your child feels very hot or is acting miserable despite receiving acetaminophen; he may also need sponging. In addition, take it before calling your physician.

With most infections, the level of fever bounces around for 2 or 3 days. Shivering (or feeling cold) means the fever is going up, a flushed (pink) appearance means the fever has peaked, and sweating means it is coming down. The main purpose of temperature taking is to determine if a fever is present or absent, not to chart its every move.

Extra Fluids • Extra fluids should be encouraged but not forced. Popsicles and iced drinks are helpful. Body fluids are lost during fevers because of sweating.

Less Clothing (Bundling Can Be Dangerous) • Clothing should be kept to a minimum, because most heat is lost through the skin. Do not bundle up your child; it will cause a higher fever. Be especially careful with infants who are unable to undress themselves if they become overheated. During the time your child feels cold or has shivering (the chills), give him a light blanket.

Reduced Activity • Discourage any vigorous activities, because they produce additional heat that the body must release. Normal play, however, is fine.

Call Your Child's Physician Later If

- The fever goes over 104°F (40°C) (especially if it stays over 104°F or your child is under 2 years old).

- The fever lasts more than 24 hours without an obvious cause or location of infection.

- The fever lasts more than 72 hours.

- You feel your child is getting worse.

  Remember: The response, or lack of response, of the fever to medicines tells us little about the severity of the infection. If your febrile child smiles, plays, and drinks adequate fluids, you need not worry about the fever.

THE TEMPERATURE: HOW TO MEASURE IT

Obtaining an accurate measurement of your child's temperature requires some practice. If you have questions about this procedure, ask a physician or nurse to demonstrate how it's done, and then observe you doing the same.

Where to Take the Temperature

- Accuracy: Using a glass thermometer, rectal temperatures are the most accurate. Oral temps are also accurate if done properly. Armpit temperatures are the least accurate, but better than no measurement.

- Under 5 years old: rectal is preferred, armpit (axillary) is a second choice.

- Over 5 years old: oral (mouth).

Taking Rectal Temperatures

- For all sites, first shake the thermometer until the mercury line is below 98.6°F (37.0°C).

- Have your child lie stomach-down on your lap.

- Lubricate the end of the thermometer and the opening of the anus with petroleum jelly.

- Carefully insert the thermometer about 1 inch, but never force it.

- Hold your child still while the thermometer is in, and press the buttocks together to stabilize it.

- Leave the thermometer inside the rectum for 2 minutes.

- Practice doing this a few times on days your child is happy rather than sick.

Taking Armpit (Axillary) Temperatures

- Place the tip of the thermometer in a dry armpit.

- Close the armpit by holding the elbow against the chest for 4 minutes (5 or 6 minutes after 2 years of age). Fevers will be missed if the thermometer is removed too soon.

- If the armpit temperature is over 98.6°F or you're uncertain about the result, recheck it with a rectal temperature.

Taking Oral Temperatures

- Be sure your child has not taken a cold or hot drink within the previous 10 minutes.

- Place the tip of the thermometer under one side of the tongue and toward the back. An accurate temperature depends on proper placement. Ask a physician or nurse to show you where it should go.

- Have your child hold it in place with the lips and fingers (not with the teeth, because it could break).

- Have your child breathe through the nose and keep the mouth closed.

- Leave the thermometer in the mouth for 3 minutes.

- If your child can't keep the mouth closed because the nose is blocked, suction out the nose.

Reading the Thermometer • Find where the mercury line ends by rotating the thermometer slightly until the line appears.

Broken Thermometer in the Rectum or Mouth • Glass thermometers rarely break. If they do, they usually cause no harm, or a superficial scratch of the lining of the mouth or rectum. The type of mercury found in thermometers is not poisonous. Call your child's physician if you can't find all the pieces of glass.

TYPES OF THERMOMETERS

Glass (with Mercury) Thermometers • This type of thermometer has been the standard since 1870. While these are the least expensive thermometers, they record the temperature slowly and are often hard to read. If you have difficulty reading a mercury thermometer, purchase one with four color zones.

Glass thermometers come in 2 forms: oral, with a thin tip; and rectal, with a rounder tip. This difference is not too important. If necessary, a rectal thermometer can be used in the mouth and an oral thermometer can be used in the rectum, as long as the thermometer is cleaned with rubbing alcohol and you are extra careful with rectal insertion.

Digital Thermometers • Digital thermometers record temperatures with a heat sensor and run on a button battery. They measure quickly, usually in less than 30 seconds. The temperature is displayed in numbers on a small screen. A study in *Consumer Reports* (January 1988) found they were more accurate than glass thermometers. The same thermometer can be used to take both rectal and oral temperatures. I encourage you to buy one for your family; they cost about $10.

Ear Thermometers • Many hospitals and medical offices now take your child's temperature using an infrared thermometer that reads the temperature of the eardrum. In general, the eardrum temperature provides a measurement that is as accurate as or more accurate than the rectal temperature. The outstanding advantage of this instrument is that it measures temperatures in less than 2 seconds. It also requires no cooperation by the child and causes no discomfort. Development of an ear thermometer for home use is in process.

Temperature Strips • Liquid crystal strips applied to the forehead and temperature-sensitive pacifiers have been studied and found to be inaccurate. They miss fevers in many children. Touching the forehead also tends to miss mild fevers, but it is fairly reliable for detecting fevers over 102°F, according to a study by Dr. L. Banco. Disposable chemical-dot oral strips are accurate, but must be kept beside the tongue for 60 seconds.

CONVERSION OF DEGREES FAHRENHEIT TO CENTIGRADE
Remember that 1°C equals 1.8°F and that 1°F equals 0.55°C. Despite attempts to learn metric, most Americans conceptualize fever in degrees Fahrenheit.

98.6°F	= 37°C	103°F	= 39.5°C
99.5°F	= 37.5°C	104°F	= 40°C
100°F	= 37.8°C	105°F	= 40.6°C
100.4°F	= 38°C	106°F	= 41.1°C
101°F	= 38.4°C	107°F	= 41.7°C
102°F	= 38.9°C		

DECREASED APPETITE WITH ILLNESS

SYMPTOMS AND CHARACTERISTICS

• Reduced food intake of recent onset

• Associated acute illness

If your child's symptoms are different, call your physician for help.

Cause • A falloff in appetite is normal with most minor illnesses. This is not harmful. It is not very helpful in assessing the seriousness or cause of the illness.

HOME CARE
Temporarily, serve your child his favorite foods. Let him decide how much he eats. Avoid the tendency to pressure him to eat more when he is sick. Usually, his fluid intake will remain normal and that is the only important aspect of diet during an illness. Look at other guidelines for information on the treatment of associated symptoms.

CALL YOUR CHILD'S PHYSICIAN

Immediately If

• Your child is under 2 months old.

• Your child is not drinking adequate fluids.

• Your child has not urinated in more than 8 hours.

During Office Hours If

- Poor appetite lasts for more than 1 week.

- You feel your child is getting worse.

INCREASED SLEEP WITH ILLNESS

Most children sleep several extra hours a day when they are sick with any infectious illness. It helps them fight the illness and speeds recovery. Increased sleep is not very useful in judging the seriousness of the illness.

CALL YOUR CHILD'S PHYSICIAN

Immediately If

- Your child is drowsy or confused when awake (rather than alert and thinking clearly).

- Your child could have taken any sleeping pills or other drugs.

- Your child is acting very sick.

During Office Hours If

- Your child is on any medicines that could cause drowsiness.

- Your child is otherwise not sick.

- Your child could be upset or depressed.

- You have other questions.

HOME CARE

Treatment • No special treatment is needed. Refer to the guidelines regarding the basic illness your child is suffering from.

Call Your Child's Physician Later If

- Your child becomes difficult to arouse or confused when awake.

- New symptoms develop that worry you.

- The increased sleeping and tiredness last for more than 1 week.

RELATED TOPIC

DELIRIUM (see page 44)

DECREASED ACTIVITY WITH ILLNESS

Most children are less active when they are sick with an infectious illness. When they are awake, most of them prefer to be out of bed, watching television, or playing with toys.

Home Care • When children are sick, it is fine for them to choose their own level of activity. If they are feeling really badly, they will want to be in bed. Children naturally decrease their activity when they are sick. We probably don't trust this survival instinct because we know too many adults who go full speed ahead when they are sick.

Bed Rest Is Not the Answer • Mandatory bed rest is no longer recommended for treating childhood illnesses. These are the reasons:

• No evidence exists that enforced bed rest is helpful for common childhood illnesses. It doesn't reduce symptoms such as fever, despite the myth that children should stay in bed until their fever is gone. It doesn't help the body heal faster. It neither shortens the length of an illness nor prevents complications.

• The only medical conditions where bed rest is helpful are heart failure and respiratory failure. Children with these serious problems elect to remain in bed because of how badly they feel.

• Enforced bed rest is impossible to achieve. If you insist that your child stay in bed and leave the room, when you return you may find him using that bed as a trampoline.

SKIN: WIDESPREAD PINK OR RED RASHES

RASHES, UNKNOWN CAUSE (WIDESPREAD)

SYMPTOMS AND CHARACTERISTICS

- Red or pink rash (erythema)
- Smooth or slightly bumpy
- Spots or solid red
- Over most of body (widespread or generalized)
- Not itchy

Similar Condition • Fever over 103 or 104°F can cause a pinkness of the skin. Sometimes it's blotchy. If it clears with fever reduction, it's normal "fever erythema." If the rash is itchy, turn directly to the guideline on ITCHING, UNKNOWN CAUSE (WIDESPREAD), page 421.

Causes of Widespread Rashes • The possible causes of a nonitchy, pink or red rash are many. If one of the following is suspected, save time by turning directly to that guideline.

AMPICILLIN RASH (see page 423)
CHICKEN POX (VARICELLA) (see page 424)
HEAT RASH (see page 434)
MEASLES (RUBEOLA) (see page 437)
MEASLES VACCINE RASH (see page 439)

NEWBORN RASHES AND BIRTHMARKS (less than 2 weeks old) (see page 108)
ROSEOLA (see page 440)
SCARLET FEVER (see page 442)
SUNBURN (see page 484)

Expected Course • Depends on the diagnosis.

CALL YOUR CHILD'S PHYSICIAN

Immediately If

• The rash is purple or blood-colored.

• It is bright red *and* tender to the touch.

• It looks like a burn.

• Your youngster is a female adolescent *and* she currently is having her menstrual period.

• Your child is acting very sick.

Within 24 Hours If

• Your child has a fever (over 100°F) or sore throat.

• The rash has been present longer than 48 hours.

• Your child is taking a medicine.

• You have other questions or concerns.

HOME CARE FOR WIDESPREAD RASHES

Treament • Widespread rashes can occur with viral illnesses. No treatment is necessary. These rashes are unimportant and usually disappear within 48 hours.

Call Your Child's Physician Later If

• The rash becomes itchy.

• It becomes purple.

• It lasts more than 48 hours.

ITCHING, UNKNOWN CAUSE (WIDESPREAD)

CAUSES OF WIDESPREAD ITCHING

The possible causes are many. If one of the following is suspected, turn directly to that guideline.

BITES, INSECT (see page 18)
CHICKEN POX (VARICELLA) (see page 424)
DRY SKIN (see page 428)
ECZEMA (ATOPIC DERMATITIS) (see page 429)
HEAT RASH (MILIARIA) (see page 434)
HIVES (URTICARIA) (see page 435)
PITYRIASIS ROSEA (see Glossary)
SCABIES (see Glossary)

CALL YOUR CHILD'S PHYSICIAN

Immediately If

• Breathing or swallowing is difficult.

• The itching started immediately after your child took medicine or was stung by an insect.

• The itching keeps your child from sleeping.

During Office Hours

All other children with a widespread itchy rash need medical consultation. (Exception: If you know the cause and can eliminate it, proceed to HOME CARE, below.)

HOME CARE FOR ITCHY, WIDESPREAD RASHES

The following measures may help to relieve itching regardless of the cause:

• Wash the skin once with soap to remove any irritants.

• Give your child cool baths without soap every 3 to 4 hours. (Exception: If the cause is dry skin, see the guideline on page 428.)

• Follow with calamine lotion (no prescription needed) or a baking soda solution (1 teaspoon in 4 ounces water). For very itchy spots, apply ½ percent hydrocortisone cream (no prescription needed). (Exception: If the cause is chicken pox, see the guideline on page 424.)

- Encourage your child not to scratch. Cut the fingernails short.

- Since sweating aggravates itching, temporarily avoid excessive heat, sunbathing, exercise, or sleeping with several blankets.

- Since they cause dry skin, also avoid soaps and swimming pools.

- Your child should not wear itchy or tight clothes.

RASHES WHILE ON DRUGS

Most children who develop a rash while on a medication have a viral rash (viral exanthem) that is unrelated to the medicine (e.g., roseola). Another common rash is the type seen in children on amoxicillin or ampicillin (see Ampicillin Rash, page 423). This is not an allergic rash (it's called a toxic rash), and the medicine can be continued.

CALL YOUR CHILD'S PHYSICIAN

Immediately If

- The rash is hives.

- The rash is very itchy.

- Breathing or swallowing is difficult.

- The tongue is swollen.

- The rash is purple or blood-colored.

- The rash is bright red *and* tender to the touch.

- The rash looks like a burn.

- Your youngster is a female adolescent *and* she currently is having her menstrual period.

- Your child is acting very sick.

During Office Hours If

- All other children who have widespread red rashes in association with drugs.

Note: Localized rashes are not due to drugs. (See the guideline on localized rashes.)

HOME CARE

1. *Stopping the Medication.* Once your child is labeled as being allergic to a medicine, he can never receive any drugs in that category (e.g., all penicillins) in the future. Hence this is a critical decision. Unless your physician tells you otherwise, have your child examined before stopping a medication.
   Exceptions: (1) If your child has a severe rash *and* is taking antiseizure or sulfa drugs, stop the drugs. (2) If you are certain your child has hives.
2. *Antibiotic Replacement.* Any time antibiotics are discontinued without completing the full course, the child must be seen within 16 hours to assess the need for a new antibiotic. Without this precaution, many children would have flare-ups of partially treated infections.

AMPICILLIN RASH

SYMPTOMS AND CHARACTERISTICS

- Pink or red spots
- The spots are small, flat, and nonitchy
- Always on the trunk
- Spreads to the face in 50 percent of cases
- Occurs while on ampicillin or amoxacillin
- Usual day of onset is day 5 from start of medicine (with a range of 1 to 16 days)

  If your child's symptoms are different, call your physician for help.

Cause • From 5 to 10 percent of children taking ampicillin get a skin rash. This is a harmless "toxic rash" and does not indicate any allergy to ampicillin or penicillin.

Expected Course • The rash usually lasts 3 days, with a range of 1 to 6 days.

CALL YOUR CHILD'S PHYSICIAN DURING OFFICE HOURS IF

- The rash looks like hives.

- The rash is itchy.

- The rash has been present more than 6 days.

- Your child has any joint pains or swelling.

- You have other questions or concerns.

HOME CARE
No treatment is necessary.

Ampicillin • Keep your child on the ampicillin until it is gone. The rash will disappear just as quickly whether or not your child continues on ampicillin. Your child can receive ampicillin in the future when necessary and probably won't get a rash next time.

Call Your Child's Physician Later If

- The rash becomes itchy.

- The rash lasts more than 6 days.

- You feel it is a drug allergy.

CHICKEN POX (VARICELLA)

SYMPTOMS AND CHARACTERISTICS

- Multiple small red bumps that progress to thin-walled water blisters, then cloudy blisters or open sores, and finally dry brown crusts (all within 24 hours)

- Repeated crops of new chicken pox for 4 to 5 days

- The sores or crusts are usually less than ¼ inch across

- Rash is on all body surfaces, but usually starts on the head and back. Occasionally the rash stays localized for the first day or two.

- Fever (The more the rash, the higher the fever. However, your child may not have any fever on the first day of chicken pox or if the rash remains mild.)

- Sores (ulcers) can also occur normally in the mouth, eyelids, and genital area.

- Exposure to a child with chicken pox 14 to 16 days previously

If your child's symptoms are different, call your physician for help. Usually the diagnosis of chicken pox is easy.

Cause • Exposure to a highly contagious virus 14 to 16 days previously. A chicken pox vaccine has been tested extensively and should be licensed in 1991 for use in healthy children. It will probably be given with the MMR vaccine at the 15-month visit.

Expected Course • New eruptions continue to crop up daily for 4 to 5 days. The fever is usually the highest on the third or fourth day. Children start to feel better and their fevers clear once they stop getting new bumps. Most children get a total of 400 to 500 chicken pox bumps. Since chicken pox often looks terrible, reassure your child that the bumps are not serious and will go away. Chicken pox rarely leaves any permanent scars unless the eruptions become badly infected with impetigo or your child repeatedly picks off the scabs. Normal chicken pox, however, can leave temporary marks on the skin that take 6 to 12 months to fade. One attack gives lifelong immunity. Very rarely, a child may develop a mild second attack.

CALL YOUR CHILD'S PHYSICIAN

Immediately If

- Your child develops a patch of red, tender skin.

- Your child develops a speckled red rash that looks like scarlet fever (page 442).

- Your child is difficult to awaken or confused.

- Your child has trouble walking.

- The neck is stiff.

- The breathing is difficult.

- Vomiting occurs 3 or more times.

• Bleeding occurs into the chicken pox.

• Your child acts or looks very sick.

Within 24 Hours If

• The scabs become soft and drain yellow pus.

• The scabs become larger in size.
(Note: Use a nonprescription antibiotic ointment on these sores until your child is seen.)

• One lymph node becomes larger and more tender than the others.

• You have other questions or concerns.

HOME CARE FOR CHICKEN POX

Itching and Cool Baths • The best treatment for skin discomfort and itching is a cool bath every 3 to 4 hours for the first few days. Baths don't spread the chicken pox. To protect the scabs, pat rather than rub your child dry. Calamine lotion can be placed on itchy spots after the bath. (Don't use Caladryl because it can cause side effects.)

If the itching is severe or interferes with sleep, give your child a nonprescription antihistamine called Benadryl. For the proper dosage of Benadryl, see Hives, page 435.

Fever • Acetaminophen may be given for a few days if your child develops a fever over 102°F (39°C). (For dosage, see FEVER, page 407.) A recent study by Dr. T. F. Doran showed that chicken pox healed up a day sooner if the fever was *not* treated. Aspirin should be avoided in children and adolescents with chicken pox because of the possible link with Reyes syndrome.

Sore Mouth • Since chicken pox sores also occur in the mouth and throat, your child may be picky about eating for a few days. Encourage cold fluids. Offer a soft diet (e.g., ice cream, eggs, pudding, Jell-O, mashed potatoes). Avoid salty foods and citrus fruits.

If the mouth ulcers become troublesome, have your child gargle or swallow 1 tablespoon of an antacid solution 4 times per day after meals.

Sores also normally occur on the eyelids; this carries no danger to vision.

Sore Genital Area • Sores normally occur in the genital area. These can be very painful. If your child (especially a girl) complains of a lot of pain or holds back her urine, buy a local anesthetic like 2.5 percent Xylocaine or 1 percent Nupercainal ointment (no prescription needed). Apply it to the genital ulcers as often as necessary to relieve the pain (every 2 to 3 hours). The cool baths should also help.

Prevention of Impetigo (Infected Sores) • To prevent the sores from becoming infected with bacteria, trim your child's fingernails short. Also, wash the hands with an antibacterial soap (such as Dial or Safeguard) frequently during the day. Discourage picking and scratching, especially of the face. For young babies who are scratching badly, you may want to cover their hands with cotton socks.

Contagiousness and Isolation • Children with chicken pox are contagious until all the sores have crusted over, usually about 6 or 7 days after the rash begins. Therefore, they should be kept out of school for about 1 week. Your child does not have to stay home until all the scabs fall off, since this may take 2 weeks.
• Avoid sunlight, since extra chicken pox will occur on sun-exposed parts of the skin.
• Most adults who think they didn't have chicken pox as a child, had a mild case. Only 4 percent of adults are not protected. If you lived in the same household with siblings who had chicken pox, consider yourself protected.
• Siblings will come down with chicken pox in 14 to 16 days. The second case in a family always has many more chicken pox bumps than the first case.
• To avoid exposing other children outside the family, try not to take your child to the physician's office. If you must, leave your child in the car with a sitter while you check in.
• If a child with a serious disease or taking steroids is exposed to chicken pox, he should see his physician promptly because he may need protection with a special kind of gamma globulin (VZIG).
• Also avoid pregnant women who have not had chicken pox because of the risk to the fetus.

Call Your Child's Physician Later If
• The scabs get any pus under them or become larger in size.

- The fever lasts over 4 days.

- The itching is severe and doesn't respond to treatment.

- Breathing becomes difficult or fast.

- Your child becomes confused or difficult to awaken.

- Your child has severe pain when passing urine.

- You feel your child is getting worse.

DRY SKIN

Dry, rough skin is mainly caused by removing the skin's natural oils through too much bathing and soap ("soapy dermatitis"). Once the oils are gone, the skin can't hold moisture. Dry climates make it worse, as does winter weather ("winter itch"). The problem is less common in teenagers, because the oil glands are more active. Dry, rough, bumpy skin on the back of the upper arms is called keratosis pilaris. Dry, pale spots on the face are called pityriasis alba. Both are complications of scrubbing dry skin with soap. The dry areas are often itchy, and this is the main symptom.

HOME CARE

Soap and Bathing • For children with dry skin, avoid all soaps. Have your child bathe or shower less often than usual—perhaps twice a week. Keep bathing time to less than 10 minutes. Avoid soaps, detergents, and bubble baths. Don't let a bar of soap just float around in the tub. For teenagers, buy a special soap for dry skin (Dove received high ratings in a recent study). Teenagers can get by with applying soap only to the armpits, genitals, and feet. Use no soap on itchy areas. Don't lather up—the outer arms are often affected for this reason. Rinse well.

Lubricating Creams • Buy a large bottle of a lubricating cream (see ECZEMA, below, for details). Apply the cream to any dry or itchy areas several times a day, especially immediately after bathing. You will probably have to continue this throughout the winter. If the itch persists after 4 days, use ½ percent hydrocortisone cream (no prescription needed) temporarily.

Humidifier • If your winters are dry, you can protect your child's skin from the constant drying effect by running a room humidifier full time. The presence of static electricity means your home is much too dry. During cold weather, have your child wear gloves outside to protect against the rapid evaporation of moisture from the hands.

Bath Oils • It does not make sense to pour bath oils into the bathwater; most of the oil goes down the drain. It also makes the bathtub slippery and dangerous. If you prefer a bath oil over hand lotion, it should be applied (usually in a diluted form) immediately after the bath. Baby oil (mineral oil) is inexpensive and keeps the skin moisture from evaporating.

Call Your Child's Physician Later If

• No improvement occurs within 2 weeks.

ECZEMA (ATOPIC DERMATITIS)

SYMPTOMS AND CHARACTERISTICS

• Red, extremely itchy rash

• Often starts on the cheeks at 2 to 6 months of age.

• Most common on flexor surfaces (creases) of the elbows, wrists, and knees. (Infants who are crawling often have more rash on the forearms and lower legs.)

• Occasionally the neck, ankles, and feet are involved

• If scratched, the rash becomes raw and weeping

• Constant dry skin

• Previous confirmation of this diagnosis by a physician is helpful

If your child's symptoms are different, call your physician for help.

Cause • Eczema results from an inherited type of sensitive skin and lowered itch threshold. A personal history of asthma or hay fever or a family history of eczema adds weight to the diagnosis. Flare-ups occur when there is contact with irritating substances (especially soaps and chlorine). While food allergies are not the underlying cause of eczema, in 30 percent of these infants a particular food may cause the eczema to flare up. If you suspect some food (e.g., cow's milk, soy formula, eggs, or peanut butter), feed it to your child as a single challenge after avoiding it for 2 weeks. If it plays any role, the eczema should become itchy or develop hives within 2 hours of ingestion. If this occurs, avoid this food in the future and talk to your child's physician about food substitutes.

Expected Course • This is a chronic condition and will usually not go away before adolescence. Eczema of the face usually clears by age 2 or 3 years. Early treatment of any itching or change in the skin is the key to preventing a severe rash.

CALL YOUR CHILD'S PHYSICIAN

Immediately If

• The rash appears to be infected and your child has a fever.

• The rash flares up after contact with someone with fever blisters (herpes).

• Your child acts or looks very sick.

Within 24 Hours If

• The rash appears to be infected, as evidenced by pus or soft yellow scabs.

• The rash is raw and bleeding in several places.

During Office Hours If

• Your child is under 2 years of age.

• The itching interferes with sleep.

• You have other questions or concerns.

HOME CARE

Steroid Cream • Steroid cream is the main treatment for eczema. Use the one your physician prescribes or nonprescription ½ percent hydrocortisone cream. Apply it up to 4 times a day when the eczema flares up. When the rash quiets down, use it at least once a day for an additional 2 weeks. After that, break the itch cycle by using it immediately on any spot that itches.

This cream should be applied in small amounts and rubbed in until it can't be seen. When you travel with your child, always take the steroid cream with you, and always leave it available for baby-sitters. If your supply starts to run out, get it renewed.

Bathing and Hydrating the Skin • Your child should have 1 bath a day (twice a day in the wintertime) for 10 minutes. Water-soaked skin is far less itchy. Don't use any soap on the areas of rash. Eczema is very sensitive to soaps. Young children can usually be cleaned without any soap. Teenagers need a soap to wash under the arms, the genital area, and the feet. They can use a nondrying soap such as Dove for these areas. Try to keep shampoo off the eczema.

Lubricating Cream • Children with eczema always have dry skin. After a 10-minute bath, the skin is hydrated and feels good. Help trap the moisture in the skin by applying an outer layer of cream to the entire skin surface while it is damp. Apply it after steroid cream has been applied to any itchy areas. Apply the lubricating cream once daily (twice a day during the winter). Some lubricating creams are Eucerin, Keri, Lubriderm, Nivea, and Nutraderm. Avoid applying any ointments, petroleum jelly, or vegetable shortening, because they can block the sweat glands, increase the itching, and worsen the rash. They cause the most trouble during hot and humid weather. Also, soap is needed to wash them off. For severe eczema, ointments may be needed temporarily to heal the skin.

Itching • At the first sign of any itching, apply the steroid cream to the area that itches. Keep your child's fingernails cut short so they are less damaging to the skin. Also, wash your child's hands with water frequently to avoid infecting the eczema. When itching is present, it is always worse at bedtime compared to the rest of the day, because your child has little else by way of distraction. Therefore, steroid cream at bedtime is important.

Call Your Child's Physician Later If

• Itching interferes with sleep.

• The rash becomes infected.

• The rash hasn't greatly improved within 7 days on this treatment.

PREVENTION

- Try to breast-feed all high-risk infants. Also avoid cow's milk products, soy, eggs, peanut butter, wheat, and fish during the first year of life.

- Clothes made of cotton, or of cotton in combination with other fibers, should be worn as much as possible.

- Avoid wool fibers and clothes made of other scratchy, rough materials. They make eczema worse.

- Avoid materials that hold in heat, such as most synthetic fibers, which can worsen the rash.

- Avoid triggers that cause eczema to flare up, such as excessive heat, sweating, excessive cold, dry air, chlorine, harsh chemicals, and soaps.

- In dry climates, place a humidifier in your child's bedroom.

- Never use bubble bath, because it can have a disastrous effect on eczema.

- Keep your child off the grass during grass pollen season (May and June).

- Keep your child away from anyone with fever blisters. The herpes virus can cause a serious skin infection in children with eczema.

FIFTH DISEASE (ERYTHEMA INFECTIOSUM)

SYMPTOMS AND CHARACTERISTICS

- Bright red rash of both cheeks for 1 to 3 days ("slapped cheek" appearance)

- Followed by pink "lacelike" (or "netlike") rash of extremities

- "Lacy" rash mainly on thighs and upper arms

- "Lacy" rash that comes and goes several times over 1 to 3 weeks

- No fever or minimal one

If your child's symptoms are different, call your physician for help. Fifth Disease was so named because it was the fifth pink-red infectious rash to be described. Despite some controversy about roseola being fourth disease, the other 4 are:

SCARLET FEVER (see page 442)
MEASLES (see page 437)
RUBELLA (see page 441)
ROSEOLA (see page 440)

See those guidelines for details.

Cause • Fifth disease is caused by the human parvovirus B19. The attack rate in schools is usually 50 percent of the students.

Expected Course • This is a very mild disease with either no symptoms or a slight runny nose and sore throat. Complications in children are very rare. The lacelike rash can come and go for 5 weeks. Heat seems to be the main precipitant; therefore it returns following warm baths, exercise, and sun exposure.

CALL YOUR CHILD'S PHYSICIAN DURING OFFICE HOURS IF

• Your child was on any medicine when the rash began.

• A fever over 101°F is present.

• The rash is itchy.

• You have other questions or concerns.

HOME CARE

Treatment • No treatment is necessary. This distinctive rash is harmless and causes no symptoms.

Contagiousness • Exposed children will come down with the rash in 10 to 14 days. Because the disease is mainly contagious during the week before the rash begins, a child who has the rash is no longer contagious and does not need to stay home from school.

Adults with Fifth Disease • Most adults who acquire Fifth Disease develop a mild pinkness of the cheeks or no rash whatever. More commonly, adults develop joint pains, especially of the knees. These pains may take 1 to 3 months to run their course. Taking a nonprescription ibuprofen product usually relieves symptoms. An arthritis workup is unnecessary for joint pains following Fifth Disease.

Pregnant Women • Recent research showed that some fetuses who are infected with Fifth Disease before birth can develop severe anemia (10%) or even die (2%). If you are pregnant and exposed to a child with Fifth Disease before he develops the rash, see your obstetrician. He or she will obtain an antibody test to see if you already had the disease and are protected. If not, your pregnancy will need to be monitored closely. The good news is that this virus doesn't cause any birth defects.

Call Your Child's Physician Later If

• It becomes itchy.

• A fever over 101°F occurs.

• You feel your child is getting worse.

HEAT RASH (MILIARIA)

A heat rash consists of tiny pink bumps, mainly of the neck and upper back. It is caused by blocked-off sweat glands. Lots of children get it during hot, humid weather when sweat glands are overworked. Infants can also get it in the wintertime with fever, overdressing, or ointments applied to the chest for coughs. It is also called prickly heat.

HOME CARE

Treatment • Heat rash will clear up completely in 2 to 3 days with techniques that cool off the skin. Give cool baths every 2 to 3 hours, without soap. Let your child's skin air-dry. Leave as many clothes off as possible. Use a fan if your child is asleep or in a playpen. Have your child lie on a towel so the face isn't constantly wet.

Calamine lotion (no prescription needed) can be applied to the worst spots. Cornstarch applied to body creases can prevent some heat rashes. Avoid all ointments or oils, because they can block off sweat glands.

Call Your Child's Physician Later If

• The rash lasts more than 72 hours on this treatment.

HIVES (URTICARIA)

SYMPTOMS AND CHARACTERISTICS

• Very itchy rash

• Raised pink spots with pale centers (hives look like mosquito bites)

• Sizes of spots range from ½ inch to several inches across

• Shapes are quite variable

• Location, size, and shape change rapidly and repeatedly

If your child's symptoms are different, call your physician for help.

Causes • Hives are an allergic reaction to a food (especially shrimp, fruits, and nuts), drug, viral infection, insect bite, or a host of other substances. Usually a child has been exposed to the substance many times in the past before developing an allergy to it. Often the cause is not found.

Expected Course • More than 10 percent of children get hives. Most children who develop hives have it only once. The hives come and go for 3 or 4 days and then mysteriously disappear. Large swellings are common about the eyes, lips, and genitals if hives occur there. Some young children become sensitized to mosquito or flea bites. They develop big hives (called papular urticaria) at the site of old and new bites that last for months.

CALL YOUR CHILD'S PHYSICIAN

Immediately If

• Breathing or swallowing is difficult.

• The tongue is swollen.

• Any abdominal pain is present.

- The hives started immediately after your child took medicine or was stung by an insect.
- Your child is on any medicine.
- Your child acts or looks very sick.

During Office Hours If

- A fever (over 100°F) is present.
- Joint swelling or pain is present.
- Your child had hives before *and* the cause wasn't found.
- You have other questions or concerns.

HOME CARE

Treatment • The best drug for hives is an antihistamine. While an antihistamine won't cure the hives, it will reduce their numbers and relieve itching. Benadryl is a good product that became available without a prescription in 1988. The main side effect is some drowsiness. If you have another antihistamine (e.g., any drug for hay fever) at home, use it until you can get some Benadryl. Give Benadryl 4 times a day in the following dosage:

Child's weight (pounds)	20	40	60	80	100	120
Benadryl liquid 12.5-mg./5-ml.	3-ml.	6	10	13	16	20
Benadryl 25-mg. tablets	—	—	1	1	1½	2

A cool bath will also make your child feel better. In the meantime, avoid anything you think might have brought on the hives. If the cause was definitely a food or drug your child swallowed in the last 4 hours, give one large dose of a laxative to speed its passage out of the body. (Such as 1 or 2 tablespoons of Milk of Magnesia.) Since hives are not contagious, your child can be with other children.

Common Mistakes • Many parents wait to give the antihistamine until new hives have re-appeared. This means your child will become itchy again. The purpose of the medicine is to keep your child comfortable until the hives go away. Therefore, give the medicine regularly until you are sure the hives are completely gone.

Call Your Child's Physician Later If

- Most of the itch is not relieved within 24 hours on the medicine.

- The hives last for more than a week.

- You feel your child is getting worse.

MEASLES (RUBEOLA)

SYMPTOMS AND CHARACTERISTICS

- 3 or 4 days of red eyes, cough, runny nose, and fever before the rash begins

- Pronounced blotchy red rash starting on the face and spreading downward over the entire body in 3 days

- White specks on the lining of the mouth, especially by the molars (Koplik's spots)

- Exposure to a child with measles 10 to 12 days earlier

  (Note: Because of the measles vaccine, this disease has become rare in our country.)

  If your child's symptoms are different, call your physician for help.

Cause • A highly contagious virus.

Expected Course • Measles can be a miserable illness, and there's not much we can do to shorten it. The Koplik's spots (which cause no symptoms) appear 1 day before the rash and are gone by day 2 of the rash. The rash usually lasts 7 days (this is why it's called 7-day measles). Your child will usually begin to feel a lot better by the fourth day of the rash. Ear infections, eye infections, and pneumonia are common complications.

CALL YOUR CHILD'S PHYSICIAN

Immediately If

- Breathing is difficult *and* no better after you clear the nose.

- Your child is confused or delirious.

- Your child is hard to awaken completely.

- Your child has a severe headache.

- Your child acts or looks very sick.

During Office Hours

All other children with suspected measles need medical consultation. This disease must be reported to the public health department to prevent spread.

HOME CARE

Fever • Use acetaminophen (for dosage, see FEVER, page 407).

Cough • Use corn syrup or honey (1 to 4 years old) or cough drops (over 4 years old). If the cough interferes with sleep, give a cough suppressant such as dextromethorphan (DM). Also, use a humidifier. (See COUGH, page 570, for further information.)

Red Eyes • Wipe your child's eyes frequently with a clean wet cotton ball. The eyes are usually sensitive to bright light, so your child may prefer the curtains drawn in his room and probably won't want to go outside for several days unless he wears sunglasses. Light exposure, however, can't damage the eyes.

Rash • The rash requires no treatment.

Diet • Offer a diet of your child's own choosing. The appetite will be poor for several days.

Contagiousness • The disease is no longer contagious after the rash is gone and your child can then see friends and go to school. This usually takes 7 days.

Measles Exposure • Any child or adult who has been exposed to your child and who has not had natural measles or the measles vaccine should call his or her physician. If given early, a measles vaccine is often protective.

Call Your Child's Physician Later If

- An earache develops.

- The eyes develop a yellow discharge.

- The nasal discharge becomes yellow for more than 24 hours.

- The breathing becomes labored *and* not due to a stuffy nose.

- Fever is still present on the fourth day of the rash.

- Fever returns after the temperature has been normal for more than 24 hours.

- You feel your child is getting worse.

MEASLES VACCINE RASH

The live measles vaccine has prevented many deaths and serious complications of the natural disease. The vaccine is given to children over 15 months of age. About 20 percent of children develop some mild symptoms 7 to 10 days after the vaccine. A slight, pink rash of the trunk usually lasts 2 or 3 days. A fever is usually 101°F to 103°F and lasts less than 72 hours. The fever rarely lasts 5 days.

HOME CARE

Treatment is not usually needed. The measles vaccine rash is harmless and not contagious.

CALL YOUR CHILD'S PHYSICIAN DURING OFFICE HOURS IF

- The rash becomes itchy.

- The rash changes to purple spots.

- The rash lasts more than 3 days.

PURPLE SPOTS

If your child develops purple to blood-red spots of the skin or unexplained bruises, call your child's physician *immediately*. The size of the bleeding into the skin can vary from small dots (petechiae) to large spots (purpura). These spots can be caused by a serious bloodstream infection such as meningococcemia or Rocky Mountain spotted fever (especially if your child also has a fever) or by a bleeding tendency.

(Note: Bruises due to injuries or blue birthmarks don't count.)

RELATED TOPIC

SKIN TRAUMA, BRUISES (see page 80)

ROSEOLA (ROSEOLA INFANTUM)

SYMPTOMS AND CHARACTERISTICS

- Age 6 months to 3 years
- Presence of a fine pink rash, mainly on the trunk
- High fever during the preceding 2 to 4 days which cleared within 24 hours before the rash appeared
- Your child was only mildly ill during the time with fever.
- Your child acts fine now.

  If your child's symptoms are different, call your physician for help.

Cause • Roseola is caused by the human herpes virus type 6.

Expected Course • The rash lasts 1 or 2 days, followed by complete recovery. Some children have 3 days of fever without a rash.

HOME CARE

Treatment • No particular treatment is necessary, since the fever is usually gone when the rash appears. Roseola is contagious, and other children under age 3 who have been with your child may come down with roseola in about 12 days. Once the rash is gone, the disease is no longer contagious.

Call Your Child's Physician Later If

- The spots become purple or blood-colored.
- The rash lasts more than 3 days.

- The rash becomes itchy.
- Any new symptoms develop that concern you.

RELATED TOPIC

RASHES, UNKNOWN CAUSE (WIDESPREAD) (see page 419)

RUBELLA (GERMAN MEASLES)

SYMPTOMS AND CHARACTERISTICS

- Widespread pink-red spots
- Starts on the face
- Moves rapidly downward, covering the body in 24 hours
- Lasts 3 to 4 days ("3-day measles")
- Associated enlarged lymph nodes at back of neck
- Mild fever
- Your child never had the rubella vaccine

The rash is not distinctive. Many other viral rashes look like it. Physicians have difficulty being certain of this diagnosis even after examining the child. Don't try to make this diagnosis at home unless there is an epidemic of it in your community.

Cause • Rubella is a viral illness. The incubation period is 14 to 21 days.

Expected Course • The disease is mild with complete recovery in 3 or 4 days. Complications are very rare except for about 10 percent of teenagers (especially girls) who develop associated joint pains. However, complications to the unborn child are disastrous and include deafness, cataracts, heart defects, growth retardation, and encephalitis. Pregnant women should avoid anyone with suspected rubella.

CALL YOUR CHILD'S PHYSICIAN DURING OFFICE HOURS IF

- Your child has a widespread, pink rash with fever.
- You think your child might have rubella.

HOME CARE

If your physician has confirmed that your child probably has rubella, the following may be helpful:

Treatment • None is probably necessary. Give acetaminophen for fever over 102°F, sore throat, or other pains. (For dosage, see FEVER, page 407.)

Avoid Pregnant Women • If your child might have rubella, keep him away from any pregnant women. He is contagious for 5 days after the start of the rash.

EXPOSURE OF ADULT WOMEN TO RUBELLA

The nonpregnant woman exposed to rubella should avoid pregnancy during the following 3 months, and the pregnant woman should see her obstetrician. If she has already received the rubella vaccine, she (and her unborn child) should be protected. If she thinks she had German measles as a child, this history is too unreliable. Even if the present exposure was minor or brief, she should have a blood test to determine her immunity against rubella.

RUBELLA VACCINE

Get your children protected against rubella at 15 months of age so we won't have to worry about pregnant women when kids get a pink or red rash. It's quite safe to immunize the child of a pregnant woman.

SCARLET FEVER

SYMPTOMS AND CHARACTERISTICS

- Reddened, sunburned-looking skin (especially of the chest and abdomen)

- On close inspection, the redness is speckled (i.e., tiny pink dots)

- Increased redness in skin folds (especially the groin, armpits, and elbow creases)

- The rash is everywhere within 24 hours

- Rough, sandpapery feeling to the reddened skin

- Flushed face with paleness around the mouth

- Sore throat and fever (usually preceding the rash by 18 to 24 hours)

  If your child's symptoms are different, call your physician for help.

Cause • Scarlet fever is a strep throat infection with a rash. The complication rate is no different from that for strep throat alone. The rash is caused by a special rash-producing toxin that is present in some strep bacteria.

Expected Course • The red rash usually clears in 4 or 5 days. Sometimes the skin peels in 1 or 2 weeks where the rash was most prominent (e.g., the groin). The skin on the fingertips also commonly peels. The skin may peel and flake for several weeks. The sore throat and fever clear after 1 or 2 days on penicillin. Your child can return to school then. The penicillin will need to be continued for 10 days to completely eliminate the strep. The rash itself is not contagious.

CALL YOUR CHILD'S PHYSICIAN

Immediately If

- Your child is drooling or having great difficulty swallowing.

- Your child also has a wound infection.

- Your child is a female adolescent *and* she is also having her menstrual period.

- The urine is red or cola-colored.

- Your child acts or looks very sick.

Within 24 Hours If

All other children with suspected scarlet fever need medical consultation. Your child's physician will advise you about a throat culture and antibiotics.

RELATED TOPIC

Sore Throat (see page 556)

SKIN: LOCALIZED PINK OR RED RASHES

RASHES, UNKNOWN CAUSE (LOCALIZED)

SYMPTOMS AND CHARACTERISTICS

- Red or pink rash (erythema)
- Smooth or slightly bumpy
- Spots or solid red
- On one part of body (localized or clustered)
- Not itchy

Similar Condition • If the rash is itchy, turn directly to the guideline for ITCHING, UNKNOWN CAUSE (LOCALIZED), page 446.

Causes of Localized Rashes • The possible causes are many. If one of the following is suspected, turn directly to that guideline:

- Scalp location
  CRADLE CAP (see page 127)

- Face location
  ACNE (see page 447)

- Fingers location
  Peeling Fingers: See your child's physician by appointment to rule out strep (see page 443).

- Genital location
  DIAPER RASH (see page 128)

- Hand and foot location
  HAND, FOOT, AND MOUTH DISEASE (see page 455)

- Nostrils (nasal openings) location
  IMPETIGO (see page 456)

- Shoulder location
  TINEA VERSICOLOR (see page 467)

- Variable location
  BOILS (see page 452)
  IMPETIGO (see page 456)
  NEWBORN RASHES (less than 2 weeks old) (see page 108)
  RINGWORM (see page 464)
  SHINGLES (see page 465)

Expected Course • Depends on the diagnosis.

CALL YOUR CHILD'S PHYSICIAN

Immediately If

- The rash is purple or blood-colored.

- It is bright red *and* tender to the touch.

- It looks like a burn.

- Red streaks that look like a spreading infection are present.

- Your child is less than 1 month old *and* has some small blisters or pimples.

- Your child acts or looks very sick.

During Office Hours If

- You have other questions or concerns.

HOME CARE FOR LOCALIZED RASHES

Treatment • Localized red rashes can be due to a chemical or plant irritant that got on your child's skin. No treatment is necessary. Wash the rash once with soap to remove any irritating substances. Thereafter cleanse it only with water. Don't apply any medicine or petroleum jelly. If the rash seems dry, apply hand lotion twice a day.

Call Your Child's Physician Later If

• The rash spreads.

• It becomes tender to the touch.

• It lasts more than 1 week.

ITCHING, UNKNOWN CAUSE (LOCALIZED)

CAUSES
The possible causes are many. If one of the following is suspected, turn directly to that guideline:

• Itching of anus
  PINWORMS (see page 602)

• Itching of eyes
  EYES, ALLERGIES (see page 502)
  EYE, ITCHY (see page 505)

• Itching of foot
  ATHLETE'S FOOT (see page 451)

• Itching of genitals
  JOCK ITCH (see page 459)

• Itching of head
  LICE (HEAD) (see page 460)
  DANDRUFF (see page 472)

• Itching of lip
  LIP, SWOLLEN (see page 555)

• Itching of variable locations
  BITES, INSECT (see page 18)
  POISON IVY (see page 464)
  RINGWORM (see page 464)

CALL YOUR CHILD'S PHYSICIAN DURING OFFICE HOURS IF

• The itching is severe.

• The rash is larger than 2 inches in size.

• You have other questions or concerns.

HOME CARE

Clarification • The itchy spot is probably due to contact with an irritant like a plant, chemicals, Fiberglas, detergents, a new cosmetic, or new jewelry (called contact dermatitis). Try to figure out what caused it and avoid this substance in the future.

Treatment • Wash the area once thoroughly with soap to remove any remaining irritants. Thereafter avoid soaps to this area. Apply cold-water compresses or ice for 20 minutes every 3 to 4 hours to reduce itching. Follow this with calamine lotion. If the itch is more than mild, apply ½ percent hydrocortisone cream (no prescription needed) every 2 hours until it feels better. Encourage your child not to scratch; cut the fingernails short.

Call Your Child's Physician Later If

• The rash spreads.

• The itching becomes worse.

• It lasts more than 1 week.

ACNE

SYMPTOMS AND CHARACTERISTICS

• Blackheads, whiteheads (pimples), or red bumps

• Face, neck, and shoulders involved

• The larger red lumps are quite painful

• Occurs during adolescent and young adult years

Cause • Acne is due to an overactivity and plugging of the oil glands. More than 90 percent of teenagers have some acne. The main cause of the changes in the oil glands is increased levels of hormones during adolescence. Heredity is also a factor. It is not caused by diet, and it is unnecessary to restrict fried foods, chocolate, or any other food. Acne is not caused by sexual activity or by dirt and not washing the face often enough. The tops of blackheads turn black because of the chemical reaction of the oil plug with the air.

Expected Course • Acne usually lasts until age 20 or even 25. It is rare for acne to leave any scars, and people worry needlessly about this.

CALL YOUR CHILD'S PHYSICIAN WITHIN 24 HOURS IF

• There are any boils.

• There are any red streaks.

• There are more than five tender, red lumps.

• You have other questions or concerns.

HOME CARE

There is no magic medicine at this time that will cure acne. However, good skin care can keep acne under control and at a mild level.

Basic Treatment for All Acne

• Soap. The skin should be washed twice a day, the most important time being at bedtime. A mild soap such as Dove should be used, because overly dry skin makes acne harder to treat. Lack of washing does not cause acne. Excessive washing can make it worse.

• Hair. The hair should be shampooed daily. Acne can be made worse by friction if the hair is too long.

• Avoid picking. Many young people pick at their acne when they are not thinking about it. This keeps it from healing. They should try not to touch the face at all during the day.

• Avoid looking in mirrors more than 1 or 2 minutes a day. Your youngster will just find something to pick and make the acne worse.

• Get out and meet people. Acne is not contagious.

Additional Treatment for Pimples • Pimples are infected oil glands. They should be treated with the following:

• Benzoyl peroxide 5 percent lotion or gel. This lotion helps to open pimples, unplug blackheads, and it also kills bacteria. It is available without a prescription. Ask your pharmacist to recommend a brand. The lotion should be applied in a thin film once a day at bedtime. In redheads and blonds, it should be applied every other day initially. Apply the lotion to the entire face (except for the sensitive skin next to the eyes and mouth), not just the areas that have currently flared up. An amount the size of a pea should cover most of the face. If the skin peels or becomes red, you are using too much of the medicine or applying it too often, so slow down. After a desirable effect has been achieved, the benzoyl peroxide lotion may be needed only every other night.

• Pimple opening. In general, "popping" pimples is discouraged; but teenagers do it anyway. Therefore, teach your youngster to open pimples safely without popping them. Never open a pimple before it has come to a head. Wash your face and hands first. Nick the surface of the yellow pimple with the tip of a sterile needle. The pus should run out without squeezing. Wipe away the pus and wash that area with soap and water. Scarring will not result from opening small pimples, but it can result from squeezing boils or other red, tender lumps. This should never be done, because it damages the skin.

Additional Treatment for Blackheads (Comedones) • Blackheads are the plugs found in blocked-off oil glands. Blackheads are not infected and should be treated with the following:

• Benzoyl peroxide. This agent is the best nonprescription medicine for removing the thickened skin that blocks the openings to oil glands. It should be used as previously described. (Note: A stronger agent for stopping blackhead formation is retinoic acid A, but a prescription is required.)

• Blackhead extractor. Blackheads that are a cosmetic problem can sometimes be removed with a blackhead or comedone extractor. This instrument costs about a dollar and is available at any drugstore. By placing the hole in the end of the small metal spoon directly over the blackhead, uniform pressure can be applied that does not hurt the normal skin. This method is much more efficient than anything you can accomplish with your fingers. Soak your face with a warm washcloth before trying to remove blackheads. If the blackhead does not come out the first time, leave it alone, and consult your physician about Retin A.

Results of Treatment • Even the best of medicines takes 4 to 6 weeks to improve acne. Success depends on your patience. There are no shortcuts. The proper treatment program will need to remain in effect for several years.

Common Mistakes in Treating Acne

- Alcohol wipes, medicated soaps, or abrasive soaps have no benefits, and they irritate the skin and block off more oil glands.

- Avoid rubbing the skin. Hard scrubbing of the skin is harmful because it breaks the walls of the oil glands, which leads to pimples and large lumps.

- Avoid applying any oily or greasy substances to the face. They make acne worse by blocking off oil glands. If you must use cover-up cosmetics, use water-based ones and wash them off at bedtime.

- Avoid hair tonics or hair creams (especially greasy ones). With sweating, these will spread to the face and aggravate the acne.

- Avoid any friction. Friction or pressure on the face, such as from headbands, scarves, turtlenecks, or resting the cheek or chin on the palm of the hand will worsen the acne in these areas.

- Avoid close shaves. Attempts to look extra good for a date usually nick the openings of the oil glands and cause the acne to flare up.

- Avoid self-medication with high dosages of zinc or Vitamin A. The former can increase the risk for strokes and the latter can cause brain swelling and bone pain.

Call Your Child's Physician Later If

- A boil develops on the face.

- Several large, tender, red lumps appear.

- Acne is not improved after treating it with benzoyl peroxide for 2 months.

- Benzoyl peroxide makes the face itchy or swollen.

ATHLETE'S FOOT (TINEA PEDIS)

SYMPTOMS AND CHARACTERISTICS

- A red, scaly, cracked rash between the toes
- The rash itches and burns
- With itching the rash becomes raw and weepy
- Scaly rash often involves the insteps of the feet
- Unpleasant foot odor
- Mainly occurs in adolescents

Similar Condition

CRACKED SKIN (see page 472)

Cause • A fungus infection that grows best on warm, damp skin. The condition is worse in summer, in people who sweat a lot (e.g., athletes), and in people who rarely take off their shoes.

Expected Course • With proper treatment, athlete's foot usually clears in 2 to 3 weeks.

CALL YOUR CHILD'S PHYSICIAN DURING OFFICE HOURS IF

- The rash is not confined to the instep and between the toes.
- Pus is draining from the rash.
- The feet are very painful.
- You have other questions or concerns.

HOME CARE

Antifungal Cream • Buy Tinactin or Micatin lotion at your drugstore (no prescription needed). Before applying, rinse the feet in plain water or water with a little white vinegar added. Dry them carefully, especially between the toes. Apply the lotion twice a day to the rash and well beyond its borders. Continue Tinactin or Micatin for several weeks, or for at least 7 days after the rash seems to have cleared.

Dryness • Athlete's foot improves dramatically if the feet are kept dry. It helps to go barefoot or wear sandals or thongs as much as possible. Canvas tennis shoes are good. Plastic or tight shoes are bad because they don't allow the feet to breathe. Cotton socks should be worn because they absorb sweat and keep the feet dry. Change the socks twice daily. Dry the feet thoroughly after baths and showers.

Foot Odor • Foot odor will often clear as the athlete's foot improves. Rinsing the feet and changing the socks twice daily are essential. If you can still smell your child coming, take off his tennis shoes and throw them in your washing machine with some soap and bleach.

Discourage Scratching • Scratching infected feet will delay a cure.

Contagiousness • The condition is not very contagious. The fungus won't grow on dry, normal skin. Your child may take gym and continue with sports. The socks don't need to be boiled, nor do shoes need to be discarded. Taking special precautions in community showers or swimming pools is pointless. If a preadolescent child has athlete's foot, usually a parent or older sibling also has it and requires treatment.

Prevention • Prevent recurrence by continuing the measures already described that keep your feet dry. Applying cornstarch powder to the feet once a day also helps.

Call Your Child's Physician Later If

• The athlete's foot is not improved in 1 week.

• It is not completely cured after 4 weeks of this treatment.

BOILS (ABSCESSES)

SYMPTOMS AND CHARACTERISTICS

• Tender, red lump in the skin

• Causes pain even when not being touched

• Usually ½ inch to 1 inch across

If your child's symptoms are different, call your physician for help.

Cause • A bacterial infection of a hair root or skin pore caused by staph (*Staphylococcus aureus*). Rubbing can cause additional boils. The back of the neck is especially vulnerable because of friction from collars.

Expected Course • Without treatment, the body will wall off the infection. After about a week, the center of the boil becomes soft and mushy (filled with pus). The overlying skin then develops a pimple or becomes thin and pale ("comes to a head"). The boil is now ready for draining. Without lancing, it will drain by itself in 3 or 4 days. Until it drains, a boil is extremely painful.

CALL YOUR CHILD'S PHYSICIAN

Immediately If

• An unexplained fever (over 100° F) is present.

• A spreading red streak runs from the boil.

• Your child acts or looks very sick.

During Office Hours

All children with boils need medical consultation to decide if antibiotics and/or lancing are needed. Boils heal faster and are less likely to recur if your child receives an antibiotic that kills the staph bacteria. Boils on the face are especially dangerous and should always be treated by a physician.

HOME CARE

Lancing or Draining the Boil • In general, it's better not to open a boil on your own child because it's a very painful procedure. However, if your physician has agreed that you can open the boil, the following information may help: Until the abscess comes to a head or becomes soft, apply warm compresses 3 times a day for 20 minutes. When the boil is ready, use a sterile needle (sterilized with alcohol or a flame), make a large opening, and squeeze very gently or not at all. Once opened, it will drain pus for 2 or 3 days and then heal up. Since this pus is contagious, the boil must be covered by a large 4-by-4-inch gauze and microporous tape. This bandage should be changed and the area washed with an antiseptic (Dial or Safeguard) soap 3 times a day.

Contagiousness • Boils are very contagious. Be certain that other people in your family do not use your child's towel or washcloth. Any clothes, towels, or sheets that are contaminated with drainage from the boils should be washed with Lysol. Any bandages with pus on them should be carefully thrown away.

Common Mistakes in the Treatment of Boils • Sometimes friends or relatives may advise you to squeeze a boil until you get the core out. The pus in a boil will come out easily if the opening is large enough. Vigorous squeezing is not only very painful, but also entails the risk of forcing bacteria into the bloodstream or causing other boils in the same area. Again, squeezing should be done very gently or not at all. A boil on the face should be treated by a physician.

Call Your Child's Physician Later If

• The boil has come to a head and needs to be opened.

• Your child develops more boils.

• A fever (over 100°F) occurs.

PREVENTION OF MORE BOILS

Boils can easily become a recurrent problem. The staph bacteria on the skin can be decreased by showering and washing the hair daily with an antibacterial soap (e.g., Dial or Safeguard). Showers are preferred to a bath because, during a bath, bacteria are just relocated to other parts of the skin. Often the staph bacteria are carried inside the nose. Eliminate them by applying Bacitracin ointment (no prescription needed) with a cotton swab twice a day for 2 weeks. Also discourage your child from picking the nose. A recent study by Dr. M. C. Weijmer found that boils are more common in people who have low serum iron levels. If your child is a picky eater or doesn't like meats, see your physician about changing the diet or adding iron supplements.

RELATED TOPICS

FINGERNAIL INFECTION (PARONYCHIA) (see page 473)
PIMPLES (see page 482)
STYE (see page 512)

HAND, FOOT, AND MOUTH DISEASE

SYMPTOMS AND CHARACTERISTICS

- Small ulcers in the mouth
- A mildly painful mouth
- Small water blisters or red spots located on the palms and soles, and between the fingers and toes (70 percent)
- 5 or fewer blisters per extremity
- Sometimes, small blisters or red spots on the buttocks (30 percent)
- Low-grade fever (over 100°F)
- Mainly occurs in children age 6 months to 4 years

If your child's symptoms are different, call your physician for help.

Similar Conditions • If one of the following is suspected, save time by turning directly to that guideline:

CANKER SORES (see page 551)
COLD SORES (see page 553)
THRUSH (see page 137)

Cause • Hand, foot, and mouth disease is always caused by a Coxackie A virus. It has no relationship to hoof and mouth disease of cattle.

Expected Course • The fever and discomfort are usually gone by day 3 or 4. The mouth ulcers resolve by 7 days, but the rash on the hands and feet can last 10 days. The only complication seen with any frequency is dehydration from refusing fluids.

CALL YOUR CHILD'S PHYSICIAN

Immediately If

- Your child has not urinated for more than 8 hours.
- The neck is stiff.
- Your child is confused or delirious.
- Your child is hard to awaken completely.
- Your child acts or looks very sick.

During Office Hours If

• Fluid intake is poor.

• The mouth pain is severe.

• The gums are red, swollen, or tender.

• You have other questions or concerns.

HOME CARE

Diet • Avoid giving your child citrus, salty, or spicy foods. Also avoid foods that need much chewing. Change to a soft diet for a few days and encourage plenty of clear fluids. Cold drinks, Popsicles, and sherbet are often well received. Have your child rinse the mouth with warm water after meals.

Fever • Acetaminophen may be given for a few days if the fever is above 102°F (39°C). (For dosage, see FEVER, page 407.)

Contagiousness • Hand, foot, and mouth disease is quite contagious and usually some of your child's playmates will develop it at about the same time. The incubation period after contact is 3 to 6 days. Because the spread of infection is extremely difficult to prevent and the condition is harmless, these children do not need to be isolated. They can return to school when the fever returns to normal range.

Call Your Child's Physician Later If

• Signs of dehydration develop.

• The fever lasts more than 3 days.

• You feel your child is getting worse.

IMPETIGO (INFECTED SORES)

SYMPTOMS AND CHARACTERISTICS

• Sores smaller than 1 inch in diameter

• Begin as small red bumps which rapidly change to cloudy blisters, then pimples, and finally sores

- Sores increase in size (any wound that doesn't heal)
- Sores often covered by a soft, yellow-brown (honey-colored) scab
- Scabs may be draining pus
- Sores increase in number
- Often starts near the nose or mouth

  If your child's symptoms are different, call your physician for help.

Cause • Impetigo is a superficial infection of the skin, caused by streptococcus (60 percent) or staphylococcus bacteria (40 percent). It is more common in the summertime when the skin, which normally is a barrier to infection, is often broken by cuts, scrapes, and insect bites.

Expected Course • With proper treatment the skin will be completely healed in 1 week. Some blemishes will remain for 6 to 12 months, but scars are unusual unless your child picks his sores.

CALL YOUR CHILD'S PHYSICIAN

Immediately If

- A red streak runs from the impetigo.
- The face is bright red *and* tender to the touch.
- Any big blisters (larger than 1 inch across) are present.
- The urine is red or cola-colored.

Within 24 Hours

All children with impetigo need medical consultation. Impetigo is an active bacterial infection, and the physician will decide if your child needs an antibiotic.

HOME CARE

Antibiotic (Oral or Injectable) • If your physician prescribes an antibiotic, be certain to take it as directed until the drug is completely gone. The following measures will also help clear up the infection.

Removing the Scabs • The bacteria live underneath the soft scabs, and until the scabs are removed, the antibiotic ointment cannot get through to the bacteria to kill them. Scabs can be soaked off initially using a warm 1:120 bleach solution (1 tablespoon of bleach to 2 quarts of water), with a little liquid soap added to help with penetration. The area may need to be gently rubbed, but it should not be scrubbed. A little bleeding is common if you remove all the crust.

Antibiotic Ointment • After the crust has been removed, antibiotic ointment should be applied to the raw surface 3 times a day. Buy Betadine or Bacitracin ointment at your drugstore (no prescription needed). Apply for 7 days, or longer if necessary. The area should be washed off with an antibacterial soap (Dial or Safeguard) each time. Any *new* thin crust that forms should not be removed, since that would delay healing. If your child has received oral or injectable antibiotics, the antibiotic ointment is needed for only 48 hours.

Preventing the Spread of Impetigo to Other Areas on Your Child's Body • Every time your child touches the impetigo and then scratches another part of the skin with that finger, a new site of impetigo can form. To prevent this, discourage your child from touching or picking at the sores. Keep the fingernails cut short, and wash the hands often with one of the antibacterial soaps.

Contagiousness • Impetigo is quite contagious. Be certain that other people in the family do not use your child's towel or washcloth. Any clothes, towels, or sheets that are contaminated with drainage from the impetigo should be washed with Lysol or bleach. Your child should be kept out of school until he or she has been on treatment for 24 hours with oral (or injectable) antibiotics, or 48 hours with antibiotic ointment alone.

Call Your Child's Physician Later If

• Other people in the family develop impetigo.

• The impetigo increases in size and number of sores after 48 hours on treatment.

• A fever or a sore throat occurs.

• Cola-colored urine or swollen eyelids occur.

JOCK ITCH

Jock itch is also called ringworm of the crotch, or *Tinea cruris.*

SYMPTOMS AND CHARACTERISTICS

- Pink, scaly, itchy rash
- Inner thighs and groin are involved
  (The penis is not involved and the scrotum is occasionally involved.)
- Occurs almost exclusively in males

If your child's symptoms are different, call your physician for help.

HOME CARE

Antifungal Medicine • Buy Tinactin or Micatin powder or spray at your drugstore. You won't need a prescription. It needs to be applied twice a day to the rash and at least 1 inch beyond the borders. Make sure you get it in all the skin creases. Continue it for several weeks, or for at least 7 days after the rash seems to have cleared.

Dryness • Jock itch will improve dramatically if the groin area is kept dry. Loose-fitting cotton shorts should be worn (avoid nylon or synthetic-fiber underwear because these fabrics don't absorb moisture). Shorts and athletic supporters should be washed frequently. After showers and baths, all creases should be carefully dried. The rash areas should be carefully cleansed once a day with plain water. Avoid using soap on the rash.

Scratching • Scratching will delay the cure, so have your child avoid scratching the area. Also keep the fingernails cut short.

Contagiousness • The condition is not very contagious. The fungus won't grow on dry, normal skin. Your child may continue to take gym and play sports.

Call Your Child's Physician During Office Hours If

- Any pimples, pus, or yellow crusts develop.
- There is no improvement in 1 week.
- The rash is not completely cured in 1 month.

LICE (PEDICULOSIS)

SYMPTOMS AND CHARACTERISTICS

- Nits (white eggs) firmly attached to hair shafts near the skin

- Unlike dandruff or sand, nits can't be shaken off

- Gray bugs (lice) are $\frac{1}{16}$-inch long, move quickly, and are difficult to see

- Itching and rash of the scalp

- The back of the neck is the favorite area

- The nits are easier to see than the lice because they are white and very numerous

  If your child's symptoms are different, call your physician for help.

Cause • Head lice live only on human beings and can spread quickly despite good health habits and regular hairwashing. They are spread by close contact or using the hat, comb, brush, or headphones of an infected person. The nits (eggs) normally hatch in about 1 week. Pubic lice ("crabs") are slightly different but are treated the same way. They can be transmitted from bedding or clothing and do not signify sexual contact. Pets can get a different type of lice, but they will not spread to humans.

Expected Course • With treatment, all lice and nits will be killed. A recurrence usually means another contact with an infected person. There are no lasting problems from having lice and they do not carry other diseases.

HOME CARE

Antilice Shampoos • Buy Nix 1 percent antilice shampoo (no prescription needed). Pour about 2 ounces of the shampoo into dry hair. Add a little warm water to work up a lather. Scrub the hair and scalp for 15 to 20 minutes, by the clock. Rinse the hair thoroughly and dry it with a towel. This shampoo kills both the lice and the nits and requires only 1 application. If any of the older pyrethrin antilice shampoos (A-200, R

& C, or Rid) are used, reapplication is necessary in 7 days to prevent reinfection.

Removing Nits • Remove the dead nits by backcombing with a fine-tooth comb or pull them out individually. The nits can be loosened using a mixture of half vinegar and half rubbing alcohol. Even though the nits are dead, most schools will not allow children to return if nits are present. Fortunately, the hair does not need to be shaved to cure lice.

Lice in the Eyelashes • If you see any lice or nits in the eyelashes, apply plain petrolatum to the eyelashes twice a day for 8 days. The lice won't survive.

Cleaning the House • Lice can't live for over 72 hours off the human body. Your child's room should be vacuumed. Combs and brushes should be soaked for 1 hour in a solution containing some anti-lice shampoo. Wash your child's sheets, blankets, pillow cases, and any clothes worn in the past 72 hours in hot water (140°F kills lice and nits). Items which can't be washed (e.g., hats, coats, or scarves) should be set aside in airtight plastic bags for 3 weeks (the longest period that nits can survive). Anti-lice sprays or fumigation of the house are unnecessary.

Contagiousness of Lice • Check the heads of everyone else living in your home. If any have scalp rashes, sores, or itching, they should be treated with the anti-lice shampoo even if lice and nits are not seen. Your child can return to school after 1 treatment with the shampoo. Reemphasize not sharing combs and hats. Also notify the school nurse so she can check other students in your child's class.

Call Your Child's Physician Later If

- Itching interferes with sleep.
- The rash is not cleared by 1 week after treatment.
- The rash clears and then returns.
- New eggs appear in the hair.
- The sores start to spread or look infected.

POISON IVY

SYMPTOMS AND CHARACTERISTICS

- Redness, swelling, and weeping blisters
- Eruption on exposed body surfaces (such as the hands)
- Shaped like streaks or patches
- Extreme itchiness
- Onset 1 or 2 days after the patient was in a forest or field

  If your child's symptoms are different, call your physician for help.

Cause • Poison ivy, poison oak, and poison sumac cause the same type of rash and are found throughout the United States (except Nevada, Alaska, and Hawaii). Over 50 percent of people are sensitive to the oil of these plants. When the plants are burned, the toxic substance becomes airborne in the smoke and soot. Some children develop a similar blistering reaction after skin contact with lime juice or celery, followed by sun exposure (called phytophotodermatitis).

Expected Course • Usually lasts 2 weeks. Treatment reduces the symptoms but doesn't cure. The best approach is prevention. Swelling or rash near the eye will not harm the eye in any way.

CALL YOUR CHILD'S PHYSICIAN

Immediately If

- The face is red or coughing begins following exposure to smoke.
- The rash involves more than one fourth of the body.
- Your child had a severe poison ivy reaction in the past.

During Office Hours If

- The face, eyes, lips, or genitals are involved.
- The itching interferes with sleep.
- Any big blisters are present.

- The rash is open and oozing.

- Signs of infection occur, such as pus or soft yellow scabs.

- You have other questions or concerns.

HOME CARE

Cool Soaks • Soak the involved area in cool water or massage it with an ice cube for 20 minutes as many times a day as necessary. Then let it air-dry. This will reduce itching and oozing.

Hydrocortisone Cream • Buy some ½ percent hydrocortisone cream (no prescription needed). If you already have a stronger steroid (the gels are the most effective), use it. Apply the cream 4 times a day or as often as the rash begins to itch. The sores should be dried up and no longer itchy in 10 to 14 days. In the meantime, cut your child's fingernails short and discourage scratching. Keep your child busy with other activities.

Contagiousness • Anything that has poison ivy oil or sap on it is contagious for several weeks. This includes the shoes and clothes you last wore into the woods, as well as any pets that may have oil on their fur. Routine laundering will remove oil from clothing and a bath with soap will cleanup "Old Yeller." The rash begins 1 to 2 days after skin contact. The fluid from the blisters, however, is not contagious. Therefore, scratching the poison ivy sores will not cause it to spread.

Call Your Child's Physician Later If

- The itching becomes severe.

- Your child can't sleep.

- The poison ivy becomes infected as suggested by pus, soft yellow scabs, or increasing tenderness.

PREVENTION

- Learn to recognize poison ivy plants. They tend to grow near river banks. At least, avoid all plants with 3 large shiny leaves. Another clue is the presence of shiny black spots on damaged leaves. On the West Coast you will need to identify poison oak.

- If your young child gets poison ivy twice, some plants are probably growing near your home. Locate and remove them.

- Wear long pants or socks when walking through woods that may contain poison ivy.

- If you think your child has had contact with poison ivy, wash the exposed areas of skin with any available soap several times. Do this as soon as possible, because after one hour, it is of little value in preventing absorption of the oil.

- Currently, allergy shots or pills are not of value for poison ivy.

RINGWORM (TINEA CORPORIS)

SYMPTOMS AND CHARACTERISTICS

- Ring-shaped pink patch
- Scaly raised border (always has scales)
- Clear center
- Usually ½ to 1 inch in size
- Ring slowly increases in size
- Mildly itchy

If your child's symptoms are different, call your physician for help.

Cause • A fungus infection of the skin, often transferred from puppies or kittens who have it. It is not caused by a worm.

Expected Course • Ringworm responds well to appropriate treatment. Without treatment, natural immunity will develop in about 4 months.

CALL YOUR CHILD'S PHYSICIAN DURING OFFICE HOURS IF

- The scalp is involved. (Reason: pills are needed for treatment.)
- More than 3 spots are present.
- You have other questions or concerns.

HOME CARE

Antifungal Cream • Buy Micatin or Tinactin cream at your drugstore (no prescription needed). Apply the cream twice a day to the rash and 1 inch beyond its borders. Continue this treatment for 1 week after the ringworm patch is smooth and seems to be gone. Encourage your child to avoid scratching the area, because scratching will delay a cure.

Contagiousness • Ringworm of the skin is not contagious to humans. Your child doesn't have to miss any school (or daycare) and can play with other children.

Treatment of Pets • Kittens and puppies with ringworm usually have no symptoms. If ringworm patches are seen, apply Micatin or Tinactin cream as described for humans. If no patches are present, treat the animal only if ringworm recurs in your child. Use Micatin or Tinactin powder and apply it to the entire fur twice a week for 3 weeks. Also have your child avoid close contact with the animal. Natural immunity also develops in animals after 4 months. Call your veterinarian for other questions.

Call Your Child's Physician Later If

• The ringworm continues to spread after 1 week on treatment.

• The rash is not cleared in 4 weeks.

RELATED TOPICS

IMPETIGO (see page 456)
POISON IVY (see page 462)
DRY SKIN (see page 428)

SHINGLES (ZOSTER)

SYMPTOMS AND CHARACTERISTICS

• A linear rash that follows the path of a nerve

• The rash occurs on only 1 side of the body

• The rash starts with clusters of red bumps, changes to water blisters, and finally becomes dry crusts

• The back, chest, or abdomen are the most common sites

• The rash usually doesn't burn or itch in children (in contrast to the adult form)

- Your child does not have a fever or feel sick

- Your child had chicken pox in the past

  If your child's symptoms are different, call your physician for help.

Cause • Zoster is caused by the chicken pox virus. The disease is not caught from other people with active shingles or chicken pox. The chicken pox virus lies dormant in the body of some people and is reactivated for unknown reasons as zoster. Children with zoster are usually over 3 years old.

Expected Course • New shingles continue to appear for several days. All the rash dries up by 7 to 10 days. Complications do not occur unless the eye is involved. Most people have shingles just once; a second attack occurs in 5 percent of children.

CALL YOUR CHILD'S PHYSICIAN DURING OFFICE HOURS IF

- The rash is very painful or very itchy.

- The rash is near the eye.

- You have other questions or concerns.

HOME CARE

Relief of Symptoms • Most children have no symptoms. For pain, give acetaminophen as necessary. (For dosage, see FEVER, page 407.) Avoid aspirin for zoster because of the possible link with Reyes syndrome. Discourage itching or picking the rash. The rash does not need any cream.

Contagiousness • Children with zoster can transmit chicken pox (but not zoster) to others. Although they are far less contagious than children with chicken pox, children with zoster should stay home from school for 7 days unless they can keep the rash covered until it crusts over. Children or adults who have not had chicken pox should avoid visiting the child with zoster (unless the rash is covered).

Call Your Physician Later If

- The rash lasts more than 14 days.

- The rash becomes infected with pus or soft yellow scabs.

- You feel your child is getting worse.

SORES

Sores are coin-sized ulcerated, weeping, or scabbed areas on the skin. Many begin as blisters which quickly break open. The possible causes are many. If one of the following is suspected, save time by turning directly to that guideline:

BURNS, THERMAL (see page 37)
CHICKEN POX (see page 424)
COLD SORES (see page 553)
IMPETIGO (see page 456)
BITES, INSECT (see page 18)
POISON IVY (see page 462)
RINGWORM (see page 464)

If the cause of the sores is unknown, call your child's physician during office hours for an appointment.

TINEA VERSICOLOR

SYMPTOMS AND CHARACTERISTICS

- The name means "multicolored ringworm"

- The condition occurs in adolescents and adults

- Numerous spots and patches on the neck, upper back, and shoulders

- The spots are covered by a fine scale

- The spots vary in size

- In summer, the spots are light and don't tan

- In winter, the spots are darker (often pink or brown) compared to normal Caucasian skin

    If your child's symptoms are different, call your physician for help.

Cause • This superficial infection is caused by a yeastlike fungus called *Malassezia furfur*. It occurs more commonly in warm, humid climates.

Expected Course • The problem tends to wax and wane for many years. Since complications do not occur, tinea versicolor is solely a cosmetic problem. Itching is uncommon.

HOME CARE

Selsun Blue Shampoo • Selsun Blue (selenium sulfide) is a nonprescription medicated shampoo that can cure this condition. Apply this shampoo once a day for 14 days. Apply it to the affected skin areas as well as 2 or 3 inches onto the adjacent normal skin. Rub it in and let it dry. Be careful to keep it off the eyes or genitals, since it is irritating to these tissues. After 20 minutes, take a shower. By 2 weeks, the scaling should be stopped, and the rash is temporarily cured. The normal skin color will not return for 6 to 12 months.

Prevention of Recurrences • Tinea versicolor tends to recur. Prevent this by applying Selsun Blue shampoo to the formerly involved areas once a month for several years. Leave it on for 1 to 2 hours. This precaution is especially important in the summer months, because this fungus thrives in warm weather.

Contagiousness • Tinea versicolor is not contagious. This fungus is a normal inhabitant of the hair follicles in many people. Only a few develop the overgrowth of the fungus and a rash.

Call Your Child's Physician Later If

• The rash is not improved with this treatment by 2 weeks.

• You feel your child is getting worse.

RELATED TOPIC

RINGWORM (see page 464)

SKIN: CONDITIONS WITHOUT A RASH

BLISTERS, FOOT OR HAND

SYMPTOMS AND CHARACTERISTICS

- Water blister on the sole or palm
- The toes or heel are most commonly involved
- Caused by friction
- Foot blisters are due to sports, hiking, or new shoes
- Hand blisters are due to prolonged use of a tool (such as a shovel) or playground equipment

HOME CARE

Treatment • Do not open the blisters, since this increases the possibility of infection. The blisters will dry up and peel off in 1 to 2 weeks. In the meantime, take the pressure off the area by placing a foam "donut" or a Band-Aid with a hole cut in the center over the blister. Also, temporarily wear a more comfortable shoe. If the blister accidentally breaks open, trim off the loose skin. Keep the surface clean by washing it twice a day with an antibacterial soap (such as Dial or Safeguard) and changing to clean socks (for foot blisters). The open blister can be covered with an antibiotic ointment (like Bacitracin), surrounded by a "donut" of foam rubber, and then the whole area patched over with tape.

Cleanse the area with warm water and reapply the ointment each day.

Call Your Child's Physician Later If

• The blister becomes infected.

PREVENTION OF FOOT BLISTERS

Avoid shoes that are too tight or too loose. If your child frequently gets blisters on certain pressure areas, cover that spot with petroleum jelly or tape before athletic activities to decrease the friction on the spot. Friction can also be reduced by wearing 2 pairs of socks if the shoes are not too tight. If blisters occur under a callus, file the callus down and lubricate it so it won't contribute to the friction.

SIMILAR CONDITIONS THAT ALSO HAVE BLISTERS

BURNS, THERMAL (see page 37)
IMPETIGO (see page 456)
POISON IVY (see page 462)

BLUISH LIPS (CYANOSIS)

If your child's lips, mouth, ears, or nail beds have become bluish or dusky, call your child's physician *immediately*. Bluish skin (cyanosis) can indicate reduced oxygen in the blood, and serious disease. If your child is bluish and very cold, check first if the normal color returns with warming. Also, normal newborns can have bluish hands and feet (acrocyanosis) from sluggish circulation until 3 or 4 days of age.

RELATED TOPIC

BREATH-HOLDING SPELLS (see page 331)

CALLUSES, CORNS, AND BUNIONS

Calluses and corns are areas of thickened, hard skin. Calluses are located on the palms or soles and are painless. They occur over areas of prolonged friction or pressure, as with walking barefoot or using a hand tool. Corns can be located anywhere on the foot except the sole, are caused by pressure from tight shoes, and are painful. Bunions occur on the side of the foot over the protruding bone at the base of the first or fifth toe. Occasionally a bunion will occur where the back of a shoe rubs against the back of the heel. A bunion is painful and often causes a swollen area due to damage to both the skin and underlying bone. Bunions can also result from tight shoes, especially narrow or pointed ones.

CALL YOUR CHILD'S PHYSICIAN DURING OFFICE HOURS IF

- A callus is quite painful.

- A callus has black dots in it.

- A bunion is extremely painful or swollen.

- An unexplained fever (over 100°F) is present.

- You have other questions or concerns.

HOME CARE

Calluses • No treatment is necessary. The callus is protective. If it cracks, see CRACKED SKIN, page 472. If a blister develops, see BLISTERS, FOOT OR HAND, page 469.

Corns • Change to properly fitting shoes. Temporarily protect the corn with donut-shaped foam pads or a Band-Aid with a hole cut from the center. The pain should resolve in 1 week.

Bunions • The key to recovery is changing to properly fitting (i.e., wider or longer) shoes. Your youngster may need to wear soft slippers for a week. While most tight shoes must be discarded, a prized shoe (if it is long enough) may be salvaged by having the constricting area stretched out by a shoemaker with a shoe punch. (Note: The leather-stretching chemicals give disappointing results.) Soak the feet in warm water for 15 minutes twice a day. Take aspirin or acetaminophen for pain. (For dosage, see FEVER, page 407.) Protect the area with donut-shaped bunion pads. The pain and swelling will take 2 to 3 months to resolve. Call your child's physician if it gets worse instead of better.

CRACKED SKIN

Cracked skin most commonly occurs on the soles of the feet, especially the heels and big toes (called juvenile plantar dermatosis). Deep cracks are painful and periodically bleed. The main cause is wearing wet shoes and socks, or swimming a lot. Cracks can also develop on the hands in children who frequently wash dishes or suck their thumbs. The lips can become cracked (chapped) in children with a habit of licking their lips or from excessive exposure to sun or wind.

HOME CARE

Even deep cracks of many years duration can be healed in about 2 weeks if they are constantly covered with an ointment (like petroleum jelly). If the crack seems mildly infected, use Bacitracin ointment (no prescription needed). Covering the ointment with a Band-Aid, socks, or gloves speeds recovery even more. For chapped lips, a lip balm can be applied frequently. Call your child's physician during office hours if any of the cracks develop pimples or yellow drainage.

DANDRUFF

Dandruff is normal shedding of the scalp. Skin is constantly regenerating. On most of the body surface, the flakes of dead skin fall to the ground without fanfare, but they can accumulate in the hair. Some children shed skin faster than others, making the dandruff more noticeable. Keep in mind that the shedding of skin cells is a normal process that occurs throughout life on the entire body surface. It is not contagious.

HOME CARE FOR DANDRUFF

Daily Shampooing • The key to fighting dandruff is removing the flakes as fast as they form by washing the hair daily. A regular shampoo usually works very well. Brush the hair before each washing. Eventually, you may be able to wash the hair every other day without seeing dandruff, but you probably won't ever be able to wash it less often than that.

Anti-Dandruff Shampoos • If the scalp is red and irritated or the scales are quite greasy, use a medicated shampoo (one that contains selenium sulfide) for 3 days in a row and then once a week. Your pharmacist can help you select one that does not require a prescription (e.g., Selsun Blue). These shampoos not only remove the dandruff but also cut down on the rate of shedding. They are used in a special way: Lather the hair, wait 3 minutes, then rinse thoroughly. Continue to use a regular shampoo on other days.

Avoid Hair Tonics • Hair tonics and creams just cover up the problem, and the dandruff eventually comes off in bigger flakes.

Call Your Child's Physician Later If

• The dandruff is not improved after 2 weeks of treatment.

FINGERNAIL INFECTION (PARONYCHIA)

SYMPTOMS AND CHARACTERISTICS

• A large pimple at the junction of the cuticle and the fingernail

• Redness and tenderness of this area

• Occasionally, pus draining from this area

If your child's symptoms are different, call your physician for help.

Cause • Paronychia are usually infected with the staphylococcus bacteria, but are occasionally due to strep bacteria. The primary event, however, is usually a break in the skin secondary to pulling or chewing on the cuticle. Thumbsucking may also contribute.

Expected Course • With proper treatment, this infection should clear up in 7 days. If not, your physician will probably prescribe an oral antibiotic.

CALL YOUR CHILD'S PHYSICIAN

Immediately If

- Fever or chills are present.

- A red streak spreads beyond the cuticle.

- The finger pad is swollen or tender.

Within 24 Hours If

- You want your physician to open the pus pockets.

- You can see pus under the base of the nail.

- The infection encircles the nail.

- This is a recurrent problem.

- You have other questions or concerns.

HOME CARE

Lancing • Open and drain any visible pus pockets with a sterile needle (sterilized with rubbing alcohol or a flame). Make a large opening where the pus pocket joins with the nail. Squeeze the pus out gently.

Antiseptic Soaks • Soak the infected finger 3 times a day for 10 minutes in a warm 120 bleach solution (1 tablespoon of bleach to 2 quarts of water) with a little liquid soap added. Do this for 4 days or longer if the wound has not healed.

Antibiotic Ointments • Apply an antibiotic ointment (Bacitracin or Betadine) 6 times a day.

Call Your Child's Physician Later If

- The infection is not improved by 48 hours on home treatment.

- The infection is not totally resolved by 7 days.

PREVENTION

Discourage any picking or chewing of hangnails (loose pieces of cuticle). Instead, cut these off with nail clippers.

RELATED TOPIC

TOENAIL, INGROWN (see page 489)

FOREIGN BODY IN SKIN (SLIVERS)

A sliver is a foreign object embedded in the skin. Most of these are wood slivers (splinters) that go in very superficially. Others are thorns or glass or metal fragments. Most slivers are painful to pressure unless they are very superficial. While organic slivers (e.g., wood) usually become infected if they are not removed, nonorganic slivers (e.g., metal) generally do not. Remember that pencil lead is actually graphite (harmless), not lead. Even colored leads are nontoxic. If appropriate, turn to the guideline on SKIN TRAUMA (SCRAPES), page 80.

CALL YOUR CHILD'S PHYSICIAN

Immediately If

- The sliver is deeply embedded (for instance, a needle or toothpick in the foot).

- It is a fish hook or anything with a barb.

- You think you won't be able to get it out.

During Office Hours If

- It was removed but went deeply (a puncture wound) *and* more than 5 years have passed since the last tetanus booster.

- You have other questions or concerns.

HOME CARE

Removing Slivers • Most slivers can be removed with a needle and tweezers. Check the tweezers beforehand to be certain the pickups meet exactly. (If they do not, bend them.) These items can be sterilized with rubbing alcohol or a flame. The skin surrounding the sliver should also be washed with soap before you try to remove the sliver. Use the needle to expose the end of the sliver fully. Then grasp the sliver firmly with the tweezers and pull it out at the same angle that it went in. Getting a good grip the first time is especially important with slivers that go in perpendicular to the skin or those trapped under a fingernail. Sometimes a wedge of the fingernail must be cut away with a fine scissors to expose the end of the sliver.

Superficial horizontal slivers (where you can see all of it) can be removed by opening the skin along the length of the sliver and flicking it out. If superficial slivers are numerous and pain-free, they can be left in. Eventually they will work their way out with normal shedding of the skin.

Cactus Spines • The following method can also be used for small Fiberglas spicules or plant stickers (e.g., stinging nettle). Usually these break when pressure is applied with a tweezers. Apply a layer of facial gel or wax depilatory (hair remover). Let it air-dry for 5 minutes, or accelerate the process with a hair dryer. Then peel it off with the spicules. White glue can also be tried, but it is less effective.

Call Your Child's Physician Later If

• You can't get it all out *and* the sliver is glass or metal.

• You can't get it all out *and* it's painful (i.e., not superficial).

• The site of penetration becomes infected. (See WOUND INFECTIONS, page 88.)

FRECKLES

Freckles are pigmented spots brought out by sunlight. Thus, they usually are confined to the face, neck, chest, and shoulders. They occur mainly in fair-skinned people and are due to an inherited tendency to have tanning pigment (melanin) scattered irregularly, rather than evenly, throughout the skin. They start around age 5, and although they fade somewhat each winter, they become prominent each summer.

HOME CARE
Sunscreens cannot prevent them, and lemon juice cannot bleach them. Therefore, the child who has freckles must learn to live with them. Family and friends can help by referring to the freckles as special and attractive. They never turn into skin cancer. People with freckles sunburn easily. They need to be extra careful about using a strong sunscreen and avoiding sun overexposure (see SUNBURN, page 484).

HAIR LOSS

Hair loss (alopecia) can occur in patches or throughout the scalp. The causes are many, including ringworm, which requires medical diagnosis and treatment.

CALL YOUR CHILD'S PHYSICIAN DURING OFFICE HOURS
All children who have hair loss should be seen by a physician with the following exceptions:

• The hair of many newborns falls out during the first few months of life. This baby hair is replaced by permanent hair.

• Babies from 3 to 6 months of age commonly rub off a patch of hair on the back of the head due to friction during head-turning against the mattresses of cribs, playpens, and infant seats. This grows back nicely once they start sitting up.

• Hair can be lost because of vigorous hairbrushing, hot combs, tight pony tails or braids, or exercising while wearing headphones.

• Stress-related hair loss. Hair follicles are very sensitive to stress. The hair begins to fall out about 3 months (100 days) after a severe stress (such as high fever, severe illnesses, psychological crisis, crash diets, surgery, or even childbirth). The hair falls out in a generalized distribution over the next 3 or 4 months. After the hair stops shedding, it takes another 6 to 8 months to return to normal. Complete hair regrowth is the rule. The whole cycle takes about 12 months. If this description fits your child, he has telogen effluvium.

JAUNDICE

A jaundiced child has yellowish skin and sclera (the white part of the eyes). The yellow color is due to the accumulation of bilirubin pigment in the blood and skin. The most common cause of jaundice is hepatitis (a liver infection). Usually these infections are not serious, but they need to be evaluated by a physician.

While jaundice occurs in over 30 percent of newborns and

is usually harmless, the follow-up of jaundiced newborns should be carried out under the direction of your baby's physician. Be certain to notify your physician if the jaundice worsens after discharge from the hospital. (See JAUNDICE OF THE NEW-BORN, page 131.)

CALL YOUR CHILD'S PHYSICIAN
Immediately If

• Your child has vomited any blood.

• Your child is confused or difficult to awaken.

• Your child acts or looks very sick.

During Office Hours

All other children with jaundice need medical consultation. Close contacts of children with hepatitis can usually be protected with a gamma globulin injection.

CAROTENEMIA: THE JAUNDICE IMITATOR

Your child has carotenemia if the following are present:

• Lemon-yellow coloration of the skin

• No yellow coloration of the sclera (white part of the eye)

• High intake of yellow and green vegetables

• Age under 2 years

Carotenemia is harmless and temporary. The yellow color is due to a pigment (carotene) found in yellow and green vegetables, as well as fruits such as oranges, apricots, and peaches. The intake of these vegetables and fruits needs to be reduced only if you want to change your child's skin tone. After a return to a more normal diet, the carotenemia color will disappear in 3 or 4 weeks. Even without dietary change, the skin color will gradually return to normal by 2 or 3 years of age.

LYMPH NODES (OR GLANDS), SWOLLEN

SYMPTOMS AND CHARACTERISTICS

- Normal nodes are smaller than ½ inch across (often the size of a pea or baked bean). The body contains more than 500 lymph nodes. They can always be felt in the neck and groin. Normal nodes are largest at age 10 to 12. At this age they can be twice the normal adult size.

- Active nodes with viral infections are usually ½ to 1 inch across. Slight enlargement and mild tenderness means the lymph node is fighting infection and succeeding.

- Active nodes with bacterial infections are usually larger than 1 inch across and exquisitely tender. If they are over 2 inches across or the overlying skin is pink, the nodes are not controlling the infection, and may contain pus.

Causes • Lymph glands stop the spread of infection and protect the bloodstream from invasion (blood poisoning). They enlarge with cuts, scrapes, scratches, splinters, burns, insect bites, rashes, impetigo, or any break in the skin. Cancer is an extremely rare cause in children. Try to locate and identify the cause of the swollen gland by remembering that the groin nodes drain lymph from the legs and lower abdomen, the armpit nodes drain the arms and upper chest, the back of the neck nodes drain the scalp, and the front of the neck nodes drain the lower face, nose, and throat. Most enlarged neck nodes are due to colds and throat infections. A disease like chicken pox can cause all the nodes to swell.

Expected Course • With the usual viral infections or skin injuries, nodes quickly swell up to a peak size in 2 or 3 days and then slowly return to normal size over 2 to 4 weeks. However, you can still see and feel nodes in most normal children, especially in the neck and groin. Don't look for lymph nodes, because you can always find some.

CALL YOUR CHILD'S PHYSICIAN

Immediately If

- The node is 2 or more inches in size.
- The node is quite tender to the touch.
- Red streaks go to the node or the overlying skin is red.
- The node is in the neck *and* there is any difficulty with breathing, swallowing, or opening the mouth.
- The node interferes with moving the neck.
- Your child acts or looks very sick.

Within 24 Hours If

- The node is 1 to 2 inches in size.
- The cause of the swollen node is unknown.
- Your baby is under 1 month old.
- The swollen node is in the neck, and your child also has a sore throat.
- An unexplained fever (over 100°F) is present.
- An explained fever lasts more than 3 days.
- You have other questions or concerns.

HOME CARE

Clarification • Minor skin infections and irritations can cause lymph nodes to double in size. It may take a month for them to slowly return to normal size. However, they won't completely disappear. The lymph nodes in the neck and groin are especially prominent. **Caution:** Poking and squeezing lymph nodes may keep them from shrinking back to normal size. Don't check them more than once a month, and be sure your child doesn't fidget with them.

Treatment • No treatment is necessary for the nodes, just for the underlying disease—for instance, remove the sliver or treat the skin rash.

Call Your Child's Physician Later If

- The node becomes quite tender.
- The node enlarges to greater than 1 inch in size.

• The node remains larger than ½ inch for more than 1 month.

• You feel your child is getting worse.

MOLES (NEVI)

Moles, or nevi, are tan, brown, or black spots on the skin. Most adults have 20 to 30 moles. They first appear around 1 year of age, and we are constantly getting new ones. They do not fade and they last throughout our lives. In general, they are harmless. Even the moles removed for the changes listed below are usually not cancerous.

CALL YOUR CHILD'S PHYSICIAN DURING OFFICE HOURS IF

• You want a mole removed for cosmetic purposes.

• The mole is pitch-black *and* your child was born with it.

• The mole is growing rapidly in size.

• The mole has bled or become an open sore.

• The mole has changed colors (especially to red or blue).

• The surface has become lumpy (a smooth surface is normal).

(Note: Moles are no longer routinely removed just because they are in areas of friction or pressure.)

PALE SKIN

The skin color is white or very pale. This concern is rarely voiced about non-Caucasian children.

Causes • Most of these children simply have a fair complexion. They have always been fair, have light hair, and usually have a parent with similar skin coloring. Another factor is lack of sun exposure; hence pallor (pale color) is noted more during winter months. Temporary paleness also occurs when someone is very cold; the normal color returns after warming up.

Pale skin (pallor) rarely is due to anemia (low red blood cell count). In anemia, the lips, gums, and nailbeds are also pale. In a child with fair complexion who is not anemic, these areas should be nice and pink.

CALL YOUR CHILD'S PHYSICIAN

Immediately If

• Your child has fainted.

• Your child becomes dizzy when standing up.

• Nosebleeds have been heavy.

• Menstrual periods have been heavy.

• Blood has been passed in stools or vomited material.

• The whites of the eyes are yellow.

• Your child acts or looks very sick.

During Office Hours If

• The paleness is of recent onset.

• The paleness is longstanding, but the cause is unclear.

• You have other questions or concerns.

PIMPLES

SYMPTOMS AND CHARACTERISTICS

Pimples (pustules or whiteheads) are small blisters filled with pus. They are caused by the staph bacteria (unlike acne). While they can occur on any part of the body, they commonly occur in areas of friction (as where a diaper rubs). Tight braids combined with pomades (perfumed ointments) are a common cause of pimples in the scalp. The tight braid injures the hair follicles and the pomade seals them off, thus predisposing them to infection. Pimples are a superficial skin infection and never leave scars.

Similar Conditions • If appropriate, turn directly to the following guidelines:

ACNE (see page 447)
BOILS (see page 452)
FINGERNAIL INFECTION (see page 473)
IMPETIGO (see page 456)

CALL YOUR CHILD'S PHYSICIAN

Immediately If

- Your child is under 4 weeks old (Exception: erythema toxicum, see under NEWBORN RASHES, page 109.)

- An unexplained fever (over 100°F) is present.

- Your child acts or looks very sick.

Within 24 Hours If

- Your child is under 1 year old.

- There are 6 or more pimples.

- The pimples are larger than ⅛ inch across.

- You have other questions or concerns.

HOME CARE

Treatment • The best inexpensive agent for killing the staphylococci that are causing the pimples is a 1:120 bleach solution, made by mixing 1 tablespoon of bleach in 2 quarts of water. Second-best is soap and water. Open any pimples that have come to a head, using a needle sterilized with rubbing alcohol or flame, and then throw the needle away. The pus should run out easily without any squeezing. Clean the pimples with the weak bleach solution before and after you do this. Do this at least twice a day; then rinse the skin with plain water. Then apply an antibiotic ointment such as Bacitracin or Betadine.

Common Mistakes • A common mistake is to cover pimples with a Band-Aid. This can cause them to spread. The application of petroleum jelly or any ointment not containing an antibiotic can also make them much worse.

Call Your Child's Physician Later If

- The pimples are not completely gone in 3 days.

- New pimples develop after 24 hours on treatment.

PREVENTION

To prevent spread, ask your child not to touch the pimples or rub the skin. Cut the fingernails short and wash the hands frequently. Give your child a shower once a day with an antibacterial soap (Dial or Safeguard). Be sure to use a separate washcloth and towel for this child. Wash your child's clothes and sheets with Lysol or bleach to remove the staph bacteria from them. For pimples of the scalp, pomades should be discontinued and braiding done loosely.

SUNBURN

Sunburn is due to overexposure of the skin to the ultraviolet rays of the sun or a sun lamp. Most people have been sunburned many times. Vacations can quickly turn into painful experiences when the power of the sun is overlooked. Unfortunately, the symptoms of sunburn do not begin until 2 to 4 hours after the sun's damage has been done. The peak reaction of redness, pain, and swelling is not seen for 24 hours.

Minor sunburn is a first-degree burn which turns the skin pink or red. Prolonged sun exposure can cause blistering and a second-degree burn. Sunburn never causes a third-degree burn or scarring because it is limited to the superficial layer of skin (epidermis).

Repeated sun exposure and suntans causes premature aging of the skin (wrinkling, sagging, and brown sunspots). Repeated sunburns increase the risk of skin cancer in the damaged areas. Each blistering sunburn doubles the risk of developing malignant melanoma, which is the most serious type of skin cancer.

CALL YOUR CHILD'S PHYSICIAN

Immediately If

- The sunburn is extremely painful *and* widespread.

- Your child is unable to look at lights because of eye pain.

- Your child has an unexplained fever over 102°F.

- Your child passes out or feels dizzy with standing.

- Your child acts or looks very sick.

Within 24 Hours If

- More than 2 blisters are present.

- Any of the blisters are broken.

- You have other questions or concerns.

HOME CARE

Pain Relief • The sensation of pain and heat will probably last for 48 hours.

- Aspirin or ibuprofen products begun within 6 hours of sun exposure and continued for 2 days can reduce the discomfort. (For dosage, see chart on page 66.)

- Nonprescription ½ percent hydrocortisone cream may cut down on swelling and pain, but only if used early. Apply 3 times a day. If you don't have any, apply a moisturizing cream.

- The symptoms can also be helped by cool baths or compresses several times a day. Add 2 or 3 tablespoons of baking soda to the tub.

- Showers are usually painful because of the force of the spray.

- Don't use any soap on the burned skin.

- Offer extra water on the first day to replace the fluids lost into the sunburn and to prevent dehydration and dizziness.

- Peeling will usually occur on the fifth to seventh day. Peeling and itching can be reduced by applying the ½ percent hydrocortisone cream or a moisturizing cream (see ECZEMA, page 429) to the involved skin once or twice a day. (Avoid petrolatum or other ointments because they keep heat and sweat from escaping.)

Common Mistakes in Sunburn Treatment

- Avoid applying ointments or butter to sunburn; they just make the symptoms worse and are painful to remove.

- Don't buy any of the common first-aid creams or sprays for burns. They often contain benzocaine, which can cause an allergic rash, and they don't relieve the pain of first-degree burns.

- Don't confuse sunscreens, which block the sun's burning rays, with suntan lotions or oils, which mainly lubricate the skin. Despite advertisements to the contrary, suntan oils cannot help your child tan faster or more deeply. Also, they offer no protection against sunburn.

Call Your Child's Physician Later If

- Blisters start to break open.
- The sunburn looks infected.
- You feel your child is getting worse.

PREVENTION OF SUNBURNS

The best way to prevent skin cancer is to prevent sunburn. Although skin cancer occurs in adults, it is caused by the sun exposure and sunburns that occurred during childhood. Every time you apply sunscreen to your child, you are preventing skin cancer down the line.

- Apply sunscreen anytime your child is going to be outside for more than 30 minutes.
- Try to keep sun exposure to small amounts early in the season until a tan builds up. (**Caution:** While people with a suntan can tolerate a little more sun, they can still get a serious sunburn.) Start with 15 or 20 minutes per day and increase by 5 minutes per day. Decrease daily exposure time if the skin becomes reddened. Because of the 2- to 4-hour delay before sunburn starts, don't expect symptoms to tell you when it's time to get out of the sun.
- About 15 percent of white people have skin that never tans but only burns. These fair-skinned children need to be extremely careful about the sun throughout their lives. The big risk factors for sunburn are red hair, blond hair, blue or green eyes, or freckles. These children are also at increased risk for skin cancer. They need to be instructed repeatedly to use a sunscreen throughout the summer and to avoid the sun whenever possible.
- The skin of infants is thinner and more sensitive to the sun. Sunscreens, longer clothing, and a hat with a brim are essen-

tial for these children. Don't apply sunscreen to areas where the infant may lick it off.

- Avoid the hours of 10:00 A.M. to 3:00 P.M., when the sun's rays are most intense.

- Don't let overcast days give you a false sense of security. Over 70 percent of the sun's rays still get through the clouds. Over 30 percent of the sun's rays can also penetrate loosely woven fabrics (for instance, a T-shirt).

- Sun exposure increases by 4 percent for each 1,000 feet of elevation. A sunburn can occur quickly when hiking above the timberline.

- Water, sand, or snow increases the sun's exposure. The shade from a hat or umbrella won't protect you from reflected rays.

- Also protect your child's eyes. Years of exposure to ultraviolet light increases the risk of cataracts. Buy sunglasses with UV protection.

- Set a good example. Did you apply your sunscreen?

Sunscreens • There are good sunscreens on the market that prevent sunburn but still permit gradual tanning to occur. The sun protection factor (SPF) or filtering power of the product determines what percent of the ultraviolet rays get through to the skin. The SPF of various products ranges from 2 to 45.

An SPF of 15 allows only $\frac{1}{15}$ (7 percent) of the sun's rays to get through and thereby extends safe sun exposure from 20 minutes to 5 hours without sunburning. For practical purposes, an SPF higher than 15 is rarely needed because sun exposure beyond 5 hours is unusual. Fair-skinned whites (with red or blond hair) need a sunscreen with an SPF of 15, or higher, darker whites need an 8 to 10, and Mediterranean whites need a 6 to 8.

Apply the sunscreen 30 minutes before exposure to the sun to give it time to penetrate the skin. Give special attention to the areas most likely to become sunburned, such as your child's nose, ears, cheeks, and shoulders. Most products need to be reapplied every 3 to 4 hours, as well as immediately after swimming or profuse sweating. A "waterproof" sunscreen stays on for about 30 minutes in water. Most people apply too little (the average adult requires 1 ounce of sunscreen per application). To prevent sunburned lips, apply a lip coating that also contains PABA. This is especially important in children who develop fever blisters after sun exposure. If your child's nose or some other area has been repeatedly burned during the summer, protect it completely from all the sun's rays with zinc oxide ointment.

SWEATING, EXCESSIVE

SYMPTOMS AND CHARACTERISTICS
The parent may be concerned because a child has a wet pillow after naps. Sometimes the entire bed is wet, since sweat glands are found throughout the body's surface. Neither of these examples is necessarily abnormal.

Your adolescent may be unduly worried about underarm perspiration. Teenagers may be reassured that sweating normally increases with exercise and tension, and this is never abnormal.

Similar Conditions • Sweating occurs with fever (so take your child's temperature). If fever is present, save time by turning directly to that guideline. (See FEVER, page 407.)

Causes • The purpose of sweating is to cool off the body by evaporation. The most common cause of sweating is overheating due to hot weather, a hot room, overdressing, or too many blankets. When a child is covered up in bed, the *only* way to release heat is through the head. Night sweats in a child who is otherwise well mean nothing. Some parents worry unduly about diseases from another era (such as tuberculosis or malaria).

CALL YOUR CHILD'S PHYSICIAN DURING OFFICE HOURS IF

• Your child is under 2 months old.

• Your child has unexplained fevers (over 100°F).

• Your child has unexplained weight loss.

• You have other questions or concerns.

HOME CARE
Turn down the heat in your home. Dress your child in lighter clothing for naps. Offer your child extra fluids in hot weather

to prevent dehydration. Adolescents, of course, need to be introduced to underarm antiperspirants/deodorants to prevent body odor. Some also need to bathe with an antibacterial soap. For foot odors from excessive perspiration, consider special shoe liners that absorb odors.

TOENAIL, INGROWN

SYMPTOMS AND CHARACTERISTICS

• Tenderness, redness, and swelling of the skin surrounding the corner of the toenail on one of the big toes

Causes • Ingrown toenails are usually due to tight shoes (such as cowboy boots) and/or improper cutting of the toenails. Children with wide feet are predisposed, since many shoes come in only one width. Ingrown toenails take several weeks to clear up.

CALL YOUR CHILD'S PHYSICIAN

Immediately If

• Fever or chills are present.

• A red streak spreads beyond the toe.

During Office Hours If

• Any pus or yellow drainage is present.

• The corner of the nail is impossible to locate.

• The problem is a recurrent one.

• You have other questions.

HOME CARE

Soaking • Soak the foot twice a day in a 1:120 bleach solution (1 tablespoon of bleach to 2 quarts of water) for 20 minutes. This solution kills most germs. Add a little liquid soap to help penetration. While soaking, massage outward the part of the cuticle (skin next to the nail) that is swollen. A "cuticle pusher" (available in most drugstores) may be helpful.

Cut Off the Corner of the Toenail • The pain is always caused by the corner of the toenail rubbing against the raw cuticle. Only this once, cut the corner off so the irritated tissue can quiet down and heal. If the corner is buried in the swollen cuticle, have your physician remove it. The main purpose of treatment is to help the nail grow *over* the nail cuticle rather than get stuck in it. Therefore, during soaks, try to bend the nail corners upward. You can try to wedge some cotton under the edge of the nail, but for practical purposes, this is impossible during the infected phase. Filing or cutting a wedge out of the center of the upper edge of the nail may help the corners bend upward.

Antibiotic Ointment • If your child's cuticle is just red and irritated, an antibiotic ointment is probably not needed. But if the cuticle is swollen or oozing, apply Neosporin ointment (no prescription needed) 5 or 6 times a day.

Shoes • Have your child wear sandals or go barefoot as much as possible to prevent pressure on the toenail. When your child must wear closed shoes, protect the ingrown toenail as follows: If the inner edge is involved, tape cotton between the first and second toes to keep them from touching. If the outer edge is involved, tape cotton to the outside of the ball of the toe to keep the toenail from touching the side of the shoe.

Call Your Child's Physician Later If

• The ingrown toenail becomes infected.

• The problem is not much better in 1 week.

• The problem is not totally resolved in 2 weeks.

PREVENTION

Prevent recurrences by making sure that your child's shoes are not too narrow. Give away those pointed or tight shoes. After the cuticle is healed, cut the toenails straight across, leaving the corners. Don't cut them too short. After baths, while the nails are pliable, bend the corners of the nails upward.

WARTS

SYMPTOMS AND CHARACTERISTICS

- Raised, round, rough-surfaced growth on the skin
- Skin-colored or pink
- Most commonly occur on the hands
- Not painful unless located on the sole of the foot (plantar wart)
- Unlike a callus, the wart has brown dots within it and clearly has a boundary with the normal skin

If your child's symptoms are different, call your physician for help.

Cause • Warts are caused by viruses (not by playing with toads).

Expected Course • Most warts disappear without treatment in 2 or 3 years. With treatment, they resolve in 2 to 3 months. There are no shortcuts in treating warts. Itching and redness mean the wart is responding to treatment. If the treatment of warts becomes painful or expensive, it may be better to step back and wait for them to go away naturally.

CALL YOUR CHILD'S PHYSICIAN DURING OFFICE HOURS IF

- Some warts are on the bottom of the feet.
- Some are on the face.
- Some are on the genital area.
- A wart is open and infected-looking.
- You have other questions or concerns.

HOME CARE

Adhesive Tape • Apply adhesive tape to cover the wart completely. Leave it on for 6½ days; then remove it for 12 hours. Repeat the procedure weekly. The total treatment usually takes 6 weeks. Don't apply the tape so tightly that it interferes with circulation. This method is surprisingly effective at turning on the body's immune system to the wart virus. Try it.

Wart-Removing Acids • If no progress is being made in 4 weeks with adhesive tape, switch to a nonprescription acid. Ask your pharmacist to recommend one. Apply it once a day to the top of the wart after soaking the wart in water for 5 minutes. Since you are using an acid, avoid getting any near the eyes or mouth. Keep the lid closed tightly so it won't evaporate. The acid will turn the wart into dead skin. The acid will work faster if it is covered with adhesive tape.

Once or twice a week, remove the dead wart material by paring it down with a razor blade. The dead wart will be softer and easier to slice if you soak the area first in warm water for 10 minutes. If the cutting causes any pain or minor bleeding, you have cut into living wart tissue. If your child won't let you cut off the dead wart material or you are afraid you might hurt the child, file it down with an emery board or have your child's physician pare down the wart.

Contagiousness • Encourage your child not to pick at the warts, because this may cause them to spread. If your child chews or sucks the wart, cover the area with a Band-Aid. Encourage your child to give up the habit of chewing on the wart, because doing so can lead to warts on the lips or face. Warts are not very contagious to other people. The incubation period is 1 to 4 months.

Call Your Child's Physician Later If

• A wart becomes open *and* looks infected.

• New warts develop after 2 weeks of treatment.

• The warts are still present after 8 weeks of treatment.

BRAIN

ALTITUDE SICKNESS

SYMPTOMS AND CHARACTERISTICS

- Headache, fatigue, dizziness, nausea
- Shortness of breath and rapid heartbeat on exertion
- Insomnia or restless sleep
- Onset at 8,000 feet elevation or higher
- Onset within 6 to 8 hours of arrival at higher altitude

  If your child's symptoms are different, call your physician for help.

Cause • Altitude sickness is caused by the lower level of oxygen in the air at higher altitudes. Many people travel to mountainous areas to hike or ski. Symptoms occur in 50 percent of nonacclimated people who go abruptly from sea level to 10,000 feet. The likelihood of symptoms increases with the altitude.

Expected Course • Most people with acute mountain sickness (the most common type of altitude sickness) feel normal in 2 or 3 days. With overexertion and ascent above 10,000 feet, 4 percent of people can develop life-threatening complications such as pulmonary edema (lung failure) or cerebral edema (swelling of the brain).

CALL A PHYSICIAN IMMEDIATELY IF

• Your child is confused.

• Your child can't talk normally.

• Your child can't walk normally.

• The lips are bluish.

• Breathing is labored or fast.

• The headache is severe.

• Vomiting has occurred 3 or more times.

• Your child acts or looks very sick.

HOME CARE

First Aid for Symptoms of Severe Altitude Sickness • Rapidly transport your child to a lower altitude. Descend at least 2,000 feet, and always go below 10,000 feet elevation. If your child cannot walk, carry him or her in a sitting position. Administer oxygen as soon as it becomes available.

Rest for Mild Symptoms • The symptoms usually respond to 2 or 3 days of rest, fluids, and a light diet. Acetaminophen can be given for the headache (aspirin may make it worse). The dizziness and headache can usually be improved by deliberately breathing *slower*. Skiing, hiking, or any other type of strenuous exercise should be postponed. Once your child feels healthy again, activity should be increased gradually. Breathing from an oxygen tank can improve symptoms temporarily, but generally this is unnecessary.

Call Your Physician Later If

• The symptoms become worse.

• The symptoms last more than 3 days.

PREVENTION

• Try to stage your mountain visit. Spend a few days at 5,000 to 7,000 feet before journeying to the high country.

- Keep all newborns below 8,000 feet for a few months.

- Take it easy on the day of arrival. Some exercise (like short walks) is important, but take rest breaks. Gradually increase the amount of exertion during days 2 and 3.

- Avoid dehydration by drinking ample fluids.

- While mountain climbing, gain only 1,000 feet per day.

- If your child has experienced severe altitude sickness before, talk to your physician about taking Diamox tablets (a prescription medicine) preventively in the future.

DIZZINESS

Dizziness is a sensation of lightheadedness, faintness, or apparent movement of stationary objects in one's environment. All people occasionally get temporary dizziness if they skip a meal, become a little dehydrated, get too much sun, get exhausted, stand up suddenly, stand for too long in one place, or have a viral illness. If the dizziness relates to riding in a car, going to an amusement park, or playing twirling games (turning somersaults, for instance), see the guideline on MOTION SICKNESS, page 500.

CALL YOUR CHILD'S PHYSICIAN

Immediately If

- Your child is unable to stand and walk.

- Your child acts or looks very sick.

During Office Hours If

- Ear pain or congestion is also present.

- Your child is taking any medicines that could be causing the dizziness.

- Dizziness is a recurrent problem for your child.

- You have other questions or concerns.

HOME CARE

Treatment • Have your child lie down with the feet elevated for the next hour and offer something to drink. Always prevent dizziness from progressing to fainting (passing out) by reminding your child early on to lie down or sit with the head between the knees.

Call Your Child's Physician Later If

• Your child passes out.

• The dizziness is still present after 2 hours of rest.

RELATED TOPIC

FAINTING (see below)

FAINTING

SYMPTOMS AND CHARACTERISTICS

Fainting (syncope) is defined as falling down and being unconscious briefly (usually less than 1 minute). The four most common causes are sudden stress (such as seeing a bad accident), severe pain, prolonged standing in one position with the knees locked, or standing up suddenly (especially after bed rest). Fainting due to these conditions quickly responds to lying horizontally for a few minutes with the feet elevated.

Similar Conditions • If appropriate, turn directly to the following guidelines:

BREATH-HOLDING SPELLS (see page 331)
COMA (remaining unconscious is an *emergency*) (see page 39)
HEAT REACTIONS (see page 53)

CALL YOUR CHILD'S PHYSICIAN

Immediately If

• The fainting followed a head injury.

• Any shaking or jerking occurred while your child was unconscious.

- The unconsciousness lasted more than 2 minutes.
- The fainting occurred during exertion or exercise.
- The cause of the fainting isn't obvious.
- Your child also acts sick.

During Office Hours If

- Fainting is a recurrent problem for your child.
- You have other questions or concerns.

HOME CARE

First Aid • Have your child lie down for 10 to 20 minutes with the feet elevated. Do not place a pillow under the head. Also, offer a glass of fruit juice when he is fully conscious. In hot weather, your child may also need several glasses of water and a cool compress to the forehead. If fainting was due to stress or fear, help your child talk about it. **Caution:** Smelling salts are unpleasant and unnecessary.

Call Your Child's Physician Later If

- Your child isn't back to normal by 1 hour.
- Your child passes out again on the same day.

PREVENTION

For fainting that occurs following prolonged standing, remind your child that keeping the knees locked interferes with recirculation of the blood. Under these circumstances, your child should pump the blood by repeatedly relaxing and retightening the leg muscles.

For fainting that occurs with standing up suddenly, have your child sit up first and take some deep breaths.

Also, feeling faint at any time or place is a warning to sit or lie down quickly.

RELATED TOPIC

DIZZINESS (see page 495)

HEADACHE

SYMPTOM

• Your child complains that his or her head hurts.

Similar Condition • If a blow to the head is suspected, save time by turning directly to the guideline for HEAD TRAUMA, page 73.

Causes • A mild headache commonly occurs as part of a cold or other viral illness. A high fever almost always causes a headache. Many children get a headache in the late afternoon when they are hungry.

   In children and adults, the most common cause of recurrent headaches is tension. Tension headaches give a sensation of tightness that completely encircles the head. The neck muscles also become sore and tight. Tension headaches can be caused by prolonged use of video games, computers, or typewriters. Many children get tension headaches as a reaction to stresses (such as pressure for better grades or unresolved disagreements with parents). Recurrent headaches can have numerous causes and deserve a medical evaluation.

Expected Course • Many headaches clear when a fever comes down. Others come and go during an illness. Tension headaches usually last 2 to 8 hours, and tend to recur.

CALL YOUR CHILD'S PHYSICIAN

Immediately If

• The pain is very severe (e.g., causes constant crying).

• Your child is confused.

• Your child is difficult to awaken from sleep.

• Speech is slurred.

• Vision is blurred or double.

• Walking is unsteady.

• Vomiting has occurred 3 or more times.

• The neck is stiff.

- The pupils are unequal in size.

- Your child acts or looks very sick.

During Office Hours If

- The headache has lasted more than 24 hours despite using a pain-relieving medicine.

- Headaches are a recurrent problem for your child

- You have other questions or concerns.

HOME CARE

Treatment • Have your child lie down and rest until he or she is feeling better. If your child is hungry, offer some food. Give a pain-relieving medicine and repeat it in 4 hours if needed. If your child also has a fever, use acetaminophen. If your child doesn't have a fever, give aspirin or acetaminophen. (See FEVER, page 407, for dosage.) Apply a cool washcloth to the forehead.

Tension Headaches: Treatment • If your child has been evaluated by a physician and has tension headaches, try the following to help ease the pain:

- When a headache occurs, your youngster should lie down and relax. Give him aspirin or acetaminophen as soon as the headache begins. It's more effective if started early.

- If something is bothering your child, help him talk about it and get it off his mind.

- Teach your child not to skip meals, if doing so brings on headaches.

- To prevent tension headaches, teach your child to take breaks from activities that require sustained concentration. During the breaks, encourage relaxation exercises.

- If overachievement causes headaches, help your child get out of the fast track.

Call Your Child's Physician Later If

- The headache lasts for more than 24 hours despite the medicine.

- It worsens after 2 hours on pain-relieving medicine.

- New symptoms develop that concern you.

RELATED TOPIC

Sinus Congestion (see page 546)

Consider this diagnosis if the pain is on one side and near the eye, the nose is runny or blocked, and your child has previously experienced sinus problems.

MOTION SICKNESS

Motion sickness is a common condition, especially in young children. The same children who get dizzy and nauseated in the car are also prone to becoming seasick, trainsick, airsick, and sick on amusement park rides. The problem is due to an inherited sensitivity of the equilibrium center found in the semicircular canals (inner ear). It is not related to emotional problems, nor can your child control it. The sensitivity to motion is usually a lifelong problem.

HOME CARE

Treatment for the Nausea • Have your child lie down, and keep a vomiting pan handy. Give only sips of clear fluids until the stomach settles down. If your child goes to sleep, all the better. Usually, children don't vomit more than once, and all symptoms disappear in about 4 hours.

PREVENTION

Anti-Nausea Medicine • Buy some nonprescription Dramamine tablets at your drugstore. They come in 50 mg tablets or 15 mg-per-teaspoon liquid. The dosage is 1 teaspoon for children 2 to 6 years old, 1 tablet for children 6 to 12 years old, and 2 tablets for children over 12. Give the Dramamine 1 hour before traveling or going to an amusement park. The tablets give 6 hours of protection and are very helpful.

Car trips • Have your child sit in the front seat and at window level. Have your child look out the front window, not the side one. Ask your child not to look at books or play games during car travel. Keep a window cracked to provide fresh air.

Amusement parks • Have your child a
the Tilt-a-Whirl). Some children can
rides without becoming sick. Your chil
on the Ferris wheel.

Sea travel • Avoid it. Boating on small lakes is

Air travel • Airsickness can be helped by selecti
the wings or center of the aircraft, since turbi
least there.

Meals • Have your child eat light meals on these days.

SOFT SPOT, BULGING

The soft spot (called the anterior fontanel) is open during the
first 12 to 18 months of life. Normally it is flat or slightly
sunken. Normally it moves up and down (pulsates) with each
beat of the heart, if the child is sitting up and quiet. It can be
slightly elevated while your child is crying. If the soft spot is
tense and bulging, the brain is under pressure. Many of the
causes are serious.

CALL YOUR CHILD'S PHYSICIAN IMMEDIATELY IF

• Your child has a bulging soft spot.

EYES

ALLERGIES OF THE EYES

SYMPTOMS AND CHARACTERISTICS

- Itchy eyes (without pain)
- Increased tearing (without pus)
- Red or pink eyes
- Mild swelling of the eyelids
- Similar symptoms during the same month of the previous year
- Previous confirmation of this diagnosis by a physician is helpful

If your child's symptoms are different, call your physician for help.

Similar Condition • If the nose is also involved, save time by turning directly to the guideline on HAY FEVER, page 540.

Causes • For cases that occur during the same season each year, the cause is pollens. For cases that are not seasonal, the allergic factor can be pets (cats, for instance), feathers, perfumes, mascara, eyeliner, and so forth.

Expected Course • Most eye allergies due to a pollen last for 4 to 6 weeks, which is the length of most pollen seasons. If the

502

allergic substance can be identified *and* avoided (a cat, perhaps), the symptoms will not recur.

CALL YOUR CHILD'S PHYSICIAN WITHIN 24 HOURS IF

• The eye allergy keeps your child from playing or sleeping.

• The eyelids are swollen tight.

• Sacs of clear yellow fluid are present between the eyelids.

• The eyelids become matted together with pus.
(Note: It's normal to awaken in the morning with some strands of sticky mucus in the eye. This mucus can often be prevented by washing the pollen off the eyelids and face the night before.)

• You have other questions or concerns.

HOME CARE

Removing Pollen • First wash the pollen off the face. Then use a clean washcloth and cool water to clean off the eyelids. Tears will wash the pollen out of the eyes. This rinse of the eyelids may need to be repeated every time your child comes in on a windy day. Pollen also collects in the hair and on exposed body surfaces. This pollen can easily be reintroduced into the eyes. Therefore, give your child a shower and shampoo every night before bedtime. Encourage your child not to touch the eyes unless the hands have been washed recently.

Vasoconstrictor Eyedrops • Usually, the eyes will feel much better after the pollen is washed out and cold compresses are applied. If they are still itchy or bloodshot (i.e., the blood vessels are swollen), instill some long-acting vasoconstrictive eyedrops (no prescription needed). Ask your pharmacist for help in choosing a reliable product. Use 2 drops every 6 to 8 hours as necessary.

Antihistamines • If these measures aren't effective, your child probably also has hay fever (i.e., allergic symptoms of the nose). Give your child an oral antihistamine. (For dosage, see HAY FEVER, page 540.)

Call Your Child's Physician Later If

- This treatment and an antihistamine do not relieve most of the symptoms in 2 or 3 days.

  Keep in mind that the pollen season lasts for 1 to 2 months. You need to continue the treatment for that length of time and start it again next year.

DARK CIRCLES UNDER THE EYES

The most common cause for dark, bluish circles under the eyes is congestion of the nose. The veins from the eyes drain into the veins of the nose. If the nose is blocked up, the veins around the eyes become larger and darker. To figure out what's going on, we need to look at the nose.

Usually the cause of the nasal congestion is nasal allergy or hay fever. That's why these dark circles are also called allergic shiners. Dark circles are also caused by chronic sinus infections, recurrent colds, or mouth breathing due to large adenoids. They're also more noticeable in children with a fair complexion. Overall, dark circles under the eyes are not a sign of poor health or troubled sleep.

Treatment • Treatment depends on the cause of the congestion. Turn directly to the guideline that pertains to your child:

- COLDS (see page 533)

- HAY FEVER (see page 540)

- SINUS CONGESTION (see page 546)

- TONSIL AND ADENOID SURGERY (if your child has snoring and mouth breathing) (see page 562)

Call Your Child's Physician During Office Hours If

- You don't know what is causing your child's dark circles.

ITCHY EYE

For itchy, watery, red eyes, the possible causes are many. If the itching begins suddenly and is intense, usually your child has been around something he's allergic to (e.g., a cat). If the cause is unclear, assume the itching is caused by a minor irritant. Irrigate the eyes with warm water as described on page 507. Turn directly to the guideline that pertains to your child.

ALLERGIES (see page 502)
CHEMICAL IN EYE (see page 48)
RED OR PINKEYE (includes minor irritants) (see below)

RED OR PINKEYE WITHOUT PUS

SYMPTOMS AND CHARACTERISTICS

• Redness of the sclera (white part of the eye)

• Redness of the inner eyelids

• A watery discharge ("watery eyes")

• No yellow discharge or matting of eyelids

• Not from crying

• Also called pinkeye, bloodshot eyes, or conjunctivitis

If your child's symptoms are different, call your physician for help.

Similar Conditions • If one of the following is suspected, save time by turning directly to that guideline:

ALLERGIES (see page 502)
CHEMICAL IN EYE (see page 48)
FOREIGN BODY IN EYE, (e.g., blowing dust or eyelash)
   (see page 49)
EYE TRAUMA (see page 67)
HAY FEVER (see page 540)
RED OR PINKEYE WITH PUS (see page 508)

Causes • Red eyes are usually caused by a viral infection, and commonly accompany colds. If a bacterial superinfection occurs, the discharge becomes yellow and the eyelids are commonly matted together after sleeping. These children need antibiotic eyedrops even if the eyes are not red. The second most common cause is getting an irritant into the eyes. The irritant can be shampoo, smog, smoke, or chlorine from a swimming pool. More commonly in young kids, it comes from touching the eyes with hands carrying dirt, soap, or food (such as cinnamon, chili powder, or other spice). Contact with mother's perfume or father's after-shave can also be irritating, as can rubbing faces with the family pet. The main symptom in children with irritants in the eye is constant rubbing and tearing of the eyes.

Expected Course • Viral conjunctivitis usually lasts as long as a cold does (4 to 7 days). Pinkeye is a mild infection and does not harm the vision. Red eyes from irritants usually are cured within 4 hours of washing out the irritating substance, unless reexposure occurs.

CALL YOUR CHILD'S PHYSICIAN

Immediately If

• The eyelids are red or swollen.

• The eyes are constantly tearing or blinking.

• Your child is complaining of pain in the eyes.

• Vision is blurred.

• Your child acts or looks very sick.

Within 24 Hours If

• Your child is under 1 month old.

• A yellow discharge develops.

• The eyelids become matted together with pus.

• The eye has been red for more than 7 days.

• You have other questions or concerns.

HOME CARE

Washing with Soap • Wash the face, then the eyelids, with a mild soap and water. This will remove any irritants.

Irrigating with Water • For viral eye infections, rinse the eyes out with warm water as often as possible, at least every 1 to 2 hours while your child is awake. Use warm (not hot) water, and use a fresh cotton ball each time. Wipe toward the inside of the eye. This usually will keep a bacterial infection from occurring. For mild chemical irritants, irrigate the eye with warm water for 5 minutes.

Vasoconstrictor Eyedrops • Viral conjunctivitis usually is not helped by eyedrops. Red eyes from irritants usually feel much better after the irritant has been washed out. If they remain uncomfortable and bloodshot, instill some long-acting vasoconstrictor eyedrops (no prescription needed). Ask your pharmacist for help in choosing a reliable product. Use 2 drops every 6 to 8 hours as necessary. Products called "artificial tears" are not helpful, since they do not contain any vasoconstrictors.

Contagiousness • If your child has pinkeye from a viral infection, the secretions can cause eye infections in other people if they get some of it on their eyes. Therefore, it is important for the sick child to have his or her own washcloth and towel. However, the infection is so mild that staying home is unnecessary. If the pinkeye is due to irritants or chemicals, obviously your child's condition is not contagious.

Call Your Child's Physician Later If

• A yellow discharge develops.

• The eyelids become matted together with pus.

• The eyelids become red or swollen.

• The redness lasts more than a week.

• The vision becomes blurred.

RED OR PINKEYE WITH PUS

SYMPTOMS AND CHARACTERISTICS

• Yellow discharge in the eye

• Eyelids stuck together with a little pus (especially after sleep) is the earliest finding

• Dried eye discharge on the upper cheek

• The eyes are also usually red or pink

• Also called runny eyes or mattery eyes (Note: Everyone can normally have a small amount of cream-colored mucus, called "sleep," in the inner corner of the eyes after sleeping.)

Causes • Caused by various bacteria. After ear infections, bacterial eye infections are the next leading complication of a cold. Red eyes without a yellow discharge, however, are more common and are due to a virus (see RED OR PINKEYE WITHOUT PUS, page 505).

Expected Course • With proper treatment, the yellow discharge should clear up in 72 hours. The red eyes (which are part of the underlying cold) may persist for several more days. These infections do not harm the vision.

CALL YOUR CHILD'S PHYSICIAN

Immediately If

• The outer eyelids are red or swollen.

• Any ulcer or sore is seen on the eyeball.

• Your child acts or looks very sick.

Within 24 Hours If

• You don't have any antibiotic eyedrops or ointment.

• Your child is under 3 years of age. (Simultaneous ear infections are very common.)

• Your infant is less than 1 month old. These children need special cultures and an antibiotic.

• There is any suggestion of an earache.

- Your child has frequent eye infections.
- You have other questions.

HOME CARE

Cleaning the Eye • Before putting in any medicines, remove all the dried and liquid pus from the eye with warm wet cotton balls. This should be done as often as you see pus in the eye, sometimes every hour. Unless this is done, the medicine will not have a chance to work. Remove the dried crusts carefully so they don't scratch the eyeball.

Antibiotic Eyedrops or Ointments • A bacterial conjunctivitis must be treated with an antibiotic eye medicine. Acceptable ones are sulfacetamide (Sulamyd), Gantrisin, Garamycin, Polysporin, or Neosporin. If you have one of these products in your home, use it. If not, you must call your physician during office hours for a prescription. Some physicians will want to examine your child before prescribing.

Holding Your Child • Putting eyedrops or ointment in the eyes of younger children can be a real battle. Ideally, it's done with two people. One person can hold the child still while the other person opens the eyelids with one hand and puts in the medicine with the other. One person *can* do it alone, sitting on the floor, holding the child's head (face up) between the knees to free both hands to put in the medicine.

Using Antibiotic Eyedrops • Put 2 drops in each eye every 2 hours while your child is awake. Do this by gently pulling down on the lower lid and placing the drops inside the lower lid. As soon as the eyedrops have been put in, have your child close the eyes for 2 minutes so the eyedrops will stay inside. If it is difficult to separate your child's eyelids, while he is lying down put the eyedrop over the inner corner of the eye. As your child opens the eye and blinks, the eyedrop will flow in. Continue the eyedrops until your child has awakened 2 mornings in a row without any pus in the eyes. If the eyedrops are stopped sooner, the infection will probably come back.

Using Antibiotic Eye Ointment (instead of eyedrops) • Eye ointment needs to be used only 4 times a day because it can remain in the eyes longer than eyedrops. Separate the eyelids and put in a ribbon of ointment from one corner to the other. If it is very difficult to separate your child's eyelids, put the ointment on the lid margins. As it melts, it will flow onto the eyeball and give equal results. Again, continue until 2 mornings have passed without any pus in the eye.

Contagiousness • The pus from the eyes can cause eye infections in other people if they get some of it on their eyes. Therefore, it is very important for the sick child to have his or her own washcloth and towel. Your child should be discouraged from touching or rubbing the eyes, because it can make the infection last longer, and it puts a lot of germs on the fingers. Therefore, your child's hands should also be washed often to prevent spreading the infection. Your child can return to school after using the eyedrops for 24 hours if the pus is minimal.

Call Your Child's Physician Later If

• The infection isn't cleared up in 72 hours.

• The eyelids become red or swollen.

• The vision becomes blurred.

• Your child develops an earache.

• The eyes become itchy or redder after eyedrops are begun.

SWELLING OF EYELID

SYMPTOMS AND CHARACTERISTICS

An insect bite near the eye can cause swelling of the eyelid. This is especially common with mosquito bites of the upper face. The eyelid is not red, but it can be pink.

Similar Conditions • If one of the following is suspected, save time by turning directly to that guideline:

EYE TRAUMA (see page 67)
ALLERGIES (see page 502)
RED OR PINKEYE (see pages 505 and 508)

CALL YOUR CHILD'S PHYSICIAN

Immediately If

- Both eyelids are swollen. (Exception: eye allergies.)
- The swollen eyelid is tender to the touch.
- The eyelid is red.
- A fever (over 100°F) is present.
- Your child also has sinus congestion.
- There is pain on movement of the eye.
- Your child acts or looks very sick.

During Office Hours If

- You are unsure of the cause of the swelling (i.e., you find no evidence for insect bites near the eye and it's the wrong season for mosquitoes in your community).
- You have other questions or concerns.

HOME CARE FOR EYELID SWELLING FROM AN INSECT BITE

Treatment • Cool compresses or ice in a washcloth help. Give your child an antihistamine to decrease the swelling and help any itching. (See HAY FEVER, page 540, for dosages.) Many common cold medicines contain antihistamines. In 2 or 3 days, the swelling from insect bites is usually gone.

Call Your Child's Physician Later If

- The swelling hasn't cleared in 3 days.
- The eyelid becomes red or tender.
- Other symptoms develop that concern you.

RELATED TOPIC

BITES, INSECT (see page 18)

STYE

SYMPTOMS AND CHARACTERISTICS

- A tender, red bump at the base of an eyelash
- A small pimple at the base of an eyelash

If your child's symptoms are different, call your physician for help.

Cause • A stye is an infection of the hair follicle of an eyelash, usually caused by staphylococcus bacteria.

Expected Course • It usually comes to a head and forms a pimple in 3 to 5 days. In a few more days, it usually drains and heals. Recurrences are common, especially in children who rub their eyes.

CALL YOUR CHILD'S PHYSICIAN

Immediately If

- The infection is spreading.
- The eyelid is red or swollen.

During Office Hours If

- Styes are a recurrent problem for your child.
- There are 2 or more styes.
- You have other questions or concerns.

HOME CARE

Warm Compresses • Wash the outer eyelids daily with an antibacterial soap (like Dial or Safeguard). Apply a warm washcloth to the eye for 10 minutes 4 times a day to help the stye come to a head. Continue to cleanse the eye several times a day even after the stye drains.

Opening the Pimple • When the stye does display a center of pus, you can open it by pulling out the eyelash that goes into the pimple with a tweezers. This will initiate drainage and healing. Your other option is just to continue warm compresses. Most styes will drain spontaneously in a few days after they have come to a head.

Antibiotic Eye Ointment • The ointments do not cure styes, but they may keep them from spreading and recurring. If your child has recurrent styes or more than 2 styes, call your child's physician, since this ointment requires a prescription. Most single styes respond to the treatment outlined.

Prevention of Recurrences • Ask your child not to touch the eyes, because rubbing can cause spread to other eyelashes.

Call Your Child's Physician Later If

• Infection seems to be spreading.

• The stye is not draining or improved by 3 days.

• The stye is not completely healed by 10 days.

• Styes recur.

EARS

EARACHE

SYMPTOMS AND CHARACTERISTICS

Your child complains of ear pain. Children too young to talk may cry several times during the night and be cranky during the day. Most of these children also have symptoms of a cold and 50 percent have a fever. The peak age range for earaches is 6 months to 2 years, but they continue to be a common complaint until age 8 or 10.

Similar Conditions • If your child is doing lots of swimming and it hurts when you move the outer ear up and down, save time by going directly to the guideline on SWIMMER'S EAR (page 528).

Cause • Most earaches are due to a middle-ear infection (acute otitis media). A middle-ear infection is a bacterial infection of the space behind the eardrum. The earache is due to the bulging of the eardrum. Most children (70 percent) have one or more ear infections, and 25 percent of these will have repeated ear infections. Ear infections are the most common complication of a cold. While colds are contagious, ear infections are not.

A temporary earache can occur for 10 to 15 minutes after being outside in cold weather. When your child comes inside, the cold air inside the middle ear warms up, expands, and causes some pain. Chewing gum or drinking fluids should relieve it. However, cold wind or weather cannot cause an ear infection.

Another cause of temporary pain in front of the ear is muscle pain from excessive chewing.

Expected Course of Ear Infection • In 5 to 15 percent of children with otitis media, the pressure in the middle ear causes the eardrum to rupture and drain. The ear drainage does not mean that the ear infection is any more serious. This small tear usually heals in a few days. Most ear infections respond nicely to a course of antibiotics. At the 2-week visit for ear recheck, about 10 percent will still be infected and need a second course of antibiotics. Another 40 percent or more will have fluid in the middle ear (serous otitis) and reduced hearing. Over the following 1 to 3 months, hearing will return to normal without treatment in most of these children. A few children will need "ventilation tubes" placed in their eardrums.

CALL YOUR CHILD'S PHYSICIAN

Immediately If

• The pain is severe (e.g., a screaming child).

• The neck is stiff.

• Your child can't walk normally.

• The earache followed injury to the ear.

• Your child acts or looks very sick.

Within 24 Hours If

• All other children with earaches that last more than 2 hours need medical consultation.

HOME CARE

Relieving Pain

• An earache is not an emergency. Until you see the physician, give acetaminophen for pain. (For dosage, see FEVER, page 407.) If your child is still uncomfortable after 1 hour, use a cough medicine containing dextromethorphan or codeine. These agents are strong anti-pain medicines. (For dosage, see COUGH, page 570.) You may also put an ice bag or ice in a wet washcloth over the painful ear for 20 minutes. Many physicians recommend a hot water bottle, but cold seems to provide greater relief.

Other Measures

• Do not use any ear drops unless your physician recommends them.

• If the ear is draining, wipe the material away as it appears.

• Don't plug the canal with cotton.

RELATED TOPICS

COLDS (see page 533)
EAR CONGESTION (see page 516)
EAR DISCHARGE (see page 518)
PULLING AT EAR (see page 527)

EAR CONGESTION

SYMPTOMS AND CHARACTERISTICS

• Sudden onset of muffled hearing

• Crackling or popping noises in the ear

• A stuffy, full sensation in the ear

• No ear pain except in cases related to airplane travel

Similar Conditions • If one of the following is suspected, save time by turning directly to that guideline:

EARACHE (see page 514)
EAR DISCHARGE (see page 518)
EARWAX, PACKED (see page 518)
HAY FEVER (see page 540)

Cause • The most common cause of ear congestion is fluid in the middle ear due to intermittent blockage of the Eustachian tube (the channel connecting the middle ear to the back of the nose) by a cold, hay fever, or overvigorous nose-blowing. Sudden increases in barometric pressure, such as occur in descent from mountain driving or airplane travel, also cause ear congestion (but usually with pain, as the eardrum is pulled inward).

CALL YOUR CHILD'S PHYSICIAN DURING OFFICE HOURS IF

- Your child could have put something in the ear canal.
- You have other questions or concerns.

HOME CARE

Treatment • Have your child chew gum, yawn frequently, and swallow (or puff out the cheeks) while the nose is pinched closed. If this isn't effective, use a long-acting decongestant nasal spray 1 hour before air travel. Ask your pharmacist to recommend a good product (no prescription needed). If your child could have water in the ear canal from a recent shower or swim, help drain it by gravity while gently pulling the ear in different directions. If your child has hay fever, an antihistamine medication should also be taken. If your child is in pain, give aspirin or acetaminophen (see FEVER, page 407, for dosage). Swimming is permitted.

Call Your Child's Physician Later If

- The ear congestion lasts more than 48 hours.
- Ear pain or fever develops.

PREVENTION OF EAR CONGESTION DUE TO ALTITUDE CHANGE •
Have your child repeatedly "pop" the ears by yawning or swallowing during the typical 30 to 60 minutes of descent. If this fails, attempt to blow the nose (and puff out the cheeks) against closed nostrils and a closed mouth. A baby can be given water to drink or a pacifier to suck on during descent, and the nose can be pinched closed periodically during swallowing. Obviously, the child should not sleep during descent.

People with recurrent problems should take an oral antihistamine and long-acting decongestant nasal spray (see HAY FEVER, page 540, and COLDS, page 533, respectively, for drug names and dosage) 1 hour before travel. If severe pain occurs despite these precautions, ask the stewardess for a hot towel to place over the ear canal. (The heat will expand the air in the middle ear and relieve the negative pressure on the retracted eardrum.)

EAR DISCHARGE

YELLOW OR CLOUDY DISCHARGE
Call your child's physician during office hours. Your child probably has an ear infection with drainage through a small tear in the eardrum.

BLOODY DISCHARGE
See the guideline on EAR TRAUMA, page 66.

EARWAX DISCHARGE
For a brown or orange discharge, see the guideline on EARWAX, PACKED, below.

CLEAR DISCHARGE

• If it followed head or ear trauma, call your child's physician immediately.

• If it followed an earache, call your child's physician within 24 hours.

• If it could be tears, bath water, or eardrops someone put in, your worries are over.

HOME CARE
Pending the office visit for a suspected ear infection, give acetaminophen for pain (For dosage, see FEVER, page 407.) Wipe away the drainage as it appears. Don't pack the ear canal closed with cotton, because this will block the natural drainage. Don't put any cotton swabs in the ear canal.

EARWAX, PACKED

Earwax is present in everyone. The color can vary from light yellow to dark brown. It has chemicals in it which can kill germs, it keeps dust off the eardrum, and it protects the lining of the ear canal. Earwax is not abnormal or dirty.

The ear canal is designed to clean itself, unless someone pushes the earwax (that's trying to get out) back in. Earwax moves outward naturally during chewing and the normal growth of the ear canal's lining. Every day or two, you may notice a little earwax at the opening of the ear canal. The amount varies from person to person, and as long as it comes out, your child can't have too much of it.

Proceed with this guideline if earwax is completely blocking one of the ear canals (i.e., impacted wax). If the hearing seems normal on that side, the blockage is only partial and you can leave it alone.

CALL YOUR CHILD'S PHYSICIAN DURING OFFICE HOURS IF

• Any discharge comes from the ear canal other than earwax.

• The eardrum has been ruptured in the past.

• Blockage from earwax is a recurrent problem for your child.

• You have other questions.

HOME CARE

Flushing Out Packed Earwax • Keep in mind that complete blockage is rare. Regular removal of earwax is not necessary to prevent wax buildup.

• If the wax is hard, soften it first. Mineral or baby oil is a good earwax softener. Put in 3 drops twice a day for 3 days. Lying with the ear against a heating pad for 20 minutes may help remove the wax by melting it.

• When the wax is soft, irrigate it out with a rubber ear syringe or Water Pik at the lowest setting. The water must be at body temperature to prevent dizziness. Irrigate several times, until the return is clear and the ear canal seems open when you look in with a light. Never put water in your child's ear if there is any chance the eardrum has a hole in it or your child has ventilation tubes.

Call Your Child's Physician Later If

• Your irrigation doesn't clear out the ear canal and return the hearing to normal.

• Any other questions come up.

PREVENTION

Earwax can usually be removed from the opening of the ear canal with the corner of a wet cloth. Don't use your fingernail, because fingernails are usually rather dirty, and too big for the job. Nothing should be put into the ear canal to try to hurry this process along, because it usually ends up packing the wax deeper. It also runs the risk of damaging your child's eardrum if he turns his head suddenly. The most common cause of earwax buildup is putting cotton swabs into the ear canal. As your child becomes older, also remind her not to clean the ears.

FOREIGN BODY IN EAR

Young children often put foreign objects in their ear canals. Some common ones are erasers, beads, food, and cotton.

FIRST AID

If a live insect is within your child's ear canal, take your child into a dark room and shine a light by the ear. The insect will often come out on its own. If this fails, kill the intruder by pouring in some alcohol. You can use 80 proof gin if you have no rubbing alcohol. Then remove the insect by irrigating the canal with water and an ear syringe (or a nasal suction bulb). For other objects, make one simple attempt at removing it. Turn the involved side down. Wiggle the ear at the same time you gently shake the head, and try to get the object to fall out with the help of gravity.

CALL YOUR CHILD'S PHYSICIAN IMMEDIATELY IF THESE MEASURES FAIL

It is critical that you do not try to remove the object by putting tweezers, fingers, or any other device into the ear canal. Also, don't try to irrigate it out at home. These attempts almost always push the object in farther and make the physician's job very difficult, even with special instruments. Watch closely that your child dosen't push it in.

ITCHY EAR

SYMPTOMS

Your child repeatedly scratches his ear or complains that it itches.

Causes • Most older children who complain of itchy ear canals have a mild otitis externa from:

• Water accumulation during swimming or showers

• Soap or shampoo retention

• Irritation from hair sprays

• Canal irritation from cotton swabs. These swabs remove the earwax that normally protects the lining of the ear canal, and this leads to itching and irritation.

Similar Conditions • If one of the following is suspected, save time by turning directly to that guideline:

SWIMMER'S EAR (see page 528)
EARACHE (see page 514)
EAR DISCHARGE (see page 518)

HOME CARE

Treatment • White vinegar has acetic acid in it and can usually restore the ear canal to its normal chemistry. Fill one ear canal at a time with white vinegar. Do this by running the vinegar down the side of the opening of the ear canal so that air doesn't get trapped under it. Leave it in for 5 minutes; then remove it by putting that side of the head down and pulling the ear in different directions to help the vinegar run out. Do this twice a day for 3 or 4 days.

Call Your Child's Physician Later If

• The canals itch for more than a week.

• The ear becomes painful.

- A discharge from the ear occurs.

- A fever (over 100°F) occurs.

PREVENTION

- Keep soap and shampoo out of the ear canal.

- Don't use cotton swabs in the ear canal.

- Do plug the openings with cotton prior to using hair spray.

- After swimming, get all water out of the ear canals by turning the head to the side and pulling the ear in different directions to help the water run out. Dry the opening to the ear canal carefully.

MUMPS

SYMPTOMS AND CHARACTERISTICS

- Swollen parotid gland, in front of the ear and crossing the corner of the jaw. (Both parotid glands are swollen in 70 percent of children with mumps.)

- Tenderness of the swollen gland

- Pain increased by jaw movement (chewing or even talking)

- Fever (over 100°F) is present

- No prior mumps vaccine

- Exposure to another child with mumps 16 to 18 days earlier adds weight to the diagnosis.

  If your child's symptoms are different, call your physician for help.

Cause • Mumps is an acute viral infection of the parotid, a gland which produces saliva and is located in front of and below each ear.

Expected Course • The fever is usually gone in 3 to 4 days. The swelling and pain are cleared by 7 days.

CALL YOUR CHILD'S PHYSICIAN

Immediately If

- Your child has a stiff neck or severe headache.
- Your child is vomiting repeatedly.
- Your child has definite abdominal pain.
- Your child acts or looks very sick.

Within 24 Hours If

- It could be an enlarged lymph node rather than mumps.
- The skin over the mumps gland is reddened.
- The gland has been swollen more than 7 days.
- In adolescent males, the testicles become tender.
- Your child received the mumps vaccine.
- Your child had mumps before.
- You have other questions or concerns.

HOME CARE

Pain and Fever Relief • Give acetaminophen. (For dosage, see FEVER, page 407.) Cold compresses (e.g., ice in a wet washcloth) applied to the swollen area may also relieve pain.

Diet

- Avoid sour foods or citrus fruits that increase saliva production and parotid swelling.
- Avoid foods that require lots of chewing.
- Consider a liquid diet if chewing is very painful.

Contagiousness • The disease is contagious until the swelling is gone (usually 6 or 7 days). Your child should be kept out of school and away from other children who have not had mumps or mumps vaccine.

Mumps Exposure • Mumps exposure can be a problem if a person has never received the mumps vaccine or had past swelling of the parotid gland (mumps). Only 10 percent of adults are really susceptible, however. Adults who as children lived in the same household with siblings who had mumps can be considered protected. People who are not protected should call their physician during office hours, if they are exposed to mumps, to see if the mumps vaccine would be helpful, based on the following guidelines:

• Children: All should receive the mumps vaccine.

• Adolescent or adult males: The vaccine is optional. There is a 2.5 percent chance of mumps infection of the testicles (orchitis).

• Adult females: The mumps vaccine is unnecessary. No serious complications occur.

Call Your Child's Physician Later If

• The swelling lasts for 8 days or more.

• The fever lasts for 5 days or more.

• The skin over the swelling becomes red.

• Your child develops a stiff neck, severe headache, or prolonged vomiting.

• You feel your child is getting worse.

RELATED TOPIC

LYMPH NODES, SWOLLEN (see page 479)

PIERCED EAR INFECTIONS

SYMPTOMS AND CHARACTERISTICS

Earrings for pierced ears have become very popular in our country. Ear piercing no longer awaits the teenage years; even infants are seen with pierced ears. For safety reasons, pierced earrings should not be worn until a child is old enough (usually past age 4) to know not to fidget with them (which can lead to infections) or take them out and put them in her mouth (which can lead to swallowing or choking on them). Ideally, the ears should not be pierced until the girl can play an active part in the decision (usually past age 8).

The most common complication of pierced ears is a bacterial infection of the channel. Signs of an infection are tenderness, a yellow discharge, redness, and some swelling.

Causes • The most common causes of infection are piercing the ears with unsterile equipment, inserting unsterile posts, or frequently touching the earlobes with dirty hands. Another frequent cause is wearing tight earrings because the post is too short (earlobes come in various thicknesses) or the clasp is applied too tightly. Tight earrings don't allow air to enter the channel through the earlobe. Also, the pressure from tight earrings reduces blood flow to the earlobe and sets it up for infection. Some inexpensive earrings have rough areas on the posts that scratch the channel and allow infection to enter. Inserting the post at the wrong angle also can scratch the channel, so a mirror should be used until insertion becomes second nature. Posts containing nickel can also cause an itchy, allergic reaction.

Expected Course • If the proper precautions are taken, most mild earlobe infections will clear up in 1 to 2 weeks. Recurrences are common if the youngster does not become conscientious in earring care.

CALL YOUR CHILD'S PHYSICIAN

Immediately If

• The earring clasp becomes embedded in the earlobe and can't be removed.

Within 24 Hours If

• An unexplained fever (over 100°F) occurs.

• The lymph node in front of or behind the earlobe becomes swollen.

• Swelling or redness spreads beyond the pierced area of the earlobe.

• You have other questions or concerns.

HOME CARE

Treating Mild Pierced Ear Infections • Remove the earring and post three times a day. Cleanse them with rubbing alcohol. Clean both sides of the earlobe with rubbing alcohol. Apply Bacitracin ointment (a nonprescription item) to the post and reinsert it. Continue the antibiotic ointment for 2 days beyond the time the infection seems cleared. Carefully review all the recommendations on preventing infections and be certain they are in effect.

Call Your Physician Later If

• Fever (over 100°F) occurs.

• The infection worsens.

• The infection is not improving after 48 hours of treatment.

PREVENTION OF INITIAL INFECTIONS

Avoid pierced ears entirely if your child has a tendency to bleed easily, form thick scars (keloids), or get staph skin infections. If none of these apply, have your child's earlobes pierced by someone who understands sterile technique and does them frequently. Using someone inexperienced can result in infections or a cosmetically poor result.

• The initial post should be 14 carat gold or stainless steel.

• Do not remove the post for 6 weeks.

• Apply the clasp loosely to allow for swelling.

• After washing the hands and cleaning both sides of the earlobe with rubbing alcohol, turn the posts approximately 3 rotations. Do this twice a day.

• By the end of 6 weeks, the lining of the channel should be healed and earrings may be changed as often as desired.

Prevention of Later Infections

• Remind your youngster not to touch the earrings except when inserting or removing them. The fingers are often dirty and can contaminate the area.

• Clean the earring, post, and earlobe with rubbing alcohol before each insertion.

• Apply the clasp loosely to prevent any pressure on the earlobe and to provide an air space on both sides.

• Polish or discard any posts with rough spots.

• At bedtime, remove the earrings to permit air exposure and drying of the channel during the night.

Prevention of Injury to the Earlobe • Remind your daughter that dangling earrings can lead to a torn earlobe requiring plastic surgery. Avoid them during sports. Also, take precautions while dancing, hair washing, or handling young children who might yank them.

PULLING AT EAR

Most young children who are pulling at or rubbing their ears, but have no other symptoms, do not have an ear infection. Many of them have an itchy ear canal from getting soap or shampoo in it. Some have just discovered their ears and are playing with them (6 months to 2 years old). If it occurs only when your child is sleepy, it may be a reassuring habit like clutching a security blanket.

CALL YOUR CHILD'S PHYSICIAN WITHIN 24 HOURS IF

- You think your child is in any pain.

- Your child has been crying without an obvious cause.

- Your child had any trouble sleeping last night.

- Your child has a fever (over 100°F) or any signs of a cold.

- You have other questions.

HOME CARE

Treatment • Mix a solution of one-half rubbing alcohol and one-half white vinegar. Place 1 to 2 drops in each ear daily for 3 days.

Call Your Child's Physician Later If

- Pulling at the ear continues beyond 3 days.

- Ear pain occurs.

- A discharge from the ear occurs.

- Any other symptoms develop that concern you.

PREVENTION

• Keep soap and shampoo out of the ear canal.

• Don't use cotton swabs in the ear canal, since they remove the earwax that protects the lining of the canal, and this can cause irritation or itching.

• After swimming, get all water out of the ear canals by turning the head to the side and pulling the ear in different directions to help the water run out. Dry the opening to the ear canal carefully.

SWIMMER'S EAR (OTITIS EXTERNA)

SYMPTOMS AND CHARACTERISTICS

• Itchy and painful ear canals

• Currently engaged in swimming

• Pain when the ear is moved up and down

• Pain when the tab of outer ear overlying the ear canal is pushed in

• The ear feels plugged

• Discharge is slight in amount and clear

If your child's symptoms are different, call your physician for help.

Cause • Swimmer's ear is an infection of the skin lining the ear canal. When water gets trapped in the ear canal, the lining becomes wet, swollen, and prone to infection. Ear canals were meant to be dry. Swimming pools are worse than lakes, because the chlorine kills all the good bacteria in the ear canal, and harmful bacteria tend to take over. However, this doesn't mean anything is wrong with the water.

Expected Course • With treatment, symptoms should be better in 3 days.

CALL YOUR CHILD'S PHYSICIAN WITHIN 24 HOURS IF

• A fever (over 100°F) is present.

• A yellow discharge issues from the ear canal.

• The canal appears full of gunk.

• The ear is very painful.

• The outer ear becomes red or swollen.

• A swollen lymph node is present behind the earlobe.

• You have other questions or concerns.

HOME CARE

Treatment • White vinegar has acetic acid in it and can usually restore the ear canal to its normal chemistry. Fill one ear canal at a time by running the vinegar down the side of the opening and moving the ear so that air isn't trapped under it. Leave it in for 5 minutes; then remove it by putting that side of the head down and pulling the ear in different directions to help the vinegar run out. Do this twice a day and following showers or baths. Use aspirin or acetaminophen for pain relief (for dosage, see FEVER, page 407). Generally, your child should not swim until the symptoms are gone. If your child is on a swim team, he or she may continue but should use a white vinegar rinse after each session.

Common Mistakes • Don't use earplugs of any kind for prevention or treatment. They tend to jam earwax back into the ear canal. Also, they don't keep all water out of the ear canals. Cotton swabs also should not be inserted in ear canals. Wax buildup traps water behind it and increases the risk of swimmer's ear. A rubbing alcohol mixture is helpful for preventing swimmer's ear but not for treating it, because it would sting too much.

Call Your Child's Physician for Prescription Eardrops Later If

• The symptoms are not cleared up in 3 days.

• The pain becomes worse after 24 hours on treatment.

• A yellow discharge from the ear canal occurs.

• A fever (over 100°F) occurs.

PREVENTION

The key to prevention is keeping the ear canals dry when your child is not swimming. After swimming, get all water out of the ear canals by turning the head to the side and pulling the ear in different directions to help the water run out. Dry the opening to the ear canal carefully. If recurrences are a big problem, rinse your child's ear canals with rubbing alcohol for 1 minute each time he or she finishes swimming or bathing.

VENTILATION TUBES SURGERY

Ventilation tubes are tiny plastic tubes that are inserted through the eardrum by an ear, nose, and throat surgeon. They are also called tympanostomy tubes, because they are placed in the tympanic membrane (eardrum). At least 1 million children in our country (most of them 1 to 3 years) have ventilation tubes placed each year. The operation costs about $300 if done in the office (only possible with older, cooperative children) and about $1,000 if it needs to be done in the hospital under brief anesthesia.

The ventilation tubes are used to drain fluid out of the middle-ear space and ventilate the area with air. The eardrum normally vibrates with sound because the space behind it (the middle ear) is filled with air. If it is filled with fluid, the hearing is muffled. This happens with ear infections. Sometimes after the infection clears, the fluid remains. This occurs if the eustachian tube (which runs from the back of the nose to the middle ear) has become blocked and no longer allows air in and fluid out. Following an ear infection, approximately 30 percent of children still have fluid in the middle ear at 1 month, 20 percent at 2 months, and 5 percent at 4 months. The main concern about prolonged fluid in the middle ear is that the associated hearing deficit may have an impact on speech development. Fluid is especially likely to persist if the first bout of ear infection occurs before 6 months of age. By age 5, the eustachian tube is wider and fluid usually doesn't persist long after ear infections are treated.

Benefits of Ventilation Tubes • Ventilation tubes allow secretions to drain out of the middle ear space and air to reenter. The risk of recurrent ear infections is greatly reduced. The hearing returns to normal with the tube in place, and speech development can get back on track. Tubes also prevent the fluid from becoming thicker (a "glue ear") and damaging the middle ear. The ventilation tubes also buy time while the child matures and the eustachian tubes begin to function better.

Risks of Ventilation Tubes • First, approximately 10 percent of children with ventilation tubes continue to have ear infections with drainage and pain. These bouts of infection, which require antibiotics, probably would have occurred anyway. Second, complications may occur around the tubes coming out. Normally the tubes come out and fall into the ear canal after about a year. Sometimes they come out too quickly and need to be replaced by another set. Rarely, they fall into the middle-ear space and need to be removed by the surgeon. If they remain in the eardrum for over two years, the ear, nose, and throat specialist may need to remove them. Third, after they come out, some leave scarring of the eardrum or a small hole (perforation) that doesn't heal. These both can cause a small hearing loss. Because of these possible complications and the requirement for an anesthetic, physcians recommend ventilation tubes only for children who definitely need them.

Dealing with Temporary Hearing Loss • As described earlier, most children with a hearing loss due to fluid in their middle ear have it on a temporary basis. During this time when you talk with your child, get close to him, get eye contact, get his full attention, and occasionally check that he understands what you have said. If not, speak in a louder voice than you normally use. A common mistake is to assume your child is ignoring you when actually he doesn't hear you. Reduce any background noise from radio or television while talking with your child. If your child goes to school, be sure he sits in front, near the teacher. (Middle-ear fluid interferes with the ability to hear in a crowd or classroom.) Keep in mind that most children's speech will catch up following a brief period of incomplete hearing.

Medical Indications for Ventilation Tubes • The surgical placement of ventilation tubes is usually indicated if several of the following conditions are met:

• The fluid has been present continuously for over 4 months.

• Both ears are involved.

- The fluid has caused a documented hearing loss. (While a loss greater than 20 Db can significantly affect speech, many children with fluid in their ears have nearly normal hearing.)

- The fluid has caused a speech delay (e.g., not using 3 words by 18 months or 20 words by 2 years).

- Recurrent ear infections have failed to respond to treatment with continuous antibiotics for several months.

Prevention of Chronic Ear Fluid • Chronic ear fluid and recurrent ear infections are usually due to a blocked eustachian tube. In some children, however, there are contributing factors:

- Exposure to adults who smoke can cause ear problems.

- Drinking a bottle while lying down (or bottle-propping) can cause milk to enter the middle-ear space.

- Children with nasal allergies have more frequent ear fluid buildup. Consider this factor if your child has associated hay fever, eczema, asthma, or food allergies.

- Children with nightly snoring due to large adenoids (see TONSIL AND ADENOID SURGERY, page 562).

  If any of these triggers are present with your child, treat or eliminate them before considering ventilation tubes.

Call Your Child's Physician During Office Hours If

- You have other questions or concerns regarding ventilation tubes.

RECOMMENDED READING
Vicki Lansky, *Ear Tubes*
(Minneapolis, Minn.: The Book Peddlers, 1990.)

NOSE

COLDS

SYMPTOMS AND CHARACTERISTICS

- Also called an upper respiratory infection (URI)
- Runny or stuffy nose
- Usually associated with fever and sore throat
- Sometimes associated with a cough, hoarseness, red eyes, and swollen lymph nodes in the neck

If your child's symptoms are different, call your physician for help.

Cause of Colds • A cold or upper respiratory infection (URI) is a viral infection of the nose and throat. The cold viruses are spread from one person to another by the mouth (kissing) or hands. Cold germs can get on your child's hands from a cold sufferer's hands or contaminated objects. Cold viruses can live on toys, phones, doorknobs, toilet handles, tables, and other objects for up to 3 hours. The virus is then transmitted to the nose or eyes, by normal face-touching habits. Airborne droplets of germs from sneezing or coughing are a rare means of cold transmission.

Once the cold germs get a foothold in the nasal passages, they start to multiply and spread downward into the throat and windpipe, causing a sore throat and cough. Since there are up to 200 cold viruses, most healthy children get at least 6 colds a year. By adolescence, the number per year starts to taper off. Cold weather, cold winds, drafts, air conditioners, and wet feet do not increase the chances of coming down with a cold.

Expected Course • Usually the fever lasts less than 3 days, and all nose and throat symptoms are gone by a week. A cough may last 2 to 3 weeks. The main things to watch for are secondary bacterial complications such as ear infections, yellow drainage from the eyes, thick pus from the nose (often indicating a sinus infection), or pneumonia. These complications may occur in 5 percent of colds because the viral infection temporarily lowers your child's resistance. In young infants, a blocked nose can interfere so much with the ability to suck, that dehydration can occur. Colds usually cause more symptoms and last longer in infants.

SIMILAR CONDITIONS

Vasomotor Rhinitis • Many children and adults have a profusely runny nose in the wintertime when they are breathing cold air. This usually clears within 15 minutes of coming indoors. It requires no treatment beyond a handkerchief and has nothing to do with infection. If you or your child must spend all day in a cold environment (for instance, on a skiing trip), you can prevent the endless nasal drip by using a long-acting vasoconstrictor spray beforehand (see under *Home Care* on page 535).

Chemical Rhinitis • Chemical rhinitis is a dry stuffy nose from excessive and prolonged use of vasoconstrictor nose drops (more than 5 days). It will be better within a day or two of stopping the nose drops.

Hay Fever • For a runny nose that sounds like an allergy, save time by turning directly to the guideline on HAY FEVER, page 540.

Sinus Infection • Suspect this complication of a cold if the nasal secretions become yellow for more than 24 hours and your child complains of sinus pressure or pain. (See SINUS CONGESTION, page 546.)

CALL YOUR CHILD'S PHYSICIAN

Immediately If

- Breathing is difficult *and* no better after you clear the nose.

- Your child acts or looks very sick.

Within 24 Hours If

- There is any suggestion of an earache or sinus pain.

- The skin under the openings of the nose is raw or scabbed over (looks like impetigo).

- The nasal discharge has been yellow (pus) for more than 24 hours.

- The discharge has been present for more than 10 days.

- The nasal discharge contains blood that is not from a simple nosebleed.

- The eyes have a yellow discharge (not just red and watery).

- The throat is quite sore (get a throat culture).

- A fever (over 100°F) has been present for more than 72 hours.

- You have other questions or concerns.

HOME CARE FOR COLDS

Remember: If you treat a cold it will be gone in a week. If you don't treat it, it will last 7 days. However, we can relieve many of the symptoms.

The Importance of Clearing the Nose in Young Infants • A child can't breathe through the mouth and suck on something at the same time. If your child is breast- or bottle-feeding, you must clear his nose out so he can breathe while he's sucking. Clearing the nasal passages is also important before putting your child down to sleep. Some babies can't breathe through the mouth during the first 6 months of life (obligate nasal breathers), so the nose must be kept open. Keep in mind that the treatment for a runny nose is quite different from that for a stuffy nose blocked with dried secretions.

Treatment for a Runny Nose with Profuse Clear Discharge • The only treatment needed is to clear the nose periodically. Sniffing and swallowing the secretions is better, because blowing the nose may force the infection into the ears or sinuses. Since most children developmentally are unable to blow the nose or sniff until age 4, use a soft rubber suction bulb to remove the secretions if they are bothering your child. Nasal discharge is the nose's way of eliminating viruses. Medicine for this stage is not recommended unless your child has a nasal allergy. However, if nasal secretions are profuse and socially inconvenient (and your child is over 1 year old), try an oral antihistamine. (See HAY FEVER, page 540, for drugs and dosages.)

Treatment for a Stuffy (Dry) Nose with Only a Little Discharge

Warm Water Nose Drops and Suctioning • Most stuffy noses are blocked by dry mucus. Suction alone or blowing the nose cannot remove most dry secretions. Warm tap-water nose drops are better than any medicine you can buy when it comes to loosening up mucus. If you prefer normal saline nose drops, mix ¼ level teaspoon of table salt in 8 ounces of water. Make up a fresh solution every few days and keep it in a clean bottle. Use a clean eyedropper or wet cotton ball to drip in drops of water.

• For the younger child who cannot blow the nose: Place 3 drops of warm water in each nostril. After 1 minute, use a soft rubber suction bulb to suck out, or a cotton swab to wipe out, the loosened mucus. Clean the bulb tip by squirting the secretions into a tissue. To remove secretions from the back of the nose, you will need to seal off both nasal openings completely with the tip of the suction bulb on one side and your finger closing the other side. You can get a suction bulb at your drugstore for about two dollars. Buy the short, stubby one with a clear-plastic mucus trap. If you cause a nosebleed, you are putting the tip of the suction bulb in too far.

• For the older child who can blow the nose: Use 3 drops as necessary in each nostril while your child is lying on her back on a bed with her head hanging over the side. Wait 1 minute for the water to soften and loosen the dried mucus. Then have your child blow her nose. This can be repeated several times in a row for complete clearing of the nasal passages.

• Errors in using warm water nose drops: The main errors are not putting in enough water, not waiting long enough for secretions to loosen up, and not repeating the procedure until the breathing is easy. The front of the nose can look open while the back of the nose is all gummed up with dried mucus. Obviously, putting in warm water nose drops without suctioning afterward is of little value.

Decongestant Nose Drops or Spray for a Stuffy Nose • If nasal congestion interferes with breathing despite warm water nose drops, buy some nonprescription vasoconstrictor nose drops.

- For 6 months to 2 years of age: ⅛ percent Neosynephrine nose drops every 2 to 3 hours as needed (especially before feeding).

- For 2 to 6 years of age: Pediatric strength, long-acting nose drops or spray every 8 to 12 hours as needed.

- Over 6 years of age: adult-strength, long-acting nose drops or spray every 8 to 12 hours as needed. (These products usually contain oxymetazoline or xylometazoline.)

Cautions:

- Use 1 drop or spray on each side.

- Do not use for children under 6 months of age.

- Use only after the nose has been cleaned out with saline or nose drops.

- Don't repeat unless nasal congestion recurs.

- Don't use for more than 5 days because they can irritate the nose and make it more congested.

- Don't use for noisy breathing unless it makes your child uncomfortable or interferes with feeding.

Treatment for Associated Symptoms of Colds

Fever • Use acetaminophen for muscle aches, headaches, or moderate fever (over 102°F). (For dosage, see FEVER, page 407.) Avoid aspirin because of the possible link with Reyes syndrome.

Sore Throat • Use hard candies and saltwater gargles for children over 4 years old.

Cough • Use cough drops for children over 4 years old, and corn syrup for younger children. Run a humidifier.

Red Eyes • Rinse frequently with wet cotton balls.

Poor Appetite • Encourage fluids of the child's choice. A recent study showed that eating chicken noodle soup loosened nasal mucus. The old saying "Feed a fever and starve a cold" has little merit. "Feeding a fever" isn't too far off the mark, since fevers do burn extra calories. If you tried to "starve a cold," however, a child could become dehydrated.

Common Mistakes • Most cold remedies or tablets are worthless. Also, oral medicines have no ability to remove dried nasal secretions. If the nose is really running, consider a pure anti-histamine such as chlorpheniramine products. (See HAY FE-VER, page 540, for dosages) or an antihistamine-decongestant product. Prescription cold medicines offer no advantages over nonprescription products. Avoid drugs that have several ingredients; they increase the risk of side effects. Avoid oral decongestants if they make your child jittery or keep the child from sleeping at night.

Use acetaminophen for a cold only if your child also has fever, sore throat, or muscle aches.

Leftover antibiotics should not be given because they have no effect on viruses and may be harmful.

The role of steam inhalation devices in treating cold symptoms gets mixed reviews in recent research.

Call Your Child's Physician Later If

• Your child is under 3 months of age *and* develops a fever.

• The fever lasts more than 3 days.

• The nasal discharge lasts more than 7 days.

• The discharge becomes consistently thick and yellow for more than 24 hours.

• The skin under the openings of the nose becomes raw or scabbed over.

• The eyes develop a yellow discharge.

• You can't unblock the nose enough for your infant to take adequate fluids.

• Breathing becomes difficult *and* not due to the stuffy nose.

• There is any suggestion of an earache or sinus pain.

- The throat becomes quite sore (get a throat culture).

- You feel your child is getting worse.

PREVENTION OF COLDS

Over the years, we all become exposed to many cold viruses and develop some immunity to them.

- Since complications are more common in children during the first year of life, try to avoid undue exposure of young babies to other children or adults with colds, to daycare nurseries, church nurseries, and crowded shopping centers. A parent can't control the majority of contact, however.

- Since the cold viruses are commonly transmitted by hand contamination, frequent hand rinsing and keeping the hands away from the nose and mouth are the most helpful steps in prevention.

- While coughing isn't contagious, sneezing is. Teach your child to cover the nose during sneezing.

- A humidifier prevents dry mucus membranes, which may be more susceptible to infections. Clean the humidifier once per week with a bleach solution.

- Nasal tissues containing virus-killing chemicals are an expensive substitute for careful disposal of regular tissues after they are used.

- Vitamin C, unfortunately, has not been shown to prevent or shorten colds. Large doses (like 2 grams) can cause diarrhea.

RELATED TOPICS

FOREIGN BODY, NOSE

Young children often put foreign objects in their nostrils and then forget about them. Favorites are food, seeds, nuts, paper, cotton, foam, stones, and beads. The body tries to reject these intruders by producing a foul-smelling yellow nasal discharge. Sometimes food particles (such as rice) end up in the nose following vomiting.

FIRST AID

Have your child blow his nose vigorously several times while closing the other nostril. Sometimes this action will expel the object. Vomited food can be removed by repeatedly blowing the nose after splashing some water into it. If you successfully remove the object, call your child's physician later only if a yellow nasal discharge occurs.

CALL YOUR CHILD'S PHYSICIAN IMMEDIATELY IF THESE MEASURES FAIL

It is critical that you do not try to remove the object by putting anything into the nose, including tweezers and fingers. This almost always pushes the object in farther and makes the physician's job very difficult, even with special instruments. Watch closely to see that your child doesn't push it in.

HAY FEVER (ALLERGIC RHINITIS)

SYMPTOMS AND CHARACTERISTICS

- Clear nasal discharge with sneezing, sniffing, and nasal itching

- Symptoms occur during pollen season

- Similar symptoms during the same month of the previous year

- Previous confirmation of this diagnosis by a physician is helpful

- Eye allergies are commonly associated

- A tickling sensation in the back of the throat can be associated

- Sinus or ear congestion are sometimes associated

- No fever

  If your child's symptoms are different, call your physician for help.

Cause • Hay fever is an allergic reaction of the nose (and sinuses) to an inhaled substance. The sensitivity is often inherited, so other family members may also have hay fever. During late April and May the most common offending pollen is from trees. From late May to mid-July, the offending pollen is usually grass. From late August to the first frost, the leading cause of hay fever is ragweed pollen. Although the inhaled substance is usually a pollen, it can also be animal dander, feathers, or other agents your child is allergic to. Cats are the most allergic of our pets. Over 30 percent of allergic people react to cats. Cat dander remains in a house for several years after the cat has moved. Cat dander will also find its way into your home on a cat owner's clothing. Hay fever is the most common allergy; over 15 percent of people have it. Skin tests or blood tests are usually unnecessary for diagnosis. These children are not allergic to hay (nor do they have a fever).

Expected Course • This is a chronic condition that will probably recur every year, perhaps for a lifetime. Therefore, learning how to control it is worth your while.

CALL YOUR CHILD'S PHYSICIAN DURING OFFICE HOURS IF

- Your child is also coughing a lot.

- The symptoms are constant rather than seasonal.

- The nasal secretions are yellow for over 24 hours.

- You have other questions or concerns.

HOME CARE FOR HAY FEVER

Antihistamine Medicine • The best drug for hay fever is an antihistamine. Some effective nonprescription ones are Chlortrimeton, Dimetane, and Teldrin. Symptoms clear up faster if antihistamines are given at the first sign of sneezing or sniffing. For children with occasional symptoms, the antihistamines can be taken on days when symptoms are present or expected. For children with daily symptoms, the best control is attained if antihistamines are taken continuously throughout the pollen season. The bedtime dosage is especially important for helping the nose repair itself during the night.

Dosages for chlorpheniramine: the short-acting liquid or tablet preparations must be given every 6 to 8 hours. For children over 20 pounds, give 1 mg. For children 3 to 6 years, give 1½ mg. For children 7 to 11 years, give 2 mg. Adolescents and adults can take 4 mg.

For convenience, children age 6 to 12 can take 8 mg long-acting pills every 12 hours for prevention of symptoms. Those over age 12 (more than 90 pounds) can take 12 mg long-acting pills of chlorpheniramine every 12 hours.

The main side effect of antihistamines is drowsiness. If your child gets drowsy, continue the drug, but temporarily decrease the dosage. In 1 to 2 weeks the regular dosage usually will be tolerated without much drowsiness. If the drowsiness becomes a problem, switch to a combination product that contains an antihistamine with a decongestant (such as pseudoephedrine or phenylpropanolamine).

Pollen Removal • Pollen tends to collect on the exposed body surface and especially in the hair. Shower your child and wash the hair any time lots of symptoms (especially itchy or burning skin) are present, following heavy exposure to pollen. At a minimum, shower your child every night before going to bed. Avoid handling pets that have been outside and are probably covered with pollen.

Eye Allergies Associated with Hay Fever • If your child also has itchy, watery eyes, some additional treatment measures are in order. Wash the face and eyelids to remove the pollen. Then apply a cold compress to the eyelids. Also, instill 2 drops of long-acting vasoconstrictor eyedrops every 8 to 12 hours as necessary (no prescription needed). Ask your pharmacist for help in choosing a reliable product.

Common Mistakes • Nose drops or nasal sprays usually do not help hay fever, because they are washed out of the nose by nasal secretions as soon as they have been instilled. Also, when used for more than 5 days, they can irritate the nose and make it more congested.

Call Your Child's Physician Later If

- The treatment does not relieve most of the symptoms.

- Your child is missing any school, work, social activities, or sleep because of hay fever.

- Your child develops symptoms of a sinus infection (see page 546).

- Any other changes concern you.

Good News • *Severe* hay fever can now usually be controlled by cromolyn or steroid nasal sprays (called Nasalcrom or Beclomethasone respectively) rather than requiring hyposensitization (allergy shots). These sprays are available by prescription. They must be used when the nose is not dripping. Antihistamines can be used first to turn it off.

PREVENTION OF HAY FEVER SYMPTOMS

- Reduce pollen exposure by closing car windows (if possible) during drives in the country, staying indoors when it is windy, closing the windows that face the prevailing winds, turning off attic fans, and not having your child near when someone is cutting the grass during pollen season (especially when the pollen count is high). Routinely keeping your child indoors during the pollen season, however, is overtreatment.

- Avoid feather pillows, pets, farms, stables, and tobacco smoke if any of them seem to bring on or accentuate symptoms of nasal allergy. If your child is allergic to one dog, usually he is allergic to all dogs. Short hair or long hair makes no difference, since the allergy is to the dog saliva, not the hair.

- If the hay fever is especially bad, you may wish to take your child to an air-conditioned store or theater for a few hours.

- For exposure you can't avoid, give an antihistamine 1 hour before and a shower immediately afterward.

Pollen-Free Vacations • If your child is allergic to ragweed, you may wish to plan an August vacation to an area that has little or no ragweed. In essence, the pollen count is highest in the Midwest, and only the coastal areas of Washington, Oregon, and California are free of ragweed pollen. You may wish to write to Abbott Laboratories, Public Affairs Section, North

Chicago, Illinois 60064, for a free map of the country with details on ragweed distribution. This booklet is called "Hayfever Holiday." Moving to another part of the country to avoid pollens is usually not worth the sacrifice, because within 3 years your child will usually develop allergies to plants in the new location.

RELATED TOPICS

EAR CONGESTION (see page 516)
EYE, ALLERGIES (see page 502)
SINUS CONGESTION (see page 546)

NOSEBLEED

Nosebleeds (epistaxsis) are very common throughout childhood. They are usually caused by dryness of the nasal lining, plus the normal rubbing and picking that all children do. Vigorous nose-blowing can also cause them. All of these behaviors are increased in children with nasal allergies. Many times they begin unexpectedly, even during sleep. If the nosebleed was caused by an injury, turn directly to the guideline on NOSE TRAUMA, page 78.

CALL YOUR CHILD'S PHYSICIAN

Immediately If

- There are any skin bruises not caused by an injury.

- Your child also has unexplained bleeding from the mouth or gums.

- Your child has fainted or feels dizzy when he or she stands up.

- A huge amount of blood has been lost.

- Your child acts or looks very sick.

During Office Hours If

- A concerning amount of blood has been lost.

- Your child is under 1 year old.

- Difficult-to-stop nosebleeds are a recurrent problem for your child.

- Your family has a history of easy bleeding.

- You have other questions or concerns.

HOME CARE

Lean Forward and Spit Out Any Blood • Have your child sit up and lean forward so he or she does not have to swallow the blood. Have a basin so your child can spit out any blood that drains into the throat. Your child's nose should be blown free of any large clots that interfere with pressure.

Squeeze the Soft Part of the Nose • Then tightly pinch the soft parts of the nose against the center wall for 10 minutes. Don't release the pressure until 10 minutes are up. If the bleeding continues, you may not be pressing on the right spot. During this time, tell your child to breathe through the mouth. Reassure your child that you can stop the bleeding.

If All Else Fails, Use Vasoconstrictor Nosedrops and Squeeze Again • If the nosebleed hasn't stopped, insert a gauze covered with vasoconstrictor nose drops (e.g., Neosynephrine) or petroleum jelly into the nostril. Squeeze again for 10 minutes. Leave the gauze in for another 10 minutes before removing it. If bleeding persists, call your physician, but continue the pressure in the meantime.

Common Mistakes

- A cold washcloth applied to the forehead, back of the neck, or under the upper lip does not help stop nosebleeds.

- Pressing on the bony part of the nose.

- Avoid packing the nose with anything, because when it is removed, bleeding usually recurs.

- Swallowed blood is irritating to the stomach. Don't be surprised or worried if it is vomited up.

Call Your Child's Physician Later If

- The bleeding has not stopped after two 10-minute attempts at pinching the nostrils closed.

- Nosebleeds occur daily even after petroleum jelly and humidification are used.

- Any other symptoms concern you.

PREVENTION

- A small amount of petroleum jelly applied twice a day to the center wall (septum) inside the nose is often helpful for relieving dryness and irritation.

- Increasing the humidity in the home by using a humidifier may also be helpful.

- If your child picks his nose a lot, help him give up this habit or at least make him more aware of it. With his permission, have him put a Band-Aid on his index finger each morning as a reminder. Also cut his fingernails weekly.

- Get your child into the habit of putting 2 or 3 drops of warm water in each nostril before blowing a stuffy nose.

- In addition, avoid aspirin temporarily. One aspirin can increase the tendency of the body to bleed easily for up to a week and can make nosebleeds last much longer.

- If your child has nasal allergies, treating them with antihistamines will help break the itching-bleeding cycle. (See HAY FEVER, page 540.)

SINUS CONGESTION

SYMPTOMS AND CHARACTERISTICS

- Sensation of fullness, pressure, or pain on the face overlying a sinus

- Pain can be above the eyebrow, behind the eye, or over the cheekbone

- Pain is usually just on one side of the face

- Runny or blocked nose

- A sensation of continuous postnasal drip

- Sinus congestion documented by a physician one or more times in the past is helpful

If your child's symptoms are different, call your physician for help.

Cause • The nose has seven bony, air-filled chambers (sinuses) that help to warm and humidify the air passing through it. Sinus congestion occurs when the sinus openings are blocked and normal sinus secretions accumulate and cause a sensation of pressure and fullness. Sinusitis occurs mainly with colds and hay fever.

Expected Course • Without treatment, the sinuses usually open after about a week. The main complication is when bacteria multiply within the blocked sinus. This leads to a yellow nasal discharge and increased pain. Sometimes the overlying skin (around the eye or cheek) becomes red or swollen. This type of sinusitis needs antibiotics. Frequent throat-clearing of postnasal secretions usually leads to a sore throat. Swallowing the sinus secretions is normal and harmless but may cause some nausea. Recent studies have shown that sinus infections can cause a chronic cough (or even wheezing).

CALL YOUR CHILD'S PHYSICIAN

Immediately If

- Redness or swelling occurs on the cheek, eyelids, or forehead.
- Your child acts or looks very sick.

Within 24 Hours If

- Your child is under 5 years old.
- A fever (over 100°F) is present.
- The nasal secretions are yellow.
- Your child is also coughing a lot.
- The pain keeps your child from getting enough sleep.
- You have other questions or concerns.

HOME CARE

Inhalation of Warm Mist • The main purpose of treatment is to open the sinuses so they can drain. Inhalation of warm moisture for 10 to 20 minutes, 4 times a day, is helpful. The easiest method is to cover the nose and mouth with a warm wet washcloth and have your child breathe through it. Another way to do this is to put warm water into a humidifier (not a vaporizer) and lean over the mist it gives off.

Decongestant Nose Drops or Spray • If the sinus still seems blocked after the inhalation of warm mist, long-acting vasoconstrictor nose drops or sprays (such as oxymetazoline) should be used. These are nonprescription items; ask your pharmacist to recommend a brand. The usual dose for adolescents is 2 drops or sprays per side twice a day. For younger children use 1 drop or spray. Use them routinely for the first 3 days of treatment. Then don't repeat them unless the sinus congestion or pain recurs. The nose should first be cleared by sniffing or nasal suction.

The openings to the sinuses are on the outer side of the nasal passages. Point the nasal spray in this direction. To deliver nose drops to this location, they must be put in while your child is lying on a bed with the head tipped back and turned to one side.

The drops or spray must be stopped for 2 days out of every 7 to prevent rebound swelling.

Pain Relief Medicines • Your child will usually need to take acetaminophen temporarily to relieve pain until the obstructed sinus is opened. The application of ice over the sinus may also help to relieve pain.

Oral Antihistamines • If your child also has hay fever, give him his allergy medicine. If your child is not allergic, avoid oral antihistamines because they can slow down the movement of secretions out of the sinuses.

Contagiousness • Sinus infections are not contagious. Your child can return to school or daycare when he or she is feeling better and the fever is gone.

Call Your Child's Physician Later If

• Your child develops a fever.

- A yellow nasal discharge occurs *and* lasts for more than 24 hours.
- Redness or swelling of the overlying skin occurs.
- The sinus discomfort persists for more than 1 week.
- The sinus pain becomes so bad that it interferes with sleep.
- You feel your child is getting worse.

PREVENTION

Jumping into the water feet first can cause sinusitis of the frontal sinuses and should be avoided unless the nose is pinched. Swimming does not worsen sinusitis, but deep diving should be forbidden unless your child wears nose plugs.

RELATED TOPICS

COLDS (see page 533)
HAY FEVER (see page 540)

MOUTH AND THROAT

BAD BREATH (HALITOSIS)

SYMPTOMS AND CHARACTERISTICS

- An unpleasant odor to the exhaled breath
- The problem can be a recent or longstanding one
- Bad breath only on awakening is normal and due to poor saliva flow at night

Causes • Causes are numerous. If your child has one of the following, turn directly to that guideline:

CANKER SORES (see page 551)
COLDS (see page 533)
SINUS CONGESTION (see page 546)
SORE THROAT (see page 556)

- If your child has dental cavities, make a dental appointment.
- If your child is forgetful about brushing her teeth, help her brush more frequently.
- If your child sucks the thumb, a blanket, or other object, the bad breath will resolve when this habit is given up. Over age 4, ask your child's physician about some ways to discourage it before the permanent teeth come in. (See THUMBSUCKING, page 325.)

CALL YOUR CHILD'S PHYSICIAN DURING OFFICE HOURS IF

• The cause of your child's bad breath remains unclear.

HOME CARE

More frequent toothbrushing improves most cases of mild bad breath. Also brush the surface of the tongue. Mouthwashes and chewable breath fresheners are heavily promoted in our society but provide temporary improvement at best. Since some products contain 20 to 30 percent alcohol, they also carry a risk of poisoning in children who swallow them. The complaint of foul breath is unusual in children, and the cause should be uncovered and dealt with directly.

CANKER SORES (MOUTH ULCERS)

SYMPTOMS AND CHARACTERISTICS

• Painful, shallow ulcers (sores) of the lining of the mouth

• The gums or inner sides of the lips or cheeks are the usual sites

• No fever

If your child's symptoms are different, call your physician for help.

Similar Condition • If thrush is suspected, save time by turning directly to the guideline for THRUSH, page 137.

Cause • The cause of canker sores is unknown, but some may be due to prolonged contact with food that gets stuck in the teeth. Others may be due to forgotten injuries from toothbrushes, toothpicks, rough foods (e.g., corn chips), hot foods or self-biting. Herpes simplex causes recurrent fever blisters (on the outside of the lip) but does not cause recurrent canker sores (of the inner mouth).

Expected Course • The white color of canker sores is the normal color of healing tissue in the mouth. This is not pus. They heal up in 1 to 2 weeks. Once begun, no treatment shortens the course. For many people they are a recurrent problem.

CALL YOUR CHILD'S PHYSICIAN

Immediately If

- Your child could have swallowed an acid or alkali.

During Office Hours If

- Four or more mouth ulcers are present.
- The gums are red, swollen, and tender.
- A raised yellow (or red) bump is present on the gums.
- A fever (over 100°F) is present.
- Fluid intake is poor.
- The eyelids or genitals have any ulcers.
- The canker sores began after taking a medicine.
- You have other questions or concerns.

HOME CARE

Pain Relief • To reduce the pain, swish 1 tablespoon of an antacid solution in the mouth for several minutes. For a single ulcer, apply an antacid tablet and let it dissolve. This can be repeated 3 or 4 times a day. Give acetaminophen as necessary for pain (especially at bedtime).

Diet • The diet can be changed to reduce the pain. Use a glass instead of a bottle if your child is a baby. Avoid giving your child salty or citrus foods and foods that need much chewing. Change to a soft diet for a few days. Cold drinks and milk-shakes are especially good. If toothbrushing is painful, have your child rinse the mouth with water after meals.

Call Your Child's Physician Later If

- The pain is severe.
- Your child can't take adequate fluids.
- The mouth ulcers increase to 4 or more in number.
- They last for more than 2 weeks.
- Your child develops a fever or other symptoms.
- You feel your child is getting worse.

PREVENTION

Canker sores tend to recur throughout life. Good attention to toothbrushing after meals may prevent some. Be careful with toothpicks and rough foods. Try to identify any offending foods. Were tomato, citrus fruit, peppermint, cinnamon, nuts, or shellfish taken within the last day? If you find a food that you think may be causing the problem, eliminate it from the diet for 2 weeks and then offer some to see whether it causes a recurrence of the canker sores. If it does, the food should be eliminated from the diet permanently.

COLD SORES (FEVER BLISTERS)

SYMPTOMS AND CHARACTERISTICS

- A cluster of painful 1-mm to 2-mm bumps or blisters on the outer lip

- On one side of the mouth only

- Tingling or burning on the outer lip where cold sores previously occurred (i.e., an early diagnosis of recurrent cold sores)

  If your child's symptoms are different, call your physician for help.

Cause • Cold sores are caused by the herpes simplex virus (usually Type I). The first bout follows contact with someone else with herpes. Recurrences occur in 2 percent of people who carry the virus in a sensory nerve. The virus is reactivated by sunburn, fever, friction, menstrual periods, or physical exhaustion.

Expected Course • The blisters go on to rupture, scab over, and dry up. The whole process takes 10 to 14 days. They do not cause scars. Treatment can shorten the course by several days.

HOME CARE

Treatment

- If you feel tingling in the usual place but blisters are not yet present, apply an ice cube or ice pack continuously for 90 minutes. This may abort the infection.

• Once you get fever blisters, you usually can't shorten the course unless you start applying an antiherpes ointment as soon as any small bumps appear. These ointments require a prescription. If you don't have an antiherpes ointment, cover the fever blisters with petroleum jelly to reduce the pain and to promote healing.

Call Your Child's Physician During Office Hours If

• You have questions about antiherpes ointments.

• The sores are spreading.

• Any sores occur near the eye.

• The sores last more than 2 weeks.

PREVENTION

Since fever blisters are often triggered by exposure to intense sunlight, prevent them in the future by using a lip balm containing sunscreen. Avoid spreading this germ to the eye, because an infection there can be serious. Therefore, discourage picking or rubbing and wash the hands frequently.

If your teenager is going skiing or to the beach and had frequent herpes flareups in the past, despite careful use of sunscreen, talk to your physician. Recent research has found that starting an antiherpes pill by mouth before such outings can prevent most flareups.

Since the condition is contagious, avoid kissing other people during this time. If your child is young and puts everything in his or her mouth, avoid sharing toys with other children for a week. In general, most children under age 6 need to stay away from other children until the sores are dry (4 or 5 days). Although one should be careful about contagion, the child with herpes should not be made to feel like a leper. Fever blisters are not a sexually transmitted disease. By age 6, more than 50 percent of children already have antibodies to the cold sore virus.

GEOGRAPHIC TONGUE

SYMPTOMS AND CHARACTERISTICS

- The tongue develops smooth red patches of various shapes and sizes

- The pattern resembles a map, and can change from week to week

- The bare spots are painless, and the sense of taste is preserved

- The condition usually occurs in children under 6 years of age and the cause is unknown, but it is not due to a vitamin deficiency

- The tongue returns to normal appearance after a period of months to years

HOME CARE

The condition is harmless and no treatment is helpful or necessary. No disease looks like geographic tongue, but if you are uncertain of the diagnosis, call your child's physician during office hours.

LIP, SWOLLEN

The sudden onset of a swollen lip without an injury is usually due to a local allergic reaction. Symptoms of itching or tingling are also present. The allergic substance can be a food, toothpaste, lipstick, lip balm, or other irritant (such as an evergreen resin) that inadvertently is transferred from the hands.

If one of the following is suspected, save time by turning directly to that guideline:

BITES, INSECT (see page 18)
COLD SORES (see page 553)
MOUTH TRAUMA (see page 77)
POISONING (see page 55)

CALL YOUR CHILD'S PHYSICIAN IMMEDIATELY IF

- Breathing or swallowing is difficult.
- The area looks like a burn.
- The swelling is tender to the touch.
- A fever (over 100°F) is present.
- Your child acts or looks very sick.

HOME CARE

Wash the lips and face with soap and water to remove any irritating substances. Apply ice to the swelling for 20 minutes out of every hour. If you have an antihistamine in your home (see HIVES, page 435, for details), give your child the correct dosage 1 or 2 times. In the future, avoid any substance you are suspicious of.

Call your child's physician if the swelling becomes worse or it lasts more than 2 days.

SORE THROAT (PHARYNGITIS)

SYMPTOMS AND CHARACTERISTICS

- Complaint of a sore throat
- In children too young to talk, a sore throat may be suspected if they refuse to eat or begin to cry during feedings
- When examined with a light, the throat is bright red

  If your child's symptoms are different, call your physician for help.

Causes • Most sore throats are caused by viruses and are part of a cold. About 10 percent of sore throats are due to strep bacteria. A throat culture or rapid strep test are the only ways to tell strep pharyngitis from viral pharyngitis. This identification of strep throat is important because without treatment some rare but serious complications (rheumatic fever or glomerulonephritis) can occur. Early treatment also prevents spread of strep to family and friends. A recent study showed that strep is not transmitted by pets.

Tonsillitis (temporary swelling and redness of the tonsils) is usually present with any throat infection, viral or bacterial. The presence of tonsillitis does not have any special meaning.

Children who sleep with their mouths open often wake in the morning with a dry mouth and sore throat. It clears within an hour of having something to drink. Use a humidifier to help prevent this problem. Children with a postnasal drip from draining sinuses often have a sore throat from frequent throat-clearing.

Expected Course • Sore throats with viral illnesses usually last 3 or 4 days. Strep throat responds nicely to penicillin. After 24 hours on medication, strep is no longer contagious, and your child can return to daycare or school if the fever is gone and the child is feeling better.

CALL YOUR CHILD'S PHYSICIAN

Immediately If

• The pain is severe.

• Your child is drooling, spitting, or having great difficulty swallowing.

• Your child can't fully open his mouth.

• Breathing is difficult *and* not due to a stuffy nose.

• Your child acts or looks very sick.

During Office Hours to Make an Appointment for a Throat Culture If

• A fever over 100°F is present.

• The sore throat has been present more than 24 hours.
  Exception: If the sore throat is very mild *and* the main symptom is croup, hoarseness, or a cough, a throat culture is probably not needed.

• There are any swollen or tender lymph glands in the neck.

• There is any associated abdominal pain.

• There was any recent contact with a person with a strep throat or impetigo.

• Your child has a sunburned-looking rash.

• You see any yellow or white spots on the tonsils while looking at them with a light.

• You have other questions.

HOME CARE

Local Pain Relief • Children over age 6 or 8 can gargle with warm salt water (¼ teaspoon salt per glass) or an antacid solution. Children over age 4 can suck on hard candy (butterscotch seems to be a soothing flavor) as often as needed. Younger children can be given a teaspoon of corn syrup or honey periodically to soothe the throat. (Avoid giving honey under 1 year of age because of the small risk of botulism in this age group).

Swollen tonsils can make some foods hard to swallow. Provide your child with a soft diet for a few days if it is preferred.

Fever • Acetaminophen may be given for a few days if your child has a fever over 102°F (39°C) or a great deal of throat discomfort. (For dosage, see FEVER, page 407.)

Common Mistakes

• Avoid expensive throat sprays or throat lozenges. Not only are they no more effective than hard candy, many also contain an ingredient (benzocaine) that may cause a drug reaction.

• Avoid using leftover antibiotics from siblings or friends. These should be thrown out because they deteriorate faster than other drugs. Unfortunately, antibiotics only help strep throats. They have no effect on viruses, and they can cause harm. They also make it difficult to find out what is wrong if your child becomes sicker.

• Avoid rapid strep tests performed in shopping malls or at home because they tend to be inaccurate. If you want a rapid strep test, contact your child's physican. These tests are helpful only if positive. If they are negative, a throat culture should be performed to pick up the 20 percent of strep infections that the rapid tests miss.

Call Your Child's Physician Later If

• A sunburned-looking rash appears.

• Breathing or swallowing becomes difficult.

• The sore throat lasts more than 48 hours (without major improvement).

• A fever (over 101°F) occurs.

RELATED TOPIC

CANKER SORES (see page 551)

SWALLOWING DIFFICULTY (DYSPHAGIA)

Difficulty in swallowing is usually due to a sore throat or mouth ulcers in a child too young to tell us what's happening. However, it can be caused by some serious conditions.

CALL YOUR CHILD'S PHYSICIAN*
Immediately If

- Your child is having any difficulty breathing.

- Your child has croup.

- Your child is drooling (or spitting) saliva and unable to swallow anything.

- This could be a reaction to a food, drug, or insect sting.

- A foreign object or bone could possibly be caught in the throat.

- Your child could have swallowed some acid, alkali, or other poison.

- Your child can't fully open his mouth.

- Your child has not urinated in more than 8 hours.

- Your child acts or looks very sick.

During Office Hours If
- You do not know the cause of your child's swallowing difficulty.

RELATED TOPICS

CANKER SORES (see page 551)
SORE THROAT (see page 556)

*Call a rescue squad (911) if your child is having serious problems breathing.

TEETHING

Teething is the normal process of new teeth working their way through the gums. "Cutting teeth" is too strong a term. The first teeth normally erupt between 6 and 10 months of age in the lower jaw. Most children have completely painless teething. The only symptoms are increased saliva, drooling, and a desire to chew on things. Teething occasionally causes some mild gum pain, but not enough to interfere with sleep. Your child won't be miserable from teething. When the back teeth (molars) come through (6 to 12 years old), the overlying gum may become bruised and swollen (an eruption hematoma). This is harmless and temporary.

Delayed eruption of primary teeth is rarely a problem. If no teeth are present by 12 months of age, contact a pediatric dentist (pedodontist).

Usually the primary (baby) tooth falls out before the corresponding permanent tooth erupts. Occasionally both teeth are temporarily present. As long as the baby tooth is a little loose, everything should go well. Have your child wiggle the baby tooth each day. The permanent tooth will find its way to the correct position once the baby tooth is out. If the primary tooth is still in place after 1 month of rocking, go to your child's dentist.

HOME CARE

Gum Massage • Find the irritated or swollen gum. Vigorously massage it with your finger for 2 minutes. Do this as often as necessary. If you wish, you may use a piece of ice to massage the gum.

Teething Rings • Your baby's way of massaging the gums is to chew on a smooth, hard object. Solid teething rings and ones with liquid in the center (as long as it's purified water) are fine. Most children like them cold. A wet washcloth placed in the freezer for 30 minutes will please many infants.

Your child may also like some ice, a Popsicle, or a frozen banana (cut it into pieces first). Avoid hard foods that your baby might choke on (like raw carrots), but teething biscuits are fine.

Diet • Avoid salty or acid foods. Your baby probably will enjoy sucking on a nipple, but if that seems to cause pain, use a cup for fluids temporarily. A few babies may need acetaminophen for pain relief for a few days.

Common Mistakes

- Since teeth erupt almost continuously from 6 months to 2 years of age, many unrelated illnesses are blamed on teething. Fevers are also common during this time because after 6 months infants lose the natural protection provided by their mother's antibodies.

- Teething does not cause fever, sleep problems, diarrhea, diaper rash, or lowered resistance to any infection. It probably doesn't cause crying. If your child has any of these symptoms, see that guideline. If your baby develops fever while teething, the fever is due to something else, so refer to the guideline on FEVER, page 407.

- Special teething gels and lotions are unnecessary. Since many contain benzocaine, there is a risk that they may cause choking due to numbing the throat or a drug reaction.

- Don't tie the teething ring around the neck. It could catch on something and strangle your child. Use a "catch-it-clip."

CALL YOUR CHILD'S PHYSICIAN DURING OFFICE HOURS IF

- You have other questions or concerns.

TONGUE-TIE

True tongue-tie, or tight tongue, is a very rare condition. The length of the lingual frenum, which is a thin band of tissue under the tongue, varies among individuals. At birth, the tongue is normally short and the band is tight. The tongue grows and the band stretches with use. After 1 year of age any tightness may be considered abnormal only if:

- The tip of the tongue can't be protruded past the teeth or gumline

- The end of the tongue becomes notched when it is protruded

Without these findings, your child's tongue is normal.

TREATMENT FOR TONGUE-TIE

If your child has these findings, mention them during your next health supervision visit. Keep in mind that a tongue with less movement than normal does not cause delay or difficulty with speech or sucking. Clipping of the band under the tongue is rarely done anymore, because it is usually unnecessary and also carries the risk of bleeding, infection, and tight scar tissue. It is never done before 1 year of age.

TONSIL AND ADENOID SURGERY

Surgical removal of the tonsils and adenoids (known as a T&A) is the most common operation performed on children in our country (400,000 per year). It has been described as "an American ritual." While as many as 30 percent of children in some communities undergo a T&A, only 2 or 3 percent of children have adequate medical indications for this procedure. Although the decision to proceed is a medical one, the frequency of questionable surgery means that parents need to be armed with more facts.

The tonsils are not just some worthless pieces of tissue that block our view of the throat. They have a purpose. They produce antibodies that fight nose and throat infections. They confine the infection to the throat, rather than allowing it to spread to the neck or bloodstream. Other beneficial functions of the tonsils and adenoids are under study.

RISKS OF A T&A

T&A procedures are not without risk. Under ideal conditions, the death rate is still 1 child per 15,000 operations. Approximately 5 percent of children bleed on the fifth to eighth postoperative day and require a transfusion or additional surgery. All the children experience throat discomfort for several days. Some children with previously normal speech develop hypernasal speech because the soft palate no longer closes completely. In addition, the operation is expensive (costing $1,500 per patient).

ERRONEOUS REASONS FOR A T&A

Many T&A's are performed for the following unwarranted reasons. By all means, don't pressure a physician to remove your child's tonsils. A few physicians have difficulty saying no. You can always find someone to perform surgery on your child; in fact, this is the main risk of "doctor-shopping."

"Large Tonsils" • Large tonsils do not mean "bad" tonsils or "infected" tonsils. The tonsils are normally large during childhood (called "physiological hypertrophy"). They can't be "too large" unless they touch each other. The peak size is reached between 8 and 12 years of age. Thereafter, they spontaneously shrink in size each year, as do all of the body's lymph tissues.

Recurrent Colds and Viral Sore Throats • Several studies have shown that T&A's do not decrease the frequency of viral upper respiratory infections. These URIs are unavoidable. Eventually your child develops immunity to these viruses and experiences fewer colds per year.

Recurrent Strep Throats • Newer studies have shown that the frequency of streptococcal infections of the throat do not decrease after the tonsils are removed unless your child experiences 7 or more per year (a rare occurrence). In children with 7 or more severe throat infections per year, some physicians would recommend daily penicillin for 6 months instead of a T&A, since penicillin can almost always eradicate the strep bacteria from the tonsils. The strep carrier state (which causes no symptoms, is harmless, and is not contagious) is not an indication for a T&A.

Recurrent Ear Infections • While formerly controversial, newer studies have shown that removal of the adenoids will not open the eustachian tube and decrease the frequency of ear infections or fluid in the middle ear. The exceptions are children who also have persistent nasal obstruction and mouth breathing due to large adenoids. Recurrent ear infections usually respond to a 3-month course of antibiotics. Persistent middle-ear fluid may need ventilation tubes inserted in the eardrums.

School Absence • If your child misses school for vague reasons (including sore throats), removing the tonsils will not improve attendance. (See SCHOOL PHOBIA OR REFUSAL, page 351.)

Miscellaneous Conditions • A T&A will not help a poor appetite, hay fever, asthma, febrile convulsions, or bad breath. There is little in medicine that has not at one time or another been blamed on the tonsils.

MEDICAL INDICATIONS FOR A T&A

Yes, sometimes the tonsils should come out. But the benefits must outweigh the risks. All of the following valid reasons are rare, with the exception of the first two. The ear, nose, and throat doctor will decide if the tonsils, adenoids, or both need removal.

Persistent Mouth-Breathing • Mouth-breathing during colds or hay fever is common. Continued mouth breathing is less common and deserves an evaluation to see if it is due to large adenoids. The open-mouth appearance results in teasing, and the mouth breathing itself leads to changes in the facial bone structure (including an overbite which could need orthodontia).

Abnormal Speech • The speech can be muffled by large tonsils or made hyponasal (no nasal resonance) by large adenoids. Although other causes are possible, an evaluation is in order.

Severe Snoring • Snoring can have many causes. If the adenoids are the cause, they should be removed. In severe cases, the loud snoring is associated with retractions (pulling in of the spaces between the ribs) and is interrupted by 30- to 60-second bouts of stopped breathing (sleep apnea). If your child has severe snoring, make a 5-minute audiotape and bring it to your physician for a listen.

Heart Failure • Rarely, large tonsils and adenoids interfere so much with breathing that blood oxygen is reduced, and the right side of the heart goes into failure. Children with this condition are short of breath, have limited exercise tolerance, and have a rapid pulse.

Persistent Swallowing Difficulties • During a throat infection, the tonsils may temporarily swell enough to cause swallowing problems. If the problem is persistent and the tonsils are seen to be touching when they are not infected, an evaluation is in order. This problem usually occurs in children with a small mouth to begin with.

Recurrent Abscess (Deep Infection) of the Tonsil • Your child's physician will make this decision.

Recurrent Abscess of a Lymph Node Draining the Tonsil • Your child's physician will make this decision.

Suspected Tumor of the Tonsil • These rare tumors cause one tonsil to be much larger than the other. The tonsil is also quite firm to the touch, and usually enlarged lymph nodes are found on the same side of the neck.

CALL YOUR CHILD'S PHYSICIAN DURING OFFICE HOURS IF

• You think your child has a valid indication for a T&A.

• You have other questions or concerns.

(*Remember:* Do not give permission for a T&A unless your child has one of the preceding indicators or until you have received a second opinion from another physician.)

TOOTHACHE

If your child complains of a painful tooth, it may just be a temporarily sensitive tooth, but usually it means decay or a cavity is present. One complication of a decaying tooth is a gumboil just below the gumline. The infection in the tooth may also spread to the face (giving a swollen cheek) or the lymph node just under the jawbone. Dental decay must be treated in both the baby and permanent teeth. Unchecked cavities in primary teeth not only cause pain, they also can damage the underlying permanent teeth.

CALL YOUR CHILD'S DENTIST

Immediately If

• The pain is very severe.

• Fever (over 100°F) is present.

• The face is swollen.

During Office Hours If

• The pain has been present for more than 24 hours.

• You can see a brown cavity in the painful tooth.

• There is a red (occasionally yellow) bump at the gumline of the painful tooth.

• You have other questions or concerns.

HOME CARE

Flossing • First use dental floss on either side of the painful tooth. The removal of a jammed piece of food may bring quick relief.

Pain Relief Medicines • For now, treat the toothache with aspirin or acetaminophen. If the pain lasts for more than 24 hours or becomes severe, call your dentist. For severe toothaches, also use dextromethorphan or codeine if you have a cough syrup containing them. (For dosage see COUGH, page 570.) An ice pack on the jaw may also help.

Oil of Cloves for Severe Toothache • If you cannot see a dentist for several days and an open cavity is visible: Clean all food out of the cavity with a toothpick, Water Pik, or water in a syringe. Buy some oil of cloves (80 percent eugenol) at a pharmacy; no prescription is needed. Place a few drops of the oil of cloves into the open pit, keeping in mind that it has no effect if applied to the tooth's surface. If the cavity is large, pack it with a small piece of cotton soaked with oil of cloves. Try to keep the oil of cloves off the tongue, because it stings. The cavity can also be temporarily sealed with melted candle wax. Just rub it in with your fingertip.

Call Your Child's Physician Later If

• You can't reach your dentist and it's an emergency.

RELATED TOPIC

TOOTH DECAY PREVENTION (page 183)

LUNGS (RESPIRATORY)

BREATHING, NOISY

CALL YOUR CHILD'S PHYSICIAN IMMEDIATELY IF

- Your child has serious and sudden difficulty in breathing. (See also BREATHING DIFFICULTY, SEVERE, page 34.)

- Wheezing is present. (See also WHEEZING, page 581.) Wheezing is a high-pitched purring or whistling sound produced during breathing out (expiration). Most squeaky sounds are wheezes.

- Stridor is present. Stridor is a harsh, raspy, low-pitched sound on breathing-in (inspiration) and is associated with a brassy, tight, hoarse cough. (See the guideline on CROUP, page 574.)

TYPES OF NONEMERGENCY NOISY BREATHING

Keep in mind that noisy breathing is due to vibrations set up somewhere in the airway (nose, throat, vocal cords, or chest). If your child's noisy breathing is intermittent and doesn't fit any of the following patterns, tape-record it and bring the tape to your physician's office.

Rattling Sounds • Rattling sounds are due to vibrations from mucus pooling in the lower throat. These gurgling sounds can be eliminated by coughing or swallowing. Many parents are needlessly concerned about a rattly chest. (See the guideline on COUGH, page 570.)

567

Snorting Sounds • Intermittent snorting sounds are due to mucus partially blocking the nasal passages. If the snorting makes your child uncomfortable, the problem can be eliminated by warm water nosedrops and nasal suction. (See the guideline on COLDS, page 533.) Increased humidity in the home will also help prevent dried secretions. During the first year of life, many babies normally make nasal sounds off and on during sleep simply because the nasal passages are so narrow. Since the sounds do not interfere with sleep, no treatment is necessary.

Snoring • Nightly snorting sounds (snoring) can be caused by partial obstruction of the nose or throat during sleep. The most common cause in children is large tonsils and adenoids. Call your child's physician during office hours. Observe your child during sleep so you can report whether or not cyanosis (bluish lips), retractions (pulling in of the spaces between the ribs), and temporary interruptions (arrests) of breathing occur during snoring.

CHEST PAIN

Your child may complain of pain in the chest. Most acute chest pain is associated with a hacking cough. Coughing can cause sore muscles in the chest wall, upper abdomen, or diaphragm. Occasionally, chest pain follows strenuous exercise, lifting, or work that involves the upper body. This type of muscle soreness often increases with movement of the shoulders. Heart disease is hardly ever the cause of chest pain in children.

The most common cause of recurrent chest pains in adolescents and adults is the precordial catch syndrome. This pain occurs just below the left nipple and comes on suddenly. The pain feels sharp or knifelike, causing the person to freeze. Usually within 1 minute, the pain is gone. Although the cause is unknown, it may be due to a pinched nerve. Although it may last for years, the precordial catch syndrome is completely harmless. Daily stretching exercises sometimes reduce these lightening pains.

CALL YOUR CHILD'S PHYSICIAN

Immediately If

• The pain is very severe (e.g., causes constant crying).

• The pain is unexplained *and* has lasted more than 2 hours.

• The breathing is difficult or fast.

• The pain prevents taking a deep breath.

• Your child also faints or feels dizzy.

• Your child acts or looks very sick.

During Office Hours If

• Coughing is also present.

• Fever (over 100°F) is present.

• The pain followed a direct blow to the chest.

• Chest pains are a recurrent problem for your child.

• You have other questions or concerns.

HOME CARE

Treatment • Treat the chest wall pains (associated with sore, strained muscles) with aspirin, acetaminophen or ibuprofen 4 times a day (for dosage, see the chart on page 66). Continue this until 24 hours have passed without pain. You can also relieve muscle spasm by applying a heating pad or warm washcloth to the area. They will probably clear within 3 days. If the pain is due to coughing, begin a cough suppressant medicine while waiting to talk with your physician. (See the guideline on COUGH, page 570.)

Call Your Child's Physician Later If

• The pains last more than 3 days on treatment.

• You feel your child is getting worse.

RELATED TOPIC

COUGH (see page 570)

CONGESTION, RESPIRATORY

Congestion means many things to different people. One of the following guidelines will probably meet your needs:

BREATHING, NOISY (see page 567)
COLDS (see page 533)
COUGH (see below)
EAR CONGESTION (see page 516)
SINUS CONGESTION (see page 546)

COUGH

SYMPTOMS AND CHARACTERISTICS

- The cough reflex expels air from the lungs with a sudden explosive noise

- Cough can be dry and hacky or wet and productive

- A coughing spasm is more than 5 minutes of continuous coughing

Similar Conditions • If one of the following is suspected, save time by turning directly to that guideline:

CROUP (see page 574)
WHEEZING (see page 581)

Causes • Keep in mind that coughing has a purpose: It clears the lungs and protects them from pneumonia.

Most coughs are due to a viral infection of the trachea (windpipe) and bronchi (larger air passages) called acute tracheitis or bronchitis. Most children get this a couple of times a year as part of a cold.

While coughs may be associated with sinus infections, they are not due to postnasal drip. People swallow while they are asleep, so secretions don't pool in the throat.

The role of milk in thickening the secretions is also doubtful, except for the 1 to 2 percent of infants with proven milk allergy.

Expected Course • Usually bronchitis gives a dry tickly cough that lasts for 2 to 3 weeks. Sometimes it becomes loose (wet) for a few days, and your child coughs up a lot of phlegm (mucus). This is usually a sign that the end of the illness is near.

CALL YOUR CHILD'S PHYSICIAN

Immediately If

• Your child is less than 1 month old. (Exception: coughs 1 or 2 times.)

• Breathing is difficult *and* not better after you clear the nose.

• The respirations are fast or labored (when your child is not coughing).

• Your child has passed out with coughing spasms.

• The lips have turned bluish with coughing spasms.

• Any blood-tinged sputum has been coughed up.

• A toy, food, or other foreign object could possibly be caught in the windpipe (especially likely if the cough came on suddenly after a choking episode *and* your child is under 3 years old).

• Your child acts or looks very sick.

During Office Hours If

• A fever (over 100°F) has lasted more than 72 hours.

• The cough has been present for more than 3 weeks.

• Your child is 1 to 3 months old *and* the cough has been present for more than 72 hours.

• The cause could be an allergy (like pollen).

• Your child also has sinus congestion.

• Coughing spasms cause lots of lost sleep.

• The coughing has caused vomiting 3 or more times.

• The coughing has caused bad chest pains.

• The cough has caused your child to miss 3 or more days of school.

• You have other questions or concerns.

HOME CARE FOR COUGH

Medicines to Thin the Secretions and Loosen the Cough

Cough Drops • Most coughs in children over age 4 can be controlled by sucking on cough drops freely.

Homemade Cough Syrup • Children under age 4 can be given a teaspoon of honey or corn syrup instead. (Avoid giving honey to babies under 1 year of age, because of the small risk of botulism for this age group.)

Warm Liquids for Coughing Spasms • Coughing symptoms are often due to sticky mucus caught on the vocal cords or windpipe. Warm, clear liquids usually relax the airway and loosen up the mucus. Start with warm lemonade, warm apple juice, or warm tea. Avoid adding any alcohol, because of the aggravation of the cough as the fumes of alcohol are inhaled into the lungs, and also the risk of intoxication from unintentional overdosage.

Cough-Suppressant Medicines • Since the cough reflex protects the lungs, cough-suppressant drugs are given in a dosage to reduce (but not eliminate) coughing. They are indicated only for dry coughs (nonproductive of mucus) that interfere with sleep, school attendance, or work. They also help children who have chest pain from coughing spasms. They should not be given to infants under 12 months of age or for wet productive coughs.

A nonprescription cough suppressant is dextromethorphan (DM). Ask your pharmacist for help in choosing a brand that contains DM without any other active ingredients. Dosage is 0.2 mg per pound of body weight, every 4 to 6 hours as needed. It usually comes as a liquid in a strength of 15 mg per teaspoon. DM is also available as a cough lozenge for easy carrying and as a long-acting (12 hour) liquid.

20-pound child	can take	4 mg of DM
30-pound child	can take	6 mg of DM
4–6 years	can take	7.5 mg of DM
7–11 years	can take	15 mg of DM
Adults	can take	30 mg of DM

Often corn syrup or honey can be given during the day, and DM given at bedtime and during the night.

Cold Mist Humidifiers • Dry air tends to make coughs worse. Dry coughs can be loosened up by encouraging a good fluid intake and using a humidifier in your child's bedroom. Don't add medicine to the water in the humidifier, because it irritates the cough in some children. The new ultrasonic humidifers not only have the advantage of quietness, they also kill molds and most bacteria that might be in the water. Distilled water is preferred over tap water.

Postural Drainage for Coughing Spasms • Some coughing spasms are due to choking on lung mucus that comes up and sticks to the vocal cords. If your child is under 3 years old and coughing up lots of mucus at night, try to improve matters by giving postural drainage at bedtime. Start by having your child breathe in warm mist from a wet washcloth over the face or a humidifier. Have your child lie stomach down on your outstretched legs, with the head lower than the rest of the body. Then gently pat your child on the back of the rib cage, working from the lower back to the shoulders. Do this for 10 minutes, and expect some productive coughing.

Vomiting with Coughing Spasms • Refeed your child after this type of vomiting. Offer smaller amounts with each feeding to reduce the chances of repeated vomiting.

Active and Passive Smoking • Since tobacco smoke agitates coughing, don't let anyone smoke around your coughing child. Better yet, try to protect your child from all passive smoking. If one parent smokes in the house, that's equivalent to your child actively smoking 30 to 40 cigarettes per year. Remind the teenager who smokes that his or her cough may last weeks longer than it normally would without smoking.

Exercise • Teenagers will find that required gym and exercise trigger coughing spasms when they have bronchitis. If so, these activities should be avoided temporarily.

Common Mistakes • Antihistamines, decongestants, and antipyretics are found in many cough syrups. These ingredients have no impact on coughs, but they can have side effects. Antihistamines are illogical for productive coughs, because they dry secretions and make them harder to cough up. While the expectorants are safe, they have recently been shown to be ineffective. Stay with the simple remedies mentioned previously, or give DM for severe coughs. Keep in mind that prescription cough medicines (unless they contain codeine) offer no advantage over nonprescription ones.

Milk does not need to be eliminated from the diet, since most sick babies want their formula, and restricting it only improves the cough if the child is allergic to milk. Never stop breast-feeding because of a cough.

Raising the head of the bed is of questionable value, since more coughing is caused by lung mucus than nasal mucus.

Lastly, physicians can usually evaluate coughs and exclude pneumonia without a chest X ray (so don't expect one).

Call Your Child's Physician Later If

• Breathing becomes labored or difficult.

• Coughing spasms cause passing out or bluish lips.

• Coughing spasms cause exhaustion or lost sleep.

• Coughing spasms occur continuously for more than 1 hour.

• Any fever lasts more than 72 hours.

• The cough lasts more than 3 weeks.

• The cough causes your child to miss 3 or more days of school.

• You feel your child is getting worse.

CROUP (CROUPY COUGH AND STRIDOR)

SYMPTOMS AND CHARACTERISTICS OF CROUPY COUGH

• A distinctive cough that occurs with infections of the voice box (larynx)

• The cough is tight, metallic, and like a barking seal

• The voice is usually hoarse

SYMPTOMS AND CHARACTERISTICS OF STRIDOR

• A harsh, raspy, vibrating sound during inspiration

• Breathing-in is very difficult

• Stridor only occurs with severe croup

- Usually only present with crying or coughing

- If the stridor occurs continuously, your child has severe respiratory distress

Similar Conditions to Croup • EPIGLOTTITIS (see page 644) is a life-threatening bacterial infection that causes stridor, fever, drooling, and difficulty swallowing. WHEEZING (see page 581)—a high-pitched meowing or whistling sound produced during expiration. If either of these is what your child has, call your physician immediately.

Cause • Croup is an infection of the vocal cords often caused by the parainfluenza virus. It is usually part of a cold. The hoarseness is due to swelling of the vocal cords. Stridor occurs as the opening between the vocal cords becomes more narrow. Croup occurs in epidemics every other year.

Expected Course • Croup usually lasts for 5 to 6 days and generally gets worse at night. During that time, it can change from mild to severe many times. The worst symptoms are seen in children under 3 years of age.

FIRST AID FOR ATTACKS OF STRIDOR WITH CROUP
If your child suddenly develops stridor or tight breathing, do the following:

Inhalation of Warm Mist • Warm, moist air seems to work best to relax the vocal cords and break the stridor. The simplest way to provide this is to have your child breathe through a warm, wet washcloth placed loosely over the nose and mouth. Another good way, if you have a humidifier (not a hot vaporizer), is to fill it with warm water (a little warmer than body temperature) and have your child put his or her face in the stream of humidity and breathe deeply through an open mouth.

The Foggy Bathroom • In the meantime, have the hot shower running with the bathroom door closed. Once the room is all fogged up, take your child in there for at least 10 minutes. Try to allay fears by cuddling your child and reading a story. Panic and crying make croup worse. If the crying can be stopped, the breathing will be easier.

If the house is closed up, an occasional child will do better if taken outside for 5 minutes. Why the fresh air should break the stridor remains a mystery.

Warm Fluids for Coughing Spasms • Coughing spasms are often due to sticky mucus caught on the vocal cords. Warm fluids may help relax the vocal cords and loosen up the mucus. Use clear fluids (ones you can see through) such as apple juice, lemonade, or tea.

Results of First Aid • Most children settle down with the above treatments and then sleep peacefully through the night. If the stridor continues in your child, call your physician immediately. If your child turns blue, passes out, or stops breathing, call the rescue squad (911).

CALL YOUR PHYSICIAN (AND ALSO BEGIN THE FIRST AID FOR STRIDOR, ABOVE)

Immediately If

- The stridor is present constantly and unresponsive to warm mist.

- Breathing is difficult.

- Your child is drooling, spitting, or having great difficulty swallowing.
  (If your child normally drools, call only if it has increased greatly.)

- Your child can't bend the neck forward.

- Your child has passed out. Also call the rescue squad (911).

- There are any retractions (tugging in) between the ribs.

- The lips are bluish or dusky.

- Your child is constantly uncomfortable.

- Your child has been unable to sleep.

- Coughing spasms occur continuously for over 1 hour.

- A toy or other small foreign object could be caught in the windpipe.

- The croup started suddenly after taking a medicine or being stung by an insect.

- Your child acts or looks very sick.

Within 24 Hours If

- Your child is under 1 year old.
- The attacks of stridor have occurred more than 3 times.
- The fluid intake is poor.
- A fever (over 104°F) is present.
- You have other questions or concerns.

HOME CARE FOR A CROUPY COUGH

Mist • Dry air tends to make coughs worse. Keep the child's room humidified. Use a cool mist humidifier if you have one. Distilled water is preferred over tap water. Have it run 24 hours a day. Be sure to empty and wash the container once a week with a dilute bleach solution made by adding 1 tablespoon of bleach to 2 quarts of water. Don't add any camphor or menthol oils to the water, because they are irritating to the cough in most children. If you don't own a humidifier, hang wet sheets or towels in your child's room.

Warm Fluids for Coughing Spasms • See page 576.

Cough Medicines • Medicines are less helpful than either mist or swallowing clear fluids. Older children can be given cough drops for the cough, and younger children can be given some corn syrup. Avoid strong cough medicines (like codeine) which could suppress the brain's respiratory center and interfere with keeping the lungs clear. If your child has a fever (over 102°F) you may give him acetaminophen. (See FEVER, page 407, for dosage.)

Close Observation • While your child is croupy, sleep in the same room temporarily. Consider bringing your child's mattress into your bedroom. Croup can be a dangerous disease.

Passive Smoking • Don't let anyone smoke around your child; smoke can make croup worse.

Contagiousness • The viruses that cause croup are quite contagious until the fever is gone or at least until 3 days into the illness. Since spread of this infection can't be prevented, your child can return to school or child care once he feels better.

CALL YOUR CHILD'S PHYSICIAN IMMEDIATELY IF

• Breathing becomes difficult.

• The lips turn bluish.

• Your child is drooling or having great difficulty swallowing.

• Your child is unable to sleep because of the croup.

• The warm mist fails to clear the stridor in 20 minutes.

• You feel your child is getting worse.

RELATED TOPICS

CHOKING (see page 10)
COUGH (see page 570)

HOARSENESS

SYMPTOMS AND CHARACTERISTICS

• The voice is raspy

• If hoarseness is severe, your child can do little more than whisper

• A cough is often associated

Similar Conditions • If appropriate, turn directly to the following guidelines:

CROUP (see page 574)
HAY FEVER (see page 540)

Causes • Hoarseness is usually caused by a cold or croup virus (laryngitis) or overuse of the vocal cords (e.g., shouting or screaming). Cheerleaders and avid sports fans are prone.

Expected Course • Hoarseness usually lasts 1 to 2 weeks. Repeated vocal cord abuse can cause thickening of the cords and a slow recovery.

CALL YOUR CHILD'S PHYSICIAN

Immediately If

- Breathing is difficult.

- A toy, food, or other foreign object could possibly be caught in the windpipe.

- Your child choked on anything recently.

During Office Hours If

- Your child is under 2 months old.

- The hoarseness has been present more than 2 weeks.

- You have other questions or concerns.

HOME CARE FOR HOARSENESS

Treatment • Have your child gargle with warm salt water and suck on hard candy or cough drops several times a day. Younger children can sip warm liquids like apple juice. Encourage your child to rest the voice and avoid the vocal strain that comes from yelling and screaming. Encourage your child to talk as little as possible for a few days. If the hoarseness gets really bad, have your child whisper or write notes. Also run a humidifier in your child's bedroom.

Call Your Child's Physician Later If

- The hoarseness gets worse.

- The hoarseness lasts more than 2 weeks.

INFLUENZA

Influenza is a viral infection of the nose, throat, trachea, and bronchi that occurs in epidemics every 3 or 4 years (e.g., Asian influenza). The main symptoms are a stuffy nose, sore throat, and nagging cough. There may be more muscle pain, headache, fever, and chills than with usual colds. Since there are many influenza viruses, and they are constantly changing, we can easily come down with influenza almost yearly. Spread is rapid because the incubation period is only 24 to 36 hours and the virus is very contagious. For most people, influenza is just a "bad" cold. The dangers of influenza for normal, healthy people (under 65 years of age) are overrated.

WHEN TO CALL YOUR CHILD'S PHYSICIAN
See the guidelines on fever, cough, colds, sore throat, sinus congestion, earache, and so forth. Ear infections, sinus infections, and pneumonia are the most common complications.

HOME CARE FOR INFLUENZA
The treatment of influenza depends on your child's main symptoms and is no different from that suggested for other viral respiratory infections. Bed rest is unnecessary.

Fever or Aches • Use acetaminophen every 4 to 6 hours. (See FEVER, page 407, for dosage.) Aspirin should be avoided in children and adolescents with suspected influenza because of the possible link with Reyes syndrome.

Cough or Hoarseness • Cough drops for children over 4 years of age and corn syrup for younger children should help. (See the guidelines on COUGH, page 570, or HOARSENESS, page 578.)

Sore Throat • Salt water or antacid solution gargles and soft diet should help. (See the guideline on SORE THROAT, page 559.)

Stuffy Nose • Warm water nose drops and suction (or nose blowing) will open most blocked noses. Vasoconstrictor nose drops or spray may be added for resistant ones. (See the guideline on COLDS, page 533.)

INFLUENZA VACCINE AND PREVENTION
The vaccine is not recommended for healthy children (unless an especially severe form of influenza comes along). One reason is that influenza vaccine gives protection for only 1 or 2 years. In addition, the vaccine itself can cause a mild fever in 20 percent and a sore injection site in 10 percent lasting 6 to 48 hours.

However, children over 6 months of age with the following conditions have a high complication rate from influenza (especially pneumonia) and need yearly influenza boosters each fall. During influenza Type A epidemics, these same children may be helped by taking an oral antiviral drug called amantadine for 2 weeks until the vaccine takes effect. The parents and siblings of high-risk children should also receive the influenza vaccine.

- Lung disease (e.g., asthma, cystic fibrosis, bronchopulmonary dysplasia)

- Heart disease (e.g., congenital heart disease, rheumatic heart disease)

- Muscle disease (e.g., muscular dystrophy)

- Metabolic disease (e.g., diabetes mellitus)

- Renal disease (e.g., nephrotic syndrome)

- Malignant and immunodeficient diseases

- Diseases requiring longterm aspirin therapy.

(*Exception:* Children allergic to eggs should not receive this vaccine.)

CALL YOUR CHILD'S PHYSICIAN DURING OFFICE HOURS IF

- You think your child needs an influenza vaccine.

- You have other questions or concerns.

WHEEZING

SYMPTOMS AND CHARACTERISTICS

Wheezing is a high-pitched purring or whistling sound produced during breathing out (expiration).

Similar Conditions • Some other respiratory sounds can be confused with wheezing. If one of the following is suspected, save time by turning directly to that guideline:

- CROUP (see page 574) or stridor gives a harsh, raspy, vibrating sound on breathing in (inspiration) and is associated with a hoarse, metallic, tight cough.

- Snorting sounds are due to mucus partially blocking the nasal passages. These sounds can be eliminated by warm water nose drops and nasal suction. (See the guideline on COLDS, page 533.)

- Rattling sounds are due to mucus in the lower throat. These sounds can be eliminated by coughing or swallowing.

WHEN TO CALL YOUR CHILD'S PHYSICIAN

If your child definitely has wheezing, call your child's physician immediately. Although asthma (reactive airway disease) is the most common cause of wheezing, there are many causes, and it can be an emergency situation. Let your physician help you sort out what is going on.

Asthma as a Cause of Wheezing • If your child has asthma, maintain close contact with the physician who coordinates your child's treatment program. Try to learn as much about asthma as you can. The most common mistake in treating asthma is delaying the start of asthma medicines. Many children wheeze soon after they get coughs and colds. If this is the case for your child, start the asthma medicine or inhaler at the first sign of any coughing. The best "cough medicines" for a child with asthma are the asthma medicines. Always keep the medicine handy, and take it with you on trips. If your supply runs low, obtain a refill.

Another mistake is not eliminating asthma triggers. Try to discover and avoid the substances that trigger attacks in your child. Routinely avoid common triggers such as feather pillows and tobacco smoke. Try to keep pets outside, or at least out of your child's room (cats cause more allergic reactions than any other pet). Learn how to dustproof your child's bedroom. Avoid wool rugs. Change the filters on your hot air heating system or air conditioner regularly. If there has been any recent contact with grass, pollen, weeds, or animals that your child might be allergic to, the pollen remaining in the hair and clothing is probably keeping the wheezing going. Have your child shower, wash his hair, and put on clean clothes.

ABDOMEN (GASTROINTESTINAL)

ABDOMINAL PAIN

SYMPTOM

- Your child complains that his stomach (abdomen) hurts

Similar Condition • For babies under 3 months old with fussy crying, see CRYING BABY (COLIC), page 239.

Causes • The causes are numerous. Usually it's something simple like overeating, gas pains from too much soda pop, or other types of indigestion. Sometimes it signals the onset of a viral gastroenteritis, and vomiting or diarrhea soon follow. In children and adults, the most common cause of recurrent abdominal pain is stress and worries. They occur in over 10 percent of children. The pain occurs in the pit of the stomach or near the belly button. The pain is low-grade but real. Recurrent stomach aches can have numerous causes and deserve a medical evaluation.

Expected Course • With harmless causes, the pain is usually better or resolved in 2 hours. With gastroenteritis, belly cramps may precede each bout of vomiting or stooling. With serious causes (such as appendicitis) the pain worsens and becomes constant.

583

CALL YOUR CHILD'S PHYSICIAN
Immediately If

- The pain is very severe (e.g., causes constant crying).

- Your child walks bent over or holding the abdomen.

- Your child is lying down and refuses to walk.

- The pain is constant *and* has lasted more than 2 hours (especially if the pain is on the lower right side, where the appendix is located).

- The pain comes and goes (cramps) *and* lasts more than 12 hours. (Exception: Vomiting or diarrhea is your child's main symptom and the stomachache clears each time your child vomits or passes a stool.)

- Your child is under 2 years old.

- The pain is in the scrotum or testicle.

- Any blood has appeared in the bowel movements.

- Poisoning with a plant, medicine, or chemical is a possibility.

- The abdomen was recently injured.

- Your child is acting very sick.

- When you press on your child's abdomen with your hand, the abdomen is quite tender to the touch.

During Office Hours If

- This is a recurrent problem for your child.

- You have other questions or concerns.

HOME CARE

Treatment • Have your child lie down and rest until feeling better. A warm washcloth or heating pad on the abdomen may speed recovery. Avoid giving your child solid foods; permit only sips of clear fluids. Keep a vomiting pan handy. Younger children are especially likely to refer to nausea as "a stomachache."

Common Mistakes • Do not give any medicines for stomach cramps unless you have talked with your physician. Painkillers (like aspirin or codeine) may mask the problem. More importantly, avoid laxatives and enemas. If your child has appendicitis, these medicines could cause the appendix to rupture.

The Worried Stomach • If your child has been evaluated by a physician and has a worried stomach, try the following to ease the pains:

• Help your child lighten up. Children with recurrent bellyaches tend to be sensitive, serious, conscientious, even model children. This makes them vulnerable to the normal stresses of life, such as changing schools or a recent move. Help your youngster talk about events that trigger his pains, and how he's going to cope with them.

• Make sure that your youngster doesn't miss any school because of stomachaches. These children have a tendency to stay home when the going gets rough.

• Teach him to use relaxation exercises for mild pains. Have him lie down in a quiet place, take deep, slow breaths; and think about something pleasant. Listening to relaxation tapes may help.

• **Caution:** Your child should have a complete medical checkup before assuming that recurrent stomachaches are due to worrying too much.

Call Your Child's Physician in 2 Hours If

• The pain is constant *and* no better.

• Call sooner if it rapidly becomes worse.

• Call in 12 hours if it's the kind of pain that comes and goes.

RELATED TOPICS
Pain with:

CONSTIPATION (see page 586)
COUGH (see page 570)
DIARRHEA (see page 591)
MENSTRUAL CRAMPS (see page 618)
URINATION (see page 612)
VOMITING (see page 608)

AMPICILLIN DIARRHEA

Ampicillin causes diarrhea in 20 percent to 30 percent of children receiving it, depending on the dosage. (Amoxicillin causes diarrhea less commonly.) This is an irritative reaction (i.e., ampicillin acts like a laxative), not an allergic one. The loose stools begin within a day or two of starting the antibiotic. Ampicillin diarrhea is usually mild and occasionally moderate in degree. Dehydration and weight loss do not occur. As soon as you finish the course of ampicillin, the BMs will return to normal.

HOME CARE

The ampicillin does not need to be discontinued. The diet does not need to be changed, unless you wish to cut back on foods like bran products, beans, and fresh fruits and vegetables. Sometimes the diarrhea causes a diaper rash. Wash the irritated area with water and then protect the skin with a thick layer of petroleum jelly or other ointment. Call your child's physician if you feel the ampicillin needs to be changed.

CONSTIPATION

SYMPTOMS AND CHARACTERISTICS

- Painful passage of stools. The best sign of constipation is the occurrence of pain or discomfort with the passage of a bowel movement.

- Inability to pass stools. These children feel a desperate urge to have a BM, have discomfort in the anal area, strain, but are unable to pass anything.

- Infrequent movements. Going more than 3 days without a BM can be considered constipation, even though this may cause no pain in some patients and even be normal for a few. *Exception:* After the second month or so of life, many breast-fed babies have normal, large, soft BMs at infrequent intervals (up to 7 days is normal). These infrequent normal stools are passed without pain or excessive straining.

Common Misconceptions in Defining Constipation • Large or hard BMs unaccompanied by any pain or discomfort are usually normal variations. Some people normally have hard BMs each day without any pain. Others have large BMs every 3 days without pain. Babies less than 6 months of age commonly grunt, push, strain, draw up the legs, and become flushed in the face during passage of bowel movements. However, they don't cry. These behaviors are normal and should remind us that it takes some time for the bowels and rectum to become coordinated. Also, it is difficult to have a bowel movement while lying down. Help your straining baby by holding the knees against the chest to simulate squatting (the natural position for pushing out a BM). In fact, some straining with BMs is normal at any age.

Causes • Constipation is usually due to a diet deficient in fiber (found in fruits, vegetables, and whole-grain foods). Fiber is not digested and makes stools larger, softer, and easier to pass. Eating or drinking too many milk products also causes constipation. Another common cause is repeated postponement of the urge to go because of embarrassment about school toilets, public toilets, or long waiting times for the home bathroom. If constipation begins during toilet training, the parent is usually applying too much pressure. (See the guideline on TOILET TRAINING, page 333.)

Expected Course • Constipation usually is easy to relieve with dietary changes. After your child is better, be sure to keep him or her on a high-fiber diet so that it doesn't happen again. On some occasions, the trauma to the anal canal causes an anal fissure (a small tear). This is confirmed by finding small amounts of bright-red blood on the toilet tissue or the stool surface.

CALL YOUR CHILD'S PHYSICIAN

Immediately for Advice About an Enema or Suppository If

• Your child is in extreme pain.

• Pain is constant *and* has persisted for more than 2 hours.

During Office Hours If

• Your child is less than 2 months old.

• Four or more days have passed without a BM.

- Your child is soiling (leaking BMs).

- You are giving suppositories or enemas.

- The anal area has any tears (fissures) that are deep or won't heal.

- Anal fissures have bled more than twice.

- Toilet training is in progress *and* there is any resistance.

- Constipation is a recurrent problem for your child.

- You have other questions or concerns.

HOME CARE

Diet Treatment for Babies Under 1 Year Old • For babies on only formula or breast milk, add fruit juices (like grape, pear, or cherry juice) twice a day. Try prune juice as a next step. Switching to soy formula may also give looser stools. If your baby is over 4 months old, add baby foods with high fiber content—peas, beans, apricots, prunes, peaches, pears, plums, spinach, or cereal—twice a day. In my experience, corn syrup usually doesn't help. (Note: If necessary, strained peas or oatmeal cereal can be added to the formula of younger babies.) Avoid strained carrots, squash, bananas, and apples (foods that make some kids constipated). Also when your child is straining, put her in a tub with warm water to help relax the anus, and hold the knees against the chest.

Diet Treatment for Children Over 1 Year Old

- Increase fruits/vegetables. Have your child eat fruits or vegetables high in fiber content at least 3 times a day (raw ones are best, and peelings are most helpful). Peas, beans, and dates are especially good because they are palatable and high in fiber. Other examples are prunes, figs, raisins, peaches, pears, apricots, cauliflower, broccoli, and cabbage. (**Warning:** Avoid any foods your child can't easily chew.)

- Increase bran. Bran is an excellent natural laxative, since it has high fiber content. Have your child eat bran daily in one of the new "natural" cereals, bran flakes, bran muffins, shredded wheat, graham crackers, oatmeal, high-fiber cookies, brown rice, or whole wheat bread. Popcorn is a high-fiber food that is acceptable to most children.

- Decrease constipating foods. Milk, ice cream, cheese, white rice, applesauce, bananas, and cooked carrots are constipating and should be kept to moderate amounts.

• Increase water. Be sure your child drinks plenty of water.

• Increase carbonated fluids. The gas from soft drinks can pass quickly through the intestines and increase the sense of fullness in the rectum. School-age children can try a can of pop each day and see if it improves their frequency of BMs.

• Exercise. If your child tends to be inactive, encourage him or her to become more outgoing in the neighborhood or join a team.

Sitting on the Toilet • Encourage your child to establish a regular bowel pattern by sitting on the toilet for 10 minutes after meals, especially breakfast. Some children and adults repeatedly get blocked up if they don't look after this. If mornings are hurried at your house, try to get up earlier so your child has time to sit on the toilet. If your child is resisting toilet training by holding back, temporarily discontinue the training and put him back in diapers. For infants who hold back, they will often release the BM while sitting in warm bathwater.

Natural Laxative Medicine • If diet alone doesn't work, a good natural laxative is Maltsupex (a malt extract from barley). No prescription is needed. It comes in liquid or powder and is best mixed with any beverage. The starting dosage is:

Infants:	½ tablespoon twice daily
Children:	1 tablespoon twice daily
Adolescents:	2 tablespoons twice daily (or 2 tablets)

Another product that can be mixed with foods (such as orange juice or applesauce) is unprocessed (unmilled) bran, available in most health food stores. The starting dosage is ½ to 1 teaspoon twice daily, depending on age. Try this for one week and then only as necessary.

Treatment for Anal Fissure • Streaks or flecks of blood noted on the surface of the stool or toilet tissue indicate that your child probably has an anal fissure. Anal fissures are prevented with the diet changes already discussed and are treated with 20-minute sitz baths in warm salt water 3 times a day, followed by ½ percent hydrocortisone cream (no prescription needed). If the pain is severe, apply 2½ percent Xylocaine ointment (no prescription needed) 4 times a day for a few days to numb the area.

Common Mistakes • Don't use any suppositories or enemas without your physician's advice. These can cause irritation or fissures (tears) of the anus, resulting in pain and stool holding. Do not use strong laxatives by mouth without asking your physician, because they can cause cramps and become somewhat habit-forming. Keep in mind that constipation will probably become a recurrent problem if the dietary changes aren't continued.

Enemas for Acute Constipation • If your child has acute rectal pain needing immediate relief and your physician has given you clearance, proceed with the following: A glycerine suppository, a gentle rectal dilation with a lubricated finger (covered with plastic wrap), or a normal saline enema will usually provide quick relief. Enemas with soapsuds, hydrogen peroxide, or tap water are dangerous. The normal saline enema is made by adding 2 teaspoons of table salt to a quart of water and is given lukewarm. Your child should lie on the stomach with knees pulled under. The enema tube should be lubricated and inserted 1½ to 2 inches into the rectum. The enema fluid should be delivered gradually by gravity, with the enema bag no more than 2 feet above the level of the anus. Your child should hold the enema until a strong need to defecate is felt (2 to 10 minutes). Occasionally the response is delayed for up to 2 hours, so don't plan any travel during that time. If you do not have an enema apparatus, you can use a rubber bulb syringe. The amount of normal saline for different ages is:

1 year:	4 ounces
1–3 years:	6 ounces
3–6 years:	8 ounces
6–12 years:	12 ounces
Adolescents and adults:	16 ounces

Call Your Child's Physician Later If

• Cramps or pains last more than 2 hours.

• Your child does not have a BM after 3 days on a nonconstipating diet.

- BMs continue to cause pain.
- Anal fissures bleed 3 or more times.
- You feel your child is getting worse.

RELATED TOPIC

STOOLS, BLOOD IN (see page 604)

DIARRHEA

SYMPTOMS AND CHARACTERISTICS

Diarrhea is the sudden increase in the frequency and loose-ness of bowel movements. Mild diarrhea is the passage of a few loose or mushy stools. Moderate diarrhea gives many watery stools. The best indicator of the severity of the diar-rhea is its frequency. A green stool also points to a very rapid passage and moderate to severe diarrhea. Keeping your child on nothing but clear fluids for more than 2 days also can cause green, watery BMs ("starvation stools").

The main complication of diarrhea is dehydration from excessive loss of body fluids. Symptoms are a dry mouth; the absence of tears; a reduction in urine production (e.g., none in 8 hours); and a darker, concentrated urine. It's dehydration you need to worry about, not the presence of diarrhea.

Causes • Diarrhea is usually caused by a viral infection of the intestines (gastroenteritis). Occasionally it is caused by bacte-ria or parasites. Occasionally it's due to excessive fruit juices or to a food allergy. If only 1 or 2 loose stools are passed, the cause often turns out to be something unusual your child ate ("indigestion"). Remember that diarrhea is the body's way of purging itself of harmful organisms until it can build up immu-nity to them.

Normal Stools in Infants • Newborns have frequent BMs that can be mistaken for diarrhea. Breast-fed babies during the first 2 months pass from 4 stools per day to 1 after each feeding. Formula-fed babies pass 1 to 8 stools per day during the first week, then 1 to 4 per day until 2 months of age. After 2 months of age, most infants (regardless of type of feeding) pass 1 or 2 stools per day (or 1 every other day) and no longer appear to have diarrhea.

Expected Course • Diarrhea stools usually last from several days to a week, regardless of the type of treatment. The main goal of therapy is to prevent dehydration by giving enough oral fluids to keep up with the fluids lost in the diarrhea. Don't expect a quick return to solid stools. Since 1 loose stool can mean nothing, don't start dietary changes until there have been at least two.

CALL YOUR CHILD'S PHYSICIAN

Immediately If

- Your child is less than 1 month old
  (**Caution:** Normal breast-fed stools can look like diarrhea.)

- Your child has not urinated in more than 8 hours.

- Crying produces no tears.

- The mouth is dry rather than moist.

- Any blood appears in the diarrhea.

- Severe abdominal cramps are present.

- More than 8 diarrhea stools have occurred in the last 8 hours.

- The diarrhea is watery *and* your child has vomited clear fluids 3 or more times.

- Your child feels dizzy with standing.

- Your child acts or looks very sick.

  If your child has vomited more than once, turn directly to the guideline on VOMITING, page 608. The treatment of vomiting takes priority over the treatment of diarrhea, until your child has gone 8 hours without vomiting.

Within 24 Hours If

- Mucus or pus is present in the stools.

- The diarrhea has caused loss of bowel control in a toilet-trained child.

- Your child was exposed to someone with bacterial diarrhea (especially in foreign travel).

- Abdominal cramps come and go for more than 12 hours.

- A fever (over 100°F) has been present for more than 72 hours.

- Your child is on any medicines that could cause diarrhea.

During Office Hours If

- The diarrhea has been present for more than 1 week.

- Diarrhea is a recurrent problem for your child.

- You have other questions or concerns.

HOME CARE
Dietary changes are the mainstay of home treatment for diarrhea. The optimal diet depends on your child's age and the severity of the diarrhea. There are 4 basic scenarios—go directly to the part that pertains to your child.

Special Diet for Diarrhea

1. MILD DIARRHEA *and* child of any age.

- Continue a regular diet with a few simple changes.

- Continue full strength formula or milk.

- Reduce the intake of fruit juices. If given, make them ½ strength with water.

- Avoid raw fruits and vegetables, beans, spicy foods and any foods that cause loose stools.

2. BOTTLE-FED INFANTS *and* frequent, watery diarrhea.
Starting oral glucose-electrolyte solutions for 6 to 24 hours.
• If your child has severe diarrhea, buy Pedialyte or Infalyte at your pharmacy or supermarket. (These special solutions are not needed for diarrhea unless it's severe.) If your child doesn't like the flavor, add a bit of Kool-Aid powder. Give as much of the liquid as your baby wants. Diarrhea makes children thirsty, and your job is to satisfy that thirst and prevent dehydration. Never restrict fluids when your child has diarrhea.
Until you get one of these special solutions, continue giving your baby full-strength formula in unlimited amounts. (Avoid giving your baby Jell-O water mixtures or sports drinks. Reason: inadequate sodium content)
If you aren't able to get an oral glucose-electrolyte so-

lution, ask your doctor about making a homemade solution as follows: Mix ½ cup of dry infant rice cereal with 2 cups (16 oz) of water and ¼ level teaspoon of salt. Be careful not to add too much salt. (Reason: risk of salt poisoning)

Continue giving your baby Pedialyte or Infalyte for at least 6 hours. Between 6 and 24 hours, switch back to formula if your baby becomes hungry, the diarrhea becomes less watery, and the child is making lots of urine.

Returning to Formula • After being given clear fluids for 6 to 24 hours, your baby will be hungry, so begin her regular formula. If the diarrhea continues to be severe, begin with a soy formula. If you give cow's milk formula and the diarrhea doesn't improve after 3 days, change to a lactose-free formula (milk-based lactose-free or a soy formula). Often there is less diarrhea with soy formulas than with cow's milk formulas because the soy formulas don't contain milk sugar (lactose). If you start giving soy formula, plan to keep your baby on the soy formula until the diarrhea is gone for 3 days.

If your baby's bowel movements are very watery, mix the formula with 1 or 2 ounces of extra water per bottle for 24 hours. Then after 24 hours go back to full-strength formula.

Adding Solids • Foods that contain a lot of starch are more easily digested than other foods during diarrhea. If your baby is over 4 months old, has had diarrhea for over 24 hours, and wants to eat solid food, give her the following starchy foods until the diarrhea is gone: any cereal, mashed potatoes, applesauce, strained bananas, strained carrots, and other high-fiber foods.

3. BREAST-FED INFANTS *and* frequent, watery diarrhea

Definition of Diarrhea • No matter how it looks, the stool of the breast-fed infant must be considered normal unless it contains mucus or blood or develops a bad odor. In fact, breast-fed babies can normally pass some green stools or stools with a water ring around them. Frequency of movements is also not much help. As previously stated, during the first 2 or 3 months of life, the breast-fed baby may normally have as many stools as one after each feeding. The presence of something in the mother's diet that causes rapid passage should always be considered in these babies (e.g., coffee, cola, or herbal teas). Diarrhea can be diagnosed if your baby's stools abruptly increase in number. Additional clues are if your baby feeds poorly, acts sick, or develops a fever.

Treatment • If your breast-fed baby has diarrhea, treatment is straightforward. Continue breast feeding, but at more frequent intervals. Breast-feeding should never be discontinued because of diarrhea. If urine production is decreased, offer Infalyte or Pedialyte between breast-feedings for 6 to 24 hours. Breast-feeding may have to be temporarily discontinued if your baby requires intravenous fluids for severe diarrhea and dehydration. Pump your breasts to maintain milk flow until nursing can be restarted (usually within 12 hours).

4. OLDER CHILDREN (over 1 year old) *and* frequent, watery diarrhea
- The choice of solids is the key factor—starchy foods are absorbed best. Give cereals (especially rice cereal), oatmeal, bread, noodles, mashed potatoes, carrots, applesauce, strained bananas, etc. Pretzels or salty crackers can help meet your child's sodium needs.
- For fluids, use water (if solids are being consumed) or ½ strength orange juice.
- Avoid apple and grape juice which usually make diarrhea worse.
- Avoid milk for 2 or 3 days. (Reason: lactose is not as easily absorbed as complex carbohydrates.) Active culture yogurt is fine.
- Infalyte or Pedialyte is rarely needed, unless diarrhea is very watery and urine production is decreased.

Common Mistakes in Treating Diarrhea • Using boiled skim milk or any concentrated solution can cause serious complications for babies with diarrhea, because they contain too much salt. Kool-Aid, soda pop, or rice water should not be used as the only food because they contain little or no salt. Fruit juices (especially apple and grape) should be avoided because they are too concentrated and can pull water out of the baby. Use only the clear fluids mentioned.

By 24 hours at the latest, add formula or solids to the diet, because your baby needs more calories than clear fluids alone can provide (that is, avoid starvation and weight loss). Also, never use diluted formula for more than 24 hours.

The most dangerous myth is that the intestine should be "put to rest"; restricting fluids can cause dehydration.

Keep in mind that there is no effective, safe drug for diarrhea and that extra water and diet therapy work best.

Diaper Rash from Diarrhea • The skin near your baby's anus can become "burned" from digestive enzymes and other chemicals found in the diarrhea stools. Wash it off after each BM and then protect it with a thick layer of petroleum jelly or other protective ointment. This protective shield is especially needed during the night and during naps. Changing the diaper quickly after BMs also helps.

Overflow Diarrhea in a Child Not Toilet Trained • For children in diapers, diarrhea can be a mess. Despite treatment, loose stools usually continue for a week. Place a cotton washcloth or a 6-inch piece of cut-up towel inside the diaper to trap some of the more watery stool. Use disposable superabsorbable diapers temporarily to cut down on cleanup time. Use the ones with snug leg bands or cover the other type with a pair of plastic pants. Wash your child under running water in the bath tub. Someday your child will be toilet trained.

Call Your Child's Physician Later If

• Any signs of dehydration occur.

• Your child vomits the clear fluids 3 or more times.

• The diarrhea becomes severe (such as a BM every hour for more than 8 hours).

• Any blood, pus, or mucus appears in the diarrhea.

• Abdominal pain develops and lasts more than 12 hours.

• The diarrhea does not improve after 48 hours on the special diet.

• Mild diarrhea lasts more than 2 weeks.

PREVENTION

Diarrhea is very contagious. Hand-washing after diaper changing or using the toilet is crucial for keeping everyone in the family from getting diarrhea. Some of the more serious diarrhea caused by bacteria can be prevented if one takes precautions preparing poultry, cleaning aquariums, and touching turtles or sick pets (see page 320).

FOREIGN BODY, SWALLOWED

Most swallowed nonfood solid items are coins. Smaller coins (dimes or pennies) usually pass with ease. Larger coins (and rarely the smaller ones) can get hung up at a narrow segment of the esophagus. Dangerous objects are pointed ones such as nails, needles, and toothpicks. Swallowed glass, on the other hand, usually passes harmlessly. A new threat to children are the button (or disk) batteries (as found in watches, calculators, and cameras). These contain acid or alkali, which can erode the lining of the intestines.

CALL YOUR CHILD'S PHYSICIAN
Immediately If
- Your child is choking or coughing severely. (Also, turn directly to the guideline on CHOKING, page 10.)

- There is any increased salivation, drooling, gagging, or difficulty swallowing.

- There is any severe discomfort in the throat or chest.

- There is any mild discomfort for over an hour.

- Your child eats slowly and cautiously.

- There is any abdominal pain or vomiting.

- The object was sharp.

- The object was longer than 1 inch.

- The object was larger than a penny.

- The object was a small button battery.

- You're not sure what your child swallowed.

- The object could be poisonous.

- You have other urgent questions.

Within 24 Hours

In all other children who have probably swallowed a foreign body. The medical evaluation of this situation is somewhat controversial. Rarely, a foreign body can become stuck in the esophagus and yet not cause any symptoms. If the swallowed object was metal, a chest X ray may be needed to be certain the foreign body has reached the stomach (even if the object is a small coin). Another approach is to obtain an X ray if the object hasn't passed within 72 hours.

HOME CARE
Diagnostic Trial of Eating • If no symptoms are present, give your child some water to drink. If this causes no symptoms such as gagging or pain, your child should eat some bread or other soft solid food. If this goes smoothly, the object is probably in the stomach. Swallowed foreign bodies almost always make it to the stomach, travel through the intestines, and are passed in a normal bowel movement in 3 or 4 days. There is nothing you can do to hurry it along.

Checking Bowel Movements • Normally, for small, smooth objects, bowel movements do not need to be checked. However, for sharp, long (larger than 1 inch), or valuable objects, the bowel movements should be collected by having your child wear a diaper or defecate on newspapers. Cut them up with a knife or strain them through a piece of screen until the object is retrieved.

Call Your Child's Physician Later If

• The stools are being checked and the foreign body hasn't passed in 7 days.

• Abdominal pain, vomiting, or blood stools develop in the next 2 weeks.

PREVENTION
Young children who put everything in their mouths must be protected from small objects they might inadvertently swal low. Check your floors periodically for coins, buttons, jewelry, small toys, pins, and the like. The new button-size batteries used for watches contain caustic chemicals and used batteries can cause intestinal damage or death if swallowed. Dispose of them carefully. Avoid pierced earrings in children under 4 years of age. Store your sewing boxes up high.

GAS, EXCESSIVE

A normal but embarrassing part of the human condition is to pass bowel gas (flatus) on a daily basis. Most people also belch or burp up stomach gas occasionally. In fact, the average adult on a regular diet passes gas 10 to 20 times a day. This amounts to approximately 1 quart of gas per day. Gas should not be considered excessive unless it occurs at more than twice the normal frequency.

Causes • The main causes of normal gas are swallowed air, gas-producing foods, and certain diseases that interfere with sugar absorption. Every baby is somewhat "gassy" because of swallowing air during sucking. This process is increased by sucking on a clogged nipple, a bottle that does not have milk in it, a pacifier, the thumb, or a blanket. Babies also swallow air during crying. Children at a later age swallow air with gum-chewing. Children with nasal allergies swallow air if they are "sniffers." Some children have a nervous habit of frequent swallowing. The carbonation in soft drinks releases gas in the stomach. Stomach gas is more likely to pass into the intestines if a child is lying down. Gas (unlike food) can pass through the gastrointestinal tract in 20 minutes.

Some foods (such as beans) are made up of complex carbohydrates that are not completely digested in the small bowel. These foods are converted into gas by bacteria in the large bowel. Eating lots of beans can increase gas production tenfold.

The most common medical condition that causes increased gas production is milk intolerance. The enzyme (lactase) that normally digests milk sugar (lactose) progressively decreases in amount between ages 4 and 20 years in large segments of our population. Those most affected people are Orientals, Blacks, and Eastern Europeans. The undigested lactose is converted into hydrogen by the bacteria in the large bowel. The amount of gas produced depends upon the amount of milk ingested. Symptoms of bloating, abdominal cramps, and increased passage of gas usually don't occur until a person drinks more than 1 quart a day.

Gas can be temporarily increased with bouts of infectious diarrhea. Gas can also build up behind constipation and be released in large amounts. The gas is often nearly odorless. Bowel gas can develop an offensive odor during a bout of infectious diarrhea or in children on a high meat diet.

CALL YOUR CHILD'S PHYSICIAN DURING OFFICE HOURS IF

- You think your child has excessive gas and you don't know the cause.

- Your child is losing weight.

- You have other questions or concerns.

HOME CARE

In general, the passage of gas causes no symptoms. By age 5 or 6 most children can be taught to release gas in a socially acceptable manner. Gas does not need to be released by inserting anything in the rectum.

Air swallowing can be reduced by eliminating some of the previously mentioned habits.

A reduced intake of beans and carbonated beverages will decrease gas production in all children.

If you feel your child has a milk intolerance (especially if your family history is positive), reduce the milk intake to 2 or 3 glasses a day. Milk does not need to be completely eliminated in most people with a lactose intolerance. Yogurt is easily digested and can be continued. If you suspect milk intolerance and symptoms persist after minor dietary change, consult your child's physician about current recommendations for this disorder.

RELATED TOPIC

DIARRHEA (see page 591)

HICCUPS

Hiccups are strange gulping sounds made by involuntary, sudden contractions (spasms) of the diaphragm, which draws in a quick gasp of air against closed vocal cords. They usually are quite uncomfortable in older children. They often accompany indigestion or an overful stomach that presses against the diaphragm. Drinking excessive carbonated beverages is a common cause of recurrent hiccups. In small infants, hiccups are normal.

HOME CARE

Treatment • Give 1 teaspoon of dry granulated sugar and have your child swallow it quickly. If this doesn't work the first time, repeat it 3 times at 2-minute intervals. For younger children, corn syrup can be used. Babies can be given a swallow of water.

Also, lying down usually helps, possibly because this position relaxes the abdominal wall. If this doesn't work, gag your child 3 or 4 times by pushing down the back of the tongue with the handle of a spoon. Other children are helped by rubbing the uvula or soft palate with a cotton swab, or by pulling the tongue outward with the fingers.

Call Your Child's Physician Later If

• The hiccups last more than 3 hours (the usual time needed to empty the stomach) and your child is uncomfortable.

NAUSEA

Nausea is an urge to vomit or a general uneasiness in the stomach. Nausea is often caused by a stomach virus and accompanied by vomiting. If so, turn directly to the guideline for VOMITING, page 608. Nausea can also be due to indigestion or fear. If nausea is your child's only symptom, it's rarely caused by anything serious.

HOME CARE

Treatment • Temporarily, serve your child clear fluids and light foods. Avoid medicines such as aspirin which can irritate the stomach.

Call Your Child's Physician Later If

• New symptoms develop that worry you.

• Your teenager could be pregnant.

• The nausea lasts more than 1 week.

RELATED TOPICS

MOTION SICKNESS (see page 500)
VOMITING (see page 608)

PINWORMS

A pinworm is a white, very thin worm, about ¼ inch long, that moves. If it doesn't wiggle it's probably lint or a thread. Pinworms are usually seen in the anal and buttock area, especially at night or early in the morning. Occasionally one is found on the surface of a bowel movement. They infect the anal area and large intestine. More than 10 percent of children have them. They do not cause any serious health problems, but they can cause considerable itching and irritation of the anal area and buttocks. Occasionally in girls, vaginal itching becomes a symptom. If the skin around the anus is red and tender, it is probably a strep infection, so call your child's physician during office hours.

HOME CARE WHEN PINWORM IS SEEN

Antipinworm Medicine • The drugs for killing pinworms all require a prescription. If you have definitely seen a pinworm, call your child's physician during office hours for a prescription. The following information may also help you.

Treatment of Other Family Members • Children are usually infected by children outside the family. If anyone else in your family has symptoms or anyone sleeps with your child, call your physician during office hours for instructions. Physicians do not agree on whether to treat everyone in the family or only those with symptoms. If any of your child's friends have similar symptoms, be sure to tell their parents to get them tested.

Call Your Child's Physician During Office Hours If

• The skin around the anus becomes red or tender (strep bacteria have a special affinity for this site).

• The anal itching is not resolved within a week after treatment.

• You have other questions or concerns.

HOME CARE FOR SUSPICIOUS SYMPTOMS WITHOUT PINWORM BEING SEEN

Suspicious Symptoms • If your child has itching or irritation of the anal area, it could mean pinworms. Keep in mind that many children get itching here solely from washing their anal area too frequently or vigorously with soap. The anal area can also become red and sore from diarrhea or local strep infections.

Check your child for pinworms as follows: First, look for a ¼-inch white, threadlike worm that moves. Examine the area around the anus, using a flashlight. Do this a few hours after your child goes to bed and first thing in the morning for 2 consecutive nights. If no adult pinworm is seen, do a Scotch-tape test for pinworm eggs.

Instructions for Scotch-tape Test • Pick up glass slides or a special pinworm lab packet at your physician's office (2 for each child) and mark your child's name on the slide. Touch a piece of clear Scotch tape (with the sticky side down) to the skin on both sides of the anus. Do this in the morning soon after your child has awakened, and definitely before any bath or shower. Do it 2 mornings in a row. Apply the piece of tape to the slide. If slides are unavailable, the transparent tape that has touched the skin can be applied to a second piece of tape. Bring the slides in for examination with a microscope. Your physician will call the results to you. If pinworm eggs are seen, a medicine will be prescribed. (See PINWORM IS SEEN, on page 602, for details on home treatment.)

HOME CARE FOR PINWORM EXPOSURE OR CONTACT

If your child had recent contact with a child with pinworms but has no symptoms, your child probably won't get them.

Pinworms are harmless and are never present very long without causing some anal itching. If you want to be sure your child doesn't have them, wait for at least a month. The swallowed egg will not mature into an adult pinworm for 3 to 4 weeks. Then contact your physician about doing a Scotchtape test for pinworm eggs. (See above, instructions on doing the Scotch-tape test.)

PREVENTION

Infection is caused by swallowing pinworm eggs. Your child can get pinworms no matter how carefully you keep the kids and your house clean. The following hygiene measures, however, can help to reduce the chances of reinfection of your child or new infections in other people. Pets don't carry pinworms.

• Have your child scrub hands and fingernails thoroughly before each meal and after each use of the toilet. Keep the fingernails cut short, because eggs can collect here. Thumbsucking and nail-biting should be discouraged.

• Don't eat food that has fallen on the floor.

• Vacuum or wet-mop your child's entire room once a week, because any eggs scattered on the floor are infectious for 1 to 2 weeks.

• Machine-washing at hot temperature will kill any eggs present in clothing or bedding.

STOOLS, BLOOD IN

SYMPTOMS AND CHARACTERISTICS

Blood in the stools (or bowel movements) is usually bright red. Rarely, blood comes out tar-black if it is from bleeding in the stomach. Swallowed blood also will look this way, so your child may have a tarry stool within 24 hours after a severe nosebleed.

Similar Condition • If your child has eaten anything red in the last 24 hours, turn first to the guideline for STOOLS, UNUSUAL COLOR OF, page 607. Most red stools are not due to blood.

CALL YOUR CHILD'S PHYSICIAN

Immediately If

- Bright-red blood is mixed throughout the stool.
- There is a large amount of bright-red blood.
- The toilet water turns red.
- There has been a tar-black stool.
- Diarrhea is also present.
- Any blood has been vomited.
- A stomachache is also present.
- Your child faints or feels dizzy with standing.
- There are any skin bruises not caused by an injury.
- Your child acts or looks very sick.

During Office Hours If

- The cause of bleeding is unknown. If you suspect an anal fissure, however, see below. More than 90 percent of children with blood in their stools have an anal fissure as the cause.

  Be sure to bring a sample of the blood in your child's stool with you to the physician's office for testing.

ANAL FISSURE

SYMPTOMS AND CHARACTERISTICS

An anal fissure is a shallow tear or crack in the skin at the opening of the anus. More than 90 percent of children with blood in their stools have an anal fissure. Your child probably has an anal fissure if the following findings are present:

- The blood is bright red.
- The blood is only a few streaks or flecks.
- The blood is on the surface of the stool or on the toilet tissue after wiping.
- Your child passed a large or hard bowel movement (BM).

- You can see a shallow tear at the opening of the anus when the buttocks are spread apart, usually at 6 or 12 o'clock. A tear cannot always be seen.

- Touching the tear causes mild pain.

  If your child's symptoms are different, call your physician for help.

Cause • Trauma to the anal canal during constipation is the usual cause of anal fissures.

Expected course • Bleeding from an anal fissure stops on its own in 5 or 10 minutes.

HOME CARE

Warm Saline Baths • Give your child warm baths for 20 minutes, 3 times a day. Have him sit in a basin or tub of warm water with about 2 tablespoons of table salt or baking soda added. Don't use any soap on the irritated area. Then gently dry the anal area.

Ointments • If it seems irritated, you can apply ½ percent hydrocortisone ointment (nonprescription). If the pain is severe, apply 2½ percent Xylocaine or 1 percent Nupercainal ointment (no prescription needed) 4 times a day for a few days to numb the area.

Diet • The most important aspect of treatment is to keep your child on a nonconstipating diet. Increase the intake of fiber with more fresh fruits and vegetables, beans, and bran products. Reduce the amount of milk products your child eats or drinks. Occasionally a stool softener (such as mineral oil) is needed temporarily.

CALL YOUR CHILD'S PHYSICIAN
Within 24 Hours If

- The bleeding increases in amount.

- The bleeding occurs more than 2 times (especially if it's painless).

During Office Hours If

- The anal fissure is not completely healed after 3 days of treatment.

- You have other questions or concerns.

RELATED TOPICS

BLOOD IN STOOLS (see page 604)
CONSTIPATION (see page 586)

STOOLS, UNUSUAL COLOR OF

Unusual colors of the stool (some color other than brown) are almost always due to food color or food additives. In children with diarrhea, the passage time is very rapid and stools often come out the same color as the Kool-Aid or Jell-O water that went in. Stool color relates more to what is eaten than to any disease.

UNUSUAL STOOL COLORS AND COMMON CAUSES

- Red: Blood, red Jell-O, red Kool-Aid, red cereals, tomato juice or soup, cranberries, beets, red medicines

- Black: Blood from the stomach, iron, bismuth (e.g., Pepto-Bismol), licorice, Oreo cookies, cigarette ashes, charcoal, grape juice

- Green: Green Jell-O, iron, spinach, diarrhea (due to rapid passage of normal bile), breast-feeding (especially during the first 2 months of life)

- Yellow-white: Aluminum hydroxide (antacids), excessive milk, hepatitis

WHEN TO CALL YOUR CHILD'S PHYSICIAN

- If stools are red without an explanation, see the guideline on STOOLS, BLOOD IN, above.

- If tar-black without an explanation, also see the guideline on STOOLS, BLOOD IN, above.

- For other unusual colors, eliminate the suspected food. If the color continues for more than 72 hours without an explanation, call your child's physician during office hours. Be prepared to bring a stool sample with you.

VOMITING

SYMPTOMS AND CHARACTERISTICS

Vomiting is the forceful ejection of a large portion of the stomach's contents through the mouth. Nausea and abdominal discomfort usually precede each bout of vomiting. The mechanism is strong stomach contractions against a closed stomach outlet.

By contrast, regurgitation is the effortless spitting up of 1 or 2 mouthfuls of stomach contents, which is commonly seen in babies under 1 year of age.

Similar Conditions • If appropriate, turn directly to the following guidelines:

COUGH (when vomiting is strictly triggered by coughing spells) (see page 570)
MOTION SICKNESS (see page 500)
SPITTING UP (REGURGITATION) (see page 133)

Causes • Most vomiting is caused by a viral infection of the stomach (stomach flu) or by your child's eating something that is hard to digest. Often the viral type is associated with DIARRHEA (see page 591). Vomiting is a protective mechanism to keep harmful substances out of the intestines.

Expected Course • The vomiting usually stops in 6 to 24 hours. Dietary changes usually speed recovery.

CALL YOUR CHILD'S PHYSICIAN

Immediately If

• Your child is less than 1 month old (exception: vomiting once or reflux).

• Your child has not urinated in more than 8 hours.

• Crying produces no tears.

• Any blood appears in the vomited material *and* it's not from a recent nosebleed.

• Any abdominal pain has persisted for more than 4 hours (especially if the abdomen is swollen).

- Your child has vomited clear fluids 3 or more times *and* has passed 3 or more diarrhea stools.
- Your child is difficult to awaken.
- Your child is confused or delirious.
- The head was recently injured (with vomiting 3 or more times).
- The abdomen was recently injured.
- A foreign object could have been swallowed and caught in the esophagus.
- Your child acts or looks very sick.

During Office Hours If

- Your child has been vomiting for more than
  12 hours (under 6 months old).
  24 hours (6 months to 2 years old).
  48 hours (over 2 years old).
- Your child is on any medicine that could cause vomiting.
- Vomiting is a recurrent problem for your child.
- You have other questions or concerns.

HOME CARE

Special Diet for Vomiting

1. FOR BOTTLE-FED INFANTS (less than 1 year old), offer Infalyte or Pedialyte for 8 hours.

- For vomiting once, offer ½ strength formula.
- For vomiting 2 or more times, offer Infalyte or Pedialyte.
- Give small amounts (1 teaspoon) every 10 minutes.
- After 4 hours without vomiting, increase the amount.
- After 8 hours without vomiting, return to formula.
- For infants more than 4 months old, also return to cereal, strained bananas, etc.
- A normal diet is OK in 24 to 48 hours.

2. FOR BREAST-FED INFANTS, reduce the amount per feeding.

- Provide breast milk in smaller amounts. Your goal is to avoid filling the stomach.
- If vomits twice, nurse on only 1 side every 1 to 2 hours.

- If vomits more than 2 times, nurse for 4 to 5 minutes every 30 to 60 minutes.

- After 8 hours without vomiting, return to regular breastfeeding

    3. FOR OLDER CHILDREN (MORE THAN 1 YEAR OLD), offer clear fluids in small amounts for 8 hours.

- Water or ice chips are best for vomiting without diarrhea because water is directly absorbed across the stomach wall.

- Other options: ½ strength flat lemon-lime soda or Popsicles. Stir soda until the fizz is gone because the bubbles can inflate the stomach.

- Give small amounts (1 Tbsp) very 10 minutes.

- After 4 hours without vomiting, increase the amount.

- For severe vomiting, rest the stomach completely for 1 hour, then start over with smaller amounts.
  For older children (more than 1 year old) add bland foods after 8 hours without vomiting.

- Stay on bland, starchy foods (any complex carbohydrates) for 24 hours.

- Start with saltine crackers, white bread, rice, mashed potatoes, etc.

- A normal diet is OK in 24 to 48 hours.

Sleep
Help your child go to sleep. Sleep often empties the stomach and relieves the need to vomit. Your child doesn't have to drink anything if he feels nauseated.

Medicines • Discontinue all nonessential medicines for 8 hours. Oral medicines can irritate the stomach and make vomiting worse. If your child has a fever over 103°F, consider using acetaminophen suppositories (no prescription necessary). Call your physician if your child needs to be taking a prescription medicine such as an antibiotic.

Common Mistakes • A common error is to give as much of clear fluids as the child wants, rather than gradually increasing the amounts. This almost always leads to continued vomiting. Another error is to force the child to drink when he or she doesn't want anything.
  Keep in mind that there is no effective drug for vomiting.

Various suppositories have caused serious reactions; in addition, they alleviate only vomiting related to anesthesia, poisoning, or motion sickness—but not the type caused by an irritated stomach lining. Diet therapy is the answer. Vomiting alone rarely causes dehydration unless you give your child drugs, milk, or too much of clear fluids at one time.

Call Your Child's Physician Later If

- Your child develops watery diarrhea *and* vomits clear fluids.

- The vomiting continues for more than 48 hours (12 hours if your child is under 6 months old, and 24 hours if between 6 and 24 months).

- Any signs of dehydration occur. (See EMERGENCY SYMPTOMS page 6.)

- Your child becomes difficult to awaken or acts confused.

- Any blood appears in the vomited material.

- Abdominal pain develops and lasts more than 4 hours.

- Your child develops a severe headache.

- You feel your child is getting worse.

VOMITING OF BLOOD

Blood in the vomited material can be bright red or the dark-brown color of coffee grounds, if it has been acted on by stomach acid.

CALL YOUR CHILD'S PHYSICIAN IMMEDIATELY

- In every case.

- *Exception:* If your child swallowed blood from a cut in the mouth or a nosebleed in the preceding 4 to 6 hours, don't call. One episode of vomited blood under these circumstances can be presumed to be due to swallowed blood and is unimportant.

- If you are asked to come in, bring a sample of the "bloody" material with you so it can be tested.

BLADDER (URINARY)

URINATION, PAIN WITH (DYSURIA)

SYMPTOMS AND CHARACTERISTICS

- Discomfort with passing urine

- Burning or stinging with passing urine

- Urgency (can't wait), frequency (passing small amounts), and straining (difficulty starting) are occasionally associated

- In children too young to talk, suspect dysuria if your child begins to cry regularly when passing urine

  If your child's symptoms are different, call your physician for help.

Causes • The most common cause of mild pain or burning with urination in young girls is an irritation and redness of the vulva (vulvitis) and opening of the urethra (urethritis). The irritation is usually caused by bubble bath, shampoo, or soap that was left on the genital area. Occasionally it is due to poor hygiene. This chemical urethritis occurs almost exclusively prior to puberty. Circumcised boys are also susceptible to urethral irritation from soap. Since 5 percent of young girls get urinary tract infections (UTI), one must always consider this diagnosis. A UTI is a bacterial infection of the bladder (cystitis) and sometimes the kidneys (pyelonephritis).

Expected Course of Bubble Bath (Chemical) Urethritis • With warm-water soaks, the pain and burning usually clear in 12 hours.

CALL YOUR CHILD'S PHYSICIAN

Immediately If

- The pain with urination is severe.
- Your child has a high fever (over 104°F) or chills.
- Any abdominal or back pain is present.
- Your child is able to pass only very small amounts of urine.
- The urine is bloody or cola-colored.
- Your child acts or looks very sick.

Within 24 Hours If

- Your child develops any fever (over 100°F).
- There is any frequency, urgency, or straining with urination.
- There is a recent onset of day or night wetting.
- Your child is a male.
- Your child is female *and* she had previous urinary tract infections.
- She has any vaginal discharge.
- You think she may have pinworms.
- You have other questions or concerns.

HOME CARE

Warm Vinegar-Water Soaks • Have your daughter soak her bottom in a basin or bathtub of warm water for 20 minutes. Put ½ cup of white vinegar in the water. Be sure she spreads her legs and allows the water to cleanse the genital area. No soap should be used. Help her dry herself completely afterward. Repeat this in 2 hours and again in 12 hours. This will remove any soap, concentrated urine, or other chemicals from the genital area. Thereafter, cleanse the genital area once a day with warm water.

Avoid Soap, Shampoo, or Bubble Bath to the Vulva Area • See *Prevention* for details (page 614).

Instructions for Collecting a Midstream, Clean-Catch Urine Specimen at Home • If you are told to bring a urine sample with you, try to collect the first one in the morning. Use a sterile jar. Wash off the genital area several times with cotton balls and warm water. Have your child then sit on the toilet seat with her legs spread widely so that the labia (skin folds of the vagina) don't touch. Have her start to urinate into the toilet, and then place the clean container directly in line with the urine stream. Remove it after you have collected a few ounces but before she stops. Catch urine from the middle of the stream without any stopping or starting. The first or last ounce that comes out of the bladder may be contaminated. Store the urine in the refrigerator until you take it to the physician's office. Bring it in on ice.

Call Your Child's Physician Later If

• The pain and burning continue more than 12 hours after a warm vinegar-water soak. (You will probably need to bring a urine specimen with you.)

PREVENTION OF RECURRENCES

• Don't use bubble bath or put any other soaps into the bath water. Don't let a bar of soap float around in the bathtub. If you are going to shampoo your child's hair, do this at the end of the bath.

• Wash the genital area with water, not soap. (The tissue inside the vaginal lips is very sensitive to soap.) If this washing causes any pain, you need to do it differently.

• Keep bath time less than 15 minutes. Have your child urinate immediately after baths.

• If this doesn't help, switch to showers.

• Teach your daughter to wipe herself correctly from front to back, especially after a bowel movement.

• Try not to let your child get constipated. (If she does, see the guideline for CONSTIPATION, page 586.)

• Encourage her to drink adequate fluids each day to keep the urine light-colored. This will increase the amount of urine she makes, and the extra urine "washes out" the kidneys and bladder.

• Encourage her to empty the bladder at least every 3 to 4

hours during the day and not to "hold back." (If she avoids public restrooms, help her overcome this reluctance.) If this doesn't help, have her empty her bladder every 2 hours.

• Have her wear loose cotton underpants. Polyester or nylon underpants, tights, or panty hose don't allow the skin to "breathe." Discourage wearing of underpants during the night.

URINE, BLOOD IN

Blood in the urine can make it pink, red, brown, or cola-colored. There are some harmless causes for these colors—beets, for instance. Keep in mind that dark-yellow (amber) urine is usually due to being a little dehydrated from a poor fluid intake, sweating, and/or fever.

If blood in the urine is suspected, your child needs to have the urine checked. Collect a specimen of the "bloody" urine in a clean container and keep it in the refrigerator until you go to your physician's office. If your child is in diapers, bring along the diaper with the pink or red spot on it. Also measure and record (in ounces) all the urine that your child passes if he or she is toilet trained.

CALL YOUR CHILD'S PHYSICIAN

Immediately If

• A headache is present.

• The eyelids are puffy.

• Your child is urinating much less than usual.

• Pain is present in the back or side.

• The back has recently been injured.

• Your child acts or looks very sick.

During Office Hours

• All other children with suspected blood in the urine need medical consultation. If your child is a young male and the opening at the tip of the penis appears to have a crack in it that is bleeding, apply petrolatum while waiting.

URINE, STRONG ODOR

SYMPTOMS AND CHARACTERISTICS

The urine has a pungent, often unpleasant odor of recent onset. The color of the urine is usually darker than normal at these times.

Similar Conditions • A dark-yellow urine may contain bilirubin; check the whites of the eyes for a yellow color change (i.e., jaundice). Urinary tract infections cause a foul-smelling urine. Blood in the urine can cause pink, red, or cola-colored urine.

If one of the following is suspected, save time by turning directly to that guideline:

JAUNDICE (see page 477)
URINATION, PAIN WITH (see page 612)
URINE, BLOOD IN (see page 615)

Causes • Most strong-smelling urine is produced when your child is mildly dehydrated. Exercise, a fever, hot weather, or a hot room can lead to slight dehydration. Children in cloth diapers can acquire a strong odor of ammonia if the bacteria in the stool have time to break down the urine. Certain drugs (e.g., penicillin and ampicillin) are excreted in the urine and cause an unusual odor. Certain foods (e.g., asparagus) or a high-protein diet lead to strong-smelling urine.

CALL YOUR CHILD'S PHYSICIAN DURING OFFICE HOURS IF

• The unusual odor has been present since birth.

• The unusual odor lasts more than 24 hours without explanation.

• You have other questions or concerns.

HOME CARE

Increase your child's water intake during warm weather or fevers. Reduce your youngster's protein intake (remember that milk is largely a protein). Refer to the guideline on DIAPER RASH, page 128, if the odor is ammonia. By and large, most of these odors are not caused by anything harmful.

GENITALS

FOREIGN BODY, VAGINA

During normal exploration of the body, young girls may put a foreign object in their vagina. Common ones are toilet tissue, a crayon, or a bead. The objects must be removed to prevent a vaginal infection. Often they are not discovered until after the girl is brought in for a bad-smelling vaginal discharge.

CALL YOUR CHILD'S PHYSICIAN

Immediately If

• The object was sharp.

• There is any bleeding.

• The object is causing any pain or discomfort.

• The object has been in the vagina for less than a day.

• You are concerned about sexual abuse.

Within 24 Hours If

• All other children need medical consultation. In the meantime, leave the object alone lest it be pushed in farther.

MENSTRUAL CRAMPS (DYSMENORRHEA)

SYMPTOMS AND CHARACTERISTICS

- Cramps during the first 1 or 2 days of a period
- Pain in lower mid-abdomen
- Pain may radiate to the lower back or both thighs
- Associated symptoms of nausea, vomiting, diarrhea, or dizziness in some girls

  If your child's symptoms are different, call your physician for help.

Cause • Menstrual cramps (dysmenorrhea) are experienced by more than 50 percent of girls and women during menstrual periods. Therefore, cramps are not abnormal. They are caused by strong contractions (even spasms) of the muscles in the womb (uterus) as it tries to expel menstrual blood. Menstrual periods usually are not painful during their first 1 to 2 years. However, once ovulation (the release of an egg from the ovary) begins, the level of progesterone and other hormones in the bloodstream increases and leads to stronger contractions and some cramps.

Expected Course • Cramps last 2 or 3 days and usually occur with each menstrual period. Current drugs usually can keep the pain to a very mild level. The cramps may be reduced after the first pregnancy and childbirth, probably due to the stretching of the opening of the womb (cervical os). Other women gain some improvement by age 25.

CALL YOUR CHILD'S PHYSICIAN

Immediately If

- The pain is so bad that your daughter is unable to walk normally.
- She also has an unexplained fever (over 100°F).
- She acts or looks very sick.

During Office Hours If

- Any school is missed because of menstrual cramps.

- Vaginal discharge was also present before the period.

- Any pain occurs with urination or bowel movements.

- The pain is located on one side only.

- Any pain persists beyond the third day of flow.

- You have other questions or concerns.

HOME CARE

Ibuprofen (Advil, Medipren, and Nuprin Are Some of the Brand Names) • Ibuprofen is a special drug for menstrual cramps. It not only decreases the pain but also decreases contractions of the uterus. Until the fall of 1984, it was available only by prescription (as Motrin). Because of an excellent safety record, it can now be obtained over the counter in 200-mg tablets, of which 1 or 2 can be given 4 or 5 times a day. (Always take 2 tablets as the first dosage.) The drug should be started as soon as there is any menstrual flow, or the day before if possible. Don't wait for the onset of menstrual cramps. Ibuprofen should make your daughter feel well enough not to miss anything important. (Note: If your daughter can't swallow pills, liquid ibuprofen is available by prescription.)

Acetaminophen and aspirin products for treating dysmenorrhea are not very helpful. Many of the nonprescription products that are advertised as providing special, fast relief for menstrual cramps are overrated. If you read the label carefully, you will notice that they contain aspirin or acetaminophen (sometimes with a small amount of caffeine).

Local Heat • A heating pad or warm washcloth applied to the area of pain may be helpful. A 20-minute warm bath twice a day may reduce the pain.

Aggravating Factors • Any type of pain will hurt more in people who are tired or upset. Avoid long hours and inadequate sleep during menstrual periods. If your daughter has undue troubles or worries on her mind, encourage her to share them with someone.

Full Activity • The main goal should be to stay active and take pain medications regularly. There are absolutely no restrictions; your child can go to school, take gym, swim, take a shower or bath, wash her hair, go outside in bad weather, date, etc., during her menstrual period. A common mistake is to go to bed; people who are busy have a better chance of repressing their pain. If the pains are limiting your daughter's activities despite using ibuprofen, ask your physician about stronger medication.

Prevention of Toxic Shock Syndrome • Over 80 percent of cases of this life-threatening disease occur in girls during a menstrual period. Most cases occur in girls who use a tampon overnight. This condition can usually be prevented if tampons are changed every 3 to 4 hours during the day and external pads are used during sleep.

Call Your Teenager's Physician Later If

• Ibuprofen does not provide adequate pain relief.
 (Note: New prescription drugs are extremely helpful for severe menstrual cramps.)

• The menstrual cramps are causing her to miss school or other important activities.

• An unexplained fever occurs.

• The pain lasts more than 3 days.

• Premenstrual weight gain or swelling occurs.

SWELLING, GROIN OR SCROTUM

SYMPTOMS
This guideline covers a swelling, bulge, or lump in the scrotum or groin in males.

Similar Conditions • If one of the following is present, save time by turning directly to that guideline:

GENITAL TRAUMA (see page 72)
LYMPH NODES, SWOLLEN (see page 479)

Causes • A hydrocele is a painless collection of clear fluid above the testicle, present at birth. (See HOME CARE OF A HYDROCELE, below.) Unlike the other conditions, both sides are commonly involved.

An inguinal hernia may be diagnosed at birth or later.

A lymph node in the groin can swell up following a rash or infection of the leg on that side. While all the other conditions cause swelling of the scrotal sac, the enlarged node is found in the groin crease.

Two emergency conditions that begin with scrotal swelling and severe pain are torsion (rotation) of the testicle, and an infected testicle (orchitis). Don't assume it's just a pulled groin muscle.

CALL YOUR CHILD'S PHYSICIAN

Immediately If

- The area is tender to the touch.
- The area is painful.

During Office Hours

- All other cases of scrotal swelling should be seen by a physician, except a hydrocele diagnosed at birth.

HOME CARE OF A HYDROCELE

Hydroceles are present in about 10 percent of normal newborn males. If your child's physician has made this diagnosis, the following information may be helpful. A hydrocele is usually caused by the pressure on the abdomen during delivery, which pushes clear fluid downward through the channel that surrounds the spermatic cord and blood vessels to the testicle. A hydrocele may take 6 to 12 months to clear completely. It is harmless, but can be rechecked during regular visits. If the swelling frequently changes in size (especially becoming larger with crying), a hernia may also be present, and you should call your physician during office hours for an appointment.

VAGINAL IRRITATION

SYMPTOMS AND CHARACTERISTICS

- Genital area pain, burning, or itching
- No pain or burning with urination

If your child's symptoms are different, call your physician for help.

Similar Conditions • If pain accompanies urination, save time by turning directly to the guideline on URINATION, PAIN WITH, page 612.

If your child also has itching of the anus and buttocks, see the guideline on PINWORMS, page 602.

Causes • Most vaginal itching or discomfort is due to a chemical irritation of the vulva or outer vagina. The usual irritants are bubble bath, shampoo, or soap left on the genital area. Occasionally it is due to poor hygiene. This chemical vulvitis occurs almost exclusively prior to puberty. If the vagina becomes infected, a vaginal discharge will be noted.

Expected Course of Chemical Vulvitis • It responds within 1 to 2 days with proper treatment.

CALL YOUR CHILD'S PHYSICIAN

Immediately If

• An unexplained fever (over 100°F) is present.

• There is any severe abdominal pain.

• Sexual abuse could be the cause.

During Office Hours If

• There is any vaginal discharge.

• You have other questions or concerns.

HOME CARE

Warm Vinegar-Water Soaks • Have your daughter soak her bottom in a basin or bathtub of warm water for 20 minutes. Put ½ cup of white vinegar in the water. Be sure she spreads her legs and allows the water to cleanse the genital area. No soap should be used. Help her dry herself completely afterward. Repeat this in 2 hours and again in 12 hours. This will remove any soap, concentrated urine, or other chemicals from the genital area. Thereafter, cleanse the genital area once a day with warm water on a washcloth.

Hydrocortisone Cream • Apply ½ percent hydrocortisone cream (no prescription needed) 4 times a day to the genital area for 2 or 3 days.

Call Your Child's Physician Later If

• The pain and itching are not cleared within 48 hours on treatment.

• Your child develops a vaginal discharge.

PREVENTION

• Don't use bubble bath or put any other soaps into the bath water. Don't let a bar of soap float around in the bathtub. If you are going to shampoo your child's hair, do this at the end of the bath.

• Wash the genital area with water, not soap. If this process causes any pain, you need to do it differently.

• Your child should wear cotton underpants. Polyester or nylon underpants, tights, or panty hose don't allow the skin to "breathe." Discourage wearing underpants during the night.

• Teach your daughter to wipe herself correctly from front to back, especially after a bowel movement.

BONES AND JOINTS

BACKACHE, ACUTE

SYMPTOMS AND CHARACTERISTICS

- Your child complains of back pain
- Usually the mid or lower back is involved
- The pain is worsened by bending
- The muscles on one side of the spine are tender and in spasm
- Mainly occurs in adolescents

Causes • Backaches are usually a symptom of a strain of some of the 200 muscles in the back that allow us to stand upright. Often the triggering event is carrying something too heavy, lifting from an awkward position, bending too far backward or sideways, or prolonged digging in the garden (overexertion of back muscles).

Expected Course • The pain and discomfort usually resolve in 1 to 2 weeks. Recurrences are common.

CALL YOUR CHILD'S PHYSICIAN

Immediately If

• The pain is very severe.

• Your child can't walk.

• The back pain shoots into the buttock or back of the thigh.

• A tingling sensation occurs in the legs.

• The backache followed an accident or injury.

• A fever (over 100°F) is present.

• Passing the urine causes pain or burning.

• Your child acts or looks very sick.

During Office Hours If

• Your child is under 5 years old.

• Your child doesn't walk normally.

• The pain interferes with sleep.

• The cause of the pain is unknown.

• Back pain is a recurrent problem for your child.

• You have other questions or concerns.

HOME CARE

Pain-Relief Medicines • Give aspirin, acetaminophen, or ibuprofen (for dosage, see the chart on page 66) 4 times a day. Continue this until 24 hours have passed without any pain. This is the most important part of the therapy, because back pain causes muscle spasm, and these medicines can greatly reduce both the spasm and the pain.

Local Heat • A heating pad or hot water bottle applied to the most painful area helps to relieve muscle spasm. Do this whenever the pain flares up. Don't allow your child to go to sleep on a heating pad, because it can cause burns.

Sleeping Position • The most comfortable sleeping position is usually on the side with a pillow between the knees. If your child sleeps on the back, it may help to place a pillow under the knees. Avoid sleeping on the adomen. The mattress should be firm or reinforced with a board.

Activity • Complete bedrest is unnecessary. Have your child avoid lifting, jumping, horseback riding, motorcycle riding, and exercise until he or she is completely well.

Call Your Child's Physician Later If

• The pain becomes worse.

• The pain begins to shoot into the leg.

• The pain is no better in 72 hours.

• The pain is still present after 2 weeks.

PREVENTION

The only way to prevent future backaches is to keep the back muscles in excellent physical condition. This will require 5 minutes of back and abdominal exercises per day, possibly for the rest of your child's life. Helpful strengthening exercises are sit-ups, 6-inch leg raises, flattening the back against the floor, and chest and leg lifts while on the abdomen. Also perform stretching exercises. The strengthening exercises should be avoided when your child is having active back pain, but the stretching exercises should be continued. Remind your child to lift objects with the leg muscles and not by bending or twisting the back.

LIMB PAIN

SYMPTOMS AND CHARACTERISTICS

• Your child complains of pains in the arms or legs

• Your child does not have a limp

• The pain is not due to a known injury

Similar Conditions • If appropriate, turn directly to the following guidelines:

LIMP (see page 628)
BONE AND JOINT TRAUMA (see page 63)

Causes • There are 2 main causes of *mild* limb pain. *Brief* pains (1 to 15 minutes) are usually due to muscle spasms. Foot or calf muscle cramps are especially common at night. *Continuous* acute pains (hours to 3 days) are usually due to overstrenuous activities or forgotten muscle injuries. Both of these normal pains have been erroneously referred to as "growing pains" (although they have nothing to do with growth). Mild muscle aches also occur with many viral illnesses.

CALL YOUR CHILD'S PHYSICIAN

Immediately If

• The limb pain is very severe (e.g., causes constant crying).

• A joint is swollen.

• A joint can't be moved fully.

• Your child acts or looks very sick.

Within 24 Hours If

• A fever (over 100°F) is present (especially if the pain is located at one site).

During Office Hours If

• The pain interferes with sleep.

• The pain has lasted more than 3 days.

• Limb pain is a recurrent problem for your child.

• You have other questions.

HOME CARE

Treatment for Muscle Cramps • Muscle cramps in the feet or calf muscles occur in a third of children. During attacks, stretch the foot and toes upward as far as they will go to break the spasm. Massage and heat to the painful muscle can also help.

Future attacks may be prevented by daily stretching exercises of the heel cords. (Lean forward at the ankles with the knees straight.) A glass of tonic (quinine) water at bedtime may prevent some of these night cramps, as will adequate fluids during sports.

Treatment for Acute Strained Muscles • Massage the sore muscles with ice for 20 to 30 minutes several times on the first day. Give aspirin, acetaminophen, or ibuprofen for pain relief. (For dosage, see the chart on page 66.) For muscle pains with fever, give acetaminophen, not aspirin.

If stiffness persists after 48 hours, have your child relax in a hot bath for 20 minutes twice a day, and gently exercise the involved part under water.

Call Your Child's Physician Later If

• Your child develops a limp, a swollen joint, or a fever.

• The pain lasts more than 3 days on treatment.

• You feel your child is getting worse.

LIMP

A limp is a painful type of walking (gait), in which the child tries to avoid putting much weight on one leg or hurries off it when walking. Some children flat-out refuse to stand or walk at all. Most of these children have limb pain but may be too young to express this in words. The most common cause of an unexplained limp in young children is a minor injury from jumping off of furniture.

CALL YOUR CHILD'S PHYSICIAN

Immediately If

• A severe limp followed a recent injury.

• Your child won't walk at all.

• A fever (over 100°F) is present.

• A joint is swollen.

• A joint can't be moved fully.

During Office Hours If

• The limp has no obvious cause. (First consider a simple cause such as tight new shoes, a sliver in the foot, a plantar wart, or an intramuscular injection within the previous 24 hours.)

• A slight limp (due to an injury) lasts more than 72 hours (as with a pulled muscle, bruised bone, stubbed toe, or scraped knee).

NECK PAIN, ACUTE

SYMPTOMS AND CHARACTERISTICS

• Your child complains of pain in the back of the neck or upper back

• Pain in the front of the neck usually is due to a sore throat or swollen lymph node

• The head is often cocked to one side

• Often the neck muscles are tender to the touch

Similar Conditon • LYMPH NODES, SWOLLEN (see page 479)

Causes • Acute neck pain (wryneck) is usually caused by sleeping in an awkward posture, painting a ceiling, reading in bed, or prolonged typing.

Serious spinal cord injury can follow diving injuries, trampoline injuries, or other accidents involving the neck. Children who have suffered such an accident should not be moved until a neck brace or spine board has been applied.

A stiff neck (in which your child can't bend forward and touch the chin to the chest) is an early finding in meningitis. (Fever should also be present.)

Expected Course • A strained neck isn't serious and usually lasts 5 to 7 days.

CALL YOUR CHILD'S PHYSICIAN

Immediately If

• The pain was caused by contact sports or an accident.
First aid: Call the rescue squad (911) and don't move your child.

• Numbness or tingling is present in the arms or upper back.

• The pain is severe.

- Your child cannot touch the chin to the center of the chest.
- A fever (over 100°F) is present.

During Office Hours If

- Your child is under 5 years old.
- The pain interferes with sleep.
- Neck pain is a recurrent problem for your child.
- You have other questions or concerns.

HOME CARE

Pain-Relief Medicines • Give aspirin, acetaminophen, or ibuprofen 4 times a day until your child has gone 24 hours without any pain. (For dosage, see the chart on page 66.) This is the most important part of therapy, because neck pain causes muscle spasm, and these medicines can interrupt this cycle.

Local Heat • A heating pad, hot water bottle, or hot shower spray applied to the most painful area helps to relieve muscle spasm. Do this whenever the pain flares up.

Sleeping Position • Instead of a pillow at night, your child may prefer a folded towel wrapped around the neck. This collar will keep the head from moving too much during sleep. (A foam cervical collar with Velcro closure can be obtained at a pharmacy.) Avoid sleeping on the abdomen.

Exercises • Your child should avoid any neck exercises until completely well.

Call Your Child's Physician Later If

- The pain becomes worse.
- The pain begins to shoot into the arms or upper back.
- The pain is no better in 72 hours.
- The pain is still present after 1 week.
- Other questions come up.

PREVENTION

If your child has had more than one neck ache, usually the child has an activity or habit that overstresses the neck muscles or bones (cervical spine). Such activities are working with the neck turned or bent backward, carrying heavy objects on the head, carrying heavy objects with one arm (instead of both arms), standing on the head, contact sports, or even friendly wrestling. Avoid these triggers. Also improve the tone of the neck muscles with 2 or 3 minutes of gentle stretching exercises per day. Helpful neck exercises are touching the chin to each shoulder, touching the ear to the shoulder, and moving the head forward and backward. Don't apply any resistance during these stretching exercises.

VII.

GLOSSARY

A GLOSSARY OF CHILDREN'S DISEASES REQUIRING PHYSICIAN CONSULTATION

All of these conditions require a physician's input for diagnosis or treatment. Therefore, they are purposely not covered in this book. Your education on how to manage them should come from your child's physician and his or her associates.

If your child is born with or develops a chronic (long-term or lifetime) disease, to best serve your child you will need to learn almost as much about symptoms and treatment as your physician. To gain such a knowledge base, you can turn to local parent support groups or a national organization, as well as medical specialists. In many cases, a parents' handbook on your child's disease is available. If your child is hospitalized, you have the right to ask the staff your questions, and they will usually be able to schedule a meeting with you once or twice a day for this purpose.

This chapter is divided into three parts: chronic diseases or conditions; severe acute illnesses usually requiring admission to the hospital; and acute illnesses usually treatable at home but requiring diagnosis by a physician or lab test.

CHRONIC DISEASES OR CONDITIONS

Acquired Immune Deficiency Syndrome (AIDS): A life-threatening disease due to markedly reduced lymphocytes and immunity. Pediatric cases are rare except for the offspring of affected adults, or children who have required multiple transfusions (hemophiliacs, for instance).

Adrenogenital syndrome: An inherited disease present at birth in which the infant has accelerated sexual development and an inability to produce steroids. Females with this disease may resemble male newborns (ambiguous genitals).

Amblyopia: Decreased vision or blindness.

Anorexia nervosa: In adolescents, excessive weight loss (more than 20 percent below ideal weight) and denial of being underweight. Over 90 percent are female. Psychotherapy is essential.

Asthma: An allergic condition of the lungs. The smaller airways (bronchioles) go into spasm and become swollen with colds and when allergens or irritants are inhaled, leading to attacks of wheezing. Occurs in 5 percent of children.

Astigmatism: Distorted vision due to variations in refractive power on different parts of the cornea.

Attention deficit disorder: The new medical term for the hyperactive child's condition. These children cannot concentrate or complete tasks. The causes are many.

Bifid uvula: A splitting of the tag of tissue hanging down from the center of the soft palate in the mouth. Looks like 2 uvulas. No symptoms except increased ear infections in some children.

Biliary atresia: Blockage of the bile ducts at birth leading to severe liver damage. Sometimes treatable with surgery.

Bronchopulmonary dysplasia (BPD): Lung damage that occurs in some prematures who needed mechanical ventilation for survival. Portable oxygen administration may be needed over the first 1 or 2 years until lung improvement occurs.

Bulimia: In adolescents, periodic food binging followed by self-induced vomiting or laxative-induced diarrhea to prevent weight gain. The weight, however, is usually kept in the normal range. Psychotherapy is essential.

Cerebral palsy: A nonprogressive motor handicap due to brain injury either before or during birth. The most common type is spastic diplegia (weakness and tightness of both legs).

Chorea: Abnormal and unexpected muscle jerks. The location of the chorea changes. Sydenham's chorea is a type seen following rheumatic fever.

Chronic Fatigue Syndrome: A new disease with symptoms of extreme fatigue and sleepiness, muscle weakness, muscle and joint pain, confusion, memory loss, and eye pain lasting 6 months or longer. Probably due to a virus, but not infectious mono.

Cleft lip and/or palate: The incomplete closure of the lip and/or roof of the mouth. Can occur in various combinations. A birth defect of unknown cause. Requires surgical repair and speech therapy.

Clubfoot: A fixed (inflexible) deformity of the foot (usually downward and inward) present at birth. Requires repeated casts or surgical correction.

Congenital heart disease: A birth defect of the heart which is usually not inherited. The defects are of many types. Surgery is frequently required.

Cow's milk allergy: An allergy to cow's milk protein resulting in the onset of diarrhea (often bloody) during the first 8 weeks of life. Responds to a non-cow's milk formula. Occurs in 1 to 2 percent of newborns and resolves spontaneously by 1 year of age in most children.

Craniosynostosis: An early closure of the sutures (growth lines) of the skull. Surgery is required if multiple sutures are involved, and should be done before 6 months of age.

Cryptorchidism: An undescended testicle that remains in the abdomen. Needs to be surgically brought down into the scrotal sac by 2 years of age.

Cystic fibrosis: An inherited disease causing very thick mucus that blocks the lungs and pancreas. The main symptoms are recurrent pneumonia, diarrhea, and poor weight gain.

Diabetes insipidus: The inability to concentrate the urine, making the child predisposed to dehydration. Symptoms of increased drinking (polydipsia) and urination (polyuria). The causes are several.

Diabetes mellitus: The inability of the pancreas to produce insulin, leading to high blood sugar and sugar in the urine. The main symptoms are increased drinking and eating, excessive urination, and weight loss. The child needs daily insulin injections.

Down's syndrome: Newborns with Down's syndrome are mentally retarded, floppy, and have a characteristic facial appearance (mongolism). They are commonly the offspring of older mothers. Caused by an extra chromosome (Trisomy 21). Can be diagnosed during pregnancy by amniocentesis.

Epilepsy: A recurrent seizure disorder. The types and causes are many. In grand mal epilepsy the child falls and the entire body jerks for several minutes. In petit mal epilepsy (staring spells) a child loses consciousness and stops what he or she is doing for 5 to 15 seconds, but doesn't fall down.

Exercise-induced bronchospasm: Attacks, lasting 20 to 30 minutes, of coughing and wheezing after (but sometimes during) exercise. Running in cold air is the main offender. Occurs in 10 to 20 percent of people (90 percent of those with asthma). Prevented by taking an asthma medicine before sports.

Fetal alcohol syndrome: Birth defects due to maternal alcohol intake in excess of 1 drink per day during pregnancy. The most common abnormalities are small eyes, a small head, low birth weight, and delayed development.

Fragile X syndrome: In males, an abnormal X chromosome. Accounts for 25 percent of mental retardation in males. Features include a long face, large jaw, large testes, and scars from hand-biting.

Galactosemia: An inherited enzyme defect that causes vomiting, diarrhea, liver damage, and mental retardation. Detection by newborn screening permits treatment with a galactose-free diet. Galactose is one of the sugars in milk.

Gastroesophageal reflux: The regurgitation or vomiting of food because the junction of the esophagus (food tube) and stomach doesn't close completely. The mild form is common in newborns and resolves by 1 year of age. The severe form can cause poor weight gain or vomited blood due to acid irritation of the end of the esophagus. This form may require surgery.

Hemophilia: An inherited bleeding tendency due to the inability to produce certain clotting factors. Mainly occurs in males.

Hip, congenital dislocation: Being born with the hip out of the socket. A brace is needed for 3 months to correct the problem. Early diagnosis is important to prevent permanent damage.

Hydrocephalus: Blockage of spinal fluid flow out of the brain; resulting in a large head if not treated early. Treatment is a surgical shunt to drain the fluid to the abdomen.

Hydronephrosis: An enlarged kidney due to obstruction of its drainage system. Usually requires surgical correction.

Hyperopia: Farsightedness. Close objects are difficult to see.

Hypertension: High blood pressure. The causes are many in children. In adolescents, the cause is usually genetic (i.e., essential hypertension).

Hypospadias: A birth defect in which the urethra opens onto the shaft of the penis rather than the end. Surgical correction is usually required.

Hypothyroidism: An underactive thyroid gland. When this condition occurs in newborns, it can cause very slow growth and development. Treated with thyroid medicine. Diagnosis before 6 weeks of age is important.

Inborn errors of metabolism: Genetic diseases that involve the absence of a particular enzyme the body requires. Examples are phenylketonuria and galactosemia.

Irritable colon of childhood: The most common cause of chronic diarrhea in infants. The loose, mushy stools do not interfere with normal weight gain. The cause is unknown but the condition miraculously clears at 2½ to 3 years of age.

Klinefelter's syndrome: In males, an extra X chromosome (i.e., XXY). Features include tall stature, borderline intelligence, breast development, small testes, and sterility.

Lactose intolerance: An inherited reduction in lactase, the enzyme needed to break down lactose in milk. Milk intake causes loose stools and gas. The condition is most common in dark-skinned races, and usually has an onset at 5 to 10 years of age.

Learning disabilities: Specific learning limitations (e.g., in mathematics or reading) in children of normal intelligence and motivation. Usually inherited. Illiteracy (the inability to read and write adequately to function in our society) is often due to untreated severe reading disability. Most schools have special programs to help these children.

Leukemia: A cancer of the white blood cells. With modern treatment, over half of children can be cured.

Malabsorption: An intestinal condition that interferes with the absorption of fat, protein, or sugar. Symptoms are severe diarrhea and weight loss. The causes are legion.

Mental retardation: An intelligence quotient (I.Q.) less than 70. Children with I.Q.'s over 50 can often learn to function independently. The causes are many.

Microcephaly: Small head size. Due to below-average brain growth. Extremely small heads are associated with mental retardation.

Migraine headaches: A headache that is incapacitating, throbbing, and on one side of the head. Nausea and vomiting are often present. Over 70 percent have a family history of similar headaches.

Minimal brain dysfunction (MBD): Twenty years ago, MBD was considered the main cause of attention deficit disorder, dyslexia, and other learning disabilities. Many physicians have discarded this simplistic, unfounded, and harmful label.

Muscular dystrophy: An inherited disease of progressive muscle weakness. Onset at age 2 to 6. In males only.

Myopia: Nearsightedness. Distant objects are difficult to see.

Neuroblastoma: A cancer of the adrenal gland located above each kidney.

Neurofibromatosis: A dominant genetic disorder characterized by 5 or more coffee-colored spots and benign tumors of the nerve sheaths (neurofibromas) or nerves (neuromas). Nervous system complications can occur.

Orthostatic proteinuria: Increased amounts of protein are released into the urine when standing but not when lying down. A harmless condition usually found in adolescent males.

Osgood-Schlatter disease: A disease causing knee pain just below the kneecap on a small normal bump called the tibial tubercle. Occurs in adolescents and lasts 1½ to 2 years. No permanent harm.

Pectus excavatum: A pulled-in or sunken breastbone (sternum). The mild form is common and causes no symptoms. The severe form of this congenital defect may interfere with heart function during exercise and requires surgery.

Peptic ulcer: An ulcer of the stomach or duodenum which causes upper abdominal pain, vomiting, or bleeding.

Phenylketonuria (PKU): An inherited enzyme defect that causes mental retardation, a light complexion, and seizures. Detection by newborn screening permits early treatment with a low-phenylalanine formula, followed by a restricted diet.

Polio: An infection of the spinal cord with serious complications like muscle paralysis and inability to breathe. Practically eliminated from our country by the polio vaccine. Occasionally causes minor epidemics (but great suffering) in religious sects that forbid immunization.

Polydactyly: Extra fingers or toes present at birth. The extra digit is usually adjacent to the little finger or toe. Dominant type of inheritance giving a 50 percent rate in offspring. Surgical removal for cosmetic reasons is fairly simple.

Prematurity: Birth of a newborn weighing less than 2,500 grams (5½ pounds). Occurs in 7 percent of births. A preterm baby is one born before 37 weeks of gestation. The smaller the baby, the higher the complication rate. Neonatal intensive care units have drastically improved survival rates and reduced complications.

Recurrent abdominal pains (RAP): Recurrent stomachaches occur in 10 percent of children. While the causes are legion, over 90 percent are on a nonphysical basis.

Retrolental fibroplasia: Damage to the retina that occurs in small prematures (less than 1,500 grams) with high oxygen therapy requirements. The name comes from overgrowth of fibrous tissue behind the lens. The result is reduced vision or blindness.

Rett syndrome: A type of mental retardation that only occurs in girls. These children start out normal but lose intellectual and motor function between 6 and 18 months of age. The most characteristic symptom is repeated wringing of the hands.

Rheumatic fever: A rare complication of an untreated strep throat. The symptoms are migrating joint pains and fever. The heart is involved over half the time and can sustain permanent damage of the valves.

Rheumatoid arthritis: An arthritis that usually involves large joints on both sides of the body. Morning stiffness is common. Joint damage is occasionally seen.

Scoliosis: A sideways curving of the spine. Usually begins at age 10. Predominantly in girls. Screened for in most schools. Bracing is needed if the curve exceeds 20 degrees.

Serous otitis media: Fluid in the middle ear due to blocked eustachian tubes. A problem of young children, sometimes requiring the insertion of ventilation (tympanostomy) tubes for 1 or 2 years.

Sickle cell anemia: An inherited type of anemia where the normally round red blood cells periodically become sickle-shaped and block off small blood vessels, causing severe pain. Also interferes with growth. Mainly occurs in Blacks at a frequency of 1 in 500.

Sickle cell trait: Children with sickle cell trait carry 1 gene for sickle cell anemia. It takes 2 genes to develop the disease. No symptoms or anemia. Present in 10 percent of Blacks.

Spina bifida: A birth defect of the spinal column and cord that causes paralysis below the level of involvement, as well as poor bladder-bowel control. Also called meningomyelocele. The cause is unknown.

Strabismus: A birth defect of the eye muscles causing crossed eyes (i.e., inward or outward turning of 1 or both eyes). Usually requires surgery. More than 90 percent of children suspected of having this actually have pseudostrabismus due to a broad nasal bridge or folds of tissue (epicanthal folds) over the inner parts of the eye. These decrease the visible sclera (white part) on the inside of the eyes and give an optical illusion of turning in.

Tay-Sachs disease: An inherited disease in which the brain degenerates. Onset at 3 to 6 months of age. Findings are blindness, arrested development, and seizures. Mainly occurs in East European Jews.

Tourette's syndrome: Frequent facial muscle jerks (tics) and irrepressible sounds (such as grunting or profanity). Onset at 2 to 6 years of age. Inherited in 50 percent of cases.

Transvestism: A preference for cross-dressing (i.e., dressing like the opposite sex). More commonly seen in heterosexuals than homosexuals. Occasional cross-dressing in preschoolers means nothing.

Turner's syndrome: In females, a missing X chromosome (i.e., X instead of XX). Features include short stature, abnormal ovaries, lack of sexual development, and infertility. The intelligence is normal.

Ulcerative colitis: Inflammation of the lining of the large bowel, which causes intermittent or continuous loose stools and cramps. Usually the stools contain mucus, pus, or blood.

Von Willebrand's disease: An inherited bleeding tendency due to problems with both platelets and clotting factor 8. Symptoms include severe nosebleeds, excessive menstrual flow, and increased bruising with trauma. Not as severe as hemophilia.

Wilson's disease: An inherited disease in which the liver can't excrete copper. The onset is after age 10, with jaundice, tremors, and deterioration in school performance.

ACUTE ILLNESSES USUALLY REQUIRING ADMISSION TO THE HOSPITAL

Anaphylactoid purpura: A disease consisting of unexplained bruises of the buttocks, hands, and feet; joint pains (70 percent), abdominal pain (30 percent); and blood in the urine (50 percent). The cause is unknown.

Apnea: An episode of cessation of breathing for 20 seconds or more, often associated with cyanosis (a bluish color of the lips). Apnea usually occurs in infants under 6 months of age. The causes are many.

Appendicitis: A blockage and infection of the appendix. The appendix is a blind pouch the size of your little finger that comes off the cecum (first part of the large bowel). Appendicitis gives constant pain in the right lower abdomen and requires surgical intervention.

Arthritis: Inflammation of a joint leading to pain, swelling, and limited motion. The causes are many.

Botulism: The most serious type of food poisoning. First symptoms are double vision, slurred speech, and swallowing problems. The cause is a toxin produced by bacteria in improperly canned vegetables. Contaminated food looks and tastes normal. During the first year of life, botulism germs can be acquired from swallowing dust or normal honey. Despite several studies, corn syrup has never been linked to a case of botulism. Progressive weakness (of suck, cry, and neck muscles) and constipation are the main symptoms in these babies.

Cellulitis: A spreading bacterial infection of the skin, often following a wound infection.

Cerebellar ataxia, acute: The abrupt onset of an unsteady gait, shaky hands, and slurred speech. Due to a viral infection of the cerebellum (balance center of the brain). Resolves in 4 to 8 weeks.

Child abuse: The mistreatment of children by adult caretakers (less commonly by strangers). The two most common types are physical abuse (inflicted injuries) and sexual abuse.

Cholecystitis: An infection of the gall bladder, often occurring because the gall bladder is blocked by gallstones. Surgical intervention is usually necessary.

Conversion reaction: The sudden onset of a physical disability (e.g., paralysis or blindness) on an emotional basis. Commonly the youngster shows lack of concern (indifference) for the symptom. Also called a hysterical reaction. Requires psychotherapy.

Diphtheria: A serious bacterial infection of the throat with complications of suffocation, heart disease, and paralysis. Preventable with DPT immunizations.

Diplopia: Double vision. Caused by drug reactions, botulism, eye muscle or brain disease.

Encephalitis: An infection of the brain caused by various viruses. Also called sleeping sickness.

Endocarditis: An infection of the valves and lining of the heart.

Epiglottitis: A life-threatening infection of the tissues surrounding the vocal cords. The cause is the *Hemophilus influenzae* bacterium. The epiglottis is the flap of tissue which normally covers the opening of the windpipe during swallowing and keeps food and drink off the larynx.

Failure-to-thrive: A malnourished, underweight condition usually occurring during the first year of life. While the causes are many, in our country over half the cases are due to underfeeding (i.e., child neglect).

Guillain-Barré syndrome: An acute progressive symmetrical paralysis that starts in the feet and moves up the body over several days. Usually follows a viral infection. Some children need to be placed on a ventilator temporarily.

Hematemesis: Vomiting up blood. The causes are many.

Hematuria: Blood in the urine. The causes are many.

Hemolytic-uremic syndrome: A combination of anemia from red blood cell breakdown (hemolysis) and kidney failure. Often preceded by bloody diarrhea. Occurs in infants. Cause unknown.

Hemoptysis: Coughing up blood. The causes are many.

Hemorrhagic disease of the newborn: A bleeding disorder that occurs on day 2 to day 7 of life. The bleeding usually occurs into the intestines, skin, or circumcision site. Due to vitamin K deficiency and preventable by routine vitamin K administration at birth. This problem is making a resurgence with home deliveries and breast-feeding.

Idiopathic thrombocytopenic purpura (ITP): The most common bleeding disorder of childhood. Due to a temporary depletion of platelets (which are needed for clotting) following various viral infections.

Intussusception: Obstruction of the bowel due to a telescoping of one segment of intestine into an adjacent one. Cases diagnosed early may become unstuck with a barium enema, but some require surgery. Usually occurs in children less than 2 years old.

Kawasaki's disease: A disease of young children characterized by a red rash, red eyes, red mouth, enlarged nodes, and a fever lasting over 5 days. The cause is unknown. Over 20 percent of the children who get it develop heart disease. Early treatment with intravenous gamma globulin can prevent some coronary artery disease. Also called mucocutaneous lymph node syndrome.

Malaria: A parasite transmitted by mosquitoes. Causes fever, shaking chills, anemia, convulsions, and coma. Affects over

200 million people worldwide and kills several million annually. The world's greatest cause of human disability. Could be eradicated if funds were provided. (Note: Doesn't occur in the United States.)

Mastoiditis: A bacterial infection of the air cells in the bone behind the ear. A complication of an untreated ear infection. Often requires surgery.

Melena: The passage of tar-colored blood in the stool. Blood darkens only if it comes from the stomach or upper intestines.

Meningitis: An infection of the meninges or thin membranes surrounding the brain and spinal cord. Usually caused by bacteria. Called aseptic meningitis when due to a virus.

Nephritis: Kidney disease where blood is passed in the urine. The causes are many, but strep throat is one of the more common forerunners. Can become chronic.

Nephrosis: Kidney disease where protein is passed in the urine, leading to swelling (edema) of the face and feet. Often becomes chronic.

Omphalitis: An infection of the navel or bellybutton. Can be serious in the first month of life.

Osteomyelitis: A bacterial infection of bone.

Papilledema: Swelling of the optic disc in the back of the eye. Reflects increased spinal-fluid pressure inside the head. Various causes, usually serious.

Pelvic inflammatory disease (PID): A bacterial infection of the Fallopian tubes—often due to gonorrhea or chlamydia. Also called salpingitis.

Pericarditis: An infection of the sac that covers the heart.

Peritonitis: An infection of the lining of the abdomen. Usually caused by a ruptured appendix.

Pertussis: A serious bacterial infection of the windpipe and lungs. Also called whooping cough because coughing spasms often end with a high-pitched whoop. Preventable with DPT immunizations.

Pneumothorax: A blowout of the lung leading to the escape of air into the space between the lung and the chest wall. Symptoms are chest pain and difficult breathing.

Pulmonary embolism: A blood clot carried through the blood stream to the lungs. Causes severe chest pain and difficult breathing.

Pyloric stenosis: An obstruction of the stomach outlet occurring in the first 4 to 8 weeks of life. Causes projectile vomiting and requires surgery.

Reyes syndrome: Abrupt swelling of the brain presenting with confusion, sleepiness, and persistent vomiting. Liver destruction also occurs. Although the cause is unknown, it sometimes follows chicken pox or influenza. Also associated with aspirin ingestion during these illnesses.

Rocky Mountain spotted fever: A life-threatening disease caused by a rickettsia that is carried by ticks. The symptoms include a purple-red rash of the extremities, fever, headache, and delirium. It responds to antibiotics.

Scalded skin syndrome: A bright-red, painful rash in which the skin peels off in sheets like a burn. The rash is caused by a toxin released by staph bacteria, often residing in the nose. The outcome is good.

Septicemia: A bacterial infection of the bloodstream in which the bacteria are actually multiplying there.

Subdural hematoma: A blood clot on the surface of the brain, usually due to direct trauma. Violently shaking a child by the shoulders so the head is snapped forward and back can also cause this life-threatening condition.

Sudden infant death syndrome (SIDS): The sudden unexplained death of a healthy infant under 12 months of age during sleep. The incidence is 2 in 1,000 live births. The cause remains unknown.

Testicular torsion: An unexplained twisting of a testicle that shuts off its blood supply and requires emergency surgical release. Presents with testicular pain and swelling.

Tetanus: A serious bacterial wound infection that progresses from local muscle spasms to total body rigidity and seizures. Preventable by DPT immunizations and tetanus boosters.

Thrombophlebitis: An infection of the lining of a vein, often the deep veins of the calf muscles.

Tonsillar abscess: An abscess deep within the tonsil that causes a severe sore throat, muffled voice, inability to open the mouth fully, and drooling. Requires surgical drainage.

Toxic shock syndrome: Symptoms include shock, fever, diarrhea, and a bright-pink (scarlet-fever like) rash. Caused by a toxin produced by a hidden staph infection. One common source of staph overgrowth is a tampon left in the vagina overnight.

Typhoid fever: A severe form of bacterial diarrhea (often bloody) that can lead to a bloodstream infection or intestinal complications. Treatable with antibiotics.

ACUTE ILLNESSES USUALLY TREATABLE AT HOME BUT REQUIRING A PHYSICIAN FOR DIAGNOSIS

Amenorrhea: The absence of menstrual periods. When regular periods stop, the most common causes are dieting, stress, or pregnancy.

Anemia: A low red-blood-cell count. While the causes are many, iron deficiency ranks first. A blood sample is needed to diagnose anemia.

Ascaris: A roundworm that causes intestinal infections. The main symptom is abdominal pain. In our country, mainly occurs in the Southeast.

Bell's palsy: An abrupt onset of weakness of the facial muscles on one side. Often associated with an ear infection, since the seventh (facial) nerve is damaged while traveling through the infected area. Usually clears in 1 to 4 weeks. Early treatment with steroids may be helpful.

Bronchiolitis: An infection of the bronchioles (small air passages) occurring in the first 2 years of life. The main symptoms are wheezing, rapid breathing, cough, runny nose, and fever. Caused by the respiratory syncytial virus.

Cat scratch fever: A swollen lymph node caused by the scratch of a young cat. Usually lasts several months. A bacterium has recently been identified as the infectious agent.

Chlamydia: A germ that causes urethral or vaginal infections. Spread by sexual contact. Can also cause eye infections or pneumonia in newborns by contact at birth.

Chondromalacia of the patella: A roughening of the underside of the kneecap causing knee pain in adolescents. Often due to excessive deep knee bends or running upstairs. Helped by rest and quadriceps-strengthening exercises.

Cold panniculitis: A lump of frozen fat tissue. Usually occurs in the fatty cheeks of infants less than 1 year of age. Due to prolonged contact with ice, Popsicles, cold metal, or cold weather. The lump can last 2 weeks and occasionally the overlying skin turns red.

Creeping eruption: A localized itchy rash consisting of a wavy red line. Caused by a tunneling young hookworm, from skin contact with dog or cat excrement. Common along the Atlantic coast. Lasts 1 to 2 months without treatment.

Ganglion: A cyst (smooth circular swelling filled with thick fluid) usually occurring on the back of the wrist. These outpouchings of the joint capsule probably result from trauma. Most eventually disappear. Surgery is necessary only if they become very large or painful.

Giardia: A small parasite that causes diarrhea. Without treatment, the diarrhea can last for months.

Goiter: An enlarged thyroid gland, found in the front of the neck. The causes are many.

Gonorrhea: A bacterium that can cause genital infections. Spread by sexual contact. Eye infections of newborns are usually prevented by routine application of silver nitrate or antibiotic eyedrops.

Granuloma annulare: Rings of little bumps, usually found at the ankle. The overlying skin looks normal. The cause is unknown. Clears spontaneously in 2 years.

Gynecomastia: The development of breast tissue in a boy. Usually mild (just breast buds) and a temporary normal condition of 14- to 16-year-old boys. Can be caused by an endocrine problem. Not to be confused with fat deposits in this area, commonly seen in overweight boys.

Heart murmur: A swishing noise heard over the heart. Due to turbulence in blood flow as it goes through the heart. While a murmur can be caused by heart disease, 99 percent are normal sounds (innocent or functional heart murmurs). Your physician can tell the difference. More than 50 percent of normal children have innocent murmurs.

Hepatitis: A viral infection of the liver leading to jaundice (yellow skin), light-colored bowel movements, and dark-colored urine.

Hernia, inguinal: A bulging in the groin due to a hole in the abdominal wall. Requires surgery.

Herpes stomatitis: A viral infection causing multiple small, painful ulcers of the gums and lining of the mouth. Associated fever. Usually occurs in young children and doesn't recur (unlike fever blisters).

Hyperventilation: Rapid, deep-breathing attacks due to emotional stress. The symptoms include a sensation of smothering, dizziness, and tingling of the mouth and fingers. Occasionally proceeds to fainting. Quickly relieved by breathing into a paper bag or deliberately slowing down to 1 breath every 5 seconds.

Hypoglycemia: Low blood sugar with symptoms of hunger, headache, trembling, and sweating. May proceed to convulsions. Commonly overdiagnosed in our country.

Infectious mononucleosis: A viral infection with fever, sore throat, swollen lymph nodes, and an enlarged spleen. Symptoms last 1 to 4 weeks.

Keloids: Overgrowth of scar tissue at sites of surgery or trauma. Some people have a tendency to produce raised scars. Plastic surgery can help.

Kyphosis: An exaggerated posterior curvature of the upper back and shoulders. Usually normal.

Labial adhesions: A fusion of the 2 labia minora by a thin membrane. Caused by irritation of the labia from soaps or a mild infection, followed by healing together. The vagina becomes covered over. Once adhesions have started, the labia are not easy to keep separated. Fortunately, the labia separate spontaneously with the onset of puberty and stay that way.

Lordosis: An exaggerated anterior curvature of the spine at the lower back. Usually normal.

Menorrhagia: Excessive or prolonged menstrual periods, often leading to anemia.

Mittelschmerz: Sharp lower abdominal pain on one side that occurs in menstruating women midway through their cycle. Lasts 1 to 2 days. Caused by small amount of blood or fluid contacting the abdominal lining when the egg is released from the ovary.

Molluscum contagiosum: Small ⅛-inch, skin-colored, waxy-looking bumps with indentations in the center. They contain a hard core. Caused by a virus and last 1 to 2 years, as with warts.

Pityriasis rosea: A rash of the chest, abdomen, and back characterized by matching oval-shaped red spots on both sides of the body. Lasts 4 to 8 weeks. Often preceded by a large scaly patch (herald patch) that resembles ringworm. Harmless and not contagious.

Pneumonia: An infection of the lungs. Generally not contagious.

Popliteal cyst: A smooth firm swelling behind the knee. Over 75 percent disappear spontaneously in 1 to 2 years. Also called a Baker's cyst. Surgery unnecessary unless it becomes painful or very large.

Pyelonephritis: A kidney infection.

Scabies: A very itchy skin rash consisting of small red bumps, pimples, and tunnels. Caused by a mite (small insect) that burrows under the skin to lay eggs. Very contagious.

Sexually transmitted diseases: Infections of the male and female genital tracts. Also called venereal diseases. Chlamydia has passed gonorrhea as the most common organism.

Shigella: A bacterium that causes severe diarrhea, often bloody. Treatable with antibiotics.

Spider nevus: A blood-vessel abnormality of the skin which looks like a spider. When the red spot in the center is pressed with a pen, all the small radiating blood vessels or spokes disappear. Occurs normally from age 6 to 12 in 50 percent of children. Clears spontaneously with puberty. Rarely associated with liver disease.

Strawberry hemangioma: A raised bright-red benign tumor that begins in the first month, grows rapidly during the first year, then slowly shrinks down until it disappears at ages 5 to 10. Surgery is unnecessary.

Strep throat: A throat infection caused by streptococcus bacteria. Usually requires a throat culture for diagnosis. Responds to penicillin.

Striae: Stretch marks on the skin occurring in areas of rapid weight gain (e.g., the thighs), rapid muscle expansion (e.g., the shoulders of weight lifters), or on the abdomen during pregnancy. Usually temporary.

Subluxation of the radial head: A partial dislocation of one of the bones of the forearm (the radius) at the elbow. Due to being suddenly lifted or pulled by the hand. An infant with this injury will not use the arm and keeps the hand turned down. Easily remedied by your child's physician.

Swimmer's itch: A widespread itchy, bumpy red rash caused by a snail parasite (schistosome) that penetrates the human skin by mistake. While the parasite quickly dies, it causes a reaction for 1 to 2 weeks. Onset following exposure in freshwater lakes. Partially prevented by toweling off immediately on emerging from the water.

Trench mouth: A bacterial infection causing red, swollen, ulcerated gums and bad breath. Responds to dental hygiene and antibiotics. Not contagious.

Trichinosis: A disease due to a small roundworm sometimes found in pork. Transmitted by undercooking the meat. The symptoms of fever, a swollen face, and muscle pains begin 1 week later.

Trichomonas: An amoebalike organism that can cause vaginal infections and discharge.

Tuberculosis: A bacterial disease of the lungs that can go on for years if not treated. Symptoms include cough, fever, and weight loss. Now rare in the United States except in immigrants.

Urethritis: An infection of the urethra, or tube that drains urine from the bladder to the body's surface.

Urinary tract infection (UTI): An infection of the bladder (cystitis) or kidneys (pyelonephritis).

Vaginitis: An infection of the vagina. At least 6 causes, but not always sexually transmitted (e.g., monilial vaginitis).

Vitiligo: A patchy loss of skin pigment giving milk-white splotches of skin. Inherited as a dominant trait. While occurring in all races, it is a major cosmetic stress for dark-skinned people. Current treatment gives unsatisfactory improvement.

INDEX